Lecture Notes in Computer Science 14355

The series Lecture Notes in Computer Science (LNCS), including its subseries Lecture Notes in Artificial Intelligence (LNAI) and Lecture Notes in Bioinformatics (LNBI), has established itself as a medium for the publication of new developments in computer science and information technology research, teaching, and education.

LNCS enjoys close cooperation with the computer science R & D community, the series counts many renowned academics among its volume editors and paper authors, and collaborates with prestigious societies. Its mission is to serve this international community by providing an invaluable service, mainly focused on the publication of conference and workshop proceedings and postproceedings. LNCS commenced publication in 1973.

Huchuan Lu · Wanli Ouyang · Hui Huang ·
Jiwen Lu · Risheng Liu · Jing Dong · Min Xu
Editors

Image
and Graphics

12th International Conference, ICIG 2023
Nanjing, China, September 22–24, 2023
Proceedings, Part I

Springer

Editors
Huchuan Lu (iD)
Dalian University of Technology
Dalian, China

Hui Huang (iD)
Shenzhen University
Shenzhen, China

Risheng Liu (iD)
Dalian University of Technology
Dalian, China

Min Xu (iD)
University of Technology Sydney
Sydney, NSW, Australia

Wanli Ouyang (iD)
University of Sydney
Sydney, NSW, Australia

Jiwen Lu (iD)
Tsinghua University
Beijing, China

Jing Dong (iD)
Institute of Automation, CAS
Beijing, China

ISSN 0302-9743   ISSN 1611-3349 (electronic)
Lecture Notes in Computer Science
ISBN 978-3-031-46304-4   ISBN 978-3-031-46305-1 (eBook)
https://doi.org/10.1007/978-3-031-46305-1

This Springer imprint is published by the registered company Springer Nature Switzerland AG
The registered company address is: Gewerbestrasse 11, 6330 Cham, Switzerland

Paper in this product is recyclable.

Preface

These are the proceedings of the 12th International Conference on Image and Graphics (ICIG 2023), which was held in Nanjing, China, on September 22–24, 2023. The Conference was hosted by China Society of Image and Graphics (CSIG), organized by Nanjing University of Posts & Telecommunications, co-organized by Nanjing University of Science & Technology and Nanjing University of Information Science and Technology, supported by Springer.

ICIG is a biennial conference that focuses on innovative technologies of image, video, and graphics processing and fostering innovation, entrepreneurship, and networking. ICIG 2023 featured world-class plenary speakers, exhibits, and high-quality peer-reviewed oral and poster presentations.

CSIG has hosted the series of ICIG conference since 2000. Details about the past conferences are as follows:

Conference	Place	Date	Submitted	Proceedings
First (ICIG 2000)	Tianjin, China	August 16–18	220	156
Second (ICIG 2002)	Hefei, China	August 15–18	280	166
Third (ICIG 2004)	Hong Kong, China	December 17–19	460	140
4th (ICIG 2007)	Chengdu, China	August 22–24	525	184
5th (ICIG 2009)	Xi'an, China	September 20–23	362	179
6th (ICIG 2011)	Hefei, China	August 12–15	329	183
7th (ICIG 2013)	Qingdao, China	July 26–28	346	181
8th (ICIG 2015)	Tianjin, China	August 13–16	345	170
9th (ICIG 2017)	Shanghai, China	September 13–15	370	172
10th (ICIG 2019)	Beijing, China	August 23–25	384	183
11th (ICIG 2021)	Haikou, China	December 26–28	421	198

For ICIG 2023, 409 submissions were received and 166 papers were accepted. To ease the search for a required paper in these proceedings, the accepted papers have been arranged into different sections according to their topic.

We sincerely thank all the contributors, who came from around the world to present their advanced work at this event. We would also like to thank all the reviewers, who carefully reviewed all submissions and made their valuable comments for improving the accepted papers. The proceedings could not have been produced without the invaluable efforts of the members of the Organizing Committee, and a number of active members of CSIG.

September 2023

Huchuan Lu
Wanli Ouyang
Hui Huang
Jiwen Lu
Risheng Liu
Jing Dong
Min Xu

Organization

Organizing Committee

General Chairs

Yaonan Wang	Hunan University, China
Qingshan Liu	Nanjing University of Posts & Telecommunications, China
Ramesh Jain	University of California, Irvine, USA
Alberto Del Bimbo	University of Florence, Italy

Technical Program Chairs

Huchuan Lu	Dalian University of Technology, China
Wanli Ouyang	University of Sydney, Australia
Hui Huang	Shenzhen University, China
Jiwen Lu	Tsinghua University, China

Organizing Committee Chairs

Yuxin Peng	Peking University, China
Xucheng Yin	University of Science and Technology Beijing, China
Bo Du	Wuhan University, China
Bingkun Bao	Nanjing University of Posts & Telecommunications, China

Publicity Chairs

Abdulmotaleb El Saddik	University of Ottawa, Canada
Phoebe Chen	La Trobe University, Australia
Kun Zhou	Zhejiang University, China
Xiaojun Wu	Jiangnan University, China

Award Chairs

Changsheng Xu	Institute of Automation, CAS, China
Shiguang Shan	Institute of Computing Technology, CAS, China
Mohan Kankanhalli	National University of Singapore, Singapore

Publication Chairs

Risheng Liu	Dalian University of Technology, China
Jing Dong	Institute of Automation, CAS, China
Min Xu	University of Technology Sydney, Australia

Workshop Chairs

Yugang Jiang	Fudan University, China
Kai Xu	National University of Defense Technology, China
Zhu Li	University of Missouri, USA
Oliver Deussen	Universität Konstanz, Germany

Exhibits Chairs

Qi Tian	Huawei Cloud, China
Wu Liu	JD.COM, China
Weishi Zheng	Sun Yat-sen University, China
Kun Xu	Tsinghua University, China

Tutorial Chairs

Weiwei Xu	Zhejiang University, China
Nannan Wang	Xidian University, China
Shengsheng Qian	Institute of Automation, CAS, China
Klaus Schöffmann	Klagenfurt University, Austria

Sponsorship Chairs

Xiang Bai	Huazhong University of Science and Technology, China
Mingming Cheng	Nankai University, China

Finance Chairs

Lifang Wu	Beijing University of Technology, China
Yubao Sun	Nanjing University of Information Science & Technology, China
Miao Hong	CSIG, China

Social Media Chairs

Zhenwei Shi	Beihang University, China
Wei Jia	Hefei University of Technology, China
Feifei Zhang	Tianjin University of Technology, China

Local Chairs

Jian Cheng	Institute of Automation, CAS, China
Xiaotong Yuan	Nanjing University of Information Science & Technology, China
Yifan Jiao	Nanjing University of Posts & Telecommunications, China

Website Chairs

Rui Huang	Chinese University of Hong Kong, Shenzhen, China
Jic Wang	Nanjing University of Posts & Telecommunications, China

Area Chairs

Yuchao Dai	Xi Peng	Yong Xia
Yulan Guo	Boxin Shi	Shiqing Xin
Xiaoguang Han	Dong Wang	Feng Xu
Tong He	Lijun Wang	Jia Xu
Gao Huang	Limin Wang	Kun Xu
Meina Kan	Nannan Wang	Yongchao Xu
Yu-Kun Lai	Xinchao Wang	Junchi Yan
Li Liu	Xinggang Wang	Shiqi Yu
Huimin Lu	Yunhai Wang	Jian Zhang
Jinshan Pan	Baoyuan Wu	Pingping Zhang
Houwen Peng	Jiazhi Xia	Shanshan Zhang

Additional Reviewers

Bingkun Bao
Yulong Bian
Chunjuan Bo
Zi-Hao Bo
JIntong Cai
Zhanchuan Cai
Mingwei Cao
Jianhui Chang
Yakun Chang
Bin Chen
Guang Chen
Hongrui Chen
Jianchuan Chen
Junsong Chen
Siming Chen
Xiang Chen
Xin Chen
Ziyang Chen
Jinghao Cheng
Lechao Cheng
Ming-Ming Cheng
Jiaming Chu
Hainan Cui
Yutao Cui
Enyan Dai
Tao Dai
Jisheng Dang
Sagnik Das
Xinhao Deng
Haiwen Diao
Jian Ding
Wenhui Dong
Xiaoyu Dong
Shuguang Dou
Zheng-Jun Du
Peiqi Duan
Qingnan Fan
Yongxian Fan
Zhenfeng Fan
Gongfan Fang
Kun Fang
Sheng Fang
Xianyong Fang

Zhiheng Fu
Wei Gai
Ziliang Gan
Changxin Gao
Qing Gao
Shang Gao
Zhifan Gao
Tong Ge
Shenjian Gong
Guanghua Gu
Yuliang Gu
Shihui Guo
Yahong Han
Yizeng Han
Yufei Han
Junwen He
Mengqi He
Xiaowei He
Yulia Hicks
Yuchen Hong
Ruibing Hou
Shouming Hou
Donghui Hu
Fuyuan Hu
Lanqing Hu
Qiming Hu
Ruimin Hu
Yang Hu
Yupeng Hu
Bao Hua
Guanjie Huang
Le Hui
Chengtao Ji
Naye Ji
Xiaosong Jia
Xu Jia
Chaohui Jiang
Haoyi Jiang
Peng Jiang
Runqing Jiang
Zhiying Jiang
Leyang Jin
Yongcheng Jing

Hao Ju
Yongzhen Ke
Lingshun Kong
Jian-Huang Lai
Yu-Kun Lai
Xingyu Lan
Yang Lang
Wentao Lei
Yang Lei
Baohua Li
Bocen Li
Boyang Li
Chao Li
Chenghong Li
Dachong Li
Feng Li
Gang Li
Guanbin Li
Guorong Li
Guozheng Li
Hao Li
Hongjun Li
Kunhong Li
Li Li
Manyi Li
Ming Li
Mingjia Li
Qifeng Li
Shifeng Li
Shutao Li
Siheng Li
Xiaoyan Li
Yanchun Li
Yang Li
Yi Li
Ying Li
Yue Li
Yunhao Li
Zihan Li
Dongze Lian
Jinxiu Liang
Junhao Liang
Tian Liang

Zhengyu Liang

Zhifang Liang

Bencheng Liao

Zehui Liao

Chuan Lin

Feng Lin

Qifeng Lin

Weilin Lin

Wenbin Lin

Xiaotian Lin

Yiqun Lin

Jingwang Ling

Qiu Lingteng

Aohan Liu

Chang Liu

Cheng-Lin Liu

Haolin Liu

Jingxin Liu

Jinyuan Liu

Kenkun Liu

Lei Liu

Long Liu

Meng Liu

Min Liu

Qingshan Liu

Risheng Liu

Shengli Liu

Shiguang Liu

Shuaiqi Liu

Songhua Liu

Wei Liu

Wenrui Liu

Wenyu Liu

Xuehu Liu

Yiguang Liu

Yijing Liu

Yipeng Liu

Yong Liu

Yu Liu

Yunan Liu

Zhenguang Liu

Zilin Lu

Weiqi Luo

Yong Luo

Zhaofan Luo

Zhongjin Luo

Yunqiu Lv

Junfeng Lyu

Youwei Lyu

Chunyan Ma

Fengji Ma

Huimin Ma

Tianlei Ma

Xinke Ma

Qirong Mao

Yuxin Mao

Wei Miao

Yongwei Miao

Weidong Min

Jiawen Ming

Weihua Ou

Jinshan Pan

Yun Pei

Zongju Peng

Hongxing Qin

Liangdong Qiu

Xinkuan Qiu

Yuda Qiu

Zhong Qu

Weisong Ren

Nong Sang

Guangcun Shan

Linlin Shen

Zhiqiang Shen

Jiamu Sheng

Jun Shi

Zhenghao Shi

Zhenwei Shi

Chengfang Song

Jiechong Song

Jifei Song

Yong Song

Zhengyao Song

Qingtang Su

Jiande Sun

Long Sun

Xuran Sun

Zhixing Sun

Gary Tam

Hongchen Tan

Jing Tan

Jiajun Tang

Jin Tang

Shiyu Tang

Minggui Teng

Yao Teng

Yanling Tian

Zhigang Tu

Matthew Vowels

Bo Wang

Dong Wang

Dongsheng Wang

Haiting Wang

Hao Wang

Jingyi Wang

Jinjia Wang

Jinting Wang

Jinwei Wang

Junyu Wang

Lijun Wang

Longguang Wang

Meng Wang

Miao Wang

Peizhen Wang

Pengjie Wang

Rui Wang

Ruiqi Wang

Ruotong Wang

Shengjin Wang

Shijie Wang

Tao Wang

Xiaoxing Wang

Xin Wang

Xingce Wang

Yili Wang

Yingquan Wang

Yongfang Wang

Yue Wang

Yun Wang

Zi Wang

Hongjiang Wei

Shaokui Wei

Xiu-Shen Wei

Ziyu Wei

Shuchen Weng

Zhi Weng
Qian Wenhua
Jianlong Wu
Lianjun Wu
Tao Wu
Yadong Wu
Yanmin Wu
Ye Wu
Yu Wu
Yushuang Wu
Di Xiao
Yuxuan Xiao
Jin Xie
Jingfen Xie
Jiu-Cheng Xie
Yutong Xie
Jiankai Xing
Bo Xu
Hongming Xu
Jie Xu
Xiaowei Xu
Yi Xu
Mingliang Xue
Xiangyang Xue
Difei Yan
Xin Yan
Yichao Yan
Zizheng Yan
Bin Yang
Cheng Yang
Jialin Yang
Kang Yang
Min Yang

Shuo Yang
Shuzhou Yang
Xingyi Yang
Xue Yang
Yang Yang
Yiqian Yang
Zhongbao Yang
Chao Yao
Chengtang Yao
Jingfeng Yao
Chongjie Ye
Dingqiang Ye
Jingwen Ye
Yiwen Ye
Xinyu Yi
Xinyi Ying
Di You
Bohan Yu
Chenyang Yu
Jiwen Yu
Runpeng Yu
Songsong Yu
Danni Yuan
Yang Yue
Lin Yushun
Qingjie Zeng
Qiong Zeng
Yaopei Zeng
Yinwei Zhan
Dawei Zhang
Guozhen Zhang
Jianpeng Zhang
Jiawan Zhang

Jing Zhang
Mingda Zhang
Pengyu Zhang
Pingping Zhang
Xiao-Yong Zhang
Xinpeng Zhang
Xuanyu Zhang
Yanan Zhang
Yang Zhang
Ye Zhang
Yuanhang Zhang
Zaibin Zhang
ZhiHao Zhang
Jie Zhao
Sicheng Zhao
Yuchao Zheng
Shuaifeng Zhi
Fan Zhong
Chu Zhou
Feng Zhou
JiaYuan Zhou
Jingyi Zhou
Tao Zhou
Yang Zhou
Zhanping Zhou
Minfeng Zhu
Mingli Zhu
Mingrui Zhu
Xu Zhu
Zihao Zhu
Shinan Zou

Contents – Part I

Computer Vision and Pattern Recognition

Computer Vision and Pattern Recognition

Attention-Based Global-Local Graph Learning for Dynamic Facial Expression Recognition

Ningwei Xie$^{(\boxtimes)}$, Jie Li, Meng Guo, Lei Yang, and Yafei Gong

China Mobile Research Institute, Beijing 100053, China
xieningwei@chinamobile.com

Abstract. Previous methods for dynamic facial expression recognition cannot jointly capture discriminative global and local features and leverage facial structural information to better understand expressions in videos with occlusions, variant poses and poor illumination. In this paper, we propose a novel global-local graph-learning method based on attention mechanisms to conduct robust recognition for these challenging cases. First, we extract high-level features from each frame by a CNN backbone. Then, to holistically describe dynamic expressions, we construct a global spatial-temporal graph (GSTG) by regarding each patch of the output feature maps as a graph node and initializing spatial and temporal connections. We employ multi-head self-attention to capture the long-range spatiotemporal relations and dynamically optimizes GSTG to generate discriminative descriptions. To capture dominant local information, we construct a local spatial-temporal graph (LSTG) by extracting intermediate CNN features of local regions based on landmark-guided attention and defining their geometric relationships. We utilize topology-learnable ST-GCNs to exploit the local dynamics and implicit relations. Finally, we design a global-local fusion unit at decision level, which adaptively controls the importance of each feature element. The proposed method achieves competitive performance on Oulu-CASIA and AFEW datasets.

Keywords: Facial expression recognition · Facial graph representation · Multi-head self-attention · Spatial-temporal graph convolutional networks · Global-local fusion

1 Introduction

Facial expression recognition (FER) has attracted increasing research interests in the field of artificial intelligence and computer vision due to its essential real-world applications in human-robot emotional interaction [1], human mental state analysis [2], etc. Early studies, such as [3–6], have been mainly conducted on static facial expression recognition (SFER) for single facial image. Recently, researchers have focused more on dynamic facial expression recognition (DFER) and developed various methods exploring the temporal cues in a image sequence (video) to better understand human emotional states.

© The Author(s), under exclusive license to Springer Nature Switzerland AG 2023
H. Lu et al. (Eds.): ICIG 2023, LNCS 14355, pp. 3–15, 2023.
https://doi.org/10.1007/978-3-031-46305-1_1

Previous methods for DFER can be divided into two categories: key-frame-selection methods and spatial-temporal methods. Most key-frame-selection methods statically extract hand-crafted features [7,8] or convolutional features [9–13] and select key frames with peak expressions to further conduct expression prediction. However, these methods cannot explicitly model the temporal dynamics and dependencies among frames. This has motivated research interests in developing spatial-temporal methods, which utilize 3D convolutional neural networks (C3D) and long-short term memory (LSTM) [14–18,39–41] to model temporal characteristics of spatial features. Unfortunately, these methods have not achieved satisfactory performance on in-the-wild expressions, due to their limitation in exploring discriminative spatiotemporal information from images with occlusions, various head poses and poor illumination.

To address the problem, there are two main research directions: geometry-based and Transformer-based methods. Geometry-based methods attempt to detect 2D or 3D facial landmarks from images as input modality [19–22], and assume that the landmark position features remain robust against occlusions and variant illumination by filtering redundant visual information. Furthermore, more recent studies utilize landmark-based graph structures to represent the facial geometry, and employ various graph neural networks to model them [23,24]. However, due to the data perturbation caused by individual diversity and landmark detection methods, the landmark features are inadequate to capture the subtle differences of facial muscle movements among confusing expressions. Liao et al. [25] and Meng et al. [26] propose to combine convolutional features with the facial graph structure in a landmark-guided manner, which has been proved to accurately distinguish similar expressions and perform well on occluded facial images. Transformer-based methods have made great progress on multiple computer vision tasks, benefiting from Transformer's strong capabilities in discriminative feature representation and contextual information modeling [27]. The basic mechanism of Transformers, multi-head self-attention (MSA), is able to model the long-range interactions among spatial features and has been demonstrated to improve the discriminatory power in the context of in-the-wild FER [5,28,29], compared with the pixel-level operators (i.e. convolutional kernels).

According to the studies of psychology and neuroscience, global description and dominant local features are both crucial and have different contributions, w.r.t. the feature selection for facial pattern recognition tasks [30]. Inspired by this intuitive idea and the strengths of both the graph representation and the MSA mechanism, we propose a novel attention-based global-local graph learning method combining the two techniques to improve the modelling of discriminative spatiotemporal characteristics for DFER. For the global branch, we first apply ResNet18 to translate each frame of the input video into a visual feature sequence. We construct the global spatial-temporal graph (GSTG), by regarding each patch of the feature maps as a graph node and initialize their connection relationships. Then, we perform the MSA mechanism in both spatial and temporal domains to dynamically optimize the nodes and edges of GSTG towards expression-specific graphs containing important structural information. For the

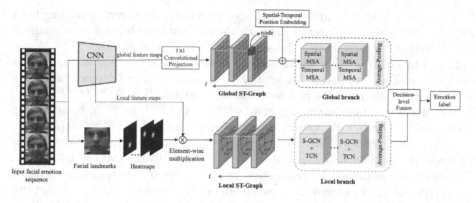

Fig. 1. Architecture of the proposed method for dynamic facial expression recognition.

local branch, we perform a landmark-guided attention to extract visual features of regions of interests from intermediate feature maps and construct the local spatial-temporal graph (LSTG) with a learnable topology. LSTG is further modeled by a sequence of ST-GCNs [31] to exploit the detailed variations and implicit relations between local regions. Finally, the global and the local information is fused by a weighted fusion unit at the decision-level to generate descriminative and robust description for expression prediction.

The main contributions of this paper are as follows:

- We propose a novel global-local facial graph representation, i.e., GSTG and LSTG to jointly model global structural information and local semantics of dynamic expressions.
- We design a global-local graph learning and fusion framework, which extracts both global-local and spatio-temporal information and fuses them for better discrimination of facial expressions.
- The proposed method demonstrates competitive performance on the lab-collected dataset Oulu-CASIA [34] and the in-the-wild dataset AFEW [35].

2   Method

The architecture of the proposed method is illustrated with Fig. 1. As for data preprocessing, we transform the raw input video into a frame sequence of fixed length T and obtain the 68 facial landmarks for each frame by [32]. We crop the face region according to the range of landmarks and resize it to 224×224.

2.1   Global Spatial-Temporal Graph Construction

The facial expression is a dynamic process consisting of various facial muscle movements cross different facial regions. To holistically represent the process, we construct the global spatial-temporal graph (GSTG) with the high-level visual features. Specifically, we first utilize ResNet18 without the average pooling layer and the fully-connected layer as the backbone network to obtain feature maps of size $H \times W$ from each frame. The sequence-level features $F_0 \in \mathbb{R}^{T \times H \times W \times C}$ are obtained by concatenating all frame-level feature maps, where C is the number of channels. Then, we flatten the spatial dimension of F_0 and project them by a 1×1 convolution, resulting in a new feature sequence $F_1 \in \mathbb{R}^{T \times (H \times W) \times d}$.

We define a fully-connected graph $G^{global} = (V^{global}, E^{global})$, by regarding each patch of the $H \times W$ feature map as a graph node. Let $V^{global} = \{v_{(t,i)} | t = 1, .., T, i = 1, ..., H \times W\}$ denote the node set, in which $v_{(t,i)}$ represents the i-th node at the time step t described by a d-length feature vector $\mathbf{f}_{(t,i)} \in F_1$. Therefore, we initialize the connection relationships of the nodes by defining three types of edges as follows: 1) spatial edges, $v_{(t,i)} \leftrightarrow v_{(t,j)} (i \neq j)$, connect two different nodes at the same time step t; 2) temporal edges, $v_{(t,i)} \leftrightarrow v_{(m,j)} (t \neq m)$, connect two nodes at different time steps; 3) self-connected edges, $v_{(t,i)} \leftrightarrow v_{(t,i)}$, connect the nodes with themselves.

We introduce learnable positional embeddings to the feature sequence F_1. The spatial embedding $\{\mathbf{p}_{(i)}^{spatial}\}$ consists of $H \times W$ vectors, indicating the spatial identity information of the nodes of length d. Similarly, the temporal embedding $\{\mathbf{p}_{(t,i)}^{temporal}\}$ is composed of $T \times (H \times W)$ vectors, representing their temporal orders. Their values are initialized by the sine and cosine functions of different frequencies following [33] and can be dynamically updated during the network optimization. The feature vector of a specific node is added to the corresponding spatial and temporal embedding vectors before fed into the spatial and temporal MSA blocks, respectively.

2.2   Spatial and Temporal Multi-head Self-attention

The GSTG is then processed by the global graph-learning branch, consisting of multiple spatial-temporal MSA blocks with residual connections. Specifically, given the feature vector of the i-th node $v_{(t,i)}$ at the time step t, the h-th spatial attention head of the spatial MSA layer $A^{spatial}$ applies three fully-connected layers to map it into three d-length vectors, Key, $Query$ and $Value$, donated by $\mathbf{K}_{(t,i)}^h$, $\mathbf{Q}_{(t,i)}^h$ and $\mathbf{V}_{(t,i)}^h$, respectively. The spatial attention head computes the attention weight between nodes $v_{(t,i)}$ and $v_{(t,j)}$ as follows,

$$u_{(t,i) \to (t,j)}^h = \frac{\left\langle \mathbf{Q}_{(t,i)}^h, \mathbf{K}_{(t,j)}^h \right\rangle}{\sqrt{d}}, \alpha_{(t,i) \to (t,j)}^h = \frac{\exp(u_{(t,i) \to (t,j)}^h)}{\sum_n^{H \times W} \exp(u_{(t,i) \to (t,n)}^h)}. \quad (1)$$

Here, $\langle \cdot, \cdot \rangle$ denotes the scaled dot-product [33]. The attention weight learned by the attention head measures the importance of information from $v_{(t,i)}$ to $v_{(t,j)}$ within the same time step, which reflects the strength of connection relationships between them. To avoid information passing through the temporal dimension, the weights between nodes in different time steps are fixed to 0. Then, the spatial attention head calculates the weighted feature $\mathbf{z}_{(t,i)}^h$ of $v_{(t,i)}$, defined as (2). In this procedure, information in nodes is transferred within same time step and aggregated based on the learned weights:

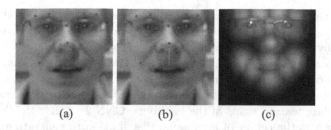

Fig. 2. The LSTG is constructed by 18 key facial landmarks shown in (a), and a defined topology illustrated in (b). The graph features are extracted from the intermediate feature maps of the CNN by landmark heatmaps, as indicated in (c).

$$\mathbf{z}^h_{(t,i)} = \sum_{j=1}^{H \times W} (\alpha^h_{(t,i) \to (t,j)} \cdot \mathbf{V}^h_{(t,j)}). \tag{2}$$

Then, the spatial MSA concatenates the spatial attention features learned by all the H spatial attention heads into a tensor, which contains multiple types of global structural information in spatial domain captured by different attention heads. Finally, the concatenated tensor is projected by a fully-connected layer with parameters $\mathbf{W}^r$ and combined with the output tensor of the former MSA layer $\mathbf{z}'_{(t,i)}$ by the residual connection:

$$\mathbf{z}_{(t,i)} = \mathbf{W}^r [\mathbf{z}^1_{(t,i)}, ..., \mathbf{z}^H_{(t,i)}]^{\mathrm{T}} + \mathbf{z}'_{(t,i)}. \tag{3}$$

The temporal MSA layer $\mathbf{A}^{temporal}$ takes the output of spatial MSA as well as the temporal position embedding as its input and applies the above-described mechanism to the temporal domain. Therefore, the result global spatial-temporal feature encodes the essential global structural information in both spatial and temporal domains carried by the input facial expression sequence. The output tensor of the last MSA block is average-pooled through the node and the temporal dimensions to generate the global feature vector.

2.3 Local Spatial-Temporal Graph Construction

The micro movements of some specific regions (i.e., eyebrows, eyes, mouth and cheeks) also provide important clues to FER. However, these details cannot be fully captured by the global branch, due to the multiple down-sampling processes of the CNN. Therefore, we design the local spatial-temporal graph (LSTG), denoted by $G^{local} = (V^{local}, E^{local}, \mathbf{A})$, to represent local informative dynamics and their geometry characteristics.

As shown in Fig. 2 (a), we select 16 key points from the 68 landmarks to locate the regions of eyebrows, eyes and mouth. We use two landmarks of the left (right) contour and the left (right) nostril to form a triangle region, and compute the center of gravity to locate the left (right) cheek [25]. The key points selected for all frames form the vertex set $V^{local} = \{v^{local}_{(t,k)} | t = 1, .., T, k = 1, ..., 18\}$. We consider three types of edges: 1) spatial edges, initialized according to the geometry relations between the key regions, as illustrated in Fig. 2 (b); 2) temporal edges connecting the same vertex across consecutive frames; 3) the self-connected edges. In the implementation, the association relationships between vertices are represented by the adjacency matrix $\mathbf{A} \in \mathbb{R}^{k \times k}$, whose element $A_{m,n}$ is set to 1 if there are connections between the m-th and the n-th vertices, and is set to 0 if there is no connection between them.

The attributes of vertices are the features of local regions extracted from the intermediate feature maps of the backbone CNN $F_3 \in \mathbb{R}^{T \times H' \times W' \times C'}$. Each vertex is taken as the center of a gaussian distribution to generate an attention heatmap, denoted by $\mathbf{H}_{(t,k)}$. As shown in Fig. 2 (c), for the time step t, given the $H' \times W'$ feature map $\mathbf{M}_t \in F_3$, the feature vector of the k-th local region is computed as follows,

$$\mathbf{f}^{local}_{(t,k)} = \mathrm{g}(\mathbf{M}_t \otimes \mathbf{H}_{(t,k)}), \tag{4}$$

where $\otimes$ represents the element-wise multiplication and g denotes the global average pooling operation.

2.4   Spatial-Temporal Graph Convolutional Networks

In the local graph-learning branch, we employ the regular spatial graph convolution [31] as the basic graph-learning component. It aggregates attributes of adjacent vertices and perform graph updating in spatial domain. Given the input local feature matrix $\mathbf{f}_{in}$ of size $(C_{in}, T, 18)$, the graph updating operation can be formulated as:

$$\mathbf{f}_{out} = \mathbf{\Lambda}^{-1/2}(\mathbf{A} + \mathbf{I})\mathbf{\Lambda}^{-1/2}\mathbf{f}_{in}\mathbf{W}. \tag{5}$$

Here, $\mathbf{I}$ is the identity matrix, $\mathbf{W}$ is the weight matrix. $\mathbf{\Lambda} = [\Lambda_{mm}]$ such that $\Lambda_{mm} = \sum_n (A_{mn} + I_{mn})$. This process is implemented by performing 2D convolutions on the graph feature vectors and multiplying the 2nd dimension of the resulting tensors with the normalized adjacency matrix $\mathbf{\Lambda}^{-1/2}(\mathbf{A} + \mathbf{I})\mathbf{\Lambda}^{-1/2}$. Furthermore, the adjacency matrix is fixed in the early stage of training and adaptively learned as parameters afterwards so that the model can leverage the implicit relations between distant local regions.

For the temporal domain, we perform a simple $K_t \times 1$ convolution on the updated graph features to add contextual information. The spatial graph updating is combined with the temporal convolution to form a basic spatiotemporal graph modelling module ST-GCN. We introduce residual connections into the non-input modules following [31]. The output tensor of the last ST-GCN is average-pooled through the temporal and the channel dimensions.

2.5   Global-Local Fusion

To combine the encoded global and local graph features, indicated by $\bar{\mathbf{z}}^{global}$ and $\bar{\mathbf{z}}^{local}$, we consider three commonly-used fusion methods: 1) sum fusion, which simply projects the two feature vectors into tensors with the same dimension and adds them up; 2) gated fusion, which learns a balancing parameter $\mathbf{t}$ to control the relative importance of the global and the local information, i.e. $\mathbf{z} = \mathbf{t} \otimes \bar{\mathbf{z}}^{global} + (1 - \mathbf{t}) \otimes \bar{\mathbf{z}}^{local}$; 3) weighted fusion, which concatenates the two feature vectors and weight the concatenated tensor by a fully-connected layer with Leaky ReLU activation. To select the appropriate integration strategy, we conduct comparison of the three methods in the following section. The fused representation is further processed by an average pooling layer and the output layer with SoftMax function to produce the classification score.

3 Experiments

3.1 Datasets

Oulu-CASIA consists of 2,880 image sequences collected from 80 subjects. Each sequence is captured with one of the two imaging systems, i.e., near-infrared (NIR) or visible light (VIS), under three different illumination conditions. Each sequence is assigned to one of the six basic expressions, i.e., anger, disgust, fear, happiness, sad, surprise. The first frame of each sequence is neutral and the last frame contains the peak expression. To make a fair comparison with other state-of-the-art methods, we employ 10-fold cross-validation experiments on the whole database. **AFEW** [35] is a temporal and multi-modal database contains video clips collected from movies with various head poses, occlusions and complicated backgrounds. Each video is labeled by seven classes including the six above-mentioned expressions and the neutral. The dataset is split into two subsets: the training set with 773 videos from 67 movies and the validating set with 383 samples from 33 movies for validation. Following the existing methods, we report the performance comparison on the validating set.

3.2 Implement Details

We use ResNet18 pretrained on MS-Celeb-1M [36] as the backbone. The number of spatial-temporal MSA blocks in the global branch, the number of attention heads in each MSA layer H, and the number of ST-GCN blocks in the local branch are empirically assigned to 2, 7 and 8, respectively. The hidden dimension d is set to 512. Each residual MSA layer is followed by a ReLU activation, a layer normalization layer and a dropout layer. Batch normalization and dropout are also applied after each graph updating layer and each temporal convolution layer of ST-GCNs.

Our model is trained with the batch-size of 16 on Oulu-CASIA and AFEW over 200 epochs and 150 epochs, respectively. The local adjacency matrix $\mathbf{A}$ is set to be learnable after 20 epochs. We optimize the model by minimizing the cross entropy loss with the SGD optimizer with an initial learning rate of 0.001. The dropout rate is set to 0.2. For Oulu-CASIA, we extract the last 7 frames and the first frame from each sequence to form a sample with 8 images. For AFEW, we divide each video clip into 8 segments and select 2 consecutive frames from the mid of each segment to form a sample with 16 images. The average accuracy on recognizing all expression classes over 10 runs serves as the evaluation metrics.

Table 1. Ablation Studies on OULU-CASIA.

Global Branch Settings		Accuracy (%)
Spatial MSA layers	Temporal MSA layers	
✗	✗	81.04
✓	✗	81.86
✗	✓	81.53
✓	✓	**83.31**
Local Branch Settings		Accuracy (%)
3-layer ST-LSTM [44]		76.41
ST-GCNs (fixed topology)		78.67
ST-GCNs (learnable topology)		**79.92**
Fusion Methods		Accuracy (%)
Sum Fusion		86.68
Gated Fusion		84.5
Weighted Fusion		**88.36**

3.3   Ablation Studies

We conduct ablation experiments to analyze the impact of each module of our model (i.e. the components of the global and local branches and different fusion methods), as shown in Table 1.

First, we conduct experiments to analyze the impact of the spatial and the temporal multi-head self-attention in the global branch. We utilize the backbone followed by a 2-layer ST-LSTM [44] as the global baseline model, which achieves the accuracy at 81.04%. Employing the spatial MSA layers improves the accuracy by 0.82% over the baseline. When simultaneously applying the spatial and temporal MSA layers, the accuracy is augmented by 2.27% over the baseline, which proves the effectiveness of the global spatial-temporal graph and the spatio-temporal modelling capability of the proposed global branch.

Then, we examine the effectiveness of the local branch settings, by comparing the following models: the local baseline model using 3-layer ST-LSTM [44], ST-GCNs with fixed graph topology, and ST-GCNs of the same structure as the former with a learnable adjacency matrix. The local baseline achieves the accuracy at 76.41%, while ST-GCNs outperform it by 2.26%. Besides, for ST-GCNs, setting the adjacency matrix as learnable parameters improves the accuracy by 1.25%, which indicates that the recognition problem may benefit from the latent relationships between distant local regions explored by the model.

Finally, we compare the global branch, the local branch and three fusion methods including the sum fusion, the gated fusion and the weighted fusion. We observe that all the three fusions of the global and local branches perform better than any of the single branch, which demonstrates that the global structural information and the local dynamics captured by the two branches reinforce each other. Among the three fusion methods, the weighted fusion outperforms the others, for it learns to adaptively control the importance of each global and local feature element according to their contribution to prediction. However, the sum fusion and the gated fusion are less flexible, for they integrate the global

Table 2. Comparison with the State-of-the-art Methods on Oulu-CASIA.

Method	Model Type	Accuracy (%)
LBP-TOP (2007) [37]	Dynamic	68.13
HOG3D (2008) [38]	Dynamic	70.63
AdaLBP (2011) [34]	Dynamic	73.54
STM-Explet (2014) [39]	Dynamic	74.59
DTAGN (2015) [19]	Dynamic	81.46
PPDN (2016) [11]	Static	84.59
DCPN (2017) [12]	Static	86.23
PHRNN (2017) [41]	Dynamic	86.25
DeRL (2018) [10]	Static	88.0
LBVCNN (2019) [42]	Dynamic	82.41
STAFER (2022) [43]	Dynamic	88.34
Ours	**Dynamic**	**88.36**

Table 3. Comparison with the State-of-the-art Methods on AFEW.

Method	Model Type	Accuracy (%)
C3D-RNN (2016) [14]	Dynamic	45.43
SSE-HoloNet (2017) [6]	Dynamic	46.48
VGG-LSTM (2017) [15]	Dynamic	48.6
C3D-LSTM (2017) [15]	Dynamic	43.2
3D ResNet18 (2018) [40]	Dynamic	46.73
C3D-GRU (2019) [17]	Dynamic	49.87
FAN (2019) [13]	Dynamic	51.18
DGNN (2020) [24]	Dynamic	32.64
DGNN+C3D-GRU (2020) [24]	Dynamic	50.65
STT (2022) [29]	Dynamic	54.35
Ours (local branch)	Dynamic	49.33
Ours (global branch)	Dynamic	53.68
Ours	**Dynamic**	**55.82**

and local feature elements in sequential order. Therefore, the effectiveness of the global-local fusion strategy and the superiority of the weighted fusion, are verified.

3.4   Comparison with State-of-the-Art Methods

As shown in Table 2, our method achieves the best performance compared to those of state-of-the-art methods on Oulu-CASIA, including hand-crafted features based methods (LBP-TOP [37], HOG3D [38], AdaLBP [34] and STM-Explet [39]), CNN-based methods (DTAGN [19], PPDN [11], DCPN [12], DeRL [10], LBVCNN [42]), the RNN-based method PHRNN [41] and the attention-based method STAFER [43]. Only PPDN [11], DCPN [12] and DeRL [10] use the static image as input, while others propose to model temporal information from image sequences.

The comparison results on AFEW are reported in Table 3. C3D-RNN [14], SSE-HoloNet [6], VGG-LSTM [15], C3D-LSTM [15], 3D ResNet18 [40], C3D-GRU [17] are CNN-based dynamic methods. DGNN [24] is a graph-learning based method based on facial landmark features, DGNN +C3D-GRU indicates the fusion of DGNN and the video-based C3D-GRU [17]. The performance of the proposed local branch is significantly better than that of DGNN [24]. Different from the landmark-based graph representation, our method constructs the LSTG combining local visual features with the local facial topology, which reduces the data perturbation caused by the raw landmarks detected from in-the-wild images, and provides informative local features and relations for ST-GCNs to model the local dynamics. Our method outperforms the Transformer-based dynamic method STT [29], for we enhance the modelling of local information that complements to the global description, and effectively fuse them to achieve better discrimination. Therefore, the advance of the proposed global-local facial graph representation and fusion framework is verified.

4   Conclusion

We propose an attention-based global-local graph-learning method for dynamic facial expression recognition. The Ablation studies show that the global information encoded by the global branch with spatial-temporal MSA and the local information captured by the local branch with topology-learnable ST-GCNs reinforce each other and are effectively fused for reliable expression representation. The comparison results with other state-of-the-arts methods prove that the proposed facial graph representation alleviate the data perturbation problem of landmark-based features and our global-local fusion framework enhances the modelling of local details of the Transformer-based method. Our method achieves recognition accuracies of 88.36% and 55.82% on Oulu-CASIA and AFEW, respectively.

References

1. Liu, Z., et al.: A facial expression emotion recognition based human-robot interaction system. IEEE/CAA J. Automatica Sinica **4**(4), 668–676 (2017). IEEE
2. Lili, N.A., Nurul Amiraa, M.R., MasRina, M., Nurul Amelina, N.: Depression level detection from facial emotion recognition using image processing. In: Alfred, R., Lim, Y. (eds.) Proceedings of the 8th International Conference on Computational Science and Technology. LNEE, vol. 835, pp. 739–750. Springer, Singapore (2022). https://doi.org/10.1007/978-981-16-8515-6_56
3. Li, S., Deng, W., Du, J.: Reliable crowdsourcing and deep locality-preserving learning for unconstrained facial expression recognition. IEEE Trans. Image Process. **28**(1), 356–370 (2018)
4. Zhao, Z., Liu, Q., Wang, S.: Learning deep global multi-scale and local attention features for facial expression recognition in the wild. IEEE Trans. Image Process. **30**, 6544–6556 (2021)
5. Ma, F., Sun, B., Li, S.: Facial expression recognition with visual transformers and attentional selective fusion. IEEE Trans. Affect. Comput. (2021)

6. Hu, P., Cai, D., Wang, S., Yao, A., Chen, Y.: Learning supervised scoring ensemble for emotion recognition in the wild. In: Proceedings of the 19th ACM International Conference on Multimodal Interaction, pp. 553–560 (2017)

7. Huang, M. W., Wang, Z. W., Ying, Z. L.: A new method for facial expression recognition based on sparse representation plus LBP. In: 2010 3rd International Congress on Image and Signal Processing, pp. 1750–1754 (2010)

8. Lee, S.H., Baddar, W.J., Ro, Y.M.: Collaborative expression representation using peak expression and intra-class variation face images for practical subject-independent emotion recognition in videos. Pattern Recogn. **54**, 52–67 (2016)

9. Liu, Y., et al.: Conditional convolution neural network enhanced random forest for facial expression recognition. Pattern Recogn. **84**, 251–261 (2018)

10. Yang, H., Ciftci, U., Yin, L. : Facial expression recognition by de-expression residue learning. In: 2018 IEEE/CVF Conference on Computer Vision and Pattern Recognition, pp. 2168–2177 (2018)

11. Zhao, X., et al.: Peak-piloted deep network for facial expression recognition. In: Leibe, B., Matas, J., Sebe, N., Welling, M. (eds.) ECCV 2016. LNCS, vol. 9906, pp. 425–442. Springer, Cham (2016). https://doi.org/10.1007/978-3-319-46475-6_27

12. Yu, Z., Liu, Q., Liu, G.: Deeper cascaded peak-piloted network for weak expression recognition. Vis. Comput. **34**, 1691–1699 (2018). Springer

13. Meng, D., Peng, X., Wang, K., Qiao, Y: Frame attention networks for facial expression recognition in videos. In: IEEE International Conference on Image Processing (ICIP), pp. 3866–3870 (2019)

14. Fan, Y., Lu, X., Li, D., Liu, Y.: Video-based emotion recognition using CNN-RNN and C3D hybrid networks. In: Proceedings of the 18th ACM International Conference on Multimodal Interaction, pp. 445–450 (2016)

15. Vielzeuf, V., Pateux, S., Jurie, F.: Temporal multimodal fusion for video emotion classification in the wild. In: Proceedings of the 19th ACM International Conference on Multimodal Interaction, pp. 569–576 (2017)

16. Ayral, T., Pedersoli, M., Bacon, S., Granger, E.: Temporal stochastic softmax for 3D CNNs: an application in facial expression recognition. In: Proceedings of the IEEE/CVF Winter Conference on Applications of Computer Vision, pp. 3029–3038 (2021)

17. Lee, M.K., Choi, D.Y., Kim, D.H., Song, B.C.: Visual scene-aware hybrid neural network architecture for video-based facial expression recognition. In: 2019 14th IEEE International Conference on Automatic Face and Gesture Recognition, pp. 1–8. IEEE (2019)

18. Chen, W., Zhang, D., Li, M., Lee, D.J.: Stcam: spatial-temporal and channel attention module for dynamic facial expression recognition. IEEE Trans. Affect. Comput. (2020)

19. Jung, H., Lee, S., Yim, J., Park, S., Kim, J.: Joint fine-tuning in deep neural networks for facial expression recognition. In: Proceedings of the IEEE International Conference on Computer Vision, pp. 2983–2991. IEEE (2015)

20. Yan, J., et al.: Multi-cue fusion for emotion recognition in the wild. Neurocomputing **309**, 27–35 (2018)

21. Fabiano, D., Canavan, S.: Deformable synthesis model for emotion recognition. In: 2019 14th IEEE International Conference on Automatic Face and Gesture Recognition (FG 2019), pp. 1–5. IEEE (2019)

22. Y. Qiu, Y. Wan: Facial expression recognition based on landmarks. In: 2019 IEEE 4th Advanced Information Technology, Electronic and Automation Control Conference (IAEAC), pp. 1356–1360 (2019)

23. Rao, T., Li, J., Wang, X., Sun, Y., Chen, H.: Facial expression recognition with multiscale graph convolutional networks. IEEE Multimedia **28**(2), 11–19 (2021)

24. Ngoc, Q.T., Lee, S., Song, B.C.: Facial landmark-based emotion recognition via directed graph neural network. Electronics **9**(5), 764 (2020)

25. Liao, L., Zhu, Yu., Zheng, B., Jiang, X., Lin, J.: FERGCN: facial expression recognition based on graph convolution network. Mach. Vis. Appl. **33**(3), 1–13 (2022). https://doi.org/10.1007/s00138-022-01288-9

26. Meng, H., Yuan, F., Tian, Y., Yan, T.: Facial expression recognition based on landmark-guided graph convolutional neural network. J. Electron. Imaging **31**(2), 023025 (2022)

27. Zhang, L., Hong, X., Arandjelović, O., Zhao, G.: Short and long range relation based spatio-temporal transformer for micro-expression recognition. IEEE Trans. Affect. Comput. **13**(4), 1973–1985 (2022)

28. Zhao, Z., Liu, Q.: Former-DFER: dynamic facial expression recognition transformer. In: Proceedings of the 29th ACM International Conference on Multimedia, pp. 1553–1561 (2021)

29. Ma, F., Sun, B., Li, S.: Spatio-temporal transformer for dynamic facial expression recognition in the wild. arXiv preprint arXiv:2205.04749 (2022)

30. Zhao, W. et al.: Face recognition: a literature survey. Technical reports of Computer Vision Laboratory of University of Maryland (2000)

31. Yan, S., Xiong, Y., Lin, D.: Spatial temporal graph convolutional networks for skeleton-based action recognition. In: Thirty-Second AAAI Conference on Artificial Intelligence (2018)

32. Yu, B., Tao, D.: Heatmap regression via randomized rounding. IEEE Trans. Pattern Anal. Mach. Intell. (2021)

33. Vaswani, A. et al.: Attention is all you need. In: Advances in Neural Information Processing Systems (2017)

34. Zhao, G., Huang, X., Taini, M., Li, S.Z., Pietikäalnen, M.: Facial expression recognition from near-infrared videos. Image Vis. Comput. **29**(9), 607–619 (2011)

35. Dhall, A.: Emotiw 2019: automatic emotion, engagement and cohesion prediction tasks. In: International Conference on Multimodal Interaction, pp. 546–550 (2019)

36. Guo, Y., Zhang, L., Hu, Y., He, X., Gao, J.: MS-Celeb-1M: a dataset and benchmark for large-scale face recognition. In: Leibe, B., Matas, J., Sebe, N., Welling, M. (eds.) ECCV 2016. LNCS, vol. 9907, pp. 87–102. Springer, Cham (2016). https://doi.org/10.1007/978-3-319-46487-9_6

37. Zhao, G., Pietikainen, M.: Dynamic texture recognition using local binary patterns with an application to facial expressions. IEEE Trans. Pattern Anal. Mach. Intell. **29**(6), 915–928 (2017)

38. Klaser, A., Marszałek, M., Schmid, C.: A spatio-temporal descriptor based on 3D-gradients. In: British Machine Vision Conference, pp. 275–1 (2008)

39. Liu, M., Shan, S., Wang, R., Chen, X.: Learning expressionlets on spatio-temporal manifold for dynamic facial expression recognition. In: Proceedings of the IEEE Conference on Computer Vision and Pattern Recognition, pp. 1749–1756 (2014)

40. Hara, K., Kataoka, H., Satoh, Y.: Can spatiotemporal 3D CNNs retrace the history of 2D CNNs and imagenet?. In: Proceedings of the IEEE Conference on Computer Vision and Pattern Recognition, pp. 6546–6555 (2018)

41. Zhang, K., Huang, Y., Du, Y., Wang, L.: Facial expression recognition based on deep evolutional spatial-temporal networks. IEEE Trans. Image Process. **26**(9), 4193–4203 (2017)

42. Kumawat, S., Verma, M., Raman, S.: LBVCNN: local binary volume convolutional neural network for facial expression recognition from image sequences. In: Proceedings of the IEEE/CVF Conference on Computer Vision and Pattern Recognition Workshops (2019)
43. Zhang, L., Zheng, X., Chen, X., Ren, X., Ji, C.: Facial expression recognition based on spatial-temporal fusion with attention mechanism. Neural Process. Lett. 1–16 (2022)
44. Liu, J., Shahroudy, A., Xu, D., Wang, G.: Spatio-temporal LSTM with trust gates for 3D human action recognition. In: Leibe, B., Matas, J., Sebe, N., Welling, M. (eds.) ECCV 2016. LNCS, vol. 9907, pp. 816–833. Springer, Cham (2016). https://doi.org/10.1007/978-3-319-46487-9_50

Implicit Representation for Interacting Hands Reconstruction from Monocular Color Images

Binghui Zuo[1,2], Zimeng Zhao[1,2], Wei Xie[1,2], and Yangang Wang[1,2(✉)]

[1] School of Automation, Southeast University, Nanjing, China
[2] Key Laboratory of Measurement and Control of Complex Systems of Engineering, Ministry of Education, Nanjing, China
yangangwang@seu.edu.cn

Abstract. Reconstructing interacting hands from monocular color images plays an important role in promoting the understanding of human behavior and the application of existing AR/VR technology. With the emergence of interacting hands datasets, numerous data-driven methods attempt to regress the MANO parameters of the left and right hand from the network. This formulation not only limits the handedness and the number of hands in the image but also introduces the deficiencies of the MANO into the interacting-hand reconstruction task. To address this obstacle, we present a novel framework for representing the surface of interacting hands with implicit functions. Our key idea is to construct an implicit neural occupancy network, which implicitly reconstructs interacting hands with image features as query strategies and conditions. The proposed query strategies only require one sample to obtain enough points on the surface. Our unified framework efficiently completes the task of reconstructing hands with the unlimited number, handedness, and interaction compactness from monocular color images.

Keywords: Interacting hands reconstruction · Implicit function · Query strategies · Query conditions

1 Introduction

Interacting hands are ubiquitous in our daily life, whether driven by a single person to express emotions or by multiple persons to collaborate. To reconstruct their states from monocular color images, those methods for isolated hand reconstruction [1,41] always become invalid since the interacting hands occupy similar space and have a similar appearance. Furthermore, due to the high degree of articulation and occlusion between interacting hands, it is more challenging to reconstruct interactions than a single hand.

Early approaches tend to leverage extra depth information [31,32] or multiviews [10] as the input. However, they always fit the input data to a specific

This work was supported in part by the Natural Science Foundation of Jiangsu Province (No. BK20220127), the National Key R&D Program of China under Grant 2018YFB1403900.

H. Lu et al. (Eds.): ICIG 2023, LNCS 14355, pp. 16–28, 2023.
https://doi.org/10.1007/978-3-031-46305-1_2

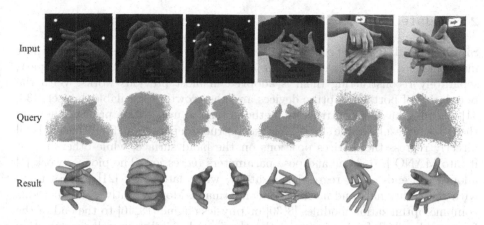

Fig. 1. Interacting hands reconstruction with implicit function. For better visualization, only partial queries are shown.

hand template without personalized variations and could not be adapted to the existing learning-based methods. The construction of Interhand2.6M [23] brings data support to this task and subsequently promotes the birth of a series of methods [4,9,28,35] for the reconstruction of interacting hands from the monocular color images. Most of these methods regress MANO [27] parameters under the assumption that only one left and right hand exist in the input image.

It is noted that existing hand parameters regression networks require the input of single-hand features extracted from the images, which is always tricky for interacting hands. To reduce the burden of feature extraction for the individual hand, our key idea is to **use a neural occupancy network to recast this task as 3D query points classification of interacting hands, while the image features are regarded as conditions and strategies in the query process**. Notably, there are no restrictions on the number of instances, the relative distance, or the left/right side of the hands in the input image, broadening the application scenes of this framework.

In contrast to existing implicit schemes [17,20,29] that reconstruct a single surface without interactions, the proposed method manages to reconstruct multiple hands that interact closely. To achieve this goal, it is designed as a framework conditioned on the *region* features. A *region* is defined as a connected component in the hand mask estimated from the input. Furthermore, we creatively use the silhouette, relative depth, and joint distribution information extracted from the region to construct a Gaussian mixture mode in 3D space and query in parallel. The efficiency of querying is significantly improved compared with [20].

In summary, we make the following contributions:

- A pioneering framework is proposed to implicitly reconstruct interacting hands as an implicit function;
- A series of novel query conditions and query strategies are devised to increase the query efficiency and reduce the query space according to the image clues;
- An unified framework with no restrictions on the number of hands, which greatly expands the scope of application.

2   Related Work

Single Hand Reconstruction. The related methods discussed in this part mainly take a monocular color image as input. When two hands are far apart, separately reconstructing them is adopted in most previous works. With the popularity of portable capture devices and the growth of available datasets [36, 41], learning-based reconstruction methods tend to utilize data prior to alleviate the extreme results in the single-view reconstruction paradigm. Some methods [6] directly regress the vertices positions on the hand surface, while others recast it into MANO [27] shape and pose parameters regression. The pioneer work [1] adopts the end-to-end regression strategy, while later ones [21] regress them with the additional hand mask or joint heatmaps. More recently, some methods combine optimization modules [8, 30] or physics engine [13, 40] to the end of the framework, which further increases the physical plausibility as well as projection consistency. Although MANO parameters are compact enough to reduce the redundancy of hand surface vertices, some researchers [22, 40] point out that this representation is difficult to perform collision detection and lacks joint DoF constraints.

Interacting Hands Reconstruction. When interacting hands entangle together, the available features in the images are further reduced due to mutual occlusions and visual similarities. Some works estimate the pose of interacting hands using multi-view [10] or extra depth information [31, 32]. As the basis, some works contribute interacting hands datasets and baseline methods using multi-view system [23, 32]. In terms of representation, most studies [4, 9, 23, 28, 35] reconstruct interaction as two independent objects and estimate two sets of MANO parameters as well as the relative offset from one to the other. Among them, [28] combines optimization modules to reduce the collision between two hands. [4] performs part segmentations to identify two hands and they consistently follow the assumption in [23] that only one left and right hand exist in the scene. In our method, we implicitly reconstruct interacting hands from the query points without restricting the handedness in the images.

Hand Representation for Reconstruction. Explicit representation of articulated objects is widely used in the community: the point clouds [5, 7, 25], the meshes [6, 27] and others [38]. [31] combines the skinned tetrahedral mesh and signed distance function of a fixed hand to create the first implicit hand representation. However, this representation is only suitable for hand-tracking applications because it relies on the hand depth map as input and cannot be applied to scenes with hand shape variations. In recent years, using neural networks to represent 3D objects [3, 20] implicitly and continuously has attracted extensive researches. Some works try to use implicit representation in the tasks of 3D registration [33], reconstruction [16, 17, 29] and free-viewpoint rendering [2]. Nevertheless, existing implicit representations suffer from a complex query process and difficulty in controlling surface continuity. We introduce the implicit representation to interacting hands as the topology structure is more flexible. Besides that, more efficient query conditions and query strategies are proposed to improve the efficiency of the reconstruction.

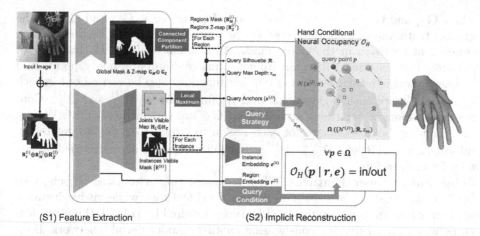

Fig. 2. Overview of our proposed method. It mainly includes two steps: extracting features from the input image and implicitly reconstructing based on the proposed query strategies and query conditions.

3 Method

An overview of our framework to reconstruct interacting hands from monocular color images is shown in Fig. 2. It consists of two main steps: extracting top-level and bottom-level hand features from the image (Sect. 3.1), sampling query points based on features from the image and building neural occupancy network to obtain occupancy value (Sect. 3.2). To enable the training of our neural occupancy, the used datasets are preprocessed as described in Sect. 3.3. All superscripts enclosed by brackets denote the index of the different features: i is used to indicate regions, j to joints, and k to hand instances.

3.1 Feature Extraction

Global and Region Features. The images containing hand features are processed sequentially at three levels: The global information corresponds to the whole image; A region is used to describe a cluster of hands that have an intersection in the image; Each instance indicates a specific hand in the region. Firstly, an input image I is divided into multiple regions $\mathbf{R}_M^{(i)}$ based on the connected components in the mask $\mathbf{G}_M$ of the segmentation of the hands. This function is implemented through a network with an encoder-decoder architecture with ResNet18 [12] as the backbone. Using an encoder-decoder architecture network, we first feed color image I into this network to generate corresponding global mask $\mathbf{G}_M$ and global Z-map $\mathbf{G}_Z$ respectively. We use MSE loss to supervise these two global features:

$$\mathcal{L}_{\text{Global}} = \|\hat{\mathbf{G}}_M - \mathbf{G}_M^*\|_2^2 + \|\hat{\mathbf{G}}_Z - \mathbf{G}_Z^*\|_2^2, \tag{1}$$

where $\hat{\mathbf{G}}_M$ and $\hat{\mathbf{G}}_Z$ are the predicted results from network, $\mathbf{G}_M^*$ and $\mathbf{G}_Z^*$ are the ground truth values from datasets. We pay more attention to each connected component partition in the global mask. As mentioned above, in this way, we decouple each intersection region from the image. Sampling query points and reconstructing hands surface using implicit functions also be carried out in each region. We mark each region mask and region Z-map as $\mathbf{R}_M^{(i)}$ and $\mathbf{R}_Z^{(i)}$. Connected component partitions according to $\mathbf{G}_M$ are further performed. We use the bounding box coordinates of each region to crop $I, \mathbf{G}_M, \mathbf{G}_Z$ to get region information, $i.e. \{\mathbf{R}_I^{(i)}\}, \{\mathbf{R}_M^{(i)}\}, \{\mathbf{R}_Z^{(i)}\}$. The following steps are performed in parallel for each region.

Joint and Instance Features. When reconstructing articulated objects, visible joint localizations are common bottom-level features, while visible instance segmentations are common top-level features. Inspired by [14, 34], these two features are extracted simultaneously using another encoder-decoder network. Both features are extracted using map-based regression [15]. The ground truth of joint localization map $\mathbf{H}_L^{(i)}$ and corresponding $\mathbf{H}_Z^{(i)}$ are similar to the pioneer work [34, 39]. In practice, this sub-network shares the encoder with the previous one and uses its own decoder, except that the last layer has more channels and the same structure as the previous one. It is worth noting that we refer to [9] to put all joints into the same channel because these features are regarded as peer information later to guide the query of neural occupancy. The precision of instance partitioning is less demanding, and it is used as a flag bit of the query to distinguish which instance of the current region is the current query object. Theoretically, there is no limit to the number of instances in each region. Considering that the number of hands in the most available datasets is always less than two, we set $k \leq 2$.

3.2   Implicit Reconstruction

Query Strategy. Different from the previous methods [16, 17, 24] that sample query points around the surface or uniformly in a cube, we propose a region-guided strategy. For a region $\{\mathbf{R}_M^{(i)}, \mathbf{R}_Z^{(i)}\}$, we first find query silhouette $\mathcal{R}$ and max query depth z_m corresponding to it. Then, using $\mathcal{R}$ as bottom area, z_m as height, we uniformly sample points in a space $\Omega(\{\mathcal{N}_j\}, \mathcal{R}, z_m)$, where $\mathcal{N}_j = \mathcal{N}(\mathbf{x}^{(j)}, \sigma)$ denotes a Gaussian mixture distribution with each visible joints coordinate $\mathbf{x}^{(j)}$ as the center and σ as the variance of each dimension, we set σ to 2.5 in our experiments. Intuitively, in this sampling space, we regard each visible joint as an anchor and sample more queries around it to obtain more surface geometry details. By concatenating the query points uniformly sampled from space and around anchors, we normalize them to a unit cube.

Query Condition. We segment each hand in a region to obtain instance mask $\{\mathbf{E}^{(k)}\}$ where k denotes the hand index. We feed each instance into an MLP to encode instance embedding $e^{(k)}$. Besides, using the encoder designed to extract features, we also extract region embedding $r^{(i)}$ for each region cropped by connected component partitions. We take these two embeddings as the conditions of implicit reconstruction and let them guide the reconstruction process. For different regions in an image, we use the same query strategy and query condition. The fewer the number of hands in an area, the less difficult it is to reconstruct. Assuming that there are two interacting hands in a specific region, using the trained network, we segment and encode each hand to obtain instance embeddings named instance embedding $e^{(1)}$ and instance embedding $e^{(2)}$. These embeddings directly influence the query target. In other words, for embedding $e^{(1)}$, which points in all queries belonging to this hand can be judged by the neural network. Furthermore, to apply our implicit representation method to more different regions, we also take the region embedding $r^{(i)}$ as one of the conditions of implicit reconstruction. Because $r^{(i)}$ denotes the characteristics corresponding to different regions. It is worth noting that we do not pay more attention to the left/right side in this region. This means in a special region, the instance features $e^{(k)}$ may represent not only one left hand and one right hand but also two left hands or two right hands.

Implicit Function. Based on the proposed query strategies and query conditions, we build a parameterized neural network $\mathcal{O}_H$, which is treated as an implicit function. The neural network takes a combination $(p, r^{(i)}, e^{(k)})$ as input and outputs a occupancy value τ:

$$\mathcal{O}_H(p \mid r, e) = \tau. \tag{2}$$

In our experiments, the interacting hands surface is implicitly represented by the isosurface of $\tau = 0.5$. It means that a query point p is regarded as outer when $\mathcal{O}_H(p) < 0.5$, and as inner when $\mathcal{O}_H(p) > 0.5$. Before training, the ground truth of occupancy value is recorded. We use the cross-entropy loss to supervise it. In addition, penetration loss is also adopted to penalize the collision on the hand surface. Considering that each query point $p \in \mathbb{R}^3$ belongs to at most one hand instance, it is defined as:

$$\mathcal{L}_{\text{pene.}} = \sum_{p \in \Omega} \sum_{k} \mathcal{O}_H\left(p \mid r, e^{(k)}\right), \text{ where } \mathcal{O}_H(\cdot) > 0.5, \tag{3}$$

where the range of k is equal to the number of hands in each region.

3.3   Data Preprocessing

Coordinate Transformation. All data is converted to the camera coordinate, and the data captured by the multi-view completes the process with the camera's external parameters. Because the implicit reconstruction usually requires image-aligned features [29], we follow the steps below to prepare the dataset for training. Since the distance between the hands and the camera is usually much larger than the focal length of the camera, we assume that the imaging process of the camera follows orthogonal projection and projects a camera coordinate $(x_c, y_c, z_c), z_c \neq 0$ onto the image (u, v) by: $(u, v, z) = (\frac{f_x}{z_c} \cdot x_c + c_x, \frac{f_y}{z_c} \cdot y_c + c_y, \frac{1}{z_c} \cdot z_c)$. This process loses depth information because the dimension corresponding to z does not perform the same scaling as the other two dimensions. So we repair it to the following formulation: $(u, v, z) = (\frac{f_x}{z_c} \cdot x_c + c_x, \frac{f_y}{z_c} \cdot y_c + c_y, \frac{f_x + f_y}{2 \cdot \bar{z}} \cdot z_c)$. Where $\bar{z}$ is the average depth of the vertices of all hands in the image. Eventually, it will also be subtracted from the minimum depth value of all vertices. After this, the effect of internal camera parameters is eliminated, and all the explicit meshes are aligned to the image coordinate with pixel units. They can be regarded as imaging results under an orthogonal projection with a focal length of 1 and an offset of 0.

Pixel-Aligned Depth Recording. The above explicit mesh is processed as point clouds according to the image coordinates. Specifically, all depth values for each ray casting from the pixel coordinates in the positive z-direction and intersecting each hand mesh are stored. To easily determine the inner and outer relationship between query points and mesh during training, we add extra faces at the wrist of the MANO model to make it watertight.

Ground Truth for Image Feature. In the training process of image feature extraction, we perform supervision on the global mask $\mathbf{G}_M$ and Z-map $\mathbf{G}_Z$, joints visible location map $\mathbf{H}_L$ and corresponding $\mathbf{H}_Z$, and instances visible mask $\mathbf{E}$. Both $\mathbf{G}_M, \mathbf{G}_Z$ and $\mathbf{E}$ are rendered by Pytorch3D [26]. The joint location maps $\mathbf{H}_L$ are prepared as the same as [15,34].

4 Experiments

In this section, we first introduce the datasets and evaluation metrics used for training and evaluating in Sect. 4.1. Comparisons with the state-of-the-art methods on benchmark datasets are shown in Sect. 4.2. We also conduct ablation experiments to evaluate the effectiveness of our key components in Sect. 4.3.

4.1 Datasets and Metrics

Datasets. We train and evaluate our method on two challenging datasets including InterHand2.6M [23] and HIC [32]. We use the latest InterHand2.6M version and the ground truth annotated by H+M. Only the subsets of HIC recording hand interaction are used, whose corresponding MANO annotations were registered by Hasson *et al.* [11].

Mesh Error. Instead of the mean per-vertex position error ($MPVPE$) with the fixed surface vertices requirement, we use chamfer distance (CD) between our queried surface points and the ground truth vertices to measure the accuracy of each reconstructed surface. To evaluate the relative state between two hands, intersection volume ($InterVol$) proposed in [16] is also adopted.

Joint Error. We use the mean per-joint position error ($MPJPE$) and the mean relative-root position error ($MRRPE$) in millimeters to measure the accuracy of interacting hands joints and relative position respectively. Considering that

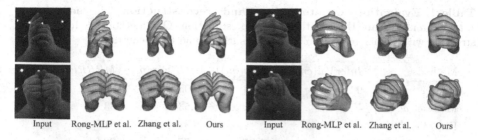

| Input | Rong-MLP et al. | Zhang et al. | Ours | Input | Rong-MLP et al. | Zhang et al. | Ours |

Fig. 3. Qualitative comparisons with SOTA methods on InterHand2.6M.

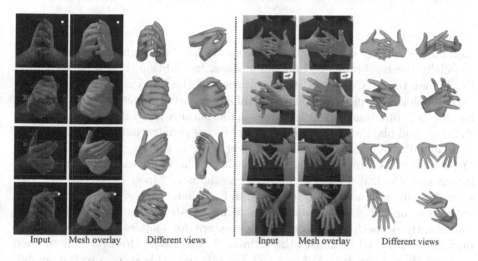

| Input | Mesh overlay | Different views | Input | Mesh overlay | Different views |

Fig. 4. Qualitative results on InterHand2.6M and HIC. For better visualization, the explicit surface is reconstructed with the marching cube [19].

the joint positions cannot be directly regressed from the vertices represented by the implicit function, we use the method proposed in [37] to estimate the joint coordinates according to the query points on the surface.

4.2   Comparisons

Implementation Details. The input and output size of the global feature extraction network is 256×256. The output size of the joint and instance feature extraction network is 64×64. We implement our method with Pytorch. The Adam optimizer [18] is used to train our network with a batch size of 64 and a learning rate of 1e-4. We train our network on a single NVIDIA GeForce RTX 3090 GPU. The architecture of the neural occupancy network is lightweight with 3 convolutional layers to encode the instance mask feature and 9 fully connected layers to represent the implicit surface.

Qualitative Results. To compare with existing methods [28,35] intuitively, we show our qualitative comparisons in Fig. 3. Benefitting from our implicit-based

Table 1. Evaluations of interacting hands reconstruction. The methods w/o *InterVol* and *CD* are those with only pose estimation. Our method produces reconstruction with higher resolution, smoother surfaces and less penetration.

Methods	$InterVol(cm^3)\downarrow$	$CD(mm)\downarrow$	$MPJPE(mm)\downarrow$	$MRRPE(mm)\downarrow$
Rong *et al.* [28]	9.24	36.74	19.05	35.56
Moon *et al.* [23]	-	-	16.53	33.14
Fan *et al.* [4]	-	-	15.37	31.73
Zhang *et al.* [35]	5.02	21.37	13.77	26.21
Ours	3.25	11.02	14.12	22.17

method, the quality of reconstructed geometry has been significantly improved, especially the resolution of the hand surface. In addition, it can be seen from Fig. 3 that the MANO-based representation of the hand is influenced by the fixed topological template, making it difficult to avoid penetration, while using the implicit function to represent the hand surface generates a flexible hand structure and plays an important role in reducing penetration. We further report more qualitative results with our framework in Fig. 4.

Quantitative Comparisons. Table 1 shows the comparison results on the InterHand2.6M [23] datasets. Since the methods of Moon *et al.* [23] and Fan *et al.* [4] only estimate hand 3D joints and not hand meshes, we only compare with them on 3D pose estimation. In terms of *MPJPE* metrics, our method significantly outperforms other methods except for [35], as the context-aware module used in [35] optimizes the estimated two hands. However, our method significantly reduces *InterVol* and *CD*. We attribute this success to the flexibility of the implicit function representation, which does not depend on a specific template.

4.3   Ablation Studies

Accuracy of Image Features. We verify the necessity of each block within the image features extractor, including the global feature extraction network and connected component partition. The reasoning structure from naïve to complex is shown in Fig. 5(a)-(c). All networks have the same input and conduct the same multi-task inference. Scheme (a) is an end-to-end extractor to perform tasks on the entire image. Scheme (b) is the version that adds global feature maps as an intermediate. Scheme (c) can be regarded as adding a connected component partition to scheme (b). Their performances in hand joint localization and instance segmentation are shown in Table 2. Scheme (a) has a lighter structure, but its performances are much lower than other schemes. Compared with scheme (b), the final version does not increase the number of parameters, but the performance has been greatly improved. Finally, scheme (c) is selected as the image extractor in our framework.

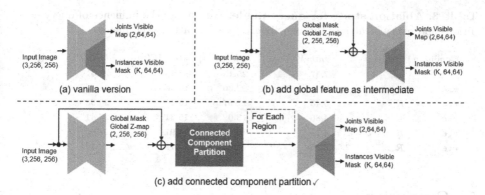

Fig. 5. Variations of image feature extraction. A variety of hand-feature extraction modules have been tried. Finally, we choose scheme (c) after ablating.

Table 2. Ablation study for image feature extractor. The three different extraction variants differ in terms of joint localization, instance segmentation and parameter amount. They are in the same order as in Fig. 5.

Extraction Scheme	(a) vanilla	(b) add global	(c) final ✓
2D-MPJPE (mm)	15.25	13.54	11.42
IoU (%)	81.3	85.8	90.6
Parameters (M)	16.9	33.7	33.7

Advantages of Implicit Representation. As the surface of interacting hands is represented by an implicit function in this work, the advantages of implicit representation can be directly derived from the comparison with existing MANO-based methods. From Row-4 and Row-5 of Table 1. In the case that the *MPJPE* is weaker than [35], our method demonstrates the superior performance on *InterVol* and *CD*, which indicates that the implicit-based methods have more advantages in solving collision, thus reducing the penetration.

Efficiency of Query Mode. The ablation of the query condition is shown in Row1-Row2 of Table 3. With the region embedding $r^{(i)}$, features extracted from different regions are distinguished, making the reconstruction more accurate than the case where only instance embedding is regarded as the condition. From Row2-Row5 of Table 3, with the consistent query conditions, we gradually refine the query strategies until the method uses all the query strategies and conditions proposed in this paper. Interestingly, with the refinement of the query space, we obtain more accurate reconstruction while ensuring more efficient queries. This may be due to the refined query space allowing the network to focus more on the hand surface, thus improving the accuracy of the reconstruction. The details of the final query strategy, i.e. different variances of Gaussian mixture distribution around visible joint coordinates, are shown in Row5-Row6.

Table 3. Ablation study for query mode. We explore the influence of query conditions and query strategies through six groups of ablation experiments.

Condition	Strategy	$InterVol(cm^3)\downarrow$	$CD(mm)\downarrow$	$MPJPE(mm)\downarrow$	$MRRPE(mm)\downarrow$
e	no	7.57	25.13	17.13	28.51
r, e	no	6.91	22.66	16.36	28.20
r, e	$\mathcal{R}$	5.43	17.57	16.11	26.98
r, e	$\mathcal{R}, z_m$	4.86	13.02	15.71	26.41
r, e	$\mathcal{R}, z_m, \sigma = 1.5$	4.15	12.44	14.97	24.96
r, e	$\mathcal{R}, z_m, \sigma = 2.5$	3.25	11.02	14.12	22.17

5   Conclusion

In this paper, a framework based on implicit representation is proposed to overcome the spatial entanglement of interacting hands. This method has fewer restrictions on the characteristics and the number of hands in the image. When performing the classification of query points, the proposed query strategies based on the image features allow us to obtain a more credible surface with fewer query times. The query conditions including region embeddings and instance embeddings enable the neural network to be reused to represent the hand surface with the variations of pose and shape. The ablation studies verify the high performance of our method. However, for those interactions with severe occlusion, using explicit representation may result in more accurate reconstructions. In the future, the most immediate migration scene for this reconstruction paradigm can be the multi-body reconstruction from monocular images.

References

1. Boukhayma, A., Bem, R.D., Torr, P.H.: 3D hand shape and pose from images in the wild. In: CVPR, pp. 10843–10852 (2019)
2. Chen, X., Zheng, Y., Black, M.J., Hilliges, O., Geiger, A.: SNARF: differentiable forward skinning for animating non-rigid neural implicit shapes. In: ICCV, pp. 11594–11604 (2021)
3. Deng, B., et al.: NASA neural articulated shape approximation. In: Vedaldi, A., Bischof, H., Brox, T., Frahm, J.-M. (eds.) ECCV 2020. LNCS, vol. 12352, pp. 612–628. Springer, Cham (2020). https://doi.org/10.1007/978-3-030-58571-6_36
4. Fan, Z., Spurr, A., Kocabas, M., Tang, S., Black, M.J., Hilliges, O.: Learning to disambiguate strongly interacting hands via probabilistic per-pixel part segmentation. In: 3DV, pp. 1–10. IEEE (2021)
5. Ge, L., Cai, Y., Weng, J., Yuan, J.: Hand PointNet: 3D hand pose estimation using point sets. In: CVPR, pp. 8417–8426 (2018)
6. Ge, L., et al.: 3D hand shape and pose estimation from a single RGB image. In: CVPR, pp. 10833–10842 (2019)
7. Ge, L., Ren, Z., Yuan, J.: Point-to-point regression PointNet for 3D hand pose estimation. In: ECCV, pp. 475–491 (2018)
8. Grady, P., Tang, C., Twigg, C.D., Vo, M., Brahmbhatt, S., Kemp, C.C.: ContactOpt: optimizing contact to improve grasps. In: CVPR, pp. 1471–1481 (2021)

9. Hampali, S., Sarkar, S.D., Rad, M., Lepetit, V.: HandsFormer: keypoint transformer for monocular 3D pose estimation of hands and object in interaction. arXiv preprint arXiv:2104.14639 (2021)
10. Han, S., et al.: MEgATrack: monochrome egocentric articulated hand-tracking for virtual reality. ACM TOG **39**(4), 87–1 (2020)
11. Hasson, Y., et al.: Learning joint reconstruction of hands and manipulated objects. In: CVPR, pp. 11807–11816 (2019)
12. He, K., Zhang, X., Ren, S., Sun, J.: Deep residual learning for image recognition. In: CVPR, pp. 770–778 (2016)
13. Huang, B., Pan, L., Yang, Y., Ju, J., Wang, Y.: Neural MoCon: neural motion control for physically plausible human motion capture. In: CVPR, pp. 6417–6426 (2022)
14. Huang, B., Zhang, T., Wang, Y.: Object-occluded human shape and pose estimation with probabilistic latent consistency. IEEE TPAMI **45**(4), 5010–5026 (2022)
15. Iqbal, U., Molchanov, P., Gall, T.B.J., Kautz, J.: Hand pose estimation via latent 2.5D heatmap regression. In: ECCV, pp. 118–134 (2018)
16. Karunratanakul, K., Spurr, A., Fan, Z., Hilliges, O., Tang, S.: A skeleton-driven neural occupancy representation for articulated hands. In: 3DV, pp. 11–21. IEEE (2021)
17. Karunratanakul, K., Yang, J., Zhang, Y., Black, M.J., Muandet, K., Tang, S.: Grasping Field: learning implicit representations for human grasps. In: 3DV, pp. 333–344. IEEE (2020)
18. Kingma, D.P., Ba, J.: Adam: a method for stochastic optimization. arXiv preprint arXiv:1412.6980 (2014)
19. Lorensen, W.E., Cline, H.E.: Marching Cubes: a high resolution 3D surface construction algorithm. ACM Siggraph Comput. Graph. **21**(4), 163–169 (1987)
20. Mescheder, L., Oechsle, M., Niemeyer, M., Nowozin, S., Geiger, A.: Occupancy networks: learning 3D reconstruction in function space. In: CVPR, pp. 4460–4470 (2019)
21. Moon, G., Lee, K.M.: I2L-MeshNet: Image-to-Lixel prediction network for accurate 3D human pose and mesh estimation from a single RGB image. In: Vedaldi, A., Bischof, H., Brox, T., Frahm, J.-M. (eds.) ECCV 2020. LNCS, vol. 12352, pp. 752–768. Springer, Cham (2020). https://doi.org/10.1007/978-3-030-58571-6_44
22. Moon, G., Shiratori, T., Lee, K.M.: DeepHandMesh: a weakly-supervised deep encoder-decoder framework for high-fidelity hand mesh modeling. In: Vedaldi, A., Bischof, H., Brox, T., Frahm, J.-M. (eds.) ECCV 2020. LNCS, vol. 12347, pp. 440–455. Springer, Cham (2020). https://doi.org/10.1007/978-3-030-58536-5_26
23. Moon, G., Yu, S.-I., Wen, H., Shiratori, T., Lee, K.M.: InterHand2.6M: a dataset and baseline for 3D interacting hand pose estimation from a single RGB image. In: Vedaldi, A., Bischof, H., Brox, T., Frahm, J.-M. (eds.) ECCV 2020. LNCS, vol. 12365, pp. 548–564. Springer, Cham (2020). https://doi.org/10.1007/978-3-030-58565-5_33
24. Park, J.J., Florence, P., Straub, J., Newcombe, R., Lovegrove, S.: DeepSDF: learning continuous signed distance functions for shape representation. In: CVPR, pp. 165–174 (2019)
25. Qin, H., Zhang, S., Liu, Q., Chen, L., Chen, B.: PointSkelCNN: deep learning-based 3D human skeleton extraction from point clouds. In: Computer Graphics Forum, vol. 39, pp. 363–374. Wiley Online Library (2020)
26. Ravi, N., et al.: Accelerating 3D deep learning with PyTorch3D. arXiv:2007.08501 (2020)

27. Romero, J., Tzionas, D., Black, M.J.: Embodied Hands: modeling and capturing hands and bodies together. ACM TOG **36**(6), 1–17 (2017)
28. Rong, Y., Wang, J., Liu, Z., Loy, C.C.: Monocular 3D reconstruction of interacting hands via collision-aware factorized refinements. In: 3DV, pp. 432–441. IEEE (2021)
29. Saito, S., Huang, Z., Natsume, R., Morishima, S., Kanazawa, A., Li, H.: PIFU: pixel-aligned implicit function for high-resolution clothed human digitization. In: ICCV, pp. 2304–2314 (2019)
30. Smith, B., et al.: Constraining dense hand surface tracking with elasticity. ACM TOG **39**(6), 1–14 (2020)
31. Taylor, J., et al.: Articulated distance fields for ultra-fast tracking of hands interacting. ACM TOG **36**(6), 1–12 (2017)
32. Tzionas, D., Ballan, L., Srikantha, A., Aponte, P., Pollefeys, M., Gall, J.: Capturing hands in action using discriminative salient points and physics simulation. IJCV **118**(2), 172–193 (2016)
33. Wang, S., Geiger, A., Tang, S.: Locally aware piecewise transformation fields for 3D human mesh registration. In: CVPR, pp. 7639–7648 (2021)
34. Wang, Y., Zhang, B., Peng, C.: SRHandNet: real-time 2D hand pose estimation with simultaneous region localization. IEEE TIP **29**, 2977–2986 (2019)
35. Zhang, B., et al.: Interacting two-hand 3D pose and shape reconstruction from single color image. In: ICCV, pp. 11354–11363 (2021)
36. Zhang, J., Jiao, J., Chen, M., Qu, L., Xu, X., Yang, Q.: 3D hand pose tracking and estimation using stereo matching. arXiv preprint arXiv:1610.07214 (2016)
37. Zhao, Z., Rao, R., Wang, Y.: Supple: Extracting hand skeleton with spherical unwrapping profiles. In: 3DV, pp. 899–909 (2021)
38. Zhao, Z., Xie, W., Zuo, B., Wang, Y.: Skeleton extraction for articulated objects with the spherical unwrapping profiles. IEEE TVCG (2023)
39. Zhao, Z., Zhao, X., Wang, Y.: TravelNet: self-supervised physically plausible hand motion learning from monocular color images. In: ICCV, pp. 11666–11676 (2021)
40. Zhao, Z., Zuo, B., Xie, W., Wang, Y.: Stability-driven contact reconstruction from monocular color images. In: CVPR, pp. 1643–1653 (2022)
41. Zimmermann, C., Ceylan, D., Yang, J., Russell, B., Argus, M., Brox, T.: Frei-HAND: a dataset for markerless capture of hand pose and shape from single RGB images. In: ICCV, pp. 813–822 (2019)

HQFS: High-Quality Feature Selection for Accurate Change Detection

Yan Xing[1], Qi'ao Xu[2], Qingyi Zhao[2], Rui Huang[2(✉)], and Yuxiang Zhang[2]

[1] College of Safety Science and Engineering, Civil Aviation University of China,
Tianjin, China
yxing@cauc.edu.cn
[2] College of Computer Science and Technology, Civil Aviation University of China,
Tianjin, China
{2021052074,2022051007,rhuang,yxzhang}@cauc.edu.cn

Abstract. High-quality features play a crucial role in achieving accurate change detection (CD). However, current CD methods often rely on simple combinations of features or the computations of feature differences between bi-temporal images, which cannot fully explore the representative capacity of features. In this paper, we design a *high-quality feature selection module*, called HQFS, to generate high-quality change-related features for accurate CD. Firstly, we analyze the pros and cons of the features utilized in recent deep learning-based CD methods. Based on this analysis, we construct a feature pool containing various change-related features. The proposed HQFS module is then employed to learn the importance of these features and assign higher weights to the high-quality features to amplify their contributions in computing the change maps. To further enhance the performance, we propose two additional components: the *fully attention enhanced feature extraction network* and the *attention pyramid fusion & change mask prediction module*. The former focuses on extracting features from images, while the latter leverages attention mechanisms and pyramid fusion techniques to generate accurate change predictions. Comprehensive experiments on three benchmark datasets demonstrate the superiority of our method over seven state-of-the-art change detectors.

Keywords: Change detection · Feature selection · High-quality features · Attention enhancement · Feature fusion

1 Introduction

Change detection (CD) aims to distinguish actual changes from background environmental changes within a bi-temporal image pair captured at different times but depicting the same scene [1]. The CD technique has wide-ranging applications in various domains, including global resources monitoring [2,3], urban management and development [4,5] and damage assessment [6].

Recent advancements in deep learning-based change detectors have shown great success in generating precise CD results by learning from a large volume of training images [7–11]. However, the extraction of change-related features remains a critical challenge in achieving high-quality CD results. Previous

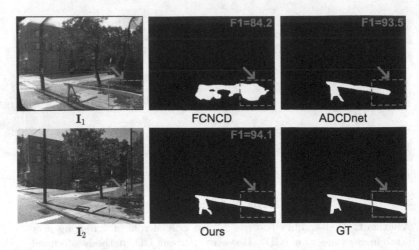

Fig. 1. Change detection results of concatenation-based method (e.g., FCNCD [12]), subtraction-based method (e.g., ADCDnet [13]) and our proposed method.

works [8,9] have proposed pre-combining two input images into a six-channeled tensor as the input of a fully convolutional network for CD, which cannot fully explore the features to distinguish changes from background and results in inferior CD results. Recent works [11,13] prone to extract features from each image through Siamese networks and then combine the features with feature difference or feature concatenation. While these methods have shown promising results in CD, they often overlook the integrity and complementary of different types of features. As shown in Fig. 1, FCNCD [12] employs concatenation operation to obtain change features, while ADCDnet [13] applies subtraction operation. We can observe that: ❶ The concatenation operation retains all the information from the image pair, but weakens the ability to represent changes accurately, leading to incorrect detection of background changes; ❷ The subtraction operation emphasizes the change, but ignores the semantic information of change objects, resulting in incomplete detection. Undoubtedly, the quality of features plays a crucial role in achieving accurate CD results. The effectiveness of feature representation directly impacts the ability to distinguish genuine changes from background changes. Therefore, it is crucial to focus on enhancing the quality of features to improve the overall performance of CD methods.

In this paper, our main objective is to achieve high-quality CD results by selecting the most informative and relevant features. To this end, we introduce a novel component called *high-quality feature selection module* (HQFS), which is used to learn the importance of the features from a feature pool. The feature pool contains various change-related features, including original convolutional features, concatenated features, absolute difference features, and so on. Additionally, we propose a *fully attention enhanced feature extraction network* that incorporates attention mechanisms to selectively highlight salient regions and capture informative details, thereby enabling effective feature extraction from input images. Furthermore, we present an *attention pyramid fusion & change mask prediction module*, which leverages attention-based fusion techniques to combine multi-scale features and generate accurate change predictions.

We have extensively evaluated our method on three benchmark datasets, showcasing its superiority over seven state-of-the-art change detectors. Our contributions are summarized as follows:

- We propose a comprehensive CD framework that focuses on selecting high-quality change-related features, and verify that the CD performance improves with these selected high-quality features.
- We introduce three key components in our framework: *high-quality feature selection, fully attention enhanced feature extraction network* and *attention pyramid fusion & change mask prediction* modules. These modules work together to effectively implement our CD method.
- We have conducted abundant experiments on three public CD datasets. The experiments demonstrate the superior performance of our method when compared to seven state-of-the-art CD methods.

2   Related Work

2.1   Change Detection

Change detection refers to the process of identifying differences in the state of an object or phenomenon by observing it at different times [14]. Traditional CD methods, such as support vector machine (SVM) [15], change vector analysis (CVA), principal component analysis (PCA) and K-means clustering [16], often face challenges in meeting the current detection requirements in terms of speed and accuracy due to their inherent limitations. Deep learning-based CD methods have gained significant attention and achieved remarkable performance by leveraging the powerful representation capabilities of deep learning.

Dault et al. [8] propose two methods for CD: directly concatenating image pairs and inputting them into a fully connected neural network; feeding them into a Siamese network followed by concatenation or subtraction. IFN [10] employs Siamese networks for feature extraction from image pairs and subsequently utilizes differential discriminant networks to detect and identify changes. ADCD-net [13] applies the absolute difference operation to the feature pairs extracted by the Siamese network, generating multi-scale change features, which are then combined and used for change prediction. ChangeFormer [17] employs hierarchical transformer encoders, based on the Transformer architecture [18], to extract long-range features and generate accurate change masks.

However, most existing CD methods process the features of image pairs in a simple manner, thus lacking of discrimination features. our work addresses this issue by constructing a feature pool consisting of various change-related features. The network is designed to evaluate the importance of these features, assign higher weights to high-quality features and enhance their contributions to accurate change map computation.

2.2   Feature Selection

Feature selection is a crucial process that involves choosing the most relevant and informative features from the original data [19]. It is essential for enhancing data understanding, reducing noise, and improving performance in various applications, such as text mining [20], image retrieval [21] and data analysis [22].

In computer vision, Peng et al. [23] employ mutual information as a feature selection technique to accomplish classification tasks successfully. Mairal et al. [24] introduce a feature selection method for color image restoration, utilizing sparse representation and leveraging singular value decomposition (SVD) for enhanced performance. Camps-Valls et al. [25] introduce a feature selection approach based on kernel independence for remote sensing data classification. Zou et al. [26] present a feature selection approach that utilizes deep belief network to address the feature reconstruction problem, enabling the image classification. Cheng et al. [27] introduce a hierarchical feature selection system that facilitates real-time image segmentation and superpixel extraction.

Previous CD methods primarily rely on simplistic strategies, such as concatenation or subtraction of image pairs, to capture the relationship between two images. However, these approaches may not be optimal for CD in diverse scene types, highlighting the need for more advanced and adaptable methods to achieve accurate and robust CD results across various scenarios. In contrast, we propose an innovation feature selection approach to process change-related features, aiming to obtain high-quality and discriminative change features. Our method improves the completeness and accuracy of change prediction results. Comparative experiments conducted on multiple datasets demonstrate the effectiveness and superiority of the proposed method.

3   Methodology

As shown in Fig. 2, we establish a deep model $\phi(\cdot)$ to transform an image pair $< \mathbf{I}_1, \mathbf{I}_2 >$ into a change mask $\mathbf{M}$ using the following equation:

$$\mathbf{M} = \phi(\mathbf{I}_1, \mathbf{I}_2), \tag{1}$$

where $\phi(\cdot)$ contains several key components, including fully attention enhanced feature extraction network, high-quality feature selection, and attention pyramid fusion & change mask prediction modules. In the upcoming sections, we provide a detailed description of the high-quality feature selection approach, followed by comprehensive explanations of our CD network and implementation details.

3.1   High-Quality Feature Selection (HQFS)

Feature Pool Construction. The feature pool $\mathcal{F}$ comprises features that capture both abstract and detailed information of changes, as discussed in Sect. 1. It has been observed that absolute difference features exhibit higher precision but lower recall, while concatenated features yield higher recall but lower precision.

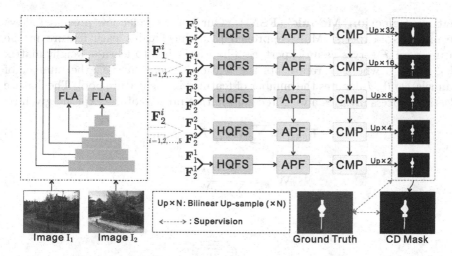

Fig. 2. Framework of the proposed HQFSnet for CD comprises the fully attentional block (FLA), high-quality feature selection (HQFS), and attention pyramid fusion (APF) & change mask prediction (CMP) modules, working synergistically to enhance CD performance.

Therefore, by combining these two types of features, we can improve both precision and recall simultaneously. Additionally, the original convolutional features extracted from the images are also valuable. Consequently, our feature pool $\mathcal{F}$ is constructed using three types of features: convolutional features from images, absolute difference features, and concatenated features. It should be noted that other types of features can also be incorporated into the feature pool if desired.

Given the convolutional features $\mathbf{F}_1^i$ and $\mathbf{F}_2^i$ extracted from the i-th convolutional layer of images $\mathbf{I}_1$ and $\mathbf{I}_2$, we calculate the absolute difference features and concatenated features using the following operations:

$$\mathbf{F}_{AD}^i = \text{Conv}_1(\text{abs}(\mathbf{F}_1^i - \mathbf{F}_2^i), 3), \qquad (2)$$

$$\mathbf{F}_{Con}^i = \text{Conv}_1(\text{Conv}_1([\mathbf{F}_1^i, \mathbf{F}_2^i], 1), 3), \qquad (3)$$

where abs($\cdot$) represents the absolute operation and $[\cdot, \cdot]$ denotes concatenation along the channel direction. Additionally, $\text{Conv}_1(\cdot, 3)$ and $\text{Conv}_1(\cdot, 1)$ refer to the computations performed by a 3×3 and 1×1 convolutional layer, respectively. We employ a convolutional layer to adjust the channel dimension of $\mathbf{F}_{AD}^i$ and $\mathbf{F}_{Con}^i$ to match that of $\mathbf{F}_1^i$ for subsequent feature selection. Note that each convolutional layer is followed by Batch Normalization and ReLU activation. Finally, we construct the feature pool as $\mathcal{F} = \{\mathbf{F}_1^i, \mathbf{F}_2^i, \mathbf{F}_{AD}^i, \mathbf{F}_{Con}^i\}$, where $\mathbf{F}_1^i$ and $\mathbf{F}_2^i$ represent the convolutional features, $\mathbf{F}_{AD}^i$ denotes the absolute difference features, and $\mathbf{F}_{Con}^i$ represents the concatenated features.

Feature Selection Module (FSM). Our feature selection process follows the mixture-of-experts (MoE) approach [28]. Specifically, each feature in the feature pool $\mathcal{F}$ serves as an expert E. The FSM aims to learn a weight matrix $\mathbf{W} \in R^{N \times M}$, where N represents the feature dimension (i.e., the number of channels), and M denotes the number of features in the feature pool. The feature selection process involves a weighted summation process of the experts, given by

$$\mathbf{F}_{\mathrm{FSM}}^{i} = \sum_{k} \hat{\mathbf{W}}_{jk} \cdot E_{k}(:,:,j), \tag{4}$$

$$\hat{\mathbf{W}}_{jk} = \frac{e^{\mathbf{W}_{jk}}}{\sum_{m} e^{\mathbf{W}_{jm}}}, \tag{5}$$

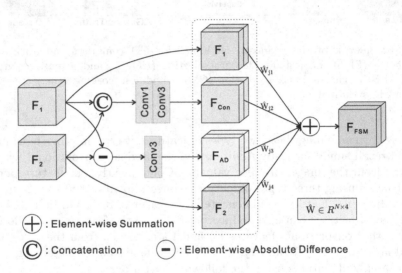

Fig. 3. The proposed HQFS module consists of two steps: constructing a feature pool and subsequently selecting features from this pool, aiming to enhance the discriminative power of feature selection for CD.

where $\mathbf{F}_{\mathrm{FSM}}^{i}$ represents the selected features from the feature selection process, $E_{k}(,:,:,j)$ denotes the j-th dimensional feature of the k-th expert. The weight matrix $\mathbf{W}$ is a learnable parameter that is updated during the network training.

3.2   Change Detection Network

Fully Attention Enhanced Feature Extraction Network. To extract multi-scale convolutional features, we employ VGG-16bn [29] as the basic feature extraction backbone and combine it with feature pyramid network (FPN) [30] structure and fully attentional block (FLA) [31] to construct a U-shaped network. This integration allows for the extraction of multi-scale features and enhances the detection performance. Specifically, we extract multiple levels of features from the feature extraction backbone in a top-down manner. Here, $\mathbf{F}^{Conv_i}$ represents the features extracted from the i-th convolutional block of the feature extraction backbone. These features then undergo the FLA and FPN processing, where the low-level features are fused with the high-level features, leading to the generation of multi-scale convolutional features. The operations are as follows:

$$\mathbf{F}^5 = \Psi_{\text{FLA}}(\mathbf{F}^{Conv_5}), \tag{6}$$

$$\mathbf{F}^4 = \text{Conv}_2([\Psi_{\text{FLA}}(\mathbf{F}^{Conv_4}), \text{Up}(\mathbf{F}^5)], 3), \tag{7}$$

$$\mathbf{F}^i = \text{Conv}_2([\mathbf{F}^{Conv_i}, \text{Up}(\mathbf{F}^{i+1})], 3), i = 3, 2, 1, \tag{8}$$

where $\Psi_{\text{FLA}}(\cdot)$ represents the calculation performed by the FLA module, $\text{Up}(\cdot)$ denotes bi-linear upsampling, and $\text{Conv}_2(\cdot, 3)$ refers to the calculation of two 3×3 convolutional layers. Interestingly, our experimental findings indicate that applying FLA solely on the fifth and fourth convolutional blocks yields superior performance compared to applying FLA on all convolutional blocks.

Attention Pyramid Fusion (APF) and Change Mask Prediction (CMP). Fusing features from different scales is a common strategy to improve the quality of CD results. In this paper, we introduce the attention pyramid fusion (APF) module, proposed in [32], to fuse the multi-scale features $\mathbf{F}^i_{\text{FSM}}$, as shown in Fig. 2. This module facilitates the integration of information across different scales, enhancing the discriminative ability and robustness in CD.

$$\mathbf{F}^5_{\text{APF}} = \Phi_{\text{APF}}(\mathbf{F}^5_{\text{FSM}}), \tag{9}$$

$$\mathbf{F}^i_{\text{APF}} = \Phi_{\text{APF}}([\text{Up}(\mathbf{F}^{i+1}_{\text{APF}}), \mathbf{F}^i_{\text{FSM}}]), i = 4, 3, 2, 1, \tag{10}$$

where $\Phi_{\text{APF}}(\cdot)$ denotes the APF module. To accelerate the training process, we add supervision on $\mathbf{F}^i_{\text{APF}}$ by producing change mask using two-layer convolutional operations $\mathbf{M}^i_{\text{APF}} = \text{Conv}_1(\text{Conv}_1(\mathbf{F}^i_{\text{APF}}, 3), 1)$. With $\mathbf{F}^i_{\text{APF}}$, we generate the multi-scale change masks through the following processing steps:

$$\mathbf{M}_i = \text{Conv}_1(\text{Conv}_1(\mathbf{F}^i_{\text{P}}, 3), 1), \tag{11}$$

$$\mathbf{F}^5_{\text{P}} = \text{Conv}_1(\mathbf{F}^5_{\text{APF}}, 1), \tag{12}$$

$$\mathbf{F}^i_{\text{P}} = \text{Conv}_1(\text{Conv}_1(\text{Up}(\mathbf{F}^{i+1}_{\text{P}}), 1) + \text{Conv}_1(\mathbf{F}^i_{\text{APF}}, 1), 1), i = 4, 3, 2, 1. \tag{13}$$

The final change mask $\mathbf{M}$ is obtained by concatenating the multi-scale change masks $\mathbf{M}_i$ and performing convolutional operations for pixel classification. This process can be represented by the following equation:

$$\mathbf{M} = \text{Conv}_1([\mathbf{M}_1, \mathbf{M}_2, \mathbf{M}_3, \mathbf{M}_4, \mathbf{M}_5], 1). \tag{14}$$

The resulting change mask $\mathbf{M}$ accurately identifies the regions of change in the input image pair.

Loss Function. We apply multi-supervision by utilizing the predicted change masks $\mathbf{M}^i_{\mathrm{APF}}, \mathbf{M}_i$ and $\mathbf{M}$. The cross-entropy loss is employed as our primary loss function, and the total loss is defined as follows:

$$\mathcal{L}_{\mathrm{Total}} = \mathcal{L}(\mathbf{M}, \mathbf{M}_{\mathrm{GT}}) + \sum_{i=1}^{5}\{\mathcal{L}(\mathbf{M}_i, \mathbf{M}_{\mathrm{GT}}) + \mathcal{L}(\mathbf{M}^i_{\mathrm{APF}}, \mathbf{M}_{\mathrm{GT}})\}. \qquad (15)$$

Please note that we utilize bi-linear upsampling operation to resize the predicted change masks to match the size of the ground truth $\mathbf{M}_{\mathrm{GT}}$. This ensures that the predicted change masks are of the same dimensions as the ground truth for accurate comparison and evaluation.

Table 1. Quantitative results of different methods on three CD datasets. The highest score is marked in bold.

Method	VL-CMU-CD					PCD					CDnet				
	P	R	F1	OA	IoU	P	R	F1	OA	IoU	P	R	F1	OA	IoU
FCNCD [12]	84.2	84.3	84.2	98.4	72.9	68.7	61.7	65.0	94.1	48.0	82.9	88.3	85.5	99.2	76.0
ADCDnet [13]	92.8	94.3	93.5	99.3	87.9	78.8	73.4	76.0	90.0	62.3	89.0	85.5	87.2	99.3	77.9
CSCDnet [33]	89.2	91.1	90.1	98.7	82.1	66.0	72.6	69.1	83.7	51.9	93.9	82.3	87.7	99.0	78.4
IFN [10]	93.1	75.9	83.6	98.1	71.4	69.5	**75.7**	72.5	87.2	57.7	93.1	80.0	86.1	98.9	75.3
BIT [11]	90.5	87.6	89.0	98.8	80.6	77.7	57.3	66.0	85.4	50.1	**95.4**	81.9	88.1	99.1	78.9
STAnet [4]	73.1	**95.8**	82.9	98.0	70.7	69.6	52.7	60.0	79.9	41.2	72.2	94.3	81.8	98.3	69.2
ChangeFormer [17]	88.0	88.6	88.3	98.7	79.2	74.0	69.2	71.5	86.6	56.4	93.4	85.9	89.5	99.2	81.3
HQFSnet (Ours)	**93.3**	95.0	**94.1**	**99.4**	**89.0**	**82.5**	71.5	**76.6**	90.1	**62.5**	93.3	**94.8**	**94.0**	**99.6**	**88.7**

3.3   Implementation Details

All experiments are conducted using PyTorch framework and trained with an NVIDIA RTX2080Ti GPU. The Adam optimizer is employed to update our model, with a momentum of 0.9 and weight decay of 0.999. We set the initial learning rate to 0.001 and batch size to 4 during training. For fair comparison, all models are trained for 20 epochs.

4   Experiments

4.1   Experimental Setups

Baselines. In this paper, we compare the proposed method with seven existing state-of-the-art methods, including FCNCD [12], ADCDnet [13], CSCDnet [33], IFN [10], BIT [11], STAnet [4] and ChangeFormer [17]. The change detector proposed in this paper is named HQFSnet. We have implemented all the methods using the PyTorch framework and trained them on the same training sets.

Datasets. To evaluate the performance of our method, we conduct experiments on three publicly available benchmark datasets, i.e., VL-CMU-CD [9], PCD [33] and CDnet [34]. VL-CMU-CD dataset contains 1362 image pairs and the labeling masks of street views with a long time span and challenging changes. The resolution of the images is 1024×768. PCD dataset has two subsets, named GSV and TSUNAMI. Each subset consists of 100 panoramic image pairs and the change masks. The resolution of the images is 1024×224. CDnet dataset contains nearly 50000 frames in 31 video sequences that captured in six different scenarios. The maximum resolution of images is 720×480. During the training process, we resize all the samples to 320×320 and convert a multi-class labeling mask to a binary change map, meaning that we only focus on changes instead of class information. In each dataset, we randomly select 80% image pairs for training and the rest for testing.

Criterion. Following the convention of previous studies, we utilize precision (P), recall (R), F1-Score (F1), overall accuracy (OA) and intersection over union (IoU) to evaluate the performance of different change detectors.

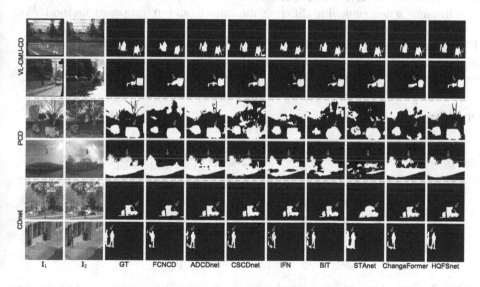

Fig. 4. Examples of CD results from various change detectors on VL-CMU-CD, PCD, and CDnet datasets. Notably, the red arrows indicate the key differences in the results. (Color figure online)

4.2   Results and Discussion

Comparison with the State-of-the-art Change Detectors. Table 1 shows the quantitative results of different change detectors on three benchmark datasets. On VL-CMU-CD, HQFSnet exhibits the best performance, and achieves 0.6%, 0.1% and 1.1% relative F1, OA and IoU improvements over the rest best method ADCDnet, respectively. The PCD presents a significant challenge for CD due to its various change types, including buildings, trees, and grass. Among the compared methods, none of them achieve F1 score higher than 76.0%. However, F1 score of our method is 76.6%, surpassing the performance of the compared methods by at least 0.6% in terms of F1 score. On CDnet, compared with ChangeFormer, the best CD method among the comparison methods, the F1, OA and IoU of HQFSnet exceed its by 4.5%, 0.4% and 7.4%. These results demonstrate the superior performance of HQFSnet in accurately detecting changes on the three benchmark CD datasets.

As shown in Fig. 4, we present several representative examples from the three CD datasets to visually demonstrate the effectiveness of our method. HQFSnet exhibits remarkable performance in accurately detecting real changes in various scenarios. It not only captures finer details of the change objects but also produces clearer boundaries compared to the other methods, as evident from the 1st, 2nd, and 4th rows. These qualitative results further reinforce the superiority of our method, aligning with the quantitative evaluations conducted.

Effectiveness of Different Modules. Table 2 presents an analysis of the performance when removing different modules from our proposed method. We use $\mathrm{Conv}_1(\cdot, 3)$ to replace $\Psi_{\mathrm{FLA}}(\cdot)$, $\mathbf{F}_{\mathrm{AD}}^i$ to replace $\mathbf{F}_{\mathrm{FSM}}^i$, and $\mathbf{F}_{\mathrm{FSM}}^i$ to replace $\mathbf{F}_{\mathrm{APF}}^i$ when removing FLA, HQFS and APF, respectively. We observe that the proposed method performs best when all modules are included, indicating the importance and effectiveness of each module in achieving superior results.

Table 2. Comparison of different modules of our method on VL-CMU-CD dataset.

FLA	HQFS	APF	P	R	F1	OA	IoU
✘	✘	✘	92.6	95.2	93.8	99.3	88.4
✘	✔	✔	93.0	94.8	93.9	99.3	88.5
✔	✘	✔	93.0	95.1	94.0	**99.4**	88.8
✔	✔	✘	92.4	**95.5**	93.9	**99.4**	88.5
✔	✔	✔	**93.3**	95.0	**94.1**	**99.4**	**89.0**

Table 3. Comparison of our method applying different approaches to obtain change features on VL-CMU-CD dataset.

Feature	P	R	F1	OA	IoU
$[\mathbf{F}_1^i, \mathbf{F}_2^i]$	92.6	**95.2**	93.8	**99.4**	88.5
$\mathrm{abs}(\mathbf{F}_1^i - \mathbf{F}_2^i)$	93.0	95.1	94.0	**99.4**	88.8
HQFS	**93.3**	95.0	**94.1**	**99.4**	**89.0**

Effectiveness of HQFS. Table 3 presents the performance of our method when utilizing three different approaches to obtain change features: concatenation, absolute difference and the proposed HQFS. It is evident that using change features selected by HQFS yields the highest values for most of the metrics, showcasing the effectiveness of our feature selection approach.

5 Conclusion

This study aims to improve the change detection performance through the application of feature selection techniques. We begin by constructing a feature pool and utilize learnable weight matrices to generate high-quality change-related features, enhancing the representation of both changes and non-changes. Additionally, we propose a fully attention enhanced feature extraction network to improve the capability of feature representation. The final change prediction is obtained through attention pyramid fusion of features and the generation of multi-scale change masks. Experimental results on three benchmark datasets demonstrate that our method outperforms seven state-of-the-art change detectors.

Acknowledgements. Thanks to the Fundamental Research Funds for the Central Universities of Civil Aviation University of China (3122022091) for funding.

References

1. Singh, A.: Review article digital change detection techniques using remotely-sensed data. Int. J. Remote Sens. **10**(6), 989–1003 (1989)
2. Khan, S.H., He, X., Porikli, F., Bennamoun, M.: Forest change detection in incomplete satellite images with deep neural networks. IEEE Trans. Geosci. Remote Sens. **55**(9), 5407–5423 (2017). https://doi.org/10.1109/TGRS.2017.2707528
3. Cai, Z., Jiang, Z., Yuan, Y.: Task-related self-supervised learning for remote sensing image change detection. In: ICASSP 2021–2021 IEEE International Conference on Acoustics, Speech and Signal Processing (ICASSP), pp. 1535–1539 (2021). https://doi.org/10.1109/ICASSP39728.2021.9414387
4. Chen, H., Shi, Z.: A spatial-temporal attention-based method and a new dataset for remote sensing image change detection. Remote Sensing **12**(10), 1662 (2020)
5. Buch, N., Velastin, S.A., Orwell, J.: A review of computer vision techniques for the analysis of urban traffic. IEEE Trans. Intell. Transp. Syst. **12**(3), 920–939 (2011). https://doi.org/10.1109/TITS.2011.2119372
6. Xu, J.Z., Lu, W., Li, Z., Khaitan, P., Zaytseva, V.: Building damage detection in satellite imagery using convolutional neural networks. arXiv preprint arXiv:1910.06444 (2019)
7. Shin, Y., Balasingham, I.: Comparison of hand-craft feature based SVM and CNN based deep learning framework for automatic polyp classification. In: 2017 39th Annual International Conference of the IEEE Engineering in Medicine and Biology Society (EMBC), pp. 3277–3280 (2017). https://doi.org/10.1109/EMBC.2017.8037556
8. Caye Daudt, R., Le Saux, B., Boulch, A.: Fully convolutional siamese networks for change detection. In: 2018 25th IEEE International Conference on Image Processing (ICIP), pp. 4063–4067 (2018). https://doi.org/10.1109/ICIP.2018.8451652

9. Alcantarilla, P.F., Stent, S., Ros, G., Arroyo, R., Gherardi, R.: Street-view change detection with deconvolutional networks. Auton. Robot. **42**(7), 1301–1322 (2018). https://doi.org/10.1007/s10514-018-9734-5

10. Zhang, C., Yue, P., Tapete, D., Jiang, L., Shangguan, B., Huang, L., Liu, G.: A deeply supervised image fusion network for change detection in high resolution bi-temporal remote sensing images. ISPRS J. Photogramm. Remote. Sens. **166**, 183–200 (2020)

11. Chen, H., Qi, Z., Shi, Z.: Remote sensing image change detection with transformers. IEEE Trans. Geosci. Remote Sens. **60**, 1–14 (2021)

12. Long, J., Shelhamer, E., Darrell, T.: Fully convolutional networks for semantic segmentation. In: Proceedings of the IEEE Conference on Computer Vision and Pattern Recognition, pp. 3431–3440 (2015)

13. Huang, R., Zhou, M., Zhao, Q., Zou, Y.: Change detection with absolute difference of multiscale deep features. Neurocomputing **418**, 102–113 (2020)

14. Shi, W., Zhang, M., Zhang, R., Chen, S., Zhan, Z.: Change detection based on artificial intelligence: state-of-the-art and challenges. Remote Sensing **12**(10), 1688 (2020)

15. Yu, M., Yu, Y., Rhuma, A., Naqvi, S.M.R., Wang, L., Chambers, J.A.: An online one class support vector machine-based person-specific fall detection system for monitoring an elderly individual in a room environment. IEEE J. Biomed. Health Inform. **17**(6), 1002–1014 (2013). https://doi.org/10.1109/JBHI.2013.2274479

16. Celik, T.: Unsupervised change detection in satellite images using principal component analysis and k-means clustering. IEEE Geosci. Remote Sens. Lett. **6**(4), 772–776 (2009). https://doi.org/10.1109/LGRS.2009.2025059

17. Bandara, W.G.C., Patel, V.M.: A transformer-based siamese network for change detection. arXiv preprint arXiv:2201.01293 (2022)

18. Vaswani, A., et al.: Attention is all you need. In: Advances in Neural Information Processing Systems 30 (2017)

19. Chandrashekar, G., Sahin, F.: A survey on feature selection methods. Comput. Electr. Eng. **40**(1), 16–28 (2014)

20. Van Landeghem, S., Abeel, T., Saeys, Y., Van de Peer, Y.: Discriminative and informative features for biomolecular text mining with ensemble feature selection. Bioinformatics **26**(18), i554–i560 (2010)

21. Rashedi, E., Nezamabadi-Pour, H., Saryazdi, S.: A simultaneous feature adaptation and feature selection method for content-based image retrieval systems. Knowl.-Based Syst. **39**, 85–94 (2013)

22. Song, Q., Ni, J., Wang, G.: A fast clustering-based feature subset selection algorithm for high-dimensional data. IEEE Trans. Knowl. Data Eng. **25**(1), 1–14 (2013). https://doi.org/10.1109/TKDE.2011.181

23. Peng, H., Long, F., Ding, C.: Feature selection based on mutual information criteria of max-dependency, max-relevance, and min-redundancy. IEEE Trans. Pattern Anal. Mach. Intell. **27**(8), 1226–1238 (2005). https://doi.org/10.1109/TPAMI.2005.159

24. Mairal, J., Elad, M., Sapiro, G.: Sparse representation for color image restoration. IEEE Trans. Image Process. **17**(1), 53–69 (2007)

25. Camps-Valls, G., Mooij, J., Scholkopf, B.: Remote sensing feature selection by kernel dependence measures. IEEE Geosci. Remote Sens. Lett. **7**(3), 587–591 (2010). https://doi.org/10.1109/LGRS.2010.2041896

26. Zou, Q., Ni, L., Zhang, T., Wang, Q.: Deep learning based feature selection for remote sensing scene classification. IEEE Geosci. Remote Sens. Lett. **12**(11), 2321–2325 (2015). https://doi.org/10.1109/LGRS.2015.2475299

27. Cheng, M.M., et al.: HFS: hierarchical feature selection for efficient image segmentation. In: Leibe, B., Matas, J., Sebe, N., Welling, M. (eds.) ECCV 2016. LNCS, vol. 9907, pp. 867–882. Springer, Cham (2016). https://doi.org/10.1007/978-3-319-46487-9_53

28. Jacobs, R.A., Jordan, M.I., Nowlan, S.J., Hinton, G.E.: Adaptive mixtures of local experts. Neural Comput. **3**(1), 79–87 (1991)

29. Simonyan, K., Zisserman, A.: Very deep convolutional networks for large-scale image recognition. arXiv preprint arXiv:1409.1556 (2014)

30. Lin, T.Y., Dollár, P., Girshick, R., He, K., Hariharan, B., Belongie, S.: Feature pyramid networks for object detection. In: Proceedings of the IEEE Conference on Computer Vision and Pattern Recognition, pp. 2117–2125 (2017)

31. Song, Q., Li, J., Li, C., Guo, H., Huang, R.: Fully attentional network for semantic segmentation. In: Proceedings of the AAAI Conference on Artificial Intelligence, vol. 36, pp. 2280–2288 (2022)

32. Elhassan, M.A., Yang, C., Huang, C., Legesse Munea, T., Hong, X.: S^2-FPN: scale-ware strip attention guided feature pyramid network for real-time semantic segmentation. arXiv e-prints pp. arXiv-2206 (2022)

33. Sakurada, K., Okatani, T.: Change detection from a street image pair using CNN features and superpixel segmentation. In: Proceedings of the British Machine Vision Conference (BMVC), pp. 61.1-61.12 (2015). https://doi.org/10.5244/C.29.61

34. Goyette, N., Jodoin, P.M., Porikli, F., Konrad, J., Ishwar, P.: Changedetection.net: a new change detection benchmark dataset. In: 2012 IEEE Computer Society Conference on Computer Vision and Pattern Recognition Workshops, pp. 1–8 (2012). https://doi.org/10.1109/CVPRW.2012.6238919

FAFormer: Foggy Scene Semantic Segmentation by Fog-Invariant Auxiliary Domain Adaptation

Ziquan Wang[✉][ID] and Zhipeng Jiang[ID]

PLA Strategic Support Force Information Engineering University, Zhengzhou 450001, Henan, China
aresdrw@163.com

Abstract. Semantic Segmentation in the Foggy Scenes (SSFS) remains a difficult problem due to uncertainties caused by imperfect observations. Considering the success of domain adaptive semantic segmentation in the clear scenes, we believe it is reasonable to transfer the knowledge from the clear images to the foggy images. Different from the previous methods which mainly focus on alignment between the clear domain and the foggy domain, we try to transfer the fog knowledge between different domains to a "teacher" segmentor, thus the latter can generate better pseudo labels to supervise the student segmentor (main segmentor) to close the domain gap. Our method achieved better performance on ACDC and Foggy Zurich benchmark compared with mainstream works.

Keywords: Foggy scene semantic segmentation · Domain adaptation · Self-training · Fog Knowledge Transferring

1 Introduction

Reliable semantic segmentation based on visual images under the adverse-weather conditions is important for scene understanding task in autonomous driving, which can save the huge cost of installing auxiliary sensors (like LiDAR). Among them, semantic segmentation in the foggy scenes (SSFS) is an significant branch. However, the segmentors trained on clear-scene datasets often generalizes bad on the foggy scenes [21] due to the visibility degradation caused by fog. Meanwhile, the cost of producing annotations directly to images under foggy scenes is much higher than to clear scenes, which makes it more difficult to solve the SSFS problem by traditional fully-supervised training strategy. At present, the main methods for the SSFS problem is to transform it into a Domain Adaptation (DA) problem [21], which tries to use the fine annotated datasets from clear scenes (such as Cityscapes [5]) as the source domain and the foggy scene datasets (such as Foggy-Zurich [21]) as the target domain, aiming at transferring the segmentation knowledge by training a DA segmentor. Unfortunately,

Supported by National Natural Science Foundation of China under Grant 42071340 and Program of Song Shan Laboratory (included in the management of Major Science and Technology of Henan Province) under Grant 2211000211000-01.

the fog in the images will cause a large domain gap between the source domain and the target domain. Thus directly using traditional domain adaptation methods (such as GAN [24]) to align feature representations between the source and target domain is not very effective (shown in Fig. 1), e.g., it's easy to generate large prediction drift at the boundary between fog and objects [21]. Recently, some works have proved that fog factors can be decoupled and optimized independently by introducing an intermediate synthetic fog domain [14]. Therefore, joint learning to segment and recognize the fog factors in training is crucial the segmentor.

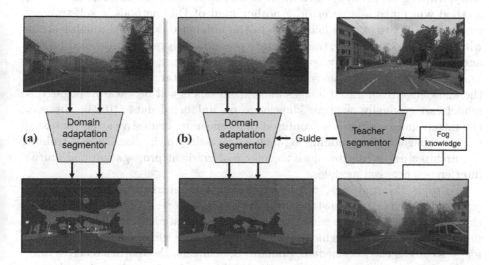

Fig. 1. The main idea of our method. (a) Original domain adaptive segmentor often confuses when dealing with the fog gap. (b) Thus we try to transfer the fog knowledge into the teacher segmentor and guide the main segmentor to perform better.

For the fog gap between the domains, the training goal is forcing the segmentor to output approximately consistent features for the same category objects under different fog conditions (fog-invariant features). There are three main methods: (1) Fog-related methods, including (a) Dehazing the foggy image and then use the traditional segmentation method [1,9,19,20,28], (b) Adding synthetic fog to the clear images [6,14,21]; (2) DA methods, including the methods based on generative adversarial network (GAN) [2,8,24,25] and the method based on self-training [10,13,18,23,27,30].

Among fog-related methods, dehazing is an ill-posed problem and easy to generate artifacts in the images which will generate prediction drift [9,20,21]. Adding synthetic fog requires extra depth data, and the modeling of synthetic fog does not fully match the real fog, which may widen the domain gap.

DA-based methods mainly include three directions: input space alignment [17], feature space alignment [2,30] and output space alignment [24,25]. Among them, the input space alignment aims to generate stylized images to narrow the domain gap thus the segmentor will be easier to close the domain and generalize. However, these stylized images may also contain unpleasant artifacts. The feature space alignment often use the "centroid" [29] to minimize the feature distance of same category objects in two domains, but this kind of alignment is difficult to fully describe the objects' changes. As for the output space alignment, which views the segmentation map as a 'structured output', attempts to constrain the segmentation of two domains by structure [24] and entropy [25]. However, the DA methods by adversarial manner rely on discriminators, which will conduct a heavy down-sampling on the feature maps to generate the discriminative proba- bility, which is very rough. Once the domain gap is large, the adversarial training method will make a large error. Another kind of DA methods is self-training, which attempts to explore knowledge in the unlabeled domain through learning with reference. Concretely, they generate pseudo labels on the unlabeled images, and then use a powerful augumentation strategy (e.g., ClassMix [18]) to mix images and labels from the source domain and the target domain. After that, the knowledge from mixed images and mixed labels will be back-propagated so model can gradually acquires knowledge on unlabeled data [10,23]. However, the mixed images often have confused pixel meaning or destroys the context of original image. Besides, adding fog-factor processing to the classical self-training DA architecture is easy to cause the chaos of gradient propagation and mutual interference between modules.

To solve the problems, we design a new Fog-invariant Auxiliary pipeline (called 'FAFormer') to construct a better teacher to generate pseudo labels on the foggy target domain, which will supervise the student segmentor (will be published as the final segmentor). FAFormer needs clear reference images of foggy scenes as the intermediate domain. Specifically, the teacher receives infor- mation from two aspects: (1) segmentation knowledge from the source domain; (2) Information used for recognize fog factor. Our method will extract fog recog- nition features from each pair of clear image & foggy image, and force a feature extractor to output fog-invariant features, and then pass the knowledge to the teacher model. Thus the latter will be better adapted to the foggy days and produce better pseudo labels.

The main contributions in this study are summarized as follows. (1) We organically combine fog-invariant feature learning and knowledge transferring for SSFS problem. (2) Our method outperforms the baseline on two widely used datasets in SSFS and shows generalization ability on other adverse scenes, such as rainy and snowy scenes.

2　Method

Suppose that there are N_s labeled images $\left\{ \left(x_s^i, y_s^i \right) \right\}_{i=1}^{N_s}$ from the clear source domain s, among them y_s^i is the label for x_s^i, and N_t unlabeled images $\left\{ \left(x_t^k \right) \right\}_{k=1}^{N_t}$ from the target foggy domain t. Our goal is to transfer segmentation knowl- edge from s to t by our proposed FAFormer. To train the for-invariant fea- ture extractor, we introduce an intermediate domain m with N_m unlabeled images $\left\{\left(x_m^j\right)\right\}_{j=1}^{N_m}$, which share similar fog influence (no fog) with the source domain and similar style variation with the target domain (same city). Figure 2 depicts the framework of our proposed method. Motivated by the success of DAFormer [10], we use the similar framework including a "student" segmentor and a "teacher" segmentor as the basic framework to train in a self-supervised manner.

Specifically, we first use the "student" segmentor to perform fully supervised learning on the labeled source domain s. For the fog-factor recognition, we input the clear intermediate domain image and the foggy target domain image into a "fog-invariant backbone", and then a fog-factor filter will calculate the Gram matrix of fog features to squeeze them into a fog feature vector. We use the distance between the two vectors as a training loss to force fog backbone to be "insensitive" to the fog factors. Then the fog-related knowledge stored in the fog backbone will be passed into the teacher model by Exponential Moving Average (EMA) updating [12]. Then we use the teacher segmentor to generate pseudo labels on the foggy target domain t. After that, the images and labels of the source domain and target domain will be mixed respectively, and semi-supervised learning will be carried out.

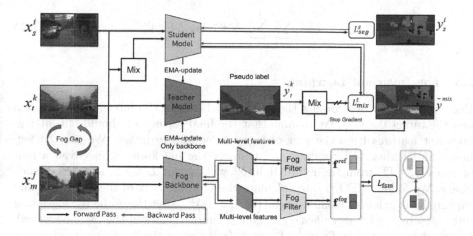

Fig. 2. The main workflow of our method. Firstly, the student segmentor will perform fully supervised learning on the labeled source domain s. Then the clear intermediate domain image and the foggy target domain image will be put into the "fog-invariant backbone" with a fog-factor filter to calculate fog feature vectors. The distance between these two vectors will be used to force fog-invariant backbone to be "insensitive" to the fog factors. Then the fog-related knowledge stored in the fog backbone will be passed into the teacher model. Then the teacher segmentor to generate pseudo labels on the foggy target domain t. After that, the images and labels of the source domain and target domain will be mixed respectively for conducting semi-supervised learning.

2.1 Sub-modules

The main workflow of our method mainly includes 4 sub-modules, i.e., (a) "student" segmentor f_θ (will be used as the final segmentor), (b) "teacher" segmentor h_φ (generates the pseudo labels on the target domain t), (c) fog-invariant backbone b_ω^{fi} (outputs fog-invariant features) and (d) Fog-factor filter $\mathcal{F}$.

All the segmentors contain backbone and decode head. The backbone follows the design of Mix Transformers (MiT) [26] to produce multi-level feature maps and the decode head follows ASPP [4] to predict segmentation map. The fog-invariant backbone b_ω^{fi} shares same architecture of MiT for subsequent knowledge transferring. The Fog pass filter $\mathcal{F}$ follows the design in FIFO [14]. The detailed architecture will be described later.

2.2 Supervised Training on Source Domain

Denote H and W as the height and width of the input image size, C as the number of classes. First, we will use the "student" segmentor f_θ to learn segmentation knowledge from labeled source domain $\{(x_s^i, y_s^i)\}_{i=1}^{N_s}$ with a categorical Cross-Entropy loss function (CE):

$$L_{seg}^s|^i = -\sum_{p=1}^{H \times W} \sum_{c=1}^{C} y_s^{(i,p,c)} \log f_\theta(x_s^i)^{(p,c)} \tag{1}$$

2.3 Fog-Invariant Learning

Here we focus on overcoming the "fog gap" between the intermediate domain and the target domain. We assume that the final segmentor should output fog-invariant features from the pair of foggy & non-foggy image. We use the fog-invariant backbone b_ω^{fi} to store and transfer the fog knowledge. Given a pair of image (I^a, I^b) from the mini-batch, b_ω^{fi} will output L layers features of each image. We follow FIFO [14] to calculate the Gram matrix of these features and capture holistic fog style knowledge $\{(\mathbf{u}^{a,l}, \mathbf{u}^{b,l})\}_{l=1}^{L}$. Let the $\mathcal{F}^l$ be the fog-factor filter attached to l^{th} layer feature. The fog factor vectors of the two images will be calculated by $\mathbf{f}^{a,l} = \mathcal{F}^l(\mathbf{u}^{a,l})$, $\mathbf{f}^{b,l} = \mathcal{F}^l(\mathbf{u}^{b,l})$ respectively. We try to close the distance of $\{(\mathbf{f}^{a,l}, \mathbf{f}^{b,l})\}_{l=1}^{L}$:

$$L_{\text{fsm}}^l(\mathbf{f}^{a,l}, \mathbf{f}^{b,l}) = \frac{1}{4d_l^2 n_l^2} \sum_{i=1}^{d_l} (\mathbf{f}_i^{a,l} - \mathbf{f}_i^{b,l})^2 \tag{2}$$

where d^l and n^l denote the dimension of their fog factors and the spatial size of the lth feature map, respectively. Then the knowledge from fog-invariant training will be also stored into the parameters in b_ω^{fi} and will be passed into "teacher" segmentor.

2.4 Know Transferring

Steps above have learned the knowledge for domain adaptation from different levels, but they need to be organically combined. Thus we use EMA-update [12] to transfer both the knowledge from the source domain s and fog-invariant backbone b_ω^{fi} to the teacher segmentor h_φ. In ablation study, we will discuss the order of EMA-updating in detail.

$$h_\varphi^{t+1} = (1-\alpha)h_\varphi^t + \alpha b_\omega^{\text{fi}|t}$$

$$h_\varphi^{t+2} = (1-\alpha)h_\varphi^{t+1} + \alpha f_\theta^t \tag{3}$$

2.5 Self-training on the Target Domain

After the knowledge transferring, the teacher segmentor h_φ are strong enough for producing better pseudo labels on the foggy target domain images $\widetilde{y}_t^{(k,p,c)}$:

$$\widetilde{y}_t^{(k,p,c)} = \left[c = \arg\max_{c'} h_\varphi(x_t^k)^{(p,c')}\right] \tag{4}$$

where [*] means the Iverson bracket. However, the quality of pseudo labels is not good enough, especially at the beginning of training, so we need to give lower weights according to their confidence. Here, we use the ratio of pixels exceeding a threshold τ of the maximum softmax probability

$$q_t^k = \frac{\sum_{j=1}^{H \times W}\left[\max_{c'} h_\varphi(x_t^k)^{(j,c')} \geq \tau\right]}{H \times W} \tag{5}$$

Then the pseudo labels and their quality estimates are used to train the segmentor h_φ additionally on the target domain:

$$L_t^j = -\sum_{p=1}^{H \times W}\sum_{c=1}^{C} q_t^k \widetilde{y}_t^{(k,p,c)} \log h_\varphi(x_t^k)^{(p,c)} \tag{6}$$

Self-training has been shown to be particularly efficient if the segmentor is trained on augmented target data. Thus we follow DACS [23], using color jitter, Gaussian blur, and ClassMix [15] as data augmentation to learn more domain-robust features.

3 Experiment

3.1 Network Architecture

For Mit-b5 backbone (used in b_ω^{fi}, h_φ and f_θ), it produces a feature pyramid with channels $[64, 128, 320, 512]$. The ASPP decoder uses $n_{che} = 256$ and the dilation rates of $[1, 6, 12, 18]$. All encoders are pretrained on ImageNet-1k [7]. The fog pass filters $\mathcal{F}$ are composed of fully connected layer and LeakyReLU layer to transfer the Gram matrix of feature maps into fog vectors.

3.2   Implementation Details

Our work is based on a Tesla v100 Graphics card with 16 GB memory, equipped by PyTorch. The main workflow is trained by AdamW optimizer, the learning rate is 6e−5 with a weight-decay of 0.01, linear learning rate warmup follows the "poly" strategy after 1.5k iterations. All the input images and labels are cropped to 512 × 512, the maximum number of the training iteration is 40k. Following the DACS [23], we use the same data augmentation parameters and set $\alpha = 0.01$ and $\tau = 0.968$.

3.3   Datasets

Cityscapes [5] is a real-world datasets composed of street scene captured in 50 different cities. The data split includes 2975 training images and 500 validation images with pixel-level label. The Cityscapes dataset will be the source domain and share the same class set with all the datasets mentioned in this paper.

Foggy Cityscapes DBF [21] has 550 synthetic foggy images including 498 training images and 52 testing images. These images are selected from Cityscapes and synthesized with fog using depth information. Note that images in Clear Cityscapes are not captured in Zurich city.

ACDC [22] contains four adverse-condition categories (fog, snow, rain and nighttime) with pixel-level annotation. Each of category contains 1000 images and is split into train set, validation set and test set for about 4:1:5 proportion. The annotation of test set is withheld for testing online. We mainly use the foggy images. Besides, ACDC dataset also provides clear reference images of each foggy image, which will be used as intermediate domain.

Foggy Zurich [6] contains 3808 real foggy road views in the city of Zurich and its suburbs. According to fog density, it is split into two categories –light and medium, consisting of 1552 and 1498 images. It has a test set: Foggy Zurich-test including 40 images with labels compatible with Cityscapes. We selected 600 images from light-fog subset as the intermediate domain of Foggy Zurich.

3.4   Performance Comparsion

We compare our method against several categories of methods, including:
1) *Backbones*: RefineNet [16], Deeplabv2 [3] and SegFormer [26];
2) *Dehazing*: MSCNN [19], DCP [9], Non-local [1], GFN [20] and DCPDN [28];
3) *DA-based*: LSGAN [17], AdaptSegNet [24], Multi-Task [11], ADVENT [25], CLAN [30], BDL [15], FDA [27], DISE [2], ProDA [29], DACS [23] and DAFormer [10]; 4) *Synthesis-based*: SFSU [21], CMAda [6] and FIFO [14]

The mean Intersection-Over-Union (mIoU) results on ACDC test set (see "FAFormer" on ACDC-fog benchmark website) and Foggy Zurich are reported in Table 1. For *Backbones* methods, we train them on Cityscapes dataset with

Table 1. Performance Comparsion. Experiments are conducted on ACDC and Foggy Zurich (FZ) datasets, measured with mean IoU (mIoU %) over all classes.

Experiment	Method	Backbone	ACDC	FZ	Experiment	Method	Backbone	ACDC	FZ
Backbone	-	DeepLabv2 [3]	33.5	25.9	DA-based	LSGAN [17]	DeepLabv2	29.3	24.4
	-	RefineNet [16]	46.4	34.6		Multi-task [11]	DeepLabv2	35.4	28.2
	-	SegFormer [26]	47.3	37.7		AdaptSegNet [24]	DeepLabv2	31.8	26.1
Dehazing	DCPDN [28]	DeepLabv2	33.4	28.7		ADVENT [25]	DeepLabv2	32.9	24.5
	MSCNN [19]	RefineNet	38.5	34.4		CLAN [30]	DeepLabv2	38.9	28.3
	DCP [9]	RefineNet	34.7	31.2		BDL [15]	DeepLabv2	37.7	30.2
	Non-local [1]	RefineNet	31.9	27.6		FDA [27]	DeepLabv2	39.5	22.2
	GFN [20]	RefineNet	33.6	28.7		DISE [2]	DeepLabv2	42.3	40.7
Synthetic	SFSU [21]	RefineNet	45.6	35.7		ProDA [29]	DeepLabv2	38.4	37.8
	CMAda [6]	RefineNet	51.1	46.8		DACS [23]	DeepLabv2	41.3	28.7
	FIFO [14]	RefineNet	54.1	48.4		DAFormer [10]	SegFormer	48.9	44.4
Our	FAFormer	Backbone	SegFormer	ACDC	**55.5**		FZ		**49.0**

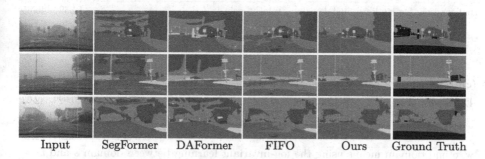

Input   SegFormer   DAFormer   FIFO   Ours   Ground Truth

Fig. 3. The qualitative comparison with the baseline methods. The input images are randomly selected from Foggy Zurich-test. Our method can better deal with the fog and details than the baseline methods.

labels and test on ACDC and Foggy Zurich to get their original performance across domains. For *Dehazing* methods, we use them to dehaze the foggy images and then use original segmentor to predict. For *DA-based* methods, we set the source domain data as clear cityscapes, s domain of our method. As for the target domain data, we use the ACDC fog images and Foggy Zurich (medium fog). For intermediate domain m, we combined the ACDC fog reference set (400 images) and manually selected 600 clear images in Foggy Zurich (light fog). For *Synthesis-based* methods, the paradigm is to finetune the segmentation model pretrained on the real clear weather images (Cityscapes) with synthetic foggy images, e.g., Foggy Cityscapes DBF [21], and labels corresponding to its clear weather images.

In Table 1, our method exceeds all the listed method categories. This suggests that neither pure defogging nor traditional DA methods can perform well in foggy scenarios with large domain gap. Our method outperforms the baseline DAFormer [10] by 6.7%, and also outperforms FIFO [14], another source of inspiration for the method, which shows that the combination of DA method and fog-invariant feature learning can achieve better results. In Fig. 3, we further demonstrate the comparison between DAFormer, FIFO and our method. The original SegFormer [26] couldn't handle the sky in the foggy scenarios. DAFormer [10] alleviates this, but there are still large artifacts in the sky. FIFO removes the effect of fog, but there is a certain degree of bias in the ground instance. In contrast, our method can remove the fog effect better and can segment more completely (Fig. 4).

Table 2. Ablation study Ablation experiments on fog-invariant learning is conducted firstly in (a). Then, we explore the effects when using different amounts of images from intermediate domain in (b). Thirdly, the order of EMA-updating is discussed in (c). Finally, we conduct the generalization test on the snowy and rainy validation set of ACDC in (d), also measured with mIoU %)

(a) Ablation Study[a]

Initialization	DAFormer		mIoU	gain
configuration	fog_inv learn	imd-domain	mIoU	gain
	✓		50.63	+1.71
		✓	53.62	+4.70
	✓	✓	55.58	+6.66

Initialization: DAFormer — 48.92 — +0.00

(b) Numbers of intermediate domain

400	600	1000[b]	1600[c]	ACDC	FZ
✓				54.39	46.65
	✓			52.36	50.12
		✓		55.58	49.03
			✓	55.42	49.36

(c) Discussion about EMA-updating order | mIoU

EMA-order	Fi->T[e]	S->T[f]	ACDC	FZ
	1	2	55.58	49.03
	2	1	55.46	48.94

(d) Generalization[d]

Method		snow	rain
	SegFormer	40.62	42.03
	DAFormer	48.27	49.19
	FAFormer	56.23	52.48

[a] w/o imd_domain means using the fog-invariant learning between domain s and t
[b] means mixing of 400 images from ACDC and 600 images from FZ.
[c] means 1000 mixing datasets adding with extra 600 images from ACDC.
[d] means from the Fog-invariant backbone to the teacher model.
[e] means from the student model to the teacher model.
[f] conducted on the rainy and snowy validation set of ACDC.

3.5   Discussion

Effectiveness of Fog-Invariant Learning. In Table 2(a), we performed the ablation study and find that 4.70% gain on mIoU could be obtained using fog-invariant learning. However, the gain is only 1.71% if the intermediate domain images are not used, which means using the intermediate domain images (with the target domain style information) can help the model recognize fog features better. In Table 2(a), we visually compare our method with the baseline model DAFormer [10]. It can be seen that DAFormer has definitely identified foggy days as artifacts (low entropy area in the middle and upper part of c), which is very unwise, indicating that DAFormer has a serious deviation in fog factor recognition during prediction. Our method can effectively identify fog and better distinguish object boundaries.

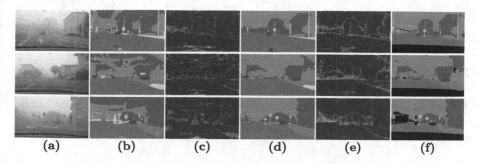

| (a) | (b) | (c) | (d) | (e) | (f) |

Fig. 4. Ablation study of our method. (a) is the input images randomly selected from Foggy Zurich-test, (b) and (d) are the prediction given by DAFormer [10] and our FAFormer. (c) and (e) are the entropy map of (b) and (d). (f) is the ground truth of (a). It can be seen that DAFormer [10] identifies the foggy sky as building definitely (low entropy area in the upper part of (c)), which is very unwise, indicating that DAFormer has a serious deviation in fog factor recognition during prediction. However, our method can effectively identify fog and better distinguish object boundaries.

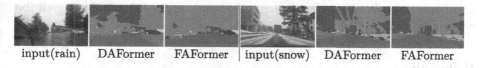

input(rain)   DAFormer   FAFormer | input(snow)   DAFormer   FAFormer

Fig. 5. Qualitative results of generalization on rainy and snowy images. These experiments are conducted on ACDC rain and snow subsets. We directly use the checkpoint acquired by this paper to test without any extra training. Our FAFormer can greatly improve the segmentation performance compared with DAFormer

Number of Images from Intermediate Domain. We try to explore the effect of intermediate domain images in Table 2(b): (1) with different amount, (2) from different datasets. Firstly, using exclusive intermediate domain does help get the best results on current dataset (400 images that strictly correspond to the foggy train set in ACDC), but it won't show the same performance on another dataset. For example, the segmentor only reached 46.65 mIoU on Foggy Zurich using the intermediate domain images from ACDC. This is due to the style variation between datasets. Secondly, in the same dataset, the number of images from intermediate domain has little influence on the final performance (using 1600 images cannot be better than 1000 images). In other words, the corresponding relationship between the clear domain and the fog domain doesn't need to be very strict, indicating the segmentor has adaptability in both fog-invariant feature learning and intermediate domain segmentation learning.

Order of EMA-Updating. EMA-updating is temporal ensembling algorithm ($a(x + b) \neq ax + b$), thus different update orders may affect the final parameters of the segmentor. In Table 2(c), we perform ablation study on EMA updating orders. It shows that different update orders related to Teacher have little effect on performance due to the cyclical training.

Generalization to Clear, Rainy and Snowy Scenes. Furthermore, we test our method on the rainy and snowy validation sets of the ACDC dataset (Table 2(d) and Fig. 5), which also shows an improvement over DAFormer, indicating the potential of our method to address the understanding of different adverse scenes.

4   Conclusion

In this paper, we propose a Fog-invariant Auxiliary domain adaptation method (FAFormer) for SSFS task. Our method outperforms classic methods on two datasets in SSFS and shows generalization ability to other adverse scenes, such as rainy and snowy scenes. We will make the code publicly available. In future studies, we will further research the fog factor and try to avoid its influence more accurately. We will also research the unified segmentor that suitable for all the adverse conditions.

References

1. Berman, D., Avidan, S., et al.: Non-local image dehazing. In: Proceedings of the IEEE Conference on Computer Vision and Pattern Recognition, pp. 1674–1682 (2016)
2. Chang, W.L., Wang, H.P., Peng, W.H., Chiu, W.C.: All about structure: adapting structural information across domains for boosting semantic segmentation. In: Proceedings of the IEEE/CVF Conference on Computer Vision and Pattern Recognition, pp. 1900–1909 (2019)
3. Chen, L.C., Papandreou, G., Kokkinos, I., Murphy, K., Yuille, A.L.: Deeplab: semantic image segmentation with deep convolutional nets, atrous convolution, and fully connected crfs. IEEE Trans. Pattern Anal. Mach. Intell. **40**(4), 834–848 (2017)
4. Chen, L.C., Zhu, Y., Papandreou, G., Schroff, F., Adam, H.: Encoder-decoder with atrous separable convolution for semantic image segmentation. In: Proceedings of the European Conference on Computer Vision (ECCV), pp. 801–818 (2018)
5. Cordts, M., et al.: The cityscapes dataset for semantic urban scene understanding. In: Proceedings of the IEEE Conference on Computer Vision and Pattern Recognition, pp. 3213–3223 (2016)
6. Dai, D., Sakaridis, C., Hecker, S., Van Gool, L.: Curriculum model adaptation with synthetic and real data for semantic foggy scene understanding. Int. J. Comput. Vision **128**, 1182–1204 (2020)
7. Deng, J., Dong, W., Socher, R., Li, L.J., Li, K., Fei-Fei, L.: Imagenet: a large-scale hierarchical image database. In: 2009 IEEE Conference on Computer Vision and Pattern Recognition, pp. 248–255. Ieee (2009)
8. Goodfellow, I., et al.: Generative adversarial networks. Commun. ACM **63**(11), 139–144 (2020)

9. He, K., Sun, J., Tang, X.: Single image haze removal using dark channel prior. IEEE Trans. Pattern Anal. Mach. Intell. **33**(12), 2341–2353 (2010)
10. Hoyer, L., Dai, D., Van Gool, L.: Daformer: improving network architectures and training strategies for domain-adaptive semantic segmentation. In: Proceedings of the IEEE/CVF Conference on Computer Vision and Pattern Recognition, pp. 9924–9935 (2022)
11. Kerim, A., Chamone, F., Ramos, W., Marcolino, L.S., Nascimento, E.R., Jiang, R.: Semantic segmentation under adverse conditions: a weather and nighttime-aware synthetic data-based approach. arXiv preprint arXiv:2210.05626 (2022)
12. Laine, S., Aila, T.: Temporal ensembling for semi-supervised learning. arXiv preprint arXiv:1610.02242 (2016)
13. Lee, D.H., et al.: Pseudo-label: The simple and efficient semi-supervised learning method for deep neural networks. In: Workshop on Challenges in Representation Learning, ICML, vol. 3, p. 896 (2013)
14. Lee, S., Son, T., Kwak, S.: Fifo: Learning fog invariant features for foggy scene segmentation. In: Proceedings of the IEEE/CVF Conference on Computer Vision and Pattern Recognition, pp. 18911–18921 (2022)
15. Li, Y., Yuan, L., Vasconcelos, N.: Bidirectional learning for domain adaptation of semantic segmentation. In: Proceedings of the IEEE/CVF Conference on Computer Vision and Pattern Recognition, pp. 6936–6945 (2019)
16. Lin, G., Milan, A., Shen, C., Reid, I.: Refinenet: multi-path refinement networks for high-resolution semantic segmentation. In: Proceedings of the IEEE Conference on Computer Vision and Pattern Recognition, pp. 1925–1934 (2017)
17. Mao, X., Li, Q., Xie, H., Lau, R.Y.K., Wang, Z., Smolley, S.P.: Least squares generative adversarial networks. Cornell University - arXiv (2016)
18. Olsson, V., Tranheden, W., Pinto, J., Svensson, L.: Classmix: Segmentation-based data augmentation for semi-supervised learning. In: Proceedings of the IEEE/CVF Winter Conference on Applications of Computer Vision, pp. 1369–1378 (2021)
19. Ren, W., Liu, S., Zhang, H., Pan, J., Cao, X., Yang, M.-H.: Single image dehazing via multi-scale convolutional neural networks. In: Leibe, B., Matas, J., Sebe, N., Welling, M. (eds.) ECCV 2016. LNCS, vol. 9906, pp. 154–169. Springer, Cham (2016). https://doi.org/10.1007/978-3-319-46475-6_10
20. Ren, W., Ma, L., Zhang, J., Pan, J., Cao, X., Liu, W., Yang, M.H.: Gated fusion network for single image dehazing. In: Proceedings of the IEEE Conference on Computer Vision and Pattern Recognition, pp. 3253–3261 (2018)
21. Sakaridis, C., Dai, D., Van Gool, L.: Semantic foggy scene understanding with synthetic data. Int. J. Comput. Vision **126**, 973–992 (2018)
22. Sakaridis, C., Dai, D., Van Gool, L.: Acdc: The adverse conditions dataset with correspondences for semantic driving scene understanding. In: Proceedings of the IEEE/CVF International Conference on Computer Vision, pp. 10765–10775 (2021)
23. Tranheden, W., Olsson, V., Pinto, J., Svensson, L.: Dacs: domain adaptation via cross-domain mixed sampling. In: Proceedings of the IEEE/CVF Winter Conference on Applications of Computer Vision, pp. 1379–1389 (2021)
24. Tsai, Y.H., Hung, W.C., Schulter, S., Sohn, K., Yang, M.H., Chandraker, M.: Learning to adapt structured output space for semantic segmentation. In: Proceedings of the IEEE Conference on Computer Vision and Pattern Recognition, pp. 7472–7481 (2018)
25. Vu, T.H., Jain, H., Bucher, M., Cord, M., Pérez, P.: Advent: adversarial entropy minimization for domain adaptation in semantic segmentation. In: Proceedings of the IEEE/CVF Conference on Computer Vision and Pattern Recognition, pp. 2517–2526 (2019)

26. Xie, E., Wang, W., Yu, Z., Anandkumar, A., Alvarez, J.M., Luo, P.: Segformer: simple and efficient design for semantic segmentation with transformers. Adv. Neural. Inf. Process. Syst. **34**, 12077–12090 (2021)
27. Yang, Y., Soatto, S.: Fda: fourier domain adaptation for semantic segmentation. In: Proceedings of the IEEE/CVF Conference on Computer Vision and Pattern Recognition, pp. 4085–4095 (2020)
28. Zhang, H., Patel, V.M.: Densely connected pyramid dehazing network. Cornell University - arXiv (2018)
29. Zhang, P., Zhang, B., Zhang, T., Chen, D., Wang, Y., Wen, F.: Prototypical pseudo label denoising and target structure learning for domain adaptive semantic segmentation. In: Proceedings of the IEEE/CVF Conference on Computer Vision and Pattern Recognition, pp. 12414–12424 (2021)
30. Zou, Y., Yu, Z., Liu, X., Kumar, B.V., Wang, J.: Confidence regularized self-training. In: The IEEE International Conference on Computer Vision (ICCV), October 2019

Video-Based Person Re-Identification with Long Short-Term Representation Learning

Xuehu Liu[1,2], Pingping Zhang[1,3], and Huchuan Lu[1,2(✉)]

[1] School of Information and Communication Engineering,
Dalian University of Technology, Dalian, China
snowtiger@mail.dlut.edu.cn, zhpp@dlut.edu.cn
[2] Ningbo Institute, Dalian University of Technology, Dalian, China
lhchuan@dlut.edu.cn
[3] School of Artificial Intelligence, Dalian University of Technology, Dalian, China

Abstract. Video-based person Re-Identification (V-ReID) aims to retrieve specific persons from raw videos captured by non-overlapped cameras. As a fundamental task, it spreads many multimedia and computer vision applications. However, due to the variations of persons and scenes, there are still many obstacles that must be overcome for high performance. In this work, we notice that both the long-term and short-term information of persons are important for robust video representations. Thus, we propose a novel deep learning framework named **Long Short-Term Representation Learning (LSTRL)** for effective V-ReID. More specifically, to extract long-term representations, we propose a **Multi-granularity Appearance Extractor (MAE)**, in which four granularity appearances are effectively captured across multiple frames. Meanwhile, to extract short-term representations, we propose a **Bi-direction Motion Estimator (BME)**, in which reciprocal motion information is efficiently extracted from consecutive frames. The MAE and BME are plug-and-play and can be easily inserted into existing networks for efficient feature learning. As a result, they significantly improve the feature representation ability for V-ReID. Extensive experiments on three widely used benchmarks show that our proposed approach can deliver better performances than most state-of-the-arts.

Keywords: Video-based person re-identification · Long-term appearance representation · Short-term motion representation

1 Introduction

Video-based person Re-Identification (V-ReID) aims to retrieve specific persons from raw videos captured by non-overlapped cameras. Due to the wide range of applications such as object tracking and scenario surveillance, V-ReID has attracted more and more attention from researchers. During the past decade, deep learning has contributed to significant improvements in V-ReID by extracting robust and discriminative features. Even so, the challenges of spatial occlusions and temporal misalignments in videos have yet to be solved. To address

H. Lu et al. (Eds.): ICIG 2023, LNCS 14355, pp. 55–67, 2023.
https://doi.org/10.1007/978-3-031-46305-1_5

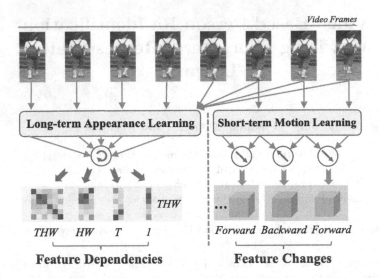

Fig. 1. Illustration of our proposed paradigm. For long-term appearance learning (left part), four granularities are captured from all the frames. For short-term motion learning (right part), feature changes are estimated in forward and backward directions. The red straight arrows indicate the execution of bidirectional motion learning, while red curved arrow indicates the mining of inter-feature dependencies. (Color figure online)

these challenges, several efforts have been made by various representation learning methods. For example, some works [18,21,26] highlight the salient visual regions of each frame, while other works [3,16,22,23] attentively aggregate the temporal diverse clues across different frames. Although effective, there are still some obvious issues. Firstly, the long-range inter-frame associations are ignored in the extraction of appearances. Secondly, the motion information is missed out, which is instrumental in identifying persons when they have similar appearances. Therefore, these methods struggle to extract long-term appearance representations effectively and fail to extract motion information efficiently.

In this work, we propose a novel **Long Short-Term Representation Learning (LSTRL)** framework for V-ReID. The illustration of our LSTRL is presented in Fig. 1. More specifically, to extract long-term representations, we design a **Multi-granularity Appearance Extractor (MAE)**, in which two local-to-local and two global-to-local dependencies are captured. With these dependencies, we highlight the meaningful local features and extract multi-granularity appearances. Further, our MAE incorporates features at multiple granularities to obtain long-term appearance representations, which contain more abundant information than the appearance of a single frame. Meanwhile, to extract short-term representations, we design a **Bi-direction Motion Estimator (BME)**, in which the motion information is extracted from consecutive frames. Distinct from the high-cost optical flow estimation, we reciprocally calculate the feature changes in a global-to-local manner, which brings two benefits.

The first is increasing the robustness for noise frames. The second is reducing the spatial misalignments caused by occlusion and scale variations.

Moreover, our MAE and BME are plug-and-play and can be easily inserted into existing networks for multi-stage long short-term feature learning. To verify the effectiveness of our method, extensive experiments are conducted on three widely used V-ReID datasets. Experimental results show that our approach performs better than most state-of-the-art methods. In summary, the main contributions of our work are as follows:

- We propose a novel Long Short-Term Representation Learning (LSTRL) framework for V-ReID.
- We design a Multi-granularity Appearance Extractor (MAE) to obtain long-term appearance representations, in which four kinds of dependencies are effectively explored from all the frames.
- We design a Bi-direction Motion Estimator (BME) to obtain short-term motion representations, in which reciprocal feature changes between consecutive frames is efficiently estimated in a global-to-local manner.
- Experimental results on three widely-used benchmarks demonstrate that our framework attains a better performance than most state-of-the-art methods.

2   Related Work

2.1   Appearance Representation Learning for V-ReID

For effective V-ReID, some works [5,12,25] aim at extracting discriminative appearance representations from spatial appearance modeling. For example, Li et al. [18] mine diverse part features which are constrained by an attention regularization. Subramaniam et al. [26] insert the co-segmentation attention module into the CNN backbone to activate salient regions of pedestrians. Zhang et al. [31] utilize the global feature to guide the extraction of multi-granularity features in each frame. Liu et al. [21] utilize human skeleton information to locate human key bodies and extract appearance information. Hou et al. [10] a bilateral complementary network for spatial complementarity modeling. Bai et al. [1] design a salient-to-broad module to enlarge the attention regions frame by frame. These methods ignore the inter-frame associations and simply focus on extracting the appearance representations of single frame. Different from them, we capture the long-range dependencies across all the frames and extract long-term appearance representations at multiple granularities.

2.2   Motion Representation Learning for V-ReID

Apart from appearance representations, the motion representation is another important clue for identifying persons. Recently, several efforts are explored to extracting motion features from videos. For example, McLaughlin et al. [24] extract optical flows to represent motion information. Liu et al. [20] accumulate motion clues of persons by recurrent feature aggregations. Li et al. [16] learn

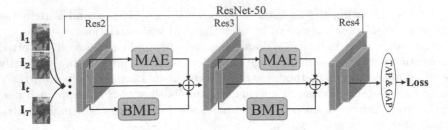

Fig. 2. The overall framework of our LSTRL.

the global-local temporal representation to exploit the multi-scale temporal cues from video sequences. Li *et al.* [19] utilize a generative model to predict the walking patterns of persons. Chen *et al.* [2] extract the coherence and motion features by temporal disentangling. Liu *et al.* [22] design a temporal reciprocal learning mechanism to model disentangled video cues. Besides, Gu *et al.* [6] model motion information based on the position and appearance changes of bodies. Different from their high-cost motion estimation, we perform a global-to-local and reciprocal motion estimator, which significantly reduces the computational complexity and increases the robustness to noise frames and spatial misalignment.

3   Our Method

Our proposed framework is presented in Fig. 2. Given a video of persons, the Restricted Random Sampling (RRS) [18] is first adopted to generate T frames $\{\mathbf{I}_1, \mathbf{I}_2, ..., \mathbf{I}_T\}$. Then, we utilize a 2D CNN, such as ResNet-50 [8], to encode the multi-scale local information of each frame. After that, our Multi-granularity Appearance Extractor (MAE) associates all the frames to extract long-term appearance representations. Meanwhile, our Bi-direction Motion Estimator (BME) links consecutive frames to extract short-term motion representations. The obtained representations from MAE and BME are added to frame-level features for subsequent feature extraction. Finally, the Global Average Pooling (GAP) and Temporal Average Pooling (TAP) are deployed after the last layer to obtain a video-level representation for retrieval. For the model training, we combine a cross-entropy loss and a batch-hard triplet loss [9] for end-to-end supervision. The details of MAE and BME are described in the following sections.

3.1   Multi-granularity Appearance Extractor

The detailed structure of our MAE is shown in Fig. 3. In MAE, four kinds of dependencies are captured respectively, including two local-local dependencies and two global-local dependencies. They are beneficial to associate meaningful local features across all the frames. With these dependencies, we can effectively extract multiple appearance features in multi-granularity, which are further incorporated to obtain long-term representations.

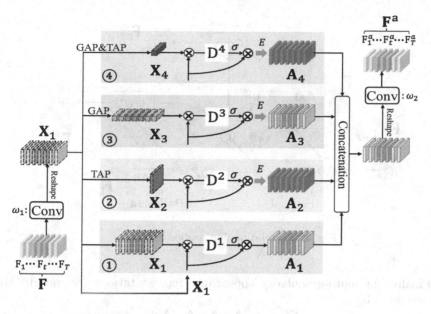

Fig. 3. The multi-granularity appearance extractor.

More specifically, after the l-th residual block of ResNet-50, we obtain the frame-level feature maps $\{\mathbf{F}_1, \mathbf{F}_2, ..., \mathbf{F}_T\}$. These frame-level features are concatenated to get $\mathbf{F} \in \mathbb{R}^{T \times H \times W \times C}$ as the input of MAE, where H, W, and C represent the height, weight and channels, respectively. Then, $\mathbf{F}$ is passed into one 1×1 convolutional layer (ω_1) for reducing its channels to one quarter. We reshape the channel-reduced feature and get one granularity feature as $\mathbf{X}_1 \in \mathbb{R}^{THW \times \frac{1}{4}C}$. Meanwhile, the GAP or TAP is deployed on $\mathbf{X}_1$ to generate multi-granularity features $\mathbf{X}_i$ ($i = 2, 3, 4$). Afterwards, as shown in Fig. 3, four kinds of dependencies are generated by

$$\mathbf{D}^i = \sigma(\mathbf{X}_i \mathbf{X}_1^\top), i = 1, 2, 3, 4, \tag{1}$$

where $\top$ denotes the transpose operator, σ is the softmax activation function. It is noted that, the dependencies $\mathbf{D}^1 \in \mathbb{R}^{THW \times THW}$ and $\mathbf{D}^2 \in \mathbb{R}^{HW \times THW}$ contain the local-to-local associations, which help to enhance local features. The dependencies $\mathbf{D}^3 \in \mathbb{R}^{T \times THW}$ and $\mathbf{D}^4 \in \mathbb{R}^{1 \times THW}$ contain the global-to-local associations, which help to highlight discriminative local features under global guidance. With these dependencies, we obtain multi-granularity appearance representations by

$$\mathbf{A}_i = \begin{cases} \mathbf{D}^i \mathbf{X}_1, & i = 1 \\ E(\mathbf{D}^i \mathbf{X}_1), & i = 2, 3, 4 \end{cases} \tag{2}$$

where E means the feature extension operation. For example, $\mathbf{D}^i \mathbf{X}_1 \in \mathbb{R}^{HW \times \frac{1}{4}C}$ is first reshaped as $\mathbb{R}^{1 \times HW \times \frac{1}{4}C}$ and then replicated T times to be $\mathbb{R}^{T \times HW \times \frac{1}{4}C}$. After that, we concatenate its temporal dimension to obtain $\mathbf{A}_2 \in \mathbb{R}^{THW \times \frac{1}{4}C}$.

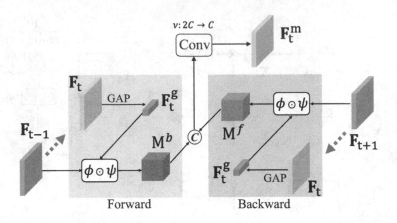

Fig. 4. The bi-direction motion estimator.

Finally, the multi-granularity appearance representations are concatenated and weighted by

$$\mathbf{F}^a = \omega_2([\mathbf{A}_1, \mathbf{A}_2, \mathbf{A}_3, \mathbf{A}_4]). \qquad (3)$$

where $[,]$ means the concatenation along channels, and ω_2 is another 1×1 convolutional layer. In this way, we obtain the long-term appearance representation $\mathbf{F}^a \in \mathbb{R}^{T \times H \times W \times C}$. Compared with single-frame learning, our MAE can effectively associate meaningful local features from all the frames. In contrast to 3D CNN-based methods, our MAE is more efficient to extract long-term representations with multi-granularity dependencies.

3.2 Bi-direction Motion Estimator

In addition, we propose a BME to extract short-term motion representations as a supplement to the appearance representations. The structure of our BME is shown in Fig. 4. After the l-th residual block of ResNet-50, our BME estimates feature changes between consecutive frames $\mathbf{F}_{t-1}$, $\mathbf{F}_t$ and $\mathbf{F}_{t+1}$.

Generally, the optical flow estimation is often used for motion prediction [13,27,32]. However, the pixel-to-pixel motion estimation is high-cost and suffers from severe spatial misalignment. Different from the pixel-to-pixel motion estimation, in our BME, we calculate motion features in a global-to-local manner, which will significantly reduces the computational complexity. Besides, the reciprocal estimation of motion information could increase the robustness to noise frames. More specifically, the global feature $\mathbf{F}_t^g \in \mathbb{R}^{1 \times 1 \times C}$ is directly generated from $\mathbf{F}_t \in \mathbb{R}^{H \times W \times C}$ by a GAP. Then, instead of the pixel-to-pixel estimation, we estimate the motion information in a global-to-local manner,

$$\mathbf{M}^f = \phi(\mathbf{F}_t^g) \odot \psi(\mathbf{F}_{t+1}), \qquad (4)$$

$$\mathbf{M}^b = \phi(\mathbf{F}_t^g) \odot \psi(\mathbf{F}_{t-1}), \qquad (5)$$

Table 1. Performance (%) comparison with state-of-the-arts on MARS and iLIDS-VID datasets. Compared methods are separated into three groups, *i.e.*, spatial learning (S), temporal learning (T), spatial-temporal (ST) learning. The texts in bold and underline highlight the best and second performances.

	Methods	MARS		iLIDS-VID	
		mAP	R-1	R-1	R-5
S	DRSA [18]	65.8	82.3	80.2	–
	COSAM [26]	79.9	84.9	77.8	97.3
	RAFA [31]	85.9	88.8	88.6	98.0
	PSTA [29]	85.8	<u>91.5</u>	91.5	98.1
	BiCNet [10]	86.0	90.2	–	–
	SINet [1]	86.2	91.0	**92.5**	–
T	RNN+Flow [24]	–	–	58	84
	AMOC+Flow [20]	–	–	68.7	94.3
	AMEM [19]	79.3	86.7	87.2	97.7
	GLTR [16]	78.5	87.0	86.0	–
	TCLNet [11]	85.1	89.8	86.6	–
	GRL [22]	84.8	91.0	90.4	<u>98.3</u>
ST	M3D [17]	74.1	84.4	74.0	94.3
	AP3D [7]	85.6	90.7	88.7	–
	SSN3D [14]	86.2	90.1	–	–
	STMN [4]	84.5	90.5	–	–
	CTL [21]	<u>86.7</u>	91.4	89.7	97.0
	STT [30]	86.3	88.7	–	–
Our	**LSTRL**	**86.8**	**91.6**	<u>92.2</u>	**98.6**

where $\odot$ presents the dot product. ϕ and ψ are two 1×1 convolutional layers, reducing the channels to half. After that, we concatenate $\mathbf{M}^f$ and $\mathbf{M}^b$, and aggregate the bi-direction motion information by

$$\mathbf{F}_t^m = \upsilon([\mathbf{M}^f, \mathbf{M}^b]), \qquad (6)$$

where υ means one 1×1 convolutional layer with ReLU. The bi-direction aggregation can realize better temporal learning, resulting in more robust motion features. By our BME, the short-term motion representation $\mathbf{F}_t^m$ can be efficiently extracted with reciprocal learning.

4 Experiments

4.1 Datasets and Evaluations

In this paper, we adopt three widely-used V-ReID benchmarks, *i.e.*, iLIDS-VID [28], MARS [33] and LS-VID [16], to evaluate our proposed method. iLIDS-VID is a small-scale dataset with 600 video sequences of 300 different identities.

MARS is one of the large-scale datasets and consists of 1,261 identities around 18,000 video sequences. LS-VID is another large-scale dataset. It comprises 4,832 sequences from 1,812 identities. Follow previous works [7,29], we compute the cumulative matching characteristic table, including R-1 and R-5, and mean Average Precision (mAP) for algorithm evaluation.

4.2 Implement Details

We conduct experiments with the Pytorch toolbox. Our experimental devices include an Intel i4790 CPU and two NVIDIA RTX3090 GPUs (24G memory). During training, we adopt the Restricted Random Sampling (RRS) [18] to sample 8 frames from one video as a sequence input. Each frame is resized to 256×128 and augmented by random cropping and erasing. In a mini-batch, 8 person identities are selected randomly, and each identity samples 4 video sequences. The Adam [15] algorithm is adopted to optimize the whole framework. Its initial learning rate is 0.0003 and decayed by 10 at every 70 epochs until 400 epochs.

4.3 Comparison with State of the Arts

We compare our LSTRL with state-of-the-art methods. The results are presented in Tables 1 and 2. It is observed that our method outperforms the most state-of-the-art methods on MARS and iLIDS-VID datasets, and attains the highest retrieval accuracy on LS-VID dataset.

In the cases of spatial appearance learning, some previous methods concentrate on a single frame and extract the salient features, such as DRSA [18], BiC-Net [10] and SINet [1]. In particular, SINet attains 91.0% ,92.5% and 87.4% R-1 accuracy on MARS, iLIDS-VID and LS-VID, respectively. Better than SINet, our method extracts the long-term appearance representations from all the frames and get higher retrieval accuracies on MARS and LS-VID. Noted that, COSAM [26] aggregates the frame-level features to activate spatial meaningful regions, and RAFA [31] learns multi-granularity representations from single-frame features. Both of them ignore the inter-frame associations. Different from them, we capture four kinds of dependencies to associate inter-frame features, which helps to extract long-term appearance representations. Thus, our method outperforms COSAM and RAFA by 6.9% and 2.8% in terms of mAP and R-1 on MARS.

Meanwhile, some works, such as GRL [22], TCLNet [11] and GLTR [16], deploy temporal learning to associate and aggregate frame-level features. However, these works hardly capture the motion information of persons. Thus, for the extraction of motion representations, previous methods, such as RNN+Flow [24] and AMOC+Flow [20], calculate the optical flow and combine RGB images as inputs. Although effective, it brings large computational complexity. Besides, some recent works, such as AMEM [19], model the walking patterns of pedestrians to capture the motion features. In our work, we perform the global-to-local and reciprocal motion extraction between consecutive frames, which consumes only a small computational cost. Combined short-term motion and long-term

Table 2. Performance (%) comparison with state-of-the-arts on LS-VID dataset.

	Methods	LS-VID	
		mAP	R-1
S	BiCNet [10]	75.1	84.6
	SINet [1]	79.6	87.4
T	GLTR [16]	44.3	63.1
	TCLNet [11]	70.3	81.5
ST	STMN [4]	69.2	82.1
	STT [30]	78.0	87.5
Our	**LSTRL**	**82.4**	**89.8**

Table 3. Ablation results (%) of key modules on MARS and LS-VID datasets.

Method	MARS		LS-VID		Param. (M)	FLOPs (G)
	mAP	R-1	mAP	R-1		
Baseline	84.2	89.4	77.8	86.9	24.79	4.09
+ MAE	86.3	90.9	81.2	89.0	26.43	4.42
+ BME	86.8	91.6	82.4	89.8	29.06	4.96

Table 4. Ablation results (%) of multi-granularity appearances on MARS and LS-VID datasets.

Mehods	MARS		LS-VID	
	mAP	R-1	mAP	R-1
Baseline+MAE	86.3	90.9	81.2	89.0
- A_1	85.9	90.6	80.8	88.4
- A_2	85.7	89.9	80.5	88.2
- A_3	85.9	90.2	80.0	88.3
- A_4	85.7	90.1	80.3	88.6

Table 5. Ablation results (%) of Motion Estimation on MARS and LS-VID Datasets.

Manner		Direction		MARS		LS-VID	
Local-	Global-	Single-	Bi-	mAP	R-1	mAP	R-1
✓			✓	86.1	90.7	82.0	88.8
	✓	✓		86.7	91.0	82.2	89.4
	✓		✓	86.8	91.6	82.4	89.8

appearance representations, our method can surpasses AMEM by 7.5% mAP and 4.9% R-1 on MARS, respectively.

Moreover, AP3D [7], CTL [21] and STT [30] model spatial-temporal information. Different from them, our method effectively extracts long-term appearance and short-term motion representations. In addition, the proposed MAE and BME can be easily inserted into existing networks for efficient learning. Results show that our method attains better performances than AP3D, CTL and STT.

4.4 Ablation Study

In this section, we conduct more experiments to investigate the effectiveness of our proposed modules.

Effectiveness of MAE and BME. We carry out incremental validation on MARS and LS-VID datasets. The experimental results are shown in Table 3. Baseline refers to the model only using ResNet-50. Then, we insert MAE into ResNet-50 at the end of the Res2 and Res3 blocks respectively. When deploying MAE, the frame-level features get enhanced. Compared with the baseline method, our MAE significantly improves the mAP by 5.7% and 2.8% on MARS and LS-VID, respectively. The improvements indicate that the extraction of long-term appearances is effective. In addition, two BMEs are deployed at the same layers and promote to gain further growth of 0.7% and 0.8% R-1 on MARS and LS-VID. These results validate the complementarity of short-term motions and long-term appearances. Meanwhile, the model complexity (Param.) and computational complexity (FLOPs) are reported in Table 3. One can see that the computational cost increase is relatively small, showing that our long short-term representation learning is efficient.

Necessities of Multi-granularity Appearance. Table 4 shows the performances of MAE on MARS and LS-VID when removing one of the four-granularity appearances. We find that the accuracies have decreased in different degrees. Especially, when the appearance feature A_2 is missing, the accuracies of R-1 and mAP drop 0.6% and 1.0% on MARS respectively. These findings account for the necessity of long-term appearances in multi-granularity.

Effects of Motion Estimation. In our BME, we perform global-to-local and bi-direction estimation to obtain short-term motion representations. As shown in Table 5, compared with the local-to-local estimation, our global-to-local estimation gains better retrieval accuracies. In the deployment of local-to-local motion estimation, the dot product is conducted between any pair-wise local features. The reciprocal temporal learning actually increases the robustness to noise frames. Thus, as shown in Table 5, our bi-direction motion estimation further raises the R-1 by 0.6% and 0.4% on MARS and LS-VID than single-direction.

Visualization Analysis. In Fig. 5, we visualize the multi-granularity dependencies, which are captured by MAE and present the inter-frame associations. One can see that D^1 associates each local feature. D^2 highlights the salient regions in spatial, such as the upper body. D^3 and D^4 tend to mine more meaningful cues under global guidance. Meanwhile, the motion feature maps M^f and M^b obtained by BME are also visualized. Comparing M^f and M^b, it can be seen that, both of them focus on the main body of persons, but there are some differences in the highlighted areas, which validate the benefits of the bi-direction estimation. Overall, these visualization results further demonstrate the effectiveness of our MAE and BME.

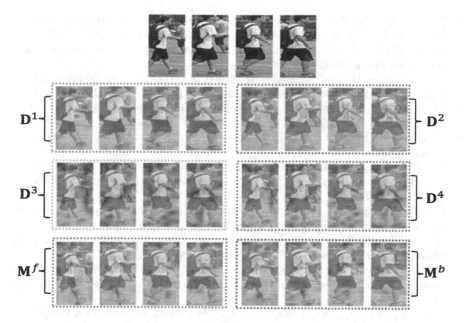

Fig. 5. The visualizations of multi-granularity dependencies ($\mathbf{D}^1$, $\mathbf{D}^2$, $\mathbf{D}^3$, $\mathbf{D}^4$) in MAE, and the motion features in forward ($\mathbf{M}^f$) and backward ($\mathbf{M}^b$) directions from BME.

5   Conclusion

In this paper, we propose a novel learning framework for video-based person Re-ID. To extract long-term representations, we propose the MAE, in which four granularity appearances are effectively captured by associating multiple frames. To extract short-term representations, we propose the BME, in which reciprocal motion information is efficiently estimated from consecutive frames. Our MAE and BME are plug-and-play and can be easily inserted into existing networks for end-to-end supervision. As a result, they significantly improve the feature representation ability for video-based person Re-ID. Experiments on three public benchmarks show that our approach outperforms most state-of-the-arts.

References

1. Bai, S., Ma, B., Chang, H., Huang, R., Chen, X.: Salient-to-broad transition for video person re-identification. In: CVPR, pp. 7339–7348 (2022)
2. Chen, G., Rao, Y., Lu, J., Zhou, J.: Temporal coherence or temporal motion: which is more critical for video-based person re-identification? In: ECCV, pp. 660–676 (2020)
3. Dai, J., Zhang, P., Wang, D., Lu, H., Wang, H.: Video person re-identification by temporal residual learning. TIP **28**, 1366–1377 (2019)
4. Eom, C., Lee, G., Lee, J., Ham, B.: Video-based person re-identification with spatial and temporal memory networks. In: ICCV, pp. 12036–12045 (2021)

5. Fu, Y., Wang, X., Wei, Y., Huang, T.: STA: spatial-temporal attention for large-scale video-based person re-identification. In: AAAI, pp. 8287–8294 (2019)
6. Gu, X., Chang, H., Ma, B., Shan, S.: Motion feature aggregation for video-based person re-identification. TIP (2022)
7. Gu, X., Chang, H., Ma, B., Zhang, H., Chen, X.: Appearance-preserving 3D convolution for video-based person re-identification. In: ECCV, pp. 228–243 (2020)
8. He, K., Zhang, X., Ren, S., Sun, J.: Deep residual learning for image recognition. In: CVPR, pp. 770–778 (2016)
9. Hermans, A., Beyer, L., Leibe, B.: In defense of the triplet loss for person re-identification. arXiv:1703.07737 (2017)
10. Hou, R., Chang, H., Ma, B., Huang, R., Shan, S.: BiCnet-TKS: learning efficient spatial-temporal representation for video person re-identification. In: CVPR, pp. 2014–2023 (2021)
11. Hou, R., Chang, H., Ma, B., Shan, S., Chen, X.: Temporal complementary learning for video person re-identification. In: ECCV, pp. 388–405 (2020)
12. Hou, R., Ma, B., Chang, H., Gu, X., Shan, S., Chen, X.: VRSTC: occlusion-free video person re-identification. In: CVPR, pp. 7183–7192 (2019)
13. Ilg, E., Mayer, N., Saikia, T., Keuper, M., Dosovitskiy, A., Brox, T.: FlowNet 2.0: evolution of optical flow estimation with deep networks. In: CVPR, pp. 2462–2470 (2017)
14. Jiang, X., Qiao, Y., Yan, J., Li, Q., Zheng, W., Chen, D.: SSN3D: self-separated network to align parts for 3D convolution in video person re-identification. In: AAAI, pp. 1691–1699 (2021)
15. Kingma, D.P., Ba, J.: Adam: a method for stochastic optimization. arXiv:1412.6980 (2014)
16. Li, J., Wang, J., Tian, Q., Gao, W., Zhang, S.: Global-local temporal representations for video person re-identification. In: ICCV, pp. 3958–3967 (2019)
17. Li, J., Zhang, S., Huang, T., so, o.: Multi-scale 3D convolution network for video based person re-identification. In: AAAI, pp. 8618–8625 (2019)
18. Li, S., Bak, S., Carr, P., Wang, X.: Diversity regularized spatiotemporal attention for video-based person re-identification. In: CVPR, pp. 369–378 (2018)
19. Li, S., Yu, H., Hu, H.: Appearance and motion enhancement for video-based person re-identification. In: AAAI, pp. 11394–11401 (2020)
20. Liu, H., et al.: Video-based person re-identification with accumulative motion context. TCSVT **28**(10), 2788–2802 (2017)
21. Liu, J., Zha, Z.J., Wu, W., Zheng, K., Sun, Q.: Spatial-temporal correlation and topology learning for person re-identification in videos. In: CVPR, pp. 4370–4379 (2021)
22. Liu, X., Zhang, P., Yu, C., Lu, H., Yang, X.: Watching you: global-guided reciprocal learning for video-based person re-identification. In: CVPR, pp. 13334–13343 (2021)
23. Liu, Y., Yuan, Z., Zhou, W., Li, H.: Spatial and temporal mutual promotion for video-based person re-identification. In: AAAI, pp. 8786–8793 (2019)
24. McLaughlin, N., Martinez del Rincon, J., Miller, P.: Recurrent convolutional network for video-based person re-identification. In: CVPR, pp. 1325–1334 (2016)
25. Sarfraz, M.S., Schumann, A., Eberle, A., Stiefelhagen, R.: A pose-sensitive embedding for person re-identification with expanded cross neighborhood re-ranking. In: CVPR, pp. 420–429 (2018)
26. Subramaniam, A., Nambiar, A., Mittal, A.: Co-segmentation inspired attention networks for video-based person re-identification. In: ICCV, pp. 562–572 (2019)

27. Sun, D., Yang, X., Liu, M.Y., Kautz, J.: PWC-Net: CNNs for optical flow using pyramid, warping, and cost volume. In: CVPR (2017)
28. Wang, T., Gong, S., Zhu, X., Wang, S.: Person re-identification by video ranking. In: ECCV, pp. 688–703 (2014)
29. Wang, Y., Zhang, P., Gao, S., Geng, X., Lu, H., Wang, D.: Pyramid spatial-temporal aggregation for video-based person re-identification. In: CVPR, pp. 12026–12035 (2021)
30. Zhang, T., et al.: Spatiotemporal transformer for video-based person re-identification. arXiv:2103.16469 (2021)
31. Zhang, Z., Lan, C., Zeng, W., Chen, Z.: Multi-granularity reference-aided attentive feature aggregation for video-based person re-identification. In: CVPR, pp. 10407–10416 (2020)
32. Zhao, S., et al.: MaskFlownet: asymmetric feature matching with learnable occlusion mask. In: CVPR, pp. 6278–6287 (2020)
33. Zheng, L., Bie, Z., Sun, Y., Wang, J., Su, C., Wang, S., Tian, Q.: MARS: a video benchmark for large-scale person re-identification. In: ECCV, pp. 868–884 (2016)

Multi-semantic Fusion Model For Generalized Zero-Shot Skeleton-Based Action Recognition

Ming-Zhe Li[1,3], Zhen Jia[3], Zhang Zhang[2,3(✉)], Zhanyu Ma[1], and Liang Wang[2,3]

[1] PRIS Lab., School of Artificial Intelligence, Beijing University of Posts and Telecommunications, Beijing, China
{limingzhe_24,mazhanyu}@bupt.edu.cn

[2] School of Artificial Intelligence, University of Chinese Academy of Sciences (UCAS), Beijing, China

[3] CRIPAC, MAIS, CASIA, Beijing, China
{zhen.jia,zzhang,wangliang}@nlpr.ia.ac.cn

Abstract. Generalized zero-shot skeleton-based action recognition (GZSSAR) is a new challenging problem in computer vision community, which requires models to recognize actions without any training samples. Previous studies only utilize the action labels of verb phrases as the semantic prototypes for learning the mapping from skeleton based actions to a shared semantic space. However, the limited semantic information of action labels restricts the generalization ability of skeleton features for recognizing unseen actions. In order to solve this dilemma, we propose a multi-semantic fusion (MSF) model for improving the performance of GZSSAR, where two kinds of class-level textual descriptions (*i.e.*, action descriptions and motion descriptions), are collected as auxiliary semantic information to enhance the learning efficacy of generalizable skeleton features. Specially, a pre-trained language encoder takes the action descriptions, motion descriptions and original class labels as inputs to obtain rich semantic features for each action class, while a skeleton encoder is implemented to extract skeleton features. Then, a variational autoencoder (VAE) based generative module is performed to learn a cross-modal alignment between skeleton and semantic features. Finally, a classification module is built to recognize the action categories of input samples, where a seen-unseen classification gate is adopted to predict whether the sample comes from seen action classes or not in GZSSAR. The superior performance compared with previous models validates the effectiveness of the proposed MSF model on GZSSAR.

Supported by the National Key R&D Program of China (2022ZD0117901), the National Natural Science Foundation of China (62106260, 62236010, 62076078, U19B2036 and 62225601), the Beijing Natural Science Foundation Project (Z200002), the Program for Youth Innovative Research Team of BUPT (2023QNTD02), and the High-performance Computing Platform of BUPT.

H. Lu et al. (Eds.): ICIG 2023, LNCS 14355, pp. 68–80, 2023.
https://doi.org/10.1007/978-3-031-46305-1_6

Keywords: Generalized Zero-Shot Learning · Skeleton-Based Action Recognition · Semantic Description · Generative Method

1 Introduction

Human action recognition is a fundamental computer vision problem with great application potentials on video surveillance [1], video retrieval [16] and human-computer interaction [25]. With the developments of advanced depth cameras and pose estimation agorithms, skeleton-based action recognition has become a hot research topic, besides the ordinary RGB video based action recognition. Skeleton-based action recognition takes the 3D skeleton sequences as input, which makes action recognition models more robust to deal with variations in illumination, camera viewpoints and other background changes. However, although there have been high-performance skeleton-based approaches [3,13,21, 28], most of these approaches are prone to overfitting and fail to generalize to the unseen classes outside the training set [5]. This is mainly because the conventional action recognition only attempts to learn a mapping that maximizes the inter-class distance, and may not be suitable of learning generalizable features for encoding new action categories.

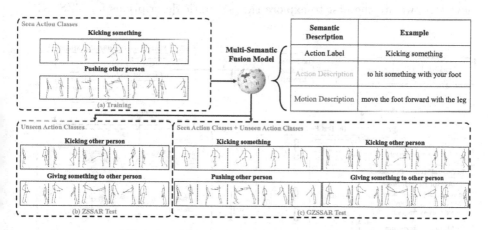

Fig. 1. A schematic diagram of ZSSAR and GZSSAR.

Therefore, there is a strong motivation for exploring the problems of zero-shot skeleton-based action recognition (ZSSAR) and generalized zero-shot skeleton-based action recognition (GZSSAR) methods. In the previous work [5], Gupta et al. set up the task of ZSSAR and GZSSAR, as the schematic diagram shown in Fig. 1. ZSSAR aims to train a model that can classify actions of unseen classes via transferring knowledge obtained from other seen classes with the help of semantic information. The setting of GZSSAR needs model to recognize samples from both seen and unseen classes simultaneously during test time, which is a more challenging issue and closer to open-world applications.

Generally, in generalized zero-shot image classification [17], the semantic information, such as language and attributes, is utilized to build a relationship between seen and unseen classes through mapping visual features and semantic features into a common space. However, the previous methods [12,27] are difficult to be directly adopted to GZSSAR. On one hand, there are not any semantic attribute based annotations or detailed language descriptions for action categories in current skeleton-based action datasets. On the other hand, as the only semantic information that can be directly utilized, the class labels which commonly are verb phrases, are too ambiguous to well distinguish the actions in skeleton modality. For example, action "reading book" and action "typing keyboard" are very similar in motion. To deal with the dilemma, auxiliary semantic descriptions are collected to better describe actions in words. The semantic descriptions include action descriptions and motion descriptions. The action descriptions are obtained by referring to the explanations of actions in the Oxford Dictionary. The motion descriptions are collected by human annotators who are asked to describe the movements of body parts when watching some examples of each action category. The class-level annotations can be completed easily with low manual costs. In this paper, the two kinds of semantic descriptions as well as the class labels are investigated to construct rich semantic representations so as to improve the learning efficacy of generalizable skeleton features. To the best of our knowledge, we are the first to explore rich semantic descriptions for GZSSAR.

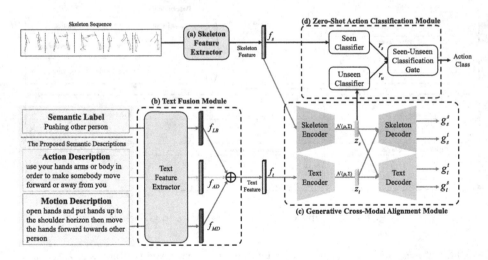

Fig. 2. Architectural diagram for the proposed Multi-Semantic Fusion model.

Since action descriptions are from textual knowledge in dictionary and motion descriptions describe the detailed movements of body parts, we design the multi-semantic fusion (MSF) model to comprehensively utilize multiple semantic information to improve the performance of GZSSAR. The overall architecture of the MSF model is shown in Fig. 2. Firstly, for the input skeleton sequences, the MSF model uses a 4 s-ShiftGCN [3] as the skeleton feature extractor to encode skeleton features. Secondly, for the input multiple semantic information, a text fusion module is designed to encode each type of semantic information and fuse them to obtain rich semantic features for each action categories. A pre-trained ViT-B/32 [18] is implemented as the text feature extractor. Thirdly, considering the superiority of the generative methods in generalized zero-shot image classification, a VAE-based generative cross-modal alignment module is designed to map the skeleton features and the rich semantic features to a common feature space. Therefore, the model is able to generate latent embeddings of unseen classes for the training of an unseen-classifier. At last, in order to achieve better GZSSAR performance, a zero-shot action classification module is implemented at the end of the model. It uses a seen-unseen classification gate to make a decision that the given sample should be classified as seen classes or unseen classes in the task setting of GZSSAR. The results of the experiments prove the effectiveness of the MSF model and the superiority of the proposed semantic descriptions.

The contributions of this paper can be summarized in threefold:

- Two kinds of class-level descriptions (*i.e.*, action descriptions and motion descriptions) are firstly explored for GZSSAR. The richer semantic information is validated effective for improving the performance of GZSSAR.
- A multi-semantic fusion model is proposed to comprehensively utilize multiple semantic information and superiority accomplish GZSSAR task. A VAE-based generative module is adopted to accomplish the cross-modal alignment between skeleton features and rich semantic features of actions.
- Extensive experiments are performed to demonstrate the proposed MSF model's state-of-the-art performance on NTU-60 [20] and NTU-120 [11] datasets.

2   Related Work

Generalized Zero-Shot Skeleton-Based Action Recognition. In recent years, there are only a few studies related to GZSSAR due to its immense difficulties in bridging the semantic gap between skeleton data and semantic labels without any prior exposure to training samples of unseen classes. Jasani et al. [7] propose to use embedding based methods [4,24] to align skeleton embeddings with their corresponding text embeddings of the class labels (*e.g.*, "take off jacket" and "put on glasses"). Gupta et al. [5] propose a model termed SynSE, which splits a class label into verbs and nouns according to its syntactic structures (*e.g.*, "drink water" can be splitted into a verb "drink" and a noun "water") and aligns the skeleton embeddings with the corresponding verb embeddings and noun embeddings. They also formally set up the task of zero-shot learning (ZSL) and generalized zero-shot learning (GZSL) in skeleton-based action recognition.

Semantic Information in Generalized Zero-Shot Learning. The most widely used semantic information for GZSL can be grouped into manually defined attributes [10] and word vectors [15]. Manually defined attributes describe the high-level characteristics of classes (*e.g.*, shape and color), which enable the models to recognize classes that never appear in the training dataset. The attribute space has been widely used in GZSL studies, however it requires human efforts in attribute annotations for each classes, which are not suitable for large-scale problems [9]. Along with the developments of foundation language models, word vector based methods can directly map the class name into a semantic embedding space and describe the similarities between seen classes and unseen ones in a more efficient way. Therefore, they are more suitable for large-scale datasets. However, for zero-shot action recognition, the class names may not reflect the detailed differences between various actions. For example, the actions "reading book" and "typing keyboard" are both related to the movement of two hands. The simple class names are not semantically abundant enough to describe the ambiguity in the two classes. Thus, in this paper, we attempt to augment the descriptions of action categories with richer semantic information.

3   Action and Motion Descriptions for GZSSAR

In generalized zero-shot image classification, the word vectors of class labels or visual attributes are used as semantic information. However, accurately representing action classes in a semantic space is still a challenging problem due to the complexity and diversity of human actions. Furthermore, for skeleton-based action recognition, there is not any other semantic information in current popular skeleton-based action datasets (*e.g.*, NTU-60 and NTU-120 datasets), except for class labels. However, the class labels (*e.g.*, "drink water" and "eat meal") are always too concise and abstract to well distinguish the actions in most cases. As shown in the previous work, the performance of GZSSAR is still limited due to the lack of transferable semantic information among different actions. To address this dilemma, action descriptions and motion descriptions are explored for GZSSAR in this paper. The examples of action descriptions and motion descriptions are demonstrated in Table 1.

Table 1. Action and Motion Description Examples

Class Labels	Action Descriptions	Motion Descriptions
brushing teeth	to clean polish or make teeth smooth with a brush	move the hand up to the head then tremble the hand
pickup	to take hold of something and lift it up	bend knees and hips to move the hand down to the ground then pinch then get up
wear on glasses	to have glasses on your head as a piece of decoration	pinch and move hands up to the head then release hands and put hands down
salute	to touch the side of your head with the fingers of your right hand to show respect	open the hand and move the hand to the side of the head then hold
drop	to allow something to fall by accident from your hand	release the hand in front of the middle of the spine

As shown in Table 1, the action descriptions are a kind of textual descriptions about actions, which are collected with reference to the explanations of actions in the Oxford Dictionary [23]. For all action categories in the NTU-60 and NTU-120 datasets, we search for the definitions of verb phrases in class labels, and form the action descritions for all action categories. Compared to class labels, the action descriptions are easier to understand and obviously contain human knowledge on various action categories which is crucial for GZSSAR. However, an unavoidable issue is that the definitions of an action category phrases may include other new abstract semantic concepts which are hard to be grounded to input skeleton samples. Therefore, the redundant new concepts may not bring benefits for the performance of GZSSAR.

Thus, we further propose the motion descriptions which are annotated with reference to the movement trajectories of relatively important body parts in skeleton sequences. To collect the annotations, we invite 10 human annotators who are graduate students in an engineering institute to describe the movement processes of all action categories in NTU-60 and NTU-120 datasets. The annotators are asked to use some simple and common verbs (*e.g.*, "move" and "put") as well as the nouns of 25 key-points (*e.g.*, "head", "shoulder" and "elbow") to describe the movements of important key-points as watching a skeleton sequence sample randomly selected from each action category. In the motion descriptions, a set of simple verbs and nouns which directly correspond to certain body parts can be shared across various action categories. Compared with class labels and action descriptions, the shared descriptions on basic movements of body parts may be more appropriate for learning transferable skeleton features across seen and unseen classes.

In summary, the proposed action descriptions contain richer vocabulary from human knowledge base. Meanwhile, the motion descriptions can better reflect the detailed movements of important skeleton joints in actions. The proposed action descriptions and motion descriptions will be available to the GZSSAR research community in the future.

4   Methodology

4.1   Problem Formulation

Assume that $S = \left\{ (x_i^s, t_i^s, y_i^s)_{i=1}^{N_s} | x_i^s \in X^s, t_i^s \in T^s, y_i^s \in Y^s \right\}$ represents the seen action class dataset, and $U = \left\{ (x_j^u, t_j^u, y_j^u)_{j=1}^{N_u} | x_j^u \in X^u, t_j^u \in T^u, y_j^u \in Y^u \right\}$ denotes the unseen action class dataset. $x_i^s, x_j^u \in \mathbb{R}^D$ indicate the D-dimensional skeleton features in skeleton feature space X, and $t_i^s, t_j^u \in \mathbb{R}^K$ indicate the K-dimensional text features in text feature space T. N_s and N_u are the numbers of seen and unseen samples. $X^u = \{x_j^u\}_{j=1}^{N_u}$ indicate the skeleton feature set of unseen action classes in X. $Y^s = \left\{ y_1^s, ..., y_{C_s}^s \right\}$ and $Y^u = \left\{ y_1^u, ..., y_{C_u}^u \right\}$ indicate the digital label sets of seen and unseen action classes in Y, where C_s and C_u are the numbers of seen and unseen action classes. $Y = Y^s \cup Y^u$ denotes all action classes and $Y^s \cap Y^u = \varnothing$. The objective of ZSSAR and GZSSAR are to learn $f_{ZSSAR} : X^u \to Y^u$ and $f_{GZSSAR} : X \to Y$, respectively.

4.2 Skeleton Feature Extractor

To complete the GZSSAR task, a crucial requirement is to acquire the discriminative features of skeleton sequences. Considering the superior performance of ShiftGCN [3] in skeleton based action recognition, the proposed MSF model adopts ShiftGCN as the skeleton feature extractor. The skeleton feature extractor in Fig. 2 (a) and the seen-classifier in Fig. 2 (d) need to be trained on the train-set (S_{train}) first in order to recognize samples in the test-set (S_{test}). S_{train} and S_{test} are two complementary and disjoint subsets partitioned from S.

4.3 Text Fusion Module

As introduced in Sect. 3, the action descriptions and the motion descriptions are complementary to each other. To comprehensively utilize these rich semantic information, the text fusion module takes multiple semantic information (*i.e.*, class labels, action descriptions and motion descriptions) as input and extracts their semantic features separately. Then, a concatenation operation is adopted to fuse the three types of semantic information together, as shown in Fig. 2 (b). Since CLIP [18] is effective in image-text matching tasks, the MSF model directly adopts the pre-trained ViT-B/32, which is the text-encoder of CLIP, as the text feature extractor to extract semantic features. The MSF model uses a simple and efficient way (*i.e.*, concatenation operation) to fuse multiple semantic information together, as shown in Eq. 1.

$$f_t = f_{LB} \oplus f_{AD} \oplus f_{MD}. \tag{1}$$

$\oplus$ indicates the concatenation operation. f_{LB}, f_{AD} and f_{MD} indicate the features of the class label, action description and motion description respectively.

4.4 Generative Cross-Modal Alignment Module

Since the skeleton feature f_s and the text feature f_t belong to two different feature spaces, it is necessary to map the f_s and the f_t to a common feature space where they are aligned with each other. For this, we employ a generative variational autoencoder (VAE) based architecture [5] to implement the mapping. The architecture of the generative cross-modal alignment module is shown in Fig. 2 (c). The module contains two branches, *i.e.*, the skeleton branch and the text branch. Since the structure of the module is symmetrical, only the skeleton branch is introduced in detail here. In the training phase, the evidence lower bound loss (ELBO) is implemented for the training of the VAE. Formally,

$$\mathcal{L}_{VAE}^s = \mathbb{E}_{q_\phi(z_s|f_s)}[\log p_\theta(f_s|z_s)] - \beta D_{KL}(q_\phi(z_s|f_s) \parallel p_\theta(z_s|f_s)), \tag{2}$$

where $p_\theta(\cdot)$ and $q_\phi(\cdot)$ denote the likelihood and the prior respectively. β is a hyper-parameter which acts as a trade-off factor between the two error terms. $q_\phi(z_s|f_s)$ obeys the multivariate Gaussian distribution $\mathcal{N}_s(\mu_s, \Sigma_s)$. The L2 loss is implemented to align the generated g_t^s with the text feature f_t. Formally,

$$\mathcal{L}_{Align}^s = \| f_t - g_t^s \|_2, \tag{3}$$

where $\| \cdot \|_2$ denotes the L2 norm. The entire loss function of the skeleton branch is formulated as follows.

$$\mathcal{L}^s = \mathcal{L}_{VAE}^s + \alpha \mathcal{L}_{Align}^s, \tag{4}$$

where α is a trade-off weight factor.

Similarly, the entire loss function of the text branch $\mathcal{L}^t = \mathcal{L}_{VAE}^t + \mathcal{L}_{Align}^t$ is calculated in text branch. Finally, the entire loss function of the generative cross-modal alignment module is formulated as follows.

$$\mathcal{L} = \mathcal{L}^s + \mathcal{L}^t. \tag{5}$$

Through this way, the encoders and the decoders are trained relying on $\mathcal{L}_{VAE}^s$ and $\mathcal{L}_{VAE}^t$. The alignment between z_s and z_t is achieved with the help of $\mathcal{L}_{align}^s$ and $\mathcal{L}_{align}^t$. After training, the generative cross-modal alignment module is able to generate latent embeddings from the input feature, in an aligned feature space.

4.5   Zero-Shot Action Classification Module

As shown in Fig. 2 (d), the zero-shot action classification module is composed of the seen-classifier, the unseen-classifier, and the seen-unseen classification gate. As mentioned in Sect. 4.2, the seen-classifier has already been trained with the skeleton feature extractor. In ZSSAR, an unseen classifier is still needed to classify the samples in U. Since samples in X^u can not be used for training, we generate z_t using $t_j^u \in T^u$ to train the unseen-classifier.

In GZSSAR, a common method is to utilize an additional classifier to classify the test samples from both seen and unseen classes. However, the prediction results obtained by this way are usually unsatisfying [2]. Therefore, a seen-unseen classification gate is implemented to predict the action classes of the input skeleton features more accurately. The classification gate is trained on a validation set, utilizing the predicted results from the seen-classifier and the unseen-classifier as inputs. It employs a logistic regression classifier to regress binary results, indicating whether the input skeleton features belong to unseen action classes or not. The validation set is partitioned from the training set based on the number of unseen classes.

5   Experimental Results

5.1   Datasets

NTU RGB+D 60 [20]. The NTU-60 dataset is a large-scale indoor dataset for 3D human action analysis. It contains 56,880 human action videos collected by three Kinect-V2 cameras. The dataset consists of 60 action classes. Only the skeleton data is used in this work. In each skeleton sequence, every frame contains no more than 2 skeletons, and each skeleton is composed of 25 joints. Two seen/unseen splits (*i.e.*, 55 (seen classes)/5 (unseen classes) and 48 (seen classes)/12 (unseen classes)) are set up in the previous work [5], in where the unseen classes are chosen randomly. In order to compare with the state-of-the-art methods, we continue to adopt the two seen/unseen splits. The selection of the unseen classes maintains the same with the previous work [5].

NTU RGB+D 120 [11]. The NTU-120 dataset is currently the largest indoor skeleton-based action recognition dataset, which is an extended version of the NTU-60 dataset. It contains a total of 114,480 videos performed by 106 subjects from 155 viewpoints. The dataset consists of 120 classes, extended from the 60 classes of the NTU-60 dataset. The seen/unseen splits are 110 (seen)/10 (unseen) and 96 (seen)/24 (unseen), also the same with the previous work [5].

5.2   Implementation Details

The training phase can be divided into 4 stages, training of the skeleton feature extractor, training of the generative cross-modal alignment module, training of the unseen-classifier and training of the seen-unseen classification gate. In stage 1, the skeleton feature extractor and the seen-classifier are trained using samples of seen classes to obtain 256-dimensional skeleton features. The specific training details of the skeleton feature extractor are the same as [3]. The 512-dimensional text features are obtained through the pre-trained text feature extractor. In stage 2, the generative cross-modal alignment module is trained using the skeleton features and the text features. The dimension of the latent embeddings is set to 100 on the NTU-60 dataset and 200 on the NTU-120 dataset. The optimizer is Adam with the learning rate $1 \times e^{-4}$, the training epoch is 1900 with the batch size of 64. In stage 3, we generate 500 latent features for each unseen class to train the unseen-classifier for 300 epochs. The learning rate is set to $1 \times e^{-3}$ with Adam optimizer. In stage 4, the logistic regression classifier is optimized using LBFGS solver with the default aggressiveness hyper-parameter ($C = 1$). [2]. All our experiments are performed on one NVIDIA GTX TITAN X GPU.

5.3   Comparisons with State-of-the-Art Methods

Since there have been a few previous work for ZSSAR and GZSSAR, Gupta et al. [5] modify representative generalized zero-shot image classification methods and implement them for GZSSAR from scratch. In this part, the proposed MSF model is compared with the state-of-the-art method SynSE [5] and the other modified GZSL methods. The evaluation protocol of the MSF model and the SynSE maintains the same. The experiments of both ZSSAR and GZSSAR are conducted. In ZSSAR experiments, the accuracy of the classification for unseen samples is reported. And in GZSSAR, the accuracy of seen classes (Acc_s), the accuracy of unseen classes (Acc_u) and their harmonic mean (H) are all reported.

Table 2. Comparisons with SOTA methods in ZSSAR accuracies (%).

Method	NTU-60		NTU-120	
	$55(s)/5(u)$	$48(s)/12(u)$	$110(s)/10(u)$	$96(s)/24(u)$
ReViSE [6]	53.91	17.49	55.04	32.38
JPoSE [26]	64.32	28.75	51.93	32.44
CADA-VAE [19]	76.84	28.96	59.53	35.77
SynSE [5]	75.81	33.30	62.69	38.70
Ours(LB)	80.01	40.80	67.33	47.57
Ours(AD)	78.91	45.81	56.03	42.99
Ours(MD)	83.26	**55.38**	60.36	45.39
Ours(LB+AD+MD)	**83.63**	49.19	**71.20**	**59.73**

Table 3. Comparisons with SOTA methods in GZSSAR accuracies (%) and harmonic mean.

Method	NTU-60						NTU-120					
	$55(s)/5(u)$			$48(s)/12(u)$			$110(s)/10(u)$			$96(s)/24(u)$		
	Acc_s	Acc_u	H	Acc_s	Acc_u	H	Acc_s	Acc_u	H	Acc_s	Acc_u	H
ReViSE [6]	74.22	34.73	29.22	62.36	20.77	31.16	48.69	44.84	46.68	49.66	25.06	33.31
JPoSE [26]	64.44	50.29	56.49	60.49	20.62	30.75	47.66	46.40	47.05	38.62	22.79	28.67
CADA-VAE [19]	69.38	61.79	65.37	51.32	27.03	35.41	47.16	19.78	48.44	41.11	34.14	37.31
SynSE [5]	61.27	56.93	59.02	52.21	27.85	36.33	52.51	57.60	54.94	56.39	32.25	41.04
Ours(LB)	69.41	57.15	62.69	53.25	34.43	41.82	56.45	58.38	**57.40**	58.96	35.71	44.48
Ours(AD)	67.34	60.69	63.84	59.42	37.52	46.00	49.87	52.87	51.33	59.66	33.45	42.87
Ours(MD)	65.04	**66.74**	65.88	50.69	**48.75**	**49.70**	58.67	52.38	55.35	58.76	32.86	42.15
Ours(LB+AD+MD)	71.73	66.15	**68.83**	58.80	40.00	47.61	46.84	**68.30**	55.57	56.84	**48.61**	**52.40**

As shown in Table 2 and Table 3, in both ZSSAR and GZSSAR, the proposed MSF model surpasses all the state-of-the-art methods by a large margin. Even if only using class labels, the MSF model achieves better performance than SynSE, due to the use of CLIP based text feature extractor. Noted, the skeleton feature extractor used in this work, *i.e.*, ShiftGCN, is also the same with the SynSE. Compared to SynSE, the most significant increase of MSF in ZSSAR accuracy reaches up to 21.03%, and the most significant increase of MSF in H reaches up to 11.36%. The increase of Acc_u in GZSSAR is particularly significant. Furthermore, in the $48(s)/12(u)$ split of NTU-60 and $96(s)/24(u)$ split of NTU-120, our method achieves greater performance improvements, which verifies the advantages of MSF on more challenging data splits.

5.4   Ablation Studies

Comparisons of Text Feature Extractors: In CLIP, there are two pre-trained text encoders that are frequently used in previous vision-language models (*i.e.*, ViT-B/16 and ViT-B/32). Both of them can be directly used as the text feature extractor. To select one of them for feature extraction, both of the two encoders are tested in ZSSAR and GZSSAR. The results are presented in Table 4 and Table 5. As shown in the two tables, in both ZSSAR and GZSSAR, ViT-

B/32 performs better than ViT-B/16 in most cases. Only under the $96(s)/24(u)$ split of NTU-120 dataset, the performance of ViT-B/32 is slightly inferior to ViT-B/16. Therefore, ViT-B/32 is more suitable as the text feature extractor in the MSF model. In the subsequent experiments, we will use ViT-B/32 as the text feature extractor.

Table 4. Comparisons of different text feature extractors in ZSSAR accuracies (%).

Model	NTU-60		NTU-120	
	$55(s)/5(u)$	$48(s)/12(u)$	$110(s)/10(u)$	$96(s)/24(u)$
ViT-B/16	83.55	43.98	69.34	**60.29**
ViT-B/32	**83.63**	**49.19**	**71.20**	59.73

Table 5. Comparisons of different text feature extractors in GZSSAR accuracies (%) and harmonic mean.

Model	NTU-60						NTU-120					
	$55(s)/5(u)$			$48(s)/12(u)$			$110(s)/10(u)$			$96(s)/24(u)$		
	Acc_s	Acc_u	H	Acc_s	Acc_u	H	Acc_s	Acc_u	H	Acc_s	Acc_u	H
ViT-B/16	71.85	65.49	68.52	55.04	36.73	44.06	46.07	67.03	54.61	57.14	**49.90**	**53.27**
ViT-B/32	71.73	**66.15**	**68.83**	58.80	**40.00**	**47.61**	46.84	**68.30**	**55.57**	56.84	48.61	52.40

Table 6. Comparisons of different semantic information in ZSSAR accuracies (%).

Method	NTU-60		NTU-120	
	$55(s)/5(u)$	$48(s)/12(u)$	$110(s)/10(u)$	$96(s)/24(u)$
LB	80.01	40.80	67.33	47.57
AD	78.91	45.81	56.03	42.99
MD	83.26	**55.38**	60.36	45.39
AD+MD	83.04	47.22	65.03	57.44
LB+AD+MD	**83.63**	49.19	**71.20**	**59.73**

Comparisons of Different Semantic Information: In Sect. 3, three different types of semantic information (*i.e.*, class label (LB), action description (AD) and motion description (MD)) are evaluated. To verify the advantages of the fusion strategy (*i.e.*, LB+AD+MD), the ablation studies with ZSSAR and GZSSAR settings are conducted. As shown in Table 6 and Table 7, generally, the fusion strategy performs superior in both ZSSAR and GZSSAR. However, under the $48(s)/12(u)$ split of NTU-60 dataset, MD performs even better than fusion. Because under this split which is proposed in the previous work [5], unseen classes have less semantical relations with seen classes when using LB or AD as semantic information. However, MD is not affected because it has more shared words. And under the $110(s)/10(u)$ split of NTU-120 dataset, LB performs better than fusion in H of GZSSAR. In this condition, compared to the fusion strategy, H benefits more from Acc_s than from Acc_u when using LB, due to the instability of the seen-unseen classification gate. Overall, the fusion strategy is the optimal choice.

Table 7. Comparisons of different semantic information in GZSSAR accuracies (%) and harmonic mean.

Method	NTU-60						NTU-120					
	$55(s)/5(u)$			$48(s)/12(u)$			$110(s)/10(u)$			$96(s)/24(u)$		
	Acc_s	Acc_u	H	Acc_s	Acc_u	H	Acc_s	Acc_u	H	Acc_s	Acc_u	H
LB	69.41	57.15	62.69	53.25	34.43	41.82	56.45	58.38	**57.40**	58.96	35.71	44.48
AD	67.34	60.69	63.84	59.42	37.52	46.00	49.87	52.87	51.33	59.66	33.45	42.87
MD	65.04	66.74	65.88	50.69	**48.75**	**49.70**	58.67	52.38	55.35	58.76	32.86	42.15
AD+MD	64.50	**72.20**	68.13	57.00	39.54	46.69	45.86	62.74	52.99	50.91	51.90	51.40
LB+AD+MD	71.73	66.15	**68.83**	58.80	40.00	47.61	46.84	**68.30**	55.57	56.84	**48.61**	**52.40**

6 Conclusion

In this paper, the action descriptions and the motion descriptions are explored for the NTU-60 and NTU-120 datasets. The multi-semantic fusion (MSF) model is proposed to integrate multiple semantic information together and accomplish the alignment between skeleton and text features. On two large-scale datasets (*i.e.*, NTU-60 and NTU-120), the experimental results show that the MSF method outperforms other state-of-the-art methods in both ZSSAR and GZSSAR.

References

1. Aggarwal, J.K., Ryoo, M.S.: Human activity analysis: a review. ACM Comput. Surv. **43**(3), 1–43 (2011)
2. Atzmon, Y., Chechik, G.: Adaptive confidence smoothing for generalized zero-shot learning. In: Proceedings of the IEEE/CVF CVPR, pp. 11671–11680 (2019)
3. Cheng, K., Zhang, Y., He, X., Chen, W., Cheng, J., Lu, H.: Skeleton-based action recognition with shift graph convolutional network. In: Proceedings of the IEEE/CVF CVPR, pp. 183–192 (2020)
4. Frome, A., Corrado, G.S., et al.: DeViSE: a deep visual-semantic embedding model. In: Advances in Neural Information Processing Systems 26 (2013)
5. Gupta, P., Sharma, D., Sarvadevabhatla, R.K.: Syntactically guided generative embeddings for zero-shot skeleton action recognition. In: 2021 IEEE ICIP, pp. 439–443 IEEE (2021)
6. Hubert Tsai, Y.H., Huang, L.K., Salakhutdinov, R.: Learning robust visual-semantic embeddings. In: Proceedings of the IEEE ICCV, pp. 3571–3580 (2017)
7. Jasani, B., Mazagonwalla, A.: Skeleton based zero shot action recognition in joint pose-language semantic space. arXiv preprint arXiv:1911.11344 (2019)
8. Kingma, D.P., Welling, M.: Auto-encoding variational Bayes. arXiv preprint arXiv:1312.6114 (2013)
9. Kodirov, E., Xiang, T., Gong, S.: Semantic autoencoder for zero-shot learning. In: Proceedings of the IEEE CVPR, pp. 3174–3183 (2017)
10. Lampert, C.H., Nickisch, H., Harmeling, S.: Attribute-based classification for zero-shot visual object categorization. IEEE TPAMI **36**(3), 453–465 (2013)
11. Liu, J., Shahroudy, A., Perez, M., Wang, G., Duan, L.Y., Kot, A.C.: NTU RGB+ d 120: a large-scale benchmark for 3D human activity understanding. IEEE TPAMI **42**(10), 2684–2701 (2019)

12. Liu, Y., et al.: Goal-oriented gaze estimation for zero-shot learning. In: Proceedings of the IEEE/CVF CVPR, pp. 3794–3803 (2021)
13. Liu, Z., Zhang, H., Chen, Z., Wang, Z., Ouyang, W.: Disentangling and unifying graph convolutions for skeleton-based action recognition. In: Proceedings of the IEEE/CVF CVPR, pp. 143–152 (2020)
14. Mikolov, T., Chen, K., Corrado, G., Dean, J.: Efficient estimation of word representations in vector space. arXiv preprint arXiv:1301.3781 (2013)
15. Mikolov, T., Sutskever, I., Chen, K., Corrado, G.S., Dean, J.: Distributed representations of words and phrases and their compositionality. In: Advances in Neural Information Processing Systems 26 (2013)
16. Poppe, R.: A survey on vision-based human action recognition. Image Vis. Comput. **28**(6), 976–990 (2010)
17. Pourpanah, F., et al.: A review of generalized zero-shot learning methods. IEEE TPAMI (2022)
18. Radford, A., et al.: Learning transferable visual models from natural language supervision. In: ICML, pp. 8748–8763. PMLR (2021)
19. Schonfeld, E., Ebrahimi, S., Sinha, S., Darrell, T., Akata, Z.: Generalized zero- and few-shot learning via aligned variational autoencoders. In: Proceedings of the IEEE/CVF CVPR, pp. 8247–8255 (2019)
20. Shahroudy, A., Liu, J., Ng, T.T., Wang, G.: NTU RGB+D: a large scale dataset for 3D human activity analysis. In: Proceedings of the IEEE CVPR, pp. 1010–1019 (2016)
21. Shi, L., Zhang, Y., Cheng, J., Lu, H.: Two-stream adaptive graph convolutional networks for skeleton-based action recognition. In: Proceedings of the IEEE/CVF CVPR, pp. 12026–12035 (2019)
22. Song, Y.F., Zhang, Z., Shan, C., Wang, L.: Constructing stronger and faster baselines for skeleton-based action recognition. IEEE TPAMI **45**(2), 1474–1488 (2022)
23. Stevenson, A.: Oxford dictionary of English. Oxford University Press, USA (2010)
24. Sung, F., Yang, Y., Zhang, L., Xiang, T., Torr, P.H., Hospedales, T.M.: Learning to compare: Relation network for few-shot learning. In: Proceedings of the IEEE CVPR, pp. 1199–1208 (2018)
25. Weinland, D., Ronfard, R., Boyer, E.: A survey of vision-based methods for action representation, segmentation and recognition. Comput. Vis. Image Underst. **115**(2), 224–241 (2011)
26. Wray, M., Larlus, D., Csurka, G., Damen, D.: Fine-grained action retrieval through multiple parts-of-speech embeddings. In: Proceedings of the IEEE/CVF ICCV, pp. 450–459 (2019)
27. Zhang, L., et al.: Towards effective deep embedding for zero-shot learning. IEEE TCSVT **30**(9), 2843–2852 (2020)
28. Zhang, P., Lan, C., Xing, J., Zeng, W., Xue, J., Zheng, N.: View adaptive neural networks for high performance skeleton-based human action recognition. IEEE TPAMI **41**(8), 1963–1978 (2019)

Toward Better SSIM Loss for Unsupervised Monocular Depth Estimation

Yijun Cao⬭, Fuya Luo⬭, and Yongjie Li$^{(\boxtimes)}$⬭

The MOE Key Laboratory for Neuroinformation,
The School of Life Science and Technology,
University of Electronic Science and Technology of China,
Chengdu 610054, China
`liyj@uestc.edu.cn`

Abstract. Unsupervised monocular depth learning generally relies on the photometric relation among temporally adjacent images. Most of previous works use both mean absolute error (MAE) and structure similarity index measure (SSIM) with conventional form as training loss. However, they ignore the effect of different components in the SSIM function and the corresponding hyperparameters on the training. To address these issues, this work proposes a new form of SSIM. Compared with original SSIM function, the proposed new form uses addition rather than multiplication to combine the luminance, contrast, and structural similarity related components in SSIM. The loss function constructed with this scheme helps result in smoother gradients and achieve higher performance on unsupervised depth estimation. We conduct extensive experiments to determine the relatively optimal combination of parameters for our new SSIM. Based on the popular MonoDepth approach, the optimized SSIM loss function can remarkably outperform the baseline on the KITTI-2015 outdoor dataset.

Keywords: Monocular Depth Estimation · Unsupervised Learning · SSIM Loss

1 Introduction

Single Image Depth Estimation (SIDE) is a critical task in the field of computer vision. It contributes to many other tasks, e.g., edge detection [2], scene reconstruction [25], object detection [15] and visual odometry [3]. Recent learning-based SIDE can be generally divided into supervised [5,12] and unsupervised approaches [3,7]. Supervised SIDE requires ground-truth depth map as training labels, whose process would be costly and time-consuming. Usupervised methods learn depth maps using photometric consistency from consecutive monocular or stereo image pairs. Recently, though unsupervised SIDE has seen great progresses, there still exists a large performance gap compared with supervised methods. We argue that this gap comes from the following four aspects: occlusion

H. Lu et al. (Eds.): ICIG 2023, LNCS 14355, pp. 81–92, 2023.
https://doi.org/10.1007/978-3-031-46305-1_7

and illumination inconsistency among adjacent images, inaccurate pose estimation (especially for the dynamic regions), loss function and network architecture.

In the past few years, researchers mainly focus on addressing the first two issues, i.e., reducing the effect of inconsistency among adjacent images [7,13] and pursuing accurate pose [3,22], while ignoring the last two issues. Thus, based on popular pixel-wise mean absolute error (MAE) and structure similarity index measure (SSIM), this work analyzes the effect of different coefficients on SSIM and designs a more suitable SSIM loss function for unsupervised SIDE. In addition, we found that the sub-pixel convolution [17] is better than conventional interpolation schemes in the processing of depth upsampling. A large number of experiments on KITTI dataset [6] demonstrates that the proposed loss function and network are better than baseline and many existing unsupervised SIDE methods.

2 Related Works

2.1 Supervised Monocular Depth Learning

With the development of convolutional Neural Networks (CNNs), a variety of models have been proposed to learn monocular depth in a supervised manner [4,12]. These approaches usually take a single image as input and use RGB-D camera or LIDAR as ground truth labels. Supervised methods were usually to design a better network for capturing structural information in monocular images, by using ranking or ordinal relation constraint [26], surface normal constraint [10] or other heuristic refinement constraint [21]. However, the supervised methods require labeled ground truth, which are expensive to obtain in natural environments.

2.2 Unsupervised Monocular Depth Learning

More recent works have begun to approach the SIDE task in a unsupervised way. A pioneering work is SfMLearner [23], which learns depth and ego-motion jointly by minimizing photometric loss in an unsupervised manner. This pipeline has inspired a large amount of follow-up works. To deal with moving objects breaking the assumption of static scenes, many works [13,20] employ the consistency of forward-backward optical [22], depth-optical [27], or depth-depth [1] flow to mask dynamic objects. Several methods developed new frameworks by changing training strategies and adding supplementary constraints [7] and collaborative competition [16]. More recently, several researchers [19,22] have tried to combine a geometric algorithm into the deep learning architecture, and obtained better depth and VO estimations by training with only two frames in a video sequence. Compared with previous works, the proposed method improves the loss function and proposes to use sub-pixel convolution [17] to replace nearest interpolation as upsampling approach aiming to obtain accurate and smooth SIDE.

3   Method

3.1   Unsupervised Depth Learning Pipeline

The aim of learning based monocular depth estimation is to predict a pixel-aligned depth map D_t with an input image I_t via a network with the parameter set θ,

$$D_t = DepthNet(I_t; \theta). \tag{1}$$

For computing re-projection error, or named photometric error, we need to calculate the ego-motion from image I_t to I_{t+1},

$$T_{t \to t+1} = PoseNet(I_t, I_{t+1}; \theta), \tag{2}$$

where $T_{t \to t'} \in \mathcal{SE}(3)$ is the ego-motion in three dimensional special euclidean group from time t to $t+1$.

Given the depth D_t and ego-motion $T_{t \to t+1}$, for a pixel p_t in I_t, the corresponding pixel p_{t+1} in I_{t+1} can be found through camera perspective projection, which are consistent for static scenes. Formally, the relationships can be written as

$$p_{t+1} = KT_{t \to t+1} D_t(p_t) K^{-1} p_t, \tag{3}$$

where K and $D_t(p_t)$ denote the camera intrinsic and the depth in p_t, respectively.

After computing the corresponding p_t and p_{t+1}, the synthetic image $I'_{t \leftarrow t+1}$ can be warped using I_{t+1}. Similarly, we can use I_{t-1} to synthesize $I'_{t \leftarrow t-1}$ with pose $T_{t \to t-1}$. Then, unsupervised training of depth is realized by minimizing the photometric error between the raw and the synthetic images, like Monodepth2 [7]:

$$\mathcal{L}_p = \frac{1}{N} \sum min(r(I_t, I'_{t \leftarrow t+1}), r(I_t, I'_{t \leftarrow t-1})), \tag{4}$$

where N is the total number of pixels in the image I_t. The function $r(\cdot, \cdot)$ is the metric between the target and synthetic images.

Pixel-level color matching alone is unstable and ambiguous. Therefore, an edge-aware smoothness term is often applied for regularization [13]:

$$\mathcal{L}_s = \frac{1}{N} \sum |\frac{\partial d_t}{\partial x}| e^{-|\frac{\partial I_t}{\partial x}|} + |\frac{\partial d_t}{\partial y}| e^{-|\frac{\partial I_t}{\partial y}|}, \tag{5}$$

where $d_t = 1/D_t$ can be considered as disparity.

3.2   Improved Photometric Error

The main loss used for training depth prediction model in unsupervised manner is photometric error (Eq. 4). Most previous works [7,13] usually define the pixel-wise image metric $r(I, I')$ using the combination of SSIM [24] with MAE,

$$r(I, I') = \frac{\kappa}{2}(1 - SSIM(I, I')) + (1 - \kappa)|I - I'|, \tag{6}$$

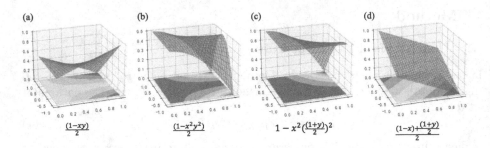

(a)   (b)   (c)   (d)

$$\frac{(1-xy)}{2} \qquad \frac{(1-x^2y^2)}{2} \qquad 1-x^2(\tfrac{(1+y)}{2})^2 \qquad \frac{(1-x)+\frac{(1+y)}{2}}{2}$$

Fig. 1. Four toy examples to illustrate the effect of different components of the SSIM on the output. x indicates luminance and contrast parts, whose outputs are in the range $[0,1]$. y indicates structure part, whose output is in the range $[-1,1]$.

where κ is the weight and usually set to 0.85 [7,13]. SSIM is the function of structure similarity index measure [24] for evaluating the similarity between two images, which is consists of three key features of the differences between two images: luminance L, contrast C and structure S,

$$SSIM = L^\alpha \cdot C^\beta \cdot S^\gamma, \tag{7}$$

where symbols SSIM, L, C and S are functions that we omit its independent variable (I and I') for a more concise description. α, β, γ represent the proportion of different characteristics in the SSIM measure. The value of SSIM is in the range of $[-1,1]$, the values closer to 1 mean the higher similarities between I and I', so to make the SSIM available for the gradient descent algorithm, we need to make a simple transformation $\frac{1}{2}(1-SSIM)$.

To measure the similarity of two images, we usually compute the metrics by sliding window across the image and then average them. Typically, most previous works has used $\alpha = 1, \beta = 1, \gamma = 1$ and set window size to 3. However, the regular settings are not always the best settings. In our experiments (see Table 1), a significant performance improvement can be obtained by simply adjusting these three weights α, β and γ. Note that luminance L, contrast C and structure components S are in the range $[0,1]$, $[0,1]$ and $[-1,1]$, respectively. If $\gamma = 1$ is set to even, then its minimum value is not unique (Fig. 1(b)) and we need to give structure component a transformation before calculating the exponent,

$$SSIM_m = 1 - L^\alpha \cdot C^\beta \cdot (\frac{1}{2}(1+S))^\gamma. \tag{8}$$

Figure 1(a–c) show three toy examples of the SSIM outputs changing with exponent weights. Compared with Fig. 1(a) and 1(c), we can see as the exponential weights get larger, their outputs become steeper near zero and more flatten out away from zero. Table 1 demonstrates that larger exponential weights result in better performances on the KITTI dataset.

The original form of SSIM is the combination of components (L, C, S) by multiplication and the weight of each component is weighted by an exponent.

It may be not a good choose as a loss function to train a deep learning model. Figure 1(a–c) show that combining by multiplication leads to the uneven gradient distribution. In some initializations, there may be some parameters that do not converge well due to the small gradients backpropagated based on the SSIM outputs. Therefore, we propose to combine the different components using addition,

$$SSIM_a = w_l(1 - L) + w_c(1 - C) + w_s(1 - \frac{1}{2}(1 + S)), \qquad (9)$$

where w_l, w_c and w_s are the weights of components L, C and S, respectively. Figure 1(d) shows the example of the function $SSIM_a$, we can see that the gradient of the result is equal everywhere by a combination with addition rather than multiplication.

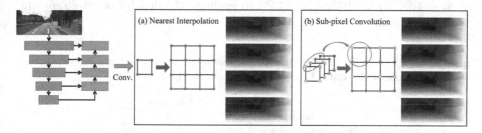

Fig. 2. The network architecture. (a) the nearest upsampling module used in the baseline network. (b) the sub-pixel convolution upsampling module used in our network.

3.3 Multi-scale Depth Estimation

The depth network is similar to the architecture in [7], which adopts encoder-decoder design with skip connections and five-scale side outputs. The encoder is ResNet18 [9] without full connection layers; at each scale, the decoder consists of 2 convolutional layers with the kernel size of 3 and 1 convolutional layer with the kernel size of 1. Different from the previous network [7], we use sub-pixel convolution [17] rather than nearest interpolation to upsample the low resolution depth map to higher.

Sub-pixel convolution [17] is the strategy converting information from channel to spatial. For example, given the original low-resolution depth map of size $H/2 \times W/2 \times r^2$, the channels of each pixel are rearranged into an $r \times r$ spatial region, so that the depth map of size $H/2 \times W/2 \times r^2$ is rearranged into a high-resolution of $H \times W \times 1$. Figure 2 shows the difference between the nearest interpolation and sub-pixel convolution method. Note that although the technique of sub-pixel convolution is already used on task of super-resolution, we introduce it to solve the unsupervised SIDE task and achieve better results compared with many previous works [7,13].

4   Experiments

Dataset. The KITTI dataset [6] commonly used for the task of depth estimation provides videos of 200 street scenes captured by RGB cameras, with sparse depth ground truths captured by laser scanner. For depth, training was done on the KITTI raw [1,7] and the frames were resized to 640×192 pixels. The depth was evaluated on the Eigen's testing split [5].

Implementation Details. The Adam [11] optimizer was used, the learning rate was set to 10^{-4}, and the batch size to 8. The training epochs was set to 20. We used warmup strategy to update learning rate, the warmup step was set to 1000. For a more fair comparision, we set the random seeds to 1234 on *PyTorch* [14] and *NumPy* [8] package.

Metrics. We adopted the standard metrics (Abs Rel, Sq Rel, RMSE, RMSE log, $\delta_1 < 1.25$, $\delta_2 < 1.25^2$, $\delta_3 < 1.25^3$) to evaluate the depth from 0–80 meters. Detailed definitions can be found in [13].

Table 1. Ablation studies on $SSIM_m$. All the methods were trained in a self-supervised manner with monocular data. Bolded numbers are the best metrics.

α	β	γ	Error				Accuracy		
			AbsRel ↓	SqRel ↓	RMS ↓	RMSlog ↓	< 1.25 ↑	< 1.25^2 ↑	< 1.25^3 ↑
Monodepth2 [7]			0.115	0.903	4.863	0.193	0.877	0.959	0.981
Baseline			0.118	0.868	4.856	0.194	0.869	0.957	0.981
2	1	1	0.115	0.860	4.895	0.193	0.871	0.957	0.981
3	1	1	0.116	0.861	4.880	0.193	0.872	0.958	0.981
1	2	1	0.115	**0.835**	**4.823**	0.193	0.871	0.958	**0.982**
1	3	1	0.116	0.856	4.894	0.194	0.871	0.957	0.981
1	1	2	**0.114**	0.836	4.862	0.193	0.873	0.958	0.981
1	1	3	0.115	0.868	4.830	**0.192**	0.874	**0.959**	0.981
2	2	2	0.115	0.838	4.834	**0.192**	0.874	0.958	0.981
3	3	3	0.115	0.829	4.826	**0.192**	0.871	0.958	0.981

4.1   Ablation Study

This part presents the ablation analysis to assess the performance of the proposed SIDE method.

Experiments on $SSIM_m$. We first test the loss function combining with $SSIM_m$ and MAE,

$$\mathcal{L}_m = (1 - w)MAE + w(1 - L^\alpha C^\beta (\frac{1}{2}(1 + S))^\gamma), \qquad (10)$$

where $w = 0.85$ is similar to previous works [7,13]. The baseline is the re-implemented Monodepth2 [7], which is trained using $\alpha = 1$, $\beta = 1$, $\gamma = 1$. Compared with the original version, the performances of re-implemented method is largely consistent with the original version.

Table 2. Ablation studies on $SSIM_a$. All the methods were trained in a self-supervised manner with monocular data. Bolded numbers are the best metrics.

				Error				Accuracy		
w_1	w_l	w_c	w_s	AbsRel ↓	SqRel ↓	RMS ↓	RMSlog ↓	< 1.25 ↑	< 1.25² ↑	< 1.25³ ↑
Monodepth2 [7]				0.115	0.903	4.863	0.193	0.877	0.959	0.981
Baseline				0.118	0.868	4.856	0.194	0.869	0.957	0.981
0.3	0.4	0.4	0.5	0.116	0.836	4.856	0.194	0.871	0.958	0.981
0.3	0.4	0.4	0.6	0.115	0.842	4.879	0.193	0.871	0.958	**0.982**
0.3	0.4	0.4	0.7	0.116	0.834	4.833	0.193	0.871	0.958	0.981
0.3	0.4	0.5	0.5	0.116	0.850	4.871	0.194	0.870	0.958	0.981
0.3	0.4	0.5	0.6	0.115	0.828	4.859	0.193	0.871	0.958	0.981
0.3	0.4	0.5	0.7	0.115	0.832	4.828	0.192	**0.873**	**0.959**	0.981
0.3	0.5	0.5	0.5	0.115	**0.816**	4.846	0.194	0.871	0.958	0.981
0.3	0.5	0.5	0.6	**0.114**	**0.816**	4.823	**0.191**	**0.873**	**0.959**	**0.982**
0.3	0.5	0.5	0.7	0.115	0.849	4.858	0.193	0.872	0.958	0.981
0.3	0.6	0.5	0.5	**0.114**	0.819	4.834	0.192	0.872	0.958	**0.982**
0.3	0.6	0.5	0.6	0.115	0.831	4.854	0.193	0.872	0.958	0.981
0.3	0.6	0.6	0.5	0.117	0.837	4.898	0.195	0.867	0.957	0.981
0.3	0.6	0.6	0.6	0.116	0.830	4.854	0.194	0.870	0.958	0.981
0.4	0.4	0.4	0.6	0.116	0.865	4.886	0.194	0.872	0.957	0.981
0.4	0.4	0.5	0.6	0.116	0.842	4.840	0.193	0.872	0.958	0.981
0.4	0.4	0.5	0.7	**0.114**	0.826	**4.822**	0.192	0.872	**0.959**	0.981
0.4	0.5	0.5	0.5	0.115	0.836	4.853	0.194	0.871	0.957	0.981
0.4	0.5	0.5	0.6	0.115	0.817	4.846	0.193	0.871	0.957	0.981
0.4	0.5	0.5	0.7	0.115	0.823	4.828	0.193	**0.873**	0.958	**0.982**
0.4	0.6	0.5	0.5	0.116	0.819	4.836	0.192	**0.873**	0.958	0.981
0.4	0.5	0.6	0.5	0.117	0.843	4.856	0.194	0.870	0.957	0.981

Table 1 shows the experimental results. We can see that most of the combinations of α, β and γ are better than setting them to 1. Compared with baseline, most of the indicators are better when the weights are simply revised. From Table 1, we can summarize the following two conclusions.

1) *The contrast C and structure S in SSIM is important than the luminance L.* From Table 1, we can clearly find that the best performance is obtained only when adjusting (increasing) the contrast and brightness weights.

2) *Increasing all the weights is not necessarily better than increasing a single weight.* From Table 1, we can find that $\alpha, \beta, \gamma = 2$ or 3 is not better than adding partial weights alone. One possible reason is that increasing α, β and γ at the same time will result in more flat areas, like Fig. 1(c). Its areas may make the gradient propagation insignificant and bring convergence difficulties.

Table 3. Ablation studies on upsampling methods.

w_1	w_l	w_c	w_s	Error				Accuracy		
				AbsRel ↓	SqRel ↓	RMS ↓	RMSlog ↓	< 1.25 ↑	< 1.25² ↑	< 1.25³ ↑
0.3	0.5	0.5	0.6	**0.114**	0.816	4.823	0.191	**0.873**	**0.959**	0.982
w/ sub-pixel conv.				0.116	**0.776**	**4.811**	**0.190**	0.862	0.957	**0.983**
0.4	0.4	0.5	0.7	**0.114**	0.826	4.822	0.192	**0.872**	**0.959**	0.981
w/ sub-pixel conv.				0.116	**0.784**	**4.793**	**0.189**	0.863	0.957	**0.983**
0.4	0.5	0.5	0.7	**0.115**	0.823	4.828	0.193	**0.873**	**0.958**	0.982
w/ sub-pixel conv.				**0.115**	**0.770**	**4.813**	**0.188**	0.863	0.957	**0.983**

Table 4. Comparing multi-scale performance of nearest upsample and sub-pixel convolution. We use combining $SSIM_a$ and MAE as training loss with $w_1 = 0.4$, $w_l = 0.5$, $w_c = 0.5$, $w_s = 0.7$.

Resolution	Bilinear	Error				Accuracy		
		AbsRel ↓	SqRel ↓	RMS ↓	RMSlog ↓	< 1.25 ↑	< 1.25² ↑	< 1.25³ ↑
1/2	✓	**0.115**	0.823	4.828	0.193	**0.873**	**0.958**	0.982
1/2		**0.115**	**0.770**	**4.813**	**0.188**	0.863	0.957	**0.983**
1/4	✓	**0.115**	0.818	4.833	0.192	**0.870**	**0.958**	0.982
1/4		**0.115**	**0.770**	**4.812**	**0.188**	0.863	0.957	**0.983**
1/8	✓	0.119	0.833	4.925	0.195	0.862	0.956	0.982
1/8		**0.115**	**0.771**	**4.820**	**0.188**	**0.863**	**0.957**	**0.983**
1/16	✓	0.130	0.943	5.203	0.203	0.844	0.952	0.981
1/16		**0.116**	**0.780**	**4.844**	**0.189**	**0.862**	**0.957**	**0.983**

Experiments on $SSIM_a$. We then test the loss function combining with $SSIM_a$ and MAE,

$$\mathcal{L}_a = w_1 MAE + w_l(1 - L) + w_c(1 - C) + w_s(1 - \frac{1}{2}(1 + S)). \tag{11}$$

Table 2 shows the experimental results. We can see that most of the combinations of w_1, w_l, w_c and w_s are better than baseline which uses multiplication rather than addition to fuse SSIM. From Table 2, we summarize the following two conclusions.

1) SSIM loss constructed by addition outperforms multiplication in terms of upper bound on performance. Compared with the best performances of Table 2 and Table 1, we can find that most of the best results come from Table 2, especially the indicator SqRel.

Fig. 3. Visualization of different upsampling methods.

Table 5. Quantitative comparison of the proposed method with existing methods. SSC denotes the $SSIM_a$ and sub-pixel convolution. Bolded and underlined numbers are respectively the best and second-best metrics.

Methods	Error				Accuracy		
	AbsRel↓	SqRel ↓	RMS ↓	RMSlog ↓	< 1.25 ↑	< 1.25² ↑	< 1.25³ ↑
SfMLearner [23]	0.183	1.595	6.709	0.270	0.734	0.902	0.959
CC [16]	0.140	1.070	5.326	0.217	0.826	0.941	0.975
EPC++ [13]	0.141	1.029	5.350	0.216	0.816	0.941	0.976
SC-SfMLearner [1]	0.137	1.089	5.439	0.217	0.830	0.942	0.975
Monodepth2 [7]	0.115	0.903	4.863	0.193	<u>0.877</u>	0.961	0.982
Zhao et al. [22]	<u>0.113</u>	**0.704**	4.581	0.184	0.871	0.961	<u>0.984</u>
3DHR [18]	**0.109**	0.790	4.656	0.185	**0.882**	<u>0.962</u>	0.983
GVO [3]	0.118	0.787	<u>4.488</u>	<u>0.183</u>	0.870	<u>0.962</u>	**0.985**
Monodepth2 + SSC	0.115	0.770	4.813	0.188	0.863	0.957	0.983
GVO + SSC	0.115	<u>0.747</u>	**4.416**	**0.181**	0.868	**0.964**	**0.985**

2) Statistics reveals that the performances is better when $w_c = 0.5$ and $w_s = 0.7$. We counted the edge distribution of all results in Table 2 and found that the performance is better when $w_c = 0.5$ and $w_s = 0.7$. The values of w_1 and w_l do not significantly affect the results of depth estimation.

Experiments on Sub-pixel Convolution. In this part, we show the experiments on upsampling method. We substitute nearest upsample with sub-pixel convolution approach. Table 3 and Table 4 show some experimental results.

1) Using sub-pixel convolution is better than nearest upsampling on most metrics. Table 3 shows four groups of experiments. We can see that the sub-pixel convolution is better than the nearest upsampling module on most metrics, especially on SqRel and RMSlog. In addition, for the accurate metric < 1.25, nearest upsampling is always better than sub-pixel convolution. This may be because the depth estimated by sub-pixel convolution is more smooth and therefore lacks precision, like the visualization results in Fig. 3.

2) Sub-pixel convolution still has good performance at small resolutions. Table 4 shows the performances at different resolutions. As we can see that the sub-pixel convolution has consistent performances at each resolutions. Since good depth estimates are learned at low resolution, it may be more difficult to learn clear contours during constant upsampling decoding. Figure 4 shows the visualization results.

4.2 Comparison with State-of-the-Art

The predicted depths are reported and compared with several methods in Table 5. When our modified loss function and upsampling module were incorporated into Monodepth2 [7] and GVO [3] (i.e., "Monodepth2 + SSC" and "GVO + SSC" in Table 5), their performances were largely improved. We can find that compared with recent methods, which use multi-frames [18] or auxiliary optical flow model [3,22], our model also performs well under some metrics. Note that the the weights of $SSIM_a$ is set to $w_1 = 0.4$, $w_l = 0.5$, $w_c = 0.5$, $w_s = 0.7$ in Table 5.

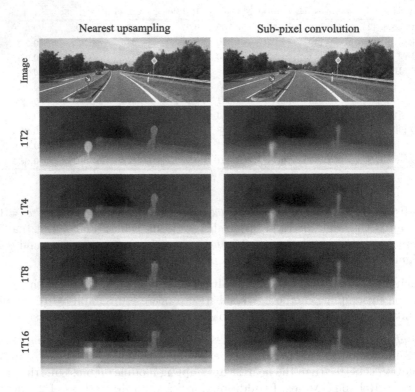

Fig. 4. Visualization of different upsampling methods at different resolution.

5   Discussion

Motivation. From the first unsupervised SIDE approach [23] to recent state-of-the-art methods [3,7], the combination of MAE with SSIM as loss function seems to be a standard option. However, we found in practice that it is difficult to reflect the change in depth through the measurement of the pixel-wise SSIM loss. In many cases, different depths will result in similar RGB values by re-projection, and large changes in depth can only lead to small shifts in SSIM values. These phenomenons drive us to find a suitable loss function for unsupervised SIDE task. Modification to the SSIM function is the simplest solution, and this work demonstrates the effectiveness of this modification from a large number of experiments. The future work is to analyze the gaps between the supervised and unsupervised manners, and design a more valid loss function.

Generalization. Although we only apply the proposed SSIM to Monodepth2 [7] and GVO [3], we think that it can be easily promoted and might improve the performances in many other unsupervised SIDE task. One reason is that there is no conflict between the proposed loss and the assumptions of the existing models, which usually develop the occlusion mask [13] and pursuing accurate pose [3, 22].

Limitation. Although the proposed SSIM is better than original version in every indicator of SIDE evaluation, the increase of performances is small. The RMS from 4.856 to 4.822 is improved by 0.7%, and the SqRel from 0.868 to 0.816 is improved by 6.4%. This shows that there is still a lot of room for further improvement in the loss function.

Sub-pixel Convolution. We argue that sub-pixel convolution might decrease the performances in the case of using more powerful model. We may be aiming for a smooth estimate when the depth is overall inaccurate, however, the edge areas, usually the most difficult part to learn, is also the pursuit of future work. Thus, how to take advantage of sub-pixel convolution and avoid its disadvantages is also a good research direction.

6   Conclusions

In this work, we explored the loss function and the upsampling approach for the task of unsupervised SIDE. Extensive experiments showed that the proposed version of SSIM loss is better than the original one, especially the form combining by addition. Further more, we proposed to use sub-pixel convolution upsampling method instead of nearest interpolation for multi-scale training. The results showed that the proposed approaches achieve a significant performance improvement compared with the baseline.

Acknowledgements. This work was supported by National Natural Science Foundation of China (62076055) and Sichuan Science and Technology Program (2022ZYD0112).

References

1. Bian, J.W., et al.: Unsupervised scale-consistent depth and ego-motion learning from monocular video. In: NeurIPS (2019)
2. Cao, Y.J., Lin, C., Li, Y.J.: Learning crisp boundaries using deep refinement network and adaptive weighting loss. IEEE T-MM **23**, 761–771 (2021). https://doi.org/10.1109/TMM.2020.2987685
3. Cao, Y.J., et al.: Learning generalized visual odometry using position-aware optical flow and geometric bundle adjustment. Pattern Recogn. **136**, 109262 (2023)
4. Eigen, D., Fergus, R.: Predicting depth, surface normals and semantic labels with a common multi-scale convolutional architecture. In: ICCV (2015)
5. Eigen, D., Puhrsch, C., Fergus, R.: Depth map prediction from a single image using a multi-scale deep network. In: NeurIPS (2014)

6. Geiger, A., Lenz, P., Stiller, C., Urtasun, R.: Vision meets robotics: The Kitti dataset. IJRR (2013)
7. Godard, C., Mac Aodha, O., Firman, M., Brostow, G.J.: Digging into self-supervised monocular depth prediction. In: ICCV (2019)
8. Harris, C.R., et al.: Array programming with numpy. Nature 585(7825), 357–362 (2020)
9. He, K., Zhang, X., Ren, S., Sun, J.: Deep residual learning for image recognition. In: CVPR (2016)
10. Hu, J., Ozay, M., Zhang, Y., Okatani, T.: Revisiting single image depth estimation: toward higher resolution maps with accurate object boundaries. In: WACV, pp. 1043–1051. IEEE (2019)
11. Kingma, D.P., Ba, J.: Adam: a method for stochastic optimization. In: ICLR (2015)
12. Liu, C., Kumar, S., Gu, S., Timofte, R., Van Gool, L.: VA-depthnet: a variational approach to single image depth prediction. In: ICLR (2023)
13. Luo, C., et al.: Every pixel counts++: joint learning of geometry and motion with 3D holistic understanding. IEEE T-PAMI 42(10), 2624–2641 (2020). https://doi.org/10.1109/TPAMI.2019.2930258
14. Paszke, A., et al.: Pytorch: an imperative style, high-performance deep learning library. In: NeurIPS (2019)
15. Peng, P., Yang, K.F., Luo, F.Y., Li, Y.J.: Saliency detection inspired by topological perception theory. Int. J. Comput. Vision 129(8), 2352–2374 (2021)
16. Ranjan, A., et al.: Competitive collaboration: joint unsupervised learning of depth, camera motion, optical flow and motion segmentation. In: CVPR (2019)
17. Shi, W., et al.: Real-time single image and video super-resolution using an efficient sub-pixel convolutional neural network. In: CVPR, pp. 1874–1883 (2016)
18. Wang, G., Zhong, J., Zhao, S., Wu, W., Liu, Z., Wang, H.: 3D hierarchical refinement and augmentation for unsupervised learning of depth and pose from monocular video. IEEE Trans. Circuits Syst. Video Technol. (2022)
19. Yang, N., Stumberg, L., Wang, R., Cremers, D.: D3vo: deep depth, deep pose and deep uncertainty for monocular visual odometry. In: CVPR (2020)
20. Yin, Z., Shi, J.: Geonet: unsupervised learning of dense depth, optical flow and camera pose. In: CVPR (2018)
21. Yuan, W., Gu, X., Dai, Z., Zhu, S., Tan, P.: Neural window fully-connected CRFs for monocular depth estimation. In: CVPR, pp. 3916–3925 (2022)
22. Zhao, W., Liu, S., Shu, Y., Liu, Y.J.: Towards better generalization: joint depth-pose learning without posenet. In: CVPR (2020)
23. Zhou, T., Brown, M., Snavely, N., Lowe, D.G.: Unsupervised learning of depth and ego-motion from video. In: CVPR (2017)
24. Wang, Z., Bovik, A.C., Sheikh, H.R., Simoncelli, E.P.: Image quality assessment: from error visibility to structural similarity. IEEE T-IP 13(4), 600–612 (2004). https://doi.org/10.1109/TIP.2003.819861
25. Zhu, Z., et al.: Nice-slam: neural implicit scalable encoding for slam. In: CVPR, pp. 12786–12796 (2022)
26. Zoran, D., Isola, P., Krishnan, D., Freeman, W.T.: Learning ordinal relationships for mid-level vision. In: ICCV, pp. 388–396 (2015)
27. Zou, Y., Luo, Z., Huang, J.-B.: DF-net: unsupervised joint learning of depth and flow using cross-task consistency. In: Ferrari, V., Hebert, M., Sminchisescu, C., Weiss, Y. (eds.) ECCV 2018. LNCS, vol. 11209, pp. 38–55. Springer, Cham (2018). https://doi.org/10.1007/978-3-030-01228-1_3

SECT: Sentiment-Enriched Continual Training for Image Sentiment Analysis

Lifang Wu, Lehao Xing, Ge Shi[✉], Sinuo Deng, and Jie Yang

Beijing University of Technology, No. 100 Pingleyuan, Chaoyang District, Beijing
100124, China
tinkersxy@gmail.com

Abstract. In recent times, pre-training models of a large scale have
achieved notable success in various downstream tasks by relying on contrastive image-text pairs to learn high-quality visual general representations from natural language supervision. However, these models typically disregard sentiment knowledge during the pre-training phase, subsequently hindering their capacity for optimal image sentiment analysis.
To address these challenges, we propose a sentiment-enriched continual
training framework (SECT), which continually trains CLIP and introduces multi-level sentiment knowledge in the further pre-training process
through the use of sentiment-based natural language supervision. Moreover, we construct a large-scale weakly annotated sentiment image-text
dataset to ensure that the model is trained robustly. In addition, SECT
conducts three training objectives that effectively integrate multi-level
sentiment knowledge into the model training process. Our experiments
on various datasets, namely EmotionROI, FI, and Twitter I, demonstrate
that our SECT method provides a pre-training model that outperforms
previous models and CLIP on most of the downstream datasets. Our
codes will be publicly available for research purposes.

Keywords: Continual training · Nature language supervision · Image
sentiment analysis

1 Introduction

Nowadays, with the proliferation of mobile devices and social networks, humans
tend to share their feelings online through images. Accurate identification of
sentimental tendencies from images, called image sentiment analysis, has implications for psychotherapy, product recommendations, and decision-making [20].

Early approaches in image sentiment analysis employed a backbone model
that is supervised classification or self-supervised learning on ImageNet, like
AlexNet or ResNet. Since these pre-training models are supervised by entity
words(e.g. dog, cat, car, etc.), the limited knowledge of entity words makes
it challenging to introduce sufficient information in the pre-training model
to directly recognize the abstract sentimental content [5]. So the traditional
works [13] tend to add a specific module to a pre-training model and fine-tune
the whole model for each downstream dataset individually based on hand-crafted
features or deep learning features.

H. Lu et al. (Eds.): ICIG 2023, LNCS 14355, pp. 93–105, 2023.
https://doi.org/10.1007/978-3-031-46305-1_8

Recently, different from conventional supervised and self-supervised pre-train-ing methods only based on images, some visual and language pre-training (VLP) models learn perception from natural language supervision. Such models have produced impressive results in various computer vision tasks, such as image classification and image retrieval, by learning general semantic features with the help of rich textual semantic information. However, these pre-training methods prioritize generic semantics representation while ignoring the sentiment information of an image. So it is hard to expect such general features to deliver optimal results for sentiment analysis. Therefore, to learn sentiment-specific representations that are capable of image sentiment analysis, we believe that integrating sentiment knowledge into pre-training models is necessary.

To address these issues, we propose a CLIP-based sentiment-enriched continual training framework (SECT), where sentiment knowledge about image-text pairs and words is included to guide the learning of the sentiment-enriched pre-training model. During the training procedure, SECT interprets the sentiment in the relevant images using the rich sentiment knowledge from sentiment-based natural language supervision, to effectively transfer sentiment knowledge cross-modal transfer. However, one significant challenge is the lack of a large-scale sentiment image-text dataset for training. To overcome this issue, SKEP proposes data selecting module. By selecting image-text pairs with significant sentiment tendencies from the large-scale dataset CC12M [3], we create the Sentiment-Rich CC12M (SR-CC12M) dataset, which includes image-text pairs with weakly-annotated sentiment labels. To address this issue, we construct Sentiment-Rich CC12M (SR-CC12M) dataset by selecting image-text pairs with significant sentiment tendencies from the large-scale dataset CC12M [3]. During the continual training process, pseudo-labeled image-text pairs in the dataset are used as sentence-level sentiment supervision. Meanwhile, words with obvious polarity in the text are filtered through sentiment mining as a form of word-level supervision.

Specifically, SECT contains image-text semantic matching and two sentiment knowledge prediction objectives, image polarity prediction, and word polarity prediction. By guiding the embedding of multi-level sentiment knowledge into the image representation with training objectives, we obtain task-specific features suitable for image sentiment analysis. Quite different from traditional sentiment analysis approaches, where complex fine-tuning schemes are designed and trained for specific datasets. SECT integrates sentiment knowledge in a pre-training model to provide a unified sentiment representation for image sentiment analysis. To validate the effectiveness of our framework, we compare the performance of CLIP and the model continually trained by SECT on the downstream datasets using zero-shot and linear probe settings. Additionally, we conduct experiments in the supervised setting and compare the results with previous models.

In summary, our contributions are summarized as follows: (1) We present a continual training framework, SECT, to incorporate sentiment knowledge into the vision-language pre-training model, making it the first pre-training model that outputs a unified sentiment representation for image sentiment analysis. (2)

We introduce the SR-CC12M dataset that offers multi-level sentiment knowledge for training models. (3) Our SECT framework outperforms CLIP in both zero-shot and linear probe image sentiment analysis tasks with superior results. After fine-tuning, our model achieves improvements compared to previous models on five datasets.

2 Related Works

Image Sentiment Analysis. With the advent of deep learning methods, traditional approaches for studying image sentiment analysis focused on fine-tuning off-the-shelf CNNs that were pre-trained on ImageNet datasets. Deng et al. [5] adopted ResNet101 as the backbone to extract global features and use them as the image sentiment representation. Furthermore, sentimental content always involves some key regions based on psychological theory. Thus, Yang et al. [13] extract information-rich local regions to fuse both holistic and localized representations as sentimental features for sentiment classification. Even though earlier studies made some progress, researchers still face challenges obtaining suitable features from images. To address this problem, researchers explore enhencing feature representations by incorporating external knowledge, like proposing a well-designed sentiment dictionary [16] or introducing different kinds of dataset-specific information [12,19]. However, such approaches concentrate on elaborating various fine-tuning methods rather than fundamentally improving the pre-training model to be more compatible with image sentiment analysis.

Task-oriented Pre-training. Pre-training models such as ImageBERT [11], Unicoder-VL [7] and CLIP, have achieved state-of-the-art(SOTA) results in diverse downstream tasks due to their focus on general semantic information. Despite their impressive performance in downstream tasks, pre-training models can face challenges while delivering optimal results for specific tasks as they do not consider task-specific knowledge during training. According to SKEP [14], sentiment knowledge that includes sentiment words and aspect-sentiment pairs is ignored in language pre-training models. Hence, it proposes a masking strategy to model the sentiment knowledge alongside a sentiment multi-objective learning algorithm. Ultimately, by integrating sentiment knowledge in various levels, SKEP achieves SOTA performance in text sentiment analysis tasks. Moreover, CLIP-event [8] finds that current VLP models emphasize image or entity comprehension, overlooking event semantics and structures. Consequently, they aim to integrate event structural information into VLP.

3 The SR-C12M Dataset

In order to ensure the model is robustly trained, we filter image-text pairs containing sentiment polarity from the large-scale image-text pairs dataset CC12M and construct a new dataset called SR-CC12M (Sentiment-Rich - Conceptual 12M). For each image-text pair in SR-CC12M, the knowledge-mining module

Datasets	SR-CC12M
Image-Text Pairs	300,000
Average words	23.82
Average sentiment words	9.08
Negative words	1,215,380
Positive words	1,508,922
Total words	7,144,558
Negative unique words	5,528
Positive unique words	5,568
Unique words	100,575

(a) Statics of SR-CC12M Dataset

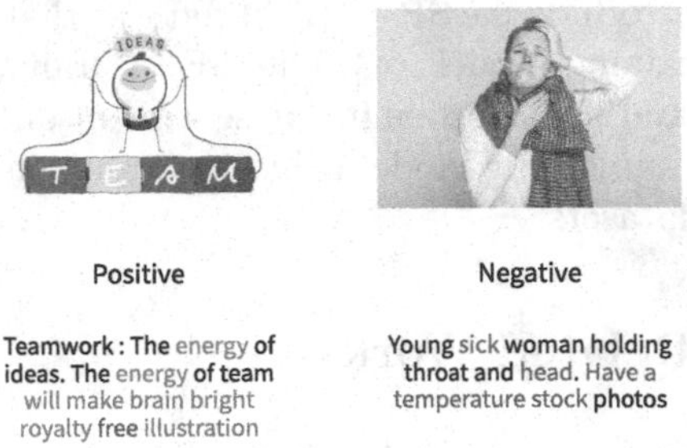

Positive

Teamwork : The energy of ideas. The energy of team will make brain bright royalty free illustration

Negative

Young sick woman holding throat and head. Have a temperature stock photos

(b) Examples of SR-CC12M Dataset

Fig. 1. (a) is the statistical information of the text in SR-CC12M. (b) is two examples of image-text pairs with sentiment polarity in SR-CC12M.

collects the following information: 1) sentiment pseudo-labels. 2) words with significant sentiment polarity in the texts. The details about the date-selecting module and knowledge-mining module are described in the following paragraphs.

3.1   Data-Selecting Module

Some works point that text sentiment is more specific and easy to distinguish. For this reason, we use the sentiment classification results of texts in the CC12M dataset to label the sentiment polarity of image-text pairs and use them to filter out image-text pairs with apparent sentiment polarity as training data. Specifically, the TWEETEVAL [2] model is applied as a text sentiment classifier to obtain positive, negative, and neutral sentiment scores of the text. The sum of these three scores is equal to 1. Texts with the highest positive score are collected and labeled as positive. Similarly, texts with the highest negative scores are collected and labeled as negative. When we get the image, we annotated it with the sentiment label of its corresponding text.

Finally, SR-CC12M consists of 300K image-text pairs with sentiment polarity, as some images no longer existed on the Internet or could not be opened in python. Specifically, there are 250K positive images and 50K negative images in SR-CC12M. And we randomly split SR-CC12M into training and testing sets with the proportion of 9:1.

3.2   Sentiment Knowledge-Mining Module

Sentence-level sentiment knowledge is mined as sentiment texts and pseudo-labels in the data-selecting module. To mine fine-grained sentiment knowledge, words with high sentiment scores are selected and labeled by querying the sentiment dictionary as word-level sentiment knowledge. SentiWordNet 3.0 [1] is a WordNet-based word sentiment dictionary that manually labels three sentiment scores indicating the degree of positively, negativity, and neutrality of words

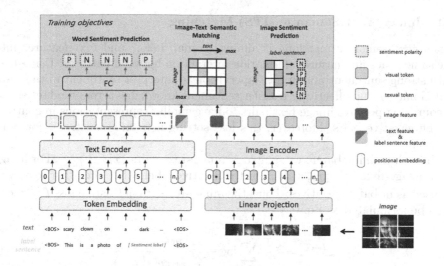

Fig. 2. Overall architecture of SECT, a dual-stream model with Transformer-based image and text encoders.

contained in synonymous phrases, as negative score S_-, neutral score S_0 and positive score S_+. A sentiment dictionary is designed specifically for the SR-CC12M dataset, which includes only words and their corresponding sentiment labels (positive, negative). Specifically, for words that recur in SentiWordNet 3.0, the corresponding scores are added and averaged to obtain the final score. Afterward, words with $S_- > S_+, S_0$ are picked out, labeled as negative word. Words with $S_+ > S_-, S_0$ are picked out, labeled as positive word.

Consequently, the mined sentiment knowledge contains a collection of sentiment image-text pairs with their polarity along with a set of sentiment words labeled by polarity. Our research focuses on the necessity of integrating sentiment knowledge in the pre-training model by a common and easy mining method.

4 Continual Training Method

As shown in Fig. 2. To learn encoders f_θ for image data I and g_ϕ for text data T with label-sentence S such that, given an image $x^I \in I$ and a text sentence $x^T \in T$, it will gets the encoded representations for image $f_\theta(x^I)$, text $g_\phi(x^T)$, and words $g_\phi(x^W)$. To better incorporate the multi-level sentiment knowledge mining in the data preprocessing stage, we utilize three training objectives: image-text semantic (ITS) matching, image polarity prediction (IP), and word polarity (WP) prediction.

4.1   Image-Text Semantic (ITS) Matching

Image-text semantic matching is aiming to map image and text features into the same space and ensure information interaction between patterns. Using text with strong sentiment polarity as supervision to interpret sentiment in the associated images and effectively transfer sentiment knowledge across modalities, by encouraging positive image-text pairs to have similar representations in contrast to the negative pairs. Moreover, this loss setting acts as a constraint for both encoders.

In each training batch, we sample N image-text pairs $\{x_k^I, x_k^T\}_{k=1}^N$. For image x_j^I in image-text pair $\{x_j^I, x_j^T\}$, x_j^T is the positive label, while the other texts will be used as in-batch negatives. Thus, the image-to-text contrastive loss $\mathcal{L}^{I \to T}$ can then be formulated as Eq. 1:

$$\mathcal{L}^{I \to T} = -\frac{1}{N} \sum_{j=1}^{N} \log \frac{exp(s_{j,j}^I/\tau)}{\sum_{k=1}^N exp(s_{j,k}^I/\tau)} \tag{1}$$

here $s_{j,k}^I$ denotes the similarity of the $j-th$ image to the $k-th$ sentence, and computed as Eq. 2, τ is a temperature parameter. This loss takes the same form as the CLIP loss, and minimizing this loss will guide the encoders to maximize the representation of modal information. Intuitively, it is an attempt to predict $\{x_j^I, x_j^T\}$ as the logarithmic loss of an N-way classifier of true pairs.

$$s_{j,k}^I = s_{j,k}^T = \frac{f_\theta(x_j^I)^{\mathbf{T}} \cdot g_\phi(x_k^T)}{\|f_\theta(x_j^I)\| \cdot \|g_\phi(x_k^T)\|} \tag{2}$$

The text-to-image contrastive loss $\mathcal{L}^{T \to I}$ is in the same way as image-to-text contrastive loss:

$$\mathcal{L}_{ITS} = \lambda \mathcal{L}_j^{I \to T} + (1 - \lambda)\mathcal{L}_j^{T \to I} \tag{3}$$

Then the final image-text semantic matching loss $\mathcal{L}_{ITS}$ is then computed as a weight combination of the two losses, as shown in Eq. 3, where λ is set as 0.5.

4.2   Image Polarity (IP) Prediction

To introduce sentence-level sentiment knowledge, we design an image polarity prediction loss function. Unlike other models, we do not use a linear layer for image sentiment classification. Instead, we directly calculate the semantic similarity between image features and sentiment categories for classification. The purpose is to reduce the training cost associated with training classification layers and to prevent the encoder from not being fully trained due to over-training of the classification layer. Specifically, the image polarity category (negative, positive) is extended by a template *"it is a photo of [polarity]"* into label-sentences $x^S = \{x^{S_n}, x^{S_p}\}$. And feed label-sentences in the text encoder to get label-sentence representation $g_\phi(x^S) = \{g_\phi(x^{S_n}), g_\phi(x^{S_p})\}$. Then we calculate the cosine similarity of image features with label-sentence features and optimize asymmetric cross-entropy loss over these similarity scores. Finally, obtain image sentiment (IP) loss $\mathcal{L}_{IP}$.

4.3   Word Polarity (WP) Prediction

To obtain the features of words $g_\phi(x^W)$, the features of tokens split from the same word are averaged in the last layer of the text encoder. Then word-level sentiment polarity analysis is performed using the learnable FC layer. And the sentiment distribution $p(\hat{y}_g = y_g | g_\phi(x^W_{g,j}), \psi)$ for predicting g-th word in j-th text, is calculated as follow:

$$p(\hat{y}_g = y_g | g_\phi(x^W_{g,j}), \psi) = h_\psi(g_\phi(x^W_{g,j})) \tag{4}$$

where $\hat{y}_g$ denotes the predict polarity, ψ stands the parameters of the FC layer h and y_g is the ground-truth. Thus, the classification is carried out by minimizing the following log likelihood function, word polarity (WP) loss L_{WP}:

$$\mathcal{L}_{WP} = -\frac{1}{N}\sum_{j=1}^{N}\frac{1}{H_j}\sum_{h=1}^{H_j}[y_g\log(h_\psi(g_\phi(x^W_{g,j})))+(1-y_g)\log(1-h_\psi(g_\phi(x^W_{g,j})))] \tag{5}$$

where H_j is the word amount in j-th sentence, and the number of words may be different for different sentences.

4.4   Joint Training

The overall training objective $\mathcal{L}_{total}$ is calculated as Eq. 6:

$$\mathcal{L}_{total} = \lambda_1\mathcal{L}_{ITS} + \lambda_2\mathcal{L}_{IP} + \lambda_3\mathcal{L}_{WP} \tag{6}$$

After test, λ_1, λ_2 are set as 1 and λ_3 is set as 0.1. With the total loss, the image encoder and text encoder can be well-optimized for the final prediction of multiple tasks.

5   Experiments and Results

5.1   Experiment Settings

Implementation Details. The model architectures follow CLIP, SECT build image encoder and text encoder based on the CLIP-ViT-B/32, both of which adopt Transformers [6,15] as basic architecture. For the input images are resized to 224×224 resolution during pre-training and the maximum length of the text is limited to 77 tokens following CLIP. To train SECT, we employ AdamW [9] optimizer with a base learning rate of $5e-7$ and weight decay of $1e-2$. And to train a fully-connected layer for word sentiment classification, we employ AdamW optimizer with a base learning rate of $1e-6$ and weight decay of $1e-2$. We train SECT for 40K steps on an NVIDIA RTX3090 GPU with a batch size of 128.

Table 1. Comparisons with CLIP and previous models. The scores of previous models come from: [1](Zhang et al., 2020) [19]; [2](Rao et al., 2019) [12]; [3](Wu et al., 2021) [16]; [4](Deng et al., 2022) [4]. The bold fonts represent the best results.

Setting	Model	EmotionROI		FI		Twitter I
		2	6	2	8	2
Linear probe	CLIP	0.8788	0.6633	0.9368	0.7801	0.8937
	CLIP+SECTL	**0.8889**	**0.6650**	**0.9372**	**0.7810**	**0.9094**
Zero-shot	CLIP	0.5976	0.3956	0.7140	0.5546	0.6535
	CLIP+SECT	**0.7407**	**0.4798**	**0.8782**	**0.6580**	**0.8661**
Supervised	Previous Model	0.8510^1	0.6041^1	0.9389^4	0.7546^2	$\mathbf{0.8965}^3$
	CLIP	0.8822	0.6886	0.9416	0.7857	0.8780
	CLIP+SECT	**0.8872**	**0.6936**	**0.9489**	**0.7921**	0.8898

Downstream Dataset. We evaluate the proposed SECT on three public affective datasets including the EmotionROI [10], the Flickr and Instagram(FI) [18], Twitter I [17].

Evaluation Criteria. We evaluate the SECT method on the binary sentiment polarity prediction and the multi-class sentiment classification on three criteria.

Zero-shot Setting: Zero-shot evaluation directly compares the effectiveness of sentiment knowledge encoding during pre-training. The prompt template, *"a photo of [label]"*, designed by CLIP for the downstream tasks is still used in the zero-shot evaluations.

Linear Probe Setting: A linear classifier is added to the last layer of the model, keeping the parameters of the pre-training model fixed, and the downstream datasets are used to train the classifier for one epoch. The effectiveness of the pre-training model at encoding sentiment knowledge is verified by classifying the image sentiment with the classifier during testing.

Supervised (Fine-tuning) Setting: To fairly compare with previous models, an FC layer is added on the top of the vision encoder. And the whole model is trained by the downstream datasets for 3 epochs.

5.2   Main Results

We compare our SECT method with the baseline CLIP and previous models in zero-shot setting, linear probe setting, and supervised setting on the downstream datasets. The results are shown in Table 1.

Comparison in Zero-Shot and Linear Probe Settings. As shown in Table 1, "CLIP+SECT" outperforms CLIP on all datasets in both zero-shot and linear probe settings, especially in zero-shot binary sentiment classification on EmotionROI dataset gets about 14.3% improvement. Moreover, although our supervised signal is about sentiment polarity, SECT achieves a boost in multi-class sentiment classification because the model introduces multi-level sentiment knowledge and focuses on fine-grained semantic information. Note that SECT gets about 9.6% improvement in zero-shot 8-class sentiment classification on the FI dataset. It suggests that pre-training scheme learning with sentiment-specific knowledge and objectives can improve the sensitivity of the model to a variety of sentimental information.

Compared to the zero-shot task, there is only a slight improvement in SECT's performance on the linear probe task. This is because the linear probe task provides task-specific, high-quality training data for the downstream task, which enhances the model's validation performance on datasets with the same distribution. As a result, the significance of the generalized sentiment information learned in the pre-training model is not emphasized, and the linear probe setting does not accurately reflect the performance of the pre-training model. Therefore, any improvements made in the final results are negligible.

Overall, the results verify the necessity of incorporating sentiment information and the effectiveness of our proposed sentiment pre-training scheme.

Comparison in Supervised Setting. The fine-tuning model is obtained by training the visual encoder and FC layer with sentiment classification loss using the downstream task-specific data as supervision. Then the results are compared with the previous models, as shown in Table 1.

From Table 1, we can draw several conclusions: 1) Compared with fine-tuning CLIP, fine-tuning SECT significantly and consistently improves the performance in the different tasks on all datasets. It indicates that the introduction of sentiment knowledge makes the model more sensitive to sentiment information, and the features are more inclined to express sentiment information. 2) Previous models only show better performance on specific datasets, but SECT provides an efficient model that achieves new state-of-the-art results on almost all datasets, which are not only for the binary sentiment classification but also for the multi-class sentiment classification. Especially, SECT outperforms previous models by 8.9% in 6-class sentiment classification on EmotionROI, and by 3.9% in binary sentiment classification on FI. This result suggests that our model can provide a more applicable sentiment representation for downstream sentiment analysis tasks compared to models using complex fine-tuning methods.

Overall, SECT provides image semantic features with distinct sentiment information in different data distributions.

5.3   Ablation Studies

To present an in-depth analysis of the effect of each component in SECT, we conduct ablation studies on the same five datasets and show the results in Table 2.

Firstly, compared with training with only image-text semantic (ITS) matching loss, adding image polarity prediction loss (ITS+IP) is more significant

Table 2. Effectiveness of objectives. IP, WP, and ITS refer to pre-training objectives: Image Polarity prediction, Word Polarity prediction, and Image-Text Semantic matching. The bold fonts represent the best results.

Setting	Loss	EmotionROI		FI		Twitter I
		2	6	2	8	2
Linear probe	CLIP	0.8788	0.6633	0.9368	0.7801	0.8937
	+ITS	0.8822	0.6582	0.9366	0.7803	0.8976
	+ITS+IP	0.8906	0.6650	**0.9377**	0.7807	0.9094
	+ITS+WP	0.8855	**0.6684**	0.9372	**0.7813**	0.8998
	+ITS+IP+WP	**0.8889**	0.6650	0.9372	0.7810	**0.9094**
Zero-shot	CLIP	0.5387	0.3805	0.7434	0.5385	0.6457
	+ITS	0.5067	0.4596	0.7463	0.6533	0.6378
	+ITS+IP	0.7391	0.4596	0.8726	**0.6618**	**0.8701**
	+ITS+WP	0.5253	0.4697	0.7507	0.6538	0.6457
	+ITS+IP+WP	**0.7407**	**0.4798**	**0.8782**	0.6580	0.8661

for binary sentiment classification. Specifically, the result shows about 22.7% improvement in zero-shot binary sentiment classification on EmotionROI. Secondly, compared with training with only image-text semantic (ITS) matching loss, adding word polarity prediction loss (ITS+WP) is more effective for multiclass sentiment classification. The results of the study indicate that incorporating sentence-level sentiment knowledge enhances the model's understanding of sentiment but makes it more difficult to distinguish between polarities. On the other hand, integrating word-level sentiment knowledge prioritizes fine-grained semantic information, enabling the model to discern subtle differences between multiple sentiments more easily. Despite this, CLIP using ITS loss further continual training on SR-CC12M only achieve the anticipated improvement in some of the classification tasks. This suggests that the coarser data selection method inevitably includes some noise in the dataset. However, the improvement in multi-class classification tasks indicates that the dataset is still effective at enhancing image sentiment analysis.

Overall, from the comparison of the objectives, we conclude that sentiment knowledge is helpful and that more diverse knowledge leads to better performance. This also encourages us to focus on more types of knowledge and use better mining methods in the future.

5.4   Visualization

A comparison of the performance between CLIP and SECT can be visualized in Fig. 3. It is observed that SECT outperforms CLIP in terms of the highest values in the diagonal of the confusion matrix for most positions in the same row and column. This result indicates that our proposed approach, with multi-level specific sentiment information, achieves better performance across various

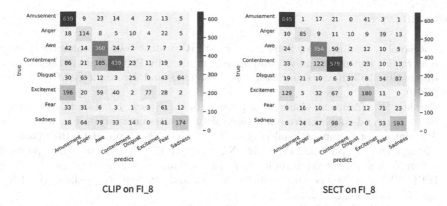

CLIP on FI_8   SECT on FI_8

Fig. 3. Visualization confusion metrics of zero-shot classified by CLIP and SECT.

datasets. In addition, Fig. 3(a) and Fig. 3(b) demonstrate that CLIP has difficulties in distinguishing the problem of sentiment belonging to the same polarity. For example, CLIP tends to predict excitement as amusement and disgust as anger. Conversely, SECT has alleviated this issue by more accurately recognizing such nuances. The SECT matrix shows that the colors of the upper left and lower right regions, which correspond to positive and negative areas, become progressively darker along the diagonal, demonstrating the more powerful capability of SECT in distinguishing between similar sentiments.

6   Conclusion

In this paper, we propose the SECT, a sentiment-enriched continual training framework. In the framework, the multi-level sentiment-specific information is integrated into the pre-training model with three training objectives under sentiment nature language supervision. Benefiting from the SECT, we get a new pre-training model that delivers fast and precise solutions for downstream image sentiment analysis based on CLIP. We carry out experiments to evaluate our framework, which shows that the model significantly outperforms the pre-training baseline and current models both in the binary- and multi-categories sentiment classification, in the zero-shot, linear probe, and supervised settings after continual training by the SECT. Our method highlights the significance of sentiment knowledge and training objectives in pre-training models and training strategies for image sentiment analysis. In the future, we aim to further increase the accuracy of sentiment mining techniques and further explore different types of sentiment knowledge by applying these methods to the SR-CC12M dataset.

Acknowledgment. This work was supported in part by the National Natural Science Foundation of China under Grant NO. 62236010, 61976010, 62106011, 62106010, 62176011.

References

1. Baccianella, S., Esuli, A., Sebastiani, F.: Sentiwordnet 3.0: an enhanced lexical resource for sentiment analysis and opinion mining. In: Proceedings of the Seventh International Conference on Language Resources and Evaluation (LREC 2010) (2010)
2. Barbieri, F., Camacho-Collados, J., Anke, L.E., Neves, L.: TweetEval: unified benchmark and comparative evaluation for tweet classification. In: Findings of the Association for Computational Linguistics: EMNLP 2020, pp. 1644–1650 (2020)
3. Changpinyo, S., Sharma, P., Ding, N., Soricut, R.: Conceptual 12m: pushing web-scale image-text pre-training to recognize long-tail visual concepts. In: 2021 IEEE/CVF Conference on Computer Vision and Pattern Recognition (CVPR), pp. 3557–3567. IEEE (2021)
4. Deng, S., Wu, L., Shi, G., Xing, L., Jian, M.: Learning to compose diversified prompts for image emotion classification. arXiv preprint arXiv:2201.10963 (2022)
5. Deng, S., Wu, L., Shi, G., Zhang, H., Hu, W., Dong, R.: Emotion class-wise aware loss for image emotion classification. In: Fang, L., Chen, Y., Zhai, G., Wang, J., Wang, R., Dong, W. (eds.) Artificial Intelligence. CICAI 2021. LNCS, vol. 13069, pp. 553–564. Springer, Cham (2021). https://doi.org/10.1007/978-3-030-93046-2_47
6. Dosovitskiy, A., et al.: An image is worth 16x16 words: transformers for image recognition at scale. In: International Conference on Learning Representations (2020)
7. Li, G., Duan, N., Fang, Y., Gong, M., Jiang, D.: Unicoder-vl: a universal encoder for vision and language by cross-modal pre-training. In: Proceedings of the AAAI Conference on Artificial Intelligence, vol. 34, pp. 11336–11344 (2020)
8. Li, M., et al.: Clip-event: connecting text and images with event structures. In: Proceedings of the IEEE/CVF Conference on Computer Vision and Pattern Recognition, pp. 16420–16429 (2022)
9. Loshchilov, I., Hutter, F.: Decoupled weight decay regularization. In: International Conference on Learning Representations (2018)
10. Peng, K.C., Sadovnik, A., Gallagher, A., Chen, T.: Where do emotions come from? predicting the emotion stimuli map. In: 2016 IEEE International Conference on Image Processing (ICIP), pp. 614–618. IEEE (2016)
11. Qi, D., Su, L., Song, J., Cui, E., Bharti, T., Sacheti, A.: ImageBERT: cross-modal pre-training with large-scale weak-supervised image-text data. arXiv preprint arXiv:2001.07966 (2020)
12. Rao, T., Li, X., Zhang, H., Xu, M.: Multi-level region-based convolutional neural network for image emotion classification. Neurocomputing **333**, 429–439 (2019)
13. She, D., Yang, J., Cheng, M.M., Lai, Y.K., Rosin, P.L., Wang, L.: WSCNet: weakly supervised coupled networks for visual sentiment classification and detection. IEEE Trans. Multimedia **22**(5), 1358–1371 (2019)
14. Tian, H., et al.: Skep: sentiment knowledge enhanced pre-training for sentiment analysis. In: Proceedings of the 58th Annual Meeting of the Association for Computational Linguistics, pp. 4067–4076 (2020)
15. Vaswani, A., et al.: Attention is all you need. In: Advances in Neural Information Processing Systems, vol. 30 (2017)
16. Wu, L., Zhang, H., Deng, S., Shi, G., Liu, X.: Discovering sentimental interaction via graph convolutional network for visual sentiment prediction. Appl. Sci. **11**(4), 1404 (2021)

17. You, Q., Luo, J., Jin, H., Yang, J.: Robust image sentiment analysis using progressively trained and domain transferred deep networks. In: Twenty-ninth AAAI Conference on Artificial Intelligence (2015)
18. You, Q., Luo, J., Jin, H., Yang, J.: Building a large scale dataset for image emotion recognition: the fine print and the benchmark. In: Proceedings of the AAAI Conference on Artificial Intelligence, vol. 30 (2016)
19. Zhang, H., Xu, M.: Weakly supervised emotion intensity prediction for recognition of emotions in images. IEEE Trans. Multimedia **23**, 2033–2044 (2020)
20. Zhao, S., et al.: Affective image content analysis: two decades review and new perspectives. IEEE Trans. Pattern Anal. Mach. Intell. **44**(10), 6729–6751 (2021)

Learn to Enhance the Negative Information in Convolutional Neural Network

Zhicheng Cai, Chenglei Peng$^{(\boxtimes)}$, and Qiu Shen

School of Electronic Science and Engineering, Nanjing University, Nanjing, China
caizc@smail.nju.edu.cn, {pcl,shenqiu}@nju.edu.cn

Abstract. This paper proposes a learnable nonlinear activation mechanism specifically for convolutional neural network (CNN) termed as LENI, which learns to enhance the negative information in CNNs. In sharp contrast to ReLU which cuts off the negative neurons and suffers from the issue of "dying ReLU", LENI enjoys the capacity to reconstruct the dead neurons and reduce the information loss. Compared to improved ReLUs, LENI introduces a learnable approach to process the negative phase information more properly. In this way, LENI can enhance the model representational capacity significantly while maintaining the original advantages of ReLU. As a generic activation mechanism, LENI possesses the property of portability and can be easily utilized in any CNN models through simply replacing the activation layers with LENI block. Extensive experiments validate that LENI can improve the performance of various baseline models on various benchmark datasets by a clear margin (up to 1.24% higher top-1 accuracy on ImageNet-1k) with negligible extra parameters. Further experiments show that LENI can act as a channel compensation mechanism, offering competitive or even better performance but with fewer learned parameters than baseline models. In addition, LENI introduces the asymmetry to the model structure which contributes to the enhancement of representational capacity. Through visualization experiments, we validate that LENI can retain more information and learn more representations.

Keywords: CNN · Nonlinear Activation · Computer Vision

1 Introduction

Since AlexNet [13] won the ILSVRC-2012, convolutional neural network (CNN) has flourished in a compelling way [8,10,11,17,20] and been successfully applied in many real scenarios. It is known that the effective utilization of the information at all layers is vital for CNNs. Typically, CNN adopts ReLU [6] as the activation function. Although ReLU is an unsaturated nonlinear function

This work was supported by National Natural Science Foundation of China under Grant 62071216 and Natural Science Foundation of Jiangsu Province of China via Grant BK20211149.

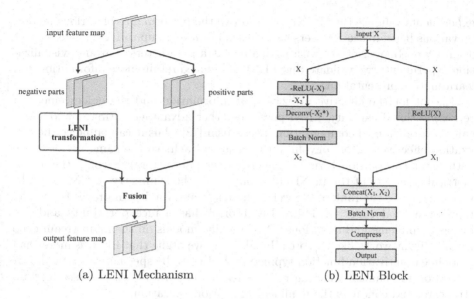

(a) LENI Mechanism   (b) LENI Block

Fig. 1. LENI mechanism and LENI block

and brings benefits for training dynamics, the forward propagation process will truncate all the negative neurons, thus the backward propagation will cause the death of these neurons. This issue is termed as "dying ReLU" [16]. Consequently, the information contained in these truncated neurons fails to be adopted effectively and the information with negative phase is completely obstructed through the network. Furthermore, the information loss will accumulate through layers, thus significantly weakening the model representational capacity. While some improved ReLUs like Leaky ReLU [15] take advantage of negative information, they inevitably lose some ReLU's original advantages. In addition, these functions may not process the negative phase information properly in that they simply multiply the negative values with relatively light weights. As proved in the later experiments, replacing ReLU with these improved ReLUs fails to improve the model's performance significantly.

This paper raises a novel nonlinear activation mechanism termed **LENI** specifically for CNN models. The core of LENI mechanism is utilizing an extra learnable transformation (termed as **LENI transformation**) to re-process the neurons cut off by ReLU. Subsequently, the information carried by the LENI neurons are fused with the positive feature maps to the further forward propagation through **Fusion**. Figure 1(a) exhibits the pipeline of LENI mechanism. **LENI block** (as exhibited in Fig. 1(b)) is utilized to realize the LENI mechanism and replace the activation layers in CNN models. LENI aims to take better advantage of the information carried by all neurons and learn to process the negative phase information more properly, it reduces the loss of information in the network flow without sacrificing the benefits that ReLU provides. In this way, LENI can enhance the model representational capacity significantly. Extensive experiments validate that LENI can improve the performance of various models on various benchmarks datasets by a clear margin (e.g., up to 1.24% higher top-1 accuracy on ImageNet-1k) with negligible extra parameters. Through visualization experiments, we validate that LENI can indeed retain more information and learn more representations.

Except for the effective utilization of information and the enhancement of representational capacity, LENI possesses other advantages. First, LENI block can act as a channel compensation mechanism [18], thus it can enhance the utilization effectiveness of convolution kernels and achieve the same performance with fewer convolution kernels (namely, fewer parameters). Second, the asymmetrical structure of the LENI block can break the symmetry of CNN models, which increases the rank of the weight matrices and further improves the model representational capacity. Third, LENI block has a nice portability and can be easily implemented in various CNN baseline models on the mainstream deep learning frameworks like PyTorch. In addition, we argue that LENI is more than a nonlinear activation function typified by ReLU, to be specific, it is a nonlinear activation mechanism which introduces learnable parameters, possesses certain structure, and conducts the nonlinear activation operation.

2   Related Work

2.1   Nonlinear Activation Functions

The nonlinear activation function follows a weight layer to conduct nonlinear operation, allowing neural networks to learn the nonlinear mapping. A common and effective nonlinear activation function is the Rectified Linear Unit (ReLU) [6]. The gradient of ReLU is either one for positive neurons or zero for negative neurons, which alleviates the issue of vanishing gradient. Besides, ReLU can accelerate the convergence and make the optimization more stable [16]. Although ReLU brings many benefits, it discards the negative neurons and executes simple truncation to the negative information, while negative neurons account for a large proportion [16] and the negative information can possess valuable features [16], thus ReLU results in the loss of information and weakens the model representational capacity. This issue is termed as "dying ReLU" [16]. In an attempt to mitigate the 'dying ReLU' issue, some researchers improve ReLU by taking advantage of negative values, such as LeakyReLU [15], PReLU [7] and so on [1,5,9,21]. However, these improved ReLUs simply multiply the negative values with light weights, which is explored insufficiently and may not be a proper treatment for the negative phase information. Besides, empirical investigations [2] validate that under certain circumstance, improved ReLUs fail to perform better than ReLU, and they inevitably lose some original advantages of ReLU.

2.2 Utilization of the Negative Information

Because of ReLU, the negative values are abandoned and the information flow in CNN is constantly positive. However, this unbalanced circumstance maybe improper for that the negative information can be valuable. Kuoet al. [4,12,14] pointed that ReLU makes CNN have its preference on images over their foreground and background reversed ones, which is termed as the issue of *sign confusion*. To tackle this issue, Saak [4] augments the kernels by duplicating the negative ones. Shang et al. [18] proved that at the shallow layers of CNN, it is sensitive to both positive and negative information, tending to capture these two kinds of information simultaneously. Thus CReLU [18] concatenated both positive and negative information simply along the channels. Although LENI may be slightly similar to CReLU, there are two great differences. Firstly, CReLU changes the width of the original model while LENI can keep the model width unchanged. Secondly, CReLU simply channel-concatenates the positive and negative feature maps without any learnable process, while LENI introduces extra trainable transformation on the negative feature maps and intends to enhance the negative information and process the negative information properly.

3 Method

3.1 LENI Mechanism and LENI Block

To process the negative neurons more properly and enhance the valuable information in the negative phase, we rethink the flow mode of negative phase information in deep CNN models and introduce a novel nonlinear activation mechanism termed LENI.

The module that introduces and implements the LENI mechanism is termed as LENI block, as Fig. 1 exhibits. Suppose X is the input of LENI block. LENI block has two parallel branches. One branch is a single ReLU, it selects the positive neurons of X and truncates the negative ones as a common practice, outputting X_1 with positive information. Simultaneously, $-X$ is input into another paralleled ReLU to screen out the negative neurons and obtains X_2^* with negative information. In order to retain the phase of the gradient, X_2^* is inverted. Then a trainable transformation is conduct on $-X_2^*$ to process the negative information and obtain X_2. In LENI block, the certain transformation consists of a depthwise separable deconvolution layer and a batch normalization layer. After that, X_1 and X_2 are concatenated along the channels and then batch normalized. To compress the doubled channels, one 1×1 convolution layer is employed after the fusion. Finally, the nonlinearly activated feature map is obtained.

In this way, negative neurons otherwise perished can be re-connected and re-processed through certain trainable transformation, therefore the negative phase information is able to propagate forward and backward effectively. LENI is superior to a function which can be simply written in the formation of normal function expression and drawn the function curve. Consequently, this operation is considered as a kind of nonlinear activation mechanism.

For implementation, we can simply replace all the original activation functions with LENI without fine-tuning the feature channels or other hyperparameters. Moreover, we observed that only utilizing the LENI in the shallow layers (or only the first layer) and keeping the rest activation layers unchanged can still enhance the accuracy higher up to 1.24% for MobileNetV3 [10] on ImageNet dataset.

3.2   Advantages of LENI

Maintain the Advantages of ReLU. LENI has two parallel branches. One of the branch only contains a single ReLU, retaining ReLU's advantages undoubtedly. The other branch conducts the ReLU before deconvolution, which works in the same way as the ReLU before the next convolution layer in normal CNN, thus still retaining ReLU's advantages. Besides, the concatenation and compression will not damage ReLU's advantages. As a result, LENI retains the ReLU's advantages.

Effective Usage of Information and Enhancement of Representational Capacity. It has been validated that features with negative phase possesses valuable information as well [15,18]. Instead of simply discarding the negative phase information like ReLU, or multiplying negative values with slight weights like improved ReLUs, or simply concatenating negative and positive values like CReLU, LENI conducts trainable transformation on the negative feature maps and fuses them with the positive feature maps. Thus LENI offers a more proper way to process and exploit the valuable negative phase information, which enables the CNN model to take full advantage of the features and reduce the loss of information, thus enhancing the model representational capacity.

Asymmetrical Structure Design. LENI block has an asymmetrical structure, breaking the model symmetrical characteristic, which is beneficial to enhancing the model representational capacity. Suppose that only a small number of neurons alter their activated values according to the different inputs while the majority of the neurons are insensitive to the different inputs, thus the order of the weight matrix is small, and the total order will be significantly decayed after the multiplication of weight matrices. Consequently, although the dimension of weight matrices is high, most of the dimensions possess little valuable information, thus weakening the model representational capacity. Such degradation problem is partially attributed to the symmetrical characteristic of the model.

Channel Compensation Mechanism. LENI is a channel compensation mechanism that enhances the efficiency of feature channels. As stated above, the lower layers of CNN are sensitive to both positive and negative information [18], while ReLU forbids the negative phase information to flow, thus requiring convolution kernels with more redundancy channels. This issue is termed as *complementary phenomenon of parameters* [18]. LENI alleviates this problem by processing the negative phase information with certain transformation and fusing both positive and negative information. Consequently, the model with LENI can utilize the kernels more effectively and achieve the same performance as that of the model

Table 1. Test accuracy of various methods on ImageNet. The number of parameters and inference speeds of these methods are also exhibited. The speed is tested on 4×3090 Ti GPUs with a batch-size of 256, measured in examples/second.

Model	LENI	Top1-Acc	↑	Params	↑	Speed	↓
VGGNet-16	--	73.34%	--	15.236M	--	1383/s	--
VGGNet-16	layer 1	73.82%	+0.48%	15.246M	+0.010M	1375/s	−8/s
VGGNet-16	layer 1,2	73.85%	+0.51%	15.256M	+0.020M	1362/s	−21/s
VGGNet-16	layer 1,2,3	73.92%	+0.58%	15.266M	+0.030M	1347/s	−36/s
ResNet-18	--	70.94%	--	11.724M	--	1492/s	--
ResNet-18	layer 1	71.29%	+0.35%	11.734M	+0.010M	1479/s	−13/s
ResNet-18	layer 1,2	71.25%	+0.31%	11.744M	+0.020M	1468/s	−24/s
ResNet-18	layer 1,2,3	71.35%	+0.41%	11.754M	+0.030M	1457/s	−35/s
MobileNetV1	--	72.08%	--	4.232M	--	1583/s	--
MobileNetV1	layer 1	72.44%	+0.36%	4.234M	+0.002M	1571/s	−12/s
MobileNetV2	--	71.68%	--	3.565M	--	1753/s	--
MobileNetV2	layer 1	71.99%	+0.31%	3.567M	+0.002M	1737/s	−16/s
MobileNetV3-S	--	61.95%	--	2.938M	--	1578/s	--
MobileNetV3-S	layer 1	63.19%	+1.24%	2.939M	+0.001M	1573/s	−5/s
MobileNetV3-L	--	71.61%	--	5.476M	--	1723/s	--
MobileNetV3-L	layer 1	71.98%	+0.37%	5.477M	+0.001M	1721/s	−2/s

with ReLU with a fewer number of parameters, which will be verified in the later experiments.

Portability. LENI is a generic activation mechanism and can be utilized in any CNNs. For implementation, we can simply utilize the LENI block to replace the original activation layers without fine-tuning the feature channels or other hyper-parameters. In addition, LENI can be easily realized on the mainstream deep learning frameworks like PyTorch.

4   Experiment

4.1   Performance Improvements on ImageNet

To verify the effectiveness of LENI, we compare the performance of various baseline models with LENI or ReLU on ImageNet. ImageNet is the most challenging and authoritative benchmark dataset for image classification, which comprises 1.28M images for training and 50K for validation from 1000 classes. The baselines include VGGNet-16 [19], ResNet-18 [8], MobileNetV1 [11], MobileNetV2 [17], and MobileNetV3 [10] with ReLU. Consider that the shallow layers of CNN are more sensitive to both positive and negative information, we only employ LENI to replace the ReLUs in shallow layers here, which also considers the trade off between the performance gain and extra computational costs. The training configuration follows the benchmark [8].

Table 1 shows the experimental results. As can be observed, the performance of all models with LENI is consistently improved by a clear margin. For example,

Table 2. Test accuracy of three baseline CNNs with different activation methods on various benchmark datasets.

Method	CIFAR-10	CIFAR-100	SVHN	MNIST	KMNIST	FMNIST	Params
VGGNet-11							
ReLU	90.39%	67.27%	93.96%	99.50%	97.06%	92.95%	5.21M
Leaky ReLU	90.43%	66.89%	93.76%	99.42%	96.64%	93.09%	5.21M
PReLU	89.38%	66.30%	93.64%	99.52%	96.97%	92.84%	5.21M
RReLU	90.66%	68.09%	94.05%	99.41%	97.09%	93.20%	5.21M
CELU	89.45%	65.62%	93.57%	99.41%	96.59%	92.76%	5.21M
GELU	87.92%	61.13%	93.50%	99.41%	96.25%	92.65%	5.21M
ELU	90.00%	65.92%	93.42%	99.41%	96.24%	92.82%	5.21M
CReLU	89.83%	66.71%	94.37%	99.41%	97.68%	93.02%	9.39M
LENI	**91.80%**	**68.41%**	**95.34%**	**99.59%**	**98.24%**	**93.66%**	6.02M
VGGNet-16							
ReLU	91.58%	68.48%	94.82%	99.55%	97.55%	93.36%	15.24M
Leaky ReLU	91.52%	68.89%	94.86%	99.51%	97.47%	93.52%	15.24M
PReLU	91.08%	68.11%	94.55%	99.50%	97.55%	93.71%	15.24M
RReLU	91.75%	69.38%	94.74%	99.48%	97.69%	93.48%	15.24M
CELU	89.55%	68.67%	94.57%	99.47%	97.43%	92.79%	15.24M
GELU	87.61%	65.02%	94.27%	99.41%	97.20%	92.71%	15.24M
ELU	90.22%	66.34%	94.31%	99.43%	97.39%	92.92%	15.24M
CReLU	92.06%	69.07%	95.37%	99.61%	97.78%	93.39%	29.68M
LENI	**93.17%**	**70.77%**	**95.81%**	**99.70%**	**98.51%**	**93.86%**	21.52M
ResNet-34							
ReLU	93.64%	74.89%	95.43%	99.57%	98.17%	94.23%	21.33M
Leaky ReLU	93.56%	74.37%	95.41%	99.51%	98.17%	94.17%	21.33M
PReLU	93.46%	72.68%	95.45%	99.50%	97.95%	94.33%	21.33M
RReLU	93.77%	74.91%	95.53%	99.48%	98.09%	94.35%	21.33M
CELU	92.52%	72.34%	95.47%	99.47%	97.63%	93.76%	21.33M
GELU	90.64%	70.22%	94.93%	99.41%	97.40%	93.88%	21.33M
ELU	92.71%	72.86%	95.01%	99.43%	97.49%	93.91%	21.33M
CReLU	93.89%	75.32%	95.67%	99.61%	98.34%	94.17%	41.85M
LENI	**94.73%**	**76.56%**	**96.72%**	**99.73%**	**99.05%**	**95.01%**	28.44M

when only replacing ReLU with LENI in the single first activation layer, the Top-1 accuracy of MobileNetV3-S is lifted significantly by 1.24%. When applying LENI in the first three activation layers, VGGNet-16 and ResNet-18 obtain the accuracy improvement of 0.58% and 0.41% respectively. The results validate that LENI can enhance the model representational capacity. In addition, LENI is cost-efficient considering that the improvement is significant while the amount of the extra parameters is so slight that can be ignored.

4.2   Comparison with Other Activation Functions

We further conduct comparative experiments of baseline CNNs with different nonlinear activation methods. We simply replace all the ReLUs in baseline models with LENI or other improved activation functions including CReLU, Leaky ReLU, PReLU, RReLU [21], CELU [1], GELU [9], and ELU [5]. The baseline models include VGGNet-11, VGGNet-16 and ResNet-34. After that, we employed the same benchmark training configurations as [8] to train these CNN models on six benchmark datasets, namely, CIFAR-10, CIFAR-100, SVHN, MNIST, KMNIST, and Fashion-MNIST. These datasets are described detailedly in [3].

As Table 2 shows, LENI enabled the CNN models to obtain significantly better results than all the other activation functions. Moreover, we can see that some improved ReLU functions performed slightly better or even poorer than the original ReLU function. The experimental results verify that LENI can enhance the model representational capacity and process the negative phase information in a more proper way.

Table 3. Test accuracy of three baseline CNNs, of which the width is halved, with ReLU, CReLU and LENI, and test accuracy of baselines with extended convolution layers.

Method	CIFAR-10	CIFAR-100	SVHN	MNIST	KMNIST	FMNIST	Params
VGGNet-11							
ReLU	90.39%	67.27%	**93.96%**	99.50%	97.06%	92.95%	5.21M
Half ReLU	88.91%	65.22%	92.91%	99.43%	96.11%	92.45%	1.30M
Half CReLU	88.62%	65.01%	93.56%	99.36%	**97.15%**	92.93%	2.35M
Half LENI	**91.19%**	**67.35%**	93.90%	**99.53%**	96.92%	**93.05%**	1.51M
Extended Conv	90.45%	66.79%	93.93%	99.54%	96.92%	93.17%	6.02M
VGGNet-16							
ReLU	91.58%	68.48%	94.82%	99.55%	97.55%	93.36%	15.24M
Half ReLU	90.45%	67.25%	94.67%	99.42%	97.56%	92.56%	3.81M
Half CReLU	90.56%	67.10%	95.11%	99.51%	97.61%	92.74%	7.42M
Half LENI	**91.74%**	**68.56%**	**95.56%**	**99.63%**	**98.27%**	**93.39%**	5.37M
Extended Conv	90.54%	67.32%	94.96%	99.54%	97.75%	93.09%	21.52M
ResNet-34							
ReLU	**93.64%**	74.89%	95.43%	99.57%	98.17%	**94.23%**	21.33M
Half ReLU	92.65%	72.66%	94.23%	99.56%	97.87%	93.57%	5.33M
Half CReLU	92.76%	73.14%	95.21%	99.54%	98.04%	93.91%	10.46M
Half LENI	93.15%	**75.23%**	**95.73%**	**99.62%**	**98.22%**	93.97%	7.10M
Extended Conv	93.67%	74.93%	95.36%	99.57%	98.21%	94.25%	28.44M

4.3   Channel Compensation Mechanism

We further design experiments that halve the model width to validate the channel compensation of LENI. Table 3 shows the experimental results, where mark

Half means the number of feature channels in all convolution layers of the model is halved. It is observed that although the model width is halved, the models with LENI still performs better than the models with ReLU which possess three times more parameters, demonstrating that LENI can enhance the utilization efficiency of the feature channels. Compared to the CReLU which is also tested as another channel compensation method, LENI obtains better results. This is attributed to that LENI conducts well-designed operation on the negative channels thus processes the negative feature channels more properly, while CReLU simply concatenates negative channels with the positive ones without any processing operations.

4.4 Further Analysis About Effectiveness

It is noted that LENI block contains more learned parameters. To validate that the more learned parameters is not the key reason for the effectiveness of LENI, we add one 3×3 depthwise convolution layer immediately after each ReLU in baselines. Row **Extended Conv** in Table 3 shows the experimental results. It is observed that these extended convolution layers fail to improve the representational capacity of the baseline models. This experimentally illustrates that the structural asymmetry that LENI block introduces is functional. In addition, CReLU widens the model by two times and doubles the parameter amount as exhibited in Table 2. CReLU utilizes both positive and negative information and is asymmetric. However, it still fails to improve the model performance significantly. This experimentally illustrates that the deconvolutional learnable transformation that LENI block introduces is vital. Thus it can be concluded that more parameters do not necessarily improve the model representational capacity which makes no contribution to the effectiveness of LENI. Consequently, we attribute the effectiveness of LENI to the proper processing (realized by certain trainable transformation) of the negative information and the well-designed asymmetric structure of LENI block.

4.5 LENI Retains More Information

Figure 2 exhibits the distribution histogram of the values in the feature maps non-activated or activated by ReLU, Leaky ReLU and LENI. The baseline model utilized is the MobileNetV3-S trained on ImageNet. We extract the pre-activated and activated feature maps of the first convolution layer. It can be observed that about half of the values in the non-activated feature maps are negative and truncated by ReLU, leading to the loss of much information. For Leaky ReLU, these negative values are multiplied with a small coefficient of 0.01, which makes the negative values cluster close to zero, thus the distribution histogram is observed similarly to that of ReLU. However, for LENI, the distribution histogram is meaningful as it is similar to the normal distribution, which is the distribution possessing the most information entropy. This phenomenon validates that LENI can retain more information, which can be attributed to the extra learnable transformation that LENI conducts to enhance the negative information.

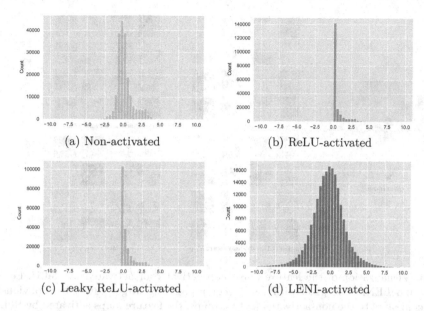

Fig. 2. Distribution histogram of the values in the feature maps non-activated or activated by ReLU, Leaky ReLU and LENI. About half of the neurons are truncated by ReLU, which loses much information. For Leaky ReLU, the negative values are multiplied with a small coefficient of 0.01, which makes the negative values close to zero, thus the distribution histogram is similar to that of ReLU. For LENI, it is similar to the normal distribution, which is the distribution possessing the most information entropy, thus validating that LENI can retain more information.

4.6   LENI Learns More Representations

Figure 3 visualizes various non-activated feature maps and the feature maps activated by ReLU, Leaky ReLU and LENI. Still, the baseline model utilized is the MobileNetV3-S trained on ImageNet and we extract the pre-activated and activated feature maps of the first convolution layer. It is obviously that, compared to the non-activated feature maps, the feature maps activated by ReLU lose many representations of significance due to the "dying ReLU" issue, specifically, the contrast of object and background is blurry and many patterns are discarded. The feature maps activated by Leaky ReLU is similar to that of ReLU (the reason is the same as stated above), there still exists the similar issue that losing meaningful representations. Consequently, Leaky ReLU fails to obtain better representational capacity than ReLU. While for LENI, it can clearly observed that the representations are more richer, for example, the edges are more clear and the textures are more distinct. This phenomenon illustrates that LENI can learn more representations through the additional learnable transformation that conducts the proper processing on the negative information.

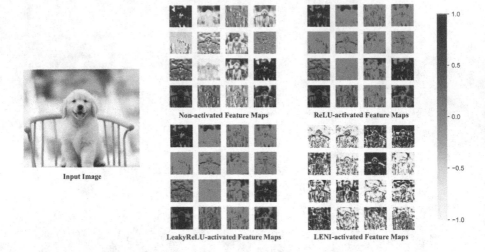

Fig. 3. Visualization of the feature maps non-activated or activated by ReLU, Leaky ReLU and LENI. The pixel with darker color possesses larger value. It is obviously that, compared to the non-activated feature maps, the feature maps activated by ReLU lose many representations of significance due to the "dying ReLU" issue. Leaky ReLU still has the similar issue that losing meaningful representations. While for LENI, it is observed that the representations are more richer, for example, the edges are more clear and the textures are more distinct. This phenomenon illustrates that LENI can learn more representations through the additional learnable transformation that conducts the proper processing on the negative information.

5   Conclusion

This paper proposes LENI, an innovative nonlinear activation mechanism, to learn to enhance the negative information and strengthen the model representational capacity. As a generic design element, LENI block can be implemented in various CNN baselines. Extensive experiments validate that LENI can produce superior performance to ReLU or improved ReLUs. Further experiments illustrate that LENI can enhance the efficiency of convolution kernels. We attribute the effectiveness of LENI to the proper processing of negative information and the well-designed asymmetric structure. Through visualization experiments, we validate that LENI can retain more information and learn more representations.

References

1. Barron, J.T.: Continuously differentiable exponential linear units. CoRR, abs/1704.07483 (2017)
2. Cai, Z., Peng, C.: A study on training fine-tuning of convolutional neural networks. In: 2021 13th International Conference on Knowledge and Smart Technology (KST), pp. 84–89. IEEE (2021)

3. Cai, Z., Peng, C., Du, S.: Jitter: random jittering loss function. In: 2021 International Joint Conference on Neural Networks (IJCNN), pp. 1–8. IEEE (2021)

4. Chen, Y., Xu, Z., Cai, S., Lang, Y., Jay Kuo, C.-C.: A saak transform approach to efficient, scalable and robust handwritten digits recognition. In: 2018 Picture Coding Symposium (PCS), pp. 174–178 (2018)

5. Clevert, D.-A., Unterthiner, T., Hochreiter, S.: Fast and accurate deep network learning by exponential linear units (elus). arXiv preprint arXiv:1511.07289 (2015)

6. Glorot, X., Bordes, A., Bengio, Y.: Deep sparse rectifier networks. Learning/statistics & Optimisation (2010)

7. He, K., Zhang, X., Ren, S., Sun, J.: Delving deep into rectifiers: surpassing human-level performance on imagenet classification. In: Proceedings of the IEEE International Conference on Computer Vision, pp. 1026–1034 (2015)

8. He, K., Zhang, X., Ren, S., Sun, J.: Deep residual learning for image recognition. In: Proceedings of the IEEE Conference on Computer Vision and Pattern Recognition, pp. 770–778 (2016)

9. Hendrycks, D., Gimpel, K.: Gaussian error linear units (gelus). arXiv preprint arXiv:1606.08415 (2016)

10. Howard, A., et al.: Searching for mobilenetv3. In: Proceedings of the IEEE International Conference on Computer Vision, pp. 1314–1324 (2019)

11. Howard, A.G., et al.: Mobilenets: efficient convolutional neural networks for mobile vision applications. arXiv preprint arXiv:1704.04861 (2017)

12. Jay Kuo, C.-C., Chen, Y.: On data-driven saak transform. J. Vis. Commun. Image Representation **50**, 237–246 (2018)

13. Krizhevsky, A., Sutskever, I., Hinton, G.E.: Imagenet classification with deep convolutional neural networks. In: Advances in Neural Information Processing Systems, pp. 1097–1105 (2012)

14. Jay Kuo, C.-C., Zhang, M., Li, S., Duan, J., Chen, Y.: Interpretable convolutional neural networks via feedforward design. J. Vis. Commun. Image Representation **60**, 346–359 (2019)

15. Maas, A.L., Hannun, A.Y., Ng, A.Y.: Rectifier nonlinearities improve neural network acoustic models. In: Proc. icml, vol. 30, p. 3(2013)

16. Parisi, L., Neagu, D., Ma, R., Campean, F.: Quantum ReLU activation for convolutional neural networks to improve diagnosis of Parkinson's disease and COVID-19. Expert Syst. Appl. **187**, 115892 (2022)

17. Sandler, M., Howard, A., Zhu, M., Zhmoginov, A., Chen, L.-C.: Mobilenetv 2: inverted residuals and linear bottlenecks. In: Proceedings of the IEEE Conference on Computer Vision and Pattern Recognition, pp. 4510–4520 (2018)

18. Shang, W., Sohn, K., Almeida, D., Lee, H.: Understanding and improving convolutional neural networks via concatenated rectified linear units. In: International Conference on Machine Learning, pp. 2217–2225 (2016)

19. Simonyan, K., Zisserman, A.: Very deep convolutional networks for large-scale image recognition. arXiv preprint arXiv:1409.1556 (2014)

20. Szegedy, C., et al.: Going deeper with convolutions. In: Proceedings of the IEEE Conference on Computer Vision and Pattern Recognition, pp. 1–9 (2015)

21. Xu, B., Wang, N., Chen, T., Li, M.: Empirical evaluation of rectified activations in convolutional network. CoRR, abs/1505.00853 (2015)

Task-Agnostic Generalized Meta-learning Based on MAML for Few-Shot Bearing Fault Diagnosis

Xitao Yang[1], Lijun Zhang[1], and Jinjia Wang[1,2](✉) [iD]

[1] School of Information and Science Engineer, Yanshan University, Qinhuangdao 066004, Hebei, China
[2] Hebei Key Laboratory of Information Transmission and Singal Processing, Yanshan University, Qinhuangdao 066004, Hebei, China
`wjj@ysu.edu.cn`

Abstract. Meta-learning methods have been widely applied to solve few-shot problems. However, the metamodels of current meta-learning methods may be too biased toward the tasks in the meta-training phase and are less adaptable to new tasks, especially when the number of new tasks is small. To reduce the bias of the metamodel and improve its generalizability, this paper proposes a Task-Agnostic Generalized Meta-Learning (TAGML) algorithm based on Model-Agnostic Meta-Learning (MAML) for few-shot bearing fault diagnosis. The algorithm improves MAML in terms of both network structure and optimization algorithm. Firstly, the quality of feature extraction is improved by adding a squeeze-and-excitation attention module to the network of MAML. Secondly, the following improvements are made in the optimization algorithm: (1) The stability of the training process is improved by using multi-step loss optimization in the optimization; (2) It is proposed to add the Task-Agnositic regular penalty term to the meta-optimization objective function to improve the task unbiasedness of the metamodel; (3) To speed up the convergence and further improve the model's ability to generalize to different tasks, an iterative updatable outer loop learning rate strategy is used. Experiments demonstrate that the algorithm is not only effective in identifying new fault tasks that do not appear in the meta-training phase but also has good recognition performance for generalized bearing fault scenarios with a mixture of seen and unseen class fault tasks.

Keywords: MAML · Task-Agnostic · few-shot · fault diagnosis

1 Introduction

Bearing fault diagnosis is a crucial task in machinery and equipment maintenance, which is of great significance to ensure normal operation and extend the life of the equipment. However, few-shot bearing fault diagnosis has become a

Supported in part by Central Funds Guiding the Local Science and Technology Development (Basic Research Projects) (206Z5001G), Hebei Natural Science Foundation (F2019203583), and Hebei Key Laboratory Project (202250701010046).

H. Lu et al. (Eds.): ICIG 2023, LNCS 14355, pp. 118–129, 2023.
https://doi.org/10.1007/978-3-031-46305-1_10

challenge due to factors such as brutal bearing fault data collection, small sample size, and insufficient markers.

In recent years, scholars have researched few-shot bearing fault diagnosis from several aspects of data augmentation, feature learning, and classifier design [1]. Among these numerous few-shot learning methods, meta-learning [2] is a well-represented approach that can be divided into three main categories: metric-based methods (e.g., Matching Networks, Prototypical Networks, and Relation Networks) [3–5], model-based methods (e.g., MANN) [6], and optimization-based methods (e.g., MAML) [7].

These three meta-learning strategies have been widely used in various fields of artificial intelligence today, but in terms of the few-shot intelligent bearing fault diagnosis field, a large amount of research has focused on metric-based methods [8]. Although the metric-based methods are simple and easy to implement, they have the following drawbacks: (a) they are very sensitive to data distribution; (b) they require sufficient training samples; (c) feature selection is complex, and (d) the models have poor generalization performance and are difficult to adapt to unknown fault types or known fault types with different data distributions. Model-based approaches usually require two or more learners for meta-optimization, and task-specific adaptation [8], and model selection is difficult. Optimization-based approaches, generally using a two-level optimization strategy, aim to provide a globally shared initialization for all given fault identification tasks, allowing the model to be quickly adapted to new tasks after fine-tuning using only a few numbers of samples, providing an improvement on the shortcomings of metric-based and model-based approaches, in particular, the MAML proposed by Finn et al. [7]. However, the problem with existing MAML meta-learning methods is that the meta-model or initial learner may be biased towards some tasks sampled in the meta-training phase, and such biased initialization models may not generalize well to unseen tasks that deviate significantly from the meta-training task, especially when there are few samples available on the new task [9].

Based on the above analysis, this paper proposes a Task-Agnostic few-shot fault diagnosis method (TAGML) with the MAML model as the infrastructure, which improves vanilla MAML in terms of both the network model and the optimization algorithm to solve the biasedness problem of MAML.

2   Related Work

2.1   Meta-agnostic Meta-learning

The basic principle of MAML is to use meta-learning methods to pre-train generic model initialization parameters so that they can be quickly adapted to new tasks and learn to perform well on a small number of samples [7]. MAML, as a typical few-shot meta-learning method, uses the task T as the training and testing object and divides the tasks in the same N-way K-shot format as [10], where each small task is a small batch of data randomly selected from the data set containing a support-set and a query-set. Specifically, the whole MAML algorithm employs two processes:

(1) Inner loop updating process

$$\theta_i^{T_j} = \theta_{i-1}^{T_j} - \alpha \nabla_\theta L_{S_{T_j}} \left(f_{\theta_{i-1}^{T_j}} \right) \tag{1}$$

where α is the learning rate, $\theta_i^{T_j}$ is the weight of the base network in task T_j after i steps of update, and $L_{S_{T_j}} \left(f_{\theta_{i-1}^{T_j}} \right)$ is the loss of task T_j on the support set after $(i-1)$ steps of update.

(2) Outer loop updating process

$$\theta = \theta - \beta \nabla_\theta \sum_{j=1}^{J} L_{T_j} \left(f_{\theta_N^{T_j}} \right) \tag{2}$$

where the batch task size is assumed to be J, β is the learning rate, and L_{T_j} is the loss of task j on the query set, using cross-entropy loss [11].

2.2   Squeeze-and-Excitation Module

The Squeeze-and-Excitation(SE) Module is a lightweight neural network module designed to improve the expressiveness of feature representations by learning the attention of channels in feature mapping [12], including both Squeeze and Excitation operations.

Squeeze compresses and reduces the feature data's dimensionality, converting the features' spatial dimensionality from high to one-dimensional using a global average pooling operation. The output $x_{input}^{SE} \in R^{W \times C}$ of the feature extraction module is used as the input to the SE module, and the global spatial information in each channel of the input features is compressed into a scalar after the Squeeze operation, as follows [13]:

$$q = F_{sq}(x) = \frac{1}{W} \left[\sum_{j=1}^{W} x(c, j) \right]_{c=1}^{C} \tag{3}$$

where $q \in R^C$, C is the number of channels. The Excitation operation, which consists mainly of fully connected layers and activation functions, aggregates the information after the Squeeze operation, allowing for the enhancement of information on channel features with solid correlation and the suppression of the rest of the information, as follows:

$$Z = F_{ex}(q) = f_{sig}(W_2 f_{relu}(W_1 q)) \tag{4}$$

where $W_1 \in R^{\frac{C}{r} \times C}, W_2 \in R^{C \times \frac{C}{r}}, z \in R^C$, r is the dimension reduction rate and f_{sig} is sigmoid activation function. The introduction of the SE module in the network model of this article essentially introduces input-conditional dynamics that help to improve the resolution of features, which can ultimately be effective in improving the quality of extracted features to ensure that the inner loop of the TAGML model can be adapted to new tasks with fewer iterative steps.

3 Metodology

3.1 Model Overview

The network structure of our proposed model is shown in Fig. 1. First, the encoder processes each sample x in the bearing fault task T_j to a preliminary feature map $X_1 \subseteq R^{W \times C}$, where W represents the size of the feature map and C represents the number of feature channels. Immediately afterward, in order to obtain more representative features, the feature map X_1 is fed into the SE module, which uses the Squeeze and Excitation operations of the SE module to perform adaptive feature weight weighting for each channel in the task and finally outputs a refined feature map $X_2 \subseteq R^{W \times C}$. The final feature map X_2 will be processed by the classifier module to obtain a probability distribution vector $Y \subseteq R^N$, where N is the number of sample categories in each task.

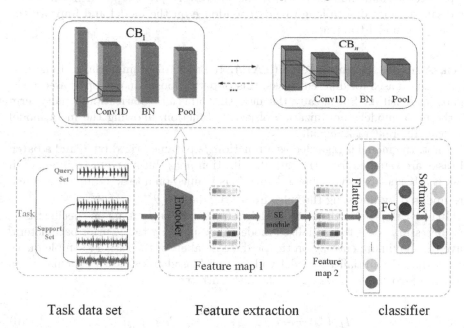

Fig. 1. The network architecture of TAGML model.

3.2 Our Proposed Method

Inner Loop Multi Step Loss Optimization (MLS). MAML works by minimizing the query set loss computed by the base network after all internal loop updates to the task support set are completed, and the base network weights are implicitly optimized by backpropagation at each step except the last step, which leads to many instability problems in MAML, such as gradient disappearance or gradient explosion [14]. To ensure a more stable training process, this paper proposes a multi step loss optimization approach, i.e., minimizing the query set loss calculated by the base network after each update step of the training task support set. More specifically, this paper proposes that the minimized loss is a weighted sum of the query set losses after each support set loss update, with the formula:

$$\theta = \theta - \beta \nabla_\theta E_{T_j \sim P(T)} \left\{ \frac{1}{m} \sum_{i=1}^m v_i L_{T_j} \left(f_{\theta_i^{T_j}} \right) \right\} \tag{5}$$

where β is the learning rate of outer loop, m is the number of steps in the inner loop iterative update, and $L_{T_j} \left(f_{\theta_i^{T_j}} \right)$ denotes the loss of the query set after step i of the meta-model task T_j update, and $v_i = i$ is the importance weight of the loss of the target set at step i.Using this method, the underlying network weights at each step receive gradients of loss from the current and subsequent steps directly and indirectly, which can effectively prevent gradient explosion or disappearance due to long-range dependence on the model and improve the stability of model training.

Task-Agnostic Regular Term (TAR). In order to obtain initial meta models that are unbiased for different tasks, this paper proposes an entropy-based task-agnostic algorithm. Specifically, the algorithm adds a regularization penalty term to the meta model's optimization objective function, allowing the meta model to treat different tasks equally.

First, the model is regarded as a function f_θ parameterized by θ, and a batch of tasks are sampled from the task distribution $p(T)$ during meta-training, each task is a K-shot N-way problem. When it is trained on a task T_j, its parameters are updated by updating the rules from θ Update to $\theta_i^{T_j}$.

In order to prevent the meta model f_θ from over-performing on specific tasks, it is necessary to let the initialized model corresponding to the prior parameter θ have the maximum entropy on the prediction labels of the task T_j sample query set so that the initialized model will not be biased towards a particular task, with the following expression for the task entropy:

$$H_{T_j} (f_\theta) = -E_{x_i \sim P_{T_j}(x)} \sum_{n=1}^N \hat{y}_{i,n} log \left(\hat{y}_{i,n} \right) \tag{6}$$

where $x_i \sim P_{T_j} (x)$ and $[y_{i,1}, ..., y_{i,N}] = f_\theta (x_i)$ are the predicted values of f_θ, which generally come from the softmax layer of classification tasks. Further, we need to maximize the task entropy $H_{T_j} (f_\theta)$ before the parameter update and minimize the task entropy $H_{T_j} \left(f_{\theta_i^{T_j}} \right)$ after the parameter update. It is therefore straightforward to maximize the entropy reduction $H_{T_j} (f_\theta) - H_{T_j} \left(f_{\theta_i^{T_j}} \right)$ for each task before and after the parameter update. Where the minimization of $H_{T_j}\left(f_{\theta_i^{T_j}}\right)$ means that after the θ parameter is updated to $\theta_i^{T_j}$, the model can be more sure of the label with higher confidence. Task entropy reduction $H_{T_j}\left(f_\theta\right) - H_{T_j}\left(f_{\theta_i^{T_j}}\right)$ is added into the objective optimization function of the meta-learner as a regular penalty term. Since this regular term is the key to improving the task unbias of the meta-model, it is named the task-agnostic regular term. The meta-optimization objective function after adding the regular penalty term is shown in Eq. 7:

$$\arg\min_\theta E_{T_j \sim P(T)}\left\{\frac{1}{m}\sum_{i=1}^{m} v_i L_{T_j}\left(f_{\theta_i^{T_j}}\right) + \lambda\left[-H_{T_j}\left(f_\theta\right) + H_{T_j}\left(f_{\theta_m^{T_j}}\right)\right]\right\} \quad (7)$$

where λ is the equilibrium coefficient of the regular term.

Outer Loop Learning Rate Update (OLR). Usually, a fixed learning rate is used in MAML models to optimize the metamodel, but using a fixed learning rate not only requires much effort to adjust the learning rate but also reduces the generalization performance of MAML [14]. In the MAML model, the training phase involves two levels of loop updates and has two different learning rates, the inner loop learning rate l_r and the outer loop learning rate β. In [11], Zhang et al. used a learnable approach to update the inner loop learning rate, but the method requires a derivative update operation for the learning rate, which consumes a large number of computational resources.

Because of this, this paper adopts an outer-loop learning rate update strategy based on the cosine annealing algorithm, with the expression:

$$\beta_t = \beta_{min} + \frac{1}{2}\left(\beta_{max} - \beta_{min}\right)\left(1 + cos\left(\frac{T_{cur}}{T_{max}}\pi\right)\right) \quad (8)$$

where β_{min} and β_{max} are the ranges of learning rates, T_{cur} denotes the total number of rounds trained, and T_{max} denotes the maximum number of training epochs. The cosine annealing algorithm dynamically adjusts the learning rate of the outer loop, eliminating the need for hyperparametric search of the learning rate on the one hand, and helping the metamodel escape from local optimality with the help of the violent fluctuations of the cosine on the other hand, allowing the model to fit the training set efficiently and thus producing higher generalization performance.

Overall Algorithm of TAGML. The MSL, TAR, and OLR strategies proposed above are jointly applied to the optimization process of MAML in [7] to obtain the overall optimization algorithm of the TAGML model finally, the specific optimization process of which is shown in Fig. 2.

The overall process of the metamodel training phase is similar to that of [7], where the inner loop achieves fast iterative adaptation to different training tasks. Each epoch of the outer loop updates the initialization parameters of the

model based on the mean gradient of the iterative average loss sum of the model
on all task query sets after the inner loop iterations, providing new initialization parameters for the inner loop of the model in the following training epochs,
enabling it to be adapted to different tasks with fewer iterative steps. After multiple epochs, the final result is a meta-knowledge θ that can be quickly adapted
to different tasks. The meta-knowledge θ is used as an initialization parameter
for the model during the testing phase of the metamodel, enabling the model to
be quickly adapted to a new few-shot bearing fault tasks.

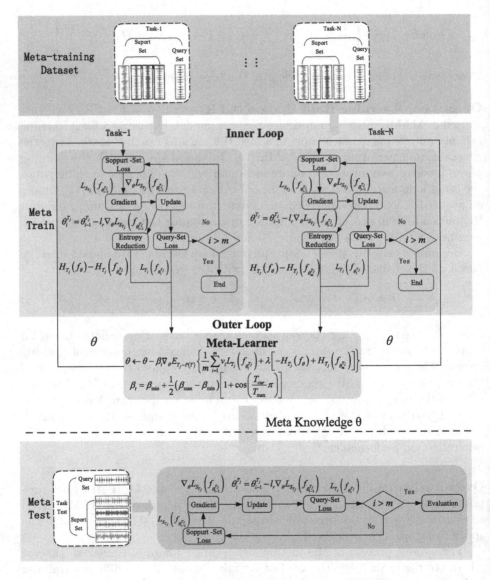

Fig. 2. General structure of the TAGML optimization algorithm.

4   Experiment

4.1   Data Set

CWRU Dataset. The CWRU data set [15] provided by the Bearing Data Center of Case Western Reserve University (CWRU) is widely used as a reference in the research of bearing fault diagnosis. This paper selected ten fault types from the CWRU dataset using the same approach as [11] based on the location and size of the bearing faults.

PU Dataset. In order to further investigate the generalization performance of the TAGML method proposed in this paper in diagnosing real bearing faults, experiments were conducted using the Paderborn dataset [16]. In the experiments in this paper, we have selected 13 types of bearing fault data in the manner described in [17] to investigate the model's ability to generalize from artificially damaged failures to actual failures. Details of these 13 bearings are shown in Table 1.

4.2   Implementation Details

The Encoder Module and SE Module implementation is modified from [3,13]. The inner and outer loops of the model are trained using the Adam [18] optimizer. By searching through the grid parameters, choose $l_r = 0.05$ as the fixed learning rate of the inner loop, set $\beta = 0.005$ as the initial learning rate of the outer loop with learning rate update, and update as in [19], and finally set the coefficient $\lambda = 0.005$ of the task unbiased regular term. Each meta-training scenario consisted of 16 tasks for training, for N-way 1-shot and N-way 5-shot iterations of the inner task loop of 3 and 1 step, respectively. All models were trained for 200 epochs.

4.3   Predicting New Bearing Faults

Artificial Bearing Faults. The experiments aim to investigate the performance of the proposed method in predicting new artificial bearing faults, using the CWRU dataset in Subsect. 4.1 as experimental data and setting up four prediction scenarios for new faults: Inner and outer ring faults and ball faults as well as combinations of maximum fault sizes for each fault position (IOR).

In this experiment, several mainstream methods for few-shot bearing fault diagnosis were selected for comparison with the proposed method in this paper under the same experimental setup, and the experimental results are shown in Table 2. The results show that the TAGML model performs excellently in all four different task scenarios. Specifically, the proposed method shows a significant performance improvement over the baseline MAML [7], especially for the 1-shot scenario, with a performance improvement of no less than 5% for all three types of faults: inner ring faults, outer ring faults, and ball faults, and the two advanced methods DSMN [20] and FSM3-MN [20] are more task biased compared to TAGML. For example, the diagnostic performance for outer ring faults is significantly lower than the other three types.

Table 1. Different types of bearing faults in the PU dataset

Artificial damages(source domain)				
Label	Name	Fault location	Cause of Failure	Severity
1	KA01	Outer Race	Electrical discharge maching	1
2	KA03	Outer Race	Electrical engraver	2
3	KA05	Outer Race	Electrical engraver	1
4	KA07	Outer Race	Drilling	1
5	KA08	Inner Race	Drilling	2
6	KI01	Inner Race	Electrical discharge maching	1
7	KI03	Inner Race	Electrical engraver	1
8	KI05	Inner Race	Electrical engraver	2
Healthy&Real damages (taget domain)				
9	K001	Healthy	-	-
10	KA04	Outer Race	Fatihue pitting	1
11	KB23	Inner + Outer	Fatihue pitting	2
12	KB27	Inner + Outer	Plastic deform: Indentations	1
13	KI04	Inner Race	Fatihue pitting	1

Actual Bearing Faults. To further explore the generalization performance of the proposed method in this paper under actual faults, the source domain data in Table 1 was used for meta-training and the target domain data for meta-testing to achieve meta-knowledge transfer from artificial faults to actual faults. A comparison was also made with several methods, and the accurate statistics of the respective tests are presented in Table 3. Where MRN is a meta-relational network model proposed by Wu et al. [17], which has achieved state-of-the-art results in typical mechanical fault diagnosis scenarios from artificial to actual faults in PU datasets, but the ones provided in [17] are all test results of MRN in frequency domain data conditions. In order to unify the experimental conditions, the open source code provided by them was used in this experiment to participate in comparison experiments in time domain data conditions. As seen in Table 4, even in the artificial to natural fault diagnosis scenario where the source and target domain data distributions differ significantly, TAGML still performs consistently well and achieves optimal results for different sample sizes.

4.4 Mixed Fault Diagnosis of Seen and Unseen Classes

The test task in this experiment is a generalized fault task that includes both seen and unseen classes of faults. This task is more closely related to fault diagnosis in real-life work scenarios and places higher demands on the task unbiasedness, generalization performance, and robustness of the metamodel. K001 and KA04 were selected from the target domain data in Table 1 and added to the source domain data set. The original KA05 and KA08 categories in the source domain were removed, and the target domain data type was kept unchanged.

Table 2. The result of artificial-to-artificial faults diagnosis

New Fault Category	Inner Race Defect		Outer Race Defect	
	1-shot	5-shot	1-shot	5-shot
Finetune Last [17]	82.22%	87.80%	75.89%	76.55%
ProtoNet [4]	78.80%	93.24%	80.07%	93.63%
RelationNet [5]	66.82%	89.50%	86.63%	91.00%
MAML [7]	90.86%	96.32%	90.57%	98.00%
DSMN [20]	96.76%	98.42%	85.44%	94.05%
FSM3-MN [20]	98.76%	100%	92.55%	98.98%
TAGML(ours)	**99.60%**	**100%**	**100%**	**100%**
New Fault Category	Ball Race Defect		IOR	
	1-shot	5-shot	1-shot	5-shot
Finetune Last [17]	67.77%	85.24%	77.33%	87.91%
ProtoNet [4]	68.80%	73.82%	85.20%	84.26%
RelationNet [5]	80.63%	88.19%	76.03%	87.03%
MAML [7]	88.56%	93.78%	95.48%	98.86%
DSMN [20]	98.45%	**99.91%**	99.95%	99.95%
FSM3-MN [20]	**99.55%**	99.20%	97.66%	100%
TAGML(ours)	99.07%	99.50%	**100%**	**100%**

The method proposed in this paper is compared with the basic MAML model. The results are shown in Table 4. It is clear from the analysis of the results that the proposed method has a significant advantage in the generalized fault scenario, but both algorithms have a decrease compared to the results in Subsect. 4.3, which may be due to the model bias towards the seen category. In addition, it can be found that in the case of 1-shot, the accuracy of MAML is even slightly better than the result of identifying new actual faults. This is due to the fact that the results in Table 4 are the total accuracy of the five categories, and the biased nature of the MAML model causes an increase in the identification accuracy of the seen category faults, thus creating the illusion of increased accuracy.

Therefore in order to further validate the proposed model's improvement on the unbiased nature of the underlying MAML, the model obtained by selecting the 3-shot case training was tested on 100 samples selected for each specific category. For the more effective performance of the results, a confusion matrix was used in the form of Fig. 3. Through the analysis of the confusion matrix, it can be found that the MAML model has an obvious bias for the two seen categories of faults K001 and KA04, except for the fact that these two classes themselves have a high recognition accuracy, other new categories will also be

Table 3. The result of artificial-to-actual faults diagnosis

Algorithms	1-shot	3-shot	5-shot	average
MAML	77.06%	89.82%	93.65%	86.84%
ProtoNet	76.50%	79.37%	88.52%	81.46%
RelationNet	66.86%	73.94%	80.29%	73.59%
MRN [17]	88.00%	88.67%	95.59%	90.75%
TAGML(ours)	**96.70%**	**99.70%**	**99.88%**	**98.76%**

Table 4. Generalized faults diagnosis results

Algorithms	1-shot	3-shot	5-shot	average
MAML	79.80%	85.67%	90.45%	85.31%
TAGML(ours)	**92.94%**	**96.45%**	**97.74%**	**95.71%**

misidentified as these two categories, and the more similar the location of the fault and the cause of the fault, the more likely it is to be misidentified. The TAGML modality not only has a high overall recognition efficiency but also does not have a bias for the seen category of faults.

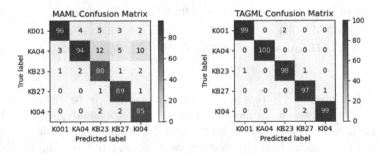

Fig. 3. 3-shot generalized faults scenario confusion matrix

5   Conclusion

In this paper, we improve the MAML model regarding the network model structure and the optimization algorithm, propose a meta-learning method TAGML with task unbiasedness, and apply the method to diagnosis from artificial-to-actual faults and a generalized fault diagnosis scenario. Experiments have demonstrated the effectiveness of our TAGML.

References

1. Zhang, T., Chen, J., Li, F., Zhang, K., Lv, H., He, S., Xu, E.: Intelligent fault diagnosis of machines with small & imbalanced data: a state-of-the-art review and possible extensions. ISA transactions (2021)
2. Li, Z., Zhou, F., Chen, F., Li, H.: Meta-sgd: Learning to learn quickly for few shot learning. ArXiv abs/1707.09835 (2017)
3. Vinyals, O., Blundell, C., Lillicrap, T.P., Kavukcuoglu, K., Wierstra, D.: Matching networks for one shot learning. In: NIPS (2016)
4. Snell, J., Swersky, K., Zemel, R.S.: Prototypical networks for few-shot learning. ArXiv abs/1703.05175 (2017)
5. Sung, F., Yang, Y., Zhang, L., Xiang, T., Torr, P.H.S., Hospedales, T.M.: Learning to compare: relation network for few-shot learning. 2018 IEEE/CVF Conference on Computer Vision and Pattern Recognition, pp. 1199–1208 (2017)
6. Santoro, A., Bartunov, S., Botvinick, M., Wierstra, D., Lillicrap, T.: Meta-learning with memory-augmented neural networks. In: International Conference on Machine Learning, pp. 1842–1850. PMLR (2016)
7. Finn, C., Abbeel, P., Levine, S.: Model-agnostic meta-learning for fast adaptation of deep networks. In: International Conference on Machine Learning (2017)
8. Feng, Y., Chen, J., Xie, J., Zhang, T., Lv, H., Pan, T.: Meta-learning as a promising approach for few-shot cross-domain fault diagnosis: algorithms, applications, and prospects. Knowl. Based Syst. **235**, 107646 (2021)
9. Jamal, M.A., Qi, G.J., Shah, M.: Task agnostic meta-learning for few-shot learning. 2019 IEEE/CVF Conference on Computer Vision and Pattern Recognition (CVPR), pp. 11711–11719 (2018)
10. Ren, M., et al.: Meta-learning for semi-supervised few-shot classification. ArXiv abs/1803.00676 (2018)
11. Zhang, S., Ye, F., Wang, B., Habetler, T.G.: Few-shot bearing fault diagnosis based on model-agnostic meta-learning. IEEE Trans. Ind. Appl. **57**, 4754–4764 (2020)
12. Hu, J., Shen, L., Albanie, S., Sun, G., Wu, E.: Squeeze-and-excitation networks. IEEE Trans. Pattern Anal. Mach. Intell. **42**, 2011–2023 (2017)
13. Feng, Y., Chen, J., Zhang, T., He, S., Xu, E., Zhou, Z.: Semi-supervised meta-learning networks with squeeze-and-excitation attention for few-shot fault diagnosis. ISA transactions (2021)
14. Antoniou, A., Edwards, H., Storkey, A.J.: How to train your maml. ArXiv abs/1810.09502 (2018)
15. Smith, W.A., Randall, R.B.: Rolling element bearing diagnostics using the case western reserve university data: a benchmark study. Mech. Syst. Signal Process. **64**, 100–131 (2015)
16. Lessmeier, C., Kimotho, J.K., Zimmer, D., Sextro, W.: Condition monitoring of bearing damage in electromechanical drive systems by using motor current signals of electric motors: a benchmark data set for data-driven classification (2016)
17. Wu, J., Zhao, Z., Sun, C., Yan, R., Chen, X.: Few-shot transfer learning for intelligent fault diagnosis of machine. Measurement **166**, 108202 (2020)
18. Kingma, D.P., Ba, J.: Adam: A method for stochastic optimization. CoRR abs/1412.6980 (2014)
19. Loshchilov, I., Hutter, F.: Sgdr: Stochastic gradient descent with warm restarts. arXiv: Learning (2016)
20. Wang, D., Zhang, M., Xu, Y., Lu, W., Yang, J., Zhang, T.: Metric-based meta-learning model for few-shot fault diagnosis under multiple limited data conditions. Mechanical Systems and Signal Processing (2021)

Weakly Supervised Image Matting via Patch Clustering

Yunke Zhang[1], Chi Wang[1], Yu Zhang[2], Hujun Bao[1], and Weiwei Xu[1]($\boxtimes$)

[1] State Key Lab of CAD and CG, Zhejiang University, Hangzhou, China
xww@cad.zju.edu.cn
[2] Nanjing University, Nanjing, China

Abstract. Image matting aims to extract the accurate foreground opacity mask for a given image. State-of-the-art approaches are usually based on encoder-decoder neural networks and require a large dataset with ground-truth alpha matte to facilitate the training process. However, the alpha matte annotation process is extremely time-consuming and labor-intensive. To lift such a burden, we propose a novel deep learning-based weakly supervised image matting method. It can simultaneously utilize data with and without ground-truth alpha mattes to boost the matting performance. The key idea is to exploit the patch-wise similarity of the alpha mattes without explicitly relying on ground-truth alpha mattes. To this end, we design a novel patch clustering module to cluster patches with similar alpha mattes and subsequently propose a new loss function to supervise the matting network by utilizing the clustering prior. Experimental results show that our proposed method can effectively cluster image patches by their corresponding alpha patches' similarity and improve the matting performance. To our knowledge, our method is the first to tackle the weakly supervised image matting problem with only trimaps as the annotation.

Keywords: Neural networks · Image matting · Weakly-supervised learning · Clustering

1 Introduction

The task of image matting is to extract the foreground object in an image accurately. It is widely used in editing applications, *e.g.*, compositing the foreground object on a new background. The resulting alpha mattes represent the opacity (in $[0, 1]$) of the foreground, where 0 and 1 represent the solid background and foreground, respectively. The fractional opacity mainly comes from the transparency or the partial coverage of the background. Specifically, the matting problem tries to solve for three types of unknowns at each pixel, *i.e.*, the foreground color F, the background color B, and the alpha value α, based on the measured pixel color C, where $C = \alpha F + (1-\alpha)B$. To facilitate image matting, it usually requires a trimap to separate an image into the foreground region, the

---

Y. Zhang and C. Wang—Equal contribution.

Supplementary Information The online version contains supplementary material available at https://doi.org/10.1007/978-3-031-46305-1_11.

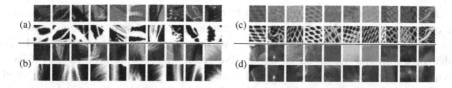

Fig. 1. Visualization of top 10 RGB patches (the first row in (a)-(e)) that are closest to four different clusters centroids. The clusters are generated by our proposed patch clustering module (PCM). The second row in (a)-(e) shows their corresponding ground-truth alpha mattes, which are not used in the training of PCM.

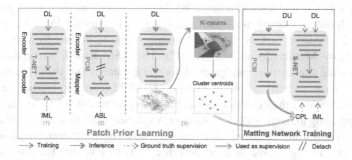

Fig. 2. The flowchart of our proposed method. The method consists of two stages named "Patch Prior Learning" and "Matting Network Training". The (1)–(3) in Patch Prior Learning stage indicates the consecutive training steps. All encoders' parameters in step (2) and (3) are initialized using the trained encoder from step (1). The parameters of S-NET are initialized with T-NET. The PCM in Matting Network Training stage is the same as the one trained in the Patch Prior Training step (3). DL: labeled data. DU: unlabeled data. PCM: Patch Clustering Module. IML: Image Matting Loss. ASL: Alpha-Similarity Loss. CPL: Cluster Prior Loss.

background region, and the unknown region. In general, the unknown region covers all area that has fractional opacity [36].

The matting problem is challenging since the matting equation above is severely under-constrained. While traditional matting methods build color and spatial relationships as priors to constrain the solution space, state-of-the-art methods leverage convolutional neural networks (CNN) to predict the alpha matte. These methods achieved much better performance by learning multi-scale high-dimensional features for unknown region pixels. However, they require a large dataset to facilitate the training process. Compared to other tasks that also leverage pixel-level annotation (*e.g.*, semantic segmentation), the annotation process for matting requires a much higher skill level and is generally much slower. It is tough on natural images without a green or blue screen setup. As a result, the most commonly used dataset DIM [37] contains only hundreds of unique foreground objects, far fewer than the tens of thousands of unique images that semantic segmentation datasets usually contain. Due to the scarcity of foreground objects, most methods use random images from other datasets (*e.g.*, COCO [19], PASCAL VOC [7]) as background images to augment the dataset during training.

On the other hand, weakly supervised learning has shown great potential in numerous computer vision tasks recently (*e.g.*, object detection and semantic segmentation). Nonetheless, there is little progress w.r.t. the weakly supervised image matting problem under the traditional trimap-based setting. We define this specific problem as follows: given a small amount of data with ground-truth alpha mattes (*i.e.* labelled data, denoted as "DL") and a large amount of data with only trimap annotations (*i.e.* unlabeled data, denoted as "DU"), the goal of trimap-based weakly supervised image matting is to utilize data from both DL and DU and predict more accurate alpha mattes than training on DL only.

In this paper, we propose a novel method to tackle the trimap-based weakly supervised image matting problem. The key contributions of our method are a novel Patch Clustering Module (denoted as "PCM") and a new Clustering Prior Loss (denoted as "CPL"). The design of CPL and the training of PCM is based on our proposed Alpha-Similarity Metric (denoted as "ASM"). The ASM is a differentiable function that describes the similarity of two given alpha matte patches and therefore can be used as a distance measurement in loss functions. The PCM learns to predict embeddings for image patches that the embeddings' distance can represent the difference between their corresponding alpha mattes described by ASM. Subsequently, it can cluster image patches with similar alpha mattes together without using their corresponding ground truth, as shown in Fig. 1. We then propose the CPL to leverage the clustering prior acquired from the PCM. We combine the conventional image matting losses and CPL to fine-tune the matting network with data from DL and DU. For better utilization of the limited data in DL, we add random non-rigid deformation and alpha jitter as the data augmentation method during training and empirically found that it can drastically improve the matting performance. To our knowledge, our method is the first to tackle the weakly supervised image matting problem with only trimaps as the annotation.

2   Related Works

Image Matting. For non-deep learning-based methods, there are mainly two different approaches. The sampling-based image matting methods [4,8,10,29] build the foreground region and background region color priors using the sampled pixels to infer the alpha values. In contrast, the affinity-based methods [1,3,9,13,14,33] propagate the alpha values from the known foreground region and background region pixels to the unknown region pixels based on affinity score and have proven to be robust when dealing with complex images. The deep learning-based matting methods usually train a convolutional encoder-decoder neural network to predict alpha values or foreground/background colors with or without user-specified trimaps [2,5,11,15–18,24,31,38,40,41]. A popular image matting dataset in this line of research is provided by Xu *et al.* [37], which consists of 431 unique foreground images. Qiao *et al.* [26] constructed a larger dataset that consists of 646 foreground images for trimap-less image matting.

Weakly-Supervised Learning. For reducing the cost of labor-intensive image annotation in deep learning, WSL methods [42] have been extensively studied as they can utilize incomplete or coarsely annotated data. Recently, they have achieved promising results for various computer vision tasks, such as object detection [27,39], semantic

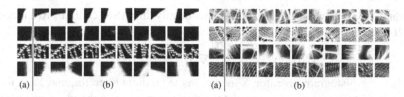

Fig. 3. Alpha matte patch retrieval results using ASM on a toy dataset that consists of 50 unique foreground objects. (a) Query patch. (b) Retrieved patches.

segmentation [12,21]. For image matting, Liu *et al.* [20] proposed a framework that uses coarse segmentation maps to boost performance on trimap-less human matting. But, unlike our method, the coarse segmentation maps are only used to supervise the semantic segmentation network for predicting a better semantic prior and thus do not provide information to the matting network. Zou *et al.* [43] proposed a weakly super-vised method for cloud image matting by taking advantage of adversarial training and the physics behind the imaging process to generate new cloud images and their corre-sponding ground truth. Note that this approach is specifically designed for cloud matting leveraging the cloud's monochromatic and mostly translucent characteristic, and thus not applicable to general image matting.

3   Our Method

Our patch clustering aims to group the image patches with both RGB and trimap chan-nels according to their alpha-similarity metrics (ASM), which enables us to improve the performance of the image matting network. It is achieved by using an additionally designed clustering prior loss (CPL) for patches in DU.

Specifically, our method consists of two training stages. In the first stage named "Patch Prior Learning", we first pretrain a conventional encoder-decoder image matting network (denoted as "T-NET") using conventional image matting losses on DL. Next, we train the patch clustering module (PCM) with an ASM-based loss utilizing patches from DL. Finally, we perform clustering on embeddings mapped by the MLP network in the PCM (denoted as "Mapper") and subsequently use the clustering centroids as the clustering prior for the CPL. In the second stage, named "Matting Network Training", we train another image matting network (denoted as "S-NET") with the same archi-tecture as T-NET on both DL and DU, utilizing both the image matting losses and our proposed CPL. Only the S-NET is used during the inference. The overall workflow of our method is shown in Fig. 2.

In the following, we will first address our proposed ASM used in Patch Prior Learn-ing stage (Sec. 3.1) and proceed to describe the design, training, and patch clustering procedure of the PCM (Sec. 3.2). Finally, we describe our proposed CPL (Sec. 3.3).

3.1   Alpha-Similarity Metric

This section describes our differentiable metric for measuring similarity between two alpha matte patches. We denote α_i and α_j as two same-sized alpha matte patches that have quantized alpha values (*e.g.* 0–255). Specifically, the ASM contains two measurements H and G:

$$H(\alpha_i, \alpha_j) = \mathcal{W}(\mathcal{H}(\alpha_i), \mathcal{H}(\alpha_j))$$
$$G(\alpha_i, \alpha_j) = \mathcal{W}(\mathcal{H}(\nabla(\alpha_i)), \mathcal{H}(\nabla(\alpha_j))) \tag{1}$$

where $\mathcal{H}$ is the histogram operator, ∇ is the image gradient operator, and $\mathcal{W}$ is the 1D Wasserstein distance. H and G represent the difference between the two alpha patches' histogram and the image gradient histogram, respectively. We base our metric on histogram since it ignores the spatial relation inside the alpha patch and only focuses on the statistical difference between the patches. An example of patch retrieval using ASM on a toy dataset can be seen in Fig. 3. It shows that our ASM can distinguish different patches with distinct alpha statistics.

Note that since both α_i and α_j have the same number of pixels, calculating the 1D Wasserstein distance between their histogram is equivalent to sorting the values and summing the differences [30]. Thus, Eq. 1 can be effectively rewritten as:

$$H(\alpha_i, \alpha_j) = \|\mathcal{S}(\alpha_i) - \mathcal{S}(\alpha_j)\|_1$$
$$G(\alpha_i, \alpha_j) = \|\mathcal{S}(\nabla(\alpha_i)) - \mathcal{S}(\nabla(\alpha_j))\|_1 \tag{2}$$

where $\mathcal{S}$ is the sorting operator. Since we eliminated the histogram operator, Eq. 2 is differentiable and consequently can be back-propagated during training. A straight-through gradient estimator can also be used for back-propagating through the alpha value quantization.

3.2   Patch Clustering Module

As shown in Fig. 2's step (2), the PCM consists of an encoder and a mapper module. In this paper, the PCM's encoder is the same as the T-NET's encoder if not stated otherwise. The mapper module is an MLP where every layer has the conventional "FC+Normalization+Activation" structure. The detailed architecture for the mapper module can be found in our supplementary material.

The PCM has two goals: (1) output embeddings whose distance can represent the difference in their corresponding alpha patches described by ASM; (2) perform patch clustering to build the clustering prior. For the first goal, we train the mapper module on DL patches using the Alpha-Similarity Loss (denoted as "ASL" in the following). For the second goal, we acquire the cluster centroids of the embeddings predicted by the trained mapper module using K-means, as seen in Fig. 2's step (3). In the following, we will describe these procedures in detail.

Training the Mapper Module on DL Patches. First, we denote the mapper module as M_T. Assuming the T-NET's encoder has an output stride of 32, and we have an image $I_{DL}^c \in \mathbb{R}^{H \times W \times 3}$ with its corresponding trimap $I_{DL}^t \in \mathbb{R}^{H \times W}$ and ground-truth alpha matte $I_{DL}^\alpha \in \mathbb{R}^{H \times W}$ from DL. First, we forward I_{DL}^c and I_{DL}^t through the T-NET's encoder, acquiring the output feature map $\mathbf{F_{DL}} \in \mathbb{R}^{(H/32) \times (W/32) \times C_e}$ where C_e is the length of the feature in the encoder feature map. Since we only focus on the unknown region of the image, we then extract features inside the unknown region $\mathbf{F_{DL}^U} \in \mathbb{R}^{M \times C}$ from $\mathbf{F_{DL}}$, where M is the number of unknown region pixels in the downsampled I_{DL}^t that has the same size as $\mathbf{F_{DL}}$. Similarly, the corresponding alpha patches $\mathbf{A}_{\mathbf{DL}}^{\mathbf{U}} \in \mathbb{R}^{M \times 32 \times 32}$ can also be extracted from I_{DL}^{α}. Finally, $\mathbf{F}_{\mathbf{DL}}^{\mathbf{U}}$ is sent into the mapper module, and our ASL is used to supervise the output embedding. Specifically, the ASL is defined as:

$$
\begin{aligned}
L_{as} &= \tau(s_p, s_n) \\
\tau(s_p, s_n) &= \log[1 + \Sigma_j \exp\left(\gamma w_n^j s_n^j\right) \Sigma_i \exp\left(-\gamma w_p^i s_p^i\right)] \\
w_p^i &= \max(1 + \theta_m - s_p^i, 0) \\
w_n^j &= \max(s_n^j - \theta_m, 0) \\
s_p &= \{\phi(M_T(f_i), M_T(f_j))\}, \\
&\quad H(\alpha_i, \alpha_j) \le \theta_H^p \wedge G(\alpha_i, \alpha_j) \le \theta_G^p \\
s_n &= \{\phi(M_T(f_i), M_T(f_j))\}, \\
&\quad H(\alpha_i, \alpha_j) > \theta_H^n \vee G(\alpha_i, \alpha_j) > \theta_G^n
\end{aligned}
\tag{3}
$$

where τ is the Circle Loss [35] and γ, θ_m are the parameters of the loss. s_p and s_n are the intra-class and inter-class pair sets. ϕ is the cosine similarity. $f_i, f_j \in \mathbf{F_{DL}}$ are the corresponding output features of the patch i and j from T-NET's encoder, and α_i, α_j are their corresponding alpha patch. $\theta_H^p, \theta_H^n, \theta_G^p, \theta_G^n$ are thresholds for pair selection. One can easily see that L_{as} is a pair similarity loss and thus could pull close features that have been classified as inter-class pairs and vice versa. We only use L_{as} during this stage of training.

Clustering on DL Patches. After training the mapper module on DL, we can forward the entire DL through the PCM to acquire the patch embedding for every patch. Once the embeddings are acquired, we use K-means to obtain K centroids $\mathbf{E} \in \mathbb{R}^{K \times C_m}$ for DL. The corresponding cluster label is $\mathbf{C} \in \{1..K\}$. The clusters is further selected and grouped in the centroid refinement process. Please refer to the companied supplemantary materials for the detail.

Please note that we do not use data from DU in this step. One underlying assumption of this design is that DL and DU should generally share the same domain, albeit DL has fewer samples than DU. Since the embedding and the cluster centroids are trained and calculated using DL, patches outside this shared domain usually have low-confident embeddings and clustering labels, thus cannot be used for building the clustering prior.

3.3   Clustering Prior Loss

Given the trained PCM and cluster centroids, it is trivial to calculate clustering labels $c_i, c_j \in \mathbf{C}$ for patch i, j. A naive approach to leverage the clustering information is to supervise the similarity of intra-class patches' features during training. However, since the clustering process does not consider pixels' spatial relationship inside the patch, there is information discrepancy between the feature similarity loss and the features. A more effective approach is supervising the statistics of the S-NET's final alpha matte predictions directly. Specifically, we utilize the top-N patches close to cluster centroids as anchor patches and use the ASM as the measurement between the predicted patches and the anchor patches. We denote the anchor patches for K cluster centroids as $\hat{\alpha} \in \mathbb{R}^{K \times N \times 32 \times 32}$. Given a minibatch of image patches from DU whose clustering labels are predicted using the trained PCM and alpha mattes α predicted by the S-NET, our

CPL can be formulated as the following:

$$L_{cp} = \sum_i \{l_i | \Phi(M_T(f_i), e_{c_i}) < \epsilon_{c_i}\}$$
$$c_i = \arg\min_j \Phi(M_T(f_i), e_j)$$
$$\epsilon_i = 0.1 \times \min_j \Phi(e_i, e_j)$$
$$l_i = \max(\theta_c - d_p^i + d_n^i, 0)$$
$$d_p^i = \max_{j,k}[D(\alpha_i, \hat{\alpha}_{jk})], j \in \mathbf{C}_P^i, k \in 1..N \tag{4}$$
$$d_n^i = \max_{j,k}[D(\alpha_i, \hat{\alpha}_{jk})], j \in \mathbf{C}_N^i, k \in 1..N$$
$$D(\alpha_i, \alpha_j) = [1 - \chi(H(\alpha_i, \alpha_j))][1 - \chi(G(\alpha_i, \alpha_j))]$$
$$\mathbf{C}_P^i = \{j | \mathbf{B}_{c_{ij}} = 1\}$$
$$\mathbf{C}_N^i = \{j | (\mathbf{B}^2)_{c_{ij}} = 0\}$$

where $f_i \in \mathbf{F}_{\mathbf{DU}}^{\mathbf{U}}, c_i \in \mathbf{C}, \alpha_i \in \alpha$ is the output feature from the T-NET's encoder, clustering label, and S-NET's predicted alpha matte for patch i. $\Phi(a, b)$ is the normalized distance using cosine similarity, $e_i \in \mathbf{E}$ is the cluster centroids computed by the PCM. ϵ_i is the maximum threshold to select valid patches for every centroid. d_p^i and d_n^i are the similarity measurements of alpha patch i to its closest intra-class and inter-class centroid's anchor patches, respectively. θ_c is the margin for d_p and d_n. $\mathbf{C}_P^i, \mathbf{C}_N^i$ are the intra-class and inter-class centroids w.r.t. c_i. $D(\alpha_i, \alpha_j)$ is the similarity measurement between two patches based on ASM. χ is a linear normalization function that squashes the raw metric to 0–1 range. One can see that at its core, L_{cp} is a margin loss that penalizes the network if the predicted alpha patch is more similar to the closest inter-class centroid's anchor patch than the closest intra-class centroid's anchor patch. Note that we only select patches whose embedding is close to the clustering centroids.

The final loss for training S-NET is the combination of two losses:

$$L_S = L_{im} + \theta_S L_{cp} \tag{5}$$

where L_{im} is the IML and θ_S is the loss weight for CPL.

4   Experimental Results

In this section, we test our method on the DIM dataset [37]. We leverage the state-of-the-art Swin Transformer [23] as our T-NET's encoder. We use the "tiny" variant of the network to reduce the computation cost. For implementation details, please refer to the companied supplementary materials. The training set consists of 431 unique foreground objects with ground-truth alpha mattes. We compose each foreground object with images randomly picked from MS-COCO [19] as background to generate the RGB image. Conventional data augmentation techniques including random scaling, rotation, flipping, cropping, color jitter, and JPEG compression is used during training. To better utilize DL, we additionally use random non-rigid deformation and alpha jitter as data augmentation. Precisely, the random non-rigid deformation consists of the classic elastic [32] and thin plate spline transform [6], and alpha jitter applies random gamma to the ground-truth alpha matte. For evaluation, we use the DIM dataset's test

Table 1. Our method compared with other state-of-the-art matting methods. † indicates that SIM [34] uses additional semantic labels. "Ours-Full" denotes we train the T-NET fully supervised. When training with only partial ground truth data as DL, all remaining data is used as DU. "Ours-T" and "Ours-S" denote our Swin Transformer-based T-NET and S-NET model. "GCA-T" and "GCA-S" denote that we use GCA [17] to replace Swin Transformer in T-NET and S-NET. The best result is in bold.

Table 2. The ablation study of our proposed method on the Composition-1k dataset. "M": Whether the mapper module is used in the PCM. "N/A" denotes not applicable. "AA": Whether the random non-rigid deformation and alpha jitter data augmentation are used. L in the brackets denotes which loss is used for supervision during S-NET's training. All experiments are conducted using 20% of the full data as DL with all remaining data as DU expect "Full" which is fully supervised. The best S-NET result is in bold.

Methods	SAD	MSE	Grad	Conn
Fully supervised				
AlphaGAN [25]	52.4	30.0	38.0	53.0
DIM [37]	50.4	14.0	31.0	50.8
IndexNet [24]	45.8	13.0	25.9	43.7
AdaMatting [2]	41.7	10.0	16.8	–
CA [11]	35.8	8.2	17.3	33.2
GCA [17]	35.3	9.1	16.9	32.5
A^2U [5]	32.2	8.2	16.4	29.3
TIMINet [22]	29.1	6.0	11.5	25.4
MG Matting [38]	28.4	5.4	11.1	24.3
SIM† [34]	28.0	5.8	10.8	24.8
Ours-Full	**26.9**	**4.9**	**9.0**	**22.5**
20% as DL				
Ours-T	35.1	7.4	13.5	32.3
Ours-S	**32.4**	**6.4**	**13.0**	**29.1**
GCA-T	43.8	12.6	17.6	42.2
GCA-S	43.1	12.2	17.6	41.3
10% as DL				
Ours-T	40.6	10.0	16.8	39.2
Ours-S	36.9	8.2	15.2	34.6

Models	M	AA	SAD	MSE	Grad	Conn
Full	N/A		27.7	5.1	9.5	23.5
	N/A	✓	26.9	4.9	9.0	22.5
T-NET	N/A		43.0	9.4	18.4	42.4
	N/A	✓	35.1	7.4	13.5	32.3
S-NET (L_{cp})		✓	36.2	7.1	14.3	34.1
S-NET (L_{con})	N/A	✓	44.3	9.4	17.6	44.6
S-NET (L_{feat})	✓	✓	36.0	7.5	15.3	33.5
S-NET (L_{cp})	✓	✓	**32.4**	**6.4**	**13.0**	**29.1**

set Composition-1k. It has 50 unique foreground images where each of the images is composited with 20 background images randomly picked from PASCAL VOC [7] to form 1000 testing images in total. For evaluation, we choose the commonly used four metrics: SAD (sum of absolution difference), MSE (mean square error), Grad (gradient error), and Conn (connectivity error) [28]. Lower values are better for all metrics.

Building DL/DU. For all 431 unique foreground objects (denoted as "full data" in the following) in DIM's training set, we first divide them into five categories: hair/fur, plants, structure (*e.g.*, nets, cloths), translucent (*e.g.*, glass, chiffon), and others; then we randomly select a fixed percentage of objects from each category as DL; the rest form DU if not stated otherwise. DL's trimaps are generated on the fly by randomly dilating the translucent area of the ground-truth alpha matte during the training process. DU's trimaps are generated using this method beforehand and fixed during training. By default, we use 20% of the full data as DL.

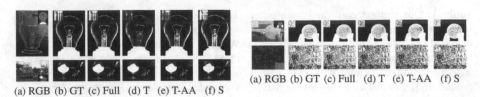

(a) RGB (b) GT (c) Full (d) T (e) T-AA (f) S

(a) RGB (b) GT (c) Full (d) T (e) T-AA (f) S

Fig. 4. The qualitative evaluations on the Composition-1k test dataset. Blowups are used to show the details of the alpha matte. (a) RGB image. The Blue box is the corresponding input trimap. (b) Ground-truth alpha matte. (c) Alpha matte prediction by T-NET trained with the full data. (d) Alpha matte prediction by T-NET trained without additional data augmentation. (e) Alpha matte prediction by T-NET trained with additional data augmentation. (f) Alpha matte prediction by S-NET. (Color figure online)

Quantitative Evaluation. Table 1 shows the quantitative comparisons between our proposed method and other image matting networks. First, we train the T-NET with all ground truth available, which dictates the upper bound of our method. Under this setting, the network achieves state-of-the-art performance due to the superior Swin Transformer [23] backbone. Next, we test our proposed weakly supervised method. With only 20% of the full data as DL, one can see that the our T-NET model has already surpassed half of the methods due to our proposed additional data augmentation techniques. The S-NET model of our method lowers the metric more. As shown in the last two rows in Table 1, with 10% of the full data as DL, the S-NET model can obtain an even higher performance gain. Furthermore, we also test our method using the network architecture from GCA [17] to replace the Swin Transformer in T-NET and S-NET. We set $\theta_J = 0.35$ in this experiment and empirically found it gives the best result. The result can be seen in the last third and fourth row in Table 1. The GCA-based S-NET model also achieved lower metrics than the T-NET model, which shows that our method can work with different matting methods. The quantitative result on the test set of alphamatting.com [28] using the T-NET and the S-NET model can be found in the companied supplementary material.

Ablation Studies. We first investigate the influence of our additional data augmentation techniques (denoted as "AA" in the following). The AA constantly improves the T-NET's performance, as shown in the first four rows in Table 2, especially with DL. Thus, AA is used in all following experiments if not stated otherwise. Next, we investigate the effect of the mapper module in the PCM in the last fourth row in Table 2. Specifically, we replace the mapper module with an identity layer and skip the initial training on DL patches (*i.e.*, step (2) in Fig. 2). In other words, we directly use the matting feature from T-NET's model for patch clustering. As one can see, without the mapper module, the model's performance decreases. One possible reason is that the matting feature is more focused on encoding details from the image, which is incompatible with our statistics-based CPL. Finally, in the last three rows of Table 2, we assess the influence of loss functions during the training of S-NET. That is, we replace L_{cp} in Eq. 5 with different loss functions. First, we use the conventional consistency-based loss widely adopted by WSL approaches. Specifically, we construct the consistency-based loss function L_{con} by augmenting different images from the sample and forwarding all augmented images through T-NET. We use the consistent part of the prediction from the T-NET as the ground truth to supervise the S-NET. The result of replacing L_{cp} with L_{con} can be seen in the last third row of Table 2. Among all three losses we used for the S-NET's training, L_{con} has the worst performance. We hypothesize that L_{con}'s supervision provides more erroneous gradients since it is more sensitive to the pixel-level error in the predicted alpha matte. On the other hand, our CPL is more robust to the errors by working at the patch-level and supervising the patch statistics directly. Second, we use the naive feature similarity loss L_{feat} described in Sect. 3.3. As one can see in the last second row of Table 2, with L_{feat}, the S-NET performs slightly worse than the T-NET, although it uses the same clustering prior as L_{cp}. The details of these two loss functions, more ablation studies on the utilization percentages of the full data during training and the selection of hyperparameters can be found in the companied supplementary material.

Qualitative Evaluation. In Fig. 4, we show that our method can improve the performance of the image matting network. First, comparing Fig. 4(e) to (d), it is clear that AA can substantially improve the detail of the alpha matte. Second, the PCM and CPL can provide both "detailed" and "regional" improvement on the alpha matte prediction, as shown in Fig. 4(f) compared to (e), respectively. Note that in cases such as the second row on the left in Fig. 4, the alpha matte predicted by the S-NET is more accurate than the network with the full data training in the highlight region of the glass (see the blowup). One possible reason is that the patch-level supervision from the CPL during training is different from the pixel-level IML. More qualitative results can be found in the companied supplementary material.

5 Conclusion

We have developed a novel weakly-supervised image matting method that can utilize data with only trimap annotation to boost matting performance. Specifically, we proposed a patch clustering module to cluster image patches with similar alpha mattes, and a clustering prior loss to supervise the matting network. We also added new data augmentation techniques to utilize data with ground-truth alpha annotation better. In the future, we would like to expand our method into an iterative process akin to the teacher-student model widely adopted in the self-training methods so that the T-NET could also utilize the information from DU.

Acknowledgements. We thank the reviewers for their constructive comments. Weiwei Xu is partially supported by "Pioneer" and "Leading Goose" R&D Program of Zhejiang (No. 2023C01181). This paper is supported by Information Technology Center and State Key Lab of CAD&CG, Zhejiang University.

References

1. Aksoy, Y., Oh, T.H., Paris, S., Pollefeys, M., Matusik, W.: Semantic soft segmentation. ACM Trans. Graph. **37**(4), 72 (2018)
2. Cai, S., et al.: Disentangled image matting. In: International Conference on Computer Vision, October 2019
3. Chen, Q., Li, D., Tang, C.K.: KNN matting. IEEE Trans. Pattern Anal. Mach. Intell. **35**(9), 2175–2188 (2013)

4. Chuang, Y.Y., Curless, B., Salesin, D., Szeliski, R.: A bayesian approach to digital matting. In: CVPR, 2001. In: Proceedings of the 2001 IEEE Computer Society Conference on, CVPR 2001, vol. 2, pp. II-II. IEEE (2001)
5. Dai, Y., Lu, H., Shen, C.: Learning affinity-aware upsampling for deep image matting. In: IEEE Conference on Computer Vision and Pattern Recognition, pp. 6841–6850. Computer Vision Foundation/IEEE (2021)
6. Duchon, J.: Splines minimizing rotation-invariant semi-norms in sobolev spaces. In: Schempp, W., Zeller, K. (eds.) Constructive Theory of Functions of Several Variables: Proceedings of a Conference Held at Oberwolfach, Germany, April 25–May 1, 1976. LNM, vol. 571, pp. 85–100. Springer, Cham (1976). https://doi.org/10.1007/BFb0086566
7. Everingham, M., Van Gool, L., Williams, C.K.I., Winn, J., Zisserman, A.: The pascal visual object classes (VOC) challenge. IJCV **88**(2), 303–338 (2010)
8. Gastal, E.S., Oliveira, M.M.: Shared sampling for real-time alpha matting. In: Computer Graphics Forum, pp. 575–584. Wiley Online Library (2010)
9. Grady, L., Schiwietz, T., Aharon, S., Westermann, R.: Random walks for interactive alpha-matting. In: Proceedings of VIIP, vol. 2005, pp. 423–429 (2005)
10. He, K., Rhemann, C., Rother, C., Tang, X., Sun, J.: A global sampling method for alpha matting. In: IEEE Conference on Computer Vision and Pattern Recognition, pp. 2049–2056. IEEE Computer Society (2011)
11. Hou, Q., Liu, F.: Context-aware image matting for simultaneous foreground and alpha estimation. In: International Conference on Computer Vision, October 2019
12. Kulharia, V., Chandra, S., Agrawal, A., Torr, P., Tyagi, A.: Box2Seg: attention weighted loss and discriminative feature learning for weakly supervised segmentation. In: Vedaldi, A., Bischof, H., Brox, T., Frahm, J.-M. (eds.) ECCV 2020. LNCS, vol. 12372, pp. 290–308. Springer, Cham (2020). https://doi.org/10.1007/978-3-030-58583-9_18
13. Levin, A., Lischinski, D., Weiss, Y.: A closed form solution to natural image matting. In: IEEE Conference on Computer Vision and Pattern Recognition, vol. 1, pp. 61–68. IEEE (2006)
14. Levin, A., Rav-Acha, A., Lischinski, D.: Spectral matting. IEEE Trans. Pattern Anal. Mach. Intell. **30**(10), 1699–1712 (2008)
15. Li, J., Zhang, J., Maybank, S.J., Tao, D.: Bridging composite and real: towards end-to-end deep image matting. Int. J. Comput. Vis. 1–21 (2021). https://doi.org/10.1007/s11263-021-01541-0
16. Li, J., Zhang, J., Tao, D.: Deep automatic natural image matting. In: Zhou, Z. (ed.) Proceedings of the Thirtieth International Joint Conference on Artificial Intelligence, IJCAI 2021, Virtual Event/Montreal, Canada, 19–27 August 2021, pp. 800–806. ijcai.org (2021)
17. Li, Y., Lu, H.: Natural image matting via guided contextual attention. In: AAAI, vol. 34, pp. 11450–11457 (2020)
18. Lin, S., Ryabtsev, A., Sengupta, S., Curless, B.L., Seitz, S.M., Kemelmacher-Shlizerman, I.: Real-time high-resolution background matting. In: IEEE Conference on Computer Vision and Pattern recognition, pp. 8762–8771, June 2021
19. Lin, T.-Y., et al.: Microsoft coco: common objects in context. In: Fleet, D., Pajdla, T., Schiele, B., Tuytelaars, T. (eds.) ECCV 2014. LNCS, vol. 8693, pp. 740–755. Springer, Cham (2014). https://doi.org/10.1007/978-3-319-10602-1_48
20. Liu, J., Yao, Y., Hou, W., Cui, M., Xie, X., Zhang, C., Hua, X.: Boosting semantic human matting with coarse annotations. In: IEEE Conference on Computer Vision and Pattern Recognition, pp. 8560–8569. Computer Vision Foundation/IEEE (2020)
21. Liu, W., Zhang, C., Lin, G., Hung, T.Y., Miao, C.: Weakly supervised segmentation with maximum bipartite graph matching. In: ACMMM (2020)
22. Liu, Y., Xie, J., Shi, X., Qiao, Y., Huang, Y., Tang, Y., Yang, X.: Tripartite information mining and integration for image matting. In: ICCV, pp. 7555–7564 (2021)

23. Liu, Z., et al.: Swin transformer: Hierarchical vision transformer using shifted windows. In: Proceedings of the IEEE/CVF International Conference on Computer Vision (ICCV), pp. 10012–10022, October 2021

24. Lu, H., Dai, Y., Shen, C., Xu, S.: Indices matter: learning to index for deep image matting. In: International Conference on Computer Vision, October 2019

25. Lutz, S., Amplianitis, K., Smolic, A.: AlphaGAN: generative adversarial networks for natural image matting. In: British Machine Vision Conference, p. 259. BMVA Press (2018)

26. Qiao, Y., Liu, Y., Yang, X., Zhou, D., Xu, M., Zhang, Q., Wei, X.: Attention-guided hierarchical structure aggregation for image matting. In: IEEE Conference on Computer Vision and Pattern Recognition, June 2020

27. Ren, Z., et al.: Instance-aware, context-focused, and memory-efficient weakly supervised object detection. In: IEEE Conference on Computer Vision and Pattern Recognition, pp. 10598–10607 (2020)

28. Rhemann, C., Rother, C., Wang, J., Gelautz, M., Kohli, P., Rott, P.: A perceptually motivated online benchmark for image matting. In: IEEE Conference on Computer Vision and Pattern Recognition, pp. 1826–1833. IEEE (2009)

29. Ruzon, M.A., Tomasi, C.: Alpha estimation in natural images. In: IEEE Conference on Computer Vision and Pattern Recognition, p. 1018. IEEE (2000)

30. Santambrogio, F.: Optimal Transport for Applied Mathematicians. PNDETA, vol. 87. Springer, Cham (2015). https://doi.org/10.1007/978-3-319-20828-2

31. Sengupta, S., Jayaram, V., Curless, B., Seitz, S.M., Kemelmacher-Shlizerman, I.: Background matting: the world is your green screen. In: IEEE Conference on Computer Vision and Pattern Recognition, pp. 2291–2300 (2020)

32. Simard, P.Y., Steinkraus, D., Platt, J.C.: Best practices for convolutional neural networks applied to visual document analysis. In: ICDAR 2003, pp. 958–962. IEEE Computer Society (2003)

33. Sun, J., Jia, J., Tang, C.K., Shum, H.Y.: Poisson matting. ACM Trans. Graph. 23(3), 315–321 (2004)

34. Sun, Y., Tang, C., Tai, Y.: Semantic image matting. In: IEEE Conference on Computer Vision and Pattern Recognition, pp. 11120–11129. Computer Vision Foundation/IEEE (2021)

35. Sun, Y., et al.: Circle loss: a unified perspective of pair similarity optimization. In: IEEE Conference on Computer Vision and Pattern Recognition, pp. 6397–6406. Computer Vision Foundation/IEEE (2020)

36. Wang, J., Cohen, M.F., et al.: Image and video matting: a survey. Found. Trends® Comput. Graph. Vis. 3(2), 97–175 (2008)

37. Xu, N., Price, B.L., Cohen, S., Huang, T.S.: Deep image matting. In: IEEE Conference on Computer Vision and Pattern Recognition, vol. 2, p. 4 (2017)

38. Yu, Q., et al.: Mask guided matting via progressive refinement network. In: IEEE Conference on Computer Vision and Pattern Recognition, pp. 1154–1163. Computer Vision Foundation/IEEE (2021)

39. Zhang, D., Han, J., Cheng, G., Yang, M.H.: Weakly supervised object localization and detection: a survey. IEEE Trans. Pattern Anal. Mach. Intell. 44(9), 5866–5885 (2021)

40. Zhang, Y., et al.: A late fusion CNN for digital matting. In: IEEE Conference on Computer Vision and Pattern Recognition, June 2019

41. Zhou, F., Tian, Y., Qi, Z.: Attention transfer network for nature image matting. IEEE Trans. Circ. Syst. Video Technol. 31(6), 2192–2205 (2020)

42. Zhou, Z.H.: A brief introduction to weakly supervised learning. Natl. Sci. Rev. 5(1), 44–53 (2018)

43. Zou, Z., Li, W., Shi, T., Shi, Z., Ye, J.: Generative adversarial training for weakly supervised cloud matting. In: ICCV, pp. 201–210 (2019)

Attention-Guided Motion Estimation for Video Compression

Siru Zhang[1,2] and Pengrui Duan[1,2(✉)]

[1] Beijing Key Lab of Intelligent Telecommunication Software and Multimedia,
Beijing, China
dpr@bupt.edu.cn
[2] Beijing University of Posts and Telecommunications, Beijing 100876, China

Abstract. Video compression is the crucial technology of video representation, transmission, and storage. Recently, learnable video compression
has received great attention from both industry and research, as a result
of the potential of neural networks. More and more researchers are developing learned-based video compression frameworks and methods. Obviously, how to represent the motion information in the video is one of the
essential questions across all of the end-to-end video compression methods. A robust and efficient motion representation could help the method
compress the video better. In this paper, we propose the Attention-guided
motion encoder (AME) to get a compact motion representation. The proposed method uses attention to guide the network in exploring the relationship between frames. Meanwhile, the proposed method leverages the
multi-scale features to realize a coarse-to-fine mechanism, which will make
the network compress the temporal information without losing the crucial spatial information. Furthermore, video compression not only needs
better performance but also costs fewer computation resources. From the
results of experiments, the proposed model outperforms existing learned
and conventional video codecs on UVG, MCL-JCV, and HEVC Standard
Test Sequences in PSNR and MS-SSIM, meanwhile, the proposed method
also brings better improvement for each parameter.

Keywords: Computer Vision · Video Compression · Vision Attention

1 Introduction

Multimedia contents are increasingly important at present and contain more
abundant information than any other format. With the growth of video and
image content, how to represent, transmit and store them becomes more and
more important, which means that compressing multimedia data may be the
core technology in this era. Before the bloom of artificial intelligence, researchers
use block-based methods to predict motion and use transform to aggregate the
information. By using this block-based hybrid prediction manner, researchers
have made many successful protocols to compress the image and video, such as
H.264 [1], H.265 [2], H.266 [3], VP8 [4], VP9 [5], AV1 [6] and so on. While, with
the rapid growth of multimedia information, traditional methods have encoun-
tered problems in dealing with various data. The reason is that the traditional

codecs are designed specifically that may not have a better generalization for wide data distribution. At the same time, the data-driven neural network has achieved great performance in other multimedia tasks, such as image classification, object detection, segmentation, and so on. As the result of that, many researchers begin using deep learning to improve the traditional methods or directly use the pure neural network to compress videos. And in our paper, we will use the pure neural network to compress the video.

The learning-based video compression can be roughly divided into two classes based on their backbone. One of them chooses the CNN as the backbone, for example, [7–9]. And the other part uses the transformer as the backbone, such as [10]. Both of them have advantages and disadvantages. For the CNN-based methods, they make full use of the local information to get a compact representation of the video, while losing the global information. When it comes to the transformer-based methods, they indeed use the global information by the attention mechanism, however, they introduce a huge complexity. And in our paper, we combine them in a reasonable manner to propose a new motion estimation module. Meanwhile, we use the experiments to support the validity of the proposed method. The main contributions of this paper are:

- Using the attention mechanism to enhance the estimation of motion information. In our proposed method, we use the attention mechanism combined with convolutions in the motion estimation module.
- Using the experiments to demonstrate the proposed method can achieve the state-of-the-art performance.
- Exploring how to design the attention module in the video compression methods.

2 Related Work

2.1 Video Compression

Video compression or multimedia compression is always the cutting-edge technology in computer vision. Decades ago, the research of video compression is flourishing. At that point, the block-based traditional video compression technology dominates the research and industry such as H.264 and H.265, and royalty-free codecs VP8 and VP9. Until now, this kind of technology is still the main research direction and still has some surprising progress such as H.266 and AV1. On the other hand, the fast development of data-driven AI methods provides some new solutions, such as convolution-based DVC [7], C2F [9], GAN-based SGANC [11], and transformer-based video compression framework VCT [10].

2.2 Vision Attention

Convolution neural network helps computer vision make huge progress in many tasks such as object detection, segmentation, and so on. While, recently, the attention-based neural network, or in other words, the transformer-based method overcomes some drawbacks of CNN, and make the model the ability to find the relationship not only between different data samples, but in the nature of itself. As the result of that, the transformer will build a much larger model than that built by CNN, such as ViT [12], SWIN [13], and so on. Meanwhile, the transformer can be used in video compression, such as VCT. Similarly, we use the attention in the proposed method to get more accurate motion information between different frames. However, we do not choose the transformer as the backbone in the proposed method. Although using the huge model may enhance the performance of the proposed method, it will damage the efficiency of the whole model. Based on the basic idea of balancing the performance and the efficiency, we just use the core idea in the transformer, i.e., the attention mechanism, instead of replacing all CNNs with transformer.

3   Methods

3.1   Introduction of Notations

Let $X = \{x_t\}_{t=1,...,T}$ denotes the current video sequence of length T, where x_t is the t-th frame. The predicted frame is denoted by $\overline{x}_t$, and the reconstructed frame is denoted as $\hat{x}_t$. m_t represents the motion information and $\hat{m}_t$ refers to the quantized motion information. $\hat{z}_t$ is the reconstructed latent representation from the motion decoder. v_t is the motion vector generated by the optical flow model and $\hat{v}_t$ is the corresponding reconstructed optical flow value. The residual information r_t between the original frame x_t and the predicted frame $\overline{x}_t$ will be transferred to Residual Encoder Network to produce the latent feature, namely y_t. For the quantized residual information and the latent feature, we use $\hat{r}_t$ and $\hat{y}_t$ to denote them, respectively.

3.2   Overview

The entire video compression pipeline in the end-to-end manner is shown in Fig. 1. Similar to the previous work, our pipeline has the module to encode and decode the motion information and residual information, the module to compensate the residual part with the motion information, the network to compress the residual information, and the bitrate estimation network. Nevertheless, we propose a new motion information estimation module, named Attention-guided Motion Encoder (AME, described in Sect. 3.3) to improve the process of extracting the robust motion information from inter-frames.

The proposed Attention-guided Motion Encoder obtains motion information m_t between the current frame x_t and the last frame x_{t-1}. After quantization of m_t, the quantized motion information $\hat{m}_t$ will be sent to Motion Decoder, as shown in Fig. 2, to obtain the corresponding reconstructed latent representation $\hat{z}_t$. Then the predicted frame $\overline{x}_t$ is achieved by Motion Compensation Network based on $\hat{z}_t$ and $\hat{x}_{t-1}$. The residual r_t will be transferred to Residual Encoder Network to calculate y_t. To improve performance for generalization, we

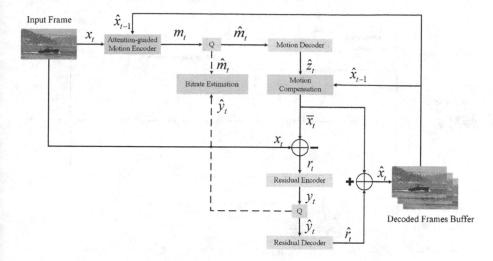

Fig. 1. Overview of the whole end-to-end video compression. The Q represents the quantization.

add uniform noise to obtain quantized $\hat{y}_t$. After Residual Decoder Network, the reconstructed residual $\hat{r}_t$ and the predicted frame $\overline{x}_t$ are added to acquire the reconstructed frame $\hat{x}_t = \overline{x}_t + \hat{r}_t$. Finally, the reconstructed frame $\hat{x}_t$ will be used to compress the next frame x_{t+1}.

We transfer motion information $\hat{m}_t$ and residual $\hat{r}_t$ to Bitrate Estimation Network [14] to estimate needed bits and use these bits to calculate Rate-Distortion Loss. For the decoder side, the reconstructed frame $\hat{x}_t$ is obtained by transferred bits, motion information, residual information, and inverse quantization.

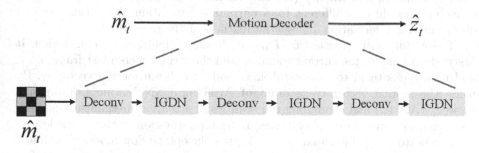

Fig. 2. The implementation of motion decoder. The motion decoder uses quantized motion information $\hat{m}_t$ as input and outputs the reconstructed latent representation $\hat{z}_t$ based on stacks of deconvolution and IGDN layers.

3.3 Attention-Guided Motion Encoder (AME)

Inspired by the capability of the attention mechanism to exploit both local and global correlations [15,16], we proposed Attention-guided Motion Encoder, as shown in Fig. 3, which has three paths to compress the whole frame.

The top path, named $F_{enhancement}$, utilizes self-attention to enhance the representation of motion estimation. It uses the current frame x_t and the last

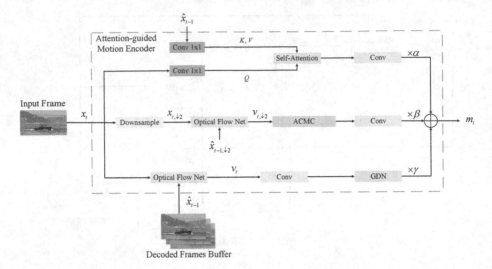

Fig. 3. The network structure of the proposed Attention-guided Motion Encoder. It uses the current frame as Query and the spatial neighbor frame as Key, Value to calculate the attention map so as to obtain temporal information while maintaining spatial information. To utilize multi-scale motion information, the proposed method downsamples input frame x_t as coarse level and the original frame x_t as fine level. After getting the motion information from the optical flow model, we leverage the Attention-CNN Motion Compression network(ACMC) to utilize the self-attention inside the optical flow map.

reconstructed frame $\hat{x}_{t-1}$ as the input. The query (Q) is projected with one 1×1 convolution and the key (K) and value (V) are projected with two 1×1 convolutions, which is different from normal self-attention. After that, we can obtain motion information and spatial features at the same time.

The middle path, denoted by F_{ACMC}, leverages multi-scale information. It firstly downsamples the current frame x_t and the reconstructed last frame $\hat{x}_{t-1}$, and then sends them to an optical flow model to obtain motion vector v_t. By using the motion vector v_t as input of Attention-CNN Motion Compression network (ACMC) and combining the abilities of attention mechanism and convolutions, we can obtain the enhanced motion information at the coarse level.

The bottom way, indicated by F_{norm}, uses the optical flow model to estimate the motion vector v_t between the current frame x_t and the last frame $\hat{x}_{t-1}$. After that, employ sequences of convolutions and GDN [17] to compress the optical flow value further.

All motion information from the above three paths is aggregated and represents the final output F_{me}.

$$F_{me} = \alpha F_{enhancement} + \beta F_{ACMC} + \gamma F_{norm} \tag{1}$$

Attention-CNN Motion Compression Network (ACMC). Motivated by the powerful capability but huge parameters of attention mechanism to exploit

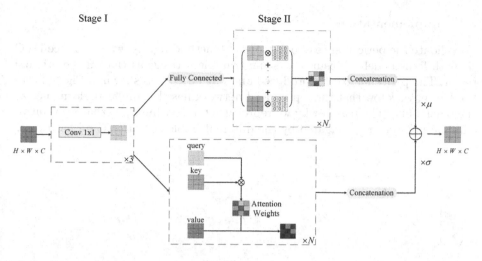

Fig. 4. The structure of Attention-CNN Motion Compression network (ACMC). At stage I, the input feature map is projected by three 1×1 convolutions. At stage II, the features are used in both Convolution and Self-Attention respectively. Finally, features from both paths are added together as the output.

global dependencies and the ability of convolutions with fitting quickly, we proposed Attention-CNN Motion Compression network (ACMC).

As shown in Fig. 4, at stage I, the input feature map is projected with three 1×1 convolutions and reshaped into $3 \times N$ pieces. At stage II, the $3 \times N$ pieces are used for convolutions and self-attention respectively. For the convolutions with kernel size k, indicated by symbol *conv*, we first employ a fully connected layer to generate k^2 feature maps. We use fixed group convolution kernels and aggregation operations to obtain corresponding features. For the self-attention path, denoted by symbol *attn*, the input of $3 \times N$ pieces are gathered into N groups. Each group contains 3 pieces from each 1×1 convolution respectively. Such that, the query (Q), key (K), and value (V) are 1 piece respectively, and serve as input for traditional multi-head self-attention modules. Finally, we add the outputs from two paths together:

$$F_{ACMC} = \mu F_{conv} + \sigma F_{attn} \tag{2}$$

4   Experiments

In this part, we will introduce the experiments. Firstly, we will describe how to implement the whole method, and then we will introduce the datasets we used. After that, we compare the performance of our proposed method with related codecs on UVG [18], MCL-JCV [19], and HEVC Standard Test Sequences(Class B, Class C, Class D, and Class E) [20]. At the end of this part, we will discuss the design of the proposed method using the ablation study.

4.1   Implementation

To validate the performance of our proposed method rightly, we reproduce DVC [7] with four models by using the same training settings as that in the original paper. The performance of reproduced and official DVC is shown in Fig. 5. From the figure, we know that the reproduced network has the similar performance as the official one. The reason why we reproduce the benchmark is that we want to eliminate the error propagated by the different implementations and hardware.

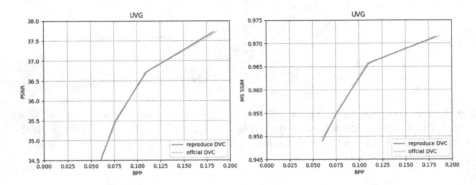

Fig. 5. PSNR and MS-SSIM results on UVG of reproduced and official DVC.

Further, we freeze the pre-trained DVC model and only train the proposed method with four different λ (λ = 256, 512, 1024, 2048) to ensure that the improvement is not obtained by the other module. For each model, we use the Adam optimizer [21] by setting the initial learning rate as 1×10^{-3}, β_1 as 0.9, and β_2 as 0.999, respectively. The proposed model is trained jointly with rate-distortion optimization, controlled by the Lagrange parameter λ to trade off bitrate and quality. The loss function is defined as follows:

$$L_{RD} = R + \lambda D \tag{3}$$

During the training process, the bitrate R is estimated by Bitrate Estimation network, and the distortion D is measured by Mean Squared Error (MSE). For a better evaluation of the proposed method, we pre-process the data during the test phase by resizing it to the same resolution, specifically 512×512. We use compressed I frames generated from H.265 as the reference frames. The GOP size for the UVG and MCL-JCV datasets is 12, and for HEVC Standard Test Sequences is 10.

Evaluation Metrics. To measure the distortion of the reconstructed frames, we use two evaluation metrics: PSNR and MS-SSIM [22]. The equation of PSNR is shown in Eq. 4. MS-SSIM correlates better with human perception of distortion than PSNR. To measure the number of bits for encoding the representations, we use bits per pixel (BPP) to represent the required bits for each pixel in the current frame.

$$PSNR = 10 \cdot \log_{10} \frac{MAX_I^2}{MSE} \tag{4}$$

4.2 Dataset

Training Dataset. We train the proposed video compression framework by using the Vimeo-90K [23], a large-scale, high-quality video dataset for low-level video processing, such as frame interpolation and video super-resolution. It consists of 89,800 high-quality video clips downloaded from Vimeo.

Validation Dataset. To validate the performance of the proposed method, we empirically evaluate our proposed video compression framework on the UVG [18], MCL-JCV [19] and HEVC Standard Test Sequences [20]. UVG is composed of 16 versatile 4K (3840 × 2160) test video sequences. Moreover, they release 1920 × 1080 test video sequences. These natural sequences were captured at either 50 or 120 frames per second (fps) and stored in raw 8-bit and 10-bit 4:2:0 YUV formats. MCL-JCV is designed to measure human perception quality. It is made up of 30 source sequences of resolution 1920 × 1080. Each video clip has a duration of 5 s but a different frame rate. HEVC Standard Test Sequences have wide ranges of resolutions and fps, from 240p (416 × 240) to 1080p (1920 × 1080) for resolutions and ranging from 24 to 60 fps. All videos are stored in raw 8-bit 4:2:0 YUV format. And, for the test phase, we convert all YUV formats to RGB ones.

4.3 Experimental Results

We will introduce the experiment results in this section. Firstly, Fig. 6 shows our proposed method's validation results on Vimeo-90K. It is obvious that our method outperforms the conventional codecs, H.264 and H.265. On the Vimeo-90K validation, compared with H.264, our proposed method achieved about 1.0 dB on PSNR and 6.0 dB on MS-SSIM (dB) at the same BPP level. It proves that our model has learned the general information used for the compression task and the great performance also represents that our model has a good generalization on the validation set.

Secondly, we also report the performance on some other datasets to show the generalization of the proposed method, so Fig. 7 and Fig. 8 show the experimental results on the UVG, MCL-JCV, and HEVC Standard Test Sequences, along with corresponding results of DVC, OpenDVC, H.264, and H.265. On most of the datasets, our proposed video compression framework outperforms the H.264 standard when measured by PSNR and MS-SSIM. In addition, our framework achieves competitive or better compression performance when compared with H.265, except in terms of MS-SSIM on MCL-JCV. It is obvious that our method outperforms the learned video compression codecs, DVC and OpenDVC.

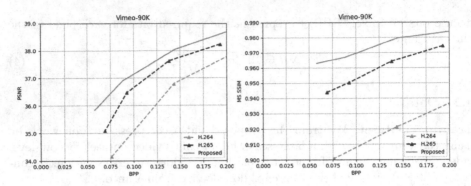

Fig. 6. PSNR and MS-SSIM results on Vimeo-90K validation dataset.

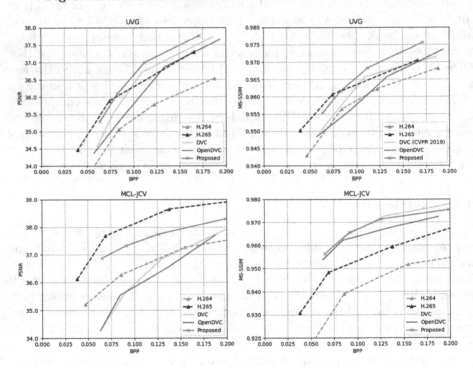

Fig. 7. PSNR and MS-SSIM results on UVG and MCL-JCV.

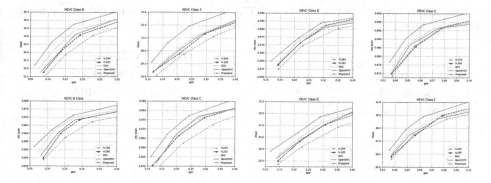

Fig. 8. PSNR and MS-SSIM results on HEVC Class B, C, D, and E.

4.4 Ablation Study

To evaluate the performance of different optical flow models on our proposed method, we practically implement our proposed motion encoder on 5 optical flow models, including RAFT [24], LiteFlowNet3 [25], IRR [26], PWCNet [27], and Spynet [28]. The PSNR and MS-SSIM results are shown in Fig. 9. In most cases of the UVG dataset, the proposed method with the RAFT model can achieve higher values on PSNR and MS-SSIM metrics. In low bitrate, LiteFlowNet3 is better than IRR. PWCNet and Spynet are worse than the three other optical flow models, which might be related to the resolution of video sequences.

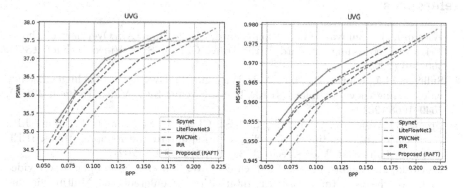

Fig. 9. Ablation study on optical flow models. PSNR and MS-SSIM results on the UVG dataset of our proposed video compression framework with different optical flow estimation methods.

Moreover, we compare our model with the transformer-based method. Table 1 shows the performance between the number of parameters and BD-rate relative to H.264 on the UVG dataset. From this table, we can know that the proposed method will bring a larger improvement for each parameter.

Table 1. The comparison between DVC, VCT, and Proposed. The indicators ↓/↑ mean the lower/higher better. - indicates that the result is unavailable.

	DVC	VCT	Proposed
#Parameters	11M	114M	11.7M
BD-Rate(%) ↓	−27.86	-	−40.58
BD-Rate improvement(%)/#Parameters(M) ↑	2.53	-	3.47

5   Conclusion

In this paper, we propose an end-to-end video compression framework with the attention-guided motion encoder. We implement the attention mechanism with CNN to exploit the advantages of these two paradigms. Furthermore, we utilize the coarse-to-fine motion estimation module to enrich the motion information. Our attention-based motion estimation encoder is feasible for the end-to-end video compression framework. Our experimental results show that the proposed framework is effective and exceeds the state-of-the-art (SOTA) rate-distortion performance. In the future, we will explore how to achieve the real-time performance for video compression.

Acknowledgement. This work was supported by the National Key Research and Development Program of China (No. 2021YFF0900702).

References

1. Wiegand, T., Sullivan, G.J., Bjontegaard, G., Luthra, A.: Overview of the h. 264/avc video coding standard. IEEE Trans. Circuits Syst. Video Technol. **13**(7), 560–576 (2003)
2. Sullivan, G.J., Ohm, J.R., Han, W.J., Wiegand, T.: Overview of the high efficiency video coding (hevc) standard. IEEE Trans. Circuits Syst. Video Technol. **22**(12), 1649–1668 (2012)
3. Bross, B., Wang, Y.K., Ye, Y., Liu, S., Chen, J., Sullivan, G.J., Ohm, J.R.: Overview of the versatile video coding (vvc) standard and its applications. IEEE Trans. Circuits Syst. Video Technol. **31**(10), 3736–3764 (2021)
4. Bankoski, J., Wilkins, P., Xu, Y.: Technical overview of vp8, an open source video codec for the web. In: 2011 IEEE International Conference on Multimedia and Expo, pp. 1–6. IEEE (2011)
5. Mukherjee, D., Han, J., Bankoski, J., Bultje, R., Grange, A., Koleszar, J., Wilkins, P., Xu, Y.: A technical overview of vp9-the latest open-source video codec. SMPTE Motion Imaging J. **124**(1), 44–54 (2015)
6. Chen, Y., et al.: An overview of core coding tools in the av1 video codec. In: 2018 picture coding symposium (PCS), pp. 41–45. IEEE (2018)
7. Lu, G., Ouyang, W., Xu, D., Zhang, X., Cai, C., Gao, Z.: DVC: an End-To-End Deep Video Compression Framework. In: 2019 IEEE/CVF Conference on Computer Vision and Pattern Recognition (CVPR) (2019)

8. Lu, G., Zhang, X., Ouyang, W., Chen, L., Gao, Z., Xu, D.: An end-to-end learning framework for video compression. IEEE Trans. Pattern Anal. Mach. Intell. **43**(10), October 2021

9. Hu, Z., Lu, G., Guo, J., Liu, S., Jiang, W., Xu, D.: Coarse-to-fine deep video coding with hyperprior-guided mode prediction. In: 2022 IEEE/CVF Conference on Computer Vision and Pattern Recognition (CVPR), New Orleans, LA, USA, June 2022

10. Mentzer, F., Toderici, G., Minnen, D., Hwang, S.J., Caelles, S., Lucic, M., Agustsson, E.: Vct: A video compression transformer. arXiv preprint arXiv:2206.07307 (2022)

11. Shukor, M., YAO, X., Damodaran, B.B., Hellier, P.: Learning perceptual compression of facial video (2022)

12. Dosovitskiy, A., et al.: An image is worth 16x16 words: transformers for image recognition at scale. arXiv preprint arXiv:2010.11929 (2020)

13. Liu, Z., Lin, Y., Cao, Y., Hu, H., Wei, Y., Zhang, Z., Lin, S., Guo, B.: Swin transformer: hierarchical vision transformer using shifted windows. In: Proceedings of the IEEE/CVF International Conference on Computer Vision, pp. 10012–10022 (2021)

14. Ballé, J., Minnen, D., Singh, S., Hwang, S.J., Johnston, N.: Variational image compression with a scale hyperprior. arXiv preprint arXiv:1802.01436 (2018)

15. Pan, X., Ge, C., Lu, R., Song, S., Chen, G., Huang, Z., Huang, G.: On the Integration of Self-Attention and Convolution. In: IEEE/CVF Conference on Computer Vision and Pattern Recognition (CVPR) (2022)

16. Zhang, G., Zhu, Y., Wang, H., Chen, Y., Wu, G., Wang, L.: Extracting motion and appearance via inter-frame attention for efficient video frame interpolation. arXiv preprint arXiv:2303.00440 (2023)

17. Ballé, J., Laparra, V., Simoncelli, E.P.: End-to-end optimized image compression. In: 5th International Conference on Learning Representations, ICLR 2017 (2017)

18. Mercat, A., Viitanen, M., Vanne, J.: Uvg dataset: 50/120fps 4k sequences for video codec analysis and development. In: Proceedings of the 11th ACM Multimedia Systems Conference, pp. 297–302 (2020)

19. Wang, H., et al.: Mcl-jcv: a jnd-based h. 264/avc video quality assessment dataset. In: 2016 IEEE International Conference on Image Processing (ICIP), pp. 1509–1513. IEEE (2016)

20. Ohm, J.R., Sullivan, G.J., Schwarz, H., Tan, T.K., Wiegand, T.: Comparison of the coding efficiency of video coding standards-including high efficiency video coding (hevc). IEEE Trans. Circuits Syst. Video Technol. **22**(12), 1669–1684 (2012)

21. Kingma, D.P., Ba, J.: Adam: a method for stochastic optimization. arXiv preprint arXiv:1412.6980 (2014)

22. Wang, Z., Simoncelli, E., Bovik, A.: Multiscale structural similarity for image quality assessment. In: The Thrity-Seventh Asilomar Conference on Signals, Systems & Computers, 2003, vol. 2, pp. 1398–1402 (2003). https://doi.org/10.1109/ACSSC.2003.1292216

23. Xue, T., Chen, B., Wu, J., Wei, D., Freeman, W.T.: Video enhancement with task-oriented flow. Int. J. Comput. Vision **127**, 1106–1125 (2019)

24. Teed, Z., Deng, J.: RAFT: recurrent all-pairs field transforms for optical flow. In: Vedaldi, A., Bischof, H., Brox, T., Frahm, J.-M. (eds.) ECCV 2020. LNCS, vol. 12347, pp. 402–419. Springer, Cham (2020). https://doi.org/10.1007/978-3-030-58536-5_24

154   S. Zhang and P. Duan

25. Hui, T.-W., Loy, C.C.: LiteFlowNet3: resolving correspondence ambiguity for more accurate optical flow estimation. In: Vedaldi, A., Bischof, H., Brox, T., Frahm, J.-M. (eds.) ECCV 2020. LNCS, vol. 12365, pp. 169–184. Springer, Cham (2020). https://doi.org/10.1007/978-3-030-58565-5_11
26. Hur, J., Roth, S.: Iterative residual refinement for joint optical flow and occlusion estimation. In: Proceedings of the IEEE/CVF Conference on Computer Vision and Pattern Recognition, pp. 5754–5763 (2019)
27. Sun, D., Yang, X., Liu, M.Y., Kautz, J.: Pwc-net: Cnns for optical flow using pyramid, warping, and cost volume. In: Proceedings of the IEEE Conference on Computer Vision and Pattern Recognition, pp. 8934–8943 (2018)
28. Ranjan, A., Black, M.J.: Optical flow estimation using a spatial pyramid network. In: Proceedings of the IEEE Conference on Computer Vision and Pattern Recognition, pp. 4161–4170 (2017)

Cloud Detection from Remote Sensing Images by Cascaded U-shape Attention Networks

Ao Li[1], Jing Yang[2], and Xinghua Li[1](✉)

[1] School of Remote Sensing and Information Engineering, Wuhan University, Wuhan, China
lixinghua5540@whu.edu.cn
[2] CCCC Second Highway Consultants Co, Ltd, Wuhan, China

Abstract. Cloud is an important meteorological information in remote sensing applications as it plays a significant role in the Earth's climate and weather patterns, but it also brings difficulties to the information extraction from optical images, especially when the underlying surface features to be analyzed are obscured. Therefore, cloud detection is an indispensable step in optical remote sensing image processing. Different from low-spatial resolution images, medium and high-resolution images contain richer geographical features, and the distribution of clouds is more scattered, which makes it necessary to enhance the network's ability on detailed features extraction. Therefore, the two cascaded U-shape attention networks (CUA-Net) model is proposed to detect the cloud in Landsat 8 images. In the first U-shape network, the up-sampling layers in path expansion integrate the information from all previous layers to make full use of multi-scale features. Additionally, the attention modules in the skip connection are added to detect the position and edges of cloud accurately. After that, the second U-shape network is utilized to optimize the preliminary segmentations from the first network, thus obtaining results closer to the ground truth. In the experiments, CUA-Net was evaluated on 38-Cloud Dataset and compared with current mainstream networks, showing significant improvements both on visual effects and quantitative indicators.

Keywords: Cloud detection · Cascaded U-shape networks · Attention module

1 Introduction

Remote sensing images play a vital role in natural disaster detection, agricultural resources management, environmental monitoring, urbanization surveys and other research fields. However, a factor that cannot be ignored in optical satellite images is cloud cover. Cloud can interfere with the remote sensing data by reflecting and absorbing the electromagnetic radiation, which leads to difficulties in data interpretation. Consequently, it is a crucial part of remote sensing field to accurately identify the cloud coverage over images for subsequent applications [1].

Cloud detection methods can be roughly grouped into classical methods and pattern recognition methods [2]. The threshold-based methods are the earliest classical methods.

© The Author(s), under exclusive license to Springer Nature Switzerland AG 2023
H. Lu et al. (Eds.): ICIG 2023, LNCS 14355, pp. 155–166, 2023.
https://doi.org/10.1007/978-3-031-46305-1_13

They mainly analyze individual pixels, such as the automatic cloud coverage evaluation [3] and Fmask [4], and they can segment cloud from images by multiple fixed thresholds. Especially, Sun et al. [5] proposed a general dynamic threshold cloud detection algorithm to solve the difficultly in fixed thresholds selection. Since those threshold-based methods are easily restricted by the spectrum, the Bayesian methods [6] and texture based methods [7] utilizing the spectral and geometric properties of cloud are proposed to leverage more features. Moreover, some methods based on statistical characteristics [8] are proposed for thin cloud detection. They mainly take advantage of the physical properties of clouds, so the results can be obtained quickly with the high-level characteristics of images ignored, which leads to detection difficulties when facing complex surface environments and ever-changing clouds.

With the development of computer hardware, pattern recognition technology has attracted the attentions. Many advanced machine learning methods to identify cloud are proposed. Among them, the early clustering [9], fuzzy clustering [10, 11] and SVM [12–14] have formed a mature system, however, the detection accuracy is relatively limited by their poor performance in large-scale training set. In recent years, artificial neural networks have emerged as a promising approach for cloud detection due to their ability to learn complex patterns and feature representations from multitudinous labeled training data. For example, the U-net [15, 16] uses a completely symmetrical network structure and skip connections to improve the accuracy of cloud detection with fewer training samples. MS-UNet [17] combines convolutions of different sizes to extract multi-scale features, thus identifying cloud of different sizes and shapes. Cloud-Net [18] proposed by Mohajerani et al. adds the residual structure to U-Net, and achieves superior results for Landsat 8 images. As time goes on, more advanced networks are proposed, Unet 3 + [19] uses full-scale skip connection to preserve spatial information and fuse features at different layers. Li et al. proposed global context-dense block U-Net (GCDB-UNet) [20] to enhance the detection capability of thin cloud. Lu et al. designed a mutual guidance module (MGM) [21] to solve the problem of rough segmentation boundaries. Although these methods have been able to detect most of cloud on remote sensing images, the thin cloud recognition and boundary identification capabilities still need to be further strengthened especially for medium and high-resolution images such as Landsat 8.

In order to better capture the complex semantic features and precisely segment the cloud in remote sensing images, the two cascaded U-shape attention networks (CUA-Net) model is proposed. Its innovations are as follows, (1) it enhances the connection between the network layers to preserve as much information as possible, (2) it makes use of the attention module to focus on relevant cloud features and to ignore irrelevant ones, which can improve the network's ability of identifying clouds in complex scenes with varying cloud and background noise, (3) a second U-shape network is designed to correct the inaccurate information gain from the previous steps. Via these structures, the features extracted from convolution blocks can be utilized effectively to recover sophisticated cloud masks and obtain higher accuracy.

2   Algorithm

The architecture is designed as two cascaded U-shape networks, as shown in Fig. 1. The first network is used to perform a preliminary segmentation by identifying the possible cloudy regions of the image. The output of the first network X_{En}^1 is then fed into the second network, which refines the edges and details by further segmenting the cloudy regions and removing false detections. After that, the preliminary results X_{En}^1 and the supplementary information X_{De}^1 are added and convolved once to obtain the final cloud detection results. The proposed CUA-Net will be introduced separately below.

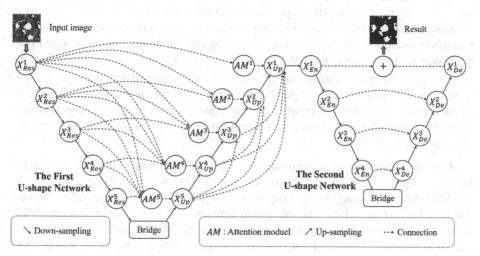

Fig. 1. The proposed Cascaded U-shape Attention Networks (CUA-Net).

2.1   The First U-shape Network

The first U-shape network consists of a contraction path for feature extraction and an expansion path for image recovery. The two parts are connected by the attention-based skip connection, which is used for transferring deep features from the contraction path to the expansion path to preserve spatial information.

Down-sampling Layer in Contraction Path. The down-sampling layer mainly uses residual structure shown in Fig. 2. Its branches on the above include two 3×3 convolutions to extract features from the input. The branches below use a small-scale skip connection, where the input firstly go through a 1×1 convolution, and then connected with itself. Finally, the results of the two branches are summed and put to a maximum pooling. This structure can avoid the gradient disappearance caused by the deep network, and make the encoder converge faster. Simultaneously, it allows the network to learn the residual mapping between the input and output feature maps, which helps to preserve the low-level features from upper layer.

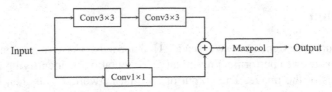

Fig. 2. Down-sampling layer in contraction path.

Attention-Based Skip Connection. In U-Net, the skip connections are used to preserve the features learned from the contraction path and improve the accuracy of segmentation. However, only layers with same depth are connected in the original U-Net architecture. To address this limitation, a modified skip connection shown in Fig. 3 is proposed, the features from all previous layers in the contracting path are concatenated and sent to the expansion path. In order to make the output from layer $X_{Res}^1, \cdots, X_{Res}^{i-1}, X_{Res}^i$ able to be connected, multiple self-connections are used to make the dimension of $X_{Res}^1, \cdots, X_{Res}^{i-1}$ as same as X_{Res}^i, and then feature graph size is unified by maximum pooling. After that, all the i layers are added and input to the subsequent attention module. This modified skip connection allows the network to capture more fine-grained details and improve cloud detection accuracy.

Convolutional block attention module (CBAM) [22] is a lightweight attention architecture composed of channel attention module (CAM) and spatial attention module (SAM). CAM focuses more on the category information. The input image will go through parallel MaxPool layer and AvgPool layer at first, and then pass by a single shared MLP to extract more comprehensive high-level features. SAM pays more attention on the spatial location of the target. It applies the average pooling and the maximum pooling along channel axis, which can effectively strengthen the spatial information.

The attention-based skip connection can preserve features extracted from all layers in contraction path and pay effective attention on the channel and spatial characteristics of the target. What's more, the number of parameters in this structural is small, which will not bring additional burden to the network.

Up-sampling Layer in Expansion Path. The up-sampling layer in the expansion path is used to increase the resolution of feature maps while reducing the number of channels, as shown in Fig. 4. The input X_{Up}^{i+1} is firstly up-sampled by a deconvolution, then combined with AM^i from corresponding skip connection and $X_{Up}^{i+2}, X_{Up}^{i+2}, \cdots, X_{Up}^5$ from the lower up-sampling layers. By this way, not only the feature maps in contraction path are used, the maps in the layers in front of expansion path are also used. Their combination will go through two convolutions to recover the semantic details and be added to the deconvolved X_{Up}^{i+1}. More complex and detailed cloud properties from deep feature maps can be recovered due to the full use of multi-scale information.

2.2 The Second U-shape Network

The second U-Shape network is mainly utilized to refine the segmentation mask generated by the first network. Although most of the cloud information can be extracted after

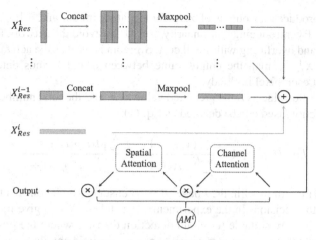

Fig. 3. Attention-based skip connection.

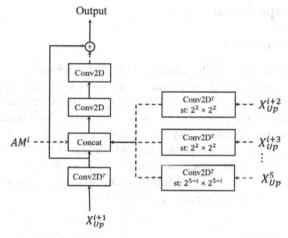

Fig. 4. Up-sampling layer in expansion path.

the anterior training, thin cloud and fragmentary cloud are easily failed to be detected, and some highlight surfaces can be mistaken as cloud. Therefore, the second U-shape network is designed to revise these incorrect detections. It consists of an encoder-decoder structure with skip connections between them, similar to a four-layer U-net. The difference is that the bridge layer in the middle takes advantage of dropout function to prevent the model from overfitting. No extra structures are added to the second network due to its complementary role and the expectation of lower network complexity.

2.3 Activation Function and Loss Function

ReLU is used as the activation function except from the last layers of the two U-shape networks and the attention module which has certain definition. It is a piecewise linear function that produces an output of zero for negative inputs and a linear output for positive inputs. By introducing non-linearity, ReLU can avoid the network from gradient disappearance and overfitting with small cost. Sigmoid is used as the activation function after X_{Up}^1 and X_{De}^1 to map the output value between 0 and 1, thus determining the probability that each pixel is cloudy.

Denote the true value as t, the predicted value as p, and the total number of pixels as N, the loss function used can be denoted as Eq. (1).

$$Loss(t, p) = 1 - \frac{\left(1 + \beta^2\right) \times \sum_{i=1}^N t(i)p(i) + \epsilon}{\sum_{i=1}^N t(i) + \beta^2 \times \sum_{i=1}^N t(i)p(i) + \epsilon} \tag{1}$$

where i means the i th pixel in the image, β is a constant which controls the weight of recall relative to precision. In the experiments, β is taken as 2 to give more weight to recall, making it more suitable for cloud detection datasets where the positive class is smaller than the negative class. ϵ is assigned as 10^{-7} to avoid any division by zero.

3 Data and Experiments

3.1 Data and Environment

The experimental data set is 38-Cloud Dataset [18] made by Sorour Mohajerani, including 18 scenes for training and 20 scenes for testing, and each scene is cut to 384×384 patches. The source of the dataset is Landsat 8 images with the resolution of 30 m, and their red, green, blue and near-infrared bands are chosen for cloud detection.

The experiments were performed on a Linux system with Python 3.6, configured with GPU versions of Tensorflow1.12.0, Keras2.2.4 and skimage 0.15.0. A Quadro RTX 5000 graphics card was used as the driver for training and prediction. The Adam optimizer with an initial learning rate of 1×10^{-4} was used during training, and when the learning rate was reduced to 1×10^{-8}, the training was finished.

3.2 Experiments Results

In order to verify the ability of the proposed CUA-Net, the comparison experiments and ablation experiments were conducted. The comparison experiments involve the performance of CUA-Net with state-of-the-art networks. On the other hand, the ablation experiments were conducted to evaluate the effectiveness of the second U-shape network and CBAM in skip connections.

Comparison Experiments. U-net [16], MS-UNet [17], Cloud-Net [18] and Unet 3 + [19] are selected for comparison, and the experimental results are shown in Fig. 5, where the black and white refers to the correctly identified clear and cloudy area, respectively, while the red means it is cloudy but falsely detected as clear, and the blue means it is clear but falsely detected as a cloudy area.

The visual effects of cloud detection from whole scene image by different methods are shown in Fig. 5(a). It can be seen that these methods can detect majority of

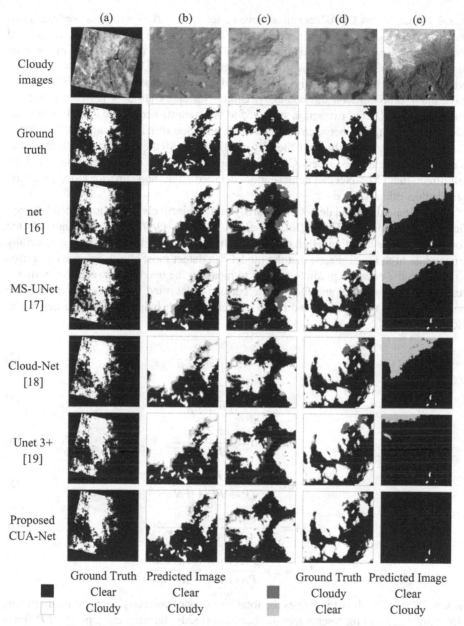

	(a)	(b)	(c)	(d)	(e)
Cloudy images					
Ground truth					
net [16]					
MS-UNet [17]					
Cloud-Net [18]					
Unet 3+ [19]					
Proposed CUA-Net					

	Ground Truth	Predicted Image		Ground Truth	Predicted Image
■	Clear	Clear	■	Cloudy	Clear
□	Cloudy	Cloudy	▦	Clear	Cloudy

Fig. 5. Visual results of cloud detection in comparison experiments.

cloudy area, but U-net, MS-UNet and Cloud-Net have more mistakes, especially for the highlighted regions in lower right corner. Although Unet 3 + can achieve better results, the performance on boundaries is still worse and the missing cloud information is more compared with CUA-Net. Figure 5(b)–Fig. 5(e) is the visual effect of local details, representing four different types of landcovers: bare land, ice land, vegetation and mountains.

Results indicate that CUA-Net can achieve better visual effect with less confusion and more clear boundaries under different surface conditions. For example, in Fig. 5(b) and Fig. 5(d) covering both thin and thick cloud, all methods can accurately detect the main cloud, but for edges and details, the results gained from CUA-Net is most consistent with the ground truth. As for Fig. 5(c) covered with ice and snow, U-net and MS-UNet have many omissions on the boundary, Cloud-Net and Unet 3 + perform better but the capability of detail extraction still need to be strengthened, while the CUA-Net can accurately distinguish between ice land and cloud due to its advantageous structures. For highlighted ground shown in the above of Fig. 5(e), all the other four methods detect it as cloud more or less except CUA-Net. Through the visual interpretation, it can be confirmed that CUA-Net can achieve more detailed edges and superior cloud detection results than other methods.

To evaluate the cloud detection accuracy more objectively, Precision, Recall, Specificity, Intersection over Union (IoU), Overall Accuracy (OA) and F1 score are selected for quantitative evaluation. High precision indicates that the detected cloud is generally true, while high recall means that the model can detect most cloud. Specificity is used to measure the negative predictions, IoU to measure the overlap between the predicted result and ground truth, and OA for the correctly classified instances. F1 score is the harmonic mean of precision and recall to measure their balance. They are defined as Eqs. (2)–(7).

$$Precision = \frac{TP}{TP + FP} \tag{2}$$

$$Recall = \frac{TP}{TP + FN} \tag{3}$$

$$Specificity = \frac{TN}{TN + FP} \tag{4}$$

$$IoU = \frac{TP}{TP + FP + FN} \tag{5}$$

$$OA = \frac{TP + TN}{TP + FP + FN + TN} \tag{6}$$

$$F1 = 2 \times \frac{Precision \times Recall}{Precision + Recall} \tag{7}$$

where TP (true positive) indicates the total amounts of correctly detected cloud pixels, TN (true negative) represents the number of correctly detected clear pixels, FP (false positive) means the amounts of clear pixels incorrectly detected as cloud pixels and the FN (false negative) on the contrary. The quantitative evaluation results are shown in Table 1.

Table 1. Accuracy evaluation results in comparison experiments (%).

Method	Precision	Recall	Specificity	IoU	OA	F1
U-net [16]	78.27	89.73	95.52	72.87	94.32	83.61
Ms-UNet [17]	78.53	89.76	95.14	71.09	94.52	83.77
Cloud-Net [18]	80.80	89.83	96.16	72.70	95.32	85.07
Unet 3 + [19]	87.33	90.68	97.52	79.77	96.13	88.97
Proposed CUA-Net	**88.58**	**91.10**	**97.80**	**80.94**	**96.72**	**89.82**

Table 1 shows that the proposed method achieves higher accuracy than the other four networks in Precision, Recall, Specificity, IoU, OA and F1, which is consistent with the judgment of visual interpretation, indicating that the proposed method performs better in most of remote sensing scenes.

Ablation Experiments. In order to verify the effect of second U-shape network (denoted as S-UNet) and CBAM in skip connections, we designed four ablation experiments: (1) only the first U-shape network used (denoted as F-UNet only), (2) the second U-shape network used without CBAM (denoted as +S-UNet), (3) the CBAM used without the second U-shape network (denoted as +CBAM), (4) both the second U-shape network and the CBAM used (CUA-Net). Their visual effect and accuracy evaluation results are shown in Fig. 6 and Table 2, respectively.

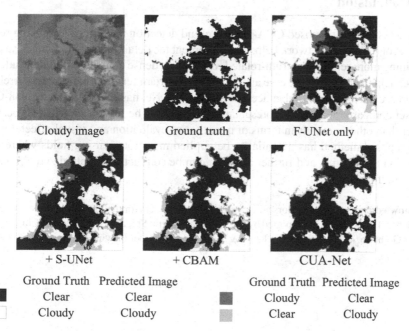

Fig. 6. Cloud detection visual results of ablation experiments.

Table 2. Accuracy evaluation results of ablation experiments (%).

Method	Precision	Recall	Specificity	IoU	OA	F1
F-UNet only	82.79	90.09	96.97	74.61	96.18	86.29
+S-UNet	85.87	88.74	97.57	76.47	95.85	87.28
+CBAM	84.66	**92.47**	96.95	78.49	96.26	88.39
CUA-Net	**88.58**	91.10	**97.80**	**80.94**	**96.72**	**89.82**

Comparing the results in groups F-UNet only and +S-UNet combined with +CBAM and CUA-Net, it is found that S-UNet leads to a slight decrease in Recall, but the Specificity, IoU and F1 scores are higher than the experiments without S-UNet, and the Precision is remarkably improved. The visual interpretation also shows that the addition of S-UNet can achieve results closer to the ground truth, as it can be a good complement to the edges and details for cloud. Comparing the results in groups F-UNet only and + CBAM combined with +S-UNet and CUA-Net, it can be confirmed that CBAM can focus well on the attributes and locations of cloud, which can improve the detection accuracy comprehensively, and reduce the probability of confusing cloudy and clear area. The overall results show that better cloud detection results can be achieved with both S-UNet and CBAM.

4 Conclusion

In conclusion, the proposed CUA-Net for cloud detection has shown promising results. The second U-shape network helps to supplement the details and cloud boundaries, thus obtaining more refined and truth-related results. The dense connections and the attention model help the network preserve and focus on important features and suppress irrelevant features, contributing to higher accuracy. The CUA-Net has been evaluated on 38-Cloud dataset compared with four representative networks. The results show that it performs better than other methods in terms of quantitative evaluation and visual effect. Overall, the proposed method has potential to be applied in remote sensing fields where cloud detection is essential, and further research can be conducted to optimize the model for better performance.

Acknowledgement. The authors are grateful to the reviewers for their attention and comments on our paper. This research is supported by the National Natural Science Foundation of China (NSFC) under Grant no. 42171302 and the Key R&D Program of Hubei Province, China (2021BAA185).

References

1. Long, C., Li, X., Jing, Y., Shen, H.: Bishift networks for thick cloud removal with multitemporal remote sensing images. Int. J. Intell. Syst.Intell. Syst. **2023**, 9953198 (2023)
2. Gupta, R., Nanda, S.J.: Cloud detection in satellite images with classical and deep neural network approach: a review. Multimed. Tools Appl. **81**(22), 31847–31880 (2022)
3. Irish, R.R., Barker, J.L., Goward, S.N., Arvidson, T.: Characterization of the Landsat-7 ETM+ automated cloud-cover assessment (ACCA) algorithm. Photogramm. Eng. Remote Sens.. Eng. Remote Sens. **72**(10), 1179–1188 (2006)
4. Zhu, Z., Woodcock, C.E.: Object-based cloud and cloud shadow detection in Landsat imagery. Remote Sens. Environ. **118**, 83–94 (2012)
5. Sun, L., et al.: A universal dynamic threshold cloud detection algorithm (UDTCDA) supported by a prior surface reflectance database. J. Geophys. Res. Atmospheres **121**(12), 7172–7196 (2016)
6. Xu, L., Wong, A., Clausi, D.A.: A novel bayesian spatial-temporal random field model applied to cloud detection from remotely sensed imagery. IEEE Trans. Geosci. Remote Sens.Geosci. Remote Sens. **55**(9), 4913–4924 (2017)
7. Başeski, E., Cenaras, Ç.: Texture and color based cloud detection. In: 7th International Conference on Recent Advances in Space Technologies, pp. 311–315. Istanbul, Turkey (2015)
8. He, X.Y., Hu, J.B., Chen, W., Li, X.Y.: Haze removal based on advanced haze-optimized transformation (AHOT) for multispectral imagery. Int. J. Remote Sens. **31**(20), 5331–5348 (2010)
9. Gómez-Chova, L., et al.: Cloud detection for CHRIS/Proba hyperspectral images. In: 10th Remote Sensing of Clouds and the Atmosphere, pp. 508–519. International Society for Optics and Photonics, Bruges, Belgium (2005)
10. Surya, S., Simon, P.: Automatic cloud detection using spectral rationing and fuzzy clustering. In: 2nd International Conference on Advanced Computing, Networking and Security, pp. 90–95. Mangalore, India (2013)
11. Bo, P., Fenzhen, S., Yunshan, M.: A cloud and cloud shadow detection method based on fuzzy c-means algorithm. IEEE J. Sel. Top. Appl. Earth Observations Remote Sens. **13**, 1714–1727 (2020)
12. Li, P., Dong, L., Xiao, H., Xu, M.: A cloud image detection method based on SVM vector machine. Neurocomputing **169**, 34–42 (2015)
13. Sui, Y., He, B., Fu, T.: Energy-based cloud detection in multispectral images based on the SVM technique. Int. J. Remote Sens. **40**(14), 5530–5543 (2019)
14. Latry, C., Panem, C., Dejean, P.: Cloud detection with SVM technique. In: International Geoscience and Remote Sensing Symposium, pp. 448–451. Barcelona Spain (2007)
15. Ronneberger, O., Fischer, P., Brox, T.: U-net: Convolutional networks for biomedical image segmentation. In: 18th International Conference on Medical Image Computing and Computer-assisted Intervention, pp. 234–241. Springer, Munich, Germany (2015)
16. Mohajerani, S., Krammer, T.A., Saeedi, P.: A cloud detection algorithm for remote sensing images using fully convolutional neural networks. In: 20th International Workshop on Multimedia Signal Processing, pp. 1–5. Vancouver, Canada (2018)
17. Kushnure, D.T., Talbar, S.N.: MS-UNet: a multi-scale UNet with feature recalibration approach for automatic liver and tumor segmentation in CT images. Comput. Med. Imaging Graph.. Med. Imaging Graph. **89**, 101885 (2021)
18. Mohajerani, S., Saeedi, P.: Cloud-Net: An end-to-end cloud detection algorithm for Landsat 8 imagery. In: 39th International Geoscience and Remote Sensing Symposium, pp. 1029–1032. IEEE, Yakohama, Japan (2019)

19. Huang, H., et al.: Unet 3+: a full-scale connected unet for medical image segmentation. In: 45th International Conference on Acoustics, Speech and Signal Processing, pp. 1055–1059. Barcelona, Spain (2020)
20. Li, X., Yang, X., Li, X., Lu, S., Ye, Y., Ban, Y.: GCDB-UNet: a novel robust cloud detection approach for remote sensing images. Knowl.-Based Syst..-Based Syst. **238**, 107890 (2022)
21. Lu, C., Xia, M., Qian, M., Chen, B.: Dual-branch network for cloud and cloud shadow segmentation. IEEE Trans. Geosci. Remote Sens.Geosci. Remote Sens. **60**, 1–12 (2022)
22. Woo, S., Park, J., Lee, J.-Y., Kweon, I.S.: Cbam: convolutional block attention module. In: 15th European Conference on Computer Vision, pp. 3–19. Munich, Germany (2018)

Ar3dHands: A Dataset and Baseline for Real-Time 3D Hand Pose Estimation from Binocular Distorted Images

Mengting Gan[1,2], Yihong Lin[1,2], Xingyan Liu[1], Wenwei Song[1,2], Jie Zeng[4], and Wenxiong Kang[1,2,3(✉)]

[1] School of Automation Science and Engineering, SCUT, Guangzhou, China
auwxkang@scut.edu.cn
[2] Pazhou Lab., Guangzhou, China
[3] School of Future Technology, SCUT, Guangzhou, China
[4] Hisense Group, Qingdao, China

Abstract. Hand pose estimation is an important technology for real-time human-computer interaction. Most existing methods neglect the distorted images captured by wide-angle cameras and tend to have high inference latency particularly without the acceleration of Graphic Process Units (GPUs). In this paper, we propose the first large multi-view distorted hand dataset, Ar3dHands, and develop a simple but effective 3D hand pose estimation algorithm for real-time binocular distorted images which make our method compatible with the wide-angled camera system equipped in miniature visual device like AR/VR glasses. Evaluation shows that our method can achieve state-of-the-art results on several datasets with lower mean 2D end point error and can realize real-time performance on embedded devices without GPUs.

Keywords: Hand pose estimation · Hand detection · Real-time application · Binocular images

1 Introduction

Recent improvements on VR and AR have made vision-based hand pose tracking an active research topic. Unlike motion controllers or game controllers usually used in VR applications, interaction with hands is more friendly and convenient. To accurately capture the interaction between hands and other objects, the hand tracking system needs to estimate the 3D coordinates of all hand keypoints precisely. Moreover, as the AR devices are increasingly mobile, the system should be able to run on the devices with limited computational capability in low latency.

Currently, 3D Hand pose estimation can be divided into non-vision-based and vision-based methods. Most researches on non-vision-based methods are based on wearable devices which present several challenges such as inconvenience in data collection, device preparation and high repair rate. Vision-based methods

Supplementary Information The online version contains supplementary material available at https://doi.org/10.1007/978-3-031-46305-1_14.

focus more on extracting image features such as color, texture, orientation and contour. Extensive work has been done on color images and depth images. Some existing vision-based hand pose tracking and estimation methods [1,3,6,9,10, 19,22] adopt depth sensors like Kinect to capture distance information for hand keypoint estimation, which are not portable enough and easy to be interfered at outdoors environment due to their narrow measurement range, high noise level and small field of view. Other solutions [2,32] use monocular RGB modality to present a cost-effective solution with simple configuration and calibration. They also avoid issues associated with depth cameras such as large light influence, small field of view and small measurement range, making it highly valuable for commercial applications.

There are two main challenges in RGB-based real-time 3D hand pose estimation. One is the significant computational resource requirements for 3D hand pose estimation. The other is the lack of large-scale public datasets collected by wide-angle camera in various distortion which are widely used in real-world. Thus, in this paper, we collect a large hand dataset Ar3dHands containing 52,560 RGB and monochrome images captured by normal cameras and fisheye cameras from 12 perspectives and propose a lightweight 3D real-time hand pose estimation algorithm for binocular RGB distorted images. Our system quickly locates and estimates the position of hands in distorted images of two views using detection and estimation technology we designed. After the distortion correction on the estimated 2D keypoints, we use camera parameters to calculate the corresponding global 3D hand keypoint coordinates relative to the main camera. Combining with the simple Kalman filter tracking algorithm, our method can achieve real-time performance without GPU on embedded devices. Our contributions can be summarized as follow:

- We propose the first large multi-view hand dataset Ar3dHands captured by both normal RGB cameras and fisheye cameras.
- We provide a simple baseline containing detection, tracking and pose estimation which can perform real-time 3D hand pose estimation from binocular distorted images on CPU-only devices.
- We conduct extensive experiments on several public hand gesture datasets and our new dataset Ar3dHands. Experimental results demonstrate that our baseline model is a state-of-the-art lightweight model that achieves exceptional performance at a relatively low computational cost.

2   Related Work

2.1   Datasets for Vision-Based 3D Hand Pose Estimation

Public datasets are one essential resource for hand pose estimation research in the era of deep learning, enabling the development of more accurate and robust models that have vast applications in various fields. [16] presented SynthHands, a photorealistic dataset that uses a merged reality approach to capture natural hand interactions, hand shape, size and color variations, object occlusions, and background variations from egocentric viewpoints. [16] also introduces a benchmark dataset EgoDexter that contains annotated sequences of challenging cluttered scenes as seen from egocentric viewpoints. FHAD [8] collects RGB-D video sequences comprised of more than 100K frames of 45 daily hand action categories, involving 26 different objects in several hand configurations. [32] introduces a large scale 3D hand pose dataset RHD based on synthetic hand models for training the involved networks. Zhang et al. designs STB [29] containing 18,000 stereo image pairs as well as the ground-truth 3D positions of palm and finger joints from different scenarios. [33] provided the first large-scale, multi-view hand dataset FreiHAND that is accompanied by both 3D hand pose and shape annotations. However, existing datasets have no distorted input images captured by wide-angled cameras like fisheye cameras which are suitable for miniature visual system like AR/VR glasses, leading to poor compatibility of most existing methods for processing high-distortion images. To our best known, our dataset Ar3dHands makes up for the lack of work in this field.

2.2 Vision-Based 3D Hand Pose Estimation Methods with Monocular RGB Modality

The early researches [11,13,28] used monocular RGB modality to estimate the 2.5D information of hand keypoints usually suffer from the scale ambiguity problem, unable to directly obtain accurate global 3D coordinates of hand keypoints. Recently, a lot of work [2,4,5,14,23,27,31,32] can directly estimate global 3D hand keypoint locations from monocular RGB images. They usually depend on an extra processing which fits the scale-normalized prediction to an articulated deformable hand model like MANO [20]. The performance of these monocular hand pose estimation networks largely depend on the dataset with high quality 3D ground truths and delicate network designs, which greatly increases development costs and is difficult to satisfy the real-time requirement of lightweight devices. Our method can directly estimate global 3D coordinates of hand keypoints in real time with no-GPU devices.

3   The Ar3dHands Dataset

3.1   Data Collection

Aiming to meet the requirements of algorithms such as hand pose estimation, hand detection and left-right hand classification, we build a large-scale hand gesture dataset including RGB and monochrome images from 12 perspectives with the annotated hand bounding boxes, 2D keypoint coordinates and 3D keypoint coordinates. As shown in Fig. 1, our equipment consists of 12 cameras, including 2 gray fisheye cameras (resolution 1280 × 960), 2 RGB fisheye cameras (resolution 1280 × 960) and 8 Realsense D435 cameras (resolution 1280 × 720, only RGB cameras are used). Four sets of fisheye cameras are installed above our heads to simulate the viewing angle of VR glasses to the greatest extent. We

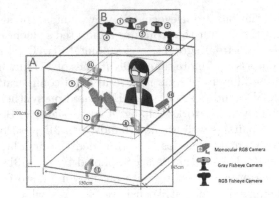

Fig. 1. Data collection system.

invited 7 volunteers and each volunteer records 60 types of hand gesture videos captured from 12 different perspectives at 15 frames per second(FPS). Before collecting each type of gesture video, volunteers were shown a template video to get familiar with that gesture. Then, they repeatedly perform the gestures with moderate speed for 5 s to provide a clear gesture video. Our new Ar3dHands dataset containing 52,560 RGB and monochrome images is the only large multi-view dataset with both strongly distorted images and weakly distorted images.

3.2   Multi-camera Calibration

According to the layout of the multi-camera system, we select a reference camera on both sides of the RGB cameras (side A in Fig. 1) and the fisheye cameras (side B in Fig. 1). The fisheye cameras use Camera 2 as the reference with the world coordinate system, while the RGB cameras use Camera 11 as the reference for reconstructing the world coordinates. Choosing the correct reference camera is crucial for the successful operation of the multi-camera system since it provides a common framework that can be used by other cameras to locate themselves. We choose the Zhang-Suen calibration method [30] for stereo calibration. Specifically, we use the kalibr calibration tool based on ROS for the combination of the two fisheye cameras and the combination of a fisheye camera and a RGB camera. For the combination of the two RGB cameras, we use the Matlab Stereo Calibration tool as it can automatically select clear images for calibration, raising calibration accuracy.

3.3   Data Annotation

To begin, we annotate all gesture images with 2D keypoints. Then, we use the camera system's internal and external parameters to obtain a candidate solution set for the corresponding 3D coordinates based on the 2D annotations from multiple perspectives. Additionally, to enhance the precision of reconstructing the

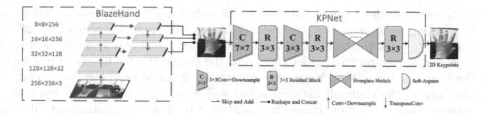

Fig. 2. Network Architecture.

3D keypoint coordinates, RANSAC [7] and Bundle Adjustment [18] is applied. Finally, upon acquiring the 2D coordinates of all nodes in various perspectives, we can automatically generate a highly accurate hand annotation detection box based on the coordinates.

4 Binocular 3D Hand Pose Estimation with Distortion Correction

The strategy of correcting distorted input images before performing normal 2D estimation is simple, but it has been found to be inefficient for real-time applications. This is because the algorithm needs to process two images for each frame, which can be time-consuming(See Sect. 5.3). To overcome this challenge, a new algorithm has been proposed that corrects the 2D keypoint coordinates estimated from distorted input images, greatly reducing the running latency.

We design our architecture from the popular top-down based keypoint estimation solutions. The pipeline of our algorithm is presented on Fig. 2. It mainly consists of three steps: 1) Locating hand bounding boxes of two views with a lightweight hand detector or a tracking module and cropping the hand images. 2) Estimating all 2D hand keypoint coordinates from cropped distorted hand images. 3) Correcting the predicted distorted 2D keypoint coordinates and calculating the corresponding global 3D coordinates with provided parameters and distortion coefficients of the binocular camera system. We will detail each step in following parts.

4.1 Hand Detection and Hand Tracking

Adapting from the lightweight palm detector named BlazePalm in MediaPipe Hands [28], we design a more lightweight version to detect complete hands named BlazeHand, containing a backbone with two stages of residual blocks and a FPN with three feature levels. To achieve higher inference speed, based on the original BlazePalm detector, we reduce the number of residual blocks and drop the highest feature level (64×64) of FPN.

We find that during actual use, the tremble or shake of the detected hand bounding boxes sometimes impact the stability of the system. To relieve this problem and further improve the hand location efficiency, we introduce detection-by-tracking strategy to our pipeline. Specifically, we apply Kalman Filter [25] tracking to assist the hand location. Kalman Filter tracking is a simple moving object tracking algorithm, which can model the motion state of hand and predict the bounding box of next frame according to the obtained hand locations so far. Considering the trade off between speed and accuracy, we design to run the detector once every three frames to update the template of the Kalman Filter tracker.

4.2   2D Hand Keypoint Estimation

Existing popular architectures [11,13] which extract a high resolution feature map with large receptive field to generate high-quality keypoint heatmaps are not lightweight enough for our application. Therefore, we create a novel lightweight 2D keypoint estimator named KPNet. We build the backbone using a series of residual blocks with Depthwise Separable Convolutions [21], and an Hourglass module [17] consisting of three stacks. These designs guarantee high inference speed and maintain high resolution feature maps as possible following the trait mentioned above. We use the soft-argmax operation to find the 2D coordinates of keypoints from heatmaps which makes the whole network can be trained end-to-end.

4.3   Hand Keypoint Correction

With short focal length and large aperture, fisheye cameras have large field of view and are usually leveraged in miniature imaging systems. Images captured by fisheye cameras have obvious distortion which means we can not directly leverage the predicted 2D hand keypoints on distorted images to calculate final 3D coordinates. Therefore, we firstly correct the distortion of predicted 2D keypoint coordinates using the provided distortion coefficients of cameras. For i-th predicted distorted 2D hand keypoint coordinate (u_i, v_i), we have:

$$\begin{cases} x_i = \frac{u_i - c_x}{f_x} \\ y_i = \frac{v_i - c_y}{f_y} \end{cases} \tag{1}$$

where (x_i, y_i) is the corresponding image plane coordinate of i-th keypoint, and f_x, f_y, c_x, c_y are focal length and principle point of the camera. Then according to the distortion model of fisheye cameras [12], we have:

$$r_d = \theta(1 + k_1\theta^2 + k_2\theta^4 + k_3\theta^6 + k_4\theta^8) \tag{2}$$

where r_d is the distance between the distorted point and the principal point, θ is the angle between the principal axis and the incoming ray, k_1, k_2, k_3, k_4 are coefficients of radial distortion of fisheye camera. We have $r_d^2 = x_i^2 + y_i^2$, thus we can solve this high order equation for θ. Once we obtain θ, we can calculate the distance between the corrected point and the principal point r and the corrected 2D coordinate $(\tilde{x}_i, \tilde{y}_i)$:

$$\begin{cases} r = \tan(\theta) \\ \tilde{x}_i = \frac{r}{r-r_d} x_i \\ \tilde{y}_i = \frac{r}{r-r_d} y_i \end{cases} \tag{3}$$

Finally we can get the corrected pixel coordinate $(\tilde{u}_i, \tilde{v}_i)$ of the i-th hand keypoint using the intrinsic parameters:

$$\begin{cases} \tilde{u}_i = \tilde{x}_i f_x + c_x \\ \tilde{v}_i = \tilde{y}_i f_y + c_y \end{cases} \tag{4}$$

With the corrected 2D keypoint coordinates from two views, we can calculate the corresponding final 3D coordinates with camera parameters according to the perspective projection of camera model.

5 Experiment

5.1 Implementation Details

Network Training. We train our hand detection networks and 2D keypoint estimation networks with batch size of 64 for 200 epochs on GeForce GTX 1080Ti GPU using an Adam optimizer with initial learning rate of 0.001. We also apply an exponential decay to learning rate with decay rate of 0.97 for each epoch. We scale and pad the complete input image to the size of 256×256 for hand detectors, and resize the cropped hand images to 128×128 for 2D keypoint estimators. We minimize the focal loss to supervise the bounding boxes classification and use Smooth-L1 Loss for regression of bounding box and hand keypoints.

Inference. To accelerate our method to a full extent for on-device applications, we convert our trained hand detectors and 2D hand keypoint estimators to Tensorflow Lite format models which tremendously reduce the inference latency by hardware acceleration and model optimization. As for the pre-process and post-process of data like image scaling and the non-maximum suppression of detector which do not belong to the part of model inference, we implement them with tensorflow APIs and leverage the AutoGraph mechanism to improve their running speed. Note that the inference latency reported in following experiments is evaluated on PC with Intel-i9 10900x CPU.

Dataset and Data Augmentation. Along with the Ar3dHands dataset, we selected widely-used hand datasets like STB, RHD and FreiHAND to assess our architecture. Furthermore, to enhance hand detection and 2D keypoint estimation, we utilized random HSV color variation and Gaussian noise. As a means of augmenting data for 2D hand keypoint estimator training, we randomly translated cropped hands.

Metric. We report Average Precision (AP) for hand detection evaluation and report the average End-Point-Error(EPE) and the Area Under the Curve(AUC) for hand estimation evaluation following [11,13,32]. Additionally, we calculate the network parameters(Params) and latency to measure the memory occupation and running efficiency of the network, which is crucial for real-time on-device applications.

5.2   Hand Detection and 2D Hand Keypoint Estimation

We first present the performance of our hand detection and 2D hand keypoint estimation on Ar3dHands and other datasets. Given the limitations in available space, we will showcase only two visual results for each dataset assessment. All the visual results demonstrated in Fig. 3 showcase the qualitative success of our hand detection and 2D hand keypoint estimation. Our visualizations effectively illustrate the effectiveness of BlazeHand and KPNet across different datasets, highlighting the universality of our approach. Additionally, we compare our 2D hand keypoint estimation methods with other state-of-the-art architectures, which also focus on real-time hand pose estimation, in terms of evaluation metrics [2]. The comparison results presented in Table 1 indicate that our KPNet outperforms other methods, exhibiting the best performance. The results of all these experiments demonstrate the robustness of our hand detection and 2D hand keypoint estimation method across various datasets, encompassing not only those without any distortion but also those containing distorted samples.

Table 1. Comparison of our 2D keypoint estimation method and other lightweight architecture on STB and RHD. Blue is the best. ↑ means the higher the better, while ↓ means the lower the better.

Dataset	Metric	SRHand Net [24]	NSRM Hand [26]	MediaPipe Hands [28]	Inter Hand [15]	Fast Hand [2]	KPNet
STB	SSE↓	-	0.7078	0.9435	0.4853	0.3490	0.0762
	EPE↓	–	0.1326	0.1522	0.1302	0.1317	0.0504
	PCK0.2↑	0.8526	0.7246	0.7032	0.8245	0.8948	0.9913
RHD	SSE↓	–	2.5613	1.9929	2.0413	0.6368	0.3137
	EPE↓	–	0.1953	0.2133	0.2630	0.0986	0.0535
	PCK0.2↑	0.5317	0.7177	0.6927	0.3910	0.8661	0.9740

(a) Hand Detection   (b) 2D Hand Keypoint Estimation

Fig. 3. Representative hand detection and 2D hand keypoint estimation results. (a) shows samples of hand detection on RHD (top) and Ar3dHands (bottom). (b) shows samples of 2D hand keypoint estimation on Ar3dHands (upper left), FreiHAND (upper right), RHD (bottom left) and STB (bottom right).

5.3   3D Hand Keypoint Estimation

We compare the running efficiency between two correction strategies: only correcting 2D keypoint coordinates and correcting the whole input image. According to our test results, only correcting 2D keypoint coordinates takes only 0.31 ms which is much faster than 77.83 ms that correcting the whole input image takes.

Table 2. Evaluation of the complete binocular 3D hand pose estimation pipeline. AP (L/R) demonstrates the Average Precision of the detection of left and right hand. EPE (average End-Point-Error) and the AUC (Area Under the Curve) are calculated for hand estimation evaluation. The best and second best results are highlighted in blue and green.

Method	AP (L/R)	2D EPE (px)	2D AUC	3D EPE (mm)	3D AUC	#Params	Latency (ms)
GT hand location + KPNet	–	8.268	0.739	13.509	0.923	1.45M	–
BlazeHand+KPNet	0.986/0.991	–	–	15.362	0.900	3.27M	272.19
BlazeHand-S+KPNet	0.980/0.987	–	–	15.395	0.899	2.31M	183.15
BlazeHand-S+KPNet-T	–	10.786	0.670	19.480	0.849	1.34M	129.78
BlazeHand-T+KPNet-T	0.961/0.972	–	–	19.642	0.844	0.70M	117.77
BlazeHand-T+KPNet-T+Aug	0.982/0.987	9.520	0.698	17.659	0.857	–	–

To achieve high inference speed to the full extent, we design multiple variants of BlazeHand and KPNet. We designed **BlazeHand-S**, a small version of Blaze-Hand, by reducing the residual blocks on each stage of the backbone and the feature channels. Similarly, we created **BlazeHand-T**, a tiny version of Blaze-Hand, by further reducing the feature channels of BlazeHand-S. For KPNet, we developed **KPNet-T**, a tiny version of KPNet, by reducing the residual blocks and feature channels, and replacing all normal 3×3 Convolutions with Depth-wise Separable Convolutions. We evaluated our binocular 3D hand pose estimation algorithm and compared its actual running latency with different schemes for combining the modules mentioned before. Table 2 provides a detailed report of the efficiency and latency of various schemes in our algorithm. All reported latencies are derived by averaging the time of each step for each frame when running our algorithm on the collected test video.

Table 3. Inference latency of the complete binocular 3D hand pose estimation pipeline with hand tracking in different deep learning frameworks. Loc. and Est. represent the latency of hand location and hand keypoint estimation respectively. The "*" superscript indicates the corresponding converted Tensorflow Lite model. Blue is the best. All results are reported in millisecond (ms).

Method	Loc.	Est.	Others	Total
BlazeHand-T+KPNet-T	55.20	61.52	1.05	117.77
BlazeHand-T+Tracking+KPNet-T	24.01	60.51	1.02	85.54
BlazeHand-T*+Tracking+KPNet-T*+Aug	12.94	20.98	1.03	34.95

We calculated the overall latency of the binocular 3D hand pose estimation pipeline with hand tracking. Afterwards, we convert our hand detectors and 2D hand keypoint estimators to Tensorflow Lite format models, resulting in significant reduction of latency. To simplify the presentation, we have only included the latencies of the two most time-consuming steps, which are hand location and 2D hand keypoint estimation; whereas, we have omitted the latencies of other steps such as data processing and 3D calculation. Based on the results presented in Table 3, our simple tracking strategy has successfully reduced the hand location latency, enabling our method to perform in real-time without the need of GPUs, with a latency of less than 40 ms per frame.

Fig. 4. One sample frame from the test result video. Left: Hand detection and 2D keypoints estimation from binocular images. Right: Reconstrucion of 3D coordinate of hand keypoints.

To showcase our work on binocular 3D hand estimation, we present a test video from Ar3dHands, demonstrating the entire process of our approach. The resulting video is available at YouTube video. Figure 4 showcases one frame from the video, which plays at 15 frames per second (FPS). Our detector tracked the hands with exceptional accuracy, effectively detecting both left and right hands. Even when the hand was distorted, our 2D keypoint estimator displayed remarkable performance in estimating the positions of hand joints. Additionally, we utilized binocular reconstruction to reconstruct the 3D hand joints in real-time.

6   Conclusion

This paper introduces a novel multi-view hand pose dataset comprising of both first-person and third-person viewpoint images captured through normal and fisheye cameras. Alongside, we present a lightweight baseline technique for real-time hand pose estimation from binocular distorted images, thereby achieving low inference latency on on-device applications without GPUs. Our approach employs a simple tracking strategy, and numerous experiments highlight its potential for high-fidelity 3D hand keypoint estimation on edge devices without GPUs.

References

1. A2j: anchor-to-joint regression network for 3D articulated pose estimation from a single depth image. In: International Conference on Computer Vision (2019)
2. An, S., Zhang, X., Wei, D., Zhu, H., Yang, J., Tsintotas, K.A.: Fast monocular hand pose estimation on embedded systems. Cornell University - arXiv (2021)
3. Bouaziz, S., Tagliasacchi, A., Schroeder, M., Botsch, M., Tkach, A.: Robust articulated-ICP for real-time hand tracking. Comput. Graph. Forum: J. Eur. Assoc. Comput. Graph. 34(5), 101–114 (2015)
4. Chen, X., et al.: MobRecon: mobile-friendly hand mesh reconstruction from monocular image (2023)
5. Chen, X., et al.: Camera-space hand mesh recovery via semantic aggregation and adaptive 2D-1D registration. In: Computer Vision and Pattern Recognition (2021)
6. Fang, L., Liu, X., Liu, L., Xu, H., Kang, W.: JGR-P2O: joint graph reasoning based pixel-to-offset prediction network for 3D hand pose estimation from a single depth image (2020)
7. Fischler, M.A., Bolles, R.C.: Random sample consensus: a paradigm for model fitting with applications to image analysis and automated cartography. Commun. ACM 24(6), 381–395 (1981)
8. Garcia-Hernando, G., Yuan, S., Baek, S., Kim, T.K.: First-person hand action benchmark with RGB-D videos and 3D hand pose annotations. arXiv Computer Vision and Pattern Recognition (2017)
9. Ge, L., Liang, H., Yuan, J., Thalmann, D.: Robust 3D hand pose estimation from single depth images using multi-view CNNs. IEEE Trans. Image Process. 27, 4422–4436 (2018)
10. Huang, W., Ren, P., Wang, J., Sun, H.: AWR: adaptive weighting regression for 3D hand pose estimation. arXiv e-prints (2020)

11. Iqbal, U., Molchanov, P., Breuel, T., Gall, J., Kautz, J.: Hand pose estimation via latent 2.5D heatmap regression. In: Ferrari, V., Hebert, M., Sminchisescu, C., Weiss, Y. (eds.) ECCV 2018. LNCS, vol. 11215, pp. 125–143. Springer, Cham (2018). https://doi.org/10.1007/978-3-030-01252-6_8

12. Kannala, J., Brandt, S.: A generic camera model and calibration method for conventional, wide-angle, and fish-eye lenses. IEEE Trans. Pattern Anal. Mach. Intell. **28**(8), 1335–1340 (2006). https://doi.org/10.1109/TPAMI.2006.153

13. Li, M., Gao, Y., Sang, N.: Exploiting learnable joint groups for hand pose estimation. In: National Conference on Artificial Intelligence (2021)

14. Meng, H., et al.: 3D interacting hand pose estimation by hand de-occlusion and removal. In: Avidan, S., Brostow, G., Cissé, M., Farinella, G.M., Hassner, T. (eds.) ECCV 2022. LNCS, vol. 13666, pp. 380–397. Springer, Cham (2022). https://doi.org/10.1007/978-3-031-20068-7_22

15. Moon, G., Yu, S.I., Wen, H., Shiratori, T., Lee, K.M.: InterHand2.6M: a dataset and baseline for 3D interacting hand pose estimation from a single RGB image. arXiv Computer Vision and Pattern Recognition (2020)

16. Mueller, F., Mehta, D., Sotnychenko, O., Sridhar, S., Casas, D., Theobalt, C.: Real-time hand tracking under occlusion from an egocentric RGB-D sensor. Cornell University - arXiv (2017)

17. Newell, A., Yang, K., Deng, J.: Stacked hourglass networks for human pose estimation. In: Leibe, B., Matas, J., Sebe, N., Welling, M. (eds.) ECCV 2016. LNCS, vol. 9912, pp. 483–499. Springer, Cham (2016). https://doi.org/10.1007/978-3-319-46484-8_29

18. Ni, K., Steedly, D., Dellaert, F.: Out-of-core bundle adjustment for large-scale 3D reconstruction. In: 2007 IEEE 11th International Conference on Computer Vision, pp. 1–8 (2007). https://doi.org/10.1109/ICCV.2007.4409085

19. Oikonomidis, I., Kyriazis, N., Argyros, A.: Efficient model-based 3D tracking of hand articulations using kinect (2011)

20. Panteleris, P., Oikonomidis, I., Argyros, A.: Using a single RGB frame for real time 3D hand pose estimation in the wild. In: 2018 IEEE Winter Conference on Applications of Computer Vision (WACV) (2018)

21. Sifre, L., Mallat, S.: Rigid-motion scattering for texture classification (2014)

22. Sridhar, S., Mueller, F., Zollhöfer, M., Casas, D., Oulasvirta, A., Theobalt, C.: Real-time joint tracking of a hand manipulating an object from RGB-D input. In: Leibe, B., Matas, J., Sebe, N., Welling, M. (eds.) ECCV 2016. LNCS, vol. 9906, pp. 294–310. Springer, Cham (2016). https://doi.org/10.1007/978-3-319-46475-6_19

23. Tang, X., Wang, T., Fu, C.W.: Towards accurate alignment in real-time 3D hand-mesh reconstruction. Cornell University - arXiv (2021)

24. Wang, Y., Zhang, B., Peng, C.: SRHandNet: real-time 2D hand pose estimation with simultaneous region localization. IEEE Trans. Image Process. **29**, 2977–2986 (2020)

25. Xin, L., Wang, K., Wei, W., Yang, L.: A multiple object tracking method using Kalman filter. In: IEEE International Conference on Information & Automation (2010)

26. Yifei, C., et al.: Nonparametric structure regularization machine for 2D hand pose estimation. In: IEEE Conference Proceedings (2020)

27. Zhang, B., et al.: Interacting two-hand 3D pose and shape reconstruction from single color image. In: International Conference on Computer Vision (2021)

28. Zhang, F., et al.: MediaPipe hands: on-device real-time hand tracking (2020)

29. Zhang, J., Jiao, J., Chen, M., Qu, L., Xu, X., Yang, Q.: A hand pose tracking benchmark from stereo matching. In: International Conference on Image Processing (2017)
30. Zhang, Z.: Flexible camera calibration by viewing a plane from unknown orientations. In: International Conference on Computer Vision (1999)
31. Zhou, Y., Habermann, M., Xu, W., Habibie, I., Xu, F.: Monocular real-time hand shape and motion capture using multi-modal data. IEEE (2020)
32. Zimmermann, C., Brox, T.: Learning to estimate 3D hand pose from single RGB images. arXiv Computer Vision and Pattern Recognition (2017)
33. Zimmermann, C., Ceylan, D., Yang, J., Russell, B., Argus, M., Brox, T.: Frei-HAND: a dataset for markerless capture of hand pose and shape from single RGB images. arXiv Computer Vision and Pattern Recognition (2019)

TANet: Adversarial Network via Tokens Transformer for Universal Domain Adaptation

Hong Wu, Zhanxiang Feng$^{(\boxtimes)}$, Quan Zhang, Jiang Wu, and Jianhuang Lai

School of Computer Science and Engineering, Sun Yat-sen University, Guangzhou, China
{fengzhx7,stsljh}@mail.sysu.edu.cn, {wuhong25,zhangq48, wujiang7}@mail2.sysu.edu.cn

Abstract. Universal Domain Adaptation (UDA) aims to transfer knowledge between two datasets. The main challenge is to distinguish "unknown" classes that do not exist in the labeled source domain but exist in the unlabeled target domain. Some existing methods have poor feature representation capability and prediction diversity. Besides, they cannot clearly discover the common label set effectively and the label sets private to each domain. In this paper, we propose an algorithm named TANet, which extracts features by a Tokens Transformer and automatically learns the classification boundaries between different classes by training a one-vs-all classifier for each class and design batch nuclear-norm maximization loss to ensure the discriminativeness of the model and the diversity of classification. Moreover, by employing adversarial and non-adversarial domain discriminators in Tokens Transformer, TANet can distinguish the source and target data in the common label set. Finally, extensive experimental results show that TANet outperforms competitors and is robust.

Keywords: Universal Domain Adaptation · Vision Transformer · Adversarial training

1 Introduction

Domain Adaptation (DA) aims to transfer source categories representations to the target domain without additional supervision. As shown in Fig. 1, several possible "category shifts" can occur, including closed-set, open-set [2], partial-set [3], or a mix of open and partial-set [19]. Since the target domain is unlabeled, it is difficult to predict which of these situations will occur in advance [19]. This is where Universal Domain Adaptation (UDA) comes in. In UDA, we must identify "unknown" classes that do not exist in the labeled source domain but are present in the unlabeled target domain. Prior works have attempted to solve the universal domain adaptation problem.

However, some existing methods have poor feature representation capability and prediction diversity. For example, Sait et al. [17] propose an adversarial learning framework, which enables the feature extractor to identify and separate

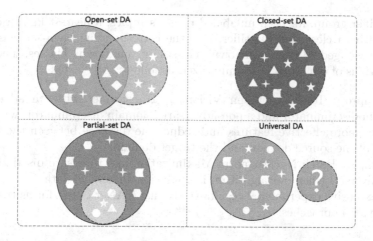

Fig. 1. Different categories of Domain Adaptation. Open-set DA means the source labels partially shared with the target domain. Closed-set DA means label sets are identical across domains. Partial-set DA means the source label set contains the target label set. Universal DA means the source label set and target label set have a certain intersection, and both have their independent parts, but we can't know it in advance.

the public and private classes of the source domain and target domain. But it used the pre-trained models of AlexNet and VGGNet on ImageNet, the models are relatively simple, which leads to poor model representation capability. Saito et al. [16] propose OVANet, which used a strong backbone likes ResNet50 and trained a classifier for each category to learn the boundaries of positive and negative categories. Though ResNet50 can effectively capture local image features, but it tends to ignore global features, which might lead to poor model representation capability too. Oppositely, ViT [5] leverages embedding and MSA mechanisms to link larger global features, but it may overlook local structural features.

Besides, even for known common categories in the target domain, its feature spaces may also be quite different from the common categories of the source domain. Saito et al. [15] introduce Domain Adaptive Neighborhood Clustering via Entropy optimization (DANCE) which makes strong assumptions about the degree to which the source categories overlap with the target domain, which limits their prediction diversity. So we can see, the traditional entropy minimization method will reduce the prediction diversity, and a few categories will have a high probability of being predicted as many categories. Cui et al. [4] prove that maximize the nuclear-norm of the prediction matrix can enforce the maximization of the F-norm, thereby enabling the model's predictions to be both discriminative and diverse. So we employ a new loss function named Batch Nuclear-norm Maximization (BNM) to ensure discrimination and diversity.

To address the above problem, we propose a novel UDA algorithm called TANet in this paper, which is shown in Fig. 2. TANet mainly consists of a feature extractor, a discriminator group, and a classifier group. We use discriminator group to enhance the feature representation capability of feature extractor. In the classifier group, for each unlabeled target samples, a nearest known class is identified by a closed-set classifier, and the corresponding open-set classifier's score is leveraged to decide "known" classes or "unknown" classes. The main contributions of our work are summarized as follows:

- We improve Tokens-to-Token Vision in Transformer with an adversarial domain discriminator and a non-adversarial domain discriminator, which can extract more effective features and reduce the distance between the feature space of the source domain and the target domain.
- We employ Batch Nuclear-norm Maximization loss to ensure discrimination and diversity when our algorithm is applied to unlabeled data.
- The extensive experimental results verify that TANet outperforms the state-of-the-art approaches.

2   Related Work

Open-Set Domain Adaptation. Open-set Domain Adaptation (ODA) is proposed for the first time in [2]. In recent years, a lot of work [1, 2, 6, 11, 17, 22, 23] has focused on the application scenarios of open-sets. Gall et al. [2] propose ATI algorithm to map the target sample to the source domain, and SVM is trained for classification. Sait et al. [17] propose an adversarial learning framework, which enable the feature extractor to identify and separate the public and private classes of the source domain and target domain and classify the private classes as "unknown" classes in the model. Separation of known and unknown classes based on self-supervised learning techniques to achieve feature space alignment. At last, Fang et al. [6] provide a strict theoretical generalization limit for ODA. Compared with Closed-set Domain Adaptation, ODA can better adapt to the actual situation of transfer learning. However, ODA may not be applicable in other scenarios such as Partial-set Domain adaptation because the target domain contains category features that do not exist in the source domain.

Universal Domain Adaptation. The idea of Universal Domain Adaptation is proposed in [19], they apply their method to a mixture of Partial-set Domain Adaptation (PDA) and ODA, which we call OPDA, where the target domain contains a subset of the source classes plus some "unknown" classes. Saito et al. [15] introduce DANCE which performs well on Universal Domain Adaptation. But it makes strong assumptions about the degree to which the source categories overlap with the target domain, which limits their prediction diversity. Liu et al. [12] focus on unknown noisy environments when transfering. Saito et al. [16] further proposed OVANet: One-vs-All Network for Universal Domain Adaptation which trains a One-vs-All classifier for each class and decides "known" or "unknown" by using the output.

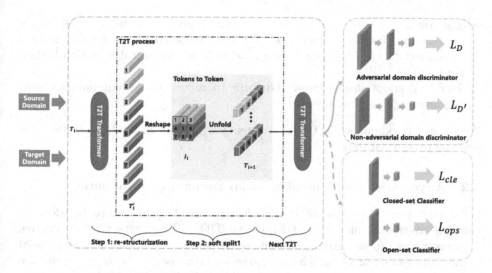

Fig. 2. The architecture of TANet. The images of the source domain and target domain are input into the feature extractor, then the feature are input into the discriminator group and the classifier group. The discriminator group is responsible for confrontational training to optimize the feature extractor, and the classifier group is responsible for the classification task. L_{cle} denotes the loss of the Closed-set Classifier, which is defined in Eq. (5). L_{ops} defined in Eq. (9) denotes the loss of Open-set Classifier. L_D defined in Eq. (1) is the loss of the Adversarial domain discriminator. $L_{D'}$ defined in Eq. (2) denotes the loss of the Non-adversarial domain Discriminator.

3   TANet

The architecture of TANet is shown in Fig. 2. We will introduce our approach in detail as follow.

Notation. We denote labeled source domain $D_s = \{(x_i^s, y_i^s)\}_{i=1}^{N_s}$ with "known" categories l_s and unlabeled target domain $D_t = \{x_i^t\}_{i=1}^{N_t}$ which contains "known" categories and "unknown" categories l_t, where l_s and l_t represent the label spaces of the source and target respectively.

3.1   T2T-ViT

An et al. [5] introduce a new network named Vision in Transformer (ViT). It divides the original images into blocks, which can combine with Transformer model to classify the images. However, ViT directly expands the image into a one-dimensional vector, which is not conducive to the modeling of image structural information (such as edges and lines). So in order to solve this problem, Li et al. [20] design a new method named tokens-to-token ViT (T2T-ViT), which combine multiple soft splits and reshape mechanisms to simultaneously consider both global and local features. T2T-ViT is briefly introduced as follows.

- The tokens are converted into tokens layer by layer, meaning that all tokens are reshaped into two dimensions. Then, an unfolded sliding window is used to connect tokens belonging to one window into a larger token, which is then fed into the ViT.
- T2T-ViT adopt deep narrow structure to reduce model computation and improve high performance.

We set our backbone as T2T-ViT. We use its pre-trained model and fine-tune training on our datasets.

3.2 Adversarial and Non-adversarial Domain Discriminator

Enhancing the robustness of the model against forged feature interference through adversarial methods, and improve T2T-ViT to extract more effective features, we design an adversarial domain discriminator D and a non-adversarial domain discriminator D', which can also reduce the distance between the feature space of the source domain and the target domain. The domain discriminator's guiding principle is straightforward: it determines if the input data originates from the source domain or the target domain. According to [19], the data $\mathbf{x}$ (from both the source domain and the target domain) is forwarded into the feature extractor to get the data feature $\mathbf{z} = F(\mathbf{x})$ and the input of the adversarial domain discriminator D is $\mathbf{z}$. Let L_D represents the loss function for adversarial domain discriminator D, which are formally defined as:

$$L_D = -\mathbb{E}_{(x_i^s, y_i^s) \sim D_s} log(D(F(x_i^s))) - \mathbb{E}_{(x_i^t) \sim D_t} log(1 - D(F(x_i^t))). \tag{1}$$

The output of the non-adversarial domain discriminator $D'(F(\mathbf{x}))$ is the domain similarity, which is a value from 0 to 1. The more likely the data $\mathbf{x}$ is from the source domain, the closer $D'(F(\mathbf{x}))$ is to 1. The closer the data $\mathbf{x}$ is to the target domain, the closer the output $D'(F(\mathbf{x}))$ is to 0. The loss function of the non-adversarial domain discriminator can be expressed as follow:

$$L_{D'} = -\mathbb{E}_{(x_i^s, y_i^s) \sim D_s} log(D'(F(x_i^s))) - \mathbb{E}_{(x_i^t) \sim D_t} log(1 - D'(F(x_i^t))). \tag{2}$$

We only employ the non-adversarial domain discriminator in the training phase, in contrast to [19], which uses it in both the training and prediction phases. Since the output of the non-adversarial domain discriminator is around 0.5 when the input data belongs to the category of the intersection of the source domain and the target domain. In order for the feature extractor to better extract category features at the intersection of source and target domains, we ignore any input that causes the output of the non-adversarial domain discriminator to be close to 1 or 0 during training. In other words, only when $D'(F(\mathbf{x}))$ meets the following conditions will it be used for gradient backpropagation to train the feature extractor:

$$1 - \delta \leq D'(F(\mathbf{x})) \leq \delta, \quad 0.5 < \delta < 1. \tag{3}$$

3.3   Closed-Set Classifier

The Closed-set classifier is designed to classify the sample categories included in the source domain. A common method to enhance the model's prediction discriminability is to limit the entropy of the model's prediction for unsupervised data. The smaller the entropy, the stronger the model's discriminative prediction (when the prediction is a one-hot vector, the entropy is at its minimum). However, this method has a drawback of being unfriendly to minority categories. This is because in order to ensure the discriminative prediction of unsupervised data, the samples of minority categories may be forced into majority categories. Consequently, the model's predicted diversity cannot be guaranteed.

Therefore, it is necessary to constrain the prediction of the model so that it has the following characteristics at the same time:

- Discriminability: it can be expressed as the certainty of prediction.
- Diversity: it can be approximately expressed as the number of predicted categories to avoid collapsing in majority categories.

Similar to [4], we employ BNM loss to ensure discrimination and diversity at the same time. With randomly sampled batch size B_t examples X^t, the classification response matrix on D^t could be denoted as $G(X^t)$. And the loss function of BNM can be expressed as:

$$L_{bnm}(X^t) = \frac{1}{B_t}||G(X^t)||_* = \frac{1}{B_t}tr\left(\sqrt{G(X^t)^T G(X^t)}\right), \quad (4)$$

where G denotes Closed-set classifier. Minimizing L_{bnm} could reduce the data density near the decision boundary without losing diversity, which is more effective than typical entropy minimization.

Therefore, combining the Eq. (4), we can define the loss function of Closed-set classifier as follow:

$$L_{cle} = \mathbb{E}_{(x_i^s, y_i^s)\sim D_s}(L_{cls}(x_i^s, y_i^s)) + \mathbb{E}_{(x_i^t)\sim D_t}(L_{bnm}(x_i^t)), \quad (5)$$

where $L_{cls}(\cdot)$ represents cross-entropy loss of Closed-set classifier and $\mathbb{E}(\cdot)$ denotes the mean function.

3.4   Open-Set Classifier

Similar to [16], we train a linear classifier (Open-set Classifier) for each class to learn the internal value of each class and the boundary between the most similar but different samples. For each classifier, the class is trained to be positive, while the other classes are negative. Each sub-classifier uses an Open-set classifier on top of the extracted features, that is, $z^k = s^k F_\theta(x)$, where F_θ and s^k represent a feature extractor and a weight of an Open-set classifier for class k respectively. Each dimension of z^k denotes the score for known and unknown respectively. We denote $p(\hat{y}^k|x) = \Lambda(z^k)$ as the output probability, where the instance x is an in-lier for class k, Λ represents softmax activation function.

Let $L_{ceh}(x^s, y^s)$ denote the Open-set classification loss for a sample (x^s, y^s):

$$L_{ceh}(x^s, y^s) = -p(\hat{y}^{y^s}|x^s)log(p(\hat{y}^{y^s}|x^s)) - \min_{i \neq y^s}(1 - p(\hat{y}^i|x^s))log(1 - p(\hat{y}^i|x^s)). \tag{6}$$

This calculates the loss for the positive class and the hardest negative class namely hard negative classifier sampling. However, if the datasets are small, this Eq. (6) converge slowly and is easy to fall into the local optimum. So we can simplify it by referring to the Eq. (7) in [16]:

$$L_{ceh}(x^s, y^s) = log(p(\hat{y}^{y^s}|x^s)) - \min_{i \neq y^s} log(1 - p(\hat{y}^i|x^s)). \tag{7}$$

Since the target sample and the source sample have different characteristics, the classifier trained on the source domain may be classified incorrectly in both Closed-set and Open-set classification. To solve this problem, we adopt the entropy minimization method to adapt the Open-set classifier to the target domain.

We apply entropy minimization training to all Open-set classifiers for each $x^t \in D_t$. We calculate the entropy of all classifiers and take the average value as expressed in Eq. (8) and train the model to minimize the entropy.

$$L_{ent}(x^t) = -\sum_{i=1}^{|l_s|} p(\hat{y}^i|x^t)log(p(\hat{y}^i|x^t)) + (1 - p(\hat{y}^i|x^t))log(1 - p(\hat{y}^i|x^t)). \tag{8}$$

Note that entropy minimization is performed by the Open-set classifier, not by the Closed-set classifier. Therefore, through this entropy minimization, the known target samples will be aligned with the source samples, while the unknown samples can be kept as "unknown", so that the model can increase its confidence.

Therefore, combining the Eq. (6) and Eq. (8), we can define the loss function of Open-set classifier as follow:

$$L_{ops} = \mathbb{E}_{(x_i^s, y_i^s) \sim D_s}(L_{ceh}(x^s, y^s)) + \mathbb{E}_{(x_i^t) \sim D_t}(\gamma L_{ent}(x_i^t)), \tag{9}$$

where $0 \leq \gamma \leq 1$ is a hyper-parameter and $\mathbb{E}(\cdot)$ denotes the mean function.

3.5 Training

Combining the above-mentioned parts, the loss function of TANet can be written in the following equation:

$$\begin{aligned} L_{all} &= L_{cle} + L_{ops} + \lambda(L_D + L_{D'}) \\ &= L_{cle} + L_{ops} + \mathbb{E}_{(x_i^s, y_i^s) \sim D_s}(\lambda L_{DD'1}) + \mathbb{E}_{(x_i^t) \sim D_t}(\lambda L_{DD'2}), \end{aligned} \tag{10}$$

where $L_{DD'1} = -log(D(F(x_i^s))) - log(D'(F(x_i^s)))$ and $L_{DD'2} = -log(1 - D'(F(x_i^t))) - log(1 - D'(F(x_i^t)))$.

The parameters of TANet are optimized to minimize the loss L_{all} to achieve Domain Adaptation.

4 Experiments

4.1 Setup

Datasets. We utilize popular datasets in DA: VisDA2017[1], DomainNet [14], and VisDA2021[2]. For VisDA2021, we use ImageNet-1K as the source domain and the target domain provided by VisDA2021 competition officials: ObjectNet, ImageNet-R, C, O, ObjectNet-ImageNet-R, C, O. For convenience, we specify as follows: I2O means ImageNet-1K to ObjectNet, I2OIC means ImageNet-1K to ObjectNet-ImageNet-R, C, O, I2IC means ImageNet-1K to ImageNet-R, C, O.

Evaluation Metric. VisDA2021 provides two evaluation metric ACC and AUROC, while ACC is calculated only on known categories and the AUROC measures "unknown" category detection by thresholding ascore that represents how likely the input belongs to an "unknown" class. In another way, it is important to consider the trade-off between the accuracy of known and "unknown" classes in evaluating universal or Open-set DA methods. So we evaluate Domain-Net and VisDA2017 using H-score [1]. H-score is the harmonic mean of the accuracy on common classes (acc_c) and accuracy on the "unknown" classes acc_t as:

$$H_{score} = \frac{2acc_c \times acc_t}{acc_c + acc_t}. \tag{11}$$

Implementation. We choose Python as our programming language to build our network. We selected a 24-layer T2T-ViT, and the obtained features were parallelly inputted into both the domain discriminator and the open-closed set classifier for training. The Adversarial and Non-adversarial Domain Discriminators are both three-layer fully connected layers, while the open-closed set classifier is a single-layer fully connected layer, as shown in Fig. 2. We set the model hyper-parameter γ as 0.1, the learning rate lr as 0.01, batch_size B as 64, and iteration step number T as 10000. All experiments are implemented on one A100 GPU.

4.2 Result

For VisDA2017 and DomainNet, we select DANCE [15], RTN [13], IWAN [21], ATI [2], OSBP [17], UAN [19], CMU [7], DCC [10], OVANet [16], EISAKA [18] and OVANet+SPA [9] as baselines. The results are shown in the Table 1. Our approach performs significantly better than other baselines in terms of H-score.

For VisDA2021, we select DANN [8], DANCE [15] and OVANet [16] as baselines. The results are shown in the Table 2. The results show that our method performs better than any of the baselines. In terms of ACC and AUROC, our method outperforms existing methods with a large margin in all three datasets, among which, I2IC get the best performance.

---

[1] http://ai.bu.edu/visda-2017/.
[2] http://ai.bu.edu/visda-2021/.

Table 1. H-score of open-partial DA using DomainNet, VisDA2017('-': it cannot be computed).

Method	DomainNet						Avg	VisDA2017
	P2R	R2P	P2S	S2P	R2S	S2R		
DANCE [15]	21.0	47.3	37.0	27.7	46.7	21.0	33.5	4.4
RTN [13]	32.3	30.3	28.7	28.7	28.6	31.9	30.1	26.0
ATI [2]	32.6	30.6	29.0	29.0	28.9	32.2	30.4	26.3
OSBP [17]	33.6	33.0	30.6	30.5	30.6	33.7	32.0	27.3
IWAN [21]	35.4	33.0	31.2	31.2	31.1	35.0	32.8	27.6
UAN [19]	41.9	43.6	39.1	38.9	38.7	43.7	41.0	30.5
CMU [7]	50.8	52.2	45.1	44.8	45.6	51.0	48.3	34.6
DCC [10]	56.9	50.3	43.7	44.9	43.3	56.2	49.2	43.0
OVANet [16]	56.0	51.7	47.1	47.4	44.9	57.2	50.7	53.1
EISAKA [18]	59.1	52.4	47.5	48.1	45.1	58.6	51.8	54.7
OVANet+SPA [9]	61.1	51.7	47.6	48.7	45.1	58.9	52.2	–
Ours	**66.1**	**57.7**	**52.0**	**55.0**	**49.8**	**63.6**	**57.4**	**60.1**

Table 2. ACC and AUROC of different UDA method.('–': it cannot be computed).

Method	I2O		I2IC		I2OIC	
	ACC	AUROC	ACC	AUROC	ACC	AUROC
DANN	0.8	–	1.5	–	1.3	–
DANCE	6.0	47.6	32.0	19.3	24.9	49.4
OVANet	22.4	54.1	35.6	15.8	32.6	48.1
Ours	**35.4**	**54.4**	**55.5**	**46.7**	**51.9**	**52.0**

4.3 Sensitivity Analysis

In order to verify the robustness of our model, we conduct hyper-parameter sensitivity analysis and set the hyper-parameters γ as several values (e.g., 0.1, 0.3, ..., 0.9), respectively. Other settings are the same as in Implementation in Sect. 4.1, and the results are shown in the Fig. 3. As can be seen from Fig. 3, for different parameters, the H-score of DomainNet and the ACC of the VisDA201 fluctuate a little on the whole. In general, H-score and ACC can reach a high value at the same time when the $\gamma = 0.1$.

4.4 Ablation Study

Table 3 shows the ablation study. We set up 5 training protocols. Protocol-1 denotes we choose OVANet as the baseline only. From protocol-2, when data augmentation is added, the ACC of OVANet is improved up to 2 points in these three datasets. From protocol-3, when the loss module is added, the ACC the performance is greatly improved up to 6 points. This shows that the BNM loss can bring good performance improvements.

From protocol-4, feature extractor is changed into T2T-ViT with domain discriminator, compared with protocol-2, the model performance is greatly

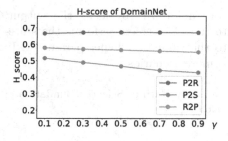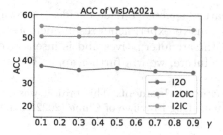

Fig. 3. Sensitivity analysis of hyper-parameter (γ) in DomainNet and VisDA2021.

improved, and the ACC of the three datasets is increased up 12 points. This shows that the introduction of a great feature extractor is very important.

From protocol-5, when the loss module is added, we can see that our overall model can achieve optimal performance. When it compared with protocol-3, the performance is greatly improved up to 13 points in I2IC, this can also show that the introduction of a great feature extractor bring good performance improvements. Besides, compared with protocol-4, the performance is greatly improved up to 6 points, which shows the effectiveness of BNM loss.

In summary, through cross-validation, the T2T-ViT with domain discriminator module and modified BNM loss are mutually reinforcing in our model and have the greatest impact on model performance.

Table 3. Ablation study (ACC)

Protocol	Ablation			I2O	I2IC	I2OIC
	T2T	Loss	DataAugmentation			
1				22.4	35.6	32.6
2			✓	23.2	38.2	34.3
3		✓	✓	31.5	41.8	40.5
4	✓		✓	29.9	50.7	45.7
5	✓	✓	✓	**35.4**	**55.5**	**51.9**

5   Conclusion

In this paper, we present a novel Universal Domain Adaptation algorithm, TANet. It trains a one-vs-all classifier for each class to automatically learn the classification boundaries between different classes and designs batch nuclear-norm maximization loss to ensure the discriminativeness of the model and the diversity of classification. Besides, we design the adversarial and non-adversarial domain discriminator to reduce the distance between source and target domain feature spaces. TANet decides "known" or "unknown" by using the output. Extensive experiments results demonstrate that TANet outperforms the state-of-the-art alternatives and is insensitive to the value of a hyper-parameter. In the future, we will further apply TANet to more scenarios.

Acknowledgement. This project was supported by Natural Science Foundation of Guangdong Province of China (2022A1515010269).

References

1. Bucci, S., Loghmani, M.R., Tommasi, T.: On the effectiveness of image rotation for open set domain adaptation. In: Vedaldi, A., Bischof, H., Brox, T., Frahm, J.-M. (eds.) ECCV 2020. LNCS, vol. 12361, pp. 422–438. Springer, Cham (2020). https://doi.org/10.1007/978-3-030-58517-4_25
2. Busto, P.P., Gall, J.: Open set domain adaptation. In: ICCV (2017)
3. Cao, Z., Ma, L., Long, M., Wang, J.: Partial adversarial domain adaptation. In: ECCV (2018)
4. Cui, S., Wang, S., Zhuo, J., Li, L., Huang, Q., Tian, Q.: Towards discriminability and diversity: batch nuclear-norm maximization under label insufficient situations. In: CVPR (2020)
5. Dosovitskiy, A., et al.: An image is worth 16×16 words: transformers for image recognition at scale. In: ICLR (2021)
6. Fang, Z., Lu, J., Liu, F., Xuan, J., Zhang, G.: Open set domain adaptation: theoretical bound and algorithm. IEEE Trans. Neural Netw. Learn. Syst. **32**, 4309–4322 (2021)
7. Fu, B., Cao, Z., Long, M., Wang, J.: Learning to detect open classes for universal domain adaptation. In: Vedaldi, A., Bischof, H., Brox, T., Frahm, J.-M. (eds.) ECCV 2020. LNCS, vol. 12360, pp. 567–583. Springer, Cham (2020). https://doi.org/10.1007/978-3-030-58555-6_34
8. Ganin, Y., Lempitsky, V.: Unsupervised domain adaptation by backpropagation. ArXiv (2015)
9. Kundu, J.N., Bhambri, S., Kulkarni, A.R., Sarkar, H., Jampani, V., et al.: Subsidiary prototype alignment for universal domain adaptation. In: Advances in Neural Information Processing Systems (2022)
10. Li, G., Kang, G., Zhu, Y., Wei, Y., Yang, Y.: Domain consensus clustering for universal domain adaptation. In: CVPR (2021)
11. Liu, H., Cao, Z., Long, M., Wang, J., Yang, Q.: Separate to adapt: open set domain adaptation via progressive separation. In: CVPR (2019)
12. Liu, X., Huang, Y., He, S., Yin, J., Chen, X., Zhang, S.: Learning to transfer under unknown noisy environments: an universal weakly-supervised domain adaptation method. In: ICME (2021)
13. Long, M., Zhu, H., Wang, J., Jordan, M.I.: Unsupervised domain adaptation with residual transfer networks. In: NeurIPS (2016)
14. Peng, X., Bai, Q., Xia, X., Huang, Z., Wang, B.: Moment matching for multi-source domain adaptation. In: ICCV (2019)
15. Saito, K., Kim, D., Sclaroff, S., Saenko, K.: Universal domain adaptation through self supervision. In: NeurIPS (2020)
16. Saito, K., Saenko, K.: OVANet: one-vs-all network for universal domain adaptation. arXiv preprint arXiv:2104.03344 (2021)

17. Saito, K., Yamamoto, S., Ushiku, Y., Harada, T.: Open set domain adaptation by backpropagation. In: ECCV (2018)
18. Wang, Y., Zhang, L., Song, R., Ma, L., Zhang, W.: Exploiting inter-sample affinity for knowability-aware universal domain adaptation. arXiv preprint arXiv:2207.09280 (2022)
19. You, K., Long, M., Cao, Z., Wang, J., Jordan, M.I.: Universal domain adaptation. In: CVPR (2019)
20. Yuan, L., et al.: Tokens-to-token ViT: training vision transformers from scratch on ImageNet. In: ICCV (2021)
21. Zhang, J., Ding, Z., Li, W., Ogunbona, P.: Importance weighted adversarial nets for partial domain adaptation. In: CVPR (2018)
22. Zhang, Q., Dang, K., Lai, J.H., Feng, Z., Xie, X.: Modeling 3D layout for group re-identification. In: CVPR (2022)
23. Zhang, Q., Lai, J., Xie, X.: Learning modal-invariant angular metric by cyclic projection network for VIS-NIR person re-identification. IEEE Trans. Image Process. **30**, 8019–8033 (2021)

GLM: A Model Based on Global-Local Joint Learning for Emotion Recognition from Gaits Using Dual-Stream Network

Feixiang Zhang[1,3] and Xiao Sun[2,3(✉)]

[1] AHU -IAI AI Joint Laboratory, Anhui University, Hefei, China
zhangfx1999@qq.com
[2] School of Computer Science and Information Engineering, Hefei University
of Technology, Hefei, China
sunx@hfut.edu.cn
[3] Institute of Artificial Intelligence, Hefei Comprehensive National Science Center,
Hefei, China
sunx@iai.ustc.edu.cn

Abstract. Gait is a distinctive human feature that can be recognized from a distance and has been widely utilized in the field of emotion recognition. In this study, we propose a novel dual-stream model (GLM) for gait emotion recognition that combines the strengths of global and local features. We extract skeleton point gait data from walking videos and process them into suitable inputs for two channels of feature extraction networks, which respectively capture global and local characteristics. To enhance the features and improve recognition accuracy, we further introduce an attention-based feature fusion module. Through experiments on benchmark datasets, our proposed model achieves high accuracy in recognizing emotions from gait data.

Keywords: Emotion recognition · Graph convolutional networks · Attention · Dual-stream network

1 Introduction

Emotions play a significant role in interpersonal communication and enable individuals to better understand others' behavioral patterns and inner feelings, thus enhancing cooperation efficiency. While non-verbal cues such as gestures [10] and eye movements [16] are crucial in expressing and understanding emotions, they can be challenging to acquire and identify from a distance. Gait recognition [8] has emerged as a viable alternative, allowing for contactless collection of data through devices such as Microsoft Kinect and video cameras. Psychological research has established a correlation between human emotions and walking

This work was supported by the National Key R&D Programme of China (2022YFC3803202), Major Project of Anhui Province under Grant 202203a05020011 and General Programmer of the National Natural Science Foundation of China (61976078).

gait, which can be used to perform emotion recognition using features such as arm swing, stride size, and head position. Combining features of different scales in multimodal emotion recognition [18] can lead to excellent results using fused features [9].

In summary, this paper makes the following main contributions:

- We propose a dual-channel feature extraction network that combines an improved network based on ST-GCN and a designed CNN-LSTM network to better capture both global and local features of the gait data.
- We introduce a self-attention module (SAM) and cross-attention module (CAM) in the feature fusion network to enhance the connection of features in two channels and improve the accuracy of emotion recognition.
- Our proposed method outperforms existing methods and achieves better accuracy in emotion recognition on the datasets used in our experiments.

2 Related Work

Depressed patients display distinct gait patterns, suggesting a potential link between gait and emotion recognition, as reported by J. Michalak's study [13]. Data processing is critical in preparing video datasets for emotion recognition, with video commonly transformed into a digital format suitable for classification, such as a sequence of images represented as silhouettes or skeleton maps. Three models are used to describe and measure emotions: the discrete categories model, the pleasure-arousal-dominance (PAD) model [12], and the appraisal approach. Recent studies propose new approaches to improve the accuracy of gait emotion recognition. Uttaran Bhattacharya et al. [2] [1] proposed a semi-supervised method that leverages hierarchical attentional focus and emotion mapping to improve average accuracy by 10%-50%. Tanmay Randhavane et al. [15] used deep features learned via LSTM to achieve 80.07% accuracy in recognizing perceived emotion. Chenyang Si et al. [17] proposed an attention-enhanced graph convolutional LSTM network (AGCLSTM) that achieved state-of-the-art performance on the NTU RGB+D dataset and Northwestern-UCLA dataset, capturing the discriminative features of spatial structure and temporal dynamics while exploring the relationship between spatiotemporal domains.

3 Approaches

In this section, we will discuss the data processing and model structure (GLM) design for gait recognition. First, we extract the most basic data from walking gait videos using methods such as *OpenPose*, which provides us with the three-dimensional coordinates of each joint point. Next, we describe the model in detail and explain the function of each module within the structure.

3.1   Extracting Original Data from Videos

This paper uses two datasets - E-Gait and ELMD - containing gait walking videos with emotional labels. Data for learning is extracted from these datasets, and an appropriate number of frames is selected to isolate walking gait using pose estimation techniques like *OpenPose*. Three-dimensional coordinates of joint key points are extracted to represent the original data within each frame. Therefore, the original data within each frame of the sequence can be represented as $\{x_i, y_i, z_i\}$, where i denotes the i_{th} joint keypoint. The original frame features can be expressed as follows:

$$feature_{original} = \{f_0, f_1, ..., f_n\}. \tag{1}$$

In order to facilitate the feature extraction when the subsequent data is input to the network, this paper adopts a standardized format for extracting joint points, and converts the walking gait picture sequences into sequences of skeleton maps with 16 joint points, as shown in Fig. 1.

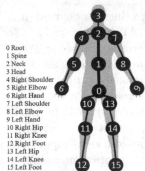

0 Root
1 Spine
2 Neck
3 Head
4 Right Shoulder
5 Right Elbow
6 Right Hand
7 Left Shoulder
8 Left Elbow
9 Left Hand
10 Right Hip
11 Right Knee
12 Right Foot
13 Left Hip
14 Left Knee
15 Left Foot

Different emotions often reflect different gaits during walking:

Happy: when people are happy, their shoulders will open when walking, and the body will swing more

Sad: when people are sad, they walk with their backs hunched over and their shoulders folded

Angry: when people are angry, their bodies will lean forward, their necks will stretch forward, and they walk in a hurry

Neutral: when people are neutral, their heads and torsos stand straight with their arms open

Fig. 1. Selection and correspondence of 16 joints from the human body for walking gait-based emotion recognition.

This paper uses emotion labels to classify gait videos into four categories: *Happy, Angry, Sad,* and *Neutral*. The labels are collected using a 5-point Likert scale and are then aggregated through statistical analysis. The paper uses maximum voting to determine the real emotion label for each video. The formula for calculating the ground-truth label is as follows:

$$Label_{emotion} = Max\left(\sum_{id=0}^{n} Score_{id}\right). \tag{2}$$

3.2   Proposed Dual-Channel Approach

This paper proposes two channels for emotion recognition: global and local features, as illustrated in Fig. 2. Skeleton joint points are mapped to an image and processed by designed CNN and LSTM for global feature extraction. Local features are obtained through an improved ST-GCN module on the topological map of the human skeleton. Features from both channels are fused with attention-based methods for improved recognition.

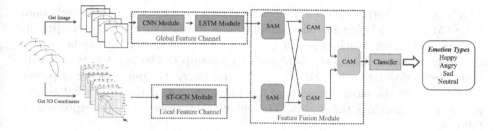

Fig. 2. The structure of our gait emotion recognition model (GLM).

3.3 Global Feature Channel

In the global feature channel, the first step is to preprocess the data to obtain the three-dimensional coordinates of the joint points of the human movement skeleton. Then, the joint points are mapped to an image, using red and blue colors to distinguish the left and right parts of the human body.

As depicted in Fig. 3, to expedite and stabilize the training process, we utilize a pre-trained CNN module for image feature extraction. Each basic block in the CNN module comprises a two-dimensional convolutional layer, a ReLU activation layer, and a batch normalization layer.

In the CNN module, each convolutional layer has a 3×3 kernel and a 1×1 stride, which extends the channels from 1 to 8, 16, and 32. Dropout layers are added between the basic blocks as necessary. The MaxPooling layers have a core size of 2×2. After passing through five basic blocks and three MaxPooling layers, the data is flattened to a size of 1600. Then, a fully connected layer is used to transform the flattened data into a vector of size 200, which allows us to extract the desired global features from the image.

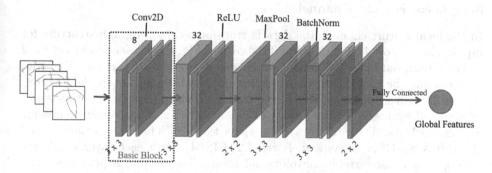

Fig. 3. The structure of the global feature channel.

Bidirectional Long Short-Term Memory (BiLSTM) was used to extract timing information in this study. This was chosen due to the cyclical nature of human walking and the little variation between each walking cycle. Using a BiLSTM, which captures both forward and backward data, improves emotion prediction. BiLSTM and LSTM have similar calculation formulas, with three gates (input, output, and forget), each of which has its own weight matrix W, updating the cell state c_t and hidden state h_t at each timestamp t. The input gate i_t selects and enters information into the next cell through x_t, the output gate o_t passes information to the hidden state, and the forget gate f_t determines what to forget from the previous timestamp. The calculation process can be expressed as follows:

$$i_t = Sigmoid\left(W_i x_t + U_i h_{t-1} + b_i\right). \tag{3}$$

$$o_t = Sigmoid\left(W_o x_t + U_o h_{t-1} + b_o\right). \tag{4}$$

$$f_t = Sigmoid\left(W_f x_t + U_f h_{t-1} + b_f\right). \tag{5}$$

$$c_t = f_t \circ c_{t-1} + i_t \circ \tanh\left(W_c x_t + U_c h_{t-1} + b_c\right). \tag{6}$$

$$h_t = o_t \circ \tanh\left(c_t\right). \tag{7}$$

where W represents the weight of the gate or cell to be entered, U represents the weight of the hidden cell state, and b represents the bias of each gate or cell.

BiLSTM enhances the original LSTM by processing the data in both forward and backward directions, resulting in a hidden state that includes both the forward and backward hidden states from the previous moment. In this paper, we use a layer of forward LSTM and backward LSTM in our BiLSTM implementation. The input size for the BiLSTM is 200×frame, and the output size is 256, which is the desired feature size for subsequent processing. The calculation process for the BiLSTM is as follows:

$$feature_{global} = Linear(h_t), h_t = BiLSTM(input_t, h_{t-1}). \tag{8}$$

3.4   Local Feature Channel

In the local feature channel, the data is transformed into a graph structure for input. The improved ST-GCN module, shown in Fig. 4, is chosen to extract local features from data because human walking gait videos have certain time series features, and the joint points when people walk also have certain spatial features.

The human skeleton maps extracted from each video frame form a time series represented by a graph with a fixed adjacency matrix. Each vertex represents a joint, with its 3D coordinates $\{x, y, z\}$ as features. The data is then passed through 3 ST-GCN layers(kernel size: 32, 64, 64), with each layer consisting of 9 spatiotemporal graph convolutional layers. The output is processed with ReLU activation and BatchNorm for normalization before being merged using an AvePooling layer. A 1×1 convolutional layer is used to compress the feature maps, followed by another BatchNorm layer. Finally, the features are fed into a fully connected layer for emotion recognition. Residual links and dropouts are used for regularization.

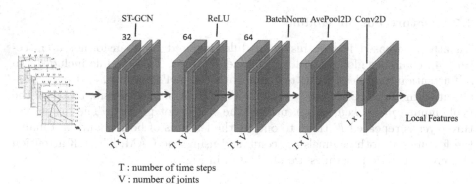

T : number of time steps
V : number of joints

Fig. 4. The structure of the local feature channel.

A gait is represented as a graph $G = (V, E)$, where V denotes the set of vertices and E denotes the set of edges. Among them, the vertex set:

$$V = \left\{ v_i^t \mid t = 1, ..., T; i = 1, ..., N \right\}. \tag{9}$$

where T is denoted as the number of time steps and N is denoted as the number of joints.

The edge set E is composed of two subsets. The first subset contains the spatial connections of joints in each frame, denoted as $E_s = \{v_{ti}v_{tj} \mid (i, j) \in H\}$, where H is set of naturally connected joints. The second subset contains frame-to-frame temporal edges that connect the same joints in the preceding and following frames, denoted as $E_f = \{v_{ti}v_{(t+1)i}\}$.

Each frame of the human walking gait video is represented as a graph with a fixed adjacency matrix A and a self-connected identity matrix I, where the body connections of joints are encoded in A. The graph convolution operation needed to extract local features from the graph is achieved using the following formula:

$$f_{out} = \Lambda^{-\frac{1}{2}} (A + I) \Lambda^{-\frac{1}{2}} f_{in} W. \tag{10}$$

where $\Lambda^{ii} = \sum_j \left(A^{ij} + I^{ij}\right)$. The weight matrix W is formed by stacking the weight vectors of multiple output channels. In practice, we can represent the input feature as a tensor of (C, V, T).

For partitioning strategies with multiple subsets, we can also use this method to solve the problem, but this time the adjacency matrix A is split into multiple matrices A_j where $A + I = \sum_j A_j$. The above formula is also rewritten as:

$$feature_{local} = f_{out} = \sum_j \Lambda_j^{-\frac{1}{2}} A_j \Lambda_j^{-\frac{1}{2}} f_{in} W_j. \tag{11}$$

where $\Lambda_j^{ii} = \sum_k (A_j^{ik}) + \alpha$, we can set $\alpha = 0.001$ to avoid empty rows in A_j.

3.5   Feature Fusion Module

An attention-based feature fusion module, inspired by Transformer architecture [4], combines global and local channel features. This module includes two self-attention modules (SAM) to refine each channel's features, and two cross-attention modules (CAM) to fuse them. The attention mechanism, based on the tuple input $(query, key, value)$, utilizes the scaled dot product. The fusion feature layer is repeated N times to output the features of both channels. Finally, the features of both channels are combined using one CAM. The self-attention and cross-attention modules are illustrated in Fig. 5.

$$Attention(Q, K, V) = softmax(\frac{QK^{\top}}{\sqrt{d_k}})V. \tag{12}$$

where the dot product operation of query matrix Q and content K calculates attention weight of Q on V. Scaling by $\sqrt{d_k}$ avoids large dot product, which yields a small gradient through $softmax()$. $softmax()$ smooths results to 0–1 interval, aiding in gradient calculation of backpropagation. Q, K, and V are the same initially, resulting from feature and position embeddings.

The multi-head attention consists of several attention modules, where each attention module seeks different relationships between objects in the sequences. The formula of the multi-head attention module is as follows:

$$MultiHead(Q, K, V) = Concat(H_1, ..., H_{n_h})W^O. \tag{13}$$

$$H_i = Attention(QW_i^Q, KW_i^K, VW_i^V). \tag{14}$$

where $W_i^Q \in \mathbb{R}^{d_{model} \times d_k}, W_i^K \in \mathbb{R}^{d_{model} \times d_k}, W_i^V \in \mathbb{R}^{d_{model} \times d_v}$ and $W^O \in \mathbb{R}^{n_h d_v \times d_{model}}$ are parameter matrices.

SAM (left side of Fig. 5) uses multi-head attention with residuals to learn information from different feature positions. Positional information of the input X is encoded using sinusoidal functions inspired by Carion et al. [3] The calculation process of SAM is as follows:

$$X_{SAM} = X + MultiHead(X + POS_X, X + POS_X, X). \tag{15}$$

where POS_X is the spatial positional encodings.

CAM (right side of Fig. 5) fuses two feature sets from different channels using cross-attention and a fully connected feed-forward neural network (FFN) that includes two linear transformations and a ReLU layer. To ensure spatial position coding consistency with SAM, we also use a sinusoidal function to encode positional information. The calculation process of CAM can be expressed as follows:

$$FFN(x) = max(0, xW_1 + b_1)W_2 + b_2. \tag{16}$$

where W represents weight matrice and b represents the basis vector.

In summary, the calculation process of CAM can be summarized as:

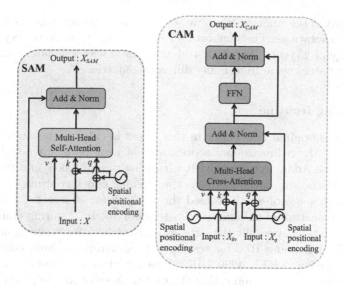

Fig. 5. The structure of the attention-based feature fusion module.

$$\tilde{X}_{CAM} = X_q + MultiHead(X_q + POS_q, X_{kv} + POS_{kv}, X_{kv}). \qquad (17)$$

$$X_{CAM} = \tilde{X}_{CAM} + FFN(\tilde{X}_{CAM}). \qquad (18)$$

where $X_q \in \mathbb{R}^{d \times N_q}$ is the input of the current channel branch, $POS_q \in \mathbb{R}^{d \times N_q}$ is the spatial position code corresponding to X_q. $X_{kv} \in \mathbb{R}^{d \times N_{kv}}$ is the input of another channel branch, and $POS_{kv} \in \mathbb{R}^{d \times N_{kv}}$ is the spatial position code corresponding to X_{kv}. The resulting $X_{CAM} \in \mathbb{R}^{d \times N_q}$ is the final output of this module.

4   Experiment Results and Analysis

4.1   Datasets Preparation

For our emotion recognition task, we selected a dataset consisting of human walking gait videos, with emotion labels assigned to each video. The input to our model consists of picture sequences from these videos. The emotion labels were obtained through objective scoring by a variety of individuals.

E-Gait Dataset [1]: Videos of real gaits were obtained from various sources, including BML [11], Human3.6M [7], ICT [14], CMU-MOCAP [6] combined. It contains 342 video clips.

ELMD Dataset [5]: Obtained from the Edinburgh Locomotion Mocap Database. It contains 1835 video clips.

Our dataset consists of 2177 real gait videos, each of which has been converted into a sequence of 16 joint skeleton point pictures of human movement. To ensure the objectivity of the emotion label, we selected the category with the most votes among the annotations. The annotators ranged in age from 20 to 28 years, with a median age of 23 years. The male-to-female ratio was 4 females and 6 males, and the annotators came from many different countries.

4.2   Training Routine

The size of the original data input in this paper is video sequence length $\times$ 16 joint points $\times$ three-dimensional coordinates of joint points. We trained their model using the Adam optimizer with a learning rate of 0.005, and the learning rate decays at the appropriate time as the training epoch continues to increase. We used a batch size of 8 and trained the network for 40 epochs. Additionally, we used a momentum of 0.9 and weight-decay of 5×10^{-4} during training.

For each dataset, we split the data into about 90% for training and validation, and the remaining 10% for testing. The experiments were conducted on an NVIDIA GeForce RTX 3090 GPU. The final testing accuracy achieved in our experiments was high, indicating the effectiveness of the proposed model for emotion recognition in human gait videos.

4.3   Our Method's Results

In terms of measuring model performance, we use macro accuracy as a measure, which is defined as follows:

$$Emotion \in \{Happy, Angry, Sad, Neutral\}. \tag{19}$$

$$Accuracy = \sum_{i=0}^{E} \frac{TP_{Emotion}}{DataCount}. \tag{20}$$

As shown in Table 1, previous research indicates that most of the previous methods have an accuracy of less than 70% on this dataset, except for Uttaran Bhattacharya et al., who used a modified graph convolutional neural network to improve the accuracy to 82.15%. Later on, the accuracy was even raised to 84.00%. However, our dual-stream model, which combines the advantages of CNN and GCN models to complement each other, achieves an accuracy of 87.50%, the highest accuracy rate among existing methods.

Table 1. Comparing our method to other existing methods.

Karg et al.	Daoudi et al.	Wang et al.	ST-GCN	Crenn et al.	LSTM	STEP	Uttaran et al.	Our Method
39.58%	42.52%	53.73%	65.62%	66.22%	74.10%	82.15%	84.00%	**87.50%**

4.4   Ablation Experiment

In the ablation experiment, we tested the accuracy of two channels as a single-stream network model for emotion recognition, and the results are shown in Table 2. We can observe that although the single-stream channel does not achieve the high accuracy of the dual-stream channel, it still improves the classification accuracy to a certain extent, indicating the effectiveness of our module. Moreover, the dual-stream channels outperform the single-stream channels, demonstrating the superiority of the dual-stream model.

Table 2. Ablation Experiment.

Single-stream Channel		Dual-stream Channel
Global Feature Channel	Local Feature Channel	
86.03%	86.96%	87.50%

4.5   Single Emotion Recognition Experiment

The confusion matrix in Fig. 6 indicates that our emotion recognition model can accurately identify each emotion label, as shown by the high diagonal values. However, the uneven distribution of emotions in the dataset affects the accuracy of recognizing each emotion label. *Happy* and *Sad* have more samples, resulting in higher accuracy, while *Angry* and *Neutral* have fewer samples, resulting in a higher probability of misidentification. *Angry* is often misidentified as *Sad*, while other emotions are less likely to be misidentified as *Neutral*. The model achieved an average accuracy of 76.82% for correctly recognizing a single emotion label in the dataset.

4.6   Robustness Experiment

As shown in Table 3, we conducted an experiment to test the robustness of our model by introducing noise to the dataset. To simulate the real-world scenario, we randomly removed some bones (edges in the image) and cleared the 3D coordinates of the joints connected to the bones, resulting in partially dirty data. Despite the noise, our model still achieved an accuracy of above 80%, indicating that our model has some degree of robustness.

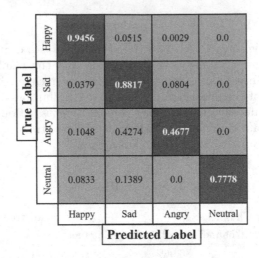

Fig. 6. Confusion Matrix: The accuracy of every single emotion of the dataset.

Table 3. Robustness Experiment.

Number of bones covered	1–3	4–6	7–9	10–12	13–15
Accuracy	85.33%	84.24%	82.64%	82.61%	80.43%

5   Conclusion

The GLM model presented in this study achieves superior results for gait emotion recognition by extracting and fusing global and local features using an attention-based feature fusion module. Our results show that our model outperforms existing methods in terms of accuracy. Multimodal approaches combining gait data with other modalities, as well as exploring emotion recognition in multi-person walking videos and continuous emotional labels, are promising directions for future research.

In summary, the proposed GLM model presents a novel approach to gait emotion recognition with promising results. Future research can focus on multimodal approaches, multi-person walking videos, and continuous emotional labels.

References

1. Bhattacharya, U., Mittal, T., Chandra, R., Randhavane, T., Bera, A., Manocha, D.: Step: spatial temporal graph convolutional networks for emotion perception from gaits. In: Proceedings of the AAAI Conference on Artificial Intelligence, vol. 34, pp. 1342–1350 (2020)
2. Bhattacharya, U., et al.: Take an emotion walk: perceiving emotions from gaits using hierarchical attention pooling and affective mapping. In: Vedaldi, A., Bischof, H., Brox, T., Frahm, J.-M. (eds.) ECCV 2020. LNCS, vol. 12355, pp. 145–163. Springer, Cham (2020). https://doi.org/10.1007/978-3-030-58607-2_9

3. Carion, N., Massa, F., Synnaeve, G., Usunier, N., Kirillov, A., Zagoruyko, S.: End-to-end object detection with transformers. In: Vedaldi, A., Bischof, H., Brox, T., Frahm, J.-M. (eds.) ECCV 2020. LNCS, vol. 12346, pp. 213–229. Springer, Cham (2020). https://doi.org/10.1007/978-3-030-58452-8_13

4. Chen, X., Yan, B., Zhu, J., Wang, D., Yang, X., Lu, H.: Transformer tracking. In: Proceedings of the IEEE/CVF conference on computer vision and pattern recognition, pp. 8126–8135 (2021)

5. Habibie, I., Holden, D., Schwarz, J., Yearsley, J., Komura, T.: A recurrent variational autoencoder for human motion synthesis. In: Proceedings of the British Machine Vision Conference (BMVC) (2017)

6. Hodgins, J.: CMU graphics lab motion capture database (2015)

7. Ionescu, C., Papava, D., Olaru, V., Sminchisescu, C.: Human3. 6 m: large scale datasets and predictive methods for 3d human sensing in natural environments. IEEE Trans. Pattern Anal. Mach. Intell. **36**(7), 1325–1339 (2013)

8. Li, B., Zhu, C., Li, S., Zhu, T.: Identifying emotions from non-contact gaits information based on microsoft kinects. IEEE Trans. Affect. Comput. **9**(4), 585–591 (2016)

9. Lian, Z., Li, Y., Tao, J., Huang, J.: Investigation of multimodal features, classifiers and fusion methods for emotion recognition. arXiv preprint arXiv:1809.06225 (2018)

10. Lin, C., Wan, J., Liang, Y., Li, S.Z.: Large-scale isolated gesture recognition using a refined fused model based on masked res-c3d network and skeleton LSTM. In: 2018 13th IEEE International Conference on Automatic Face & Gesture Recognition (FG 2018), pp. 52–58. IEEE (2018)

11. Ma, Y., Paterson, H.M., Pollick, F.E.: A motion capture library for the study of identity, gender, and emotion perception from biological motion. Behav. Res. Methods **38**(1), 134–141 (2006)

12. Mehrabian, A.: Pleasure-arousal-dominance: a general framework for describing and measuring individual differences in temperament. Curr. Psychol. **14**, 261–292 (1996)

13. Michalak, J., Troje, N.F., Fischer, J., Vollmar, P., Heidenreich, T., Schulte, D.: Embodiment of sadness and depression-gait patterns associated with dysphoric mood. Psychosom. Med. **71**(5), 580–587 (2009)

14. Narang, S., Best, A., Feng, A., Kang, S.h., Manocha, D., Shapiro, A.: Motion recognition of self and others on realistic 3d avatars. Comput. Anim. Virt. Worlds **28**(3–4), e1762 (2017)

15. Randhavane, T., Bhattacharya, U., Kapsaskis, K., Gray, K., Bera, A., Manocha, D.: Identifying emotions from walking using affective and deep features. arXiv preprint arXiv:1906.11884 (2019)

16. Schurgin, M., Nelson, J., Iida, S., Ohira, H., Chiao, J., Franconeri, S.: Eye movements during emotion recognition in faces. J. Vis. **14**(13), 14–14 (2014)

17. Si, C., Chen, W., Wang, W., Wang, L., Tan, T.: An attention enhanced graph convolutional LSTM network for skeleton-based action recognition. In: Proceedings of the IEEE/CVF Conference on Computer Vision and Pattern Recognition, pp. 1227–1236 (2019)

18. Tang, J., Li, K., Jin, X., Cichocki, A., Zhao, Q., Kong, W.: CTFN: hierarchical learning for multimodal sentiment analysis using coupled-translation fusion network. In: Proceedings of the 59th Annual Meeting of the Association for Computational Linguistics and the 11th International Joint Conference on Natural Language Processing (Volume 1: Long Papers), pp. 5301–5311 (2021)

HuMoMM: A Multi-Modal Dataset and Benchmark for Human Motion Analysis

Xiong Zhang[1], Minghui Wang[1], Ming Zeng[1], Wenxiong Kang[1,2,3(✉)],
and Feiqi Deng[1]

[1] School of Automation Science and Engineering, South China University of
Technology, Guangdong 510641, China
auwxkang@scut.edu.cn
[2] School of Future Technology, South China University of Technology, Guangdong
510641, China
[3] Pazhou Laboratory, Guangzhou 510335, China

Abstract. Human motion analysis is a fundamental task in computer
vision, and there is an increasing demand for versatile datasets with the
development of deep learning. However, how to obtain the annotations
of human motion, such as 3D keypoints and SMPL parameters, requires
further research. In this work, we design a multi-view human motion
capture system and develop a toolchain to generate multi-modal motion
annotations. Additionally, we contribute HuMoMM, a large-scale multi-
modal dataset which has the following characteristics: 1) multiple modalities, including two data formats, i.e., RGB and depth images, and four
annotation formats, i.e., action categories, 2D keypoints, 3D keypoints,
and SMPL parameters; 2) large-scale with 18 subjects, 30 actions, 3.5k
sequences, and 262k frames; 3) multi-task for action recognition, 2D keypoint detection, 3D pose estimation and human mesh recovery. Furthermore, we provide a benchmark on HuMoMM to test the performance
of popular methods in several related tasks. The experimental results
demonstrate that HuMoMM holds significant research value. We expect
HuMoMM can contribute to human motion-related research, and it is
available at https://github.com/SCUT-BIP-Lab/HuMoMM.

Keywords: Human motion analysis · Human pose estimation ·
Human mesh recovery · Multi-modal dataset · Benchmark

1 Introduction

Human motion analysis is a longstanding research area in computer vision and
one of the fundamental techniques in virtual reality, avatar creation, gaming, etc.
In recent years, many datasets [1–6] have contributed significantly to human
motion analysis research. However, how to obtain the annotations of human

H. Lu et al. (Eds.): ICIG 2023, LNCS 14355, pp. 204–215, 2023.
https://doi.org/10.1007/978-3-031-46305-1_17

motion (e.g., 3D keypoints, SMPL parameters) needs further study. Most existing 3D pose estimation and 3D mesh recovery datasets [2–4] rely on expensive optical or inertial motion capture systems to obtain 3D keypoints and SMPL parameters. In this work, we design a novel multi-view vision-based human motion capture system and a toolchain for generating multi-modal motion annotations. Our system uses five RGB-D cameras, including a time-of-flight (TOF) camera and four binocular cameras, to capture a diverse range of RGB images and depth sequences. To generate multi-modal motion annotations, we develop a comprehensive toolchain that includes manual and automatic 2D keypoint annotation, 3D keypoint triangulation, and multi-stage SMPL fitting.

We contribute HuMoMM, a large-scale multi-modal human motion analysis dataset with the following characteristics: 1) Multiple modalities. HuMoMM contains two data formats, including RGB and depth images, and four annotation formats, including action categories, 2D keypoints, 3D keypoints, and SMPL parameters. 2) Large scale. HuMoMM considers action categories and video duration, collecting a dataset of 18 subjects, 20 single-person actions, 10 multi-person actions, 3.5k sequences, and 262k frames. 3) Multiple tasks. HuMoMM has multi-modal annotations, allowing it to be applied in various tasks like action recognition, 2D/3D keypoint detection, human mesh recovery, etc.

To facilitate research on HuMoMM, we provide a benchmark for various domains, including action recognition, 2D keypoint detection, 3D pose estimation, and human mesh recovery. We evaluate several popular methods in various domains on HuMoMM, adopting three dataset division protocols and standard evaluation metrics. Our experiment results demonstrate that HuMoMM holds considerable potential for advancing research in human motion-related tasks.

In summary, our contributions can be summarized as follows:

- We design a multi-view vision-based human motion capture system and develop toolchain for generating multi-modal motion annotations.
- We contribute HuMoMM, a large-scale multi-modal human motion analysis dataset with two data formats, four annotations, 18 subjects, 30 actions, 3.5k sequences, and 262k frames.
- We provide a benchmark and evaluate popular methods in various domains on HuMoMM to facilitate research on human motion analysis.

2   Related Works

2.1   2D and 3D Pose Estimation

Human pose estimation is a fundamental task in computer vision that can be divided into 2D and 3D human pose estimation. For 2D human pose estimation, there are several single-frame image datasets, such as MPII [11], coco [1], which provide a variety of images and 2D keypoint annotation. Video-based 2D human pose estimation datasets like Posetrack [12] and Penn Action [13],

Table 1. Comparisons of HuMoMM with published datasets. HuMoMM provides a competitive scale of the subjects(Subj), actions(Act), sequence(Seq), frames(Frame) and persons(Person). Moreover, HuMoMM provides multiple data modalities and support multiple tasks. "RGB" denotes RGB sequences; "Depth" denotes depth image sequences; "Act" denotes action classes; "K2d" denotes 2d keypoints; "K3d" denotes 3d keypoints; "SMPL" denotes SMPL parameters; "–" denotes the data are not applicable or reported.

Dataset	Subj	Act	View	Seq	Frame	Person	RGB	Depth	Act	K2d	K3d	SMPL
UCF101 [7]	–	101	–	13k	–	single	✓	–	✓	–	–	–
AVA [8]	–	80	–	437	–	multi	✓	–	✓	–	–	–
NTU RGBD [9]	40	60	–	56k	–	multi	✓	✓	✓	–	✓	–
NTU RGBD 120 [10]	106	120	–	114k	–	multi	✓	✓	✓	–	✓	–
MPII [11]	–	410	–	–	24k	multi	✓	–	✓	✓	–	–
COCO [1]	–	–	–	–	104k	multi	✓	–	–	✓	–	–
PoseTrack [12]	–	–	–	>1.35k	>46k	multi	✓	–	–	✓	–	–
Penn Action [13]	–	15	–	2.32k	–	single	✓	–	✓	✓	–	–
HumanEva [14]	4	6	7	–	37k	single	✓	–	–	✓	✓	–
Human3.6M [2]	11	17	4	839	3.6m	single	✓	✓	✓	✓	✓	–
CMU panoptic [3]	8	5	31	65	154m	multi	✓	✓	–	✓	✓	–
MPI-INF-3DHP [15]	8	8	14	16	1.3m	single	✓	–	–	✓	✓	–
3DPW [4]	7	–	–	60	51k	multi	✓	–	–	–	✓	✓
AMASS [5]	344	–	–	>11k	>16.88m	single	–	–	–	–	✓	✓
AIST++ [16]	30	–	–	1.40k	10.1m	single	✓	–	–	✓	✓	✓
HuMoMM (ours)	18	30	5	3.5k	262k	multi	✓	✓	✓	✓	✓	✓

provide sequence-based 2D keypoint annotations. Most 3D human pose estimation datasets provide indoor scene and multi-view 3D keypoint annotations using expensive equipment. For example, Human3.6M [2] deploys motion capture cameras to obtain 3D keypoint, while MPI-INF-3DHP [15] utilizes a commercial motion capture system to obtain ground truth keypoints. Compared to the above datasets, we provide a markless motion capture system and a comprehensive toolchain for generating ground truth labels.

2.2 3D Human Mesh Recovery

Skinned Multi-Person Linear Model (SMPL) [17] has many applications in the avatar-driven gaming industry, various datasets [2,4,5] provide SMPL parameters. However, obtaining SMPL parameters still need to be further studied. Mosh [18] is applied to Human3.6M [2] to obtain SMPL parameters, and 3DPW [4] uses inertial measurement units (IMUs) to acquire SMPL parameters. Compared with these datasets, HuMoMM obtains SMPL parameters through less costly multi-stage SMPL fitting methods.

2.3 Action Recognition

Action recognition is of great importance for understanding human behaviors. Several fine-grained action datasets [7–10] have been recently collected, such as

NTU-RGBD 120 [10], which contains 120 action categories and 3D keypoint annotations. However, its 3D keypoints are derived from Kinert and are prone to inaccuracy. HuMoMM contains 30 actions with 2D and 3D keypoints, which can be used in skeleton-based action recognition.

3 Hardware Setup

We develop a motion capture system consisting of 5 RealSense RGB-D cameras. The primary camera, RealSense L515, is a time-of-flight (TOF) depth camera, while the four auxiliary cameras, RealSense D455, are binocular depth cameras. The cameras are positioned at 5 different perspectives to capture multi-view RGB-D sequences, as illustrated in Fig. 1. To calibrate the cameras, we apply a two-by-two calibration approach, where Zhang's calibration method [19] and Matlab's stereo calibrator toolbox are employed for camera pairs (#2, #0), (#2, #1), and (#2, #3) of the same type, while kalibr toolbox are used for camera pair (#2, #4) with different camera type. We implement hardware synchronization for cameras #0, #1, #2, and #3 using a synchronization cable that provides a unified clock signal. For camera #4, which has a different triggering method, we employ software synchronization by setting a synchronization variable in the collection software. Finally, we capture video at a frame rate of 15 FPS.

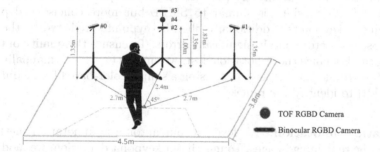

Fig. 1. Hardware setup. An overview of our data collection system, indicating the size of the collection area and the location of cameras.

4 Toolchain

We develop a comprehensive toolchain to complete the entire annotation generation process. A diagram of the pipeline is shown in Fig. 2.

4.1 2D Keypoint Annotations

For the annotation of 2D keypoints, we design our keypoint definition and divide the annotation procedure into two stages: manual annotation and automatic annotation.

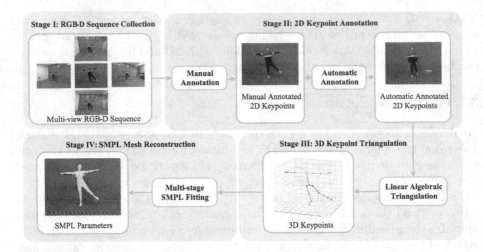

Fig. 2. Pipeline of generating multi-modal annotations.

Manual Annotation. Recent datasets [3,6] apply pose estimators like HRNet [20] to predict 2D keypoints as ground truth labels. However, the open-source pose estimator cannot accurately produce the 2D keypoints due to our specific keypoint definition, which is similar to SMPL but more concise and precise, comprising 21 keypoints. Additionally, the 2D keypoints predicted by the open-source pose estimator contain significant errors. To ensure the quality of the 2D keypoints and balance the annotation cost, we employ experts to manually annotate 20% keyframes for subjects 0–4, using a simple color-based frame difference method [21] to identify keyframes.

Automatic Annotation. We leverage our automatic annotation method to annotate the remaining images. To match our keypoint definition, we modify the number of output keypoints of the HRNet [20] and finetune it on our manually annotated keyframe data. The finetuned model achieved a validation accuracy of AP 0.987 and AR 0.995. Eventually, we infer the finetuned HRNet on the remaining images to obtain the full 2D keypoint annotations.

4.2   3D Keypoint Triangulation

With the intrinsic and extrinsic parameters of the multi-view camera through calibration, we apply linear algebraic triangulation to obtain the coordinates of the 3D keypoints. Linear algebraic triangulation [22] is a basic method in multi-view geometry where the 3D coordinates are obtained from observation points in two or more camera views. Taking two views as an example, we have the measurement $P_{2d}^1 = H_1 P_{3d}$ and $P_{2d}^2 = H_2 P_{3d}$, and these equations can be combined into a form $A \cdot P_{3d} = 0$, with

$$A = \begin{bmatrix} x_1 H_1^{3T} - H_1^{1T} \\ y_1 H_1^{3T} - H_1^{2T} \\ x_2 H_2^{3T} - H_2^{1T} \\ y_2 H_2^{3T} - H_2^{2T} \end{bmatrix}, \tag{1}$$

where H^{iT} are the rows of H. After solving the equation $A \cdot P_{3d} = 0$, we can get the 3D point P_{3d}. In our task, we construct 20 matching pairs of 2D keypoints and use them to triangulate 20 corresponding 3D keypoints, then average the 3D keypoints to obtain the initial 3D keypoint $\hat{P}_{3d}$. Furthermore, the bundle adjustment method [23] can be used to revise the triangulated 3D keypoints.

4.3 SMPL Mesh Reconstruction

We formulate the problem of obtaining SMPL parameters as an optimization task, that is, we take the shape parameter $\beta \in \mathbb{R}^{n \times 10}$, the pose parameter $\theta \in \mathbb{R}^{n \times 72}$, and the translation parameter $T \in \mathbb{R}^{n \times 3}$ as the parameters to be optimized, and use energy functions as the optimization objective.

Single-Person SMPL Reconstruction. Subject 0–14 belongs to the single-person action, so we employ the single-person SMPL parameter reconstruction method. Referring to Easymocap [24, 25], we divide the SMPL parameter reconstruction into several steps: 1) 3D keypoint triangulation. We utilize a multi-view triangulation scheme to obtain the 3D keypoints by directly associating all the projection equations. 2) 3D keypoint fitting. We fit the SMPL model to 3D keypoints by minimizing the error between the ground truth 3D keypoint and the regressed 3D keypoint. The objective is

$$E(\beta, \theta, T) = E_J(\beta, \theta, T; K, J_{reg}^{3d}, J_{gt}^{3d}) + \lambda_\theta E_\theta(\theta) + \lambda_a E_a(\theta) + \lambda_\beta E_\beta(\beta), \tag{2}$$

where $E_J(\beta, \theta, T; K, J_{reg}^{3d})$ is a penalty on the distance between regressed keypoints J_{reg}^{3d} and ground truth J_{gt}^{3d}. $E_\theta(\theta)$, $E_a(\theta)$, $E_\beta(\beta)$ are gaussians pose prior, unnatural pose prior, quadratic shape prior, respectively. 3) 2D kyepoint fitting. After fitting to 3D keypoints, we can fit the SMPL model to 2D keypoints to finetune the parameters, the objective is

$$E(\beta, \theta, T, K) = E_J(\beta, \theta, T, K; J_{rep}^{2d}, J_{gt}^{2d}) + \lambda_\theta E_\theta(\theta) + \lambda_a E_a(\theta) + \lambda_\beta E_\beta(\beta), \tag{3}$$

where $E_J(\beta, \theta, T, K; J_{rep}^{2d}, J_{gt}^{2d})$ is a penalty on the distance between reprojected keypoints J_{rep}^{2d} and ground truth J_{gt}^{2d}. It is worth noting that intrinsic and extrinsic camera parameters can optionally be optimized.

Multiple-Person SMPL Reconstruction. For multi-person SMPL parameter reconstruction, we must address the multi-view correspondences and temporal tracking problems before applying the abovementioned single-person reconstruction method. Multi-view correspondences mean that the 2D keypoints detected in different views must be matched, i.e., we need to identify which person the multiple 2D keypoints in each view belongs to. Similarly, the temporal tracking refers to the problem of tracking each 3D poses in the temporal sequence and identifying which person it belongs to. Referencing easymocap [24,26], we compute the affinity matrix for the multi-view correspondence problem to obtain the similarity of keypoints under multiple views. To tackle the temporal tracking problem, we leverage the Geometry-Guided Association method [26] to compute the distance of the 3D poses within the temporal window and identify each 3D keypoint sequence.

5   Dataset

Data Modalities: Based on the above hardware setup and toolchain, we can finally collect multi-modal data, including RGB and depth images, and provide multi-modal annotations, including 2D keypoints, 3D keypoints, SMPL parameters and action categories. The multi-modal data and annotations are shown in Fig. 3.

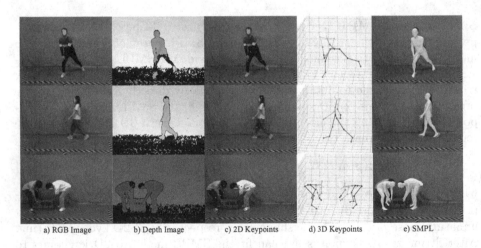

a) RGB Image   b) Depth Image   c) 2D Keypoints   d) 3D Keypoints   e) SMPL

Fig. 3. HuMoMM provides multiple modalities of data format and annotations, including a) RGB Images, b) Depth Images, c) 2D Keypoints, d) 3D Keypoints, e) SMPL Paramenters.

Action Set: For the action set, the designed actions should cover as much of the pose space as possible, and for multiplayer actions, interaction and occlusion must occur. Therefore, we design 30 actions and divide them into two groups: 1) Single-person actions. We design 20 single daily actions, including waving hands, running, lunging leg press, etc. 2) Multi-person actions. We design 10 multi-person actions, including talking, shaking hands, lifting heavy things, etc. Some action categories are shown in Fig. 4.

Subjects: We invite 18 volunteers, 15 males and 3 females, to collect our data. They are diverse in age, height, and appearance, as shown in Fig. 4. Due to our wearless collection method, the volunteers can wear their daily clothes to ensure a diverse appearance.

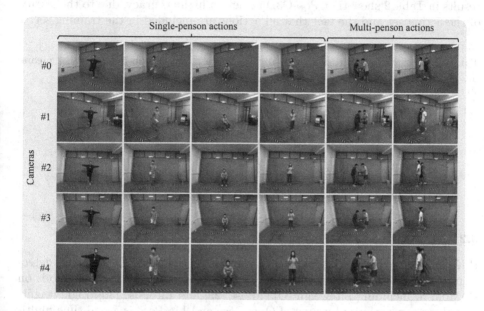

Fig. 4. HuMoMM contains a diversity of views, subjects, and actions. We select some samples for illustration here.

6   Experiments

In this section, we evaluate popular methods in various domains, including action recognition, 2D keypoint detection, 3D pose estimation, and human mesh recovery on HuMoMM.

Referring to the division in HuMMan [6] and NTU RGB-D [10], we utilize 3 protocols to divide the training and test sets. Protocol 1 (P1): split by subjects. We split subject 0–9 and 15–17 as training sets, subject 10–14 and 18–19 as testing sets. Protocol 2 (P2): split by action. We split action 0–9 and 20–24 as training sets, action 10–19 and 25–29 as testing sets. Protocol 3 (P3): split by view. We split view 0–2 as training set, and view 3–4 as testing sets. The experiments under P1, P2 and P3 aim to evaluate models' cross-subject, cross-action, and cross-view performance, respectively.

6.1   Action Recognition

We provide 30 action categories containing daily actions that can be used for the action recognition task. We evaluate popular skeleton-based action recognition methods (STGCN [27] and PoseC3D [28]) on HuMoMM. The experimental results in Table 2 show that PoseC3D achieve a high accuracy, due to the clarity of the action set and the fact that all actions are included in the training set.

Table 2. Action Recognition. Top-1: top-1 accuracy, Top-5: top-5 accuracy. ↑ means the higher the better.

Methods	P1(cross-subject)		P3(cross-view)	
	Top-1 (%) ↑	Top-5 (%) ↑	Top-1 (%) ↑	Top-5 (%) ↑
ST-GCN [27]	83.1	97.8	81.5	96.8
PoseC3D [28]	94.9	99.9	98.8	100.0

6.2   2D Keypoint Detection

HuMoMM provides 2D keypoint annotations to support 2D keypoint detection task. We evaluate the effectiveness of two popular lightweight methods on HuMoMM, including Liteweight-OpenPose [29] and LitePose [30]. Lightweight-OpenPose is a optimized verson of OpenPose and LitePose is a real-time multi-person pose estimator on edge. The experimental results in Table 3 show that both lightweight-openpose and LitePose achieve high AP and AR, it may be that our background is relatively clean and lacks distracting factors. Nonetheless, we plan to employ background enhancement methods to enhance the background diversity.

Table 3. 2D Keypoint Detection. AP: average precision, AR: average recall. ↑ means the higher the better.

Methods	P1(cross-subject)		P2(cross-action)		P3(cross-view)	
	AP ↑	AR ↑	AP ↑	AR ↑	AP ↑	AR ↑
Liteweight-OpenPose [31]	0.956	0.965	0.907	0.917	0.967	0.975
LitePose [30]	0.967	0.978	0.987	0.997	0.974	0.985

6.3   3D Human Pose Estimation

HuMoMM provides 3D keypoint annotations that can be used in 3D pose estimation task. We evaluate popular 2D-to-3D lifting methods: Videopose3D [32] and GastNet [33]. Videopose3D utilizes a temporal convolutional network to capture the temporal relationship, while GastNet introduces graph convolution to capture the relationship between joints. As shown in Table 4, the performance of these models on HuMoMM is worse than that on Human3.6M [2] (on which Videopose3D obtains MPJPE of 51.8mm), highlighting the significant research potential of HuMoMM.

Table 4. 3D Pose Estimation. MPJPE: Mean per joint position error, PA-MPJPE: Procrustes-aligned MPJPE. ↓ means the lower the better.

Methods	P1(cross-subject)		P2(cross-action)		P3(cross-view)	
	MPJPE↓	PA-MPJPE↓	MPJPE↓	PA-MPJPE↓	MPJPE↓	PA-MPJPE↓
Videopose3D [32]	62.6	42.2	89.1	66.7	87.5	47.1
GastNet [33]	59.5	40.5	84.5	63.5	99.8	53.1

6.4 Human Mesh Recovery

We provide SMPL parameter annotations so that HuMoMM can be used for human mesh recovery task. We evaluate the latest method ROMP [34] on HuMoMM. ROMP is a one-stage model for multi-person human mesh recovery that can directly regress SMPL parameters for multiple people. The experimental results in Table 5 show that the MPJPE and PA-MPJPE for multiple-person actions are significantly higher than those for single-person actions due to occlusion problems, which negatively impact the regression performance of the model. This suggests that HuMoMM is particularly challenging for human mesh recovery tasks.

Table 5. Human Mesh Recovery. MPJPE: Mean per joint position error, PA-MPJPE: Procrustes-aligned MPJPE. ↓ means the lower the better.

Methods	P1(cross-subject)		P2(cross-action)		P3(cross-view)	
	MPJPE↓	PA-MPJPE↓	MPJPE↓	PA-MPJPE↓	MPJPE↓	PA-MPJPE↓
ROMP(Single-person)	73.95	52.30	83.65	65.45	67.38	48.07
ROMP(Multi-person)	85.11	64.90	121.9	80.3	88.36	60.90

7 Conclusion

We present a large, multi-modal dataset, HuMoMM, which contains two data formats and four multimodal annotations for human motion analysis. By providing a fundamental benchmark for testing the performance of popular models across various tasks, we demonstrate that HuMoMM holds significant research value. We expect HuMoMM can contribute to the research in human action recognition, human pose estimation, human mesh recovery, and other areas to facilitate human motion analysis.

Acknowledgements. This work was supported in part by the National Natural Science Foundation of China under Grant 61976095 and in part by the Natural Science Foundation of Guangdong Province of China under Grant 2022A1515010114.

References

1. Lin, T.-Y., et al.: Microsoft COCO: common objects in context. In: Fleet, D., Pajdla, T., Schiele, B., Tuytelaars, T. (eds.) ECCV 2014. LNCS, vol. 8693, pp. 740–755. Springer, Cham (2014). https://doi.org/10.1007/978-3-319-10602-1_48
2. Ionescu, C., Papava, D., Olaru, V., Sminchisescu, C.: Human3.6M: large scale datasets and predictive methods for 3D human sensing in natural environments. IEEE TPAMI **36**(7), 1325–1339 (2013)
3. Joo, H., et al.: Panoptic Studio: a massively multiview system for social motion capture. In: IEEE ICCV, pp. 3334–3342 (2015)
4. Von Marcard, T., Henschel, R., Black, M.J., Rosenhahn, B., Pons-Moll, G.: Recovering accurate 3D human pose in the wild using IMUs and a moving camera. In: ECCV, pp. 601–617 (2018)
5. Mahmood, N., Ghorbani, N., Troje, N.F., Pons-Moll, G., Black, M.J.: AMASS: archive of motion capture as surface shapes. In: IEEE ICCV, pp. 5442–5451 (2019)
6. Cai, Z., et al.: HuMMan: multi-modal 4D human dataset for versatile sensing and modeling. In: ECCV, pp. 557–577. Springer, Cham (2022). https://doi.org/10.1007/978-3-031-20071-7_33
7. Soomro, K., Zamir, A.R., Shah, M.: UCF101: a dataset of 101 human actions classes from videos in the wild. arXiv preprint arXiv:1212.0402 (2012)
8. Gu, C., et al.: AVA: a video dataset of spatio-temporally localized atomic visual actions. In: IEEE CVPR, pp. 6047–6056 (2018)
9. Shahroudy, A., Liu, J., Ng, T.T., Wang, G.: NTU RGB+D: a large scale dataset for 3D human activity analysis. In: IEEE CVPR, pp. 1010–1019 (2016)
10. Liu, J., Shahroudy, A., Perez, M., Wang, G., Duan, L.Y., Kot, A.C.: NTU RGB+D 120: a large-scale benchmark for 3D human activity understanding. IEEE TPAMI **42**(10), 2684–2701 (2019)
11. Andriluka, M., Pishchulin, L., Gehler, P., Schiele, B.: 2D human pose estimation: new benchmark and state of the art analysis. In: IEEE CVPR, pp. 3686–3693 (2014)
12. Andriluka, M., et al.: PoseTrack: a benchmark for human pose estimation and tracking. In: IEEE CVPR, pp. 5167–5176 (2018)
13. Luvizon, D.C., Picard, D., Tabia, H.: 2D/3D pose estimation and action recognition using multitask deep learning. In: IEEE CVPR, pp. 5137–5146 (2018)
14. Sigal, L., Balan, A.O., Black, M.J.: HumanEva: synchronized video and motion capture dataset and baseline algorithm for evaluation of articulated human motion. Int. J. Comput. Vis. **87**(1–2), 4 (2010)
15. Mehta, D., et al.: Monocular 3D human pose estimation in the wild using improved CNN supervision. In: International Conference on 3D Vision (3DV), pp. 506–516. IEEE (2017)

16. Li, R., Yang, S., Ross, D.A., Kanazawa, A.: AI choreographer: music conditioned 3D dance generation with AIST++. In: IEEE ICCV, pp. 13401–13412 (2021)
17. Loper, M., Mahmood, N., Romero, J., Pons-Moll, G., Black, M.J.: SMPL: a skinned multi-person linear model. ACM Trans. Graph. (TOG) **34**(6), 1–16 (2015)
18. Loper, M., Mahmood, N., Black, M.J.: MoSh: motion and shape capture from sparse markers. ACM Trans. Graph. **33**(6), 220–1 (2014)
19. Zhang, Z.: A flexible new technique for camera calibration. IEEE Trans. Pattern Anal. Mach. Intell. **22**(11), 1330–1334 (2000)
20. Sun, K., Xiao, B., Liu, D., Wang, J.: Deep high-resolution representation learning for human pose estimation. In: IEEE CVPR, pp. 5693–5703 (2019)
21. Calic, J., Izuierdo, E.: Efficient key-frame extraction and video analysis. In: Proceedings. International Conference on Information Technology: Coding and Computing, pp. 28–33. IEEE (2002)
22. Wrobel, B.P.: Multiple view geometry in computer vision. Künstliche Intell. **15**, 41 (2001)
23. Förstner, W., Wrobel, B.P.: Bundle Adjustment. In: Photogrammetric Computer Vision. GC, vol. 11, pp. 643–725. Springer, Cham (2016). https://doi.org/10.1007/978-3-319-11550-4_15
24. Easymocap - make human motion capture easier. Github (2021). https://github.com/zju3dv/EasyMocap
25. Bogo, F., Kanazawa, A., Lassner, C., Gehler, P., Romero, J., Black, M.J.: Keep It SMPL: automatic estimation of 3D human pose and shape from a single image. In: Leibe, B., Matas, J., Sebe, N., Welling, M. (eds.) ECCV 2016. LNCS, vol. 9909, pp. 561–578. Springer, Cham (2016). https://doi.org/10.1007/978-3-319-46454-1_34
26. Dong, J., et al.: Fast and robust multi-person 3D pose estimation and tracking from multiple views. IEEE TPAMI **44**(10), 6981–6992 (2021)
27. Han, H., et al.: STGCN: a spatial-temporal aware graph learning method for poi recommendation. In: 2020 IEEE International Conference on Data Mining (ICDM), pp. 1052–1057. IEEE (2020)
28. Duan, H., Zhao, Y., Chen, K., Lin, D., Dai, B.: Revisiting skeleton-based action recognition. In: IEEE CVPR, pp. 2969–2978 (2022)
29. Osokin, D.: Real-time 2D multi-person pose estimation on CPU: lightweight openpose. arXiv preprint arXiv:1811.12004 (2018)
30. Wang, Y., Li, M., Cai, H., Chen, W.M., Han, S.: Lite Pose: efficient architecture design for 2D human pose estimation. In: IEEE CVPR, pp. 13126–13136 (2022)
31. Osman, A.A.A., Bolkart, T., Black, M.J.: STAR: sparse trained articulated human body regressor. In: Vedaldi, A., Bischof, H., Brox, T., Frahm, J.-M. (eds.) ECCV 2020. LNCS, vol. 12351, pp. 598–613. Springer, Cham (2020). https://doi.org/10.1007/978-3-030-58539-6_36
32. Pavllo, D., Feichtenhofer, C., Grangier, D., Auli, M.: 3D human pose estimation in video with temporal convolutions and semi-supervised training. In: IEEE CVPR, pp. 7753–7762 (2019)
33. Liu, J., et al.: A graph attention spatio-temporal convolutional network for 3D human pose estimation in video. In: 2021 IEEE International Conference on Robotics and Automation (ICRA), pp. 3374–3380. IEEE (2021)
34. Sun, Y., Bao, Q., Liu, W., Fu, Y., Black, M.J., Mei, T.: Monocular, one-stage, regression of multiple 3D people. In: IEEE ICCV, pp. 11179–11188 (2021)

Enhanced Frequency Information
for Image Dehazing

Fei Guo, Junkai Fan, Jun Li[✉], and Jian Yang[✉]

PCA Lab, School of Computer Science and Engineering,
Nanjing University of Science and Technology, Nanjing 210094, China
{feiguo,junkai.fan,junli,csjyang}@njust.edu.cn

Abstract. The restoration of images affected by severe weather conditions such as heavy fog is a trending topic in the field of computer vision. Despite the fact that many image dehazing methods have achieved impressive performance, it is common that frequency information attenuation is overlooked in both feature space and frequency domain. In this paper, we propose a novel frequency guidance (FG) framework for image dehazing, which contains a recurrent frequency enhancement (RFE) module and a reconstruction module. To begin with, we develop a multi-scale decomposition (MD) block to separate the feature map into high-frequency and low-frequency components. Subsequently, both components are enhanced using the same network guided by the attention map, but with different weights. In addition to enhancing the frequency information within the feature space, we introduce a Fourier frequency loss (FFL) to provide guidance in the frequency domain, obtained via the fast Fourier transform. Extensive experiments demonstrate that our method achieves state-of-the-art performance on multiple dehazing datasets.

Keywords: Image dehazing · Frequency guidance · Recurrent frequency enhancement · Fourier frequency loss

1 Introduction

The presence of fog has a detrimental effect on many computer vision tasks, such as object detection, semantic segmentation, *etc.* Therefore, it is of great significance to improve the performance of image dehazing. Single image dehazing aims to restore a clear image from a hazy image, and this process is modeled as an atmospheric scattering model [20] by researchers as follows:

$$I(x) = J(x)t(x) + A(1 - t(x)), \tag{1}$$

where $I(x)$ and $J(x)$ represent the hazy image and the haze-free image, respectively. A is the global atmospheric light, and $t(x)$ is the transmission map determined by scattering coefficient of the atmosphere β and scene depth $d(x)$, which can be specifically formulated as $t(x) = e^{-\beta d(x)}$.

Single image dehazing methods can be roughly divided into prior-based methods and learning-based methods. Prior-based image dehazing mainly depends

H. Lu et al. (Eds.): ICIG 2023, LNCS 14355, pp. 216–228, 2023.
https://doi.org/10.1007/978-3-031-46305-1_18

on priors (*e.g.*, dark channel prior and color attenuation prior) and atmospheric scattering model. Learning-based image dehazing leverages CNN or ViT to learn the translation from hazy image to dehazed image or the estimation of A and $t(x)$ in the atmospheric scattering model. Although these methods have good performance on image dehazing, they did not consider the decay of frequency information during image dehazing, leading to unbridgeable gap between dehazed image and ground truth. In the process of image dehazing, the frequency information has some degree of attenuation either in the feature space or in the frequency domain of the image itself. As shown in Fig. 1, we use the Gaussian blur to separate the clean image and the hazy image into high and low frequencies respectively, and it can be seen that the presence of fog destroys the high-frequency information that describes the edge and the low-frequency information that represents the texture. Hence, it is reasonable to provide frequency guidance for image dehazing.

To solve these problems, we propose a frequency guidance (FG) framework containing a recurrent frequency enhancement (RFE) module. Firstly, we divide the feature map extracted from input hazy image into a high-frequency map and a low-frequency map by a multi-scale decomposition (MD) block, which mainly consists of convolutions with different kernel sizes. In the frequency space of an image, information exists in the form of different frequencies. Similarly, the feature map can also be viewed as consisting of the high-frequency map describing the details and the low-frequency map representing the global texture. We enhance the high-frequency map and the low-frequency map separately with the same network but different weights. Both the decomposition and enhancement for frequency information are performed recurrently.

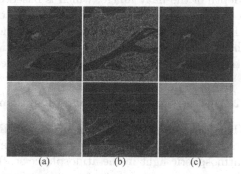

(a)   (b)   (c)

Fig. 1. Visual frequency information obtained by Gaussian blur on the RS-Haze dataset. (a) Clear image & Hazy image, (b) High-frequency component, and (c) Low-frequency component.

Also, we introduce a Fourier frequency loss (FFL), which is designed to assist the frequency enhancement. Different from the RFE module related to the high-frequency feature and low-frequency feature, FFL focuses on differences in frequency domain of the image itself. The FFL is calculated from the phase and amplitude obtained by the fast Fourier transform.

In summary, the main contributions of our work are as follows:

- We develop a recurrent frequency enhancement (RFE) module to recurrently decompose and enhance the frequency information in the feature space.
- We propose a Fourier frequency loss (FFL) calculated by the fast Fourier transform in order to provide the guidance in the frequency domain.

- Extensive experiments demonstrate that our work outperforms state-of-the-art methods on multiple dehazing datasets.

2 Related Work

2.1 Prior-Based Image Dehazing

The prior-based methods mainly depend on priors and atmospheric scattering model. He *et al.* [12] proposed the dark channel prior (DCP) to estimate the transmission map, which is based on the observation that most non-sky patches in haze-free images contain some pixels which have very low intensities in at least one color channel. Several methods [13] have been proposed to refine the DCP. Zhu *et al.* [30] proposed the color attenuation prior to model the scene depth of the hazy image, which is based on the assumption that the brightness of the image increases with the increase of haze but the saturation is opposite. There are many other prior-based methods [9]. However, the performance of haze removal is poor only depending on various priors and the estimation of transmission map and global atmospheric light.

2.2 Learning-Based Image Dehazing

The learning-based methods leverage CNN or ViT to learn the translation from hazy image to dehazed image or the estimation of transmission map and global atmospheric light in the atmospheric scattering model. Some methods [16] have been proposed to inject the atmospheric scattering model into the network in order to learn the estimation of transmission map and global atmospheric light. Park *et al.* [21] proposed an end-to-end network based on GAN, and there are similar methods [8]. As ViT has achieved good performance on various computer vision tasks, some methods [11,25] based on ViT have been proposed. Although a few methods [7,10] consider frequency as a kind of prior, they do not notice the attenuation of frequency information in feature space and frequency domain during image dehazing.

3 Method

In this section, we introduce our frequency guidance (FG) framework for image dehazing in Fig. 2. The high and low frequency information in the feature space needs to be decomposed and separately enhanced. To achieve this goal, we develop a recurrent frequency enhancement (RFE) module that contains a multi-scale decomposition (MD) block. In addition, we propose a Fourier frequency loss (FFL) calculated by the fast Fourier transform to compute the difference in frequency domain.

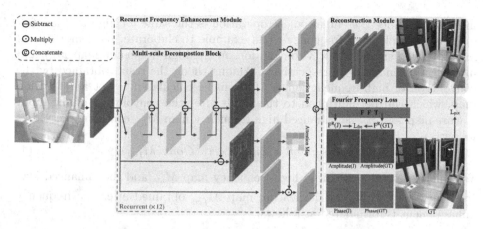

Fig. 2. The pipeline of our FG framework. It consists of a yellow RFE module and a green reconstruction module. The RFE module contains a pink MD block designed for frequency separation and a block to enhance both high-frequency and low-frequency components of the feature map. The gray FFL denotes a Fourier frequency loss for enhancing the information in frequency domain. (Color figure online)

3.1 Recurrent Frequency Enhancement

As shown in Fig. 2, our proposed FG framework contains a MD block which naturally decomposes low and high frequencies in the feature space. The high frequency information of a image mainly represents the details like edges and low frequency information describes global texture and color. Similarly, the output feature maps of a convolutional layer can also be decomposed into high-frequency maps and low-frequency maps. Inspired by the deep contrastive network [29] designed for depth super-resolution, we get different frequency components with high quality shown in Fig. 3 (b) and (c) by the MD block. Given a feature map M_{fea} extracted from input hazy image, we use convolutions with different kernel sizes to obtain high-frequency map M_{hf}, which extracts accurate and complete edge information. There are three stages to obtain the high-frequency map, which are identical except for the size of the convolution kernels, and within a stage the size of the convolution kernels is also different denoted as k and k'. The first stage can be expressed as follows:

$$M_{hf} = Sigmoid(ReLU(Conv_k(M_{fea})) - ReLU(Conv_{k'}(M_{fea}))), \quad (2)$$

For the second and the third stage, the input is the output high-frequency map of the previous stage.

Then the low-frequency map M_{lf} is calculated by subtracting the high-frequency map from input feature map M_{fea}:

$$M_{lf} = M_{fea} - M_{hf}, \quad (3)$$

After MD block, we get different frequency components with high quality. Both high-frequency map M_{hf} and low-frequency map M_{lf} will be fed into enhancement block. Since the enhancement operation is the same for high and low frequencies, we take high frequency as an example to elaborate. As demonstrated in Fig. 2, we perform a 3×3 convolution on the high-frequency map M_{hf} and input feature map M_{fea}, respectively. Among them, the result obtained by the convolution of high-frequency map M_{hf} can be calculated to get an attention map, which can be multiplied to the result after the convolution of the input feature map M_{fea}. The enhanced high-frequency map M'_{hf} can be expressed as follows:

$$M'_{hf} = Sigmoid(Conv(M_{hf})) \cdot Conv(M_{fea}), \tag{4}$$

We concatenate the enhanced high-frequency map M'_{hf} and the enhanced low-frequency map M'_{lf}, and the feature map M'_{fea} obtained after the frequency enhancement is formulated as follows:

$$M'_{fea} = Concat(Conv(M'_{hf}), Conv(M'_{lf})), \tag{5}$$

As shown by the red dashed line in Fig. 2, number of recurrences is set to 12 for both decomposition and enhancement in order to make the frequency enhancement more thorough. The RFE module provides an accurate frequency guidance, that is, the feature representation as the output of the RFE module is richer shown in Fig. 3 (d) and (e), which is beneficial for the reconstruction in the next stage.

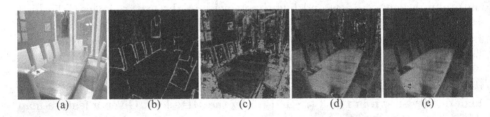

Fig. 3. Visual feature maps. (a) Hazy image, (b) High-frequency map obtained by MD block, (c) Low-frequency map obtained by MD block, (d) Feature map as input to the RFE module, and (e) Feature map as output of the RFE module.

3.2   Fourier Frequency Loss

Different from the RFE module related to the frequency information in the feature space, our proposed FFL focuses on frequency domain. Considering the limitation of pixel domain, we use fast Fourier transform (FFT) to translate the image from pixel domain to frequency domain. We apply FFT on a image I of size $H \times W$:

$$F(I)(u, v) = \frac{1}{HW} \sum_{h=0}^{H-1} \sum_{w=0}^{W-1} e^{-j2\pi(\frac{hu}{H} + \frac{wv}{W})} \cdot I(h, w), \tag{6}$$

where $u = 0, ..., H - 1$, $v = 0, ..., W - 1$.

The frequency domain $F(I)(u, v)$ of the image I can be denoted as:

$$F(I)(u, v) = Re(I)(u, v) + jIm(I)(u, v), \tag{7}$$

where $Re(I)(u, v)$ and $Im(I)(u, v)$ denote the real and imaginary parts of $F(I)(u, v)$, respectively.

The real and imaginary parts can be used to calculate the amplitude $A(I)(u, v)$ and phase $P(I)(u, v)$ formulated as:

$$A(I)(u, v) = [Re^2(I)(u, v) + Im^2(I)(u, v)]^{\frac{1}{2}}, \tag{8}$$

$$P(I)(u, v) = \tan^{-1}(Im(I)(u, v)/Re(I)(u, v)), \tag{9}$$

Inspired by the reconstruction loss in the Fourier space [2] designed for image translation, we convert the complex number domain to the real number domain and use a logarithmic function for stable training. In addition, we scale the radian value of the phase to (0,1] as the coefficient multiplied by the logarithmic term. Obviously, we take both amplitude and phase into account to fully enhance the frequency information:

$$F^R(I) = \alpha \cdot \log(\sqrt{Re^2(I)(u, v) + Im^2(I)(u, v) + \epsilon}), \tag{10}$$

$$\alpha = P(I)(u, v)_{\sim(0,1]}, \tag{11}$$

where $\epsilon = 1 \times 10^{-8}$ is an additional term for numerical stability.

We calculate the frequency information $F^R(J)$ and $F^R(GT)$ of the dehazed image J and ground truth GT, respectively, and the Fourier frequency loss computed by L1 loss is defined as:

$$Loss_{fre} = \left\| F^R(J) - F^R(GT) \right\|_1, \tag{12}$$

3.3   Training Loss

In addition to calculating the difference in the frequency domain using FFL, we also measure the pixel-level distinction by $Loss_{pix}$, which is computed by L1 loss between the dehazed image J and ground truth GT:

$$Loss_{pix} = \left\| J - GT \right\|_1, \tag{13}$$

The total training loss function is a weighted sum of $Loss_{pix}$ and $Loss_{fre}$ denoted as:

$$Loss = Loss_{pix} + \lambda Loss_{fre}, \tag{14}$$

where λ is the weight coefficient and set to 1 empirically.

4   Experiment

In this section, we perform quantitative and visual comparisons with the state-of-the-art methods on the RESIDE [17], Haze-4K [19] and RS-Haze [25] datasets. In addition, we conduct ablation studies to demonstrate the effectiveness of the key modules in our FG framework.

4.1   Experimental Setting

Datasets. We evaluate the proposed method on the RESIDE-IN, RESIDE-6K, Haze-4K and RS-Haze datasets. For the RESIDE-IN dataset, we use the ITS with 13,990 image pairs as the training set and the indoor set with 500 image pairs of the SOTS as the test set. RESIDE-6K mixes 3,000 image pairs from ITS and 3,000 image pairs from OTS for training and uses both indoor set with 500 image pairs and outdoor set with 500 image pairs of the SOTS for testing. Also as a synthetic dataset, Haze-4K is more realistic than RESIDE. Haze-4K contains 4,000 image pairs, of which there are 3,000 in the training set and 1,000 in the test set. RS-Haze is a remote sensing dehazing dataset, which contains 54,000 image pairs, of which there are 51,300 in the training set and 2,700 in the test set.

Implementation Details. Our FG framework is implemented by PyTorch with 4-card RTX-3090. We use ADAM [15] optimizer with $\beta_1 = 0.9$ and $\beta_2 = 0.999$. The initial learning rate is set to 9×10^{-4}, and the learning rate is adjusted by the cosine annealing strategy [14].

4.2   Quantitative Comparison

Table 1 shows the quantitative comparison with SOTA methods on multiple datasets. It can be observed that the proposed FG framework outperforms the SOTA methods with highest PSNR and SSIM scores. When evaluated on the RESIDE-IN and Haze-4K datasets, our method exhibits a PSNR increase of approximately 2 points compared to DEA-Net [4], which was identified as having the highest metrics among other methods. Despite FFA-Net [22] being the best-performing method on the RESIDE-6K and RS-Haze datasets among previous approaches, our method achieves superior PSNR and SSIM scores.

The quantitative comparison demonstrates that our method achieves superior metrics on all four datasets. Since high-frequency and low-frequency components represent different information in the image, providing high-frequency guidance is helpful in removing heavy fog, while low-frequency guidance is more effective in dissipating lighter fog. Although the four datasets used in our experiments are synthetic, they exhibit varying concentrations of fog, thereby demonstrating the robustness of frequency guidance.

4.3   Visual Comparison

We provide the visual comparison with SOTA methods on the RESIDE-IN dataset in Fig. 4. According to the region marked by the red box in Fig. 4, we can see that the color and illumination of the dehazed images of our FG framework are closer to those of ground truth, while other methods suffer from color distortion. The comparison on the RESIDE-6K dataset is shown in Fig. 5. Our method has much less residual fog than other methods. Figure 6 shows the visual

Table 1. Quantitative comparison with SOTA methods on multiple datasets.

Methods	RESIDE-IN		RESIDE-6K		Haze-4K		RS-Haze	
	PSNR	SSIM	PSNR	SSIM	PSNR	SSIM	PSNR	SSIM
(TPAMI'10) DCP [12]	16.62	0.818	17.88	0.816	14.01	0.760	17.86	0.734
(TIP'16) DehazeNet [1]	19.82	0.821	21.02	0.870	19.12	0.840	23.16	0.816
(ECCV'16) MSCNN [23]	19.84	0.833	20.31	0.863	14.01	0.510	22.80	0.823
(ICCV'17) AOD-Net [16]	20.51	0.816	20.27	0.855	17.15	0.830	24.90	0.830
(CVPR'18) GFN [24]	22.30	0.880	23.52	0.905	–	–	29.24	0.910
(WACV'19) GCANet [3]	30.23	0.980	25.09	0.923	–	–	34.41	0.949
(ICCV'19) GDNet [18]	32.16	0.984	25.86	0.944	23.29	0.930	36.40	0.960
(CVPR'20) MSBDN [5]	33.67	0.985	28.56	0.966	22.99	0.850	38.57	0.965
(ECCV'20) PFDN [6]	32.68	0.976	28.15	0.962	–	–	36.04	0.955
(AAAI'20) FFA-Net [22]	36.39	0.989	29.96	0.973	26.96	0.950	39.39	0.969
(CVPR'21) AECR-Net [27]	37.17	0.990	28.52	0.964	–	–	35.69	0.959
(ECCV'22) PMNet [28]	38.41	0.990	–	–	33.49	0.980	–	–
(Arxiv'22) gUNet-T [26]	37.99	0.993	29.54	0.972	31.60	0.984	38.80	0.967
(Arxiv'23) DEA-Net [4]	41.31	0.995	–	–	34.25	0.990	–	–
Ours	43.39	0.997	30.37	0.975	36.05	0.992	39.91	0.972

comparison of multiple methods on the Haze-4K dataset. Obviously, compared with other methods, our FG framework does not have artifacts, especially for white objects such as the cabinet door marked with red box in the second row of images. As for the RS-Haze dataset, it is a remote sensing dehazing dataset in which each image describes a large scene, so we enlarge the details of the images as shown in Fig. 7. We pick gUNet-T [26], which performs well among the other methods, for comparison. It can be seen that for scenes affected by heavy fog, our method recovers better.

The visual comparison confirms the effectiveness of the proposed FG framework. Our method enhances high-frequency information, which is critical for highlighting edges. Thick fog often damages the edge information in the image, and therefore enhancing the high-frequency information proves beneficial in thick fog removal. On the other hand, low-frequency information represents global texture and color, and enhancing it helps alleviate issues of color distortion and residual fog.

4.4 Ablation Study

Effect of RFE Module. Table 2 presents ablation studies of the RFE module and FFL in our FG framework. The proposed RFE module is used to decompose the frequency information into high and low components and enhance them. The initial row in Table 2 illustrates the baseline model, which employs an end-to-end approach to dehazing without any frequency guidance. The second row in the table has a large increase in PSNR and SSIM compared to the first row, indicating that the RFE module can significantly improve the performance of baseline. While the distribution of fog in the RESIDE-IN and Haze-4K datasets varies, quantitative metrics indicate a significant improvement, highlighting the universal applicability of the RFE module.

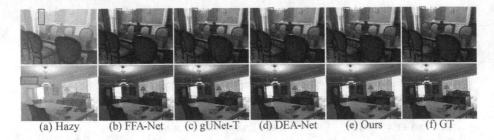

(a) Hazy   (b) FFA-Net   (c) gUNet-T   (d) DEA-Net   (e) Ours   (f) GT

Fig. 4. Visual comparison on the RESIDE-IN dataset. (Color figure online)

(a) Hazy   (b) DCP   (c) GCANet   (d) gUNet-T   (e) Ours   (f) GT

Fig. 5. Visual comparison on the RESIDE-6K dataset. (Color figure online)

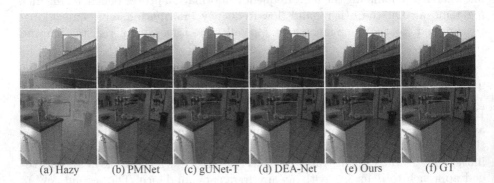

(a) Hazy   (b) PMNet   (c) gUNet-T   (d) DEA-Net   (e) Ours   (f) GT

Fig. 6. Visual comparison on the Haze-4K dataset. (Color figure online)

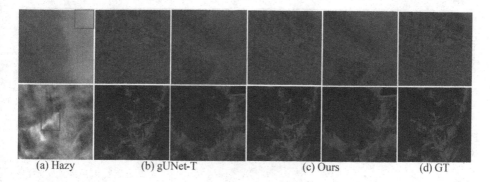

(a) Hazy   (b) gUNet-T   (c) Ours   (d) GT

Fig. 7. Visual comparison on the RS-Haze dataset. (Color figure online)

Effect of FFL. The proposed FFL aims to enhance the frequency information obtained by the fast Fourier transform. The third row in Table 2 shows a significant improvement in both PSNR and SSIM compared to the second row, thus confirming the effectiveness of FFL. The RFE module enhances the frequency information in the feature space, while the FFL provides guidance to the model for greater precision and accuracy in the frequency domain. The second and third rows in Table 2 show that both the RFE module and the FFL are essential.

Number of Recurrences. In order to investigate the effect of different number of recurrences of RFE on the experimental results, we conduct ablation studies on the Haze-4K dataset, as shown in Fig. 8. It can be found that the performance of the proposed FG framework increases with the increase of the number of recurrences. When the number of recurrences is greater than 12, the performance of the method improves slowly but the computational cost and the number of parameters increase significantly, so we choose to set the number of recurrences to 12. It proves that frequency information with higher quality helps to obtain more accurate frequency guidance, which is more beneficial for subsequent reconstruction.

Table 2. Ablation study of the FG framework on the RESIDE-IN and Haze-4K datasets.

Model	RESIDE-IN		Haze-4K	
	PSNR↑	SSIM↑	PSNR↑	SSIM↑
baseline	39.67	0.995	32.48	0.986
baseline + RFE	41.28	0.996	33.22	0.988
baseline + RFE + FFL	**43.39**	**0.997**	**36.05**	**0.992**

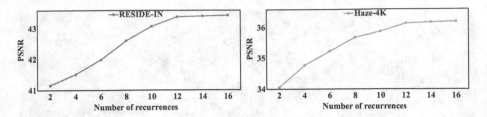

Fig. 8. Ablation study of the RFE module with different number of recurrences on the RESIDE-IN and Haze-4K datasets.

5   Conclusion

In this paper, we proposed a novel frequency guidance (FG) framework for image dehazing. The proposed FG framework consists of a recurrent frequency enhancement (RFE) module and a reconstruction module. The RFE module contains a multi-scale decomposition (MD) block for frequency separation and a frequency enhancement block. Different from the RFE module which considers frequency information in the feature space, the proposed Fourier frequency loss (FFL) focuses on the frequency information of the image itself in frequency domain. In addition, the FFL uses both amplitude and phase obtained by the fast Fourier transform. Extensive experiments on multiple dehazing datasets demonstrate the good performance of our framework compared to the state-of-the-art methods.

References

1. Cai, B., Xu, X., Jia, K., Qing, C., Tao, D.: DehazeNet: an end-to-end system for single image haze removal. IEEE Trans. Image Process. **25**(11), 5187–5198 (2016)
2. Cai, M., Zhang, H., Huang, H., Geng, Q., Li, Y., Huang, G.: Frequency domain image translation: more photo-realistic, better identity-preserving. In: Proceedings of the IEEE/CVF International Conference on Computer Vision, pp. 13930–13940 (2021)
3. Chen, D., et al.: Gated context aggregation network for image dehazing and deraining. In: 2019 IEEE Winter conference on Applications of Computer Vision, pp. 1375–1383. IEEE (2019)
4. Chen, Z., He, Z., Lu, Z.M.: DEA-Net: Single image dehazing based on detail-enhanced convolution and content-guided attention. arXiv preprint arXiv:2301.04805 (2023)
5. Dong, H., et al.: Multi-scale boosted dehazing network with dense feature fusion. In: Proceedings of the IEEE/CVF Conference on Computer Vision and Pattern Recognition, pp. 2157–2167 (2020)
6. Dong, J., Pan, J.: Physics-based feature dehazing networks. In: Vedaldi, A., Bischof, H., Brox, T., Frahm, J.-M. (eds.) ECCV 2020. LNCS, vol. 12375, pp. 188–204. Springer, Cham (2020). https://doi.org/10.1007/978-3-030-58577-8_12
7. Dong, Y., Liu, Y., Zhang, H., Chen, S., Qiao, Y.: FD-GAN: generative adversarial networks with fusion-discriminator for single image dehazing. In: Proceedings of the AAAI Conference on Artificial Intelligence. vol. 34, pp. 10729–10736 (2020)

8. Fan, J., Guo, F., Qian, J., Li, X., Li, J., Yang, J.: Non-aligned supervision for real image dehazing. arXiv preprint arXiv:2303.04940 (2023)
9. Fattal, R.: Dehazing using color-lines. ACM Trans. Graph. **34**(1), 1–14 (2014)
10. Fu, M., Liu, H., Yu, Y., Chen, J., Wang, K.: DW-GAN: a discrete wavelet transform GAN for nonhomogeneous dehazing. In: Proceedings of the IEEE/CVF Conference on Computer Vision and Pattern Recognition, pp. 203–212 (2021)
11. Guo, C.L., Yan, Q., Anwar, S., Cong, R., Ren, W., Li, C.: Image dehazing transformer with transmission-aware 3D position embedding. In: Proceedings of the IEEE/CVF Conference on Computer Vision and Pattern Recognition, pp. 5812–5820 (2022)
12. He, K., Sun, J., Tang, X.: Single image haze removal using dark channel prior. IEEE Trans. Pattern Anal. Mach. Intell. **33**(12), 2341–2353 (2010)
13. He, K., Sun, J., Tang, X.: Guided image filtering. IEEE Trans. Pattern Anal. Mach. Intell. **35**(6), 1397–1409 (2012)
14. He, T., Zhang, Z., Zhang, H., Zhang, Z., Xie, J., Li, M.: Bag of tricks for image classification with convolutional neural networks. In: Proceedings of the IEEE/CVF Conference on Computer Vision and Pattern Recognition, pp. 558–567 (2019)
15. Kingma, D.P., Ba, J.: Adam: A method for stochastic optimization. arXiv preprint arXiv:1412.6980 (2014)
16. Li, B., Peng, X., Wang, Z., Xu, J., Feng, D.: AOD-Net: all-in-one dehazing network. In: Proceedings of the IEEE/CVF International Conference on Computer Vision, pp. 4770–4778 (2017)
17. Li, B., et al.: Benchmarking single-image dehazing and beyond. IEEE Trans. Image Process. **28**(1), 492–505 (2018)
18. Liu, X., Ma, Y., Shi, Z., Chen, J.: GridDehazeNet: attention-based multi-scale network for image dehazing. In: Proceedings of the IEEE/CVF International Conference on Computer Vision, pp. 7314–7323 (2019)
19. Liu, Y., et al.: From synthetic to real: Image dehazing collaborating with unlabeled real data. In: Proceedings of the 29th ACM International Conference on Multimedia, pp. 50–58 (2021)
20. Nayar, S.K., Narasimhan, S.G.: Vision in bad weather. In: Proceedings of the IEEE/CVF International Conference on Computer Vision. vol. 2, pp. 820–827. IEEE (1999)
21. Park, J., Han, D.K., Ko, H.: Fusion of heterogeneous adversarial networks for single image dehazing. IEEE Trans. Image Process. **29**, 4721–4732 (2020)
22. Qin, X., Wang, Z., Bai, Y., Xie, X., Jia, H.: FFA-Net: feature fusion attention network for single image dehazing. In: Proceedings of the AAAI Conference on Artificial Intelligence. vol. 34, pp. 11908–11915 (2020)
23. Ren, W., Liu, S., Zhang, H., Pan, J., Cao, X., Yang, M.-H.: Single image dehazing via multi-scale convolutional neural networks. In: Leibe, B., Matas, J., Sebe, N., Welling, M. (eds.) ECCV 2016. LNCS, vol. 9906, pp. 154–169. Springer, Cham (2016). https://doi.org/10.1007/978-3-319-46475-6_10
24. Ren, W., et al.: Gated fusion network for single image dehazing. In: Proceedings of the IEEE/CVF Conference on Computer Vision and Pattern Recognition, pp. 3253–3261 (2018)
25. Song, Y., He, Z., Qian, H., Du, X.: Vision transformers for single image dehazing. arXiv preprint arXiv:2204.03883 (2022)
26. Song, Y., Zhou, Y., Qian, H., Du, X.: Rethinking performance gains in image dehazing networks. arXiv preprint arXiv:2209.11448 (2022)

27. Wu, H., et al.: Contrastive learning for compact single image dehazing. In: Proceedings of the IEEE/CVF Conference on Computer Vision and Pattern Recognition, pp. 10551–10560 (2021)

28. Ye, T., et al.: Perceiving and modeling density is all you need for image dehazing. arXiv preprint arXiv:2111.09733 (2021)

29. Yuan, J., Jiang, H., Li, X., Qian, J., Li, J., Yang, J.: Recurrent structure attention guidance for depth super-resolution. arXiv preprint arXiv:2301.13419 (2023)

30. Zhu, Q., Mai, J., Shao, L.: A fast single image haze removal algorithm using color attenuation prior. IEEE Trans. Image Process. **24**(11), 3522–3533 (2015)

Energy-Efficient Robotic Arm Control Based on Differentiable Spiking Neural Networks

Xuanhe Wang, Jianxiong Tang, and Jianhuang Lai[✉]

School of Computer Science and Engineering, Sun Yat-Sen University, Guangzhou,
People's Republic of China
{wangxh223,tangjx6}@mail2.sysu.edu.cn,
stsljh@mail.sysu.edu.cn

Abstract. Robotic arm control using deep neural networks (DNNs) has gained attention due to its high precision and flexibility, but requires significant computational resources and results in massive energy consumption. In contrast, spiking neural networks (SNNs) are energy-efficient, but their discretized activation function and gradient mismatch pose challenges. To address these issues, this paper proposes a hardware-independent control scheme for robotic arms based on differentiable SNNs (DSNNs). Our approach utilizes binary spike sequences generated by the DSNN to significantly reduce the cost of inference. The output of spiking neurons in DSNNs is refactored, enabling direct backpropagation training while gradually approaching a pulse function. In addition, a hand gesture dataset is created as the controlling input. Simulations and experiments on a virtual robotic arm platform demonstrate that our approach achieves high efficiency and accuracy in controlling the robotic arm with gestures, while consuming less energy compared to other methods.

Keywords: Robotic Arm Control · Spiking Neural Network · Deep Learning

1 Introduction

With the advent of intelligent manufacturing, robotic arms have emerged as indispensable tools for industrial production, such as assembly tasks [3], spray painting [10], machine loading [2]. A robotic arm consists of a sequence of joints, articulations, and manipulators [8] that collaborate to emulate the functionality of a human arm. Traditional control methods for robotic arm operation are typically based on pre-set programs, which exhibit limited scalability when the device operates in diverse environments. In recent years, deep learning has made significant breakthroughs in various fields [12,18,24], and convolutional neural networks (CNNs) have notably enhanced the performance of robotic arm control [7,21]. Nonetheless, CNN-based controls demand abundant computational resources and rely on high energy costs. To optimize the advantages of industrial production, it is imperative to develop energy-efficient neural models for robotic arm control.

Inspired by the integrate-and-fire mechanism of biological neurons, spiking neural networks (SNNs) present a promising model for low-power hardware, especially for neuromorphic chips [11,14]. Integrate-and-Fire (IF) neurons [19] and Leaky Integrate-and-Fire (LIF) neurons [9,22] are two widely used spiking neurons for SNN modeling. Both IF and LIF neurons integrate input stimuli to the membrane potential (MP) over time. If the accumulated MP exceeds the firing threshold, the IF/LIF neuron generates a binary spike. Otherwise, the neuron outputs 0. Consequently, the SNN transmits information using binary spiking sequences, which yields computational efficiency for inference. Despite the energy-saving benefits of spiking neuron binary outputs, the non-differentiability of these neurons hinders the use of the backpropagation (BP) algorithm for training SNNs. Several techniques have been developed to enable SNN learning. Recent proposals have focused on either converting a pre-trained artificial neural network (ANN) to its SNN version (ANN-to-SNN or ANN2SNN), or directly training the SNN using spike-based backpropagation (BP) algorithms [4,13]. Pre-trained ANN to SNN conversions benefit from the generalization of the ANN and achieve considerable performance in many cases. However, these conversions require spiking neurons to simulate the ANN activation, resulting in numerous time steps for inference. Although normalization techniques and code mechanisms have been proposed to decrease the time steps, the inference of many ANN2SNN conversions is still slow. Spike-based BP introduces surrogate gradients to enable backpropagation for spiking neurons, allowing SNNs to be trained using backpropagation through time (BPTT) algorithms [1,20]. Thanks to the spatial-temporal dynamics captured by spike-based training, SNNs require only a few time steps for inference. However, spike-based BP training is sensitive to the chosen surrogate gradient, and using an unsuitable gradient may result in the mismatching gradient problem [5,15].

In this paper, we propose a novel approach to enable energy-efficient control of robotic arms by designing a differentiable spiking neural network (DSNN). To achieve this, we utilize the differentiable IF (DIF) neuron, which approximates the binary spike during training, eliminating the need for any surrogate gradient during training. We then model the control problem of the robotic arm based on a gesture dataset and the DSNN. The low spike rate of the DSNN enables energy-efficient control of the robotic arm while achieving optimal performance.

The main contributions of this paper are summarized below:

- To control the robotic arm, we propose a DSNN that extracts spiking features from a gesture image and generates a decision signal. We also design a gesture dataset that is used to train and evaluate the performance of the DSNN in controlling the robotic arm. The decision signal generated by the DSNN is then used to control the behavior of the robotic arm.
- Experiment results demonstrate that the proposed DSNN achieves complete performance and saves more energy compared to the ANN, ANN2SNN, and spike-based BP models.

2   Related Work

2.1   Integrate-and-Fire Neuron

Actually, for the purpose of designing a differentiable spiking neural network (DSNN), we use a different type of spiking neuron, which is called differentiable IF (DIF) neuron. Supposing W^n and $o^{t,n-1}$ are the synaptic weights and spiking input of layer n, the dynamic of the IF neuron can be described as:

$$u^{t+1,n} = u^{t,n}(1 - o^{t,n}) + W^n o^{t,n-1}, \tag{1}$$

$$o^{t,n} = \begin{cases} 1, & \text{if } u^{t,n} > V_{th}. \\ 0, & \text{otherwise.} \end{cases} \tag{2}$$

If the accumulated MPs $u^{t,n}$ exceed the threshold V_{th}, the IF neuron will generate a spike $o^{t,n}$ at t. Otherwise, the IF will be inactive, and $u^{t,n}$ will be integrated into the accumulated MPs of $t+1$-th step. Benefiting from the binary outputs of the IF neuron, the SNNs achieve energy-efficient for inference. In addition, the spatial-temporal dynamics of IF neurons enable SNNs to capture the features of the input through time and space. However, the binary property of the spiking features disables the popular BP training for SNNs.

2.2   Spike-Based BP Training

The gradient of spiking outputs with respect to the MPs is almost zero everywhere, which disables the use of backpropagation (BP) training for SNNs. As a result, the spike-based BP training introduces surrogate gradient techniques to enable gradient calculation for IF neurons. The most popular spike-based BP algorithm for SNNs is the Spatial-Temporal BP (STBP) training, which designs a rectangle function to approximate the gradient of spikes with respect to the MPs:

$$\frac{\partial o^{t,n}}{\partial u^{t,n}} = \frac{1}{a} Sign(|\boldsymbol{u}^{t,n} - V_{th}| < \frac{a}{2}), \tag{3}$$

where $a > 0$ is a scalar factor to adjust the gradient. Many surrogate gradients have been designed to enable BP training for SNNs [6,16,23]. However, it is important to note that spike-based BP training is sensitive to the choice of surrogate gradient. An unsuitable surrogate gradient may result in vanishing or exploding gradients, which can lead to poor performance of SNNs.

3   Approaches

In this section, we outline our approach for controlling the robotic arm through a differentiable spiking neural network (DSNN). To begin, we focus on the design of the differentiable IF (DIF) neuron. Afterward, we proceed to model the spiking neural networks based on the DIF neurons. Finally, we provide an elaborate description of the training process involved in our approach.

3.1 Differentiable if Neuron

In this section, we introduce the differentiable spike [15] to model the IF neuron in a differentiable manner. Specifically, we relax the outputs of the IF neuron as follows:

$$\tilde{o}^{t,n}(u^{t,n}, e) = \frac{\tanh(e(u^{t,n} - V_{th}))}{2\tanh(eV_{th})} + \frac{1}{2}, \tag{4}$$

where e denotes the training epoch, and $V_{th} > 0$ is the firing threshold. Obviously, Eq. (4) is a smooth function of $(u^{t,n}, e)$ and satisfies the following property:

$$\lim_{e \to +\infty} \tilde{o}^{t,n}(u^{t,n}, e) = \begin{cases} 1, & u^{t,n} > V_{th}, \\ 0.5, & u^{t,n} = V_{th}, \\ 0, & u^{t,n} < V_{th}. \end{cases} \tag{5}$$

Combing Eq. (1) and (4), we obtain the differentiable IF neuron (DIF), and the gradient of $\tilde{o}^{t,n}$ w.r.t $u^{t,n}$ is

$$\frac{\partial \tilde{o}^{t,n}}{\partial u^{t,n}} = \frac{e}{2\tanh(eV_{th})}(1 - \tanh^2(e(u^{t,n} - V_{th}))). \tag{6}$$

Figure 1 presents the relationship between training epoch and the output of DIF neuron, and the gradient of DIF neuron is plot in Fig. 2. As the training epoch increases, the DIF output gradually approaches the Heaviside function.

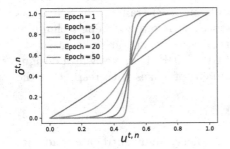

Fig. 1. The output of the DIF neuron.

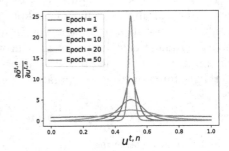

Fig. 2. The gradient of the DIF neuron.

3.2 Differentiable SNN for Robotic Arm Control

The IF/LIF neurons generate the spikes as the features of SNN in every time step. Therefore, Eq. (2) can be regarded as the activation function of SNN at step t. The binary spiking features guarantee that the forward propagation of SNN only involves the float-pointing (FP) addition operations. However, the binary features disable the BP training for SNNs. To address this problem, we design a differentiable SNN (DSNN) by replacing Eq. (2) with Eq. (4) in the training process. Supposing $\mathcal{L}$ is the training loss function for the control of arm robotic, the synaptic weights of layer n in DSNN can be updated by the BPTT:

$$\frac{\partial \mathcal{L}}{\partial W^n} = \sum_{t=1}^{T} \frac{\partial \mathcal{L}}{\partial \tilde{o}^{t,n}} \frac{\partial \tilde{o}^{t,n}}{\partial u^{t,n}} \frac{\partial u^{t,n}}{\partial W^n}$$

$$= \sum_{t=1}^{T} \frac{\partial \mathcal{L}}{\partial \tilde{o}^{t,n}} \frac{\partial \tilde{o}^{t,n}}{\partial u^{t,n}} ((1 - \tilde{o}^{t-1,n}) \frac{\partial u^{t,n}}{\partial u^{t-1,n}} \frac{\partial u^{t-1,n}}{\partial W^n} + \frac{\partial W^n \tilde{o}^{t,n-1}}{\partial W^n}), \quad (7)$$

where T denotes the total inference time steps. The gradient of $\tilde{o}^{t,n}$ w.r.t $u^{t,n}$ is calculated based on Eq. (6) and is changing with the training epoch. Since the output of DIF is an approximation of the spiking outputs when the training epoch is large. Once the training is finished, we replace Eq. (2) with Eq. (4) for inference. Figure 3 presents the architecture of DSNN. The encoder consists of N convolution blocks and a full connection (FC) block and encodes the input image to the features. Then, the last FC layer integrates the features to generate the decision signal, and the robotic arm responds accordingly. The DIF neuron is used to drive the integrate-and-fire network, and batch normalization is applied to remove variation in the convolution outputs. To enlarge the receptive field, we use a max-pooling layer to under-sample the feature maps.

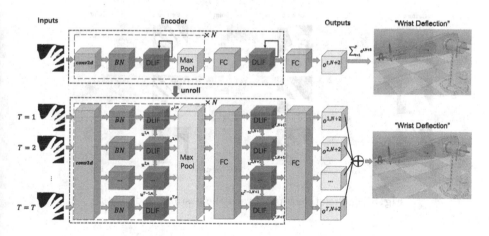

Fig. 3. The architecture of DSNN.

4   Experiments

4.1   PUMA-560 Robotic Arm

We conducted experiments to evaluate the effectiveness of our approach using the Virtual Robot Experimentation Platform (V-REP) and the PUMA-560 multi-joint robot. This robot simulates the basic structure of the human waist to arm and has six joints: waist (joint1), shoulder (joint2), elbow (joint3), wrist flip (joint4), wrist pitch (joint5), and wrist deflection (joint6). The model and joints of the PUMA-560 are shown in Fig. 4.

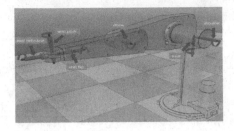

Fig. 4. The PUMA-560 Robotic Arm. The red arrows denotes the active directions of the joints. (Color figure online)

4.2 Dataset

The gesture dataset is composed of 9 gesture classes, including "None", "Start", "Stop", and "Joint1" to "Joint6". These gestures correspond to different joint movements of the PUMA-560 robotic arm, as shown in Fig. 5. The dataset consists of 200 samples for each class, with each sample being a grayscale image of size $28 \times 28 \times 1$. This dataset is used for training and validating the DSNN for controlling the robotic arm through computer vision.

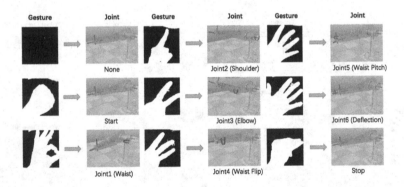

Fig. 5. The relationship between the gestures and joints.

4.3 Experiment Setting

Loss Function. To model the training error between the predictions of DSNN and the ground truth of the joints, we apply the mean square error (MSE) loss for training:

$$\mathcal{L} = \frac{1}{2S} \sum_{i=1}^{S} \| y_i - \frac{1}{T} \sum_{t=1}^{T} \tilde{o}^{t,N+2} \|_2^2, \tag{8}$$

where S is the total number of the training samples, and y_i is the ground truth of sample i. Equation (8) applies the average spiking outputs to predict the control of the joint.

Training Setting. We used a network architecture similar to the one given in Fig. 3. Specifically, we set $N = 2$ and used 3×3 kernels for each convolution layer with 128 output channels. The first FC layer reduced the input features to a $128 \times 4 \times 4$ vector at each time step, and the last FC layer acted as the predictor. During the training process, we set V_{th} to 0.5, applied SGD with a 0.01 learning rate, and trained the DSNN for 15 epochs. The dataset contained $1,800$ samples, and we used 5-fold cross-validation for our experiments.

To validate the effectiveness of our DSNN, we use the following metrics to evaluate the model:

$$\text{Accuracy} = \frac{TP + TN}{TP + TN + FP + FN},$$

$$\text{Precision} = \frac{TP}{TP + FP},$$

$$\text{Recall} = \frac{TP}{TP + FN},$$

and

$$F_1 = \frac{2 \times \text{Precision} \times \text{Recall}}{\text{Precision} + \text{Recall}}$$

where TP, TN, FP, and FN are the samples of true positive, true negative, false positive, and false negative, respectively.

4.4 Performance

In this section, we evaluate the performance of the DSNN using the mentioned metrics and compare it with other models such as ANN, ANN2SNN, LIF-SNN, and IF-SNN with the same network architecture. Table 1 summarizes the experimental results.

According to the experimental results, the DSNN achieves the best metrics among all SNN models. Although the ANN2SNN model outperforms others, except for the DSNN, it requires 100 steps for inference. By setting $T = 20$, the average accuracy of DSNN is 5.85%, 7.07%, and 7.71% higher than that of ANN2SNN, LIF-SNN, and IF-SNN, respectively. Furthermore, when $T = 20$, all metrics of DSNN outperform other SNNs. The confusion matrix of the DSNN with $T = 20$ shown in Fig. 6 demonstrates that the DSNN effectively discriminates the control signal for the robotic arm.

4.5 Energy Analysis

Following [17], we estimate the energy efficiency based on the energy of ANN versus SNNs. The energy is computed based on the layer-wise spike rate and the following equation:

$$\frac{E_{ANN}}{E_{SNN}} = \frac{4.6 \times \sum_{n=1}^{L} \# \, A_{ops,n}}{\sum_{n=1}^{L} \# \, S_{ops,n} \times 0.9}, \tag{9}$$

Table 1. Performance comparison among DSNN, ANN, ANN2SNN, and IF/LIF-SNN

Method	Time Steps	Acc(%)	Pre(%)	Rec(%)	F1(%)
ANN	–	98.86 ± 1.04	87.37 ± 0.81	78.42 ± 1.02	79.26 ± 1.37
IF-SNN	20	89.61 ± 1.18	79.58 ± 0.93	70.47 ± 1.05	72.62 ± 0.78
	100	93.72 ± 1.84	81.44 ± 1.31	71.73 ± 1.4	73.28 ± 1.01
LIF-SNN	20	90.25 ± 0.72	79.38 ± 1.36	69.36 ± 0.96	70.28 ± 0.85
	100	93.80 ± 1.95	81.78 ± 1.17	72.37 ± 1.17	72.89 ± 1.12
ANN2SNN	20	91.47 ± 1.03	80.47 ± 0.89	70.82 ± 1.0	73.46 ± 1.13
	100	95.47 ± 1.02	84.73 ± 1.14	73.20 ± 0.93	76.74 ± 0.94
This Work	5	88.70 ± 1.63	79.36 ± 1.59	70.34 ± 1.21	71.08 ± 1.12
	10	90.82 ± 0.73	81.05 ± 0.98	70.92 ± 1.25	72.40 ± 0.78
	15	93.47 ± 0.73	79.65 ± 1.07	72.33 ± 1.28	73.86 ± 1.42
	20	**97.32±1.75**	**85.47±1.21**	**74.63±0.78**	**77.24±1.17**

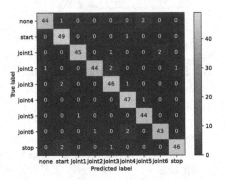

Fig. 6. The confusion matrix of the DSNN with $T = 20$.

where $\# A_{ops,n}$ and $\# S_{ops,n} = SpikeRate \times \# A_{ops,n}$ are the MAC operations of the layer n of ANN and SNN, respectively. In the 45nm CMOS technique, the cost of the MAC operation of SNN is $0.9pJ$ since the SNN only requires additional operations, while the cost of the MAC operation of ANN is $4.6pJ$. The energy comparisons are presented in Table 2, and we report the energy based on the models with the best performance. In most cases, the DSNN achieves the least layer-wise spike rate and the best energy-efficient.

Table 2. The compute energy of ANN versus IF-SNN. LIF-SNN, ANN2SNN, and DSNN.

Method	Layer	Spike Rate(%) ↓	E_{ANN}/E_{SNN} ↑
IF-SNN ($T = 100$)	layer1	3.9	6.86
	layer2	4.21	
	layer3	2.42	
	layer4	3.23	
LIF-SNN ($T = 100$)	layer1	3.84	6.52
	layer2	4.49	
	layer3	**2.38**	
	layer4	3.74	
ANN2SNN ($T = 100$)	layer1	4.12	6.12
	layer2	3.73	
	layer3	3.82	
	layer4	3.42	
This Work ($T = 20$)	layer1	**3.43**	**7.67**
	layer2	**2.52**	
	layer3	3.57	
	layer4	**3.12**	

4.6 Feature Visualization

To show the learning capability of the DSNN, we present the first layer spiking features Fig. 7. We can find that the DSNN captures different patterns from the input images, indicating that the DSNN controls the robotic arm based on various features.

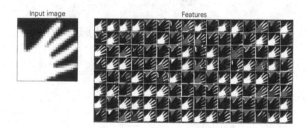

Fig. 7. The spiking features of the 1-st layer of DSNN.

4.7 Convergence

We can observe from Fig. 8 and Fig. 9 that the training and testing losses of all models decrease and eventually converge as the number of training epochs increases. Similarly, the training and testing accuracies of all models increase with the progression of epochs. Notably, the DSNN exhibits faster convergence compared to the other models, which can be attributed to the utilization of DIF neurons. These neurons facilitate the propagation of float features during training, leading to enhanced learning capabilities.

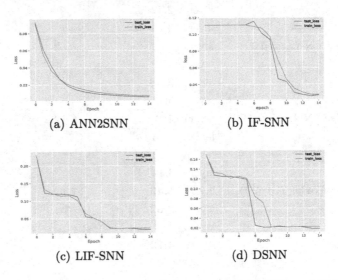

Fig. 8. The loss curves of ANN2SNN, IF-SNN, LIF-SNN, and DSNN.

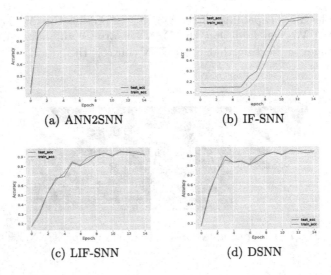

Fig. 9. The accuracy curves of ANN2SNN, IF-SNN, LIF-SNN, and DSNN.

5   Conclusion

In conclusion, our proposed DSNN offers an efficient and effective approach for controlling robotic arms based on computer vision. By leveraging DIF neurons and direct BP training, the DSNN achieves faster convergence and superior performance compared to other SNN models. Furthermore, the DSNN's low energy consumption makes it a compelling choice for practical applications involving robotic arms.

Acknowledgements. This work was supported in part by the Key-Area Research and Development Program of Guangzhou (202007030004).

References

1. Bohnstingl, T., Woźniak, S., Pantazi, A., Eleftheriou, E.: Online spatio-temporal learning in deep neural networks. In: IEEE Transactions on Neural Networks and Learning Systems (2022)
2. Chen, L., Sun, H., Zhao, W., Yu, T.: AI based gravity compensation algorithm and simulation of load end of robotic arm wrist force. Math. Probl. Eng. **2021**(8), 1–11 (2021)
3. Chen, T.Y., Chiu, Y.C., Bi, N., Tsai, R.T.H.: Multi-modal chatbot in intelligent manufacturing. IEEE Access **9**, 82118–82129 (2021)
4. Chen, Y., Qu, H., Zhang, M., Wang, Y.: Deep spiking neural network with neural oscillation and spike-phase information. In: Proceedings of the AAAI Conference on Artificial Intelligence. vol. 35, pp. 7073–7080 (2021)
5. Deng, S., Li, Y., Zhang, S., Gu, S.: Temporal efficient training of spiking neural network via gradient re-weighting. In: International Conference on Learning Representations (2021)
6. Hagenaars, J., Paredes-Vallés, F., De Croon, G.: Self-supervised learning of event-based optical flow with spiking neural networks. In: Advances in Neural Information Processing Systems. vol. 34 (2021)
7. Jeong, J.H., Shim, K.H., Kim, D.J., Lee, S.W.: Brain-controlled robotic arm system based on multi-directional CNN-BiLSTM network using EEG signals. IEEE Trans. Neural Syst. Rehabil. Eng. **28**(5), 1226–1238 (2020)
8. Jie, L., Sen, T., Ghani, N.M., Abas, M.F.: Automatic control of color sorting and pick/place of a 6- DOF robot arm. J. Européen des Systèmes Automatisés **54**, 435–443 (2021)
9. Kamal, N., Singh, J.: A highly scalable junctionless fet leaky integrate-and-fire neuron for spiking neural networks. IEEE Trans. Electron Devices **68**(4), 1633–1638 (2021)
10. Kiran, J.S., Prabhu, S.: Robot nano spray painting-a review. In: IOP Conference Series: Materials Science and Engineering. vol. 912, p. 032044. IOP Publishing (2020)
11. Koo, M., Srinivasan, G., Shim, Y., Roy, K.: sBSNN: stochastic-bits enabled binary spiking neural network with on-chip learning for energy efficient neuromorphic computing at the edge. IEEE Trans. Circuits Syst. I Regul. Pap. **67**(8), 2546–2555 (2020)

12. Lăzăroiu, G., Andronie, M., Iatagan, M., Geamănu, M., Ştefănescu, R., Dijmărescu, I.: Deep learning-assisted smart process planning, robotic wireless sensor networks, and geospatial big data management algorithms in the internet of manufacturing things. ISPRS Int. J. Geo Inf. **11**(5), 277 (2022)

13. Lee, C., Sarwar, S.S., Panda, P., Srinivasan, G., Roy, K.: Enabling spike-based backpropagation for training deep neural network architectures. Front. Neurosci. **14**, 119 (2020)

14. Li, Y., et al.: One transistor one electrolyte-gated transistor based spiking neural network for power-efficient neuromorphic computing system. Adv. Func. Mater. **31**(26), 2100042 (2021)

15. Li, Y., Guo, Y., Zhang, S., Deng, S., Hai, Y., Gu, S.: Differentiable spike: rethinking gradient-descent for training spiking neural networks. Adv. Neural. Inf. Process. Syst. **34**, 23426–23439 (2021)

16. Neftci, E.O., Mostafa, H., Zenke, F.: Surrogate gradient learning in spiking neural networks: bringing the power of gradient-based optimization to spiking neural networks. IEEE Signal Process. Mag. **36**(6), 51–63 (2019)

17. Panda, P., Aketi, S.A., Roy, K.: Toward scalable, efficient, and accurate deep spiking neural networks with backward residual connections, stochastic softmax, and hybridization. Front. Neurosci. **14**, 653 (2020)

18. Park, K.B., Choi, S.H., Lee, J.Y., Ghasemi, Y., Mohammed, M., Jeong, H.: Hands-free human-robot interaction using multimodal gestures and deep learning in wearable mixed reality. IEEE Access **9**, 55448–55464 (2021)

19. Paudel, B.R., Itani, A., Tragoudas, S.: Resiliency of SNN on black-box adversarial attacks. In: 2021 20th IEEE International Conference on Machine Learning and Applications (ICMLA), pp. 799–806. IEEE (2021)

20. Skatchkovsky, N., Jang, H., Simeone, O.: Spiking neural networks-part II: detecting spatio-temporal patterns. IEEE Commun. Lett. **25**(6), 1741–1745 (2021)

21. Sreekar, C., Sindhu, V., Bhuvaneshwaran, S., Bose, S.R., Kumar, V.S.: Positioning the 5-DOF robotic arm using single stage deep CNN model. In: 2021 Seventh International conference on Bio Signals, Images, and Instrumentation (ICBSII), pp. 1–6. IEEE (2021)

22. Yang, J.Q., et al.: Leaky integrate-and-fire neurons based on perovskite memristor for spiking neural networks. Nano Energy **74**, 104828 (2020)

23. Zenke, F., Vogels, T.P.: The remarkable robustness of surrogate gradient learning for instilling complex function in spiking neural networks. Neural Comput. **33**(4), 899–925 (2021)

24. Zuo, C., et al.: Deep learning in optical metrology: a review. Light Sci. Appl. **11**(1), 1–54 (2022)

Uncover the Body: Occluded Person Re-identification via Masked Image Modeling

Kunlun Xu[1,2], Yuxin Peng[1,2], and Jiahuan Zhou[1,2(✉)]

[1] Wangxuan Institute of Computer Technology,
Peking University, Beijing 100871, China
jiahuanzhou@pku.edu.cn
[2] National Key Laboratory for Multimedia Information Processing,
Peking University, Beijing 100871, China

Abstract. Person re-identification (ReID) has attracted tremendous attention and achieved significant progress on holistic data where the whole body of a pedestrian is completely presented. However, in a more realistic scenario where pedestrians are partially occluded, the discriminative ability of the existing ReID methods is severely limited since the visual information of the pedestrians becomes noisy and unreliable. To alleviate this issue, current solutions mostly pay more attention to visible body parts for extracting fine-grained features. Nevertheless, different occluded parts on different images of the same pedestrian always result in inaccuracy matching. In this paper, we propose an Uncover the Body Network (UBN) which exhibits the ability to remove the occlusion and attempt to restore the full body of a pedestrian. The proposed UBN can alleviate the noise brought by occlusions and extract more robust feature representations. To achieve this, we propose a MIM (Masked Image Modeling) based method for its powerful representation of partial images to the whole. Instead of randomly masking the images, we propose a Mask Prediction Module (MPM) to readily locate the occluded patches, and an occlusion-guided masking strategy is adopted to facilitate the learning. Extensive experimental results on both the occluded and holistic ReID benchmarks have demonstrated the superiority of UBN against the state-of-the-art approaches.

Keywords: Occluded Person Re-identification · Masked Image Modeling · Retrieval

1 Introduction

Person Re-Identification (ReID) has played an important role in many practical computer vision tasks such as video surveillance [1], forensic tracking [2], and so on. Over the past years, most of ReID methods [3–6] concentrated on processing holistic data where the whole body of a pedestrian is completely visible. However, in a more realistic scenario where pedestrians are partially occluded by various obstacles, the discriminative ability of the existing ReID methods is

© The Author(s), under exclusive license to Springer Nature Switzerland AG 2023
H. Lu et al. (Eds.): ICIG 2023, LNCS 14355, pp. 241–253, 2023.
https://doi.org/10.1007/978-3-031-46305-1_20

severely limited since the visual information of the pedestrians becomes noisy and unreliable, leading to deteriorated performance for occluded ReID [7,8].

To mitigate the influence of occlusions, various occluded ReID methods [8–11], have been proposed which can be roughly categorized into two groups: keypoint-based methods and feature pyramid-based ones. The former group [9,11] focuses on extracting informative features from the visible keypoint parts estimated by off-the-shelf pose estimation models. The latter group [8,10] aims to extract multi-scale features from both the query and gallery images to alleviate the influence of occlusions. However, both groups rely on the visible person region matching across query and gallery images, which is sensitive to the occlusion distribution between different images.

In this paper, by thoroughly exploring the visible parts of a pedestrian image, we propose to suppress the adverse effects of occlusions by uncovering the occluded parts. Motivated by the recent Masked Image Modeling (MIM) research [12], deep networks have exhibited the superior ability to recover factual visual information only based on the remaining visible parts, even if the proportion of the visible parts is small. Therefore, we propose an Uncover the Body Network (UBN) which exhibits the ability to remove the occlusion and attempt to restore the full body of a pedestrian. A novel Occlusion-aware Mask Prediction Module (MPM) and a Masked Image Reconstruction Module (MIR) are designed accordingly where the MPM can automatically generate mask maps to determine the dropping patches with respect to the occlusion obstacles. Moreover, the proposed MPM utilizes learnable embedding to replace masked patches for mask map generation. As for MIR, it takes the aforementioned masked images as inputs to reconstruct the holistic person images.

Our proposed UBN can readily mitigate the above issues in existing occluded ReID methods. On the one hand, our UBN can benefit the keypoint-based approaches by recovering the occluded parts, which will enhance the ability of pose estimation models and enrich the keypoints for discriminative feature extraction. On the other hand, the proposed UBN will benefit the feature pyramid-based methods by eliminating the adverse influence of occlusion obstacles which can enhance the discriminative ability of the obtained features via recovering reasonable appearance information. Extensive experimental results have demonstrated that our UBN achieves state-of-the-art performance on various ReID benchmarks, exceeding the latest baselines by a large margin. To sum up, our contributions are three-fold:

- A novel occluded ReID model named Uncover the Body Network (UBN) is proposed which consists of a Mask Prediction Module (MPM) and a Masked Image Reconstruction Module (MIR). Thus, the MPM generates mask maps to automatically decide the occluded parts in images for masking and the MIR takes the masked images as inputs to reconstruct reasonable holistic person images.
- To facilitate MPM and MIR learning, four mask supervision strategies are readily designed. Both the subjective and objective evaluation results

demonstrate that all strategies could simultaneously promote the ReID performance and the mask prediction results.

- The conducted extensive experimental experiments on various ReID benchmarks have demonstrated that our UBN achieves state-of-the-art performance against the latest baselines by a large margin.

2   Related Work

2.1   Holistic Person ReID

Person ReID aims to identify the same pedestrian captured by different cameras at different locations and different time. Most existing ReID methods [4,6,13] focus on holistic data where the whole body of a pedestrian is clearly presented. Although performs well on holistic data, they suffer serious performance degradation when they are applied to partial and occluded person images, which indeed appear frequently in a more realistic application scenario. Different from them, our proposed UBN can not only tackle the holistic ReID task, but also makes a breakthrough in the scenario with heavy occlusions.

2.2   Occluded Person ReID

Existing occluded ReID methods either utilize human pose [9,11] or extract the feature pyramid [8,10] to facilitate part-level person matching. However, these methods can not accurately predict the occluded body parts which is not coherent with how humans tackle occlusion scenarios. and most of them are sensitive to fine-grained extra cues and are not robust to variation of occlusions. Compared with the aforementioned methods, In contrast, our proposed UBN manages to remove the occlusion obstacles and uncover the full body. Therefore, a more robust and discriminative feature representation can be obtained.

2.3   Masked Image Modeling

Recently, Masked Image Modeling (MIM) [12,14–18] becomes an effective self-supervised pre-training manner to provide initial weights with strong representation capacity for downstream tasks [15]. The recent works MAE [17] and Sim-MIM [12] have demonstrated that with partial visible patches, an image with complete structural information could be successfully reconstructed. This motivates us that the occluded body parts of a pedestrian could be reconstructed based on the remaining visible parts, which could lead to a complete feature representation for ReID. However, existing MIM approaches aim to recover all the patches in the original images, which means that the occluded patches will keep being occluded in the reconstructed images. Therefore, it's vital to redesign the pipeline that guides the network to reconstruct the human body preferentially.

3   Methodology

Given a query set $Q = \{q_1, q_2, ..., q_n\}$ and a galley set $G = \{g_1, g_2, ..., g_m\}$, the goal of ReID is to compute the match scores of each image in Q and G. For the sake of convenience, we reasonably assume that the width and height of a query or galley image is W and H respectively.

3.1   Algorithm Overview

The overall pipeline of our proposed UBN is demonstrated in Fig. 1. Our model mainly contains three crucial parts including an Occlusion-aware Mask Prediction Module (MPM), a Masked Image Reconstruction Module (MIR), and a TransReID-based feature extractor. More specifically, MPM processes the original occluded images by generating the occlusion-aware mask maps. Then, MIR aims to recover the complete visual appearance according to MPM's input images and predicted masks. Finally, a TransReID-based feature extractor module is adopted to leverage the recovered contextual information from MIR to facilitate feature learning.

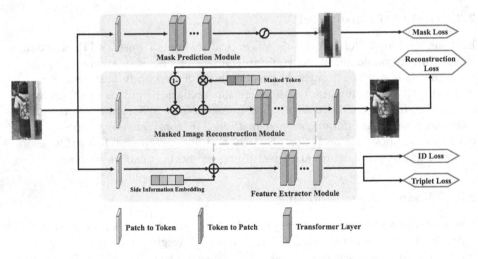

Fig. 1. The overall architecture of our proposed Uncover the Body Network (UBN).

3.2   MPM: Occlusion-Aware Mask Prediction Module

Recall existing MIM methods [12,16,17], all of them randomly mask image patches or pixels and then force the model to reconstruct the masked areas. In occluded ReID, we expect to leverage the visible person parts to predict the occluded body parts. To do so, we propose a Mask Prediction Module (MPM) to learn the occlusion-aware mask maps according to the global context. As illustrated in Fig. 1, the proposed MPM consists of a patch-to-token layer along with multiple transformer layers [3,19] in which the ultimate transformer will generate token-level mask predictions. The patch-to-token operation follows the standard ViT [19] that divides the given image into non-overlapping patches and then maps each patch into a token vector representation, after which the positional information would be added.

3.3   MIR: Masked Image Reconstruction Module

Based on the predicted occlusion-aware mask maps from MPM, our UBN will further recover the occluded patches to complete the holistic person images. Therefore, a Masked Image Reconstruction Module (MIR) is designed for holistic person generation which mainly contains three components: MIR Input, MIR Encoder and MIR Head.

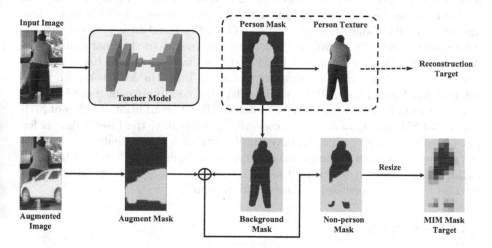

Fig. 2. An example of reconstruction target and MIR mask target generation. The image is from the holistic PRID dataset. The teacher model is a pre-trained instance segmentation model. Person mask is the biggest person mask in the image. Person texture is extracted from the image according to the person mask. Augmented image is generated by pasting a external object and it serves as the input image of MPM and MIR. The Augment mask is the mask map of pasting area. The background mask is the opposite of person mask. Non-person mask is the pixel-wise binary sum of the Augment mask and background mask. MIR mask target is sub-sampled from Non-person mask in order to fit the resolution of tokens.

MIR Input: Given a token t_i generated from the original image, we generate a MIM input token t'_i by

$$t'_i = Mask_i * t^m + (1 - Mask_i) * t_i, \qquad (1)$$

where $Mask_i$ is the Mask score of ith token and t^m is the learnable mask token. When $Mask_i$ is 0 or 1, Eq. (1) is equivalent to the mask operation of SimMIM and MaskFeat in which the original token information is totally kept or dropped. When $Mask_i \in (0, 1)$, it denotes ith token partly contribute to person construction.

MIR Encoder: Similar to MAE, MaskFeat and SimMIM, we also use transformer layers as the basic module of feature encoder. The transformer parameters follow the default setting of ViT-B [19, 20].

MIR Head: We use a simple linear layer as MIR Head to map the tokens from the encoder into RGB pixels.

3.4   FEM: TransReID-Based Feature Extractor Module

Once the occluded person images are recovered by the proposed MPM and MIR modules, a TransReID-based [3] Feature Extractor Module (FEM) is utilized to obtain the final feature representations for the given images. FEM is an efficient and effective backbone that adapts the ViT to the ReID task to construct the data stream from the original occluded person images to the final embedding. As shown in Fig. 1 the proposed FEM firstly utilizes a patch-to-token layer to map the original image into several tokens T_{reid}. Then the MIR token and Side Information Embedding (SIE) are added to T_{reid} to supplement more information such as holistic human body and camera IDs. The addition weights of MIR token and SIE are λ_{mir} and λ_{sie} respectively. Moreover, the fused token is fed to l transformer layers which will eventually extract a discriminative and robust feature representation for cross-image similarity calculation. Therefore, based on FEM, our proposed method can readily leverage the holistic information recovered by MIR to supplement occluded information.

3.5   Model Training

The MPM and MIR together formulate a complete pipeline for recovering the helpful information of the occluded parts. Therefore, the key issue here is how to guide MPM to identify which token should be dropped and meanwhile promote MIR to generate a holistic person image without occlusions. To tackle the above issue, both the MPM and MIM are pre-trained using holistic person images and then the whole model with all the three proposed modules will be jointly trained to accomplish effective Person ReID.

MPM and MIR Pre-training. Given an input holistic person image x, our method automatically generates an occluded image x^a by introducing an external object to x as the occlusion obstacle. To guide the model to reconstruct a holistic person without occlusions, we adopt an instance segmentation model, i.e. CBNetV2 [21], as the teacher model to generate person mask $M_p = \mathbb{R}^{H \times W}$. We use M_p to get the visible person areas and adopt these areas as the reconstruction target. Given original image x and reconstructed image x', the Reconstruction loss is calculated by:

$$L_R = ||(x' - x) * M_p||. \tag{2}$$

To accomplish MPM learning, we provide four kinds of supervision strategies:

1) Non-person supervision. Given person mask M_p, the background mask M_{bk} can be calculated simply by $M_{bk} = 1 - M_p$. Besides, after implementing occlusion augmentation, the augmentation mask M_{aug} could also be obtained. Therefore, the non-person mask M_{non-p} could be calculated by $M_{non-p} = M_p + M_{aug}$. The Non-person supervision takes M_{non-p} resized to $H/K \times W/K$ as the target, where K is the patch size of each token. The core idea of this supervision is to drop the patches not containing the person and keep the patches containing the person.

2) Occlusion supervision. The occlusion mask M_{occ} is calculated by $M_{occ} = M_p \times M_{aug}$. The Occlusion supervision takes M_{occ} resized to $H/K \times W/K$ as the target and the key idea is to drop the occluded patches.

3) All-drop supervision. In this setting, the target is a mask map with each element set to 1, which means that no image information should be kept. However, since MIR needs vital image patches, such as those containing human body parts, to reconstruct a holistic person, it will drive MPM to output a lower mask score in those areas. Eventually, the learned mask map will have larger values in occluded and background patches, and smaller values in visible body patches.

4) All-keep supervision. This setting is the opposite strategy of 3). The target is a mask map with each element set to 0, which means that all image information should be kept. In such condition, MIR will drive MPM to drop the patches harmful to holistic person reconstruction. Eventually, the learned mask map will have bigger values at occlusion patches and smaller valves at the visible body patches and background patches.

Figure 2 illustrates an example of the reconstruction target and target generation pipeline for Non-person supervision. For the above four supervision strategies, we adopt Binary Cross Entropy Loss to calculate Mask Loss L_m. The performance of each strategy is discussed in the **Ablation Studies**.

The overall loss of MPM and MIR Pre-training is calculated by:

$$L_{pre} = L_R + \lambda_1 L_m, \tag{3}$$

where λ_1 is super parameter to balance the loss weight of MPM and MIR. In our experiments, λ_1 is set to 1 for strategy 1) and 2), and for strategy 3) and 4), λ_1 is set to 0.001.

Joint Training. The Joint Training procedure aims to train a RRID model robust to occlusion. Given a wild occluded image, as illustrated in Fig. 1 we pass the image through MPM, MIR, and FEM successively. For supervision, we only adopt ID loss and triplet loss at the last layer of the FEM. The ID loss refers to cross entropy loss, which calculated by

$$L_{ID} = -y_i \log \left(\frac{\exp(W_i f_i)}{\sum_{j=1}^{ID_s} \exp(W_j f_j)} \right),   \quad (4)$$

where y is the ground truth, f is the extracted feature, W is a linear projection matrix.

The triplet loss is soft-margin loss which minimizes the gap between positive samples and maximizes the gap between positive and negative samples. Functionally, the loss can be presented as:

$$L_{Tri} = log(1 + e^{\|f_a - f_p\|_2^2 - \|f_a - f_n\|_2^2})   \quad (5)$$

$$L = L_{ID} + L_{Tri},   \quad (6)$$

where $\langle a, p, n \rangle$ is a triplet set $\langle anchor, positive\ sample, negative\ sample \rangle$.

4   Experiments

4.1   Datasets and Evaluation Metrics

Datasets. We conduct all experiments on four ReID datasets, including two holistic datastes Market1501 [22] and DukeMTMC-reID [23] as well as two occluded datasets Occluded-DukeMTMC [9] and Occluded-REID [7].

Evaluation Metrics. To perform a fair comparison with existing methods, all experiments follow the common evaluation settings in person ReID methods. The Cumulative Matching Characteristic (CMC) and mean Average Precision (mAP) are adopted to evaluate the performance. All experiments are performed in the single query setting.

4.2   Implementation

In our experiments, images are resized to 256×128. During MPM and MR pre-training, we collect the images from three holistic datasets: Market1501, DukeMTMC-reID and MSMT17. The basic pre-training augmentation includes Horizontal-Flipping, Random-Crop, Random-Rotation, and Colorjitter. Besides, we also adopt occlusion augmentation which randomly pasted external objects on the image. The external objects are extracted from MS-COCO valset [24]. We use four Nvidia 3090 GPU to pre-train MPM and MIR for 400 epochs.

During Person ReID training, we first augment the training images by random horizontal flipping, padding, random cropping and random erasing. The batch size is set to 64 and each one concludes 16 identities. And we train the whole network for 160 epochs using the SGD optimizer with a momentum of 0.9 and weight decay of 1e−4. And the initial learning rate is 0.008 with cosine learning rate decay. We embed the MIR-feature into the TransReID baseline using the token-level feature fusion approach and the weight of SIE (λ_s) and the weight of MIR token embedding (λ_m) are respectively set to 3.0 and 1.0. Furthermore, PRID training experiments are conducted on one Nvidia 3090 GPU.

Table 1. Performance comparison with state-of-the-art methods on four datasets, including Occluded-DukeMTMC (O-Duke), Occluded-REID (O-REID), Market1501 and DukeMTMC-reID (DukeMTMC).

Method	O-Duke		O-REID		Market1501		DukeMTMC	
	mAP	R1	mAP	R1	mAP	R1	mAP	R1
PCB [25]	33.7	42.6	38.9	41.3	77.4	92.3	66.1	81.8
RE [26]	30.0	40.5	–	–	71.3	87.1	62.4	79.3
FD-GAN [27]	–	40.8	–	–	77.7	90.5	64.5	80.0
DSR [28]	30.4	40.8	62.8	72.8	75.6	91.3	68.7	82.4
SFR [29]	32.0	42.3	-	–	81.0	93.0	71.2	84.8
FRR [30]	–	–	68.0	78.3	86.6	95.4	78.4	88.6
ISP [31]	52.3	62.8	–	–	88.6	95.3	80.0	89.6
PGFA [9]	37.3	51.4	–	–	76.8	91.2	65.5	82.6
HOReID [10]	43.8	55.1	70.2	80.3	84.9	94.2	75.6	86.9
OAMN [8]	46.1	62.6	–	–	79.8	92.3	72.6	86.3
PAT [32]	53.6	64.5	72.1	**81.6**	88.0	95.4	78.2	88.8
TransReID [3]	55.7	64.2	67.3	70.2	88.2	95.0	80.6	89.6
Ours (UBN)	**57.3**	**65.2**	**74.8**	79.9	**88.6**	**95.5**	**81.1**	**90.2**

4.3 Comparison with State-of-the-Art Methods

As shown in Table 1, we compare our method with the state-of-the-art approaches on four datasets, including Market-1501, DukeMTMC-reID, Occluded-DukeMTMC, and Occlude-REID. The results demonstrate we can achieve excellent results on both occluded and holistic datasets.

On Occluded Datasets. On the challenging Occluded-DukeMTMC, UBN achieves state-of-the-art performance with an mAP of 57.3% and R1 of 65.2%. This performance surpasses classical hand-crafted methods such as PCB [25] and FD-GAN [27], which use keypoints of pedestrians, by 23.6% and 22.6%, respectively. The performance also surpasses PGFA [9], a famous pose-guided approach based on a CNN backbone, by 20.0% and 13.8%. Moreover, the UBN model outperforms the transformer-based PAT by 3.7%/0.7% and TransReID by 1.6%/1.0%.

As for Occluded-REID, which can only be used for testing, we evaluate on it with our model trained on Market1501. The model achieved an mAP of 74.8% and R1 of 79.9%, which outperforms most recent methods. Notably, the achieved mAP of 74.8% on this dataset is state-of-the-art performance. However, as transformer-based architectures struggle to obtain strong generalization results on small training sets [33], the UBN model failed to achieve the highest R1 accuracy on this dataset.

On Holistic Datasets. On Market-1501, we obtain 0.4% (mAP) and 0.5% (R1) improvement over TransReID. On DukeMTMC, we also achieve 0.5% (mAP) and 0.6% (R1) improvement. As far as we know, we are the first to achieve R1 over 90% on DukeMTMC-reID among approaches focusing on occluded PRID. Therefore, UBN is also capable of promoting model learning on holistic datasets, albeit with smaller improvements compared to the occluded ones. This demonstrates that the uncovering occlusion design can benefit overall PRID performance.

4.4   Ablation Studies

Ablation Study of Mask Supervision Strategies. In Sect. 3.5, we introduce four mask supervision strategies: non-person supervision, occlusion supervision, all-drop supervision and all-keep supervision. In Table 2, we conduct comparison experiments of our four strategies (line 2–5) with the baseline TransReID (line 1). The results show that all supervision strategies are effective and could promote the performance consistently and significantly.

Table 2. Performance on the baseline and different mask supervision strategies.

Setting	Occ-Duke			
	mAP	R1	R5	R10
TransReID	55.7	64.2	–	–
non-person supervision	57.3	65.2	79.0	84.2
occlusion supervision	57.5	64.3	79.2	84.5
all-drop supervision	57.2	64.9	78.7	83.8
all-keep supervision	57.2	65.1	78.8	83.6

Table 3. Performance analysis of different fusion approaches. Comparing with the baseline TransReID, all fusion approaches would effectively promote performance. Best performance would be achieved once token-level fusion is adopted.

Fusion Approaches	Occ-duke			
	mAP	R1	R5	R10
TransReID	55.7	64.2	–	–
input-level	56.7	64.4	79.0	83.0
token-level	57.3	65.2	79.0	84.2
semantic-level	57.3	65.0	78.7	83.8

Ablation Study of Fusion Approaches. We discuss various approaches for integrating the MIR feature into the FEM, including input-level, token-level, and semantic-level integration. The input-level integration denotes the output of the MIR Module is directly used as the input of FEM. The token-level integration means that the MIR feature is regarded as a new embedding and added to input sequence embeddings. And the semantic-level integration refers to adding the MIR-feature to the output of FEM. As shown in Table 3, we claim that the token-level fusion method is better. The mAP/R1 of the method achieves 57.3%/65.2%, higher than the input-level one (56.7%/64.4%) and the semantic-level one (57.3%/65.0%). Since the MIR-feature is used for reconstructing the occluded pedestrian, it primarily reflects the contour, edge, shape features, and other low-level representations of the image. So it's reasonable that fusing the MIR feature and the original information at the token level is more suitable. In this way, on the one hand, the MIR-feature can provide more valuable clues for low-level information filtering out the occlusion, and on the other hand, it can make full use of the high-level semantic representational capacity of the transformer-based model.

4.5 Visualization Results

The retrieval results of TransReID [3] and our proposed UBN on Occlude-REID dataset are illustrated in Fig. 3. It is obvious our UBN achieves significantly better retrieval performance compared with the TransReID, especially when serious occlusion appears.

Fig. 3. Retrieval comparison of TransReID and our UBN. The images on the left are from the Occlude-REID query dataset. The images in green and red boxes indicate the correctly and wrongly retrieved instances respectively. The retrieval results are arranged from left to right in descending order of matching scores. (Color figure online)

5 Conclusion

In this paper, we present Uncover the Body Network (UBN), a MIM-based occluded person re-identification network. UBN is inspired by recent MIM models that can recover the whole image with partly known patches. Instead of randomly masking the images, UBN uses a Mask Prediction Module (MPM) to readily locate the occluded patches and then applied them to an occlusion-guided Masked Image Reconstruction Module (MIR) to reconstruct the holistic person images. Experimental results on both the occluded and holistic ReID benchmarks have demonstrated the superiority of UBN over the state-of-the-art approaches.

Acknowledgments. This work was supported by the National Natural Science Foundation of China (61925201, 62132001).

References

1. Zheng, L., et al.: MARS: a video benchmark for large-scale person re-identification. In: Leibe, B., Matas, J., Sebe, N., Welling, M. (eds.) ECCV 2016. LNCS, vol. 9910, pp. 868–884. Springer, Cham (2016). https://doi.org/10.1007/978-3-319-46466-4_52
2. Wang, S., Xin, X., Liu, L., Tian, J.: Multi-level feature fusion model-based real-time person re-identification for forensics. J. Real-Time Image Proc. **17**(1), 73–81 (2020)
3. He, S., Luo, H., Wang, P., Wang, F., Li, H., Jiang, W.: Transreid: transformer-based object re-identification. In: ICCV, pp. 15013–15022 (2021)
4. Zang, X., Li, G., Gao, W., Shu, X.: Learning to disentangle scenes for person re-identification. IVC **116**, 104330 (2021)
5. Sun, Y., et al.: Perceive where to focus: learning visibility-aware part-level features for partial person re-identification. In: CVPR, pp. 393–402 (2019)
6. Yao, H., Zhang, S., Hong, R., Zhang, Y., Changsheng, X., Tian, Q.: Deep representation learning with part loss for person re-identification. TIP **28**(6), 2860–2871 (2019)
7. Zhuo, J., Chen, Z., Lai, J., Wang, G.: Occluded person re-identification. In: ICME, pp. 1–6. IEEE (2018)
8. Chen, P., et al.: Occlude them all: occlusion-aware attention network for occluded person re-id. In: ICCV, pp. 11833–11842 (2021)
9. Miao, J., Wu, Y., Liu, P., Ding, Y., Yang, Y.: Pose-guided feature alignment for occluded person re-identification. In: ICCV, pp. 542–551 (2019)
10. Wang, G., et al.: High-order information matters: learning relation and topology for occluded person re-identification. In: CVPR, pp. 6449–6458 (2020)
11. Gao, S., Wang, J., Lu, H., Liu, Z.: Pose-guided visible part matching for occluded person reid. In: CVPR, pp. 11744–11752 (2020)
12. Xie, Z., et al.: Simmim: a simple framework for masked image modeling. In: CVPR, pp. 9653–9663 (2022)
13. Zhou, K., Yang, Y., Cavallaro, A., Xiang, T.: Omni-scale feature learning for person re-identification. In: ICCV, pp. 3702–3712 (2019)
14. Chen, M., et al.: Generative pretraining from pixels. In: ICML, pp. 1691–1703. PMLR (2020)
15. Doersch, C., Gupta, A., Efros, A.A.: Unsupervised visual representation learning by context prediction. In: ICCV, pp. 1422–1430 (2015)
16. Pathak, D., Krahenbuhl, P., Donahue, J., Darrell, T., Efros, A.A.: Context encoders: feature learning by inpainting. In: CVPR, pp. 2536–2544 (2016)

17. He, K., Chen, X., Xie, S., Li, Y., Dollár, P., Girshick, R.: Masked autoencoders are scalable vision learners. In: CVPR, pp. 16000–16009 (2022)
18. Wei, C., Fan, H., Xie, S., Wu, C.-Y., Yuille, A., Feichtenhofer, C.: Masked feature prediction for self-supervised visual pre-training. In: CVPR, pp. 14668–14678 (2022)
19. Dosovitskiy, A., et al.: An image is worth 16x16 words: transformers for image recognition at scale. arXiv preprint arXiv:2010.11929 (2020)
20. Bao, H., Dong, L., Wei, F.: Beit: BERT pre-training of image transformers. arXiv preprint arXiv:2106.08254 (2021)
21. Liang, T., et al.: Cbnetv2: a composite backbone network architecture for object detection. arXiv preprint arXiv:2107.00420 (2021)
22. Zheng, L., Shen, L., Tian, L., Wang, S., Wang, J., Tian, Q.: Scalable person re-identification: a benchmark. In: ICCV, pp. 1116–1124 (2015)
23. Zheng, Z., Zheng, L., Yang, Y.: Unlabeled samples generated by GAN improve the person re-identification baseline in vitro. In: ICCV, pp. 3754–3762 (2017)
24. Lin, T.-Y., et al.: Microsoft COCO: common objects in context. In: Fleet, D., Pajdla, T., Schiele, B., Tuytelaars, T. (eds.) ECCV 2014. LNCS, vol. 8693, pp. 740–755. Springer, Cham (2014). https://doi.org/10.1007/978-3-319-10602-1_48
25. Sun, Y., Zheng, L., Yang, Y., Tian, Q., Wang, S.: Beyond part models: person retrieval with refined part pooling (and a strong convolutional baseline). In: Ferrari, V., Hebert, M., Sminchisescu, C., Weiss, Y. (eds.) ECCV 2018. LNCS, vol. 11208, pp. 501–518. Springer, Cham (2018). https://doi.org/10.1007/978-3-030-01225-0_30
26. Zhong, Z., Zheng, L., Kang, G., Li, S., Yang, Y.: Random erasing data augmentation. In: AAAI, vol. 34, pp. 13001–13008 (2020)
27. Ge, Y., et al.: FD-GAN: pose-guided feature distilling GAN for robust person re-identification. In: NeurIPS, vol. 31 (2018)
28. He, L., Liang, J., Li, H., Sun, Z.: Deep spatial feature reconstruction for partial person re-identification: alignment-free approach. In: CVPR, pp. 7073–7082 (2018)
29. He, L., Sun, Z., Zhu, Y., Wang, Y.: Recognizing partial biometric patterns. arXiv preprint arXiv:1810.07399 (2018)
30. Lingxiao He, Yinggang Wang, Wu Liu, He Zhao, Zhenan Sun, and Jiashi Feng. Foreground-aware pyramid reconstruction for alignment-free occluded person re-identification. In ICCV, pages 8450–8459, 2019
31. Zhu, K., Guo, H., Liu, Z., Tang, M., Wang, J.: Identity-guided human semantic parsing for person re-identification. In: Vedaldi, A., Bischof, H., Brox, T., Frahm, J.-M. (eds.) ECCV 2020. LNCS, vol. 12348, pp. 346–363. Springer, Cham (2020). https://doi.org/10.1007/978-3-030-58580-8_21
32. Li, Y., He, J., Zhang, T., Liu, X., Zhang, Y., Wu, F.: Diverse part discovery: occluded person re-identification with part-aware transformer. In: CVPR, pp. 2898–2907 (2021)
33. Wang, Z., Zhu, F., Tang, S., Zhao, R., He, L., Song, J.: Feature erasing and diffusion network for occluded person re-identification. In: CVPR, pp. 4754–4763 (2022)

Enhancing Adversarial Transferability from the Perspective of Input Loss Landscape

Yinhu Xu, Qi Chu$^{(\boxtimes)}$, Haojie Yuan, Zixiang Luo, Bin Liu, and Nenghai Yu

University of Science and Technology of China, Hefei, China
{xyh1998,doubihj,zxluo}@mail.ustc.edu.cn,
{qchu,flowice,ynh}@ustc.edu.cn

Abstract. The transferability of adversarial examples enables the black-box attacks and poses a threat to the application of deep neural networks in real-world, which has attracted great attention in recent years. Regarding the adversarial example generation as the dual optimization process of model training, existing works mainly focus on better optimization algorithm and model augmentation to improve the transferability of adversarial examples. Despite the impressive performance, the explanation on the transferability improvement is still underexplored. In this paper, recalling that weight loss landscape is a widely used indicator to characterize the generalization ability of neural networks, we investigate the effect of input loss landscape on adversarial transferability. Through abundant analysis, we find a clear correlation between the flatness of input loss landscape and adversarial transferability: existing adversarial transferability improvements all implicitly flatten the input loss landscape and the better transferability one method achieves, the flatter input loss landscape it has. Motivated by this, we propose a simple yet effective *Adversarial Pixel Perturbation (APP)* method to explicitly flatten the input loss landscape during the adversarial example generation process. Extensive experiments demonstrate the effectiveness of the proposed method in improving the adversarial transferability. By incorporating the proposed *APP* into existing attack methods, we achieve a record of 97.0% attack success rate on average against six defense models, outperforming the state-of-the-art attack method by a clear margin of 4.0%.

Keywords: Neural Network · Image Classification · Adversarial Example · Black-box Attack

1 Introduction

Deep neural networks (DNNs) have achieved great success in various computer vision tasks, but are shown to be vulnerable to adversarial examples, which are

This work is supported by the National Natural Science Foundation of China (No. 62002336, No. U20B2047) and the Fundamental Research Funds for the Central Universities.

H. Lu et al. (Eds.): ICIG 2023, LNCS 14355, pp. 254–266, 2023.
https://doi.org/10.1007/978-3-031-46305-1_21

generated by adding human-imperceptible perturbations on the clean inputs [19]. A key property of adversarial examples is their *transferability*, i.e., adversarial example crafted for one model could fool other models with high probability [11], which enables black-box attacks and poses a threat to the application of DNNs in real-world [2,6,8,16]. On the other hand, adversarial examples can help evaluate the robustness of DNNs [3] and improve the robustness of models by adversarial training [12,23,27]. Therefore, how to craft adversarial examples has attracted a lot of attention in recent years.

In the white-box setting where the attacker has full access to the knowledge of the target model, generating adversarial examples is relatively easy and existing adversarial attacks have exhibited great effectiveness [1,3]. However, adversarial examples crafted by these methods demonstrate weak transferability for unknown models, especially for models with defense mechanisms [9,20,25]. To address this issue, recent works focus on improving the transferability of adversarial examples.

Lin et al. [10] proposed to view the process of generating adversarial examples as an optimization problem which is similar to training neural networks. In the optimizing phase, the white-box model being attacked to optimize the adversarial examples can be viewed as the training data on the training process, and the adversarial examples being optimized can be viewed as the training parameters of the neural network. From this perspective, the transferability of adversarial examples is similar to generalization ability of the trained neural network. Better optimization algorithm and data augmentation are two main directions for enhancing the generalization ability of DNNs.

Hence, a lot of methods have been proposed, which can come down to two ideas: (1) better optimization algorithms to prevent optimization from falling into local optimum, such as Momentum [4], Nesterov [10], Variance Tuning [21]; (2) model augmentation to mitigate overfitting of the surrogate model that the adversarial examples are generated from, such as various kinds of input transformation methods [5,10,22,26,28] and ensemble model attack [11]. Recently, in order to mitigate overfitting of the surrogate model, Qin et al. [14] proposed to seek adversarial example at a region with unified low loss value, formulating a min-max bi-level optimization problem. By injecting the worst-case perturbation into each iteration of the optimization procedure, they find more stable adversarial examples that locate at regions with unified lower loss and they think examples here are less sensitive to the changes of decision boundary, mitigating the overfitting problem. Although these methods successfully improve the adversarial transferability, the deeper explanation on the transferability improvement and the impact of loss landscape are still underexplored.

In this paper, inspired by that the weight loss landscape is widely used to characterize the generalization ability of DNNs, we systematically study the role of input loss landscape in adversarial example generation scenario. After thorough analysis, we find a clear correlation between the flatness of input loss landscape and adversarial transferability. Existing adversarial transferability improvements, such as DIM [26] and TIM [5], all implicitly flatten the input loss landscape and the better transferability one method achieves, the flatter input loss landscape it has. Based on these observations, we propose a simple yet effective method, named *Adversarial Pixel Perturbation (APP)*, to explicitly regularize the flatness of input loss landscape during the adversarial example generation process. *APP* can be easily incorporated into existing adversarial attack methods to boost their adversarial transferability. The main contributions are summarized as follows:

- We systematically study the role of input loss landscape in adversarial example generation scenario from both experimental and theoretical perspectives.
- We provide a comprehensive explanation for the transferability improvement of various kinds of attack methods from a theoretical point of view.
- We propose *Adversarial Pixel Perturbation (APP)* to explicitly flatten the input loss landscape during the adversarial example generation process.
- We conduct extensive experiments and the experimental results demonstrate the proposed *APP* can indeed bring flatter input loss landscape and consistently improve the adversarial transferability of various existing adversarial attack methods.

2   Related Work

2.1   Adversarial Attacks

Notations. Let x denote a clean example and y denote its corresponding ground-truth label. Given a classifier $f(\cdot)$, adversarial attack generates x^{adv} that is visually close to x but fools the classifier, *i.e.*, $f(x^{adv}) \neq y$. In order to ensure x and x^{adv} are visually close, we often use the L_p norm to constraint the distortion between them as $\left\| x - x^{adv} \right\|_p \leq \epsilon$, *i.e.*, $x^{adv} \in B_\epsilon(x)$, where p could be $0, 1, 2, \infty$ and ϵ is the size of maximum perturbation. In this paper, we use the L_∞ norm. We define the logits of input x as $l(x)$ and the loss function of classifier as $J(l(x), y)$, then the adversarial example generation can be formulated as the following optimization problem:

$$\arg \min_{x^{adv}} L(l(x^{adv}), y), \text{ s.t. } \left\| x^{adv} - x \right\|_\infty \leq \epsilon. \tag{1}$$

where $L(l(x), y) = -J(l(x), y)$. For brevity, we abbreviate $L(l(x), y)$ to $L(x)$ or $L(x, y)$ when there is no ambiguity.

Basic Iterative Method (BIM) [8] iteratively conducts gradient descent updates with a small step size to generate an adversarial example x^{adv} as:

$$x^{adv}_{t+1} = x^{adv}_t - \alpha \cdot \text{sign}(\nabla_x L(l(x^{adv}_t), y)), \tag{2}$$

where x^{adv}_t denotes the generated adversarial example at iteration t and $x^{adv}_0 = x$. Generally, $\alpha = \epsilon/T$, with T being the number of iterations. BIM performs well when attacking white-box models but exhibits poor transferability.

Later, a lot of improvements are proposed based on it, which can be roughly categorized into two aspects: better optimization algorithm to escape local optimum and model augmentation to mitigate overfitting. On the optimization side, Momentum Iterative Method (MIM) [4] and Nesterov Iterative Method (NIM) [10] integrate momentum and Nesterov accelerated gradient into BIM respectively to stabilize the update direction and Variance Tuning (VT) [21] proposes to reduce the gradient variance between iterations. Other lines of works focus on applying various differentiable transformations on input images to improve adversarial transferability. Considering the differentiable transformations and the original model together as a new model, these methods can be regarded as model augmentation that effectively derives an ensemble of models from the single original model. For example, Diverse Input Method (DIM) [26] applies random resize-padding transformations to the input image, Translation-Invariant Method (TIM) [5] uses a set of translated images, Scale-Invariant Method (SIM) [10] computes on the scale copies of an image, Diversity-Ensemble Method (DEM) [28] adopts a multi-branch resize-padding-resize transformation on the input image and Admix Attack Method (AAM) [22] mixes the original image with images from other categories. Recently, instead of using model augmentation techniques, Reverse Adversarial Perturbation (RAP) [14] formulates a min-max bi-level optimization problem to seek adversarial examples that locate at a region with unified low loss value to avoid overfitting of surrogate model.

2.2 Explanation on Adversarial Transferability

Although plenty of methods have been proposed to improve the adversarial transferability, the explanation on transferability improvements of existing works remains intuitive and qualitative. Some works [4, 21] blame the weak transferability of adversarial examples to the attack's convergence to a poor local minima and attempt to design better optimization algorithm to help escape from poor local minima. Model augmentation methods [5, 10, 26, 28] usually explain the poor adversarial transferability from the perspective of overfitting the white-box model. TIM [5] qualitatively illustrates that defense models tend to make predictions based on different discriminative regions compared to normally trained models and the adversarial example crafted on a normal model is highly correlated with its discriminative region, making it hard to transfer to other defense models. In this paper, we attempt to provide a empirical/quantitative explanation on the adversarial transferability from the perspective of input loss landscape.

3 Correlation Between Input Loss Landscape and Adversarial Transferability

In this section, we first introduce a simple method to characterize the input loss landscape and then investigate it from two perspectives: (1) same attack with different strengths; (2) different attack methods. In this way, we successfully establish a connection between input loss landscape and adversarial transferability.

Visualization. Like [24], we visualize the input loss landscape by plotting the loss change when moving the input x along a random vector d sampled from $U[-(32/255)^d, (32/255)^d]$ ($U[a^d, b^d]$ stands for the uniform distribution in d dimensions) with magnitude α:

$$g(\alpha) = E_x[\rho(x + \alpha d) - \rho(x)] = \frac{1}{n}\sum_{i=1}^{n}[\rho(x_i + \alpha d) - \rho(x_i)] \quad (3)$$

where $\rho(x) = \frac{1}{m}\sum_{i=1}^{m}L(l_i(x), y)$ is the empirical loss with respect to x, $l_i(x)$ represents the logits output of the i−th model f_i, m is the number of white-box surrogate models and n is the number of samples used.

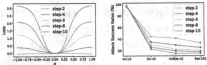 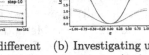 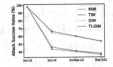

(a) Investigating with BIM of different steps (*Left*: Input loss landscape; *Right*: Attack success rates on four models)

(b) Investigating under different adversarial attacks (*Left*: Input loss landscape; *Right*: Attack success rates on four models)

Fig. 1. Investigating the connection between input loss landscape and adversarial transferability. The adversarial examples are crafted on Inc-v3 model.

Input loss landscape under same attack with different strengths. It's well known that BIM [8] with less steps has worse white-box attack performance but shows better transferability. Here, we visualize the input loss landscape of adversarial examples generated by BIM with various values of steps on Inc-v3 model. As shown in Fig. 1(a), BIM with more steps has a sharper input loss landscape and shows worse transferability correspondingly.

Input loss landscape under different adversarial attacks. We explore whether the correlation between input loss landscape and adversarial transferability still exists across different adversarial attacks. Here, we choose 10 steps of MIM [4], DIM [26], TIM [5], TI-DIM, 100 steps of RAP [14] to visualize. Figure 1(b) demonstrates that more transferable adversarial attacks tend to have a flatter input loss landscape, *e.g.*, DIM has better transferabity than MIM and also has a flatter input loss landscape correspondingly.

From the above investigations, it can be concluded that there exists a strong positive correlation between the flatness of input loss landscape and adversarial transferability.

4   Adversarial Pixel Perturbation

In this section, we propose *Adversarial Pixel Perturbation (APP)* to explicitly flatten the input loss landscape via injecting perturbations into input pixels. As discussed above, to generate transferable adversarial examples, we need to focus on both the original optimization objective and the flatness of input loss landscape. Thus, we have the new objective:

$$\min_{x}\{\rho(x) + \lambda \cdot \max(E_{\nu}[\rho(x + \nu)] - \rho(x),\ 0)\} \tag{4}$$

where $\rho(x) = \frac{1}{m}\sum_{i=1}^{m} L(l_i(x),\ y)$ is the empirical loss with respect to x, $l_i(x)$ represents the logits output of the ith model f_i, and m is the number of white-box models. $E_{\nu}[\rho(x + \nu)] - \rho(x)$ is a term to characterize the flatness of input loss landscape where ν is a random perturbation. λ is a balance factor. The $\max(\cdot)$ function controls the optimization to focus on finding x with lower loss when $E_{\nu}[\rho(x + \nu)] - \rho(x) < 0$ and x at somewhere like a peak. Actually, we can omit the $\max(\cdot)$ function to get a neat optimization objective because the optimization is dominated by the first term $\rho(x)$ in early optimization stage and the second term quickly exceeds 0. Hence, the optimization objective finally becomes:

$$\min_{x}\{\rho(x) + \lambda \cdot (E_{\nu}[\rho(x + \nu)] - \rho(x))\} \tag{5}$$

To estimate the expected term $E_{\nu}[\rho(x + \nu)]$, S perturbations are randomly sampled and we calculate the mean, *i.e.*, $E_{\nu}[\rho(x + \nu)] = \frac{1}{S}\sum_{i=1}^{S}\rho(x + \nu_i)$. Hence, the optimization objective can be written as:

$$\min_{x}\left\{\rho(x) + \lambda \cdot \left[\frac{1}{S}\sum_{i=1}^{S}\rho(x + \nu_i) - \rho(x)\right]\right\} \tag{6}$$

where ν_i is a random perturbation sampled from a uniform distribution or a Gaussian distribution.

We conduct first-order optimization for the proposed objective 6 in an iterative manner like previous methods [4,8]. Thus, a specific update step follows:

$$x \leftarrow x - \alpha \cdot \mathrm{sign}\left(\nabla_x\left(\rho(x) + \lambda \cdot \left[\frac{1}{S}\sum_{i=1}^{S}\rho(x + \nu_i) - \rho(x)\right]\right)\right) \tag{7}$$

4.1   Theoretical Analysis

In this subsection, we try to explain why previous methods that are based on advanced optimization algorithm or model augmentation and our APP work from a theoretical perspective.

Based on previous work which uses PAC-Bayes bound and sharpness to explain generalization in deep learning [13] and the duality between training neural networks and adversarial attacks, we bound the expected loss of an adversarial example to all possible models, which can reflect its transferability, with three important terms.

Let x be an arbitrary input adversary, ν be a random perturbation drawn from a distribution denoted Q. Given a 'prior' distribution P over the input adversary x, with probability at least $1-\delta$ over the draw of m white-box models, the expected loss can be bounded as follows:

$$E_\nu[\hat{\rho}(x+\nu)] \leq \rho(x) + \underbrace{E_\nu[\rho(x+\nu)] - \rho(x)}_{\text{flatness}} + 4\sqrt{\frac{1}{m}\left(KL(x+\nu \parallel P) + \ln\frac{2m}{\delta}\right)}$$

(8)

where $E_\nu[\hat{\rho}(x+\nu)] = E_\nu\{E_f[L(l_i(x+\nu), y)]\}$ is the expected loss with respect to perturbations and models which can represent the transferability of x (smaller is better). $E_\nu[\rho(x+\nu)] = E_\nu[\frac{1}{m}\sum_{i=1}^{m}L(l_i(x+\nu), y)]$ is the empirical loss computed on m white-box models. $l_i(x)$ represents the logit output of the ith model f_i.

The first term $\rho(x)$ in Eq. 8 is related to the optimization algorithm, and better optimization algorithm can escape from poor local minima and find better x. Given a determined distribution P, $KL(x+\nu \parallel P)$ becomes a constant and then the last term becomes $4\sqrt{\frac{1}{m}\left(c + \ln\frac{2m}{\delta}\right)}$ which is monotonically decreasing when $m \geq 1$ given $\delta \leq \frac{2}{e}$, where c is a constant. Therefore, model augmentation actually increases m and decreases the last term, leading to a lower bound for the expected loss, and finally improves the transferability of x. When the optimization algorithm and model augmentation are fixed, there still exists a second term which can also affect the bound of expected loss. Since this term can reflect the flatness of input loss landscape, it reveals the correlation between adversarial transferability and input loss landscape. However, this has been overlooked in recent adversarial attacks. Hence, we propose the Adversarial Pixel Perturbation method to explicitly regularize the second term and decrease the bound. Finally, APP can obtain a flatter input loss landscape and achieve stronger transferability.

4.2 Discussions

In this subsection, we discuss the difference between RAP [14] and the proposed APP. RAP proposes to seek adversarial examples located at a region with unified low loss and tries to solve it by optimizing the worst-case problem. The major differences between RAP and the proposed APP are as follows. Firstly, RAP aims to avoid overfitting of the surrogate model, while our method aims to obtain flatter input loss landscape and modifies the loss, which is totally different in both motivations and solutions. The objective of RAP can lead to a region with lower loss while our APP method can ensure a region with flatter loss. Secondly, RAP applies about 8 additional forwards and backwards steps to compute the worst-case point and needs more than 100 iterations to converge, which is about 80 times slower than our APP method using only 10 iterations. Finally, experiments show our APP method outperforms RAP by a clear margin on all models especially on defense models.

5   Experiments

In this section, we present extensive experiments on ImageNet dataset to validate the effectiveness of the proposed APP method. We first specify the experimental setup in Sect. 5.1. Then in Sect. 5.2, we evaluate the improvements of APP under single model setting. We further demonstrate better adversarial transferability on defense models with ensemble model attack in Sect. 5.3.

5.1   Experimental Settings

Dataset. Following previous work [5,26,28], we use an ImageNet-compatible dataset[1] [15] comprised of 1,000 images, which was used in the NIPS 2017 adversarial competition. The image size is $299 \times 299 \times 3$.

Models. We use four normally trained models, Inception v3 (Inc-v3) [18], Inception v4 (Inc-v4), Inception Resnet v2 (IncRes-v2) [17], and ResNet v2-101 (Res-v2-101) [7], as white-box models to generate adversarial examples. For evaluation, we use 3 ensemble adversarially trained models, Inc-v3ens3, Inc-v3ens4, IncRes-v2ens [20], and top 3 defenses of NIPS 2017 adversarial competition, HGD [9], R&P [25] and rank-3 submission[2] (NIPS-r3).

Baselines. APP can be integrated into most recently proposed iterative transferable attacks. In the experiments, we take almost all iterative attack methods as our baselines, including MIM [4], DIM [26], TIM [5], SIM [10], DEM [28], VT [21] and AAM [22].

Hyper-Parameters. Following Wang et al. [21], we set the maximum perturbation as $\epsilon = 16$, the number of iterations as $T = 10$, step size as $2/255$. For MIM, we set the decay factor as $\mu = 1.0$. For TIM, we adopt the Gaussian kernel with kernel size 7×7. For DIM, the transformation probability is set to 0.5. For SIM and DEM, the number of diversity scales is set to $K = 5$. For VT, we set $N = 20$ and $\beta = 1.5$. For RAP, we set inner iterations as 8, outer iterations as 100 by default. For the proposed method, the perturbation ν is from $U[-(32/255)^d, (32/255)^d]$, perturbation number $S = 3$ and $\lambda = 1$ unless otherwise stated.

Devices. Our algorithms are implemented using TensorFlow and conducted on Titan XP GPUs. We set the batch size to 2.

5.2   Single Model Attacks

We first perform three adversarial attacks, namely MIM [4], MIM-RAP [14], the proposed APP based method MIM-APP, on a single neural network.We craft

---

[1] https://github.com/tensorflow/cleverhans/tree/master/cleverhans_v3.1.0/
examples/nips17_adversarial_competition.
[2] https://github.com/anlthms/nips-2017/tree/master/mmd.

Table 1. Attack success rates (%) and computation time per example consumes (s) on seven models with adversaries crafted by MIM, MIM-RAP and MIM-APP on Inc-v3 model. * indicates white-box attacks.

Attack	Inc-v3	Inc-v4	IncRes-v2	Res-101	Inc-v3ens3	Inc-v3ens4	IncRes-v2ens	Time
MIM	97.9*	43.5	40.2	36.0	18.2	15.5	8.0	0.6
MIM-RAP	98.0*	58.4	58.2	46.6	14.7	13.6	6.1	**44.0**
MIM-APP	**98.3***	**72.3**	**68.1**	**62.1**	**37.0**	**36.1**	**21.6**	0.7

adversarial examples on Inc-v3 and test them on 4 normal models and 3 defense models. The attack success rates are shown in Table 1. We can see that MIM-APP consistently outperform MIM and MIM-RAP on all models. Especially, our MIM-APP outperform MIM-RAP by a large margin on defense models, which is more valuable.

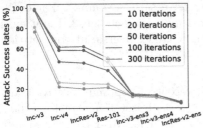

(a) Attack success rates (%) of RAP with different iterations

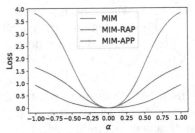

(b) Visualization of loss landscape generated by MIM, MIM-RAP and MIM-APP

Fig. 2. Attack success rates (%) of RAP and loss landscape visualization.

Besides, we find that RAP based methods need more iterations to generate transferable examples. As shown in Fig. 2(a), RAP needs more than 100 iterations to converge and each iteration takes about 8 times longer than our APP method, which is consistent with the results reported in [14]. Therefore, RAP is about 80 times slower than our APP method theoretically. What's more, Fig. 2(b) shows that the APP method flattens the input loss landscape best. These experimental results demonstrates the high efficiency and effectiveness of the proposed APP method.

Then we consider several transformation based methods, *e.g.*, DIM [26], TIM [5], SIM [10] and AAM [22]. Previous work [10,22] have shown that the combination of DIM,TIM and SIM named SI-TI-DIM could help the attack achieve great transferability and the combination of DIM, TIM and AAM named AA-TI-DIM is currently the most transferable transformation based attack. As shown in Table 2, when combined with our method, the attack success rates could be further improved on various models. For example, SI-TI-DIM equipped with APP has a remarkable improvement about 20% on IncRes-v2ens defense model, which

Table 2. Attack success rates (%) on seven models with adversaries crafted by various methods on Inc-v3 model. * indicates white-box attacks.

Attack	Inc-v3	Inc-v4	IncRes-v2	Res-101	Inc-v3ens3	Inc-v3ens4	IncRes-v2ens
SI-TI-DIM	98.0*	85.1	80.0	75.4	63.0	61.2	45.6
SI-TI-DIM-APP	98.5*	88.3	85.7	82.7	78.4	78.7	65.4
AA-TI-DIM	98.6*	88.4	86.4	82.0	73.5	70.4	52.7
AA-TI-DIM-APP	99.0*	89.0	87.8	84.0	80.7	80.4	68.3
VT-SI-TI-DIM	98.7*	89.2	86.3	83.0	79.4	77.6	66.4
VT-SI-TI-DIM-APP	98.8*	89.4	88.2	84.5	81.7	81.8	71.5

exceeds the state-of-the-art AA-TI-DIM by about 13%. AA-TI-DIM equipped with APP also gets further improvement.

Finally, the combination of advanced optimization, flatter input loss landscape and model augmentation, *i.e.*, VT-SI-TI-DIM-APP obtains the best single model attack performance which brings an improvement of 5.1% against IncRes-v2ens defense model.

5.3 Multi-Model Attacks

As proposed by Liu et al. [11], attacking multiple models simultaneously could improve the transferability of the generated adversarial examples, which we also explains from a theoretical perspective in Sect. 4.1. In this subsection, following previous work [4,10,21,22], we adopt the ensemble attack method in [4], which fuses the logits output of different models. Specifically, we attack the ensemble of four normally trained models, *i.e.*, Inc-v3, Inc-v4, IncRes-v2 and Res-101 by averaging the logit outputs of the models. We test the adversarial transferability on six defense models introduced in Sect. 5.1, *i.e.*, Inc-v3ens3, Inc-v3ens4, IncRes-v2ens and top 3 defenses of NIPS 2017 adversarial competition.

As shown in Table 3, when combined with the APP method, all attacks outperform their baselines. For example, DIM integrated with APP outperforms its baseline by about 21% on average. Specifically, DE-TIM integrated with the APP method achieves a high average success rate of 97.0%, exceeding the current state-of-the-art performance by around 4.0%.

Table 3. Attack success rates (%) on six defense models in the multi-model setting with adversaries crafted by various methods. The adversarial examples are generated on the ensemble models, *i.e.* Inc-v3, Inc-v4, IncRes-v2 and Res-101.

Attack	Inc-v3ens3	Inc-v3ens4	IncRes-v2ens	HGD	R&P	NIPS-r3	AVG
DIM	60.7	58.6	43.2	51.6	46.5	57.0	52.9
DIM-APP	**78.8**	**77.9**	**68.4**	**66.7**	**71.0**	**77.1**	**73.3**
TIM	63.2	59.9	50.8	62.4	50.3	55.4	57.0
TIM-APP	**86.2**	**85.3**	**80.8**	**82.6**	**79.7**	**82.8**	**82.9**
SI-TI-DIM	92.4	91.2	88.0	92.4	89.0	90.8	90.6
SI-TI-DIM-APP	**94.0**	**93.3**	**92.0**	**93.0**	**91.8**	**92.5**	**92.8**
AA-TI-DIM	93.6	92.1	90.2	93.7	90.8	92.4	92.1
AA-TI-DIM-APP	**94.1**	**93.5**	**91.0**	**94.4**	**91.8**	**93.1**	**93.0**
VT-SI-TI-DIM	93.1	92.4	91.2	93.0	91.6	92.4	92.3
VT-SI-TI-DIM-APP	**94.5**	**93.9**	**92.5**	**94.3**	**92.8**	**93.3**	**93.6**
DE-TIM	94.7	94.5	89.1	93.2	92.7	93.9	93.0
DE-TIM-APP	**97.6**	**97.9**	**96.0**	**96.2**	**96.7**	**97.4**	**97.0**

6   Conclusion

In this paper, we first identify the relation between input loss landscape and adversarial transferability. We find that more transferable adversarial examples tend to have a flatter input loss landscape and most transferable attacks implicitly flatten the input loss landscape. Besides, we try to explain the transferability improvement with the help of generalization theory in deep learning. Based on these observations, we propose a simple yet effective *Adversarial Pixel Perturbation (APP)* method to explicitly flatten the input loss landscape and improve the adversarial transferability. Extensive experiments are provided to demonstrate its generality and effectiveness.

References

1. Athalye, A., Carlini, N., Wagner, D.: Obfuscated gradients give a false sense of security: circumventing defenses to adversarial examples. In: International Conference on Machine Learning, pp. 274–283. PMLR (2018)
2. Athalye, A., Engstrom, L., Ilyas, A., Kwok, K.: Synthesizing robust adversarial examples. In: International Conference on Machine Learning, pp. 284–293. PMLR (2018)
3. Carlini, N., Wagner, D.: Towards evaluating the robustness of neural networks. In: 2017 IEEE Symposium on Security and Privacy (SP), pp. 39–57 (2017)
4. Dong, Y., et al.: Boosting adversarial attacks with momentum. In: Proceedings of the IEEE Conference on Computer Vision and Pattern Recognition, pp. 9185–9193 (2018)

5. Dong, Y., Pang, T., Su, H., Zhu, J.: Evading defenses to transferable adversarial examples by translation-invariant attacks. In: Proceedings of the IEEE Conference on Computer Vision and Pattern Recognition, pp. 4312–4321 (2019)
6. Eykholt, K., et al.: Robust physical-world attacks on deep learning visual classification. In: Proceedings of the IEEE Conference on Computer Vision and Pattern Recognition, pp. 1625–1634 (2018)
7. He, K., Zhang, X., Ren, S., Sun, J.: Identity mappings in deep residual networks. In: Leibe, B., Matas, J., Sebe, N., Welling, M. (eds.) ECCV 2016. LNCS, vol. 9908, pp. 630–645. Springer, Cham (2016). https://doi.org/10.1007/978-3-319-46493-0_38
8. Kurakin, A., Goodfellow, I., Bengio, S.: Adversarial examples in the physical world. In: International Conference on Learning Representations (2017)
9. Liao, F., Liang, M., Dong, Y., Pang, T., Hu, X., Zhu, J.: Defense against adversarial attacks using high-level representation guided denoiser. In: 2018 IEEE/CVF Conference on Computer Vision and Pattern Recognition, pp. 1778–1787 (2018). https://doi.org/10.1109/CVPR.2018.00191
10. Lin, J., Song, C., He, K., Wang, L., Hopcroft, J.E.: Nesterov accelerated gradient and scale invariance for adversarial attacks. In: International Conference on Learning Representations (2020)
11. Liu, Y., Chen, X., Liu, C., Song, D.: Delving into transferable adversarial examples and black-box attacks. In: International Conference on Learning Representations (2017)
12. Madry, A., Makelov, A., Schmidt, L., Tsipras, D., Vladu, A.: Towards deep learning models resistant to adversarial attacks. In: International Conference on Learning Representations (2018)
13. Neyshabur, B., Bhojanapalli, S., McAllester, D., Srebro, N.: Exploring generalization in deep learning. In: Advances in Neural Information Processing Systems, vol. 30 (2017)
14. Qin, Z., et al.: Boosting the transferability of adversarial attacks with reverse adversarial perturbation. arXiv preprint arXiv:2210.05968 (2022)
15. Russakovsky, O., et al.: Imagenet large scale visual recognition challenge. Int. J. Comput. Vision 115(3), 211–252 (2015)
16. Sharif, M., Bhagavatula, S., Bauer, L., Reiter, M.K.: Accessorize to a crime: real and stealthy attacks on state-of-the-art face recognition. In: Proceedings of the 2016 ACM SIGSAC Conference on Computer and Communications Security, pp. 1528–1540 (2016)
17. Szegedy, C., Ioffe, S., Vanhoucke, V., Alemi, A.: Inception-v4, inception-ResNet and the impact of residual connections on learning. In: Proceedings of the AAAI Conference on Artificial Intelligence (2017)
18. Szegedy, C., Vanhoucke, V., Ioffe, S., Shlens, J., Wojna, Z.: Rethinking the inception architecture for computer vision. In: Proceedings of the IEEE Conference on Computer Vision and Pattern Recognition, pp. 2818–2826 (2016)
19. Szegedy, C., et al.: Intriguing properties of neural networks. In: International Conference on Learning Representations (2014)
20. Tramèr, F., Kurakin, A., Papernot, N., Goodfellow, I., Boneh, D., McDaniel, P.: Ensemble adversarial training: attacks and defenses. In: International Conference on Learning Representations (2018)
21. Wang, X., He, K.: Enhancing the transferability of adversarial attacks through variance tuning. In: Proceedings of the IEEE/CVF Conference on Computer Vision and Pattern Recognition, pp. 1924–1933 (2021)

22. Wang, X., He, X., Wang, J., He, K.: Admix: enhancing the transferability of adversarial attacks. In: Proceedings of the IEEE/CVF International Conference on Computer Vision, pp. 16158–16167 (2021)
23. Wang, Y., Zou, D., Yi, J., Bailey, J., Ma, X., Gu, Q.: Improving adversarial robustness requires revisiting misclassified examples. In: International Conference on Learning Representations (2020)
24. Wu, D., Xia, S.T., Wang, Y.: Adversarial weight perturbation helps robust generalization. In: Advances in Neural Information Processing Systems, vol. 33, 2958–2969 (2020)
25. Xie, C., Wang, J., Zhang, Z., Ren, Z., Yuille, A.: Mitigating adversarial effects through randomization. In: International Conference on Learning Representations (2018)
26. Xie, C., et al.: Improving transferability of adversarial examples with input diversity. In: Proceedings of the IEEE Conference on Computer Vision and Pattern Recognition, pp. 2730–2739 (2019)
27. Zhang, H., Yu, Y., Jiao, J., Xing, E., El Ghaoui, L., Jordan, M.: Theoretically principled trade-off between robustness and accuracy. In: International Conference on Machine Learning, pp. 7472–7482. PMLR (2019)
28. Zou, J., Pan, Z., Qiu, J., Liu, X., Rui, T., Li, W.: Improving the transferability of adversarial examples with resized-diverse-inputs, diversity-ensemble and region fitting. In: Vedaldi, A., Bischof, H., Brox, T., Frahm, J.-M. (eds.) ECCV 2020. LNCS, vol. 12367, pp. 563–579. Springer, Cham (2020). https://doi.org/10.1007/978-3-030-58542-6_34

Local-Fusion Diffusion Model for Enhancing Few-Shot Image Generation

Jishuai Hou, Lei Luo, and Jian Yang[✉]

Nanjing University of Science and Technology, Nanjing, China
{jshou,cslluo,csjyang}@njust.edu.cn

Abstract. In recent research, few-shot generation models have attracted increasing interest in computer vision. They aim at generating more data of a given domain, with only a few available training examples. Although many methods have been introduced to handle few-shot generation tasks, most of them are usually unstable during the training process and can only generate cookie-cutter images. To alleviate these issues, we propose a novel few-shot generation method based on the classifier-free conditional diffusion model. Specifically, we train an autoencoder on seen categories and then use patch discriminator adversarial training to achieve better reconstruction quality. Subsequently, for the k-shot task, we extract k image features and calculate the conditional information to guide the training generation of the diffusion model. To avoid the singularness of conditional information caused by the prototype model, we use the latest Feature Fusion module (LFM) to learn various features. We conduct extensive experiments on three well-known datasets and the experimental results clearly demonstrate the effectiveness of our proposed method for few-shot image generation.

Keywords: Few-shot generation · Diffusion model · Local representation fusing

1 Introduction

Few-shot image generation aims to generate new images for a certain category with few samples of the same category. The episodic training mechanism [1] served as the inspiration for this task. The generation model is first trained on a sufficiently large auxiliary dataset in this mechanism. Once the model is trained, it is given only a few samples of an unseen category, and it is expected to generate a wide range of diverse images for that category. The generative model can acquire generalization ability by learning from thousands of simulated few-shot image generation tasks. This capacity is achieved despite the disjoint label spaces between the seen auxiliary and unseen test datasets.

Existing few-shot image generation methods can be divided generally into three categories: transformation-based [2], optimization-based [3], and fusion-based [4,5]. Transformation-based methods utilize intra-category transformations on the available samples to produce novel images. However, the apove two approaches may be limited in handling complex generation tasks. Optimization-based methods adopt meta-learning

H. Lu et al. (Eds.): ICIG 2023, LNCS 14355, pp. 267–278, 2023.
https://doi.org/10.1007/978-3-031-46305-1_22

paradigms [6] to learn initial optimization strategies for unconditional image generation but are also effective only for simple generation tasks. Fusion-based methods define the task as a conditional generation problem, where an encoder in the generation model learns to map several input images into a latent space before performing a fusion operation. The fused feature is then decoded back into an output image of the same category.

Fusion-based few-shot image generation methods can produce diverse outputs while maintaining high image quality and label consistency. GMN [7] implements this by combining Matching Network [1] with VAE [8] through the appending of a decoder after the matching process. MatchingGAN [9] uses a generative adversarial network instead to generate natural images for the first time, although it still struggles with complex natural images. F2GAN [5] proposed a fuse-and-fill strategy to improve the generation ability, but its generation space is limited and imprecise. LoFGAN [4] introduces a new approach called "local feature fusion" to fusion-based few-shot image generation. This approach selects one of the few available images randomly as a base image and designates the others as reference images that serve as a bank of numerous available local representations. The base image determines the basis of the generation, while the reference images offer many local representations that can be utilized. Compared with F2GAN, the generation process of LoFGAN is more targeted and leads to fewer artifacts in the resulting images.

Fig. 1. Limitations of LoFGAN method. The first three columns of images serve as reference images, while the rest images represent the ground truth in the reconstruction loss during training.

However, LoFGAN can only partially remove artifacts, and there are still two problems with it: Firstly, due to the linear weighted combination of target images in the reconstruction loss, the generated images often have unavoidable artifacts. Secondly, LoFGAN's generated images lack diversity and exhibit high similarity with the base image. Figure 1 illustrates the limitations of the LoFGAN method, where the three left images are reference images, while the five right images are target images used in reconstruction loss during the training process. Obviously, the target images remain basically the same as one of the reference images, and only part of the patches are replaced. This causes inevitable artifacts in the generated results and severely limits the diversity of results.

To tackle the above problems, we decompose the few-shot image generation task into two sub-tasks: the first stage involves obtaining fused features, while the second stage involves using the obtained fused features as class semantic information to generate diverse images of the same class. Accordingly, we propose a two-stage approach for few-shot image generation using diffusion models. In the first stage, we train a VQVAE in an autoregressive manner to extract and discretize the features of the images. For better reconstruction quality, we introduce a patch discriminator [10] to supervise training. In the second stage, for the k-shot generation task, we first extract the features of the k images and then use the LFM module in LoFGAN [4] to obtain fused features. Then we use them as conditional information to guide the diffusion model in training. Since the fused features do not exist in the latent space of the image, we map them to the corresponding latent space of the actual image through the diffusion model. Then, we generate the images through the decoder.

Our contributions can be summarized as follows:

- We propose *Local-Fusion Diffusion Model(LoFDiffusion)* for few-shot image generation, which introduces a denoising diffusion model to achieve better generation quality and diversity.
- We use *local feature fusion module (LFM)* to obtain new features as conditional information, significantly improving the quality and diversity of the generated images.
- Extensive experiments demonstrate that our *LoFDiffusion* achieves comparable performance to state-of-the-art methods on multiple datasets.

2   Related Work

2.1   Diffusion Denoising Probabilistic Models

Denoising diffusion probabilistic models [7] are a novel form of generative model that has demonstrated remarkable success in a range of tasks, surpassing generative adversarial nets (GANs) [8]. This parameterized Markov chain optimizes the lower variational bound on the likelihood function to create actual distribution-matching samples. Ho et al. [11] originally proposed diffusion models, and later, Dhariwal and Nichol [12] showcased their potential by achieving superior image sample quality on the ImageNet dataset compared to other generative models. As a result, diffusion models have garnered much attention from researchers. Saaharia et al. [13] achieved success in superresolution using diffusion models. Similarly, Pattle [14] explored diffusion models on image-to-image translation tasks, such as colorization, inpainting, uncropped, and JPEG decompression. More interestingly, contemporary works by [15, 16] utilized diffusion models for text-to-image generation problems. Overall, diffusion models are promising within the realm of generative models, with their varied applications showing their versatile use in image and text-related image generation.

2.2 Few-Shot Image Adaptation

Few-shot image adaptation aims to generate new images for a certain category giving a few images from the same category by learning with sufficient labeled samples from a set of seen classes. It means that the generation model trained from the source classes needs to be adapted to both new classes and new domains, with few samples from the target classes [17]. Estimating a distribution from limited observations is naturally subject to bias and inaccuracy, especially for GANs. In order to address the challenge of insufficient data, some methods employ transfer learning [18]. The underlying concept is to utilize a source model that has been pre-trained on a large dataset and fine-tune it to a target domain with limited data. This can be accomplished by making minimal changes to the network parameters to preserve as much information as possible or artificially augmenting the training data [19].

These approaches mentioned above use auxiliary data, typically for pre-training purposes, to adapt a pre-trained GAN to a different image domain by adjusting the model parameters [20,21]. DCL [22] utilizes contrastive learning to push away the generated samples from natural images and maximize the similarity between corresponding image pairs in the source and target domain. Yan H [23] makes the first attempt to adapt the few-shot image translation method to the few-shot image generation task and can produce images of higher diversity and fidelity for unseen categories than previous methods. DDPM-PA [24] combines DDPMs to solve this. They proposed using a pairwise similarity loss to preserve the relative distances between generated samples. However, their research was done only under ten shots, and the generated images had weak category information.

2.3 Few-Shot Image Generation

Few-shot image generation aims to generate new images given a small number of samples, and there are broad practical applications in the real world. Although it looks like few-shot image generation, it is actually two very different tasks. Adversarial learning combined with meta-learning approaches has been utilized in optimization-based methods such as the FIGR [3] and DAWSON [25] models, which have limited generation quality. On the other hand, fusion-based methods like GMN [7] and MatchingGAN [9] utilize VAE and GAN with a generalized matching network from few-shot classification tasks to accomplish few-shot image generation. The F2GAN [5] model enhances MatchingGAN by adding a non-local attentional fusion module to fuse and fill different levels of features to generate images. However, these approaches tend to fuse high-level image features with a global coefficient, which often results in more aliasing artifacts and less diversity in the generated images. To tackle this, LoFGAN [4] designed a local fusion module that is based on local feature matching and replacing to produce semantically aligned deep features and a local reconstruction loss which aligns corresponding semantic areas for the input images and better guides the model training.

Although diffusion models have aroused widespread attention due to their powerful performance in recent years [11,15,26,27], there are few new techniques designed in a data-limited regime. As far as we know, FSDM [28] is the first work introducing the diffusion model into a few-shot image generation task. The well-designed context network using a vision transformer extracts information from patch-based input, then the extracted feature is fed into the diffusion model to generate new images. FSDM achieves competitive performance in a series of experiments.

3 Few-Shot Image Generation Enhanced with Diffusion Models

3.1 Overall

The few-shot image generation task aims to generate new images for a particular category given a few reference images. To achieve this, we divide the dataset into seen categories $\mathbb{C}_s$ and unseen categories $\mathbb{C}_u$, with null intersections. Figure 2 shows the overall framework of our method under the 3-shot image generation setting.

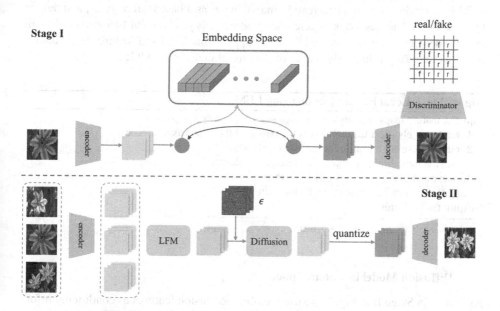

Fig. 2. LoFDiffusion framework: A comprehensive two-stage approach for few-shot image generation. Stage I consists of the VQVAE and Patch Discriminator, responsible for training high-quality reconstruction networks. Stage II consists of LFM and the diffusion model, during which we use the LFM extracts features which are then fed into the diffusion model to generate new images.

In stage I, we train VQVAE on $\mathbb{C}_s$ in a self-supervised manner. The input images are fed into the encoder to extract features, which are then quantified in the embedding space before being reconstructed by the decoder. To acquire a better quality of image reconstruction, we utilize a patch discriminator to augment the training process. Once the VQVAE is trained, it is then used for stage II.

In Stage II, we first extract deep features $\mathbb{F}$ by employing a pre-trained encoder E. Next, we utilize the LFM module to generate a semantically aligned fused feature

$\widetilde{\mathbb{F}}$, which is generated by taking $\mathbb{F}$ and a random coefficient vector α as inputs. The conditional diffusion model takes the concatenation of $\widetilde{\mathbb{F}}$ and random Gaussian noise ϵ as input and generates the feature corresponding to actual images. Finally, generated features are quantized and decoded to get generated images.

Stage II depicted in Fig. 2 represents the meta-testing process flow. Regarding meta-training, it is imperative to understand the construction of training sample pairs. Precisely, the fusion features acquired are duplicated k times, and they are then paired with k input images respectively to produce k sets of sample pairs for training purposes.

3.2   Local Feature Fusion

Given a set of encoded feature maps $F = E(X) \in R^{k \times w \times h \times c}$. Each $w \times h \times c$ tensor in F can be viewed as a set of $h \times w$ local representations of dimension c. The idea behind LFM is to randomly assign one feature map from F as a base feature f_{base}, and denote the rest $k - 1$ features maps as reference features F_{ref}. The local fusion module will take the select f_{base} as a basis and the rest F_{ref} as a bank of local features to produce a fused feature. Algorithm 1 shows the procedure of the LFM module.

Algorithm 1. Local Feature Fusion using LFM

Input k feature maps and random coefficient $\alpha = [\alpha_1, \alpha_2, \cdots, \alpha_k]$
  1. randomly choose a feature map as the base and the others as references.
  2. randomly select n feature for base denoted as ϕ_1;
  3. find the most similar feature from references, denote as $\phi_2, \cdots, \phi_k$
  4. linear combine $\phi_1, \phi_2, \cdots, \phi_k$ by α to get $\overline{\phi}$
  5. replace $\overline{\phi}$ back into base to get fusion feature $\overline{f}$
Output fusion feature $\overline{f}$

3.3   Diffusion Model in Latent Space

As shown in Stage II in Fig. 2, we use the obtained fusion features as conditional information to guide the training of the diffusion model in latent space. To train the conditional diffusion model, we follow the classifier-free guidance mechanism [29]. The method employs two types of diffusion models known as the unconditional denoising diffusion model $p_\theta(x)$, which is parameterized with a score estimator $\epsilon_\theta(x_t, t)$, as well as the conditional model $p_\theta(x|y)$, which is parameterized with $\epsilon_\theta(x_t, t, y)$. By using a single neural network, we can efficiently learn both models. Specifically, the paired data (x, y) is used to train the conditional diffusion model $p_\theta(x|y)$, whilst periodically discarding the conditioning information y, i.e. $\epsilon_\theta(x_t, t) = \epsilon_\theta(x_t, t, y = 0)$. By doing so, the model is also equipped to generate unconditional images. The gradient of an implicit classifier can be represented as:

$$\nabla_{\mathbf{x}_t} \log p(y \mid \mathbf{x}_t) = \nabla_{\mathbf{x}_t} \log p(\mathbf{x}_t \mid y) - \nabla_{\mathbf{x}_t} \log p(\mathbf{x}_t)$$

$$= -\frac{1}{\sqrt{1 - \bar{\alpha}_t}} (\epsilon_\theta(\mathbf{x}_t, t, y) - \epsilon_\theta(\mathbf{x}_t, t)) \tag{1}$$

$$\bar{\epsilon}_\theta\left(\mathbf{x}_t, t, y\right) = \epsilon_\theta\left(\mathbf{x}_t, t, y\right) - \sqrt{1 - \bar{\alpha}_t} w \nabla_{\mathbf{x}_t} \log p\left(y \mid \mathbf{x}_t\right)$$
$$= \epsilon_\theta\left(\mathbf{x}_t, t, y\right) + w\left(\epsilon_\theta\left(\mathbf{x}_t, t, y\right) - \epsilon_\theta\left(\mathbf{x}_t, t\right)\right) \qquad (2)$$
$$= (w + 1)\epsilon_\theta\left(\mathbf{x}_t, t, y\right) - w\epsilon_\theta\left(\mathbf{x}_t, t\right)$$

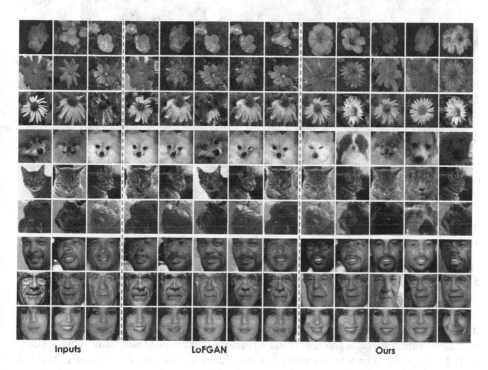

Inputs   LoFGAN   Ours

Fig. 3. Images generated by LoFGAN and our LofDiffusion on Flowers, Animal Faces, and VGGFace. The first three columns are input images; the rest are generated images.

The parameter w controls the strength of the condition signals here. When $w = -1$, the model performs unconditional image generation. On the other hand, when $w = 0$, the model operates as a wholly conditional image generation model.

4 Experiments

4.1 Setup

Datasets. We conducted experiments on three datasets: **Flowers** [30], consisting of 102 categories that we divided into 85 seen categories for training and 17 unseen categories for evaluation, with each category having a fixed number of 40 images. **Animal Faces** [31], containing 149 categories from which we selected 119 categories for training and 30 categories for evaluation, with 100 images per category. **VGGFace** [32] consisting

Fig. 4. Unconditional image generation results on Flower dataset with $w = -1$. The three images on the left are reference images, and those on the right are generated through our method.

of 1802 categories for training and 552 categories for evaluation, each category having 100 images.

Implementation Details. The VQVAE used in this study has a codebook capacity of 512 and a feature vector dimension of 3. It contains six residual blocks with a variable dimension of 32. The encoder outputs a feature dimension of 128, which is mapped to three dimensions using a 1×1 convolution. The balance factor beta is set to 0.25. The discriminator adopts a patch discriminator with four convolution blocks, each consisting of a convolution layer, a batch norm layer, and a leaky ReLU activation with a slope of 0.2. The initial convolution layer has 64 channels that are subsequently doubled sequentially.

For pre-training, the model is trained for 40,000 steps using a batch size of 64 and a learning rate of 3e-4. The quantization uses a sigmoid activation function. For meta-training, the learning rate is set to a constant value of 1e-4, with the optimizer set to Adam. The LofGAN rate is set to 0.5, and the conditional probability is set to 0.9. The model is trained for 400,000 steps using a linear scheduler with a timestep of 1000 for the beta of the diffusion model. During inference, the DDIM approach is used with the number of timesteps set to 50.

4.2 Qualitative Evaluation

Figure 3 shows a comparison of generated images of our method with those from Lof-GAN on all three datasets. In each row, we show five generated images for both methods. As can be seen, images generated by LoFGAN lack diversity compared with our method.

Our method is capable of generating unconditional images, as demonstrated in Fig. 4, which displays the generated images that are not dependent on reference images.

Furthermore, Fig. 5 shows generated images entirely dependent on reference images. Notably, our method generates images of high fidelity and diversity in both situations.

4.3 Quantiative Evaluation

We compared our method with several existing few-shot generation techniques, including FIGR [3], GMN [7], DAWSON [25], DAGAN [33], MatchingGAN [9], F2GAN [5], and LoFGAN [4]. For quantitative evaluation, we adopted a 3-way generation setting for both training and testing purposes. We evaluated the quality of the generated images using the Frechet Inception Distance (FID) and Learned Perceptual Image Patch Similarity (LPIPS) scores. We conducted our experiments following the same setting as [4].

Fig. 5. Conditional image generation results on Flower dataset with $w = 0$. The three images on the left are reference images, and those on the right are generated through our method.

Table 1 shows that our method achieved the best LPIPS score, indicating our model's ability to generate more diverse images. While our approach exhibits slightly weaker FID indicators than the LoFGAN model, the visual results presented in the previous section demonstrate that our generated images have high clarity and realism. It is worth noting that FID indicators have certain limitations, as they can only measure the generative model's quality to a certain extent. Despite our model's relatively high FID value, we could still produce clear and realistic images.

4.4 Ablation Study

Table 2 displays the results of an ablation experimental study. The first column indicates the initial experimental result utilizing the default VQVAE setting [34], with features extracted using the prototype method. In this setting, the effect was poor, and the model

Table 1. Comparison of quantitative evaluation on FID and LPIPS. We quote the results of the seven methods from the LoFGAN paper [4].The best and second-best results are highlighted.

Method	Type	Flowers		Animal		VGGFace	
		FID	LPIPS	FID	IPIPS	FID	LPIPS
FIGR [3]	Optimization	190.12	0.0634	211.54	0.0756	139.83	0.0834
DAWSON [25]	Optimization	188.96	0.0583	208.68	0.0642	137.82	0.0769
DAGAN [33]	Transformation	151.21	0.0812	155.29	0.0892	128.34	0.0913
GMN [7]	Fusion	200.11	0.0743	220.45	0.0868	136.21	0.0902
MatchingGAN [9]	Fusion	143.35	0.1627	148.52	0.1514	118.62	0.1695
F2GAN [5]	Fusion	120.48	0.2172	117.74	0.1831	109.16	0.2125
LoFGAN [4]	Fusion	**79.33**	0.3862	**112.81**	0.4964	**20.31**	0.2669
Ours	Fusion	95.48	**0.4494**	135.65	**0.5785**	27.9	**0.3702**

Table 2. Ablation Studies of our LoFDiffusion Design, demonstrating the impact of patch discriminator and LFM module on FID and LPIPS metric.

	Default	+Patch Discriminator	+LFM
FID	434.98	157.92	95.48
LPIPS	0.03	0.3592	0.4494

did not converge well. The second column added the patch discriminator in the pre-training phase, and both the FID and LPIPS indicators showed significant improvement. In the third column, we replaced the prototype method with LFM, further improving the two metrics. The ablation experiments described above demonstrate the effectiveness of our proposed method.

5   Conclusion

This paper presented a novel approach by integrating diffusion models into few-shot image generation for achieving high-quality and highly diverse image generation. We combined the conditional diffusion model of classifier-free with the advanced feature fusion method LoFGAN, using the *LFM module* in LoFGAN to generate rich and representative information guiding the training of the conditional diffusion model. Our experiments on three natural image datasets confirmed that our method generates realistic images with fewer aliasing artifacts and better diversity. Nonetheless, our approach still has limitations, and several issues need to be addressed. One of our method's challenges is that the diffusion model's training is time-consuming, despite operating under a few-shot scenario. In future work, it would be meaningful to investigate ways to redesign the diffusion models to reduce computation time. Furthermore, there is room for improvement regarding generation quality and diversity. We plan to tackle these issues in future work.

References

1. Vinyals, O., Blundell, C., Lillicrap, T., Wierstra, D., et al.: Matching networks for one shot learning. In: Advances in Neural Information Processing Systems, vol. 29 (2016)
2. Ding, G., et al.: Attribute group editing for reliable few-shot image generation. In: Proceedings of the IEEE/CVF Conference on Computer Vision and Pattern Recognition, CVPR2022, pp. 11194–11203 (2022)
3. Clouâtre, L., Demers, M.: FIGR: Few-shot Image Generation with Reptile. arXiv preprint arXiv:1901.02199 (2019)
4. Gu, Z., Li, W., Huo, J., Wang, L., Gao, Y.: LoFGAN: fusing local representations for few-shot image generation. In: Proceedings of the IEEE/CVF International Conference on Computer Vision, CVPR2021, pp. 8463–8471 (2021)
5. Hong, Y., Niu, L., Zhang, J., Zhao, W., Fu, C., Zhang, L.: F2GAN: fusing-and-filling gan for few-shot image generation. In: Proceedings of the 28th ACM International Conference on Multimedia, pp. 2535–2543. ACM Multimedia 2020 (2020)
6. Finn, C., Abbeel, P., Levine, S. : Model-agnostic meta-learning for fast adaptation of deep networks. In: International Conference on Machine Learning, pp. 1126–1135. PMLR (2017)
7. Bartunov, S., Vetrov, D.: Few-shot generative modelling with generative matching networks. In; International Conference on Artificial Intelligence and Statistics, pp. 670–678. PMLR (2018)
8. Kingma, D.P., Welling, M.: Auto-encoding variational Bayes. arXiv preprint arXiv:1312.6114 (2013)
9. Hong, Y., Niu, L., Zhang, J., Zhang, L.: MatchingGAN: matching-based few-shot image generation. In: 2020 IEEE International Conference on Multimedia and Expo (ICME), ICME2020, pp. 1–6. IEEE (2020)
10. Esser, P., Rombach, R., Ommer, B.:Taming Transformers for High-Resolution Image Synthesis, CVPR2021 (2021)
11. Ho, J., Jain, A., Abbeel, P.: Denoising diffusion probabilistic models. In: Advances in Neural Information Processing Systems, NeurIPS2020, vol. 33, pp. 6840–6851. Curran Associates Inc (2020)
12. Dhariwal, P., Nichol, A.: Diffusion models beat GANs on image synthesis. Adv. Neural. Inf. Process. Syst. **34**, 8780–8794 (2021)
13. Saharia, C., Ho, J., Chan, W., Salimans, T., Fleet, D.J., Norouzi, M.: Image super-resolution via iterative refinement IEEE Trans. Pattern Anal. Mach. Intell. (2022)
14. Saharia, C., et al.: Palette: image-to-image diffusion models. In; ACM SIGGRAPH 2022 Conference Proceedings, pp. 1–10 (2022)
15. Rombach, R., Blattmann, A., Lorenz, D., Esser, P., Ommer, B.: High-Resolution Image Synthesis with Latent Diffusion Models, CVPR2022. arXiv:2112.10752 (2022)
16. Nichol, A., et al.: Glide: Towards photorealistic image generation and editing with text-guided diffusion models. arXiv preprint arXiv:2112.10741 (2021)
17. Zhao, A., et al.: Domain-adaptive few-shot learning. In: Proceedings of the IEEE/CVF Winter Conference on Applications of Computer Vision, pp. 1390–1399 (2021)
18. Robb, E., Chu, W.S., Kumar, A., Huang, J.B.: Few-shot adaptation of generative adversarial networks. arXiv preprint arXiv:2010.11943 (2020)
19. Ojha, U., et al.: Few-shot image generation via cross-domain correspondence. In: Proceedings of the IEEE/CVF Conference on Computer Vision and Pattern Recognition, pp. 10743–10752 (2021)
20. Li, Y., Zhang, R., Lu, J., Shechtman, E.: Few-shot image generation with elastic weight consolidation. arXiv preprint arXiv:2012.02780 (2020)

21. Zhao, M., Cong, Y., Carin, L.: On leveraging pretrained GANs for generation with limited data. In: International Conference on Machine Learning, pp. 11340–11351. PMLR (2020)

22. Zhao, Y., Ding, H., Huang, H., Cheung, N.M.: A closer look at few-shot image generation. In: Proceedings of the IEEE/CVF Conference on Computer Vision and Pattern Recognition, CVPR2022, GAN Adaptation, pp. 9140–9150 (2022)

23. Hong, Y., Niu, L., Zhang, J., Zhang, L.: Few-shot Image Generation Using Discrete Content Representation. arXiv preprint arXiv:2207.10833. ACM MM (2022)

24. Zhu, J., Ma, H., Chen, J., Yuan, J.: Few-shot image generation with diffusion models. arXiv preprint arXiv:2211.03264 (2022)

25. Liang, W., Liu, Z., Liu, C.: Dawson: A domain adaptive few shot generation framework. arXiv preprint arXiv:2001.00576 (2020)

26. Nichol, A.Q., Dhariwal, P.: Improved denoising diffusion probabilistic models. In: ICML2021 (2021)

27. Wang, W., et al.: SinDiffusion: Learning a Diffusion Model from a Single Natural Image. arXiv:2211.12445 [cs] (2022)

28. Giannone, G., Nielsen, D., Winther, O.: Few-Shot Diffusion Models. Technical report arXiv:2205.15463 (2022)

29. Ho, J., Salimans, T.: Classifier-free diffusion guidance. arXiv preprint arXiv:2207.12598 (2022)

30. Nilsback, M.E., Zisserman, A.: Automated flower classification over a large number of classes. In: 2008 Sixth Indian Conference on Computer Vision, Graphics & Image Processing, pp. 722–729. IEEE (2008)

31. Liu, M.Y., et al.: Few-shot unsupervised image-to-image translation. In: Proceedings of the IEEE/CVF International Conference on Computer Vision, pp. 10551–10560 (2019)

32. Cao, Q., Shen, L., Xie, W., Parkhi, O.M., Zisserman, A.: Vggface2: a dataset for recognising faces across pose and age. In: 2018 13th IEEE International Conference on Automatic Face & Gesture Recognition (FG 2018), pp. 67–74. IEEE (2018)

33. Antoniou, A., Storkey, A., Edwards, H.: Data augmentation generative adversarial networks. arXiv preprint arXiv:1711.04340 (2017)

34. Van Den Oord, A., Vinyals, O., et al.; Neural discrete representation learning. In: Advances in Neural Information Processing Systems, vol. 30 (2017)

Table Structure Recognition of Historical Dongba Documents

Jingcheng Zhang[1], Hongjian Zhan[1,2], Xiao Tu[1], and Yue Lu[1(✉)]

[1] Shanghai Key Laboratory of Multidimensional Information Processing, East China Normal University, Shanghai, China
xtu@cee.ecnu.edu.cn, ylu@cs.ecnu.edu.cn
[2] Chongqing Institute, East China Normal University, Chongqing 401120, China

Abstract. The analysis of table structures in historical documents has been a crucial area of research. Its objective is to identify the location of tables within the documents and segment each table cell. However, this process is often hindered by irregular structures and damage caused by inadequate preservation. Similarly, analyzing historical records written in the pictographic Dongba script of the Naxi people presents significant challenges. In this paper, we propose a novel method for extracting the table structure of historical Dongba documents. Our approach involves annotating the document image with specific patterns and applying an object detection model to precisely locate the regions of interest in the image. We then extract the table structure using a set of post-processing techniques. We evaluate the effectiveness of our proposed method by conducting experiments using various object detection models and providing a detailed analysis of our dataset in the Experiments section. Our results demonstrate that our approach is highly beneficial.

Keywords: Table structure recognition · Historical document · Historical Dongba document

1 Introduction

Tables are a commonly used form of presenting organized data. In historical Dongba documents, tables are used to separate sentences rather than the way we do it today. The accurate extraction of table structure from historical Dongba documents is crucial. However, there are several challenges associated with this task. These challenges are primarily due to natural and man-made defects in the preservation process, such as missing pages and indistinct printing caused by paper deterioration. Furthermore, the drawing process for the tables in historical Dongba documents involved slanted and bent lines, making it challenging to locate the tables accurately. Additionally, electronic images of some ancient Dongba documents may be blurry due to the limitations of document scanning technology from decades ago. The analysis of the Dongba script is particularly challenging because it is a type of pictograph, and the characters are unevenly distributed in the tables. This uneven distribution makes some methods that use text area coordinates as prior knowledge ineffective for identifying tables in Dongba documents.

In recent years, deep learning techniques have advanced significantly, and several deep learning-based methods for recognizing table structures have been proposed. Notably, some methods use convolutional neural networks (CNNs) for table structure recognition, such as TabStructNet [1] and LGPMA [2]. These techniques are superior to traditional rule-based approaches in terms of effectiveness and accuracy. In these approaches, each cell of the table is considered a target to be detected.

Accurately identifying the table structures in historical Dongba documents is of great significance to historians, archaeologists, and researchers. These documents contain valuable historical information, and by identifying and reconstructing the table structures, we can gain a better understanding of the organizational structure, trade activities, population statistics, and other important historical events in ancient societies. This contributes to our research and understanding of Dongba culture and promotes the development of the field of ancient civilization studies.

Furthermore, the recognition of table structures in historical Dongba documents can provide valuable data resources for fields such as natural language processing and information extraction. By automating the extraction of table structures and data, we can build more accurate Dongba language corpora and provide better training data for natural language processing algorithms. This will help improve the performance of tasks such as machine translation, information retrieval, and text analysis.

In this paper, we present a framework for the extraction of table structure in historical documents written in Dongba script. The proposed framework consists of three main stages: object detection, corner point locating, and table structure analysis. In the object detection stage, an object detection network is utilized to detect the table corners, characters, and separators in historical Dongba document pages. Various detection models were experimented with to identify the most effective one for the task. As a result, a set of regions of interest (ROIs) are obtained. However, these ROIs alone are insufficient to determine the specific structure of the table. Therefore, a method based on x-y projection is proposed to precisely position the corner points of the table. Finally, utilizing the information from the previous stages, the A* algorithm is applied to achieve precise extraction of the table structure.

The main contributions of this paper are as follows:

- 325 historical Dongba document images were annotated based on the key patterns we developed, and the dataset was examined based on image quality.
- We proposed a novel framework for table structure recognition based on pattern detection, which can accurately segment the table structure of historical Dongba documents. The experimental results proved the effectiveness of the method.

Fig. 1. Three patterns we formulated as targets to be detected in the detection stage. **red box**: character, **blue box**: separator, **green box**: cell corners (Color figure online)

2   Related Works

2.1   Traditional Table Structure Recognition Methods

Early methods [3,4] for table structure recognition relied primarily on hand-crafted features and heuristic rules, which can be broadly divided into three stages: pre-processing, feature recognition, and post-processing. The pre-processing stage involves denoising and enhancement of the features to be recognized, such as table lines and characters. The denoising process is essential to eliminate noise and artifacts from the input image, which can interfere with subsequent analysis. In the feature recognition stage, hand-crafted features are recognized using a bottom-up approach, which progressively identifies characters, words, and phrases in the table through connected component analysis. The Hough transform is applied to detect horizontal and vertical lines, which are further processed to determine the table structure. In the post-processing stage, the complete structure of the table is obtained based on the detected pattern by applying designed heuristic rules which are designed to handle different table layouts, such as merged cells and nested tables.

2.2   Deep Learning-Based Table Structure Recognition Methods

The table structure recognition method based on deep learning far surpasses the traditional method in terms of efficiency and accuracy. Deep learning based methods can be divided into three categories: detection&segmentation-based method, generation-based method, and graph structure-based method.

Detection and Segmentation-Based Method. The detection-based approach to table recognition involves identifying specific elements within the table, such as horizontal and vertical lines, table vertices, or directly detecting table cells. Recent developments in this field have incorporated deep learning models to enhance table structure recognition performance. Schreiber et al. [5] applied a Faster R-CNN model to identify the table region in an image, followed by a segmentation model based on the Fully Convolutional Network (FCN) architecture to segment the rows and columns of the table. They then determined the specific structure of the table using a series of post-processing techniques. Subsequent studies [6–8] have also treated table recognition as a semantic segmentation problem, improving the structure of the segmentation network. In [9] and [10], the recognition target was either the table cells or the contents of the cells.

Generation-Based Method. The encoder-decoder architecture is commonly used in generation-based methods. Deng et al. [11] proposed a novel dataset, TABLE2LATEX-450K, which utilizes Long Short-Term Memory (LSTM) networks as the decoder of the model, and outputs the result in LateX format. Meanwhile, PubTabNet [12] annotate images in HTML format. Similarly, an encoder-decoder architecture-based model is applied to directly predict the table structure. The generation-based approach enables end-to-end training and direct markup generation of tables. However, the aforementioned frameworks necessitate millions of images during the training process and face difficulties in dealing with tables with complex structures.

Graph Structure-Based Method. The approach that utilizes graph structure [13–15] treats the table structure as a graph, where the content or cell in each unit is considered a node on the graph. The relationship between nodes is then determined using a graph neural network (GNN) [16] or a classification network [15], thereby identifying the table structure. The network architectures presented by Chi et al. [13] and Li et al. [14] follow a similar process. Initially, text regions in the table are detected using an object detection network, and features of the entire image are extracted using Convolutional Neural Networks (CNN). Subsequently, the detected regions are viewed as graph nodes, and the extracted features are combined to determine whether nodes belong to the same row, column, or cell, ultimately resulting in the structure of the table. In contrast, Xue et al. [15] categorized the relationships between nodes into multiple types and employed a classification network instead of a graph network to determine the relationship between two nodes.

3   Method

3.1   YOLO Key Pattern Detector

The whole architecture is shown in Fig. 2. In the first stage of our framework, we have identified three specific patterns that serve as object detection targets in Dongba documents. These patterns are composed of the characters and corners of the table cells, as well as the unique separator of Dongba script, which is shown in Fig. 1. By detecting the corners of each cell, we can accurately locate the region of each cell, while the separator in Dongba acts as a dividing line between two table cells. Moreover, we have also incorporated the detection of Dongba characters as one of our targets for two reasons. Firstly, the detection

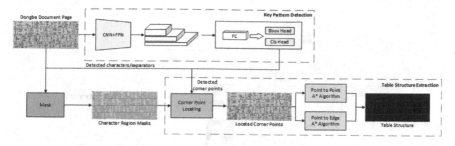

Fig. 2. Illustration of the overall framework. In the key pattern detection stage (the upper part of the figure), we detect three types of patterns we have formulated. Based on the detection results, we locate the exact coordinates of the corner points and extract the structure of the given document page (the lower part of the figure).

of Dongba characters can minimize the error rate of table extraction in subsequent processing by masking the detected character. Secondly, the inclusion of an additional detection target can enhance the complexity of the task during the detection stage, thereby allowing for the extraction of more robust features during model training. Our experiments have confirmed that the use of these detection targets has significantly improved the performance of our detection model.

Contrary to methods such as [10] and [9], which detect entire table cells, we did not adopt such strategies in our framework. This is because historical Dongba documents are handwritten documents, and the lines of the document are often slanted and curved. As a result, the tables are not strictly rectangular or only approximately rectangular, rendering direct table cell detection meaningless and not contributing to the performance of our framework. Moreover, since our dataset is labeled in the form of rectangular bounding boxes, direct table cell detection does not align with our labeling strategy.

In our study, we evaluated various object detection architectures, including the widely used Faster R-CNN [17], for their efficacy in table structure recognition tasks. However, our findings indicated that the performance of these models was suboptimal, primarily due to the limited amount of training data available (only 325 images). Specifically, the models exhibited unsatisfactory precision and regression rates. Conversely, we observed that the YOLO series of detectors outperformed the other models in this task. Consequently, we selected YOLOv8, which demonstrated superior performance compared to the other models, as the detecting model for our study. A detailed analysis of the performance of various detection models in this task is presented in Sect. 4 of our paper.

3.2 Corner Point Locating

After the detection stage, we get three types of bounding boxes: characters, cell corners, and separators. In this stage, we only need to operate on the cell corners, so we first mask the cell corners and separator area to avoid affecting

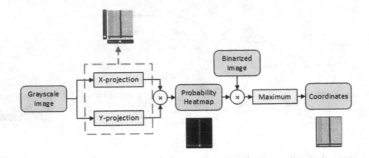

Fig. 3. The process of corner point locating, the red dot in the rightmost image represents the detected corner point. (Color figure online)

the accuracy of corner point locating. Let C denote the grayscale image of a detected cell corner and C_{binary} denote the binarized image, they are all of size $M \times N$. Let $C_{m,n}$ be the pixel in the m-th column and n-th row of the matrix C, and we get:

$$x_i = \sum_{n=i-2}^{i+2} \sum_{m=0}^{M} C_{m,n}, \quad y_j = \sum_{m=j-2}^{j+2} \sum_{n=0}^{N} C_{m,n}$$

Here, x_i represents the sum of all pixels in i^{th} column and y_j represents the sum of all pixels in j^{th} column. After normalizing all x_i and y_j, we get two arrays $\mathbf{X} = \{x_1, x_2, \cdots, x_N\}$, $\mathbf{Y} = \{y_1, y_2, \cdots, y_M\}$. Each element in these two arrays represents the sum of the pixel values of a given row&column and its two neighboring rows&columns in the image. Let

$$C' = \mathbf{Y}^\top \times \mathbf{X}$$

Obviously, C' is the same size as C. Since all the corners fall in the lower gray part of the image, we need to apply and calculate the matrix C' with the binarized matrix C^{bin}. We define the probability matrix as follows:

$$C_{i,j}^{prob} = \frac{exp(C'_{i,j} \cdot C_{i,j}^{bin})}{\sum_M^{m=0} \sum_N^{n=0} exp(C'_{m,n} \cdot C_{m,n}^{bin})}$$

The above equation is in the form of a softmax function. Each element in C^{prob} represents the probability that the corresponding pixel in the image is a corner point. We take the point with the highest probability as the predicted corner point.

3.3   Table Structure Analysis

In the table structure analysis stage, we consider the table structure analysis problem as a set of problems of solving the shortest path in the static road network, the problem is defined as follows

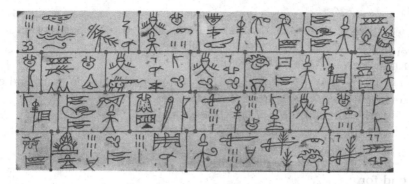

Fig. 4. In the detection stage, the corner points marked in **blue** in the figure are not detected. Therefore, an additional method is needed to extract the structure of the outermost table cells. (Color figure online)

Problem Definition. *Given a binary matrix A where 0 represents blocked cells, and a list of coordinates $[(x_1, y_1), (x_2, y_2), \cdots, (x_n, y_n)]$. Search for the shortest path between these coordinates, and the shortest path from the peripheral points to the edge of the image matrix. Subject to the constraint that the path must not pass through any cells other than those within a Euclidean distance of 50 units from any of the given coordinates.*

It is important to note that in the historical Dongba document image, the boundaries of the image coincide with the outer boundary of the table. During the detection stage, the outermost layer of the corner point remains indeterminate, as depicted in Fig. 4. Therefore, it is imperative to determine the structure of the outermost table cell by finding the shortest path from the peripheral points to the edge of the image. The computed paths represent the boundaries of each table cell in the image. To achieve this, we employ the A* algorithm, utilizing the Manhattan distance as a heuristic function. The following pseudo-code outlines the entire process:

Algorithm 1. Table Line Segmentation

Input: A binary matrix A, a coordinates list $P = [(x_1, y_1), (x_2, y_2), \cdots, (x_n, y_n)]$
Output: A list *Paths* storing all paths
    for $i = 0 \to len(P)$ **do**   ▷ Calculate the shortest path between points
        for $j = i + 1 \to len(P)$ **do**
            ▷ Replace the 50×50 area around other points except $P[i]$ and $P[j]$ with 0
            $ATemp \leftarrow A$
            for $k = 0 \to len(P), k \neq i, j$ **do**
                $ATemp[P[k].x - 25 : P[k].x + 25, P[k].y - 25 : P[k].y + 25] \leftarrow 0$
            end for
            $path = Astar(A, P[i], P[j])$ ▷ Manhattan distance as a heuristic function
            if $path \neq None$ **then**

$Paths.append(path)$
    end if
  end for
end for
for $i = 0 \rightarrow len(P)$ **do** ▷ Calculate the shortest path between point and edge
  for $dst \in (top, left, right, bottom)$ **do**
    $path = Astar(A, P[i], P[j])$
    if $path \neq None$ **then**
      $Paths.append(path)$
    end if
  end for
end for

---

4 Experiments

4.1 Datasets

Overview. The dataset utilized in our study comprises 325 scanned images of historical Dongba documents. These images are segmented into several areas by means of handwritten lines, with each area containing a single sentence. Additionally, a separator is present at the beginning of each paragraph.

Image Quality. A statistical analysis has been conducted on the image quality of a dataset consisting of 325 images. The average resolution of all images in the dataset is 1824×754. The dataset includes two types of quality issues: blurred images and paper stains. Specifically, 10 images were found to have partial blurring caused by the scanning equipment, while 21 images exhibited severe paper stains, as depicted in Fig. 5

Label Distribution. As mentioned above, we have annotated three types of labels: characters, corners of table cells, and separators. There is a long-tail problem in the label distribution, as shown in Table 1.

Table 1. Statistics of the historical Dongba datasets.

	Characters	Cell corners	Separators
Num	31117	6457	79
Proportion	82.64%	17.15%	0.21%

4.2 Detection Evaluation

We present experimental results on mainstream object detection baselines, which are currently considered state-of-the-art in the field. Object detection algorithms rely on data-driven approaches, using Convolutional Neural Networks (CNNs) to extract feature maps from input images. Recently, some Transformer-based approaches have been proposed for object detection, incorporating transformers in the encoding and decoding stages of the detection framework [18,19]. However, these methods heavily rely on large amounts of data, which can hinder effective training of the model.

To evaluate the performance of our dataset, we compared it against five commonly used baselines: Faster R-CNN [17], RetinaNet [20], YOLOv7 [21], and YOLOv8. To ensure a fair comparison, we pre-trained all backbones on the ImageNet [22] and annotated our datasets with rectangular bounding boxes. The experimental results show that YOLO provides the best overall performance (i.e. the highest F1 score). Therefore, for the subsequent experiments, we use YOLOv8 as the detection model.

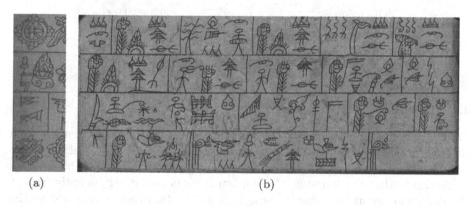

(a)   (b)

Fig. 5. (a) Blurry image; (b) stains and damages of paper

4.3 Training Details

We employed YOLOv8-x, the YOLOv8 model with the largest number of parameters and superior performance, as a detection network, and conducted the entire training procedure using MMdetection. To ensure uniformity of the input size for all images, we resized them to 640 × 640. In order to enhance the quality and diversity of the training data, we applied a range of data augmentation techniques, including random blur, random affine, HSV augment, and mosaic [23]. The dataset was randomly partitioned into 195 training sets, 65 test sets, and 65 validation sets. We employed the Stochastic Gradient Descent (SGD) optimizer for all training procedures, with an initial learning rate of 0.01 and a linear learning rate decay. Specifically, at each epoch, the learning rate was reduced by a factor of 0.1, with the final learning rate set to 0.001. We set the momentum to 0.937 and trained the model for a total of 500 epochs.

Table 2. Performance of different detection models for the pattern detection task on historical Dongba dataset.

Method	Precision	Recall	F1 score
Faster R-CNN + ResNet50	66.8	70.4	0.686
Faster R-CNN + ResNet101	66.6	70.4	0.684
Faster R-CNN + ResNext101	66.8	70.0	0.684
RetinaNet + ResNet50	65.8	69.3	0.675
RetinaNet + ResNet101	66.2	69.6	0.679
RetinaNet + ResNext101	66.7	70.1	0.684
YOLOv7-x	99.3	99.1	0.992
YOLOv7-e	99.6	**99.7**	0.996
YOLOv8-m	99.7	99.5	0.996
YOLOv8-x	**99.8**	99.6	**0.997**

4.4   Results and Discussion

Table 2 presents the outcomes of the detection stage. As the dataset suffers from the long-tail distribution problem, we conducted a separate analysis of the detection results for three distinct pattern types, as presented in Table 3. Our findings demonstrate that the long-tail distribution issue does not significantly impact the detection accuracy across classes. This observation can be ascribed to the absence of complicated backgrounds in the historical Dongba document images, as well as the simple style of separators. Consequently, the model can acquire the necessary features even with limited data. In our dataset, each image contains a considerable number of small targets that require detection. On average, there are approximately 116 targets per image that need to be identified. In YOLOv8, the Mosaic data argumentation on the input side, the PAN+FPN architecture in the neck, and the CIOU Loss are all effective in improving the performance of the detection on small targets.

During the Corner Point Locating stage, our framework ensures that all corner points detected fall within the intersection of the horizontal and vertical grid lines. However, as the detection model cannot achieve complete accuracy, the absence of a detected cell corner may result in errors during the table structure analysis stage. To evaluate the robustness of the framework, we designed an experiment to simulate scenarios where n corner points are randomly deleted from the detected corner points. The purpose of this experiment is to assess the framework's ability to maintain complete table structure extraction when the detection model fails to identify a limited number of corner points. The final outcome of the table structure extraction is presented in the figure, which reveals that our framework can still achieve a complete table structure even when a small number of corner points are undetected. This finding demonstrates the robustness of the framework and its ability to cope with the limitations of the detection model.

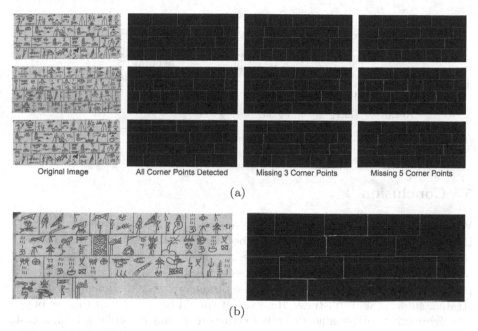

Fig. 6. (a) Randomly delete n detected corner points before applying A* algorithm for table structure analysis, and each column from left to right represents: the original image, without deleting corner points, deleting 3 detected corner points, and deleting 5 detected corner points. (b) Failure case.

The A* algorithm can successfully navigate through undetected corner points during the path calculation process, which can lead to a complete table structure. However, in certain cases, some corner points may remain undetected, resulting in the generation of small connected components where multiple paths pass through the same table line, as depicted in Fig. 6(a). To ensure the accuracy and reliability of the table structure analysis, it is necessary to perform a range comparison and eliminate any small connected components before determining the final table structure. This process effectively prevents the small connected components from interfering with the results of the table structure analysis. However, as shown in Fig. 6(b), the excessive density of characters arranged in close proximity to the boundaries of table lines leads to the omission of certain table lines. This phenomenon arises from the substantial occlusion of table lines during the masking process of the other two patterns.

In general, the performance on the proposed dataset is nearly perfect. We attribute this to several factors. First, during the detection stage, the absence of complex backgrounds in our dataset enables the detection model to achieve a high level of accuracy through training. Additionally, the blurry and damaged elements in historical documents do not significantly distort the line segments of tables in the images. Therefore, even a simple binarization algorithm can successfully extract a portion of the table lines.

Table 3. Performance of YOLOv8-x in detecting three patterns.

	Characters	Cell corners	Separators (Total 16 in validation set)
Precision	99.89	99.07	94.1
Recall	99.70	99.53	100

5   Conclusion

We proposed a novel framework for the analysis of table structure in historical Dongba documents. The proposed method involves the detection of three patterns formulated through an object detection model. The table structure is then obtained through a series of post-processing techniques based on the detected patterns. The effectiveness of the proposed framework is experimentally demonstrated, showing its robustness. However, it should be noted that the use of the A* algorithm to determine the table structure incurs a significant time cost, resulting in an overall low efficiency. Therefore, future work will aim at developing an end-to-end model to improve the efficiency of the entire framework.

References

1. Raja, S., Mondal, A., Jawahar, C.V.: Table structure recognition using top-down and bottom-up cues. In: Vedaldi, A., Bischof, H., Brox, T., Frahm, J.-M. (eds.) ECCV 2020. LNCS, vol. 12373, pp. 70–86. Springer, Cham (2020). https://doi.org/10.1007/978-3-030-58604-1_5
2. Qiao, L., et al.: LGPMA: complicated table structure recognition with local and global pyramid mask alignment. In: Lladós, J., Lopresti, D., Uchida, S. (eds.) ICDAR 2021. LNCS, vol. 12821, pp. 99–114. Springer, Cham (2021). https://doi.org/10.1007/978-3-030-86549-8_7
3. Liu, Y., Bai, K., Mitra, P., Giles, C.L.: Improving the table boundary detection in PDFs by fixing the sequence error of the sparse lines. In: 2009 10th International Conference on Document Analysis and Recognition, pp. 1006–1010. IEEE (2009)
4. Rastan, R., Paik, H.-Y., Shepherd, J.: TEXUS: A unified framework for extracting and understanding tables in PDF documents. Inf. Process. Manage. **56**(3), 895–918 (2019)

5. Schreiber, S., Agne, S., Wolf, I., Dengel, A., Ahmed, S.: DeepDeSRT: deep learning for detection and structure recognition of tables in document images. In: 2017 14th IAPR International Conference on Document Analysis and Recognition (ICDAR), vol. 1, pp. 1162–1167. IEEE (2017)
6. Siddiqui, S.A., Khan, P.I., Dengel, A., Ahmed, S.: Rethinking semantic segmentation for table structure recognition in documents. In: 2019 International Conference on Document Analysis and Recognition (ICDAR), pp. 1397–1402. IEEE (2019)
7. Khan, S.A., Khalid, S.M.D., Shahzad, M.A., Shafait, F.: Table structure extraction with bi-directional gated recurrent unit networks. In: 2019 International Conference on Document Analysis and Recognition (ICDAR), pp. 1366–1371. IEEE (2019)
8. Tensmeyer, C., Morariu, V.I., Price, B., Cohen, S., Martinez, T.: Deep splitting and merging for table structure decomposition. In: 2019 International Conference on Document Analysis and Recognition (ICDAR), pp. 114–121. IEEE (2019)
9. Hashmi, K.A., Stricker, D., Liwicki, M., Afzal, M.N., Afzal, M.Z.: Guided table structure recognition through anchor optimization. IEEE Access **9**, 113521–113534 (2021)
10. Ma, C., Lin, W., Sun, L., Huo, Q.: Robust table detection and structure recognition from heterogeneous document images. Pattern Recogn. **133**, 109006 (2023)
11. Deng, Y., Rosenberg, D., Mann, G.: Challenges in end-to-end neural scientific table recognition. In: 2019 International Conference on Document Analysis and Recognition (ICDAR), pp. 894–901. IEEE (2019)
12. Zhong, X., ShafieiBavani, E., Jimeno Yepes, A.: Image-based table recognition: data, model, and evaluation. In: Vedaldi, A., Bischof, H., Brox, T., Frahm, J.-M. (eds.) ECCV 2020. LNCS, vol. 12366, pp. 564–580. Springer, Cham (2020). https://doi.org/10.1007/978-3-030-58589-1_34
13. Chi, Z., Huang, H., Xu, H.-D., Yu, H., Yin, W., Mao, X.-L.: Complicated table structure recognition. arXiv preprint arXiv:1908.04729 (2019)
14. Li, Y., Huang, Z., Yan, J., Zhou, Y., Ye, F., Liu, X.: GFTE: graph-based financial table extraction. In: Del Bimbo, A., et al. (eds.) ICPR 2021. LNCS, vol. 12662, pp. 644–658. Springer, Cham (2021). https://doi.org/10.1007/978-3-030-68790-8_50
15. Xue, W., Li, Q., Tao, D.: ReS2TIM: reconstruct syntactic structures from table images. In: 2019 International Conference on Document Analysis and Recognition (ICDAR), pp. 749–755. IEEE (2019)
16. Scarselli, F., Gori, M., Tsoi, A.C., Hagenbuchner, M., Monfardini, G.: The graph neural network model. IEEE Trans. Neural Netw. **20**(1), 61–80 (2008)
17. Ren, S., He, K., Girshick, R., Sun, J.: Faster R-CNN: towards real-time object detection with region proposal networks. In: Advances in Neural Information Processing Systems, vol. 28 (2015)
18. Carion, N., Massa, F., Synnaeve, G., Usunier, N., Kirillov, A., Zagoruyko, S.: End-to-end object detection with transformers. In: Vedaldi, A., Bischof, H., Brox, T., Frahm, J.-M. (eds.) ECCV 2020. LNCS, vol. 12346, pp. 213–229. Springer, Cham (2020). https://doi.org/10.1007/978-3-030-58452-8_13
19. Zhu, X., Su, W., Lu, L., Li, B., Wang, X., Dai, J.: Deformable DETR: deformable transformers for end-to-end object detection. arXiv preprint arXiv:2010.04159 (2020)
20. Lin, T.-Y., Goyal, P., Girshick, R., He, K., Dollár, P.: Focal loss for dense object detection. In: Proceedings of the IEEE International Conference on Computer Vision, pp. 2980–2988 (2017)
21. Wang, C.-Y., Bochkovskiy, A., Liao, H.-Y.M.: YOLOv7: trainable bag-of-freebies sets new state-of-the-art for real-time object detectors. arXiv preprint arXiv:2207.02696 (2022)

22. Deng, J., Dong, W., Socher, R., Li, L.-J., Li, K., Fei-Fei, L.: ImageNet: a large-scale hierarchical image database. In: 2009 IEEE Conference on Computer Vision and Pattern Recognition, pp. 248–255. IEEE (2009)
23. Bochkovskiy, A., Wang, C.-Y., Liao, H.-Y.M.: YOLOv4: optimal speed and accuracy of object detection. arXiv preprint arXiv:2004.10934 (2020)

LE2Fusion: A Novel Local Edge Enhancement Module for Infrared and Visible Image Fusion

Yongbiao Xiao, Hui Li[✉], Chunyang Cheng, and Xiaoning Song

International Joint Laboratory on Artificial Intelligence of Jiangsu Province,
School of Artificial Intelligence and Computer Science, Jiangnan University,
Wuxi 214122, China
lihui.cv@jiangnan.edu.cn

Abstract. Infrared and visible image fusion task aims to generate a fused image which contains salient features and rich texture details from multi-source images. However, under complex illumination conditions, few algorithms pay attention to the edge information of local regions which is crucial for downstream tasks. To this end, we propose a fusion network based on the local edge enhancement, named LE2Fusion. Specifically, a local edge enhancement (LE2) module is proposed to improve the edge information under complex illumination conditions and preserve the essential features of image. For feature extraction, a multi-scale residual attention (MRA) module is applied to extract rich features. Then, with LE2, a set of enhancement weights are generated which are utilized in feature fusion strategy and used to guide the image reconstruction. To better preserve the local detail information and structure information, the pixel intensity loss function based on the local region is also presented. The experiments demonstrate that the proposed method exhibits better fusion performance than the state-of-the-art fusion methods on public datasets.

Keywords: Image fusion · Local edge enhancement · Feature extraction · Pixel intensity

1 Introduction

Image fusion is a technique to fuse images acquired by sensors of different types into a single informative image. As an important image enhancement technique, it has a wide range of applications in object tracking [5,7,13], object detection [10], *etc.* In this work, we focus on the infrared and visible image fusion.

Due to the complementary characteristics of the infrared and visible image fusion and the development of deep learning, many learning-based fusion methods have been proposed, and the performance of these methods has been greatly improved. Some methods use a single network structure to directly generate

Supplementary Information The online version contains supplementary material available at https://doi.org/10.1007/978-3-031-46305-1_24.

| (a) Infrared | (b) Visible | (c) DenseFuse | (d) PIAFusion | (e) Ours |

Fig. 1. An example of infrared and visible image fusion. Our method preserves edge information and details of bicycle mark.

the fused image. Although promising results can be obtained, the simple network structure may not effectively preserve useful details. Therefore, in order to retain more details and salient features in the fused images, some methods separately design enhancement modules and include them in the fusion network.

On the other hand, few learning-based algorithms pay much attention to the local edge information and salient features under complex illumination conditions. As shown in Fig. 1, compared with the illumination-aware method PIA-Fusion [12], our result can fully present the sign of the bicycle on the ground. This issue indicates that the enhancement module in the PIAFusion are not robust.

To address the aforementioned problem, we propose a novel fusion network for the infrared and visible image fusion based on the local edge enhancement module, which is termed as LE2Fusion. In LE2Fusion, a local edge enhancement module is designed to simultaneously enhance the local edge information and preserve the salient features. After that, a multi-scale residual attention module is applied into feature extractor and the rich features of source images can be obtained. Besides, a set of enhancement weights are utilized to guide the fusion stage and the reconstruction of the fused image. Finally, we innovatively design a pixel intensity loss function based on the local region, which enables the network to preserve more local structural features and thermal radiation information from the infrared modality. In this way, regardless of the illumination conditions, our method can produce promising fusion results. In summary, the major contributions of this study are summarized as follows:

- A local edge enhancement module is devised to extract the local edge intensity information. A set of enhancement weights generated by this module are used to guide the fusion and reconstruction process of the final output.
- A multi-scale residual module based on the attention mechanism is introduced in the feature extractor to obtain more rich deep features of source images.
- We design a new pixel intensity loss function based on the ideas of preserving the structural features and pixel intensity in the local region.
- Qualitative and quantitative experiments on multiple infrared and visible image fusion benchmarks demonstrate the superiority of the proposed method.

2   Related Work

In this section, we first review the image fusion algorithms without the enhancement module. After that, we briefly introduce some methods based on the enhancement module.

Algorithms Without the Enhancement Module: Without applying the enhancement modules, current algorithms only improve and optimize the network itself. DenseFuse [4] uses dense blocks during the encoding phase to extract image features. In addition to the dense connections, Li *et al.* introduce a multi-scale encoder-decoder network and the nested connections to extract more comprehensive features of source images (RFN-Nest [6]). On the other hand, IFCNN [15] is a representative general fusion network. In this work, the convolutional layers are used to extract salient features of source images. Then, the combined convolutional features are reconstructed to yield the fused images. Although these methods can achieve promising results, the design of the network structure is too simple to fully extract the robust features of the images. Besides, the coarse-grained loss function design cannot meet the requirements to focus on the details and structural information of source images.

Algorithms With the Enhancement Module: Since the use of a single network cannot achieve the desired result, some approaches introduce additional modules to enhance the fusion results. SeAFusion [11] designs a gradient residual dense block to enhance fine-grained spatial details. DIVFusion [10] designs two modules to remove the illumination degradation and enhance the contrast and texture details of the fused features respectively. In MUFusion [1], a new memory unit architecture based on the intermediate fusion results collected in the training phase is introduced to further supervise the fusion process. However, although some modules are used in their methods, the enhancement performance is not promising. Thus, we need fine-grained design to improve current enhancement-based methods.

3   Method

In this section, the proposed fusion network is presented. Firstly, we give the details of our framework. Then, the loss functions for training phase are introduced. Finally, the detail settings of our network will be given.

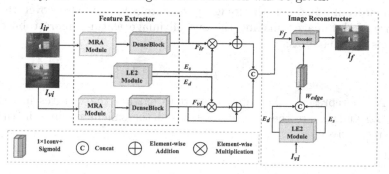

Fig. 2. The framework of the proposed method.

3.1 Framework

As we discussed, most image fusion methods ignore the local region edge information in the feature extraction process. To solve this problem, we design a fusion
network based on the local edge enhancement module. The framework is shown
in Fig. 2. Our method combined with two architectures ("Feature Extractor" and
"Image Reconstructor") in which the LE2 is utilized in these two modules simultaneously. In feature fusion strategy, the attention and the concatenation are
introduced to preserve the complementary features.

Local Edge Enhancement Module. As shown in Fig. 3, considering the
imbalance of illumination will degrade the image feature extraction, a local edge
enhancement module is proposed to avoid this drawback. The LE2 module contains five convolutional layers and one normalization operation to generate the
illumination-aware matrices (E_d and E_s).

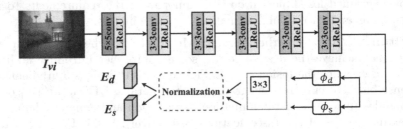

Fig. 3. The detailed structure of the local edge enhancement module (LE2).

Given a visible image I_{vi}, the LE2 module is formulated as:

$$\{\phi_d, \phi_s\} = N_{edge}(I_{vi}) \tag{1}$$

where N_{edge} denotes the edge enhancement network, ϕ_d and ϕ_s are the extracted
edge intensities and salient features.

Besides, compared with the general methods that only focus on the pixel
intensity of the source images, the features of the 3×3 region extracted by our
method not only focus on the image pixel intensity, but also cover the local
structure of the images, making the overall image features more robust. This
process is formulated as:

$$L_c = N_{local}(\phi_c), \quad c \in \{d, s\} \tag{2}$$

where N_{local} represents the network used to extract the features in the local
region, L_d and L_s are the edge intensity and the salient features in the local
region, respectively.

Meanwhile, we use a simple normalization function to calculate the final weights which also indicate the local region edge information from the source images, the formula is defined as follows,

$$E_c = \frac{L_c}{\sum_{i\in\{d,s\}} L_i}, \quad c \in \{d,s\} \tag{3}$$

where E_d and E_s indicate the edge-aware matrices which represent the edge information of local region.

Feature Extractor. In this section, we introduce the multi-scale residual attention network [2] into the feature extractor to obtain richer image features (Fig. 4).

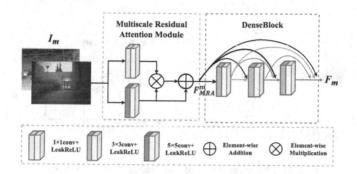

Fig. 4. The detailed structure of feature extractor.

In Fig. 4, the MRA contains several convolution layers which have different kernel size (3×3 and 5×5), these layers are utilized to extract multi-scale features to enhance the image features. Then the DenseBlock is applied into feature extractor to preserve abundant detail information. Specifically, we first extract the features of source images through the MRA module,

$$F^m_{MRA} = conv_{5\times5}(I_m) \oplus (conv_{5\times5}(I_m) \otimes conv_{1\times1}(I_m)), \quad m \in \{ir, vi\} \tag{4}$$

where $conv_{n\times n}(\cdot)$ represents several convolutional operations with the kernel size of $n \times n$, $\oplus$ refers to the element-wise summation, $\otimes$ indicates the element-wise multiplication. F^{ir}_{MRA} and F^{vi}_{MRA} are the features of the infrared and visible images obtained by the MRA module.

Then, we send these features into the DenseBlock, which is formulated as:

$$F_m = N_{Dense}(F^m_{MRA}), \quad m \in \{ir, vi\} \tag{5}$$

where N_{Dense} represents the DenseBlock. F_{ir} and F_{vi} are the obtained rich features of source images.

Fusion Strategy. In this part, the edge-aware matrices is utilized as the weights to enhance the multi-modal features, in which the attention and concatenation are applied.

Firstly, we combine the rich features extracted by the feature extractor together. It is specifically denoted as:

$$F_f = concat\left((F_{ir} \oplus (F_{ir} \otimes E_s)), (F_{vi} \oplus (F_{vi} \otimes E_d))\right), \tag{6}$$

where $concat\,(\cdot)$ represents the concatenation in the channel dimensions.

Image Reconstructor. As shown in Fig. 5, in the image reconstruction process, we use a set of enhancement weights generated by the LE2 module (consistent with the above structure) to guide this process.

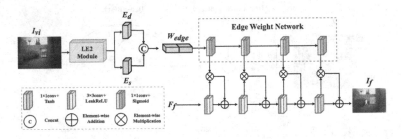

Fig. 5. The framework of the image reconstructor.

We use F_f^i and W_{edge}^i to denote the features reconstructed by the ith convolutional layer from the F_f and W_{edge}, respectively. The above image reconstruction process is defined as:

$$F_f^i = F_f^{i-1} \oplus (F_f^{i-1} \otimes conv_{1\times1}(W_{edge}^{i-1})) \tag{7}$$
$$s.t.\quad W_{edge} = concat(E_d, E_b).$$

3.2   Loss Function

A well-designed loss function enables different modules to learn specific information and make the network suitable for a specific fusion task. To make our network extract more local edge features and detail information, our fusion loss is formulated as follows,

$$L_{fusion} = \lambda_1 \cdot L_{ssim} + \lambda_2 \cdot L_{region} + \lambda_3 \cdot L_{texture}. \tag{8}$$

where the λ_1, λ_2 and λ_3 indicate the balance parameters.

Specifically, the SSIM loss function is obtained by the following formulation:

$$L_{ssim} = 1 - SSIM\,(O, I) \tag{9}$$

where $SSIM(\cdot)$ represents the structural similarity operation.

Unfortunately, for the local edge features, the structural similarity loss function is not promising. To this end, we innovatively design a pixel intensity loss function based on the local regions, which is defined as follows,

$$L_{region} = \frac{1}{HW} \| I_f - max(I_{reg}^{ir}, I_{reg}^{vi}) \|_1, \tag{10}$$

where H and W are the height and width of the source images. I_{reg}^{ir} and I_{reg}^{vi} are image features extracted from the 3×3 regions with the average operation.

Besides, we expect the fused image to preserve salient texture details of source images. Thus, we specially introduce the texture loss, which is defined as follows,

$$L_{texture} = \frac{1}{HW} \| |\nabla I_f| - max(|\nabla I_{ir}|, |\nabla I_{vi}|) \|_1, \tag{11}$$

where ∇ denotes the Sobel operator.

In summary, the design of our loss function is based on the idea of preserving meaningful information from source images.

3.3   Network Architecture

Local Edge Enhancement Network. The specific structure of the local edge enhancement module is shown in Fig. 3, which has six convolutional layers. The kernel of the first convolutional layer is 5×5, and the kernels of the remaining five layers is 3×3. Leaky Rectified Linear Unit (LReLU) activation function is used in all the convolutional layers.

Feature Extractor. The feature extraction network consists of the multi-scale residual attention module and the DenseBlock. The MRA module is composed of a 1×1 convolutional layer with the LReLU activation function and a 5×5 convolutional layer. This module can fully extract the multi-scale image features.

The output of the MRA module will be the input of the DenseBlock, which contains three 3×3 convolutional layers, and the output of each layer is cascaded with the input of the next layer. Compared with the general networks, the introduction of the DesnBlock enables our network to obtain richer image features. [1]

Image Reconstructor. In our approach, the image reconstructor is guided by a set of enhancement weights. Four 1×1 convolutional layers are utilized to capture the edge information. The image reconstructor contains three convolutional layers with the kernel size of 3×3 and one 1×1 layer used to decrease the channels. LReLU is used as the activation function for all convolutional layers in the image reconstructor, but the activation function of the last layer is the Tanh.

---

[1] More details of network architecture, please refer to our supplementary material.

4   Experimental Results and Analysis

In this section, we first introduce the details of our implementation configurations. After that, we compare our method with several SOTA image fusion algorithms by performing qualitative and quantitative experiments. In addition, we analyze the edge features. Finally, some ablation studies are conducted to verify the effectiveness of the proposed modules.

4.1   Experimental Settings

To comprehensively evaluate the proposed algorithm, we perform qualitative and quantitative experiments on the MSRS dataset [12] with all the 361 image pairs, the RoadScene dataset [14] with randomly selected 44 image pairs and the LLVIP dataset [3] with randomly selected 44 image pairs. We compare our method with six state-of-the-art (SOTA) approaches, including DenseFuse [4], FusionGAN [9], U2Fusion [14], PIAFusion [12], SwinFusion [8] and MUFusion [1]. The implementations of these approaches are publicly available.

Five statistical evaluation metrics are selected in the quantitative experiments, including standard deviation (SD), entropy (EN), mutual information (MI), the sum of correlations of differences (SCD) and Q_{abf}. SD reflects the visual effect of the fused image. EN is used to represent the image detail retention. MI measures the amount of information transferred from the source images to the fused image. SCD reflects the level of correlation between the information transmitted to the fused image and corresponding source images. Q_{abf} measures the amount of edge information. Moreover, a fusion algorithm with larger SD, EN, MI, SCD and Q_{abf} indicates better fusion performance.

Our model is trained on the MSRS dataset, which contains 1,444 resized 256×256 image patches. For the RGB images, we first convert the visible images to the YCbCr color space. Then, the Y channel of the visible images and the infrared images are fused by our proposed method. Finally, the fused image is converted back to the RGB color space via concatenating the Cb and Cr channels of the visible images.

The batch size and epochs are set as 30 and 4, respectively. The hyperparameters λ_1, λ_2, and λ_3 in the Eq. 8 are set as 3, 7, and 49, respectively. The model parameters are updated by using the Adam optimizer with the learning rate first initialized to 0.001 and then decayed exponentially. All the involved experiments are conducted on an NVIDIA RTX 3090Ti GPU and Intel Core i7-10700 CPU.

4.2   Comparative Experiments

In order to comprehensively evaluate the performance of our method, we compare our method with other six SOTA methods on the MSRS and the LLVIP datasets[2].

---

[2] For more experiments, please refer to our supplementary material.

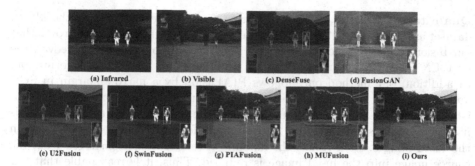

Fig. 6. Qualitative comparison of our method with six SOTA methods on the MSRS dataset.

Qualitative Results. Qualitative experiments performed on the MSRS dataset are shown in Fig. 6. As shown in the red highlighted regions, SwinFusion and FusionGAN are barely able to observe the details of the fence. Moreover, DenseFuse and U2Fusion weaken the target details. For the MUFusion, it blurs the edges of the fence. Only our method and PIAFusion can better preserve the detail information. As illustrated in the green box, there is a mismatch issue between target and overall image light condition in FusionGAN, SwinFusion and MUFusion. In addition, DenseFuse and U2Fusion weaken the infrared targets, resulting in suboptimal fusion results.

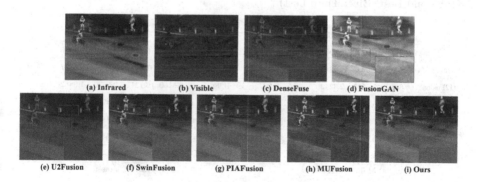

Fig. 7. Qualitative comparison of our method with six SOTA methods on the LLVIP dataset.

The visualization results of different methods on the LLVIP dataset are shown in Fig. 7. The selected nighttime images can demonstrate the superiority of our approach. As shown in the green box, DenseFuse, FusionGAN, U2Fusion, and MUFusion fail to clearly show the sidewalk in the dark, and FusionGAN fails to retain the sharp edges of the targets, suffering from the overall blurred issues. Only our method, SwinFusion and PIAFusion preserve the texture information of the sidewalks well. Besides, as shown in the red box, only our method can clearly present the bicycle mark.

Quantitative Results. The quantitative results of five metrics on the MSRS dataset are presented in Table 1 (a). The highest performance on SD proves that our fusion results are more in line with human visual perception. Moreover, the best EN means that our fused image contains more meaningful information. In addition, our method only follows PIAFusion by a narrow margin in SCD and Q_{abf}, which indicates that our fusion results can also contain more realistic information and edge information. For the MI, although the advantage is not particularly significant, our method can effectively remove the artifacts in the fused images. As a result, the amount of information transferred from the source image into the fused image is reduced. Thus, it is reasonable that our performance on MI has lower ranking.

The comparison results of different methods on the LLVIP dataset are shown in Table 1 (b). Our method ranks first on the metric of SD, which indicates that our method has satisfactory visual effects. Although our method has the second best performance on EN and MI, the margin between our method and the best is tiny. It demonstrates that our fusion results can contain more edge information and structure information. In addition, our method only follows SwinFusion and PIAFusion by a narrow margin on SCD and Q_{abf}. This is due to the reason that our method will sacrifice part of the information and reduce the noise when extracting the edge features of the local region, so as to produce a visually pleasing fused image.

Table 1. Quantitative results from MSRS [12] and LLVIP [3] datasets. (**Bold**: Best, Red: Second Best, Blue: Third best)

Methods	SD	EN	MI	SCD	Q_{abf}
DenseFuse	7.4237	5.9340	2.5905	1.2489	0.3572
FusionGAN	7.1758	5.9937	1.4315	0.3129	0.2110
U2Fusion	6.8217	5.5515	2.3242	1.2955	0.2972
SwinFusion	6.0518	5.2846	**4.1432**	0.5631	0.2942
PIAFusion	8.2822	6.4971	4.0022	**1.6421**	**0.6486**
MUFusion	6.9233	5.9682	1.6537	1.2548	0.4110
Ours	**8.3093**	**6.5364**	3.7766	1.5803	0.5996

(a) MSRS dataset

Methods	SD	EN	MI	SCD	Q_{abf}
DenseFuse	8.6065	6.4398	2.7610	1.0946	0.3426
FusionGAN	9.1167	**6.9251**	1.9305	0.5557	0.2479
U2Fusion	8.5160	6.1217	3.0870	1.0862	0.2983
SwinFusion	8.7054	6.7909	**3.8292**	1.3733	0.5927
PIAFusion	8.9390	6.7592	3.4146	**1.4105**	**0.6222**
MUFusion	8.3623	6.5243	2.5435	1.0618	0.4194
Ours	**9.2720**	6.8516	3.4509	1.3242	0.4574

(b) LLVIP dataset

4.3   Ablation Studies

Edge Features Analysis. In Fig. 8, we visualize a pair of feature maps generated by the LE2 module. We can clearly observe that the edge information are highlighted in the feature maps. When dealing with the edge features of the local regions, we use a normalization formula, making two images complementary in brightness. In our method, E_d enhances the edge information and E_s enhances other salient features. As shown in the contrast of the trees and the sky in the edge feature map, the LE2 module extracts the meaningful information from the local edge regions.

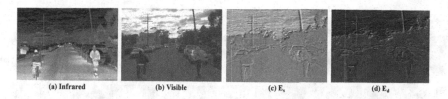

Fig. 8. Visualized results of images and feature maps.

LE2 Module Analysis. Considering the extraction of edge information in local regions, we design the LE2 module. In ablation experiment, we design two removal methods, one is to remove the LE2 module during feature reconstruction, but retain it in the fusion layer (Fig. 9(b) and Fig. 9(g)). The other approach is to remove the LE2 module completely (Fig. 9(c) and Fig. 9(h)). From the green box, we can clearly find that they weaken the salient target. Moreover, artifacts are also introduced in the enlarged red box in (g) and (h). In addition, the results of the fusion layer with the LE2 is obviously better than the results without the LE2 module, which also demonstrates that the LE2 module plays an important role in guiding the image reconstruction.

MRA Module Analysis. We introduce the MRA module into the DenseBlock to better preserve rich features from the source images. To demonstrate its effectivenesss, we conduct ablation experiments on this module. From (d), we can observer that the fused image without MRA module weakens the infrared salient target, and the sky also produces some artifacts. From (i), more artifacts occurring on the door in the red box. Moreover, the thermal target of the pedestrian is degraded in the green box. In contrast, our MRA module can effectively reduce the artifacts and preserve abundant texture details.

Analysis of the Pixel Intensity Loss Function. Considering the different illumination conditions, we design the pixel intensity loss function based on local region to guide the network training, which makes the fused images contain more meaningful informaiton from the source images. From Fig. 9(e) and Fig. 9(j), we can find that fused images weaken the salient target of the pedestrians. Compared with other experimental settings, our loss function can make network focus on the local region edge information, which achieves better overall image quality.

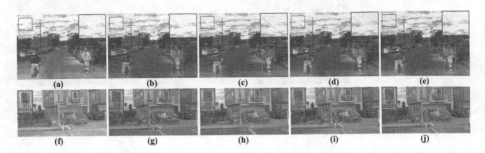

Fig. 9. Visualized results of ablation studies. From left to right: fused results of our method, LE2 module in the fusion layer but not in the image reconstructor, without LE2 module completely, without MRA module and without pixel intensity loss.

5   Conclusion

In this work, we propose an infrared and visible image fusion network based on local edge enhancement module (LE2Fusion). Specifically, we design a local edge enhancement module to enhance the edge information of the local regions and preserve salient information from the source images. After that, it can generate a set of enhancement weights for guiding the feature fusion and image reconstruction processes. To better guide the network training, we design a novel pixel intensity loss function based on the local regions, which enables our fusion results to maintain high correlation with source images in perspectives of the pixel intensities and the structure information. Moreover, we introduce the multiscale residual attention module into the DenseBlock to extract rich features. Our method achieves comparable or better performance in terms of the visualization effects and quantitative evaluation. Ablation experiments demonstrate the effectiveness of different components of the proposed method.

Acknowledgements. This work was supported by the National Social Science Foundation of China(21&ZD166), the National Natural Science Foundation of China (62202205), the Natural Science Foundation of Jiangsu Province, China(BK20221535), and the Fundamental Research Funds for the Central Universities (JUSRP123030).

References

1. Cheng, C., Xu, T., Wu, X.J.: Mufusion: a general unsupervised image fusion network based on memory unit. Inf. Fusion **92**, 80–92 (2023)
2. Fu, J., et al.: MDRAnet: a multiscale dense residual attention network for magnetic resonance and nuclear medicine image fusion. Biomed. Signal Process. Control **80**, 104382 (2023)
3. Jia, X., Zhu, C., Li, M., Tang, W., Zhou, W.: Llvip: a visible-infrared paired dataset for low-light vision. In: Proceedings of the IEEE/CVF International Conference on Computer Vision, pp. 3496–3504 (2021)
4. Li, H., Wu, X.J.: Densefuse: a fusion approach to infrared and visible images. IEEE Trans. Image Process. **28**(5), 2614–2623 (2018)

5. Li, H., Wu, X.J., Durrani, T.: NestFuse: an infrared and visible image fusion architecture based on nest connection and spatial/channel attention models. IEEE Trans. Instrum. Meas. **69**(12), 9645–9656 (2020)
6. Li, H., Wu, X.J., Kittler, J.: RFN-Nest: an end-to-end residual fusion network for infrared and visible images. Inf. Fusion **73**, 72–86 (2021)
7. Li, H., Xu, T., Wu, X.J., Lu, J., Kittler, J.: LRRNet: a novel representation learning guided fusion network for infrared and visible images. IEEE Trans. Pattern Anal. Mach. Intell. (2023)
8. Ma, J., Tang, L., Fan, F., Huang, J., Mei, X., Ma, Y.: SwinFusion: cross-domain long-range learning for general image fusion via swin transformer. IEEE/CAA J. Autom. Sinica **9**(7), 1200–1217 (2022)
9. Ma, J., Yu, W., Liang, P., Li, C., Jiang, J.: FusionGAN: a generative adversarial network for infrared and visible image fusion. Inf. Fusion **48**, 11–26 (2019)
10. Tang, L., Xiang, X., Zhang, H., Gong, M., Ma, J.: DIVFusion: darkness-free infrared and visible image fusion. Inf. Fusion **91**, 477–493 (2023)
11. Tang, L., Yuan, J., Ma, J.: Image fusion in the loop of high-level vision tasks: a semantic-aware real-time infrared and visible image fusion network. Inf. Fusion **82**, 28–42 (2022)
12. Tang, L., Yuan, J., Zhang, H., Jiang, X., Ma, J.: PIAFusion: a progressive infrared and visible image fusion network based on illumination aware. Inf. Fusion **83**, 79–92 (2022)
13. Tang, Z., Xu, T., Li, H., Wu, X.J., Zhu, X., Kittler, J.: Exploring fusion strategies for accurate RGBT visual object tracking. Inf. Fusion, 101881 (2023)
14. Xu, H., Ma, J., Jiang, J., Guo, X., Ling, H.: U2fusion: a unified unsupervised image fusion network. IEEE Trans. Pattern Anal. Mach. Intell. **44**(1), 502–518 (2020)
15. Zhang, Y., Liu, Y., Sun, P., Yan, H., Zhao, X., Zhang, L.: IFCNN: a general image fusion framework based on convolutional neural network. Inf. Fusion **54**, 99–118 (2020)

Complex Glyph Enhancement for License Plate Generation

Yu-Xiang Chen[1], Qi Liu[1], Song-Lu Chen[1], Fang Zhou[1(✉)], Yan Liu[1],
Feng Chen[2], and Xu-Cheng Yin[1]

[1] University of Science and Technology Beijing, Beijing, China
{yuxiangchen,qiliu7}@xs.ustb.edu.cn, zhoufang@ies.ustb.edu.cn,
xuchengyin@ustb.edu.cn
[2] EEasy Technology Company Ltd., Zhuhai, China

Abstract. The complex glyphs of license plates usually comes with a long-tail distribution, leading to poor recognition performance of the tail class. Supplementing the training data with generated license plates is an effective solution for this issue. However, for complex glyphs, the previous methods are prone to generate incomplete structures and blurry strokes. The first reason is that the small portion of complex glyphs on the license plate contributes little to the overall loss. Secondly, due to the complex structure and dense strokes, the glyphs are prone to be generated inaccurately. To solve the above problems, firstlly, we propose a divide-and-conquer method that generates complex and simple glyphs separately and then fuses them into a complete license plate, thus enhancing the generation of complex glyphs in loss computation. Secondly, we increase the generated resolution of complex glyph to enable the model to learn dense structures and fine strokes. Besides, considering the computational cost, low-resolution generation is used for the rest of the simple glyphs. Extensive experiments demonstrate that our method can significantly enhances the realism of the complex glyph, and generated images can boost recognition performance by 3% on SYSU. Additionally, we provide a dataset of 30,000 generated Chinese license plates with uniform Chinese distribution to promote research (https://github.com/ICIG2023-91/GCLPD).

Keywords: License plate generation · Generative adversarial network · Complex glyph · License plate dataset

1 Introduction

The performance of recognition models relies on the training data. And the complex glyphs of license plates usually come with a long-tail distribution, leading to poor license plate recognition performance of the tail class. However, generated license plates can effectively address this issue. Although previous license plate generation methods [14,16,17,21] have promising results, this work often results in blurred and incomplete glyphs when it comes to generating plausible complex glyphs.

H. Lu et al. (Eds.): ICIG 2023, LNCS 14355, pp. 306–318, 2023.
https://doi.org/10.1007/978-3-031-46305-1_25

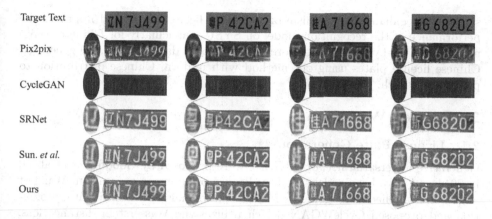

Fig. 1. Comparison of Pix2pix [7], CycleGAN [24], SRNet [18], Sun et al. [15] and our method on Chinese license plate generation.

To address these issues, Sun et al. [15] proposed a method to decouple the generation of foreground and background, alleviating the interference of the background during foreground generation. However, as shown in the Fig. 1, they still suffer from incomplete glyphs and blurred strokes. Furthermore, there are some generation methods for complex glyphs [2,6,8,11]. However, since these methods generate a single font without a background, they are not suitable for generating license plates. Therefore, enhancing the realism of the complex glyph in generated license plates remains challenging.

Poor license plate generation is attributed to several factors. Firstly, license plates contain fewer complex glyphs than simple alphanumeric glyphs. For instance, Chinese license plates feature only one complex Chinese character compared to six simple alphanumeric characters, reducing the model's focus on generating complex glyphs. Secondly, complex glyphs are characterized by denser strokes and intricate structures, making them more challenging to generate accurately alongside simple glyphs, which may result in missing strokes and incorrect structures.

Based on the above analysis, we proposed a license plate generation method to tackle the challenge of generating complex glyphs. Our method adopts a divide-and-conquer strategy, dividing the license plate into two regions based on the position of the characters: the complex glyph region and the simple glyph region. By generating complex glyphs separately, we increase their contribution to the loss of backpropagation, facilitating the learning process. Moreover, we increase the resolution of the generation network for complex glyphs to improve their realism, while keeping the rest of the generation at a lower resolution to reduce computational costs. Then, the complex glyph region and the simple glyph region are fused to generate the complete plate, followed by a trace optimization module that refines the image details and results in a more realistic generation of complex glyphs. Extensive experiments demonstrated that our method significantly enhances the realism of generated license plates and improves the performance of the recognition model on SYSU, particularly for Chinese recognition accuracy by 3%. Furthermore, we released a dataset of 30,000 generated Chinese license plates using our method with uniform Chinese distribution to promote research.

2 Related Work

2.1 License Plate Generation

Generative adversarial networks (GAN) were proposed by Goodfellow et al. [4] in 2014 and have been widely used for license plate image generation. Wang et al. [16] first applied GAN-generated license plate images to license plate recognition and proposed CycleWGAN, which utilizes the Wasserstein distance loss. To improve the realism of the generated license plates, Wu et al. [17] proposed CycleWGAN-GP to address the issue of pattern collapse. To overcome data imbalance, Sun et al. [14] introduced the P and U modules for paired and unpaired images, respectively, and Zhang et al. [21] proposed AsymCycleGAN for license plate data balancing. Moreover, Sun et al. [15] enhance the overall realism of generated license plates by decoupling the generation of foreground and background. However, these methods still need a better generation of complex glyph characters (e.g., Chinese or Korean). To address this issue, we propose a divide-and-conquer method that generates complex and simple glyphs separately, as described earlier.

2.2 Glyph Generation

After the success of GAN in various fields, it was applied to glyph generation for font design. This task involves generating new glyphs from some reference glyphs, particularly suitable for characters with high structural fineness like Chinese. Lyu et al. [11] proposed to generate Chinese glyphs based on a generic image generation model. Hassan et al. [6] used CycleGAN [24] to enhance the stability of the generated Chinese glyphs. SC-Font [8] constrained the stability of strokes through semantic information at the stroke level. DG-Font [2] used deformable convolution to process glyph features and learn the offset and deformation of strokes. Although these methods can generate Chinese glyphs with accurate strokes, they cannot learn the background of the corresponding image and can only generate a single glyph. Therefore, they are not suitable to license plate generation. On the other hand, our proposed method generates complex glyphs of license plates with backgrounds by text substitution, which allows for the generation of complete license plates with realistic complex glyphs.

3 Methodology

3.1 Overview

Our model aims to improve the generation of complex Chinese glyphs in license plates, using Chinese as an example, as shown in Fig. 2.

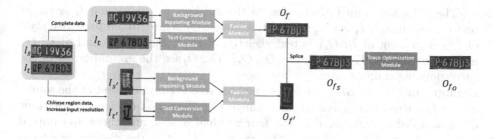

Fig. 2. The overall architecture of our method.

To achieve complex glyph generation, we proposed a method that utilizes two text substitution networks with the same structure: one for generating the complete license plate (TSN-CLP) and the other for generating the Chinese character region (TSN-CGC). Different input resolutions are used for these two regions. After generating the images of the two regions separately, they are spliced together to form a complete license plate with spliced trace. Finally, the trace optimization network generated the final complete license plate.

In the following sections, we will provide detailed descriptions of each module.

3.2 Text Substitution Network

Our method utilized two text substitution networks, TSN-CLP and TSN-CGC, which have the same network structure as depicted in Fig. 3. TSN-CLP generated complete license plates, while TSN-CGC generated Chinese characters region. The network comprised three parts, illustrated in Fig. 3 (TSN-CLP is used as an example). Adversarial generation is used as the basis for the network, where clean license plate backgrounds and license plate text images are generated separately and then fused to produce a new license plate image. To balance realism and speed, high resolution is utilized for generating complex glyphs, while a low resolution is utilized for generating simple glyphs.

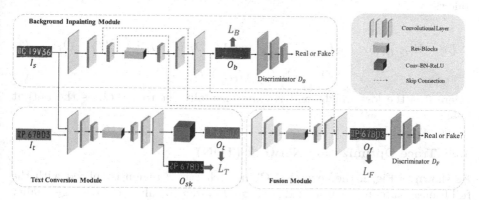

Fig. 3. The overall structure of text substitution network.

The following is an introduction to the symbols in the model: I_t is target text content image; I_s is target text style image; O_t is foreground text with style of I_s and content of I_t; O_{sk} is text skeleton of O_t; O_b is background of I_s; O_f is final output. T_t, T_{sk}, T_b, T_f are O_t, O_{sk}, O_b, O_f are the ground truth in the corresponding training data.

Background Erase Module is designed to erase the text content of the source image I_s to produce a background image O_b. This module consists of three down-sampled convolutional layers, four residual blocks, and three up-sampled transposed convolutional layers. The generator G_B and the discriminator D_B are alternately trained using generative adversarial loss and L1 loss. The loss function L_B for this module is defined as follows:

$$L_B = E_{(T_b, I_s)} \left[\log D_B (T_b, I_s) \right] + E_{I_s} \log \left[1 - D_B (G_B (I_s), I_s) \right] \\ + \beta \| T_b - G_B (I_s) \|_1 \tag{1}$$

where β is the loss weight and is experimentally set to 10.

Text Conversion Module is designed to extract the text style features in I_s and the text content features in the I_t and generated a foreground text O_t with style of I_s and content of I_t. The module contains three down-sampling convolutional layers, four residual blocks, three up-sampling transpose convolutional layers, and a Conv-BN-ReLU block. The loss function L_T for this module is defined as follows:

$$L_T = \| T_t - G_T (I_t, I_s) \|_1 + \alpha \left(1 - \frac{2 \sum_i^N (T_{sk})_i (O_{sk})_i}{\sum_i^N (T_{sk})_i + \sum_i^N (O_{sk})_i} \right), \tag{2}$$

where N is the number of pixels, G_T, refers to the text conversion module, and α is the loss weight parameter and is experimentally set to 1.

Fusion Module is designed to fuse the foreground text image O_t and the erased clean background image O_b to generate a license plate. This module consistent with the background erase module. Then the generator G_F and discriminator D_F are trained alternately. The loss function L_F for this module is defined as follows:

$$L_F = E_{(T_f, I_t)} \left[\log D_F (T_f, I_t) \right] + E_{I_t} \log \left[1 - D_F (O_f, I_t) \right] + \theta \| T_f - O_f \|_1 \tag{3}$$

$$O_f = G_F (G_T (I_t, I_s), G_B (I_s)) \tag{4}$$

where θ is the loss weight and is experimentally set to 10. O_f is the output image.

3.3   Trace Optimization Network (TON)

As shown in Fig. 2, the generated Chinese character region is spliced with the full license plate image at a fixed position. In order to enhance the image quality by removing the spliced traces and improving the global realism, we proposed the Trace Optimization Network (TON).

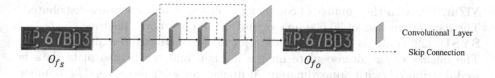

Fig. 4. Trace Optimization Network construction.

The TON module utilized a U-Net [12] structure, which includes three down-sampled and three up-sampled convolutional layers. Moreover, skip connections are used between the feature maps with the same size to better preserve the image details. The network structure is shown in Fig. 4. The TON module removes spliced traces, optimizes the license plate details, and enhances the overall realism of the final license plate image.

We adopted VGG loss to optimize TON, including perceptual loss [9] and style loss [3]. VGG-loss L_{vgg} can be expressed as follows:

$$L_{vgg} = \theta_2 \mathrm{E} \left[\sum_i \frac{1}{\mathrm{M}_i} \|\phi_i(T_{fo}) - \phi_i(O_{fo})\|_1 \right] + \theta_3 \mathrm{E}_j \left[\left\| \mathrm{G}_j^\phi(T_{fo}) - \mathrm{G}_j^\phi(O_{fo}) \right\|_1 \right] \tag{5}$$

where θ_2 and θ_3 are best to set to 1 and 500 [18]. ϕ_i is the activation map obtained in each activation layer of the VGG19 model. M_i is the element size of their map obtained in the i layer, and G is the Gram matrix.

The loss function of TON L_O is L1 loss of the output and VGG loss, as follows:

$$L_O = \|T_{fo} - G_O(O_{fs})\| + L_{vgg} \tag{6}$$

4   Experiments

4.1   Datasets

Synthetic Dataset is synthesized by SynthText [5] and contains 50,000 synthetic similar license plate images. This dataset is synthesized by randomly generating a text and background and rendering the text to the background images. And this dataset is used for model pretrain.

YiZhi2000 [15] contains 2000 horizontal license plate images. However, the data distribution of license plates is unbalanced, with the number of license plates in each province ranging from 0 to 70, this means that complex glyph characters are unevenly distributed.

SSAD30000 is a license plate text editing dataset produced by a supervised synthesis algorithm [15]. The training data for the supervised synthesis algorithm is YiZhi2000, and therefore the data distribution of SSAD30000 is consistent with

YiZhi2000, with the number of complex glyph characters unevenly distributed. The dataset consists of 30,000 images and is used for model finetune.

SYSU [22] contains license plate data for all 31 provinces in mainland China. The quality of the license plate images is high, and the license plate data is well-distributed, with approximately 70 images for each province. The number of complex glyph characters is evenly distributed. However, the dataset is not annotated, and license plates are obtained through manual labelling.

4.2   Implementation Datails

Our experiments used the Adam optimizer [10] to train our model. First, we pre-trained TSN-CLP and TSN-CGC using the synthetic dataset, and then fine-tuned them using the SSAD30000 dataset (original data size: 150 × 48). TSN-CLP was trained using the complete SSAD30000 dataset with an input resolution of 200 × 64 (input image enlarged by 1.33 times). TSN-CGC, on the other hand, was trained using the Chinese region of the SSAD30000 data images (the leftmost 24 × 48 pixels for each picture) with an input resolution of 64 × 128 (input image enlarged by 2.67 times). For TON, the input image size was adjusted to 400 × 128. The batch size was uniformly set to 8, and the initial learning rate was set to 1×10^{-4}, maximum iteration is 50,000.

4.3   Evaluation Metrics

We utilized several image metrics to assess the quality of the generated license plates, including the following: 1) FID [1], which measures the distance between the actual image and the generated image in the latent space; 2) MSE, also known as L2 loss; 3) PSNR, which calculates the peak signal-to-noise ratio of the image; 4) SSIM [23], which calculates the average structural similarity index between two images. Lower FID and MSE and higher PSNR and SSIM indicate that the generated image is closer to the ground truth.

4.4   Qualitative Experiments

We compared several license plate generation methods, including Pix2pix [7], CycleGAN [24], SRNet [18], Sun et al. method [15] and our method, using the same training superparameters. The above methods generated license plates, as shown in Fig. 1.

The license plates generated by Pix2pix have unrealistic text with the text and background intertwined, while the Chinese effect generated by CycleGAN is poor. Due to the lack of real license plate data, the text strokes generated by SRNet are also blurred, and the character size is larger than the real size. Also pre-trained with the synthetic dataset, Sun et al. method generates accurate alphanumeric characters. However, for complex Chinese, the generated strokes are not realistic and plausible enough, or even completely blurred. And our method, regardless of simple or complex glyphs, have a better generation effect than previous methods. In particular, our method generates complex Chinese forms with complete structure, accurate strokes, and a more realistic overall effect. This is because our method emphasizes the generation of complex glyphs.

4.5   Quantitative Experiments

Image Evaluation. We used the Supervision Synthesizing Algorithm [15] and SYSU [22] dataset to create a test dataset. Specifically, the test dataset includes style images and target text images synthesized by the algorithm as inputs, and actual license plates corresponding to the target text as ground truth. We then computed image metrics to compare the quality of the output image and the actual license plate image.

As shown in Table 1, compared to previous methods, our method have a significant improvement in almost all metrics, achieving best performance. It demonstrates the effectiveness of our divide-and-conquer strategy and trace optimization network. While our method has not achieve the best FID score, it is in close proximity. Moreover, FID alone does not fully capture the generation quality [13]. As demonstrated in Fig. 1, our method generates more accurate complex glyphs. This experiment demonstrates that our method generate Chinese on license plates more accurately and produce more realistic license plates compared to previous methods.

Table 1. Quantitative results of different image synthesizing models.

Methods	FID↓	MSE↓	PSNR↑	SSIM↑
Pix2pix [7]	182.238	0.3280	11.130	0.0553
CycleGAN [24]	145.983	0.2165	13.306	0.0888
SRNet [18]	54.211	0.1762	14.173	0.2520
Sun et al. [15]	**20.439**	0.0575	19.717	0.5805
Ours	20.739	**0.0495**	**20.353**	**0.6059**

Enhancement of Recognition. We implemented a rapid and efficient recognition network that relies on a parallel visual attention module [20]. Subsequently, we employed license plates generated by different methods to train the recognition network and compared the effectiveness of these methods in the license plate recognition task. Where augmentation of real data refers to traditional augmentation methods such as random Gaussian noise and rotation. The training dataset for all methods consisted of 62,000 images with the same target text, and the test dataset is SYSU.

In this experiment, we evaluated the effectiveness of license plates generated by various methods for training a recognition model using recognition accuracy (RA) and character recognition accuracy (CRA) as primary metrics. We also defined CRA-C as the accuracy of recognizing Chinese on license plates. The quality of the training data is crucial for the recognition model, especially for Chinese characters. Therefore, the realism and completeness of the text on the generated license plates are directly related to RA and CRA-C. Training the model with license plates with real glyphs and complete strokes in Chinese characters can significantly enhance recognition accuracy.

Table 2 demonstrates that traditional data augmentation methods can improve recognition accuracy with a small amount of data. However, Pix2pix, CycleGAN, and SRNet methods show poor improvement in recognition due to the large visual discrepancy between the generated images and real license plates. Although Sun et al.'s method improves overall recognition performance, it still needs further improvement for RA and CRA-C. However, our method achieves the best results and shows the most significant improvement in RA and CRA-C. In addition, our results demonstrate that the license plates generated by our method have more realistic glyphs. Therefore, utilising them for training recognition models is more effective than previous methods, significantly improving recognition performance.

Table 2. Accuracy of recognition models trained on datasets generated by different methods (%).

Methods	RA↑	CRA↑	CRA-C↑
Real data (augmentation)	87.31	98.16	87.71
Pix2pix [7]	66.84	94.95	71.22
CycleGAN [24]	0.44	50.92	4.59
SRNet [18]	20.73	80.08	45.23
Sun et al. [15]	95.18	99.28	96.58
Ours	**98.11**	**99.71**	**99.03**

Table 3 shows the CRA-C of the models trained with different generated data for some complex glyphs (parts). Traditional data augmentation cannot generate complex glyphs that are not present in the real data. Meanwhile, the complex glyphs generated by previous methods exhibit poor realism. Therefore, the performance improvement achieved by using these generated data for recognition models is insignificant. In contrast, our method generates more realistic complex glyphs. As a result, the recognition model can perform better on various complex glyphs, especially in Tibet and Guangxi.

Table 3. The enhancement of recognition (CRA-C) by the different complex glyphs generated. Tibet, Jiangxi, and Guangxi each represent a complex glyph character.

	Tibet	Jiangxi	Guangxi
Real data (augmentation)	0.00	100.00	0.00
Pix2pix [7]	65.00	71.88	46.27
CycleGAN [24]	3.75	1.56	0.00
SRNet [18]	35.00	59.36	0.00
Sun et al. [15]	38.75	90.63	83.58
Ours	**86.25**	**100.00**	**100.00**

4.6 Ablation Experiment

This paper proposed a novel license plate generation method that emphasizes the generation of complex glyphs. Furthermore, we adopted a divide-and-conquer method with varying input resolutions for different networks of the model. There are several reasons for this design choice, rather than directly generating complete license plates using a high-resolution TSN-CLP.

Firstly, directly generating the complete license plate using high-resolution TSN-CLP would significantly increase the model inference time. Meanwhile, our method achieved the same generation effect with a much shorter training time. Secondly, the high-resolution TSN-CLP is inclined to focus on alphanumeric generation rather than complex glyphs, resulting in low-quality Chinese characters. As shown in Fig. 5, TSN-CLP generates Chinese characters with incorrect details and inaccurate strokes, in both high and low resolution. In contrast, our method excels at generating accurate Chinese characters while being computationally efficient. This experiment demonstrates the significant improvements of our method.

Fig. 5. Our proposed method achieve the best generation results.

5   Generated Chinese License Plate Dataset(GCLPD)

We have created a dataset of generated Chinese license plates (https://github.com/ICIG2023-91/GCLPD) based on our method. To enhance the realism of the license plates in GCLPD, we trained our model using two datasets: YiZhi2000 [15] and SUSY [22]. This method solves the data scarcity issue of Chinese characters (complex glyphs) in some provinces. As a result, all the Chinese characters in GCLPD are real and clear. Some examples of license plate images in GCLPD are shown in Fig. 6.

Fig. 6. Examples of license plate in GCLPD.

Uneven Chinese distribution is a prevalent issue in current license plate datasets. For example, 90% of the license plates in CCPD2019 [19] are from the same province. This may lead to poor recognition network performance. However, GCLPD comprises approximately 1000 license plates per province from 31 provinces in mainland China, with each province corresponding to a complex Chinese character. As shown in Fig. 7, the Chinese character distribution in GCLPD is balanced and comparable, providing evenly-distributed data. CCPD2019, on the other hand, has an uneven data distribution on Chinese characters. Therefore, GCLPD can supplement training data for license plate recognition networks and improve the model's performance.

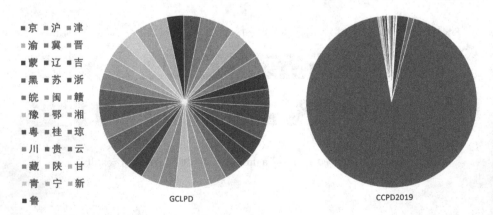

Fig. 7. The proposed dataset GCLPD has a balanced distribution of Chinese characters.

6   Conclusion

In this work, we proposed a divide-and-conquer license plate generation method that generates complex and simple glyphs separately and then fuses them into a complete license plate. This method can effectively assist the training of license plate recognition models. Furthermore, we release a dataset comprising 30,000 generated Chinese license plates. In the future, we aim to enhance the model's ability to automatically extract and refine the complex glyphs.

Acknowledgement. The research is supported by National Key Research and Development Program of China (2020AAA0109700), National Natural Science Foundation of China (62076024, 62006018, U22B2055).

References

1. Barratt, S.T., Sharma, R.: A note on the inception score. CoRR abs/1801.01973 (2018)
2. Chen, X., Xie, Y., Sun, L., Lu, Y.: DGFont++: robust deformable generative networks for unsupervised font generation. CoRR abs/2212.14742 (2022)
3. Gatys, L.A., Ecker, A.S., Bethge, M.: Image style transfer using convolutional neural networks. In: 2016 IEEE Conference on Computer Vision and Pattern Recognition, pp. 2414–2423 (2016)
4. Goodfellow, I.J., et al.: Generative adversarial networks. CoRR abs/1406.2661 (2014)
5. Gupta, A., Andrew Zisserman, A.V.: Synthetic data for text localisation in natural images. In: 2016 IEEE Conference on Computer Vision and Pattern Recognition, pp. 2315–2324 (2016)
6. Hassan, A.U., Ahmed, H., Choi, J.: Unpaired font family synthesis using conditional generative adversarial networks. Knowl. Based Syst. **229**, 107304 (2021)
7. Isola, P., Zhu, J., Zhou, T., Efros, A.A.: Image-to-image translation with conditional adversarial networks, pp. 5967–5976 (2017)
8. Jiang, Y., Lian, Z., Tang, Y., Xiao, J.: SCFont: structure-guided Chinese font generation via deep stacked networks. In: The Thirty-Third AAAI Conference on Artificial Intelligence, AAAI 2019, pp. 4015–4022. AAAI Press (2019)
9. Johnson, J., Alahi, A., Fei-Fei, L.: Perceptual losses for real-time style transfer and super-resolution. In: Computer Vision - ECCV 2016–14th European Conference, vol. 9906, pp. 694–711 (2016)
10. Kingma, D.P., Ba, J.: Adam: a method for stochastic optimization. In: 3rd International Conference on Learning Representations (2015)
11. Lyu, P., Bai, X., Yao, C., Zhu, Z., Huang, T., Liu, W.: Auto-encoder guided GAN for Chinese calligraphy synthesis. In: 14th IAPR International Conference on Document Analysis and Recognition, ICDAR 2017, pp. 1095–1100. IEEE (2017)
12. Ronneberger, O., Fischer, P., Brox, T.: U-Net: convolutional networks for biomedical image segmentation. In: Medical Image Computing and Computer-Assisted Intervention, vol. 9351, pp. 234–241 (2015)
13. Sajjadi, M.S.M., Bachem, O., Lucic, M., Bousquet, O., Gelly, S.: Assessing generative models via precision and recall. CoRR abs/1806.00035 (2018)

14. Sun, M., Zhou, F., Yang, C., Yin, X.: Image generation framework for unbalanced license plate data set. In: 2019 International Conference on Data Mining Workshops, pp. 883–889 (2019)

15. Sun, Y.F., Liu, Q., Chen, S.L., Zhou, F., Yin, X.C.: Robust Chinese license plate generation via foreground text and background separation. In: Image and Graphics - 11th International Conference, vol. 12890, pp. 290–302 (2021)

16. Wang, X., Man, Z., You, M., Shen, C.: Adversarial generation of training examples: applications to moving vehicle license plate recognition. CoRR abs/1707.03124 (2017)

17. Wu, C., Xu, S., Song, G., Zhang, S.: How many labeled license plates are needed? In: Pattern Recognition and Computer Vision - First Chinese Conference, vol. 11259, pp. 334–346 (2018)

18. Wu, L., Zhang, C., Liu, J., Han, J., Liu, J., Ding, E., Bai, X.: Editing text in the wild. In: Proceedings of the 27th ACM International Conference on Multimedia, pp. 1500–1508 (2019)

19. Xu, Z., et al.: Towards end-to-end license plate detection and recognition: A large dataset and baseline. In: Computer Vision - ECCV 2018–15th European Conference, vol. 11217, pp. 261–277 (2018)

20. Yu, D., Li, X., Zhang, C., Liu, T., Han, J., Liu, J., Ding, E.: Towards accurate scene text recognition with semantic reasoning networks. In: 2020 IEEE/CVF Conference on Computer Vision and Pattern Recognition, pp. 12110–12119 (2020)

21. Zhang, L., Wang, P., Li, H., Li, Z., Shen, C., Zhang, Y.: A robust attentional framework for license plate recognition in the wild. IEEE Trans. Intell. Transp. Syst. **22**(11), 6967–6976 (2021)

22. Zhao, Y., Yu, Z., Li, X., Cai, M.: Chinese license plate image database building methodology for license plate recognition. J. Electron. Imaging **28**(1), 013001 (2019)

23. Zhou, W., Bovik, A.C., Sheikh, H.R., Simoncelli, E.P.: Image quality assessment: from error visibility to structural similarity. IEEE Trans. Image Process. **13**(4), 600–612 (2004)

24. Zhu, J.Y., Park, T., Isola, P., Efros, A.A.: Unpaired image-to-image translation using cycle-consistent adversarial networks. In: IEEE International Conference on Computer Vision, pp. 2242–2251 (2017)

High Fidelity Virtual Try-On via Dual Branch Bottleneck Transformer

Xiuxiang Li, Guifeng Zheng, Fan Zhou, Zhuo Su, and Ge Lin$^{(\boxtimes)}$

School of Computer Science and Engineering, National Engineering Research Center
of Digital Life, Sun Yat-sen University, Guangzhou 510006, China
linge3@mail.sysu.edu.cn

Abstract. Image-based virtual try-on aims to fit an in-shop garment
into a reference person image. To achieve this, a key step is garment
warping, which aligns the target garment with the corresponding parts of
the reference person and warps it reasonably. Previous methods typically
adopt unweighted appearance flow estimation, which inherently makes it
difficult to learn meaningful positions and generates unrealistic warping
when the reference and the target have a large spatial difference. To overcome this limitation, a novel weighted appearance flow estimation strategy is proposed in this work. First, we extract the fusion latent vector
of the reference and the target via Dual Branch Bottleneck Transformer.
This enables us to take advantage of a latent vector to encode the global
context. Then, we enhance the realism of appearance flow by performing sparse spatial sampling. This strengthens the communication of local
information and applies constraints to warping. Experiment results on
a popular virtual try-on benchmark show that our method outperforms
the current state-of-the-art method in both quantitative and qualitative
evaluations.

Keywords: Virtual Try-On · Appearance Flow · Bottleneck
Transformer · Sparse Spatial Sampling

1 Introduction

Imaged Based Virtual Try-On (VTON) aims to fit an in-shop garment (target)
into a reference person image which has attracted increasing attention in areas
such as e-commerce, fashion recommendation and image editing. It can also be
applied in intelligent community scenarios. Existing methods can be roughly classified into 3D-based methods [1, 2] and 2D-based methods [3–5]. 3D-based methods achieve excellent control over the material and garment warping through
complex rendering. However, these methods heavily rely on complex data representations and consume massive computational resources. In contrast, 2D-based
methods are more suitable for real-world scenarios due to the lightweight data,
which have made significant progress in generating realistic try-on results. Nevertheless, most existing methods still suffer from large misalignment or glaring
artifacts when dealing with intricate poses and large deformation.

© The Author(s), under exclusive license to Springer Nature Switzerland AG 2023
H. Lu et al. (Eds.): ICIG 2023, LNCS 14355, pp. 319–331, 2023.
https://doi.org/10.1007/978-3-031-46305-1_26

Fig. 1. Comparison with some parser-free based methods, such as PF-AFN [5] and Style-Flow [6], our method shows certain advantages in handling occlusions (e.g. the arm in the first row) and large differences between the target and reference images (e.g. the collar in the second row).

Style-Flow [6] utilizes a global style vector extracted from the reference and target images for global guidance, which generates more realistic results. However, they treat the reference image and the target garment independently, and therefore the global style vector cannot effectively guide the subsequent garment warping. In addition, most of the existing methods [4–7] do not effectively utilize local attention when predicting appearance flow [8], which leads to poor generalization performance. Specifically, when there is a large spatial difference between the reference garment and the target, the warping of the target tends to be closer to the reference garment, as shown in the neckline in the second row of Fig. 1, which is unrealistic.

To overcome these limitations, we propose a novel appearance flow estimation strategy, called Dual Branch Bottleneck Transformer VTON (DT-VTON), shown in Fig. 2. Inspired by the feature cross-fusion strategy for multi-stream inputs in UMT [9], we introduce the dual-branch Bottleneck Transformer [10] to fuse features from the reference and target images. The lowest resolution feature maps of the reference and the target will be input to Latent Extraction, shown in Fig. 2, to extract a fused latent vector. This vector represents the global context of both and will be used in each block of the Warping Module for guidance. Besides, We introduce the sparse spatial sampling strategy proposed in Deformable DETR [11] to increase attention on surrounding sampling points to build long-term associations. It strengthens the constraints on the warping of the target garment when the spatial difference between the reference garment and the target is large.

The main contributions of this work are as follow:

- We propose a Latent Extraction module. This module extracts a latent vector representing the global context by fusing the feature maps of the reference image and the target garment, which makes our results preserve more details.
- Sparse spatial sampling is applied during garment warping to build long-term connections with local attention. By this way, our results are more robust, especially when the reference garment and the target have a large spatial difference.
- A novel VTON model is built, which applies the Latent Extraction module and Sparse Spatial Sampling. And experiments show that our method is superior to the current state-of-the-art method in terms of detail preservation and shape constraints.

2   Related Work

We will introduce this section from three parts: Image Based Virtual Try-On, Appearance Flow and Visual Attention Mechanism.

2.1   Image Based Virtual Try-On

Image based virtual try-on can be divided into two categories based on whether they rely on human parser during the inference stage: parser-based methods and parser-free methods.

Most of parser-based methods [3,4,12–16] adopt the framework proposed by VITON [3]. First of all, they use human parsing results to remove clothing regions from the reference person, generating a clothing-agnostic human representation. Then, both the target garment and the representation are fed into the network to predict try-on results. However, the heavy dependence on human parser will make these methods very sensitive to inaccurate human parsing results [5,7].

As for parser-free methods [5,7], they only require the reference and the target images as inputs during the inference stage. These methods are primarily developed to avoid bad try-on results due to inaccurate human parsing results. Since these methods do not rely on any pre-defined human parsers during the inference stage, they are less sensitive to human parsers and can generate try-on results that are more robust and accurate. WUTON [7] is one of the pioneering works that proposed the knowledge distillation approach for VTON. In their method, they use the teacher model's result as the ground-truth for the student model. Instead of regarding it as the ground-truth, PF-AFN [5] proposed a novel distillation approach that directly leverages the output of the teacher model as additional input to the student model, which performs better in VTON.

2.2   Appearance Flow

In VTON, ClothFlow [17] first proposed the appearance flow [8] which refers to 2D coordinate vectors that indicate which pixels in the source can be used to synthesize the result. As a sampling grid for garment warping, appearance flow is information lossless and superior in detail preservation. Beyond VTON, appearance flow is also popular in other tasks [1,18].

ClothFlow [17] utilized a cascade strategy to predict a dense flow field and employed flow variation regularization to enhance the smoothness of the flow field. PF-AFN [5] proposed to add second-order smoothness constraints to encourage the co-linearity of neighboring flow vectors, which can further improve the smoothness and consistency of the flow field. Style-Flow [6] used style modulation to use a global style vector as guidance for appearance flow estimation, so that the appearance flow can better handle large misalignment. These improvements make the garment warping smoother, but do not perform well when the target and the reference clothing have a large spatial difference. Our global latent vector extracted by Latent Extraction performs better in this condition.

2.3   Visual Attention Mechanism

Attention mechanisms have become increasingly popular in many computer vision tasks, including virtual try-on. UMT [9] leverages the power of BoTNet [10] for multimodal feature extraction and fusion tasks. It has shown significant improvements over previous methods on various multimodal benchmarks and datasets. We believe that this feature fusion strategy can be transplanted to two different inputs of the same modality.

Besides, Deformable DETR [11] is a recent extension of DETR [19] that leverages deformable convolutional networks (DCNs) to improve the performance of object detection tasks. In particular, Deformable DETR introduces the concept of "Deformable Attention", where the backbone features are first sampled at a fixed set of key positions. Most of the previous VTON methods cannot focus on effective areas, resulting in poor generalization when the reference and the target clothing are quite different. By focusing on a fixed set of key positions and their surrounding regions, our method can effectively leverage the contextual information and long-term dependencies between different points, and produce more accurate and robust results.

3   Methodology

In this section, we will introduce the overall framework of our proposed method, called DT-VTON, and then we will introduce the cores of our proposed method, Latent Extraction Module and Warping Module.

3.1   Architecture

First, we will train a parser-based teacher model called $\mathcal{M}^{PB}$. Then, we will use the output of $\mathcal{M}^{PB}$ as one of the inputs for the parser-free student model called $\mathcal{M}^{PF}$.

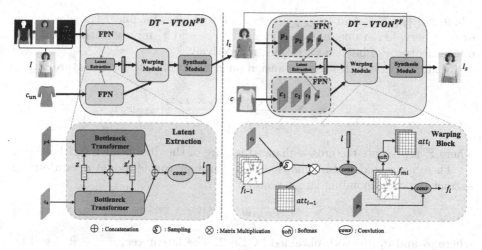

Fig. 2. The training pipeline of DT-VTON. $DT-VTON^{PB}$ is a pretrained parser-based model. Its output will be fed into the parser-free model $DT-VTON^{PF}$, along with the target. Then $DT-VTON^{PF}$ will generate the final try-on results as I_s. Both models share the same structure.

Concretely, the input of $\mathcal{M}^{PB}$ consists of two parts: the keypoint map[1], segmentation map, and DensePose map of the reference image I and an unpaired in-shop garment c_{un} which is randomly selected. The output of $\mathcal{M}^{PB}$ is an image I_t where the person in the reference image is wearing c_{un}. I_t will be one of the inputs to $\mathcal{M}^{PF}$, and another input is the in-shop garment c that corresponds to the garment in I. The output of $\mathcal{M}^{PF}$ is the final virtual try-on result I_s.

3.2 Latent Extraction Module

We are inspired by UMT's strategy of feature fusion and extraction. We leverage the shared information and structure between the reference image and the target. This approach can be particularly useful when dealing with low-quality inputs.

We first use the FPN [20] to encode the reference image I and the target garment c. The corresponding feature maps are represented as $\{p_i\}_1^N$ and $\{c_i\}_1^N$, respectively. The feature maps p_N and c_N from the last layer of the two FPNs will be input to the Latent Extraction Module. In Fig. 2, we set $N = 4$ for ease of presentation. p_4 and c_4 will be fed into the dual branch bottleneck transformer for feature fusion and extraction. Following UMT, we introduce a learnable parameter set $\{z_i\}_{i=1}^{N_b}$, where N_b is a much smaller number than the feature dimension C of p_4. We compress the features of each branch, as:

$$z_i' = z_i + w_z \sum_{j=1}^{C} \frac{exp(w_q z_i \times w_k x_j)}{\sum_{m=1}^{C} exp(w_q x_i \times w_k x_m)} w_v x_j, \tag{1}$$

---

[1] Obtained By Openpose, https://github.com/CMU-Perceptual-Computing-Lab/openpose.

where $x \in \{p_4, c_4\}$. And $w_{\{q,k,v,z\}}$ denotes the weights for linear transformation of the query, key, value, and output matrix. z_i and z_i' represent the input and output features of bottleneck tokens, respectively.

Next, we perform feature expansion on z_i' to obtain the fused feature x':

$$x_i' = x_i + w_z \sum_{j=1}^{C} \frac{exp(w_q x_i \times w_k z_j)}{\sum_{m=1}^{C} exp(w_q x_i \times w_k z_m)} w_v z_j, \tag{2}$$

where x_i' represents the cross-enhanced feature of the dual branch for the clip i.

These extracted feature maps will go through convolutional operations to extract the corresponding latent vector:

$$l = conv([p_4', c_4']), \tag{3}$$

where p_4' and c_4' are both obtained by Eq. 2. The latent vector, $l \in \mathbb{R}^C$, will be used as global guidance for subsequent appearance flow estimation.

3.3   Warping Module

This part is mainly responsible for warping the target c according to the shape of the garment in I. In Fig. 2, there are 4 Warping Blocks in total that make up the Warping Module. The input of the Warping Module consists of three parts: $\{p_i\}_1^N$, $\{c_i\}_1^N$ and l. Then, the appearance flow is predicted in a cascaded manner to finally obtain a warping garment c_w.

Specifically, in each Warping Block, we first use modulated convolution to obtain the intermediate flow f_{mi}:

$$f_{mi} = conv_m(\mathcal{S}(c_i, f_{i-1}) \cdot att_{i-1}, l), \tag{4}$$

where $\mathcal{S}(\cdot, \cdot)$ is a sampling operation. att_{i-1} is the feature map obtained through sparse spatial sampling, as:

$$att_i = softmax(\{f_{mi}\}_{C-K}^C), \tag{5}$$

where K represents the fixed sampling points number, and we start sampling from the last feature dimension of f_{mi}.

Next, f_{mi} is convolved with p_i to obtain the final flow $f_i = conv(f_{mi}, p_i)$.

3.4   Synthesis Module

The input of the Synthesis Module is I and the final warping block's appearance flow f_N. And the module generates the final try-on result:

$$I_s = \mathcal{G}([\mathcal{S}(c, f_N), I]), \tag{6}$$

where the generator $\mathcal{G}$ has an encoder-decoder architecture with skip connections in between.

3.5 Learning Objectives

During the training phase, we minimize $\mathcal{L}$ to optimize the parameters of the Warping Module and Synthesis Module:

$$\mathcal{L} = \lambda_p \mathcal{L}_p + \lambda_{warp} \mathcal{L}_{warp} + \lambda_{sec} \mathcal{L}_{sec} + \lambda_D \mathcal{L}_D, \tag{7}$$

where λ_p, λ_{warp}, λ_{sec} and λ_D are hyperparameters that balance the four losses.

$\mathcal{L}_p$ represents the perceptual loss between the try-on result I_s and the ground truth I_{gt}:

$$\mathcal{L}_p = \sum_i \|\phi_i(I_s) - \phi_i(I_{gt})\|, \tag{8}$$

where ϕ_i represents the ith block of the pre-trained VGG model. $\mathcal{L}_{warp}$ is used to supervise the Warping Module loss:

$$\mathcal{L}_{warp} = \|\mathcal{S}(c, f_N) - m_c \cdot I_{gt}\|, \tag{9}$$

where m_c represents the clothing mask corresponding to I_{gt}, which is obtained through human parsing. To better preserve the details of the warping garment, we use the second-order smooth constraint:

$$\mathcal{L}_{sec} = \sum_i \|\varDelta f_i\|, \tag{10}$$

where $\varDelta f_i$ is the generalized charbonnier loss function.

Finally, considering that the teacher model may have certain errors due to inaccurate human parsing results, if the student model is not trained with discrimination, the results may still be incorrect. Therefore, we need to add a distillation loss to enable the student model to have certain discrimination ability:

$$\mathcal{L}_D = \sum_i \|p_{ti} - p_{si}\|, \tag{11}$$

where p_{ti} represents the ith block of the person encoder in the teacher model, and p_{si} represents the ith block of the person encoder in the student model.

4 Experiments

We conducted experiments on the VITON [3] dataset and compared existing methods in terms of clothing warping methods and whether using a human parser or not. Furthermore, in terms of qualitative comparison, we compared our method with ACGPN [4], PF-AFN [5] and Style-Flow [6]. Finally, we also performed ablation study on the two modules proposed in this work.

4.1 Datasets

The VITON dataset includes a training set of 14,221 image pairs and a test set of 2,032 image pairs, each of which consists of a front-facing female photo and a high-resolution clothing image with a resolution of 256 × 192. Most of the previous works trained and evaluated their methods on this dataset.

Fig. 3. Qualitative results from different models (ACGPN [4], PF-AFN [5], Style-Flow [6] and ours) on VITON testing dataset.

4.2   Implementation Details

Both the teacher and the student models contain the Latent Extraction Module, Warping Module, and Synthesis Module, and they share the same structure. The two FPNs include 5 layers, and the convolutional stride of each layer is 2. The Warping Module contains 5 Warping Blocks.

We use a single Nvidia RTX 3090 GPU to train our model. We train the model with Adam optimizer. The entire training process consists of four stages. The first stage is the garment warping of the teacher model, with 100 epochs, a batch size of 8, and a learning rate of $1e-3$. The second stage is the try-on result synthesis of the teacher model, with 100 epochs, a batch size of 8, and a learning rate of $1e-3$. The third stage is the garment warping of the student model, with 200 epochs, a batch size of 8, and a learning rate of $6e-4$. The fourth stage is the try-on result synthesis of the student model, with 100 epochs, a batch size of 8, and a learning rate of $1e-3$. All learning rates will be linearly reduced halfway through the experiment. We set $K=6$ in the experiment.

4.3   Main Results

Following the design of [6], we evaluated our model using Structure Similarity (SSIM) [21] and Frechet Inception Distance (FID) [22] to measure its perfor-

Table 1. Quantitative results of different models on VITON dataset. Parser represents whether human parsing is required during inference.

Methods	Parser	SSIM↑	FID↓
VITON [3]	Y	0.74	55.71
CP-VTON++ [12]	Y	0.75	21.04
Cloth-flow [17]	Y	0.84	14.43
ACGPN [4]	Y	0.84	16.64
PF-AFN [5]	N	0.89	10.09
Zflow [15]	Y	0.88	15.17
Style-Flow [6]	N	**0.91**	8.89
Ours	N	**0.91**	**8.79**

mance, which mainly capture the similarity of the generated image to the real image (i.e. the reference image). For FID, a smaller FID score means a higher quality result.

Our method was compared with other methods, including VITON [3], CP-VTON++ [12], Cloth-flow [17], ACGPN [4], ZFlow [15]. We also compared our method with parse free method PFAFN [5] and the current SOTA Style-Flow [6].

The quantitative results on the VITON test dataset are shown in Table 1. Compared with parser-based methods, our method achieves significantly better FID scores. This is mainly attributed to the use of knowledge distillation, which effectively weakens the negative impact of inaccurate human parsing results on the final results. Compared with parser-free methods, our method achieves comparable SSIM scores but reduces FID scores by 0.1. This is mainly attributed to our more advanced global context extraction strategy and sparse spatial sampling, which have resulted in better results and improved model robustness.

The qualitative results can be seen in Fig. 3. As shown in the first row of Fig. 3, when the reference garment and the target have a large spatial difference, such as the collar in this case, the collar generated by ACGPN [4] and Style-Flow [6] is almost the same as that in the reference garment, but obviously it is not realistic for the target. This is mainly because their methods do not add constraints to the warping. The sparse spatial sampling establishes long-term local attention connections, which achieves this constraint. In addition, it can be observed from the second row of Fig. 3 that there exist residual reference garment in the model's arms for the baseline models, while our method generates more detailed results by fusing features from the reference image and the target garment to obtain the global latent vector.

4.4 Ablation Study

In this experiment, we validate the Latent Extraction Module (LE) and the Sparse Spatial Sampling (SS) in the Warping Block. We removed att_i from Eq. 4 to verify the effectiveness of Latent Extraction. This result is denoted as f_l.

Then, we replaced the Latent Extraction Module with a single convolutional layer with a kernel size of $(8, 6)$, and denoted the result as f_{att}.

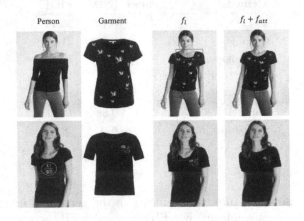

Fig. 4. Comparison between f_l and $f_l + f_{att}$.

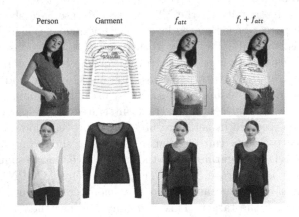

Fig. 5. Comparison between f_{att} and $f_l + f_{att}$.

The quantitative results are shown in Table 2. It can be seen that both LE and SS achieve comparable SSIM scores as LE+SS, while their FID scores are lower than our baseline Style-Flow [6]. This indicates that the two proposed modules are more advanced. As shown in Fig. 4, our model lacks shape constraints in garment warping without sparse spatial sampling, and the shape of the collar becomes unrealistic. This is mainly because without sparse spatial sampling, there is no long-term association between local regions, resulting in a lack of constraints on the warping of the clothing.

Table 2. The ablation study results on the VITON test dataset. LE denotes Latent Extraction, and SS denotes Sparse Sampling.

Methods	SSIM↑	FID↓
LE	0.91	8.87
SS	0.91	8.85
LE+SS	**0.91**	**8.79**

Latent Extraction also plays a crucial role in our model, as shown in Fig. 5. When only using sparse sampling, it can be observed that the overall receptive field of the model is missing, such as the clothing edges in the first row and the arm parts in the second row. This indicates that the use of the latent vector provides global guidance for appearance flow, making the try-on results more detailed. Through ablation study, it can be found that our model not only performs better when dealing with large differences between reference and target clothing, but also preserves more details.

5   Conclusion

In this paper, we have proposed a novel appearance flow strategy for fashion recommendation and some intelligent community scenarios. We first extract a latent vector that can represent the global context through a dual branch bottleneck transformer and use it for subsequent appearance flow estimation. During estimation, we reinforce the weight of the current point around its neighbors through sparse spatial sampling to achieve shape constraint when there are large shape differences. Our method achieves improvement in the evaluation metrics. Through testing on the VITON dataset, our model has good robustness in warping when there are large differences between reference and target clothing. We conducted multiple experiments to validate our design.

Acknowledgment. This research is supported by the National Key R&D Program of China (No. 2021YFF0900900).

References

1. Zhao, F., Xie, Z., Kampffmeyer, M., et al.: M3D-VTON: a monocular-to-3D virtual try-on network. In: Proceedings of the IEEE/CVF International Conference on Computer Vision, pp. 13239–13249 (2021)
2. Santesteban, I., Otaduy, M.A., Casas, D.: SNUG: self-supervised neural dynamic garments. In: Proceedings of the IEEE/CVF Conference on Computer Vision and Pattern Recognition, pp. 8140–8150 (2022)
3. Han, X., Wu, Z., Wu, Z., et al.: VITON: an image-based virtual try-on network. In: Proceedings of the IEEE Conference on Computer Vision and Pattern Recognition, pp. 7543–7552 (2018)

4. Yang, H., Zhang, R., Guo, X., et al.: Towards photo-realistic virtual try-on by adaptively generating-preserving image content. In: Proceedings of the IEEE/CVF Conference on Computer Vision and Pattern Recognition, pp. 7850–7859 (2020)

5. Ge, Y., Song, Y., Zhang, R., et al.: Parser-free virtual try-on via distilling appearance flows. In: Proceedings of the IEEE/CVF Conference on Computer Vision and Pattern Recognition, pp. 8485–8493 (2021)

6. He, S., Song, Y.Z., Xiang, T.: Style-based global appearance flow for virtual try-on. In: Proceedings of the IEEE/CVF Conference on Computer Vision and Pattern Recognition, pp. 3470–3479 (2022)

7. Issenhuth, T., Mary, J., Calauzènes, C.: Do not mask what you do not need to mask: a parser-free virtual try-on. In: Vedaldi, A., Bischof, H., Brox, T., Frahm, J.-M. (eds.) ECCV 2020, Part XX. LNCS, vol. 12365, pp. 619–635. Springer, Cham (2020). https://doi.org/10.1007/978-3-030-58565-5_37

8. Zhou, T., Tulsiani, S., Sun, W., Malik, J., Efros, A.A.: View synthesis by appearance flow. In: Leibe, B., Matas, J., Sebe, N., Welling, M. (eds.) ECCV 2016, Part IV. LNCS, vol. 9908, pp. 286–301. Springer, Cham (2016). https://doi.org/10.1007/978-3-319-46493-0_18

9. Liu, Y., Li, S., Wu, Y., et al.: UMT: unified multi-modal transformers for joint video moment retrieval and highlight detection. In: Proceedings of the IEEE/CVF Conference on Computer Vision and Pattern Recognition, pp. 3042–3051 (2022)

10. Srinivas, A., Lin, T.Y., Parmar, N., et al.: Bottleneck transformers for visual recognition. In: Proceedings of the IEEE/CVF Conference on Computer Vision and Pattern Recognition, pp. 16519–16529 (2021)

11. Zhu, X., Su, W., Lu, L., et al.: Deformable DETR: deformable transformers for end-to-end object detection. arXiv preprint arXiv:2010.04159 (2020)

12. Minar, M.R., Tuan, T.T., Ahn, H., et al.: CP-VTON+: clothing shape and texture preserving image-based virtual try-on. In: CVPR Workshops, vol. 3, pp. 10–14 (2020)

13. Yu, R., Wang, X., Xie, X.: VTNFP: an image-based virtual try-on network with body and clothing feature preservation. In: Proceedings of the IEEE/CVF International Conference on Computer Vision, pp. 10511–10520 (2019)

14. Minar, M.R., Ahn, H.: CloTH-VTON: clothing three-dimensional reconstruction for hybrid image-based virtual try-on. In: Proceedings of the Asian Conference on Computer Vision (2020)

15. Chopra, A., Jain, R., Hemani, M., et al.: ZFlow: gated appearance flow-based virtual try-on with 3d priors. In: Proceedings of the IEEE/CVF International Conference on Computer Vision, pp. 5433–5442 (2021)

16. Bai, S., Zhou, H., Li, Z.: Single stage virtual try-on via deformable attention flows. In: Avidan, S., Brostow, G., Cissé, M., Farinella, G.M., Hassner, T. (eds.) ECCV 2022, Part XV. LNCS, vol. 13675, pp. 409–425. Springer, Cham (2022). https://doi.org/10.1007/978-3-031-19784-0_24

17. Han, X., Hu, X., Huang, W., et al.: ClothFlow: a flow-based model for clothed person generation. In: Proceedings of the IEEE/CVF International Conference on Computer Vision, pp. 10471–10480 (2019)

18. AlBahar, B., Lu, J., Yang, J., et al.: Pose with Style: detail-preserving pose-guided image synthesis with conditional styleGAN. ACM Trans. Graph. (TOG) 40(6), 1–11 (2021)

19. Carion, N., Massa, F., Synnaeve, G., Usunier, N., Kirillov, A., Zagoruyko, S.: End-to-end object detection with transformers. In: Vedaldi, A., Bischof, H., Brox, T., Frahm, J.-M. (eds.) ECCV 2020, Part I. LNCS, vol. 12346, pp. 213–229. Springer, Cham (2020). https://doi.org/10.1007/978-3-030-58452-8_13

20. Lin, T.Y., Dollár, P., Girshick, R., et al.: Feature pyramid networks for object detection. In: Proceedings of the IEEE Conference on Computer Vision and Pattern Recognition, pp. 2117–2125 (2017)
21. Wang, Z., Bovik, A.C., Sheikh, H.R., et al.: Image quality assessment: from error visibility to structural similarity. IEEE Trans. Image Process. 13(4), 600–612 (2004)
22. Heusel, M., Ramsauer, H., Unterthiner, T., et al.: GANs trained by a two time-scale update rule converge to a local nash equilibrium. In: Advances in Neural Information Processing Systems, vol. 30 (2017)

A Road Damage Segmentation Method for Complex Environment Based on Improved UNet

Pengyu Liu[1,2,3(✉)], Jing Yuan[1,2,3], and Shanji Chen[4]

[1] Faculty of Information Technology, Beijing Institute of Technology, Beijing 100124, China
liupengyu@bjut.edu.cn
[2] Beijing Laboratory of Advanced Information Networks, Beijing 100124, China
[3] Beijing Key Laboratory of Computational Intelligence and Intelligent System, Beijing University of Technology, Beijing 100124, China
[4] School of Physics and Electronic Information Engineering, Qinghai Minzu University, Xining 810007, China

Abstract. Detecting and repairing road damage timely is crucial for ensuring traffic safety and reducing hazards. Cracks and potholes are the primary indications of early-stage road damage. However, existing deep learning-based methods for road damage detection often have limited feature extraction capabilities and only perform well in specific detection environments. To address these challenges, this paper proposes an improved UNet-based road damage segmentation method for complex environments. This method incorporates Atrous Spatial Pyramid Pooling (ASPP) and Coordinate Attention (CA) into the network, enhancing its ability to capture features of various sizes and to localize feature information. The proposed model effectively detects both cracks and potholes under different road environments, such as concrete, asphalt, and gravel. Experimental results demonstrate that the proposed network achieves 78.8% and 88.57% segmentation Intersection over Union (IoU) for cracks and potholes, respectively, outperforming classical semantic segmentation networks such as UNet, PSPNet, Attention UNet, UNet++, DANet, SegFormer, and TransUNet. This model can be applied to intelligent road inspection and maintenance to improve inspection efficiency.

Keywords: Road Damage · Cracks · Potholes · UNet

1 Introduction

Roads are an essential component of modern comprehensive transportation systems and serve as a link connecting social production, circulation, and consumption [1]. China's mountainous areas account for about 2/3 of the land area, road works are mainly mountain works. Due to factors such as construction technology or materials, roads are susceptible to damage after being put into use, under the influence of traffic load, frost, rain, snow, and other climatic conditions, resulting in road damage. Potholes and cracks are the two main types of early-stage road damage that are prone to occur [2]. Once road damage forms, it is irreversible and intensifies over time. Failure to maintain and repair these damages timely will reduce the durability and load-bearing capacity of the road, resulting in significant traffic safety hazards [3]. Therefore, there is an urgent need for a safe, low-cost, and efficient road damage detection method to solve this problem and provide a scientific basis for road managers to carry out timely road maintenance work.

Road damage detection can be divided into three main methods: manual detection methods, physical methods, and deep learning methods. Traditional manual detection methods for road damage are both inefficient and unsafe [4]. To improve detection efficiency, Yamada et al. [5] used a mobile robot equipped with a 2D laser scanner to measure the road and detect road damage. Chen et al. [6] deployed a Driving Video Recorder (DVR) on a vehicle to detect vehicle shaking and then determine whether the shaking was caused by road damages or artificial speed bumps and classified the cause. Puspita et al. [7] accomplished road damage detection using built-in sensors on smartphones. Although the above two methods can achieve road damage detection, they rely on detection equipment, are costly, and detection efficiency still requires further improvement.

With the rapid development of deep learning technology, it has become possible to monitor and recognize road damage quickly, safely, and accurately. Compared to manual and physical methods, the use of deep learning-based machine vision techniques can effectively reduce costs and improve detection efficiency [8, 9]. Currently, methods for detecting road damage based on deep learning can be divided into those based on the Siamese Convolutional Neural Network (SCNN) and those based on encoder-decoder architecture. Iraldi et al. [10] developed a classification system based on SCNN for classifying road images. In this method, the dataset images contain two types of damage: potholes and cracks. They are first converted into grayscale images, then image segmentation and Canny edge detection are applied to the grayscale images, and finally, SCNN is used for image classification. SCNN can measure the distance between features in two input images and transform the learning task into a differential evaluation problem, but it is sensitive to changes in the surrounding environment and lacks robustness. The encoder-decoder-based detection method can overcome this drawback. Wang et al. [11] proposed an improved road crack algorithm based on I-UNet, in which dilated convolutions are used to expand the receptive field of the convolution. Different scales of image features are extracted and multi-scale feature fusion is performed using methods such as "Inception". Mouzinho et al. [12] proposed a method that uses a hierarchical structure for semantic segmentation. This method divides the input image into two levels. The first level of the layer classifies the paved road and background, while the second level detects potholes, cracks, and markings identified in the first level on the road. Subha et al. [13] used a neural network based on an autoencoder architecture to improve the accuracy of detecting two types of road damage, cracks and potholes, by using a large number of loss functions and a voting process based on different weights. Chen et al. [14] proposed a locally enhanced cross-shaped windows transformer (LECSFormer) for detecting road cracks using an encoder-decoder structure. This method uses a well-designed encoder-decoder structure, and the encoder uses window-based transformer blocks to model long-term dependencies.

The above deep learning-based detection techniques have been used to identify differ-ent types of road damage, but their ability to extract different features is still insufficient and cannot adapt well to the detection of various road damages under complex condi-tions such as rainwater, gravel, and reflections. To overcome these limitations, this paper proposes an improved UNet road damage detection method that combines the Atrous Spatial Pyramid Pooling (ASPP) and coordinate attention (CA) blocks. This method can improve the model's feature extraction ability and accurately segment the two main types of road damage, cracks and potholes, on concrete, asphalt, and gravel roads. The exper-imental results show that the proposed method outperforms classic semantic segmenta-tion networks such as Unet, PSPNet, Attention UNet, UNet++, DANet, SegFormer, and TransUNet in evaluation metrics such as F1-Score and IoU.

2 Methodology

2.1 Network Structure

UNet network is a semantic segmentation network proposed after the FCN network, which was initially used to solve the problem of small number of biomedical images due to its ability to obtain good segmentation results on smaller datasets, and was later widely used in other fields [15].

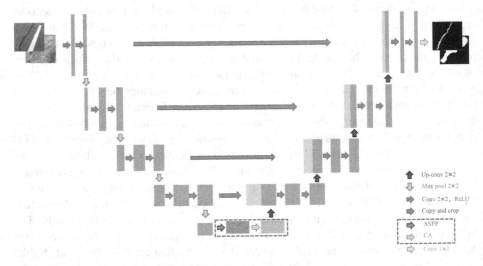

Fig. 1. Overall network architecture

The UNet network is a typical encoder-decoder architecture, where the encoding part is mainly responsible for pooling the input image to extract features, while the decoding part corresponds to the upsampling process, which restores the high-level semantic feature maps obtained from downsampling to the original image resolution. In the process of feature extraction, the deeper the network layer, the larger the receptive field of the obtained feature maps, but some edge features may also be lost. UNet addresses this issue by concatenating feature maps from different levels to fuse features from both shallow and deep layers, thereby reducing the loss of feature information. However, since UNet uses pooling operations to extract feature maps from input images, some edge features are lost while obtaining high-level semantic features. In addition, some detailed information may also be lost during the upsampling process, leading to a decrease in the model's detection accuracy.

To address these issues, this research adds ASPP and CA blocks to UNet to reduce the loss of detailed information and improve the model's feature capture ability. The improved network architecture is shown in Fig. 1. Specifically, the ASPP block and CA block added to the improved network are described as follows.

2.2 Atrous Spatial Pyramid Pooling Block

Receptive Field (RF) refers to the size of the mapping area on the input image for the pixel points on the feature map output by each layer of a Convolutional Neural Network (CNN), and the size of the RF determines the network's performance. In the UNet network, the extensive use of pooling layers for downsampling increases the size of the RF but also leads to a loss of spatial resolution and a significant amount of information in the image.

Atrous convolution, or dilated convolution, is a technique that controls the RF by adjusting the dilation rate while maintaining the feature map size, allowing for the extraction of multi-scale information. The larger the expansion rate, the larger the receptive field of the model. Standard convolution can be considered as a special case of atrous convolution with a dilation rate of 1.

The ASPP block enhances the RF of the model by adding atrous convolutions with different dilation rates. Its structure, as shown in Fig. 2, consists of four parts: a 1×1 convolution, a pooling pyramid, ASPP pooling, and feature map concatenation.

The pooling pyramid in ASPP block consists of three 3×3 dilated convolutions with different dilation rates, whose rates can be customized to achieve flexible multi-scale feature extraction.

In the ASPP pooling module, the feature maps from different channels are first compressed to 1×1 by an AdaptiveAvgPool layer to extract features and obtain global context. Then, a convolutional layer is applied to further extract and reduce the dimensionality of the features obtained from the pooling layer. Finally, the feature maps are restored to their original size. These steps enable the ASPP block to extract both multi-scale and global contextual features.

The feature maps input into the ASPP block undergo the following steps:

1. Dimensionality reduction via a 1×1 convolutional layer;
2. Extraction of features of different sizes using three dilated convolutions with different rates;
3. Extraction of global features using the ASPP pooling module;
4. Concatenation of the feature maps obtained from the above steps, followed by convolutional adjustment of the number of channels to obtain the final output.

Through this design, ASPP block outputs feature maps of multiple sizes, which enables the improved UNet network to learn feature information from feature maps of different sizes, and enhances the model's ability to capture features.

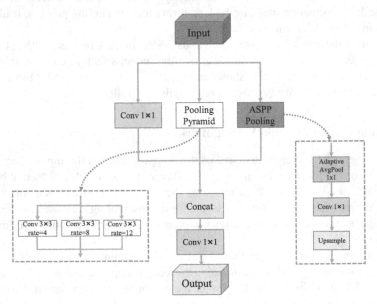

Fig. 2. ASPP block structure

2.3   Coordinate Attention Block

Attention Mechanisms have been introduced into computer vision systems inspired by the ability of the human visual system to naturally and efficiently find important regions in complex scenes. Attention Mechanisms reduce the computational complexity of image processing while improving performance by introducing a block that focuses on specific regions of an image rather than the entire image, and have been used with great success in various computer vision tasks.

Attention mechanisms can be classified into various types such as channel attention mechanisms, spatial attention mechanisms, and mixed attention mechanisms. Channel attention mechanisms are a representative class that selects more critical channels by generating attention masks in the channel domain, dynamically adjusting the weights for different channels, and weakening unimportant ones. By converting feature tensors into individual feature vectors through 2D global pooling, channel attention mechanisms enhance model performance. However, this approach often leads to the loss of location information, which is critical for vision tasks that require capturing target structures.

CA block is a novel and effective coordinate attention that enhances feature representation by embedding location information into channel attention, whose structure is shown in Fig. 3. It uses two one-dimensional global pooling operations to aggregate the input features in vertical and horizontal directions into two independent direction-aware feature maps, respectively, which are then encoded into two attention maps. This approach enables the two attention maps to capture remote dependencies along one spatial direction of the input feature maps while retaining accurate location information along the other spatial direction, thereby effectively integrating spatial coordinate information into the generated attention maps. The CA block not only captures cross-channel information, but also direction-aware and location-sensitive information, which helps the model to more accurately locate and identify the objects of interest.

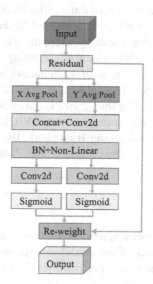

Fig. 3. CA block structure

The CA block achieves accurate position localization primarily through two steps:

1. Coordinate information embedding: for a given input image, each channel is first encoded along the horizontal and vertical coordinates using a pooling kernel of size (H,1) or (1,W) to obtain a pair of direction-aware feature maps, respectively;
2. Coordinate Attention generation: as shown in Eq. (1), the feature map obtained after the above transformation is subjected to the concatenate operation, and then sent to the shared convolutional block with a 1×1 convolutional kernel for dimensionality reduction, and the feature map F_1 processed by batch-normalization is then subjected to the nonlinear operation to obtain the intermediate feature map $\mathbf{f}$. Then, the feature map with the same number of channels is obtained by 1×1 convolution, and the attention weights of the feature map in height and width are obtained by sigmoid activation function, and the final feature map with attention weights in width and height is obtained by multiplicative weighting on the original feature map.

$$\mathbf{f} = \delta\left(F_1\left(\left[z^h, z^w\right]\right)\right) \tag{1}$$

where, [] is the concatenate operation along the spatial dimension, δ is the nonlinear activation function, $\mathbf{f}$ is the intermediate feature map that encodes the spatial information in the horizontal and vertical directions, z^h and z^w are the feature maps obtained along the horizontal and vertical coordinates in the previous step.

3 Experiments

3.1 Implementation Detail

The experimental dataset consisted of road damage images collected using web crawlers, cell phone photography, and downloading some public datasets. The obtained dataset was pre-processed with screening, cleaning, cropping, etc., and then manually labeled using Labelme software, and finally augmented according to data enhancement methods such as rotation and flip to obtain a total of 4220 dataset images, including 3060 crack images and 1160 pothole images. The dataset images are trained, validated and tested in the ratio of 8:1:1, and the training image size is uniformly scaled to 256×256.

The deep learning model was trained on an NVIDIA GeForce RTX 3090 GPU using PyTorch 1.10 as the deep learning framework, the training epoch = 30, Batch size = 10, Learning rate = 0.0005, the optimizer uses AdamW, and the loss function is BCEWithLogitsLoss.

3.2 Evaluation Metrics

In this paper, four evaluation metrics, namely Precision, Recall, F1-score and IoU, are used to evaluate the performance of the model, and the most widely used is the IoU as the main metric to measure the model performance. The calculation equation is shown as follows:

$$\text{Precision} = \frac{\text{TP}}{\text{TP} + \text{FP}} \times 100\% \tag{2}$$

$$\text{Recall} = \frac{\text{TP}}{\text{TP} + \text{FN}} \times 100\% \tag{3}$$

$$\text{F1-score} = 2 \times \frac{\text{Precision} \times \text{Recall}}{\text{Precision} + \text{Recall}} \times 100\% \tag{4}$$

$$\text{IoU} = \frac{\text{TP}}{\text{TP} + \text{FP} + \text{FN}} \times 100\% \tag{5}$$

where, TP (True Positive) indicates the number of correctly segmented road damage feature pixels; FP (False Positive) indicates the number of incorrectly segmented road damage feature pixels; and FN (False Negative) indicates the number of incorrectly segmented non-road damage feature pixels.

3.3 Parameter Selection Experiments

The pooling pyramid in the ASPP block consists of three 3×3 dilated convolutions with different dilation rates. In order to select the optimal dilation rates, comparison experiments were conducted for different combinations of dilation rates, and the experimental results are shown in Fig. 4. As can be seen from the figure, when the dilation rates of the three dilated convolutions in the pooling pyramid are 4, 8, and 12, respectively, the proposed model achieves the best segmentation IoU for both cracks and potholes.

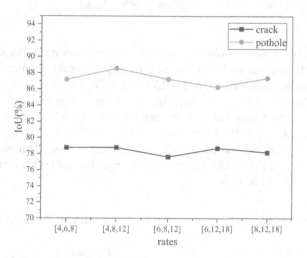

Fig. 4. Comparison results of different combinations of expansion rates

3.4 Ablation Study

To demonstrate the effectiveness of the ASPP block and CA block added in this research, the two blocks were replaced with the convolutional block used in the UNet network. The same experimental parameters and environment were used to train and test the model on the dataset, and the experimental results are presented in Table 1

The table shows that adding the ASPP block alone increases detection indexes such as the IoU, while adding the CA block alone results in varying degrees of decrease in the detection accuracy of cracks and potholes. However, the performance of the network reaches its optimum when both the ASPP and CA blocks are added simultaneously, which indicating that adding both blocks is beneficial for improving the network's performance.

3.5 Comparison with Existing Methods

Quantitative Analysis. The proposed network was compared to mainstream semantic segmentation networks, including UNet, PSPNet [16], Attention UNet [17], UNet++ [18], DANet [19], SegFormer [20], and TransUNet [21], under the same experimental conditions and parameters. The results are shown in Table 2.

Table 1. Comparison of testing performance of ablation study.

Models	Crack(%)				Pothole(%)			
	F1-score	Precision	Recall	IoU	F1-score	Precision	Recall	IoU
UNet	85.27	92.58	81.42	76.09	91.37	93.04	90.82	84.79
UNet_ASPP	86.22	**93.57**	81.44	77.42	93.34	94.45	**93.38**	88.17
UNet_CA	83.68	84.61	87.5	74.43	89.42	89.53	90.47	81.87
UNet_ASPP_CA	**87.01**	90.67	**86.26**	**78.8**	**93.63**	**95.07**	93.14	**88.57**

Comparison with these classical semantic segmentation networks shows that the proposed model has certain advantages. Specifically, for crack segmentation, the segmentation IoU of the proposed method is 2.71%, 6.11%, 3.08%, 4.16%, 7.52%, 3.52%, and 3.69% higher than UNet, PSPNet, Attention UNet, UNet++, DANet, SegFormer, and TransUNet, respectively. For pothole segmentation, the IoU is improved by 3.78%, 2.46%, 11.87%, 1.6%, 1.19%, 4.59%, and 9.69%, respectively. The proposed method performs optimally for both crack and pothole segmentation tasks, demonstrating that the addition of ASPP and CA blocks effectively enhances the network's feature extraction ability for both types of damage.

Table 2. Comparison between the proposed model and the mainstream segmentation networks.

Models	Crack(%)				Pothole(%)			
	F1-score	Precision	Recall	IoU	F1-score	Precision	Recall	IoU
UNet	85.27	92.58	81.42	76.09	91.37	93.04	90.82	84.79
PSPNet	83.08	92.48	77.26	72.69	92.27	93.28	91.82	86.11
Attention UNet	85.1	93.39	80.56	75.72	86.36	82.7	91.27	76.7
UNet++	83.97	92.65	79.77	74.64	92.78	93.11	93.19	86.97
DANet	81.78	93.66	74.8	71.28	92.84	93.55	93.29	87.38
SegFormer-b2	84.78	**94.02**	78.66	75.28	90.94	91.45	91.58	83.98
TransUNet	84.68	87.13	85.07	75.11	87.4	82.79	**94.76**	78.88
Ours	**87.01**	90.67	**86.26**	**78.8**	**93.63**	**95.07**	93.14	**88.57**

Qualitative Analysis. The segmentation results of the proposed model and the classical methods are visualized in Fig. 5. As illustrated by the experimental result images, the proposed model can better restore the shape and contour of cracks and potholes than the classical models, and can more accurately capture the detailed information of cracks. Even under complex conditions such as rainwater, gravel, reflections, and different types of road surfaces including concrete, asphalt, and gravel, it is still able to accurately segment the two types of road damage and exhibit superior detection performance.

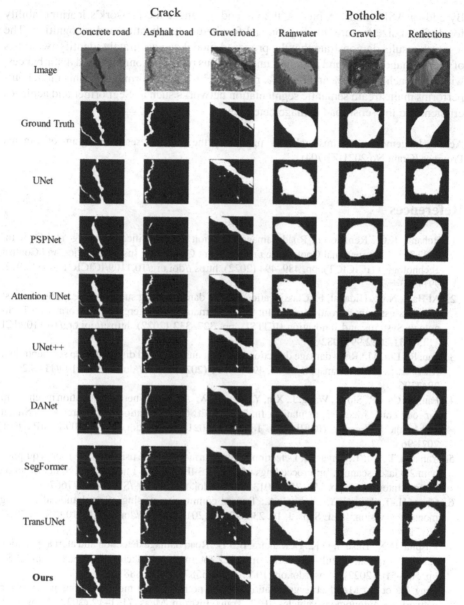

Fig. 5. Visualization results of the comparison between the proposed model and the classical models

4 Conclusion

For the existing road damage segmentation field for road damage detection environment is relatively simple, feature extraction capability is insufficient, this paper proposes an improved UNet road damage detection method that incorporates ASPP and CA blocks.

By adding ASPP and CA blocks, the method enhances the network's learning ability for different size feature information and for feature localization and recognition. The research results demonstrate that the proposed model can accurately identify two types of road damage, cracks and potholes, under various road environments and disturbances, with IoU reaching 78.8% and 88.57%, respectively. The performance of this model outperforms mainstream semantic segmentation networks such as SegFormer and achieves efficient and low-cost road damage detection.

Acknowledgement. This research was funded by the Basic Research Program of Qinghai Province (Grant No.2021-ZJ-704).

References

1. Rehana, K.C., Remya, G.: Road damage detection and classification using YOLOv5. In: 2022 Third International Conference on Intelligent Computing Instrumentation and Control Technologies (ICICICT), pp. 489–494 (2022). https://doi.org/10.1109/ICICICT54557.2022.9917763
2. Al Haqi, N.N., Hidayat, F.: Classification of road damage using supervised learning to assist visual assessment of road damage. In: 2022 International Conference on Information Technology Systems and Innovation (ICITSI), pp. 327–332 (2022). https://doi.org/10.1109/ICITSI56531.2022.9971082
3. Fan, R., Liu, M.: Road damage detection based on unsupervised disparity map segmentation. IEEE Trans. Intell. Transp. Syst. **21**, 4906–4911 (2020). https://doi.org/10.1109/TITS.2019.2947206
4. Fan, X., Cao, P., Shi, P., Wang, J., Xin, Y., Huang, W.: A nested Unet with attention mechanism for road crack image segmentation. In: 2021 IEEE 6th International Conference on Signal and Image Processing (ICSIP), pp. 189–193 (2021). https://doi.org/10.1109/ICSIP52628.2021.9688782
5. Yamada, T., Ito, T., Ohya, A.: Detection of road surface damage using mobile robot equipped with 2D laser scanner. In: Proceedings of the 2013 IEEE/SICE International Symposium on System Integration, pp. 250–256 (2013). https://doi.org/10.1109/SII.2013.6776679
6. Chen, H.-T., Lai, C.-Y., Shih, C.-A.: Toward community sensing of road anomalies using monocular vision. IEEE Sens. J. **16**, 2380–2388 (2016). https://doi.org/10.1109/JSEN.2016.2517194
7. Puspita, D.N., Basuki, D.K., Dewantara, B.S.B.: Road damage detection and alert application using smartphone's built-in sensors. In: 2022 International Electronics Symposium (IES), pp. 506–510 (2022). https://doi.org/10.1109/IES55876.2022.9888366
8. Feng, Z., et al.: MAFNet: segmentation of road potholes with multimodal attention fusion network for autonomous vehicles. IEEE Trans. Instrum. Meas. **71**, 1–12 (2022). https://doi.org/10.1109/TIM.2022.3200100
9. Zhang, B., Liu, X.: Intelligent pavement damage monitoring research in China. IEEE Access. **7**, 45891–45897 (2019). https://doi.org/10.1109/ACCESS.2019.2905845
10. Iraldi, F., Al Maki, W.F.: Damage classification on roads using machine learning. In: 2021 International Conference on Data Science and Its Applications (ICoDSA), pp. 151–156 (2021). https://doi.org/10.1109/ICoDSA53588.2021.9617520
11. Wang, L., Ma, X., Ye, Y.: Computer vision-based road crack detection using an improved I-UNet convolutional networks. In: 2020 Chinese Control and Decision Conference (CCDC), pp. 539–543 (2020). https://doi.org/10.1109/CCDC49329.2020.9164476

12. Mouzinho, F.A.L.N., Fukai, H.: Hierarchical semantic segmentation based approach for road surface damages and markings detection on paved road. In: 2021 8th International Conference on Advanced Informatics: Concepts, Theory and Applications (ICAICTA), pp. 1–5 (2021). https://doi.org/10.1109/ICAICTA53211.2021.9640296

13. Subha, T.D., Sasirekha, N., Shamitha, C., Radhika, S., Tamilselvi, M.: Analysis of deep learning methods for fracture segmentation of road surface under on encoder and decoder. In: 2022 International Conference on Innovative Computing, Intelligent Communication and Smart Electrical Systems (ICSES), pp. 1–9 (2022). https://doi.org/10.1109/ICSES55317.2022.9914306

14. Chen, J., Zhao, N., Zhang, R., Chen, L., Huang, K., Qiu, Z.: Refined crack detection via LECSFormer for autonomous road inspection vehicles. IEEE Trans. Intell. Vehicles **8**, 2049–2061 (2022). https://doi.org/10.1109/TIV.2022.3204583

15. Ronneberger, O., Fischer, P., Brox, T.: U-net: Convolutional networks for biomedical image segmentation. In: Navab, N., Hornegger, J., Wells, W.M., Frangi, A.F. (eds.) MICCAI 2015. LNCS, vol. 9351, pp. 234–241. Springer, Cham (2015). https://doi.org/10.1007/978-3-319-24574-4_28

16. Zhao, H., Shi, J., Qi, X., Wang, X., Jia, J.: Pyramid scene parsing network. In: 30th IEEE Conference on Computer Vision and Pattern Recognition, CVPR 2017, July 21, 2017 - July 26, 2017, Honolulu, HI, United states, pp. 6230–6239. Institute of Electrical and Electronics Engineers Inc. (2017). https://doi.org/10.1109/CVPR.2017.660

17. Oktay, O., et al.: Attention U-Net: learning where to look for the pancreas (2018)

18. Zhou, Z., Siddiquee, M.M.R., Tajbakhsh, N., Liang, J.: UNet++: redesigning skip connections to exploit multiscale features in image segmentation. IEEE Trans. Med. Imaging **39**, 1856–1867 (2020). https://doi.org/10.1109/TMI.2019.2959609

19. Fu, J., et al.: Dual attention network for scene segmentation. In: 32nd IEEE/CVF Conference on Computer Vision and Pattern Recognition, CVPR 2019, June 16, 2019 - June 20, 2019, pp. 3141–3149. IEEE Computer Society, Long Beach, CA, United states (2019). https://doi.org/10.1109/CVPR.2019.00326

20. Xie, E., Wang, W., Yu, Z., Anandkumar, A., Alvarez, J.M., Luo, P.: SegFormer: simple and efficient design for semantic segmentation with transformers. In: 35th Conference on Neural Information Processing Systems, NeurIPS 2021, December 6, 2021 - December 14, 2021, pp. 12077–12090. Neural information processing systems foundation, Virtual (2021)

21. Chen, J., et al.: TransUNet: transformers make strong encoders for medical image segmentation (2021)

Structural Reparameterization Network on Point Cloud Semantic Segmentation

ZhiJian Li⊙, Kebin Jia$^{(\boxtimes)}$ ⊙, YuXuan Zhao, and WeiWei Huang

Beijing Laboratory of Advanced Information Networks, Beijing Key Laboratory of
Computational Intelligence and Intelligent System, Beijing University of Technology,
Beijing 100124, China
kebinj@bjut.edu.cn

Abstract. In recent years, 3D point cloud semantic segmentation has made
remarkable progress. However, most existing work focuses on designing intricate structures to aggregate local features, resulting in a significant number of
parameters and computational demands. In this Paper, we combine the idea of
structural reparameterization in 2D convolution to propose RPNet, which can
effectively reduce the number of parameters while fully extracting the point cloud
features. Specifically. We first design the multi-branch structure SRLFA (Structure
Re-parameterization Local Feature Abstract) module based on the reparameterization to fully extract the local features of the point cloud, and design the PFA (Point
Feature Abstract) module to extract the features of the point itself. Then, by decoupling the training and inference phases, the multi-branch structure is fused into an
equivalent single-branch structure through the idea of structural reparameterization during training and inference, which ensures the feature extraction capability
while effectively reducing the number of parameters. Finally, the proposed method
is trained and tested on several public data, and the results demonstrate that the
proposed method achieves advanced performance in mIoU and OA with effective
control of the number of model parameters.

Keywords: Point Cloud · Structural Reparameterization · Semantic
Segmentation

1 Introduction

The growing popularity of 3D sensors such as 3D laser scanners and RGB-D cameras has
brought attention to the fundamental task of semantic segmentation of point clouds in 3D
computer vision. Unlike 2D images, point clouds offer richer spatial information, including coordinates, colors, and reflectance intensity. Consequently, point cloud semantic
segmentation has gained wide-spread use in autonomous driving, robotics, and augmented reality. However, point clouds are often sparse, irregular, and unordered, which
poses challenges for processing them using powerful convolutional neural networks
(CNNs).

In recent years, there have been numerous efforts to efficiently extract features from
point clouds in order to gain a more comprehensive understanding of them. PointNet

© The Author(s), under exclusive license to Springer Nature Switzerland AG 2023
H. Lu et al. (Eds.): ICIG 2023, LNCS 14355, pp. 344–355, 2023.
https://doi.org/10.1007/978-3-031-46305-1_28

[1] was one of the earliest works to use a multilayer perceptron (MLP) for direct processing of point clouds, while PointNet++ [2] expanded upon this by introducing Set Abstraction (SA) and Furthest Point Sampling (FPS) to extract local information and hierarchical feature characteristics. Subsequently, several methods have been proposed [3–6], with most of them focusing on designing complex local feature extraction modules for improved performance. However, these structures often aggregate neighboring points, which leads to a significant increase in the number of parameters computed and computational volume when the data dimension has K more neighboring points. This is not ideal for practical applications. Although these methods have shown significant improvements compared to PointNet and PointNet++, their complexity hinders their applicability in realistic scenarios.

To alleviate the growing complexity of local feature extraction for point cloud semantic segmentation and the resulting increase in computational parameters, we propose a novel local feature extraction module, SRLFA, that leverages the unique features of point clouds to fuse coordinate and feature information. SRLFA enables comprehensive point cloud local feature extraction during training while significantly reducing the number of parameters and computational effort. In addition to local feature extraction, it is crucial to extract features from the points themselves, which is often overlooked in many models that focus solely on local feature extraction or use MLPs to update point features. Therefore, we introduce the PFA structure, which employs a multi-branching plus residual structure to fully extract point features without increasing the number of inference parameters or computational effort. In summary, the main contributions of this paper are as follows:

1. To the best of our knowledge, this is the first study to apply the idea of structural reparameterization on point cloud semantic segmentation, and we propose the SRLFA module for local feature extraction while controlling the number of inference parameters.
2. We propose the PFA module to further enhance the features of point after aggregating local features of points.
3. Combining the SRLFA and PFA structures, we propose a new point cloud semantic segmentation network called RPNet, and evaluate the performance of our network on multiple public datasets.

2 Related Work

According to the form of representation of the point cloud data, there are three types of methods for processing point clouds: projection-based methods, voxel-based methods, and point-based methods.

2.1 Projection-Based Methods

Due to the irregularity and disorder of point clouds, the already maturely developed image convolutional neural networks cannot be directly applied to point cloud processing. Therefore, a straightforward approach to processing point clouds is to project irregular point clouds into regular 2D picture. Methods [7, 8] such as RangeNet converts the point cloud into a depth image, extracts features from the depth image using a fully convolutional network, and then maps the segmentation result back to the original point cloud. The projection-based approach is a promising solution for structuring the processing of point cloud data. However, this method may result in the loss of point cloud details, particularly when used in large-scale view projection.

2.2 Voxel-Based Methods

An alternative approach for converting irregular point clouds into regular representations is 3D voxelization. The voxel structure is similar to a unitary cube, allowing for the processing of voxelized point cloud data through 3D convolution. However, the voxel-based methods suffers from sparsity, and the proportion of non-empty voxels is relatively low. Using dense convolution on spatially sparse data is inefficient and generates excessive unnecessary computation and memory consumption. To address this issue, OctNet [9] proposed a non-equilibrium lattice-octree structure, which was further improved by Graham et al. [5] who proposed a new sparse convolution operation that only convolves at non-empty voxels. This reduces memory consumption and improves point cloud processing efficiency. Although the voxel-based approach has achieved greatly results, it still cannot solve the problem of geometric information loss due to point cloud transformation.

2.3 Point-Based Methods

Due to the inherent limitations of both projection-based and voxel-based methods, the direct processing of point clouds has become a consensus research direction. PointNet [1] is a pioneering work that directly processes point clouds, extracting point cloud features through a multilayer perceptron (MLP), addressing the permutation invariance of point clouds using the T-Net structure, and addressing the ordering invariance of point clouds through pooling layers that aggregate global features. However, PointNet cannot effectively extract local features of point clouds. PointNet++ [2] proposed set abstraction and hierarchical sampling structures to reduce computation and increase point cloud receptive fields. On this basis, many methods have been proposed [3, 4, 10, 11]. KPConv [3] defines convolution kernels and proposes fixed and deformable kernel point convolutions for simple and complex tasks. PAConv [4] proposes adaptive learning of eight weight matrices as a weight bank to globally assign different weight coefficients to the features of points. In addition, many studies have combined point clouds with graph convolutions. DGCNN [10] uses a graph network formed by point cloud nodes to extract local features of point clouds and dynamically updates the graph to learn hierarchical features. DeepGCN [11] investigates the advantages of using depth information for three-dimensional scene understanding in graph convolution networks.

2.4 Structural Reparameterization

In the field of 2D images, multi-branch structures are widely used due to their ability to extract more comprehensive features and carry richer information compared to single-branch structures. However, this comes at the cost of increased parameter and computational complexity. To address this problem, RepVGG [12] proposed the concept of structural reparameterization to decouple the training and inference processes. During inference, RepVGG converts the complex multi-branch structure into a single-branch structure through parameter fusion equivalence. This largely solves the problem of contradiction between model feature extraction ability and model volume, and can effectively reduce the number of parameters. DBB [13] extends the diversity of structural fusion on this basis, including 1×1 and $k \times k$ Conv-bn cascades, Concatenation of parallel Conv-bn branches, Conv-bn and average pooling connections, etc.

3 Methods

3.1 Local Feature Abstract Module

A point cloud is a collection of N points, is composed of its inherent coordinate information $p \in R^{N \times 3}$ (represented by 3 for xyz coordinates), as well as additional features information $f \in R^{N \times d}$ (represented by d for feature dimension), such as color, reflection intensity, and normal vectors. From the perspective of a single point, its coordinates and features are two distinct attributes. To extract feature information for each individual point, we typically employ Multi-Layer Perceptron (MLP) or 1D 1×1 convolution. Meanwhile, we use MLP or 2D 1×1 convolution to extract local geometric feature information of each point, which is relatively more important, and the feature extraction structure is more complex. For a central point $p_i(f_i \in R^{N \times d})$, in order to extract its local features, the information of K neighboring points is often aggregated by Knn or Ball-Query, and then extract geometric features via a local feature extraction module, at this point the feature dimension $f_{ik} \in R^{N \times K \times 3}$. If a 1D convolution with a kernel size of 1×1 and a 2D convolution are used to operate on features and coordinates respectively, the computational complexity differs by a factor of $\frac{d \times d \times K \times N}{d \times d \times N} = K$. This results in simple models being unable to effectively extract local features, and models that can extract local features well have a large volume, making them difficult to deploy in applications.

To alleviate this issue, we propose the SRLFA module which utilizes the reparameterization method [17, 30] as shown in Fig. 1. During the training phase, the SRLFA module adopts a dual-branch structure, where a Conv-bn unit serves as a basic component, and each branch contains two Conv-bn units with the same number of intermediate channels as the input channels. The input, which is composed of relative coordinates and feature summation, is first fused with the relative coordinates and feature information separately in each of the two branches. The output of the two branches is then summed, passed through a ReLU activation function, and fed to the Conv-bn-relu to further fuse double-branch features and enhance local feature extraction. During inference, to reduce the number of parameters and computation, we merge the basic Conv-bn units into a single Conv unit, as illustrated in Fig. 1-(b). Then, the cascaded two fused convolutions are further merged into a single convolution, as shown in Fig. 1-(c). Note that this fusion is only feasible when the first convolution is a 1×1 convolution [13], which is the case for point cloud processing. Finally, we merge the two parallel convolutions into the final convolution. This fusion decreases the number of parameters by approximately four times, while maintaining the same point cloud feature information.

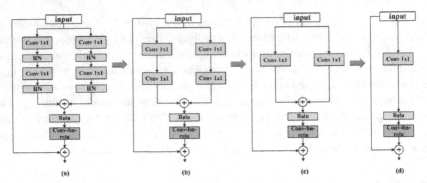

Fig. 1. (a) shows the SRLFA structure at training time; (b) shows the structure after fusing Conv-BN into Conv; (c) shows the structure after fusing two 1×1 Conv in cascade into one 1×1 Conv; (d) shows the structure after fusing two 1×1 Conv in parallel into one 1×1 Conv. Compared to (a), the number of parameters is reduced by a factor of about four.

3.2 Point Feature Abstract Module

In recent years, research on improving point cloud semantic segmentation performance has mainly focused on designing structures for point cloud local feature extraction, while neglecting the importance of point feature extraction, which is critical for improving segmentation accuracy. Therefore, we propose the PFA module for point feature extraction, as shown in Fig. 2-(b). The PFA module consists of four branches, two of which are similar to the SRLFA structure. Each branch consists of two cascaded 1D Conv-bn layers used to extract deeper-level features of the points, while one branch consisting of only one 1D Conv-bn layer is used to extract shallow-level features of the points. To enhance the model's learning and convergence capabilities and to preserve the original features of the points, a residual branch is added. The outputs of the four branches are then added and fully fused through a 1D Conv-bn-relu layer. After the points with locally aggregated features $f \in R^{N \times d}$ pass through the PFA for feature extraction, their outputs remain unchanged at $f \in R^{N \times d}$.

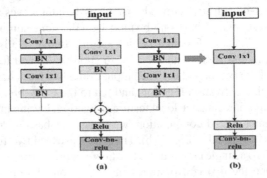

Fig. 2. (a) Structure of the PFA during training; (b) Structure of the PFA during inference.

3.3 RPNet

Based on the SRLFA and PFA modules, and following the classic encoder-decoder architecture in the segmentation field, combined with the PointNeXt network structure, we propose RPNet, as shown in Fig. 3. The input point cloud is divided into two parts, coordinates $p \in R^{N \times 3}$ and features $f \in R^{N \times d} (d = 4)$. Firstly, the input features f are projected to the high dimensional $f \in R^{N \times 32}$ through the feature embedding layer, which helps the model to learn subsequent features and accelerate the convergence. Then, the point cloud coordinates and features are fed into four feature extraction stages. Each stage consists of a Sample & Group layer and a Feature Abstract layer. The Sample & Group layer mainly down-samples the number of points through Sample layer using FPS (four times from the first stage $p \in R^{N/4 \times 3}$), reducing computation and expanding the receptive field of points. At the same time, it obtains K (=32) nearest point features $f_{ik} \in R^{N \times d \times K}$ and relative coordinates $p_{ik} \in R^{N \times K \times 3}$ within a radius of 0.1 through BallQuery. Since the points are highly correlated in 3D Euclidean distance space, in order to train the model to be location-aware, we explicitly project the relative coordinates through a 2D convolution to the feature dimension $p_{ik} \in R^{N \times d \times K}$ to further extract coordinate features, and then summing them to the SRLFA module to extract local features. Compared with Concat, the addition operation can more explicitly connect features and coordinates, and does not increase the number of channels. The local features of points are aggregated through a max pooling layer.

The structure of the Feature Abstract layer is similar to that of the Sample & Group layer, but without the need for downsampling. The input from the Sample & Group layer is first subjected to the Group operation, followed by the addition of the relative coordinates. The resulting input is then passed to the SRLFA module to fuse the two features. After aggregating local features in the pooling layer, the PFA module enhances the points' own features.

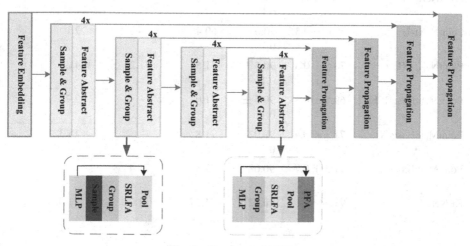

Fig. 3. Structure of RPNet.

4 Experiment

In this section, we evaluate the performance of RPNet on three public datasets, S3DIS [14], ScanNetv2 [15] for verifying semantic segmentation, and ShapeNetPart [16] for part segmentation.

Table 1. Semantic segmentation on the S3DIS (Area 5) and ScanNetV2 datasets. The term before "/" represents the number of parameters during training, and the term after "/" represents the number of parameters after fusion.

Method	S3DIS Area-5		ScanNet V2		Params.
	mIoU (%)	OA (%)	Val mIoU (%)	Test mIoU (%)	M
PointNet [1]	41.1	–	–	–	3.6
PointCNN [17]	57.3	85.9	–	45.8	0.6
DGCNN [10]	47.9	83.6	–	–	1.3
DeepGCN [11]	52.5	–	–	–	3.6
KPConv [3]	67.1	–	69.2	68.6	15.0
RandLA-Net [18]	–	–	-	64.5	1.3
BAAF-Net [6]	65.4	88.9	–	–	5.0
PointTransformer [19]	70.4	90.8	70.6	–	7.8
CBL [20]	69.4	90.6	–	70.5	18.6
PointNeXt-S [21]	63.4 ± 0.7	87.9 ± 0.3	64.5	–	0.8
PointNeXt-B	67.3 ± 0.2	89.4 ± 0.1	68.4	–	3.8
PointNeXt-L	69.0 ± 0.5	90.0 ± 0.1	69.4	–	7.1
PointNeXt-XL	70.5 ± 0.3	90.6 ± 0.1	71.5	71.2	41.6
PointMetaBase-L [22]	69.5 ± 0.3	90.5 ± 0.1	71.0	–	2.7
PointMetaBase-XL	71.1 ± 0.4	90.9 ± 0.1	71.8	–	15.3
PointMetaBase-XLL	71.3 ± 0.7	90.08 ± 0.6	72.8	71.4	19.7
RPNet	**71.34**	**90.72**	71.37	71.22	11.089/**4.91**

4.1 Datasets

S3DIS: A complete point cloud was obtained without human intervention using a Matterport scanner. The dataset consists of 271 rooms from 6 large-scale indoor scenes from 3 different buildings (total area of 6020 m^2). These areas mainly include offices, educational exhibition spaces, meeting rooms, etc. We used the mean class-wise intersection over union (mIoU), and the overall point-wise accuracy (OA) for evaluation, and provide the test results for Area 5.

ScanNet: ScanNet is also a well-known dataset for indoor segmentation, containing 3D indoor scenes with 20 semantic categories and multiple rooms. The dataset is divided into 3 parts: training, validation, and testing, corresponding to 1201, 312, and 100 scans, respectively. Following PointNeXt [21], we do not use any voting strategy. For the evaluation metrics, we provide the results of validation mIoU and test mIoU.

ShapeNetPart: The ShapeNetPart dataset is used for 3D object part segmentation, consisting of 16880 models of 16 shape categories, with 14006 models used for training and 2874 for testing. There are 50 different parts with 2 to 6 parts per category. For the evaluation metrics, we provide the results of the class mIoU and instance mIoU.

Fig. 4. Visualization of semantic segmentation results on the S3DIS dataset.

4.2 Implementation details

RPNet was trained using the PyTorch framework, utilizing the AdamW optimizer with a weight decay of 10^{-4} and an initial learning rate of 0.01. To prevent overfitting, we employed cross-entropy loss with label smoothing and a cosine decay strategy. In the case of the S3DIS dataset, we downsampled point clouds by voxelization with a size of 0.04 m, and trained for 100 epochs with a fixed sample size of 24,000 points per batch and a batch size of 4. For the ScanNet dataset, we used a voxel size of 0.02 m and input 64,000 points, implementing a multi-stage learning rate decay with a decay rate of 0.1 at epochs 70 and 90. Label smoothing was not used in this case. Lastly, for the ShapeNetPart dataset, we trained and tested with 2,048 randomly sampled points and a batch size of 8, over 400 epochs.

4.3 Result

S3DIS: The test results for Area 5 are reported in Table 1. During the training phase, our model had 11.058M parameters, which reduced to 5.638M after fusion, bringing a reduction of 5.32M parameters. This further demonstrates that the idea of structural reparameterization can effectively reduce the number of model parameters. Compared with PointMetaBase-L, our model achieves an improvement of 1.54–1.84 mIoU and 0.12–0.22 OA. Compared with PointMetaBase-XL, RPNet achieves comparable performance with only 72.5% and 32% of the parameters used in training and inference. Due to the limitation of computing power during training, we did not make any attempt to expand the model size. To further demonstrate the superiority of RPNet, some of the visualization results are shown in Fig. 4.

ScanNet: As shown in Table 1, compared to PointMetaBase-L, RPNet achieves better val mIoU by 0.32. Compared to PointNeXt-XL, RPNet achieves comparable performance with only 26.7% and 11.8% of the parameters used in training and inference.

ShapeNetPart: In order to demonstrate the generalization ability of RPNet, we conducted experiments on ShapeNetPart. Due to the relatively small size of the dataset, overly deep models can lead to overfitting. Therefore, following the PointMetaBase, we increased the width and reduced the depth of the model. The results are shown in Table 2, and our model achieves comparable performance to PointMetaBase-S (C = 64).

4.4   Ablation Experiments

To show the efficacy of each component in RPNet, a multitude of ablation experiments were performed and their results were presented in Tables 3 and 4. For the purpose of enhancing interpretability of the comparisons, experiments were exclusively conducted on S3DIS dataset using PointMetaBase-L as the baseline. Firstly, the effectiveness of SRLFA was validated in Table 3. The incorporation of SRLFA module significantly improve mIoU by 1.32–1.62, despite the substantial increase in the number of parameters. This could be attributed to the complete fusion of coordinate features and point cloud characteristics. Additionally, through the utilization of the PFA module, the salient features were further accentuated, bringing to a 0.2 mIoU improvement with minimal parameter increase during inference. This is attributed to the superior information-carrying capacity of multi-branching when compared to single-branching.

Furthermore, we conducted several experiments to explore different SRLFA architectures, as shown in Table 4. Two-B represents a dual-branch structure, i.e., an SRLFA module, and 2 × Channel is the doubling of the number of channels between two cascaded conv-bn, resulting in twice the number of input channels. Thr-B denotes a parallel triple-branch structure, while Thr-Conv represents three cascaded Conv-bn structures in each branch. It is evident that increasing the complexity of the SRLFA model not

Table 2. Part segmentation on the ShapeNetPart datasets; The term before "/" represents the number of parameters during training, and the term after "/" represents the number of parameters after fusion.

Method	ins. mIoU (%)	cls. mIoU (%)	Params. (M)
PointNet [1]	83.7	80.4	3.6
DGCNN [10]	85.2	82.3	1.3
KPConv [3]	86.4	85.1	–
CurveNet [23]	86.8	–	–
ASSANet-L [24]	86.1	–	–
Point Transformer [19]	86.6	83.7	7.8
Stratifiedformer [25]	86.6	85.1	–
PointNeXt-S [21]	86.7 ± 0.0	84.4 ± 0.2	1.0
PointNeXt-S (C = 64)	86.9 ± 0.1	84.8 ± 0.5	3.7
PointNeXt-S (C = 160)	87.0 ± 0.1	85.2 ± 0.1	22.5
PointMetaBase-S [22]	86.7 ± 0.0	84.3 ± 0.1	1.0
PointMetaBase-S (C = 64)	86.9 ± 0.0	84.9 ± 0.2	3.8
PointMetaBase-S (C = 160)	87.1 + 0.0	85.1 ± 0.3	22.7
RPNet	86.8	84.7	5.8/3.46

Table 3. Ablation studies about the effectiveness of SRLFA and PFA

Method	mIoU (%)	OA (%)	Params. (M)
PointMetaBase-L	69.5 ± 0.3	90.5 ± 0.1	2.7
+SRLFA	71.12	90.59	8.16/4.9
+PFA	71.34	90.72	11.09/4.9

Table 4. Ablation studies about different structural designs of SRFLA

Method	mIoU (%)	OA (%)	Params. (M)
Two-B	71.12	90.59	8.16/4.9
2 × Channel	70.88	90.53	12.48/4.9
Thr-B	69.88	90.47	10.32/4.9
Thr-Conv	70.44	91.12	10.32/4.9

only increases the number of parameters but also does not improve accuracy. We believe this is due to excessive feature extraction, leading to redundant feature information and resulting in either a decrease or no improvement in performance.

5 Conclusion

The Paper introduces RPNet, a novel method for semantic segmentation of point clouds, which firstly introduces the concept of structural reparameterization into the realm of point cloud semantic segmentation. This innovative contribution is a significant advancement in the field, as it effectively decouples the training and inference phases, leading to a substantial reduction in the number of parameters during inference. Furthermore, RPNet enables the extraction of local features from point clouds, thus mitigating the challenges posed by large model size and complex deployment. To achieve comprehensive feature extraction from point clouds, we propose the SRLFA and PFA modules. The former utilizes a dual-branch residual structure to fuse coordinate and feature information, while the latter employs a four-branch structure to explore point-specific features. Our experimental findings indicate that RPNet yields superior performance on various commonly used datasets.

Acknowledgement. This research was funded by the Basic Research Program of Qinghai Province (Grant No. 2021-ZJ-704) and Beijing Natural Science Foundation (GrantNo. 4212001).

References

1. Qi, C.R., Su, H., Mo, K., Guibas, L.J.: PointNet: deep learning on point sets for 3D classification and segmentation (2017). http://arxiv.org/abs/1612.00593
2. Qi, C.R., Yi, L., Su, H., Guibas, L.J.: PointNet++: deep hierarchical feature learning on point sets in a metric space, p. 14 (2017)
3. Thomas, H., Qi, C.R., Deschaud, J.-E., Marcotegui, B., Goulette, F., Guibas, L.: KPConv: flexible and deformable convolution for point clouds. In: 2019 IEEE/CVF International Conference on Computer Vision (ICCV), pp. 6410–6419. IEEE, Seoul, Korea (South) (2019). https://doi.org/10.1109/ICCV.2019.00651
4. Xu, M., Ding, R., Zhao, H., Qi, X.: PAConv: position adaptive convolution with dynamic kernel assembling on point clouds. In: 2021 IEEE/CVF Conference on Computer Vision and Pattern Recognition (CVPR), pp. 3172–3181. IEEE, Nashville, TN, USA (2021). https://doi.org/10.1109/CVPR46437.2021.00319
5. Graham, B., Engelcke, M., van der Maaten, L.: 3D semantic segmentation with submanifold sparse convolutional networks. In: Proceedings of the IEEE Conference on Computer Vision and Pattern Recognition (2018)
6. Qiu, S., Anwar, S., Barnes, N.: Semantic segmentation for real point cloud scenes via bilateral augmentation and adaptive fusion (2021). http://arxiv.org/abs/2103.07074
7. Singh, G., Gupta, S., Lease, M., Dawson, C.: Range-net: a high precision streaming SVD for big data applications. arXiv preprint arXiv:2010.14226 (2020)
8. Wei, X., Yu, R., Sun, J.: View-GCN: view-based graph convolutional network for 3D shape analysis. In: Proceedings of the IEEE/CVF Conference on Computer Vision and Pattern Recognition (2020)

9. Riegler, G., Osman Ulusoy, A., Geiger, A.: OctNet: learning deep 3D representations at high resolutions. In: Proceedings of the IEEE Conference on Computer Vision and Pattern Recognition (2017)

10. Phan, A.V., Nguyen, M.L., Nguyen, Y.L.H., Bui, L.T.: DGCNN: a convolutional neural network over large-scale labeled graphs. Neural Netw.Netw. **108**, 533–543 (2018). https://doi.org/10.1016/j.neunet.2018.09.001

11. Li, G., Muller, M., Thabet, A., Ghanem, B.: DeepGCNs: can GCNs go as deep as CNNs? In: Proceedings of the IEEE/CVF International Conference on Computer Vision (2019)

12. Ding, X., Zhang, X., Ma, N., Han, J., Ding, G., Sun, J.: RepVGG: making VGG-style ConvNets great again (2021). http://arxiv.org/abs/2101.03697

13. Ding, X., Zhang, X., Han, J., Ding, G.: Diverse branch block: building a convolution as an inception-like unit (2021). http://arxiv.org/abs/2103.13425, https://doi.org/10.48550/arXiv.2103.13425

14. Armeni, I., Sax, A., Zamir, A.R., Savarese, S.: Joint 2D-3D-semantic data for indoor scene understanding (2017)

15. Dai, A., Chang, A.X., Savva, M., Halber, M., Funkhouser, T., Niessner, M.: ScanNet: richly-annotated 3D reconstructions of indoor scenes. In: 2017 IEEE Conference on Computer Vision and Pattern Recognition (CVPR), pp. 2432–2443. IEEE, Honolulu, HI (2017). https://doi.org/10.1109/CVPR.2017.261

16. Chang, A.X., et al.: ShapeNet: an information-rich 3D model repository (2015). http://arxiv.org/abs/1512.03012, https://doi.org/10.48550/arXiv.1512.03012

17. Li, Y., Bu, R., Sun, M., Wu, W., Di, X., Chen, B.: PointCNN: convolution on x-transformed points. In: Advances in Neural Information Processing Systems. Curran Associates, Inc. (2018)

18. Hu, Q., et al.: RandLA-net: efficient semantic segmentation of large-scale point clouds (2020). http://arxiv.org/abs/1911.11236

19. Zhao, H., Jiang, L., Jia, J., Torr, P.H.S., Koltun, V.: Point Transformer. https://doi.org/10.1109/ICCV48922.2021.01595

20. Tang, L., Zhan, Y., Chen, Z., Yu, B., Tao, D.: Contrastive boundary learning for point cloud segmentation. In: 2022 IEEE/CVF Conference on Computer Vision and Pattern Recognition (CVPR), pp. 8479–8489. IEEE, New Orleans, LA, USA (2022). https://doi.org/10.1109/CVPR52688.2022.00830

21. Qian, G., et al.: PointNeXt: revisiting PointNet++ with improved training and scaling strategies (2022). http://arxiv.org/abs/2206.04670

22. Lin, H., et al.: Meta architecture for point cloud analysis (2022). http://arxiv.org/abs/2211.14462

23. Xiang, T., Zhang, C., Song, Y., Yu, J., Cai, W.: Walk in the cloud: learning curves for point clouds shape analysis (2021). http://arxiv.org/abs/2105.01288

24. Qian, G., Hammoud, H.A.A.K., Li, G., Thabet, A., Ghanem, B.: ASSANet: an anisotropic separable set abstraction for efficient point cloud representation learning (2021). http://arxiv.org/abs/2110.10538

25. Lai, X., et al.: Stratified transformer for 3D point cloud segmentation. https://doi.org/10.1109/CVPR52688.2022.00831

Physical Key Point Detection Algorithm Based on Multi-scale Feature Fusion

Xiao Wang[1,2,3], Pengyu Liu[1,2,3](✉), Peng Zhao[4], and A. Jiancuo[5]

[1] School of Information Science, Beijing University of Technology, Beijing 100124, China
liupengyu@bjut.edu.cn
[2] Advanced Information Network Beijing Laboratory, Beijing 100124, China
[3] Beijing Key Laboratory of Computational Intelligence and Intelligent Systems, Beijing University of Technology, Beijing 100124, China
[4] China Institute of Sport Science, Beijing 100061, China
[5] Qinghai Red Cross Hospital, Xining 810000, Qinghai, China

Abstract. Physical posture is a reflection of the orderly arrangement of the body's bones and the proper functioning of its muscle tissue, and it is also a guarantee of good health. Evaluating physical posture generally involves detecting key points on the human body, which is essentially a dense detection task in machine vision. This paper proposes a new key point detection method for evaluating physical posture, based on multi-scale feature fusion and self-attention mechanism. The self-attention mechanism is added in the algorithm to capture global feature dependencies, while the patching merging down-sampling structures help reduce information loss during the down-sampling process. Additionally, a deconvolution module is added in the prediction phase to generate higher quality feature maps and improve the spatial accuracy of the key points. The proposed algorithm achieves an average mAP of 85.5% on key point detection models for the front, side, and back of the body on a self-built dataset. The results demonstrate the algorithm's good performance in the field of physical posture health evaluation.

Keywords: Physical Posture Health Evaluation · Key Point Detection · Multi-Scale Feature Fusion · Self-Attention Mechanism

1 Introduction

In modern living environments, abnormal physical posture issues have become increasingly prominent, particularly among children and adolescents, due to bad behavior habits. Early symptoms of abnormal physical posture are often not obvious and can worsen over time, even posing a threat to life [1–3]. Research by Brezk et al. [4] found that bad habits such as carrying heavy school bags and unbalanced straps can lead to abnormal trunk development in preschool children. Among 155 testers between the ages of 7 and 9, 35.3% of girls and 60.9% of boys having such issues.

Supported by Qinghai Provincial Science and Technology Program-Key Research and Transformation Program under Grants No. 2023-SF-118

To address this growing problem, the General Administration of Sports of China released "Indicators and Methods for Testing Physical Posture of Children and Adolescents" in February 2022, which proposed using the relative position relationship of physical posture key points to evaluate abnormal physical posture problems. However, existing detection methods generally rely on manual measurement [5] or imaging using radiographic equipment, which are highly dependent on medical equipment and professionals, costly, time-consuming, and unsuitable for large-scale screening.

Key point detection in physical posture health assessment belongs to the dense prediction task in machine vision. In recent years, deep learning technology has made remarkable progress in visual tasks, and many researchers have conducted in-depth studies in the field of key point detection, finding that convolutional neural networks can accurately complete the task. While Convolutional Pose Machines (CPM) [6] and Hourglass [7] have been developed to predict key points, they have limitations such as insufficient key point accuracy due to using only low-scale features to predict or insufficient consideration of the dependence relationship around key point features. While HRNet [8, 9] employs a multi-scale parallel network structure and multi-scale feature fusion to maintain a high-scale feature branch, which retains rich image spatial information and improves the accuracy of key point prediction, it may still fall short in detecting key points accurately due to insufficient consideration of the dependence relationship around these features. Therefore, further network optimization is required to enhance the accuracy of key point detection in certain parts of the body.

To address these limitations, this paper proposes a novel key point detection network based on multi-scale feature fusion and attention mechanism, which improves key point detection accuracy and addresses limitations in existing methods. The proposed algorithm performs better than mainstream detection algorithms such as HRNet and Hourglass.This work has implications for addressing the growing problem of abnormal physical posture issues, particularly among children and adolescents.

2 Related Works

Recent studies have shown that incorporating attention mechanism into convolutional neural networks can significantly enhance feature extraction accuracy by focusing on feature dependencies [10–12]. Microsoft Asia Research Institute developed the Swin Transformer [13] in 2021, which introduces multi-scale processing and shift window ideas based on self-attention, leading to global attention and substantial improvements in neural network detection accuracy.

To enhance the accuracy of our key point detection model, this paper proposes a multi-scale parallel network structure based on multi-scale feature fusion, coupled with an attention mechanism module inspired by Swin Transformer. This attention module replaces the traditional residual feature extraction module, allowing for better detection accuracy of the model.

3   Methods

The key point detection network structure proposed in this article is shown in Fig. 1, which is mainly divided into two parts: the feature extraction structure with multi-scale fusion and the prediction structure.

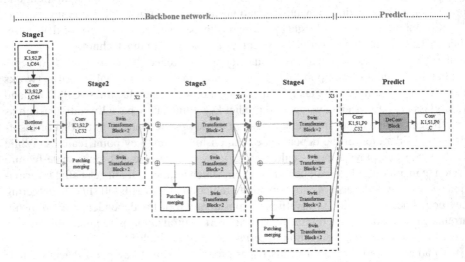

Fig. 1. The key point detection network structure in this article.

3.1   The Feature Extraction Structure with Multi-scale Fusion

The key point detection network proposed in this article adopts a multi-scale branch parallel feature extraction structure based on multi-scale feature fusion, which preserves both high-scale and low-scale features throughout the process to obtain prediction feature maps with both rich semantic and accurate spatial information. The high-scale features are maintained throughout the process via a blue arrow branch (as shown in Fig. 1), which ensures the preservation of precise spatial information.

The backbone network comprises four stages. In the first stage, input features are convolved and the channel number is expanded, after which a residual structure consisting of four Bottleneck modules [14] is used to extract early features from the raw input image. The subsequent stages (i.e., second to fourth stages) include Down-Sampling, feature extraction with attention, and multi-scale Feature Fusion, which combine rich spatial information from high-scale features and semantic information from low-scale features to obtain precise feature maps.

Down-Sampling. To reduce information loss caused by pooling layers in down-sampling, this article adopts a Patching merging down-sampling structure that is more effective at retaining spatial information. As illustrated in Fig. 2., the Patching merging down-sampling structure takes out feature map patches at pixel intervals and concatenates them into blocks of the same size. These blocks are then concatenated in the depth direction and passed through a LayerNorm layer for normalization. Finally, a fully connected layer is applied to perform linear transformation in the depth direction of the feature map, doubling the number of channels while halving the width and height. This approach maintains the semantic information from low-scale features while preserving spatial information, resulting in feature maps with both rich semantic and accurate spatial information.

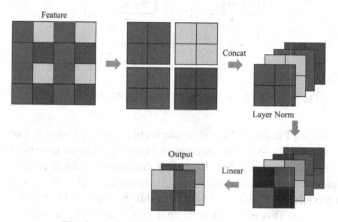

Fig. 2. Structure of down-sampling module

Feature Extraction with Fusion Attention. In this paper, detailed feature extraction was performed on each multiscale branch to capture the dependency relationships between the features around key points, which is crucial for improving the accuracy of key point detection. However, traditional residual convolution is limited in establishing long-range dependency relationships between features that are far apart. To address this issue, we incorporated Swin-Transformer modules for feature extraction in each scale branch. Swin-Transformer modules can better preserve local image information and establish long-range dependency relationships, resulting in richer semantic information. In stages 2, 3, and 4, each scale feature is passed through two consecutive Swin-Transformer attention modules, as shown in Fig. 3.

The Swin-Transformer attention module employed in this work employs a local window self-attention mechanism for feature extraction. It consists of two stages. In the first stage, the input features undergo a windowed multi-head self-attention (W-MSA) operation, which divides the features into multiple non-overlapping windows before performing self-attention. However, this operation may lead to a lack of information interaction between windows. To address this issue, a shifted window multi-head self-attention (SW-MSA) operation is used in the second stage. This operation shifts the original window lines to the right and down (shifted windows) before performing self-attention, enabling inter-window information exchange and maintaining locality. This approach preserves local image information while establishing long-range dependency relationships, enriching the semantic information extracted by the network.

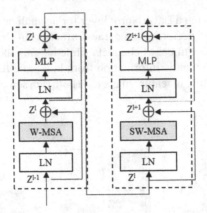

Fig. 3. Two consecutive Swin-Transformer attention modules

Multi-scale Feature Fusion. The high-scale feature maps are adept at capturing spatial information, whereas low-scale feature maps excel in semantic information extraction but lack in detailed representation. By using multi-scale feature fusion methods, the model can learn semantic information at different scales. Therefore, after each Swin-Transformer module, the multi-scale fusion module is employed to combine the features from different scales. This fusion module enables the model to extract the spatial information from high-scale features and the semantic information from low-scale features, leading to an enriched and comprehensive feature map.

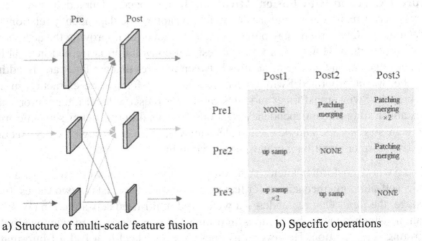

a) Structure of multi-scale feature fusion   b) Specific operations

Fig. 4. Structure of multi-scale feature fusion and Specific operations

The multi-scale feature fusion structure, depicted in Fig. 4a), involves three scale branches. The feature map before fusion is denoted as "pre", and after fusion as "post". The operations between the different scale features are illustrated in Fig. 4b). For generating post1, pre1 is unchanged, pre2 is up-sampled by 2 ×, and pre3 is up-sampled by 4 ×. For generating post2, pre1 is down-sampled by a 3 × 3 convolution, pre2 is unchanged, and pre3 is up-sampled by 2 ×. For generating post3, pre1 is down-sampled by two consecutive 3 × 3 convolutions, pre2 is down-sampled by a 3 × 3 convolution, and pre3 is unchanged.

3.2 Prediction Module

To obtain accurate key point detection results, the feature maps from the four sub-scales are fused using a multi-scale fusion module that combines the spatial information of high-scale features and the semantic information of low-scale features. Furthermore, a Deconvolution Module [15] is introduced to double the scale of the fused feature map, improving the accuracy of key point localization.

The Deconvolution Module structure, as illustrated in Fig. 5, begins with a transposed convolution layer that generates high-quality feature maps with a scale of 1/2 of the original input scale. The output of the transposed convolution layer is then fed into two residual structures, each composed of basic blocks, to perform detailed feature extraction.

Finally, the higher-scale feature map is used to generate a two-dimensional Gaussian heatmap [16]. The strong spatial generalization ability and high accuracy of the heatmap are utilized to obtain precise key point coordinates. By combining the multi-scale feature fusion and the Deconvolution Module, the proposed key point detection network achieves state-of-the-art accuracy.

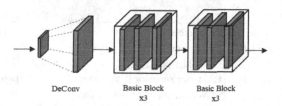

Fig. 5. Structure of Deconvolution Module

4 Experiments

4.1 Analysis of Dataset and Experimental Environment

Aiming to address commonly occurring physical posture problems, we conducted research and developed national standards for collecting physical posture image data, as well as a dataset construction plan. Following the standards and plan, we collected physical posture image data in three body positions (front, side - including left and right - and back), covering different age groups, clothing, and resolutions. To ensure a uniform sample data distribution, we annotated the dataset using pixel point annotation and identified three types of images (front, side, and back), each with a total of 27 key points [17–20].

Under the guidance of experts, we constructed a nationally large-scale physical posture image dataset with consistent resolution. The dataset consists of 7,608 images, including 2,224 front images, 3,272 side images, and 2,112 back images. Table 1 shows the key point locations in the self-built dataset.

Table 1. Explanation of key point locations in the self-built dataset.

Sample	Front	Side(Left and Right)	Back
Image			
Point Description	1 eyebrow center ; 2. 3 Right and left eyes; 4. 5 Right and left mouth corners; 6 clavicular; 7. 8 Right and left shoulder peak; 9 navel; 10. 11 Right left anterior superior iliac spine; 12.The midpoint of the right and left patella; 14. 15 Right and left lateral ankle.	1 Ear screen; 2 The seventh cervical spine; 3 Shoulder peak; 4 Anterior superior iliac spine; 5 Posterior superior iliac spine; 6 The greater trochanteric point of the femur; 7 The midpoint of the patella; 8 Outer ankle.	1 The seventh cervical spine; 2 Point of spinous process of the twelfth thoracic vertebra; 3. 4 Right and left posterior superior iliac spine.

To prevent overfitting during network training, a variety of data augmentation techniques such as left-right flipping, translation, rotation, and cropping were applied to increase the dataset size. The initial dataset was expanded from 7,608 to 20,000 images, comprising of 6,000 frontal, 8,000 side-view, and 6,000 back-view images. The augmented dataset was then divided into training, validation, and testing sets at a ratio of 8:1:1, and the input image size was uniformly set to 256 × 192 for consistency.

The hardware used for the training process included an Intel i7-10875 CPU and an NVIDIA GeForce RTX 3090 GPU, running on Ubuntu18.02 operating system. Due to differences in key point locations for detection in different views, separate models were trained for frontal, side-view, and back-view images. The HRNet architecture was employed for training, using a transfer learning strategy with pre-trained weights on the COCO dataset [21]. The models were trained with an initial learning rate of 0.00001, a batch size of 32, and an adam_w optimizer for 100 epochs.

4.2 Evaluation Criteria

The validation standard of the experiment was verified by the Object Key point Similarity (OKS) method specified by the COCO dataset, which is formulated in Eq. (1).

$$OKS = \sum_i \left[\frac{e^{\left(-d_i^2/2s^2k_i^2\right)} \delta(v_i > 0)}{\sum_i [\delta(v_i > 0)]} \right] \tag{1}$$

In the equation, d_i represents the Euclidean distance between the predicted key point and the true key point, s represents the square root of the area of the detection target's bounding box, which is formulated in Eq. (2). The upper left and lower right coordinates of the bounding box are (x_1, y_1) and (x_2, y_2), respectively. k_i is the normalization factor for the i-th key point, which is obtained by calculating the standard deviation of all true values in the self-built dataset. $\delta(v_i > 0)$ represents the selection of visible key points.

$$s = \sqrt{(x_2 - x_1)(y_2 - y_1)} \tag{2}$$

AP index is used as the main evaluation metric, which represents the proportion of correctly detected human bodies among all human bodies when the OKS index is given. AP^{50} (the prediction accuracy when OKS = 0.5), AP^{75} (the prediction accuracy when OKS = 0.75), and mAP (the average of all prediction accuracies between OKS = 0.5, 0.55,...,0.90, 0.95) are used in the experiment according to the standard OKS method.

4.3 Comparative Experiment

Qualitative Analysis. To evaluate the effectiveness of the proposed algorithm, we conducted a comparative experiment on a self-built dataset using commonly used algorithms such as Hourglass and HRNet for three body orientations (front, side (left and right), and back). The results are summarized in Table 2. Comparison with Ground Truth, other algorithms suffer from inaccuracies in key point detection, as highlighted by the blue dashed boxes in Front and Back for the anterior superior iliac spine point and posterior superior iliac spine point. In contrast, Our Method demonstrates significantly better detection results. Therefore, we can conclude that the proposed method in this paper outperforms other commonly used key point detection algorithms in the field of physical posture health assessment.

Table 2. Comparison of subjective effects of different algorithms

Sample	Front	Left	Right	Back
Ground Truth				
Hour-glass				
HRNet				
Our Method				

Quantitative Analysis. To evaluate the performance of our proposed method compared to other key point detection algorithms in the field of physical posture health assessment, we selected AP^{50} and AP^{75} as evaluation metrics and validated our method on our custom dataset to measure its accuracy. The experimental results are presented in Fig. 6 (the accuracy of the front, side, and back models were averaged in Our Method).

Compared to Hourglass and HRNet, Our Method achieved an 8.40% and 4.09% improvement in AP^{50}, a 13.5% and 7.20% improvement in AP^{75}, and a 20.6% and 6.34% improvement in mAP, respectively. These results demonstrate the superiority of our proposed method. Therefore, we conclude that Our Method is suitable for key point detection tasks in the field of physical posture health assessment.

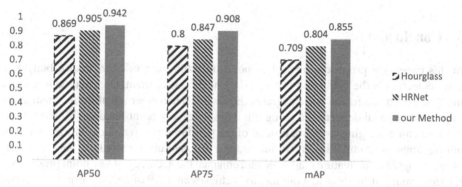

Fig. 6. Comparative Experimental Results of Accuracy of Different Algorithms

4.4 Ablation Experiment

To demonstrate the effectiveness of the proposed modules, an experiment was conducted by adding the proposed modules to the baseline HRNet. The results are shown in Table 3, which shows that the performance of the original network improved after adding the proposed modules. The AP^{50} and AP^{75} on the self-built dataset reached 94.2% and 90.8%, respectively, and mAP reached 85.5%. This validates the effectiveness of the proposed method in the key point detection task of physical posture health evaluation.

Table 3. Ablation experiments of different modules in our method

Model	AP^{50}/%	AP^{75}/%	mAP/%
HRNet	90.5	84.7	80.4
HRNet + patching merging	90.9	85.1	80.49
HRNet + Swin-Transformer block	92.9	88. 8	84.1
HRNet + Deconvolution Module	91.2	87.2	82.5
HRNet + patching merging + Deconvolution Module	92.1	87.6	83.6
HRNet + patching merging + Deconvolution Module + Swin-Transformer block	94.2	90.8	85.5

5 Conclusion

In this paper, we propose a novel key point detection network for precise body key point detection in the field of physical posture health assessment. Our method leverages multi-scale feature fusion and integrates the Swin Transformer attention mechanism to improve the global dependence recognition ability of key point features. Moreover, we use a patching merging structure instead of the pooling layer to reduce information loss during down-sampling. Finally, we introduce a deconvolution module in the prediction phase to increase the feature map scale and enhance the accuracy of key point prediction. Experimental results show that our method achieves an mAP of 85.5%, surpassing existing state-of-the-art approaches and demonstrating its ability to meet the high precision requirements of body key point detection in physical posture health assessment.

References

1. Badhe, P.C., Kulkarni, V.: A review on posture assessment. IOSR J. Sports Phys. Educ. **5**(5), 08–15 (2018)
2. Penha, P.J., João, S.M.A., Casarotto, R.A., et al.: Postural assessment of girls between 7 and 10 years of age. Clinics **60**, 9–16 (2005)
3. Fukuichi, A., Sugamura, G.: Sitting posture and moral impression formation: a focus on traditional Japanese sitting posture (Seiza). J. Phys. Educ. Sport **22**(2), 503–511 (2022)
4. Brzęk, A., Dworrak, T., Strauss, M., et al.: The weight of pupils' schoolbags in early school age and its influence on physical posture. BMC Musculoskelet. Disord. **18**(1), 1–11 (2017)
5. Kendall, F.P., McCreary, E.K., Provance, P.G., et al.: Muscles: Testing and Function, with Posture and Pain. Lippincott Williams and Wilkins, Pennsylvania (1993). Determination of footedness. J. Phys. Med. Rehabil. **2**, 835–841 (1983)
6. Wei, S.E., Ramakrishna, V., Kanade, T., et al.: Convolutional pose machines. In: Proceedings of the IEEE conference on Computer Vision and Pattern Recognition, Las Vegas, pp. 4724–4732. IEEE (2016)
7. Newell, A., Yang, K., Deng, J.: Stacked hourglass networks for human pose estimation. In: Leibe, B., Matas, J., Sebe, N., Welling, M. (eds.) ECCV 2016. LNCS, vol. 9912, pp. 483–499. Springer, Cham (2016). https://doi.org/10.1007/978-3-319-46484-8_29

8. Sun, K., Xiao, B., Liu, D., et al.: Deep high-resolution representation learning for human pose estimation. In: Proceedings of the IEEE/CVF Conference on Computer Vision and Pattern Recognition, Long Beach, pp. 5693–5703. IEEE (2019)

9. Yu, C., Xiao, B., Gao, C., et al.: Lite-HRNet: a lightweight high-resolution network. In: Proceedings of the IEEE/CVF Conference on Computer Vision and Pattern Recognition, Virtual, pp. 10440–10450. IEEE (2021)

10. Vaswani, A., Shazeer, N., Parmar, N., et al.: Attention is all you need. In: Advances in Neural In-Formation Processing Systems 30 (2017)

11. Dosovitskiy, A., Beyer, L., Kolesnikov, A., et al.: An image is worth 16x16 words: transformers for image recognition at scale. In: 9th International Conference on Learning Representations, OpenReview.net, Virtual Event (2021)

12. Yuan, Y., Fu, R., Huang, L., et al.: HRformer: high-resolution vision transformer for dense predict. Adv. Neural. Inf. Process. Syst. **34**, 7281–7293 (2021)

13. Liu, Z., Lin, Y., Cao, Y., et al.: Swin transformer: hierarchical vision transformer using shifted windows. In: Proceedings of the IEEE/CVF International Conference on Computer Vision, Montreal, pp. 10012–10022. IEEE (2021)

14. He, K., Zhang, X., Ren, S., et al.: Deep residual learning for image recognition. In: Proceedings of the IEEE Conference on Computer Vision and Pattern Recognition, Las Vegas, pp. 770–778. IEEE (2016)

15. Neff, C., Sheth, A., Furgurson, S., et al.: EfficientHRNet: efficient and scalable high-resolution networks for real-time multi-person 2D human pose estimation. J. Real-Time Image Proc. **18**, 1037–1049 (2021)

16. Tompson, J.J., Jain, A., LeCun, Y., et al.: Joint training of a convolutional network and a graphical model for human pose estimation. Adv. Neural. Inf. Process. Syst. **27**, 1799–1807 (2014)

17. Watson, A.W.S., Mac Donncha, C.: A reliable technique for the assessment of posture: assessment criteria for aspects of posture. J. Sports Med. Phys. Fitness **40**(3), 260 (2000)

18. Azadinia, F., Hosseinabadi, M., Ebrahimi, I., et al.: Validity and test–retest reliability of photo-grammetry in adolescents with hyperkyphosis. Physiotherapy Theory Pract. **38**(13), 3018–3026 (2022)

19. Hida, M., Hasegawa, A., Kamitani, S., et al.: Coronal spinal postural alignment screening tool using markerless digital photography. Adv. Sci. Technol. Eng. Syst. J. **6**(2), 965–970 (2021)

20. Ribeiro, A.F.M., Bergmann, A., Lemos, T., et al.: Reference values for human posture measurements based on computerized photogrammetry: a systematic review. J. Manipulative Physiol. Ther. **40**(3), 156–168 (2017)

21. Lin, TY., Maire, M., Belongie, S., et al.: Microsoft COCO: Common objects in context. In: Fleet, D., Pajdla, T., Schiele, B., Tuytelaars, T. (eds.) Computer Vision–ECCV 2014: 13th European Conference, vol. 8693, pp.740–755, Springer, Cham (2014). https://doi.org/10.1007/978-3-319-10602-1_48

Skeleton Based Dynamic Hand Gesture Recognition using Short Term Sampling Neural Networks (STSNN)

Aamrah Ikram[✉] [iD] and Yue Liu[iD]

Beijing Institute of Technology, No.5 Zhongguancun South Street, Haidian, Beijing 100811, China
aamrahikram@yahoo.com

Abstract. This research introduces an innovative framework for real-time dynamic hand gesture recognition in the field of Human-Computer Interaction (HCI). The framework combines depth learning networks with the integration of multiple datasets to extract both short-term and long-term features from video input. A significant contribution of this research lies in the integration of Convolutional Neural Networks (CNNs) into a specialized short-term memory network (STSNN), enabling the capture of long-term contextual information for accurate gesture recognition. The proposed framework is thoroughly evaluated using two hand-held databases, namely the 14/28 dataset and the LDMI database. By leveraging the computational power of depth learning networks and the fusion of diverse datasets, our model outperforms previous methods, establishing its efficacy in real-time dynamic hand gesture recognition tasks. The outcomes of this research significantly contribute to the advancement of HCI, providing a robust and technically sophisticated solution for gesture-based interfaces. The findings hold promise for enhancing user experiences and facilitating seamless integration of gesture-based interaction techniques across various domains, ultimately improving the efficiency and effectiveness of human-computer interactions.

Keywords: Human-Computer Interaction · Dynamic Hand Gesture Recognition · Depth Sensor · Augmented Reality

1 Introduction

Human gestures, particularly hand gestures, play a crucial role in non-verbal communication, conveying information, expressing emotions, and substituting spoken language in various contexts. The advancement of information technology and computer science has led to a growing interest in touchless Human-Computer Interaction (HCI), specifically in recognizing and interpreting hand gestures for controlling computer systems [1]. Hand gesture recognition techniques can be broadly classified into non-vision-based and vision-based approaches. Non-vision-based methods utilize wearable devices with specific optical or mechanical sensors, capturing hand motion and converting it into electrical signals for gesture recognition. While these techniques can achieve high recognition

© The Author(s), under exclusive license to Springer Nature Switzerland AG 2023
H. Lu et al. (Eds.): ICIG 2023, LNCS 14355, pp. 368–379, 2023.
https://doi.org/10.1007/978-3-031-46305-1_30

accuracy, the need for continuous device-wearing poses convenience issues, and static hand gestures may not be detected effectively.

In contrast, vision-based methods rely on cameras or body motion sensors, enabling practical and natural interaction by capturing hand gestures using visual input. Vision-based approaches have gained significant attention due to their ability to recognize both dynamic and static hand gestures, making them widely adopted in gesture recognition studies.

Presently, the majority of researchers in hand gesture recognition focus on vision-based techniques, exploring various algorithms and models to extract features from visual input and accurately classify hand gestures [2]. These methods leverage computer vision and machine learning algorithms to achieve promising results in real-time gesture recognition applications. Dynamic hand gesture recognition can be considered a subset of action recognition, which focuses on analyzing the context of an entire video sequence rather than individual frames [3, 4]. Researchers have explored deep learning techniques for video classification, extracting spatial features from individual frames using pre-trained 2D convolutional neural networks (CNNs) and incorporating temporal information to capture the dynamics of actions [5].

While the UCF101 and Sports-1M datasets have been widely used as benchmarks for evaluating video classification models, the need for more comprehensive benchmarks and standardized evaluation protocols persists to further advance the field [6]. The architecture of this approach is depicted in Fig. 1, where the spatial features are extracted from each frame using a 2D CNN, and the temporal information is integrated to capture the temporal evolution of the actions.

Dynamic hand gesture recognition poses challenges in capturing spatial and temporal information from video sequences. Deep learning techniques, such as 2D CNNs

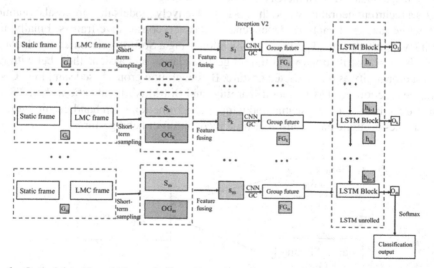

Fig. 1. Optimizing Neural Network Short-Term Samples: Input frames divided into m groups, each with randomly selected color and optical flow frames. CNN extracts group features, while FC and LSTM modules refine separable group characteristics.

and material fusion methods, show promise in addressing this task. However, further improvements are necessary, particularly in terms of benchmark datasets and computational efficiency. Continued research in this area will contribute to the development of more accurate and efficient dynamic hand gesture recognition systems.

2   Proposed Model

The proposed model introduces the Short-Term Sampling Neural Network (STSNN) and transfer learning as key components to enhance the efficiency and accuracy of hand gesture recognition systems. The STSNN is designed to extract short-term features from sampled frames, leveraging the capabilities of deep learning techniques. It aims to capture the distinctive characteristics of each gesture within a short interval, enabling more accurate recognition. By focusing on short-term features, the model can effectively represent the dynamics and nuances of hand gestures.

2.1   STSNN Architecture

The STSNN design consists of four modules: group-based sampling, CNN feature extraction, LSTM temporal learning, and result layer for classification. First, the video input is divided into m groups to ensure an even distribution of frames. Each group represents a subset of frames and promotes balanced representation across different video durations. The CNN module extracts spatial features from the frames within each group, capturing local patterns and visual cues specific to hand gestures. It processes frames independently and generates feature maps representing learned spatial features. The LSTM module then learns long-range temporal dependencies from the sequence of feature maps obtained from the CNN as depicted in Fig. 2.

As a recurrent neural network, the LSTM effectively models the temporal dynamics of hand gestures and captures dependencies between consecutive frames. Finally, the result layer performs hand gesture classification using a SoftMax classifier. It calculates the probability distribution over different gesture classes and assigns the label with the highest probability as the predicted gesture. By integrating group-based sampling, CNN feature extraction, LSTM temporal learning, and SoftMax classification, the STSNN design effectively captures spatial and temporal information from hand gesture videos. This enables accurate and robust real-time recognition of hand gestures.

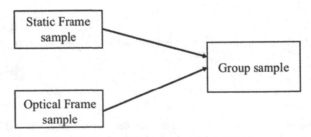

Fig. 2. The sample grouping through fusion.

3 Methodology

The proposed model incorporates the Inception V2 transfer learning method to leverage the benefits of pre-trained models and improve training performance while reducing training costs. Transfer learning is based on the concept that a model trained on one domain or task can be applied to another field or study if they share similar data characteristics and distributions. In the proposed model, the Inception V2 architecture with Batch Normalization is utilized [10, 11]. The Inception V2 model is known for its balanced efficiency and accuracy, making it suitable for the hand gesture recognition task. The inclusion of Batch Normalization helps in reducing the risk of overfitting, resulting in better generalization and improved performance on testing data. To address the overfitting issue further, a dropout layer is added after the pooling layer in the Inception V2 model [12]. Dropout is a regularization technique that randomly sets a fraction of the input units to zero during training. This helps prevent over-reliance on specific features and encourages the model to learn more robust and generalizable representations.

By incorporating the Inception V2 model with Batch Normalization and dropout layers, the proposed model benefits from the pre-trained weights and architectures of Inception V2 while mitigating the risk of overfitting. This combination enhances the model's ability to capture relevant features from hand gesture data and improves its performance and generalization capabilities [11].

3.1 Datasets

The LDMI dataset serves as the primary dataset in the experiments conducted for this research. It is a comprehensive collection of hand gesture sequences designed to evaluate the proposed algorithm's performance and effectiveness. The dataset comprises a wide range of hand gestures captured using the LMC. Each gesture sequence in the dataset is carefully labeled and annotated to provide ground truth for evaluation purposes.

Figure 4, showcases the framework and structure of the LDMI dataset, illustrating the diversity of hand gestures included. The dataset covers a variety of gestures, including both static postures and dynamic movements, allowing for a comprehensive assessment of the proposed method's capability to recognize and classify different types of gestures accurately. Utilizing the LDMI dataset ensures that the experimental evaluation is conducted on a realistic and representative set of hand gestures, providing a robust basis for performance comparison and validation of the proposed algorithm. These datasets are carefully selected based on their relevance to the research objectives and are available for evaluation (Fig. 3).

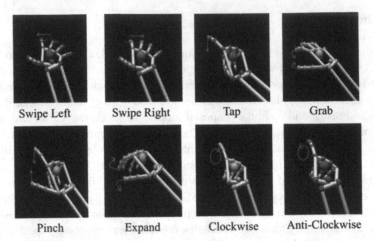

Fig. 3. LDMI dataset [16]. Eight hand gestures Swipe Right, Swipe Left, Grab, Expand, Tap, Pinch, Clockwise and Counter Clockwise. The blue arrows shows the hand motion trail.

4   Experimental Setup

Figure 4, illustrates the framework of the proposed system, which consists of three main components: the input module, the preprocessing module, and the recognition module.

The input module is responsible for capturing the image sequence of a hand gesture performed by the user. The system captures the frames at 12 frames per second when the user initiates a gesture. The supported gestures include expand (E), grab (G), pinch (P), tap (T), clockwise (C/W), anticlockwise (AC/W), swipe left (S/L), and swipe right (S/R). The image sequence is uploaded when the user presses the "space" key and stops capturing when the "space" key is pressed again. This lets the user record a hand gesture between these two consecutive keystrokes.

The captured image sequence is then passed to the preprocessing module, which performs two main tasks. First, it computes the optical flow to capture the motion information in the series. This helps in understanding the dynamic nature of the hand gesture. Second, the data is standardized to ensure consistency in the input data format. These preprocessing steps prepare the image sequence for further analysis and recognition.

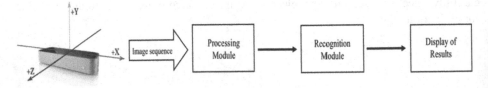

Fig. 4. Experimental system setup.

The proposed system implements the recognition and training framework using Python 3.5, PyTorch 1.0, and CUDA 10.0. In terms of hardware, the experimental setup includes the following components: Processor: Intel (R) Core (TM) i7–8700 with a clock speed of 3.20 GHz. This powerful processor ensures efficient computation and processing of deep learning algorithms. System memory: 16GB with a speed of 2400 MHz. Sufficient memory capacity and high-speed memory ensure smooth execution of the recognition and training tasks. GPU: NVIDIA Corporation GTX 1070 with 7 GB of memory. The GPU provides parallel processing capabilities, enabling accelerated training and inference of the deep learning models.

4.1 Experiment (Training and Testing)

In the training process, the cross-entropy loss function is used to measure the performance of the classification model. The mini-batch stochastic gradient descent (SGD) algorithm optimizes the network parameters. The mini-batch size is set to 16, and a momentum value of 0.9 is utilized for faster convergence. A dropout rate of 0.5 is applied to prevent overfitting and improve generalization.

The learning rate is initially set to 0.001 and is reduced by a factor of 0.1 if the loss fails to decrease significantly compared to the previous training iteration. This strategy helps the model to fine-tune its parameters and converge to an optimal solution. The maximum number of training epochs is 50 to ensure sufficient training iterations.

To strike a balance between model accuracy and computational cost, different numbers of groups (3, 5, 7, 9, 11, 13, and 15) are considered, and the classification accuracy is evaluated for each configuration. The rotation augmentation randomly rotates the image within 0 to 45 degrees. This introduces variations in the orientation of the hand gesture, mimicking real-world scenarios where the hand may be slightly turned during the gesture execution. The crop augmentation randomly crops a portion of the image within a range of 75% to 100% of the original size. This simulates different hand positions or scales within the gesture, making the model more resilient to variations in hand placement.

By applying these data augmentation techniques, the model is exposed to a wider range of variations in the training data, which helps improve its generalization capability and reduces the risk of overfitting to the specific examples in the original dataset.

4.2 Model Implementation on Different Datasets

The 14/28 DHG dataset is a benchmark for researchers to evaluate and compare their hand gesture recognition models. Numerous research groups, including the proposed model, have tested their models on this dataset. Among the top 60 models, the recognition accuracy ranges from 97.10% to 90.07%. The proposed model achieves an accuracy of 93.45%, which is 2% lower than the top-ranked model [12, 13].

In comparison to the 3D CNN architecture that achieved a precision of 95.85%, the proposed methodology only requires training a CNN architecture that has been pre-trained on the ImageNet dataset. Despite this more straightforward approach, the proposed model demonstrates higher recognition accuracy than the 3D CNN, as shown in Table 1. This suggests that the integration of short-term and long-term temporal features through the STMN framework, along with the transfer learning from the Inception V2 model, contributes to the improved performance of the proposed methodology. It is

Table 1. Comparison with other approaches on 14/28 datasets.

Model	Acc. %
Mobile Net + NL + Slow-fast	97.10%
Fusion + TSN + LSTM	90.07%
MFFS	96.08%
ResNet 101	93.45%
3D-CNN	95.85%
STSNN	97.22%

worth noting that achieving high accuracy on the DHG dataset is challenging due to the complexity and variability of hand gestures (Fig. 5).

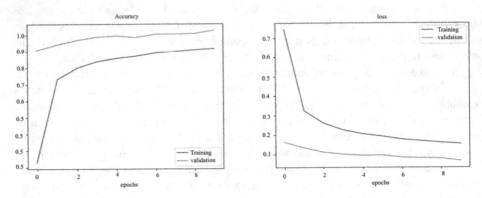

Fig. 5. Accuracy and Loss plot.

Table 2, presents a comparative analysis between the proposed model trained without transfer learning and other state-of-the-art approaches that use color and optical flow to recognize hand gestures. While the accuracy of the model trained without transfer learning is slightly lower than that of R3DCNN and MFFs, when transfer learning is applied, it achieves exceptional performance on this benchmark with a mean accuracy value of 85.13%. Furthermore, Nvidia conducted a human evaluation to assess the accuracy of human gesture recognition by providing six labels for the gesture videos in the test set after watching the colored videos. The results show that the proposed model's accuracy is comparable to the human evaluation, indicating that the model performs at a level similar to human observers when recognizing hand gestures from colored videos.

4.3 Results and Comparison

Figure 6, demonstrates the loss trend during the training cycle of the model. The loss is measured using the cross-entropy loss function, and the goal is to minimize this loss to improve the model's accuracy and performance.

Table 2. Comparison with other approaches on LDMI datasets.

Model	Acc. %
Two stream CNN [10]	67.60%
IDT [47]	93.01%
STSNN without transfer learning	88.08%
R3DCNN [48]	84.70%
MFFs [36]	85.05%
STSNN with transfer learning	85.122%

As the figure shows, the loss values gradually decrease over the training iterations. This decreasing trend indicates that the model is learning and progressing in fitting the training data. The gradient descent algorithm is used to update the network parameters iteratively, moving in the direction that minimizes the loss. The descending pattern of the loss curve indicates an effective training process. It suggests that the model is successfully adjusting its parameters better to represent the relationships and patterns within the training data.

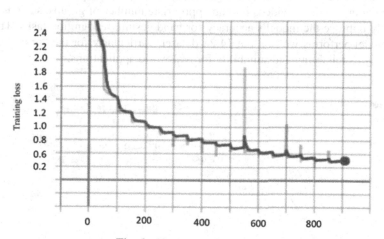

Fig. 6. Change in training loss.

Figure 7, illustrates the experiments' results to determine the optimal number of groups for segmenting the input videos. The classification accuracy is evaluated for groups ranging from 3 to 15. The results show that the model's accuracy improves as the number of groups increases from 3 to 9. This indicates that dividing the input videos into a moderate number of groups enhances the model's ability to capture and learn temporal information from the gestures.

Based on the experimentation, the presented model achieves the highest accuracy of 95.73% when the input videos are segmented into nine groups. This optimal number of groups balances computational cost and classification performance. Additionally,

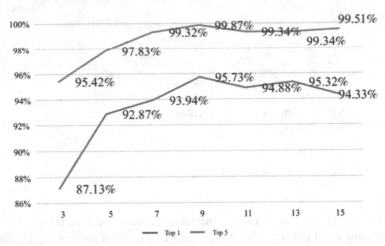

Fig. 7. Results in a 14/28 database data validation set with different group numbers, x-axis number for groups, y-axis: accuracy.

Fig. 8, highlights the model's performance specifically for the "grab gesture" on the 14/28 dataset. The accuracy achieved for this gesture is 95.39%. The experiments demonstrate that segmenting the input videos into an appropriate number of groups, such as 9, can effectively improve the model's accuracy for hand gesture recognition tasks. The presented model performs well on the 14/28 dataset, particularly for the "grab gesture", showcasing its reliability and suitability for real-world applications.

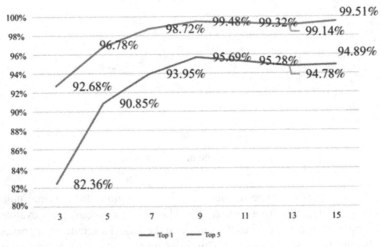

Fig. 8. Results in a 14/28 database data validation set for "grab gesture" with different group numbers, x-axis number for groups, y-axis: accuracy.

Figure 9, displays the confusion matrix of the STMN model on the 14/28 DHG validation dataset. The confusion matrix provides insights into the model's performance by showing the distribution of predicted labels compared to the existing brands.

In the confusion matrix, the rows represent the actual gesture names, while the columns represent the predicted labels. Each cell in the matrix represents the number of instances where a particular gesture was expected. The diagonal elements, where the row and column indices are the same, indicate correct predictions, while off-diagonal elements represent misclassifications. According to the confusion matrix, the STMN model tends to make errors in recognizing the "turning hand clockwise", "turning hand counter-clockwise swiping right", and "swiping left" gestures. These gestures may share similar motion patterns or visual appearances, leading to confusion during classification.

Gestures	0	1	2	3	4	5	6	7	8	9
0	0.9	0	0	0	0.0	0	0.3	0	0	0
1	0	1.0	0	0	0	0	0	0.4	0.7	0
2	0.15	0.25	0.9	0	0	0	0	0	0	0
3	0	0.05	0.1	0.9	0.7	0	0	0	0	0
4	0	0	0	0	1.0		0	0	0	0.7
5	0.13	1.0	0	0	0	1.0	0.4	0	0	0
6	0	0	0	0	0	0	1.0	0	0	0
7	0.05	0	0	0	0	0	0	1.0	0	0
8	0	0	0	0	0	0.8	0	0	1.0	0.1
9	0	0	0	0	0	0	0	0.5	0	1.0

Fig. 9. Confusion matrix for STMN model for DHG detection in 14/28 dataset.

However, despite these errors, the performance of the STMN model on the testing dataset is excellent. Most gestures are correctly classified, as indicated by the high values along the diagonal of the confusion matrix. This demonstrates the model's ability to recognize and differentiate between various hand gestures accurately. The confusion matrix provides valuable information for understanding the model's strengths and weaknesses in gesture recognition. It highlights specific gestures requiring further attention and improvement in future model iterations.

5 Conclusion

This study presents a novel approach for dynamic hand gesture recognition using the STMN. The experimental results demonstrate the effectiveness of the proposed model in accurately detecting and classifying hand gestures. The model is trained and evaluated on two datasets, the 14/28 DHG dataset, and the LDMI dataset, showcasing its robustness and generalizability. The STMN model combines the power of Convolutional Neural Networks (CNNs) and Short-Term Long Memory (LSTM) networks to extract spatial and temporal features from hand gesture videos. By segmenting the video inputs into groups and sampling representative frames from each group, the model effectively captures the dynamic nature of hand gestures. The CNN module extracts discriminative features from the sampled frames, while the LSTM module learns the long-range temporal dependencies, enabling accurate classification of the hand gestures.

The results obtained on the 14/28 DHG and LDMI datasets demonstrate the high accuracy achieved by the STMN model, ranging from 91\% to 97\% and 95.69\%, respectively. These results outperform previous models and indicate the effectiveness of the proposed approach in dynamic hand gesture recognition. Furthermore, the model is also tested on the Nvidia dataset, achieving an impressive classification precision of 85.13\%. The experimental evaluation showcases the robustness and generalization capabilities of the STMN model, making it suitable for real-world applications in HCI. The model's performance on different datasets highlights its potential to handle various hand gestures in different contexts and environments.

References

1. Nguyen, T.-N., Huynh, H.-H., Meunier, J.: Static hand gesture recognition using principal component analysis combined with artificial neural network. J. Autom. Control Eng. **3**(1), 40–45 (2015)
2. Ahuja, M.K., Singh, A.: Static vision based hand gesture recognition using principal component analysis. In: 2015 IEEE 3rd International Conference on MOOCs, Innovation and Technology in Education (MITE), pp. 402–406 (2015)
3. Maqueda, A.I., del Blanco, C.R., Jaureguizar, F., et al.: Human–computer interaction based on visual hand-gesture recognition using volumetric spatiograms of local binary patterns. Comput. Vis. Image Underst. **141**, 126–137 (2015)
4. Pomboza-Junez, G., Terriza, J.H.: Hand gesture recognition based on sEMG signals using support vector machines. In: 2016 IEEE 6th International Conference on Consumer Electronics-Berlin (ICCE-Berlin), pp. 174–178 (2016)
5. Lowndes, A.B.: Deep Learning with GPU Technology for Image & Feature Recognition [D]. [S. l.]: Tesis de Grado]. University of Leeds (2015)
6. Ghauri, J.A., Jomma, H.S.: Master of Science in Data Analytics (2019)
7. Adler, P.: Porous media: geometry and transports. Elsevier (2013)
8. Sapienza, S., Ros, P.M., Guzman, D.A.F., et al.: On-line event-driven hand gesture recognition based on surface electromyographic signals. In: 2018 IEEE International Symposium on Circuits and systems (ISCAS), pp. 1–5 (2018)
9. Tavakoli, M., Benussi, C., Lopes, P.A., et al.: Robust hand gesture recognition with a double channel surface EMG wearable armband and SVM classifier. Biomed. Signal Process. Control **46**, 121–130 (2018)

10. Poon, G., Kwan, K.C., Pang, W.-M.: Occlusion-robust bimanual gesture recognition by fusing multi-views. Multimedia Tools Appl. **78**, 23469–23488 (2019)
11. Park, H., Moon, H.-C., Lee, J.Y.: Tangible augmented prototyping of digital handheld products. Comput. Ind. **60**(2), 114–125 (2009)
12. Moon, H.-C., Park, H.-J.: Resolving hand region occlusion in tangible augmented reality environments. Korean J. Comput. Des. Eng. **16**(4), 277–284 (2011)
13. Betancourt, A., Morerio, P., Barakova, E.I., Marcenaro, L., Rauterberg, M., Regazzoni, C.S.: A dynamic approach and a new dataset for hand-detection in first person vision. In: Azzopardi, G., Petkov, N. (eds.) CAIP 2015. LNCS, vol. 9256, pp. 274–287. Springer, Cham (2015). https://doi.org/10.1007/978-3-319-23192-1_23
14. Yingxin, X., Jinghua, L., Lichun, W., et al.: A robust hand gesture recognition method via convolutional neural network. In: 2016 6th International Conference on Digital Home (ICDH), pp. 64–67 (2016)

Face Anti-spoofing Based on Client Identity Information and Depth Map

Yu Wang[1], Mingtao Pei[1(✉)] [iD], Zhengang Nie[2], and Xinmu Qi[3]

[1] Beijing Laboratory of Intelligent Information Technology,
School of Computer Science, Beijing Institute of Technology,
Beijing, China
peimt@bit.edu.cn

[2] School of Information and Electronics, Beijing Institute of Technology,
Beijing, China

[3] Stony Brook Institute, Anhui University, Stony Brook, USA

Abstract. Face anti-spoofing (FAS) is an essential prerequisite for face recognition. In most methods, FAS is usually performed before face recognition and the client identity information is not utilized. Since presentation attacks (PAs) are always aimed at a certain client, the client identity information can provide useful clues for FAS task. In this paper, we propose a face anti-spoofing method based on client identity information using Siamese network. We applied FAS after face recognition to utilize the client identity information. As the real face and fake face have different properties, we use different weights for the two subnetworks of the Siamese network to extract features for real face and fake face, respectively. In addition, we employ depth map as auxiliary information to improve the performance. We perform experiments on SiW, CASIA-FASD and Replay-Attack datasets to demonstrate the validity of our method.

Keywords: Face anti-spoofing · Client identity information · Siamese network · Depth map

1 Introduction

Face recognition has been applied in many real scenarios such as face payment and entrance guard system. However, most existing face recognition systems are vulnerable to presentation attacks (PAs). Typical PAs include print attack, replay attack and 3D-mask attack, and etc. Therefore, face anti-spoofing (FAS) methods are essential for detecting PAs and ensuring the security of face recognition systems.

Most previous FAS methods discriminate spoof and live faces before face recognition [1,3,14], and the client identity information is not utilized. However, the real face image of the client is usually available from the face recognition system and PAs are always aimed at a certain client. Therefore, the client identity information can provide useful clues for FAS task. Hao et al. [15] proposed to employ client identity information for FAS task by using a Siamese network to discriminate spoof and live face with the same client identity. In their method, the two subnetworks of the Siamese network share the same weights. However, as the real face and fake face have different properties, using the same subnetwork may not extract meaningful features.

At the same time, CNN based method only uses appearance features, which makes the model not robust enough. Auxiliary clues, such as depth information [1,20] and rPPG signal [20], can provide useful supervision for the FAS task, and improve the generalization ability of the FAS methods.

Motivated by the above observations, we propose a face anti-spoofing method based on client identity information using Siamese network. We use different weights for the two subnetworks of the Siamese network to extract features for real face and fake face, respectively, as the real face and fake face have different properties. In addition, we employ depth map as auxiliary information to improve the generalization of the model.

2 Related Work

Existing FAS methods can be roughly divided into two categories: handcrafted feature based methods and CNN based methods. On the one hand, traditional handcrafted feature based methods can discriminate spoof and live faces using color [3], texture [13,21], eye-blinking [22], face moving [2,24] and other clues. Classical handcrafted descriptors (e.g., LBP [3,12], SIFT [23], SURF [4], HOG [17] and DOG [25]) are designed for extracting effective spoofing patterns from various color spaces (RGB, HSV and YCbCr). On the other hand, CNN based methods [18,28] usually utilize softmax loss as the supervision to train a binary classifier.

A CNN with softmax loss may find any clues that can distinguish live and spoof faces, such as screen bezel. But it can not distinguish the essential difference between them, which leads to disadvantage generalization. To solve this issue, some researchers have utilized auxiliary supervision in the training process. Atoum et al. [1] applied face depth map to FAS for the first time and proposed a two-stream CNN-based method by extracting local face features and depth maps. Liu et al. [20] utilized spatial (depth map) and temporal (rPPG signal) information as auxiliary supervision. Besides depth map and rPPG signal, binary mask label [14] and 3D point cloud maps [19] are typical pixel-wise auxiliary supervisions.

The deployment of client identity information for FAS task has been limited to just a few studies [8–10,29]. These methods use the client identity information in a one-class anomaly detection paradigm. Ivana et al. [8] used identity information to build two client specific FAS solutions, one relying on a generative and another one on a discriminative paradigm. Our method collects image pairs from the same client to train the model. Hao et al. [15] proposed to employ client identity information for FAS task by using a Siamese network trained by image pairs of the same client. Different with [15], the Siamese network we used employs different subnetworks to extract features for real face and fake face, respectively. We also employ depth map as auxiliary information to improve the generalization of the model.

3   Proposed Method

Although attackers may spoof face recognition systems using photos, videos or 3D masks, the attacker's goal is to convince the face recognition system that he is a client of the system. Usually, the face recognition system has the real image of the client, so we can make use of the client identity information to distinguish spoof and live faces. We propose a FAS method based on the client identity using Siamese network, and we use depth map as auxiliary supervision to improve the generalization of the model. Fig. 1 shows the pipeline of our method.

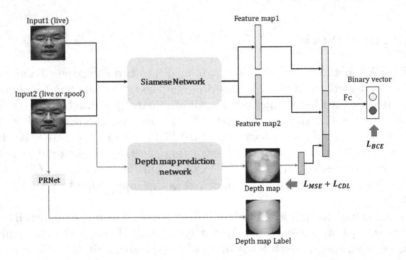

Fig. 1. The pipeline of the proposed method. It consists of two main parts: appearance feature extraction, and depth map extraction. We feed image pairs into Siamese network to extract appearance features and feed the test image into the depth map prediction network to obtain the depth map. The two parts are trained together in an end to end manner.

3.1   Preprocessing

Firstly, MTCNN [32] is used to detect faces in the input image. Then the detected faces are cropped and resized to a resolution of 224×224. We use the pretrained Dense face alignment PRNet [11] to generate the depth maps of real faces as the ground truth in a range of $[0, 1]$. We set the depth maps of spoof faces as 0. The size of depth map is 32×32.

We extract frames from the videos. Then we generate image pairs for training. Each image pair consists of two face images from the same client. The two face images can be a live face image and a spoof face image, or two live face images. If two face images are both live, it is a positive pair. Otherwise, it is a negative pair.

3.2 Network Architecture

The overall structure of the proposed network consists of two parts. One part is the appearance feature extraction module which is a Siamese network, the other part is the depth map prediction module.

In the training stage, image pairs are fed into the Siamese network, and the features of face images are extracted respectively. Then the unknown face image (live or spoof) of the image pair is input into the depth map prediction network. We splice the predicted depth map together with the two feature maps, and input them into the fully connected layer. We train the two parts together in an end to end manner. The trained network can classify the input image pair as "two live" or "one live one spoof".

In the testing stage, the test face image is identified by the face recognition system firstly. Then the real face image of the test client is retrieved, and an image pair is formed by the retrieved real face image and the test face image. The image pair is fed into our network for classification. If the image pair is classified as "two live", the test face image is a real face image. Otherwise, it is a fake face image.

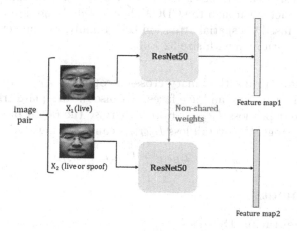

Fig. 2. The architecture of Siamese network

Siamese Network. To make use of the client identity information, we use the Siamese network. Siamese network [5] is used to measure the similarity between two inputs. It is a network architecture consisting of two or more subnetworks, which can be the same or different. In our method, ResNet50 [16] is used as the two subnetworks. As the real face and fake face have different properties, we use different weights for the two subnetworks to extract features for real face and fake face, respectively. As shown in Fig. 2, the input of the Siamese network is an image pair (X_1, X_2). X_1 is the live face image and X_2 is the unknown face image (live or spoof). $X_1 and X_2$ are from the same client. The two subnetworks use different weights to extract features for real face and fake face, respectively.

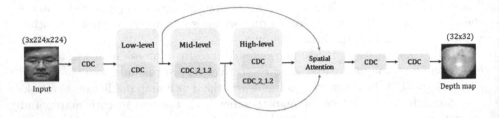

Fig. 3. The architecture of depth map prediction network

Depth Map Network. We utilize depth map as auxiliary supervision to distinguish spoof and live faces based on 3D shape. We take advantage of the network structure CDCN++ [31] designed by Yu et al. Fig. 3 shows the architecture of depth map prediction network. The unknown face image (live or spoof) of the image pair with size $3 \times 224 \times 224$ is fed into the network. Low, mid and high-level features are extracted through the CDC. Then low-mid-high level CDC features are refined and fused via spatial attention [27]. Finally, we can get the predicted grayscale face depth map with size 32×32.

Loss Function. We use the binary cross-entropy loss L_{BCE} to supervise the model to distinguish spoof and live faces, and use mean square error loss L_{MSE} and contrastive depth loss L_{CDL} [26] to supervise the depth prediction model. In the training stage, the overall loss $L_{overall}$ can be formulated as:

$$L_{overall} = L_{BCE} + L_{MSE} + L_{CDL} \tag{1}$$

4   Experiments

4.1   Implementation Details

Our method is implemented with Pytorch. In the training stage, the loss function is minimized using Adam Optimizer and the learning rate is set as 1×10^{-4} with a weight decay parameter of 0.1. The batch size is 32, and the network is trained for 30 epochs on a Nvidia 3090 GPU. The weights of ResNet50 model are initialized by the pretrained ResNet50 model. The weights of depth map prediction network are randomly initialized.

Table 1. The results of intra testing on three protocols of SiW.

Prot.	Method	APCER (%)	BPCER (%)	ACER (%)
1	Auxiliary [20]	3.58	3.58	3.58
	STASN [30]	–	–	1.00
	FAS-TD [26]	0.96	0.50	0.73
	Ours	0.27	0.27	0.27
2	Auxiliary [20]	0.57 ± 0.69	0.57 ± 0.69	0.57 ± 0.69
	STASN [30]	–	–	0.28 ± 0.05
	FAS-TD [26]	0.08 ± 0.14	0.21 ± 0.14	0.15 ± 0.14
	Ours	0.07 ± 0.05	0.10 ± 0.06	0.09 ± 0.05
3	Auxiliary [20]	8.31 ± 3.81	8.31 ± 3.80	8.31 ± 3.81
	STASN [30]	–	–	12.10 ± 1.50
	FAS-TD [26]	3.10 ± 0.81	3.09 ± 0.81	3.10 ± 0.81
	Ours	3.78 ± 3.29	4.56 ± 3.82	4.17 ± 3.56

4.2 Datasets and Metrics

Datasets. We evaluate our method on SiW [20], CASIA-FASD [33] and Replay-Attack [7]. SiW is a high-resolution dataset, containing three protocols to demonstrate the generalization of the model. SiW is used for intra testing. CASIA-FASD and Replay-Attack are datasets which contain low-resolution videos. They are used for cross-dataset testing.

Evaluation Metrics. In SiW dataset, we follow the original protocols and metrics. Evaluation indicators include Attack Presentation Classification Error Rate (APCER) [6], Bona Fide Presentation Classification Error Rate (BPCER), and ACER, which is the mean of APCER and BPCER:

$$ACER = (APCER + BPCER)/2 \qquad (2)$$

Half Total Error Rate (HTER) is used in the cross-dataset testing between CASIA-FASD and Replay-Attack, which is the mean of False Rejection Rate (FRR) and False Acceptance Rate (FAR):

$$HTER = (FRR + FAR)/2 \qquad (3)$$

4.3 Intra Testing

We perform intra testing on SiW dataset following the three protocols. Protocol 1 is designed to evaluate the generalization of the FAS methods under different face poses and expressions. Protocol 2 evaluates the generalization capability on cross medium of the same spoof type. Protocol 3 is designed to evaluate the performance on unknown PA. Table 1 shows the comparison results on SiW dataset.

4.4 Cross-Dataset Testing

To demonstrate the robustness of our proposed method, we perform cross-dataset testing between CASIA-FASD and Replay-Attack dataset. We train on CASIA-FASD, test on Replay-Attack and vice versa. Table 2 shows the comparison results of cross-dataset testing.

Table 2. The results of cross-dataset testing between CASIA-FASD and Replay-Attack. The evaluation metric is HTER (%)

Method	Train	Test	Train	Test
	CASIA-FASD	Replay-Attack	Replay-Attack	CASIA-FASD
LBP-TOP [12]	49.7		60.6	
LBP [3]	47.0		39.6	
Motion-Mag [33]	50.1		47.0	
Auxiliary [20]	27.6		28.4	
STASN [30]	31.5		30.9	
FAS-TD [26]	17.5		24.0	
Proposed method	23.9		38.0	

4.5 Ablation Study

We perform ablation experiments on the three protocols of the SiW dataset to prove that the client identity information and depth map are useful in FAS task. The experimental results are shown in Table 3. Model 1 is the commonly used binary classification method based on ResNet50, which does not take advantage of the client identity information. Model 2 is the method which employs the client identity information using Siamese network. Model 3 is the method using Siamese network and depth map, and the two subnetworks of Siamese network share the same weights. Model 4 is similar to Model 3, but the Siamese network in Model 4 employs different subnetworks.

The results of Model 2 are better than Model 1, which indicates that the client identity information can improve the performance of the model. The results of Model 3 is better than Model 2, which shows that the depth map can improve the generalization of the model. The results of Model 4 are better than Model 3, suggesting that using Siamese network with different subnetworks can extract more discriminative features for real and fake faces.

Table 3. The ablation study on three protocols of SiW. The evaluation metric is ACER (%)

Method	Prot 1	Prot 2	Prot 3
Model 1: Binary classification based on ResNet50	0.45	0.20	11.83
Model 2: Siamese network (shared weights)	0.39	0.17	9.08
Model 3: Siamese network (shared weights) and depth map	0.30	0.11	4.58
Model 4: Siamese network (non-shared weights) and depth map	0.27	0.09	4.17

4.6 Discussions

From the above experimental results, we can see that our method performs well in distinguishing live and spoof faces, which proves that the client identity information and depth map are useful in FAS task. In SiW dataset, the result of protocol 3 is worse than protocol 1 and protocol 2. The reason may be that the purpose of protocol 3 is to identity unknown PAs, so it requires higher robustness of the model than protocol 1 and protocol 2. In cross-dataset testing, the result of training on Replay-Attack is worse than training on CASIA-FASD. The reason may be that the resolution of the images in CASIA-FASD is higher than images in Replay-Attack.

5 Conclusions and Future Work

In this paper, we propose a FAS method based on the client identity information using Siamese network. Compared with directly detecting the authenticity of a face image, we use image pairs to train the network and use a real face image of the client as a reference. The Siamese network employs different subnetworks to extract features for real face and fake face respectively. In addition, We utilize depth map as the auxiliary supervision information, which is the essential difference between live and spoof faces. It can improve the generalization of the model. According to our experimental results, both client identity information and depth map are useful in FAS task. However, it can be seen from the results of cross-dataset experiments that the generalization of our method needs to be improved. In future work, we will consider temporal information and use multiple frames as input to improve the performance of FAS algorithm.

References

1. Atoum, Y., Liu, Y., Jourabloo, A., Liu, X.: Face anti-spoofing using patch and depth-based CNNs. In: 2017 IEEE International Joint Conference on Biometrics (IJCB), pp. 319–328. IEEE (2017)
2. Bao, W., Li, H., Li, N., Jiang, W.: A liveness detection method for face recognition based on optical flow field. In: 2009 International Conference on Image Analysis and Signal Processing, pp. 233–236. IEEE (2009)

3. Boulkenafet, Z., Komulainen, J., Hadid, A.: Face anti-spoofing based on color texture analysis. In: 2015 IEEE International Conference on Image Processing (ICIP), pp. 2636–2640. IEEE (2015)
4. Boulkenafet, Z., Komulainen, J., Hadid, A.: Face antispoofing using speeded-up robust features and fisher vector encoding. IEEE Sig. Process. Lett. **24**(2), 141–145 (2016)
5. Bukovčiková, Z., Sopiak, D., Oravec, M., Pavlovičová, J.: Face verification using convolutional neural networks with Siamese architecture. In: 2017 International Symposium ELMAR, pp. 205–208. IEEE (2017)
6. Busch, C.: Standards for biometric presentation attack detection. In: Marcel, S., Fierrez, J., Evans, N. (eds.) Handbook of Biometric Anti-Spoofing. Advances in Computer Vision and Pattern Recognition, pp. 571–583. Springer, Singapore (2023). https://doi.org/10.1007/978-981-19-5288-3_21
7. Chingovska, I., Anjos, A., Marcel, S.: On the effectiveness of local binary patterns in face anti-spoofing. In: 2012 BIOSIG-proceedings of the International Conference of Biometrics Special Interest Group (BIOSIG), pp. 1–7. IEEE (2012)
8. Chingovska, I., Dos Anjos, A.R.: On the use of client identity information for face antispoofing. IEEE Trans. Inf. Forensics Secur. **10**(4), 787–796 (2015)
9. Edmunds, T., Caplier, A.: Fake face detection based on radiometric distortions. In: 2016 Sixth International Conference on Image Processing Theory, Tools and Applications (IPTA), pp. 1–6. IEEE (2016)
10. Fatemifar, S., Arashloo, S.R., Awais, M., Kittler, J.: Client-specific anomaly detection for face presentation attack detection. Pattern Recogn. **112**, 107696 (2021)
11. Feng, Y., Wu, F., Shao, X., Wang, Y., Zhou, X.: Joint 3D face reconstruction and dense alignment with position map regression network. In: Ferrari, V., Hebert, M., Sminchisescu, C., Weiss, Y. (eds.) Computer Vision – ECCV 2018. LNCS, vol. 11218, pp. 557–574. Springer, Cham (2018). https://doi.org/10.1007/978-3-030-01264-9_33
12. de Freitas Pereira, T., Anjos, A., De Martino, J.M., Marcel, S.: Can face anti-spoofing countermeasures work in a real world scenario? In: 2013 International Conference on Biometrics (ICB), pp. 1–8. IEEE (2013)
13. Garcia, D.C., de Queiroz, R.L.: Face-spoofing 2D-detection based on Moiré-pattern analysis. IEEE Trans. Inf. Forensics Secur. **10**(4), 778–786 (2015)
14. George, A., Marcel, S.: Deep pixel-wise binary supervision for face presentation attack detection. In: 2019 International Conference on Biometrics (ICB), pp. 1–8. IEEE (2019)
15. Hao, H., Pei, M., Zhao, M.: Face liveness detection based on client identity using Siamese network. In: Lin, Z., et al. (eds.) PRCV 2019. LNCS, vol. 11857, pp. 172–180. Springer, Cham (2019). https://doi.org/10.1007/978-3-030-31654-9_15
16. He, K., Zhang, X., Ren, S., Sun, J.: Deep residual learning for image recognition. In: Proceedings of the IEEE Conference on Computer Vision and Pattern Recognition, pp. 770–778 (2016)
17. Komulainen, J., Hadid, A., Pietikäinen, M.: Context based face anti-spoofing. In: 2013 IEEE Sixth International Conference on Biometrics: Theory, Applications and Systems (BTAS), pp. 1–8. IEEE (2013)
18. Li, L., Feng, X., Boulkenafet, Z., Xia, Z., Li, M., Hadid, A.: An original face anti-spoofing approach using partial convolutional neural network. In: 2016 Sixth International Conference on Image Processing Theory, Tools and Applications (IPTA), pp. 1–6. IEEE (2016)

19. Li, X., Wan, J., Jin, Y., Liu, A., Guo, G., Li, S.Z.: 3DPC-net: 3D point cloud network for face anti-spoofing. In: 2020 IEEE International Joint Conference on Biometrics (IJCB), pp. 1–8. IEEE (2020)

20. Liu, Y., Jourabloo, A., Liu, X.: Learning deep models for face anti-spoofing: binary or auxiliary supervision. In: Proceedings of the IEEE Conference on Computer Vision and Pattern Recognition, pp. 389–398 (2018)

21. Määttä, J., Hadid, A., Pietikäinen, M.: Face spoofing detection from single images using micro-texture analysis. In: 2011 International Joint Conference on Biometrics (IJCB), pp. 1–7. IEEE (2011)

22. Pan, G., Sun, L., Wu, Z., Lao, S.: Eyeblink-based anti-spoofing in face recognition from a generic webcamera. In: 2007 IEEE 11th International Conference on Computer Vision, pp. 1–8. IEEE (2007)

23. Patel, K., Han, H., Jain, A.K.: Secure face unlock: spoof detection on smartphones. IEEE Trans. Inf. Forensics Secur. 11(10), 2268–2283 (2016)

24. Singh, A.K., Joshi, P., Nandi, G.C.: Face recognition with liveness detection using eye and mouth movement. In: 2014 International Conference on Signal Propagation and Computer Technology (ICSPCT 2014), pp. 592–597. IEEE (2014)

25. Tan, X., Li, Y., Liu, J., Jiang, L.: Face liveness detection from a single image with sparse low rank bilinear discriminative model. In: Daniilidis, K., Maragos, P., Paragios, N. (eds.) ECCV 2010. LNCS, vol. 6316, pp. 504–517. Springer, Heidelberg (2010). https://doi.org/10.1007/978-3-642-15567-3_37

26. Wang, Z., et al.: Exploiting temporal and depth information for multi-frame face anti-spoofing. arXiv preprint arXiv:1811.05118 (2018)

27. Woo, S., Park, J., Lee, J.-Y., Kweon, I.S.: CBAM: convolutional block attention module. In: Ferrari, V., Hebert, M., Sminchisescu, C., Weiss, Y. (eds.) ECCV 2018. LNCS, vol. 11211, pp. 3–19. Springer, Cham (2018). https://doi.org/10.1007/978-3-030-01234-2_1

28. Yang, J., Lei, Z., Li, S.Z.: Learn convolutional neural network for face anti-spoofing. arXiv preprint arXiv:1408.5601 (2014)

29. Yang, J., Lei, Z., Yi, D., Li, S.Z.: Person-specific face antispoofing with subject domain adaptation. IEEE Trans. Inf. Forensics Secur. 10(4), 797–809 (2015)

30. Yang, X., et al.: Face anti-spoofing: model matters, so does data. In: Proceedings of the IEEE/CVF Conference on Computer Vision and Pattern Recognition, pp. 3507–3516 (2019)

31. Yu, Z., et al.: Searching central difference convolutional networks for face anti-spoofing. In: Proceedings of the IEEE/CVF Conference on Computer Vision and Pattern Recognition, pp. 5295–5305 (2020)

32. Zhang, K., Zhang, Z., Li, Z., Qiao, Y.: Joint face detection and alignment using multitask cascaded convolutional networks. IEEE Sig. Process. Lett. 23(10), 1499–1503 (2016)

33. Zhang, Z., Yan, J., Liu, S., Lei, Z., Yi, D., Li, S.Z.: A face antispoofing database with diverse attacks. In: 2012 5th IAPR International Conference on Biometrics (ICB), pp. 26–31. IEEE (2012)

Attention-Based RGBD Fusenet for Monocular 3D Body Geometry and Pose Reconstruction

Pengle Jin, Miaopeng Li, and Xinguo Liu$^{(\boxtimes)}$

State Key Lab of CAD&CG, Zhejiang University, Hangzhou, China
xgliu@cad.zju.edu.cn

Abstract. This paper introduces a fully automatic method for reconstructing 3D body geometry and pose from a single RGBD image. Initially, the method combines the RGB image and the depth image to perform pose-related multi-task regression. A novel mutual-attention module is proposed, which adaptively fuses RGB and depth information while regressing multiple human features using a multi-task end-to-end deep neural network. Subsequently, the method automatically reconstructs full-body geometry and motion pose in near real-time based on these diverse features. Experimental results demonstrate that the proposed RGBD fusion network effectively extracts relevant information and eliminates ambiguous information from the two-modal inputs, significantly improving prediction accuracy in cases of appearance ambiguity, local occlusion, motion blur, and noisy input.

Keywords: RGBD Fusing Network · Mutual Attention · Motion Capture · Human Pose Estimation · Multi-task Regression

1 Introduction

Acquiring accurate 3D motion data of the human body is crucial for applications such as film production, game animation, and human-computer interaction. Traditional motion capture systems often require a dedicated motion lab and can be complex, expensive, and operationally intensive. In contrast, real-time applications necessitate the capture of human motion on-the-fly without intrusive body markers. Consequently, the automatic acquisition of human body geometry and motion information from images and videos has emerged as a popular research topic in computer science. Unlike traditional motion capture systems, image/video-based methods are compact, portable, and easy to operate without the need for cumbersome sensors and complex systems.

Deep learning has been widely applied to numerous computer vision tasks, yielding promising results and encouraging researchers to utilize deep neural networks for 3D human motion capture. However, most of these methods [7,21] rely on a single RGB modality, neglecting the integration of multiple heterogeneous modalities, such as RGB and depth. Each modality possesses unique characteristics; for instance, depth modality provides rich 3D structural information but

H. Lu et al. (Eds.): ICIG 2023, LNCS 14355, pp. 390–402, 2023.
https://doi.org/10.1007/978-3-031-46305-1_32

lacks vital texture appearance information, whereas the RGB modality offers the opposite. Although RGB and depth-based methods have been extensively researched for human motion capture [18], few studies employ both RGB and depth as CNN inputs to address the human motion capture problem. In this work, we reconstruct body geometry and pose from RGBD images and investigate a novel deep learning framework that learns a conjoint representation of both modalities, which is subsequently used to predict multiple human pose-related tasks.

This paper introduces an automatic system for reconstructing human body geometry and pose from single RGBD images. The primary focus is on effectively integrating both RGB and depth information to enhance the system's reliability and robustness, particularly in addressing the failure cases of pure RGB or depth systems. We propose a mutual-attentional RGBD fusion network that adaptively combines RGB and depth information for real-time prediction of various human features. For the first time, an RGBD image serves as the input for a neural network in human pose related multi-task learning. Results indicate that, compared to pure RGB or depth networks, the prediction accuracy of the RGBD fusion network is significantly improved, especially in cases of left-right ambiguities, background ambiguity, partial occlusion, motion blur, and noisy input.

Lastly, based on the network's predictions, we adopt an optimization-based algorithm from Deep3DPose [10] for accurate full-body shape modeling and kinematic pose reconstruction. As a result, we present a self-contained, near-real-time system that reconstructs 3D human poses and full-body geometry models from single images.

In summary, the contributions of this paper are:

- A novel and efficient attention-based scheme for fusing RGB and depth information. We propose a mutual-attentional feature fusion transformer that learns a conjoint cross-modal feature representation from RGB and depth images.
- An end-to-end RGBD-based multi-task network for learning seven pose-related tasks, encompassing 2D and 3D features as well as sparse and dense features.

2   Related Work

In recent years, significant advancements have been achieved in estimating 3D geometric body models from single images. These advancements are closely tied to the maturation of 2D pose estimation and 3D skeletal pose estimation algorithms, deep learning techniques, and large-scale training data. To our knowledge, almost all methods [7,10,11,13,15,21,25] learn human pose-related tasks from a single RGB modality. In this work, we incorporate multiple modalities, specifically RGB and depth, as inputs for learning various human pose-related tasks. While RGB images provide rich appearance features and texture details of objects, depth images offer abundant geometric information. Given the high complexity of environments and object appearances, depth information can reduce ambiguity and uncertainty in RGB images under challenging conditions. Consequently, designing an efficient model to fuse RGB and depth modalities is crucial for achieving higher accuracy.

Numerous studies have demonstrated significant improvements in the accuracy of tasks such as semantic segmentation [4,5,8,19,22]. Deng et al. provide a comprehensive overview of various existing RGBD fusion strategies [5]. Early fusion strategies involve simple concatenation of the RGB and depth images by channel, subsequently inputting them into a traditional single-stream neural network [4]. However, this approach does not sufficiently account for the disparities between the two modalities or exploit their complementary characteristics. Some methods introduce adaptive fusion operations [5,14,16], enabling the network to dynamically fuse features from both modalities based on the current input image's attributes, thereby facilitating the learning of richer cross-modality features.

The Transformer [23], a fully attention-based architecture, has been employed in several computer vision tasks, such as object detection [2], semantic segmentation [24], image generation [20], and image enhancement [3], yielding exceptional performance.

This paper presents a mutual-attention-based RGBD fusion network for human pose related multi-task estimation. The experimental results indicate that the network can adaptively fuse the effective information from both RGB images and depth images while filtering out noisy and ambiguous information.

3   Method

Our method accepts a single image as input, capturing the pose of a single person using a monocular RGBD camera, and reconstructs the 3D body geometry and pose for each frame. Figure 1 provides an overview of our method. Initially, the RGB and depth inputs are fused using an RGBD-based fusion module to generate a conjoint cross-modality feature. This feature is then processed by a multi-task prediction module to obtain predictions for seven human pose-related tasks. Lastly, following the Deep3DPose [10] approach, we use these predictions to reconstruct the 3D body geometry and pose.

3.1   RGBD-Based Fusion Module

In this section, the input RGB image and the encoded depth image are fed into distinct feature extractors to obtain separate modal features $\mathbf{F}_r$ and $\mathbf{F}_d$, where r represents RGB and d denotes depth. Finally, the mutual-attentional fusion module facilitates interaction between the two types of features, $\mathbf{F}_r$ and $\mathbf{F}_d$, and fuses them to produce the conjoint cross-modality feature.

Depth Image Encoding. When used as the input of a neural network, the depth image usually is encoded as a gray image, surface normal image, HHA image (Height above ground, Horizontal disparity, pixel-wise Angle between a

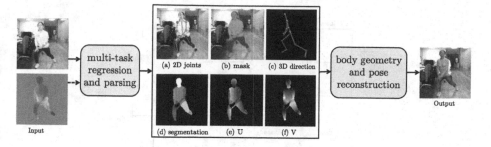

Fig. 1. The overview of our method.

surface normal and the gravity direction) [6], pseudo-color map, 3D voxel-based on a truncated symbol distance function, 3D point cloud. To enable real-time conversion, our method transforms the depth image into a pseudo-color image for network input. Specifically, given a depth image captured by the Kincct camera, we first perform human foreground extraction using the Kinect's API and then generate a three-channel color map according to the predefined mapping from the depth value to the pseudo-color values.

Mutual-Attentional Feature Fusion. As illustrated in the Fig. 3, we feed the RGB image and the depth images to the two-branch ResNet50 [9] featurc extractors to generate the intermediate features of RGB and depth modalities $\mathbf{F}_r$ and $\mathbf{F}_d$. Both types of features have their advantages and disadvantages, making it crucial to design a smart module capable of learning an efficient cross-modality representation for improved multi-task prediction.

We propose a mutual-attentional fusion module to interact and fuse features from different modalities. As depicted in Fig. 2, the proposed module comprises two mutual-attentional layers and a feature fusion operation. Analogous to the query vector $\mathbf{Q}$, the key vector $\mathbf{K}$, the value vector $\mathbf{V}$ in the standard transformer [23], $\mathbf{Q}_r$, $\mathbf{K}_r$, $\mathbf{V}_r$ correspond to the query matrices, key matrices and value matrices computed from the RGB feature $\mathbf{F}_r$ through linear operations. Similarly, $\mathbf{Q}_d$, $\mathbf{K}_d$, $\mathbf{V}_d$ are computed from the depth feature $\mathbf{F}_d$. The mutual attention is applied to retrieve the contextual information of the RGB stream (key $\mathbf{K}_r$ and value $\mathbf{V}_r$) related to the query matrix of depth stream $\mathbf{Q}_d$, and vice the verse. In other words, the RGB attention matrix $\mathbf{A}_r$ is computed by multiplying the depth query matrix $\mathbf{Q}_d$ and RGB key matrix $\mathbf{K}_r$. Then, the RGB attentional feature $\mathbf{F}'_r$ is obtained by multiplying the RGB attention matrix $\mathbf{A}_r$ and the RGB value matrix $\mathbf{V}_r$. Similarly, we also obtain the depth attentional feature $\mathbf{F}'_d$.

Following the mutual attentional layer, attentional features from both modalities $\mathbf{F}'_r$ and $\mathbf{F}'_r$ are fused via a simple feature addition operation to produce the conjoint cross-modality features $\mathbf{F}_c$. These features are then fed into a subsequent sub-network for multi-task prediction. The entire process of mutual-attentional

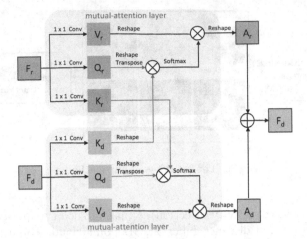

Fig. 2. The proposed mutual-attentional fusion module. The $\otimes$ denotes matrix multiplication, the $\oplus$ denotes element-wise addition. The softmax operation is performed on each row. Features embeddings from RGB and depth modalities are fed to the mutual-attention layer to exchange the information. Then the attentional features $\mathbf{A}_r$ and $\mathbf{A}_d$ are fused to obtain the conjoint representation $\mathbf{F}_m$.

feature fusion can be expressed as follows:

$$(\mathbf{F}'_r, \mathbf{F}'_d) = \mathrm{MutAtten}(\mathbf{F}_r, \mathbf{F}_d)$$

$$\mathbf{A}_r = \mathbf{Q}_d \otimes \mathbf{K}_r^T, \quad \mathbf{F}'_r = \mathbf{A}_r \otimes \mathbf{V}_r$$

$$\mathbf{A}_d = \mathbf{Q}_r \otimes \mathbf{K}_d^T, \quad \mathbf{F}'_d = \mathbf{A}_d \otimes \mathbf{V}_d$$

$$\mathbf{F}_c = \mathbf{F}'_r \oplus \mathbf{F}'_d$$

where $\otimes$ denotes matrix multiplication, $\oplus$ denotes element-wise addition. The mutual-attentional fusion module effectively integrates and balances the contributions of both RGB and depth modalities, allowing the network to learn more expressive and informative features for multi-task human pose estimation.

3.2   Multi-task Regression

In this section, the RGBD conjoint cross-modality feature $\mathbf{F}_c$ is processed through the multi-task predictor to get the predictions of seven human pose related tasks [10].

Multi-task Prediction Sub-network. Taking the fused RGBD feature $\mathbf{F}_c$ as input, the multi-task prediction sub-network outputs: the 2D confidence maps of joints $\mathbf{S} \in \mathbb{R}^{J \times w \times h}$, where $J = 18$ is the number of joints, the visibility maps of joints $\mathbf{V} \in \mathbb{R}^{J \times w \times h}$, the 2D direction fields of limbs $\mathbf{L}_{2d} \in \mathbb{R}^{2l \times w \times h}$, where $l = 17$ is the number of limbs, the 3D direction fields of limbs $\mathbf{L}_{3d} \in \mathbb{R}^{3l \times w \times h}$, the

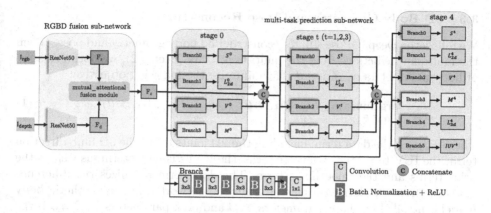

Fig. 3. The network structure.

foreground probability map $\mathbf{M} \in \mathbb{R}^{w \times h}$, the part segmentation probability maps $\mathbf{P} \in \mathbb{R}^{(c+1) \times w \times h}$, where $c = 24$ is the number of body parts, UV coordinate maps $\mathbf{U} \in \mathbb{R}^{2c \times w \times h}$, where different part segmentation regions correspond to different UV coordinate maps.

The structure of the multi-task prediction sub-network is shown in Fig. 3. First, the RGBD feature $\mathbf{F}_c$ passes through a cascaded four-branch network to predict the 2D confidence maps of joints $\mathbf{S}$ (Fig. 3 Branch0), the 2D direction fields of limbs $\mathbf{L}_{2d}$ (Fig. 3 Branch1), the visibility maps of joint $\mathbf{V}$ (Fig. 3 Branch2), the foreground probability map $\mathbf{M}$ (Fig. 3 Branch3). The common characteristics of these four tasks are that they are all 2D tasks, which are relatively simple, and there are public datasets or the ground-truth labeling is relatively easy. Then, the feature $\mathbf{F}_c$ and the outputs of these four tasks are simultaneously sent to a six-branch network to predict all tasks, including the above four tasks and the 3D direction fields of limbs $\mathbf{L}_{3d}$ (Fig. 3 Branch4), the part segmentation probability maps $\mathbf{P}$, and the UV coordinate maps $\mathbf{U}$. Among them, the same branch is used to predict the part segmentation probability map $\mathbf{P}$ and the UV coordinate maps $\mathbf{U}$, collectively called $\mathbf{IUV}$ (Fig. 3 Branch5).

Loss Functions. For the outputs of the 2D confidence maps of joints $\mathbf{S}$, the 2D direction fields of limbs $\mathbf{L}_{2d}$, the 3D direction fields of limbs $\mathbf{L}_{3d}$, and the UV coordinate maps $\mathbf{U}$, we employ l_2 loss. For the foreground probability map $\mathbf{M}$ and the visibility maps of joint $\mathbf{V}$, we employ binary cross-entropy loss. For the part segmentation probability maps $\mathbf{P}$, we employ multivariate cross-entropy loss. Where the loss weight of each task is set as follows: $w_{\mathbf{S}} = 0.5$, $w_{\mathbf{L}_{2d}} = 0.5$, $w_{\mathbf{M}} = 0.1$, $w_{\mathbf{V}} = 0.3$, $w_{\mathbf{L}_{3d}} = 0.5$, $w_{\mathbf{P}} = 0.05$, $w_{\mathbf{U}} = 0.5$. For the task of the part segmentation, the channels of different categories are applied with different weights according to their area of regions, the larger the area, the small the weight. For the task of UV coordinates, the loss for a different channel is calculated only in the corresponding part region.

3.3   3D Body Geometry and Pose Reconstruction

We follow the Deep3DPose [10] to reconstruct 3d body geometry and pose. Given the multiple predictions from the multi-task CNN (Sect. 3.2), we optimize a set of body parameters α, β and θ that minimize the following objective:

$$\arg\min_{\alpha,\beta,\theta}(w_{data}E_{data}(\alpha,\beta,\theta) + w_{prior}E_{prior}(\alpha,\beta,\theta)), \qquad (1)$$

where E_{data} is the data term, including the 2D joints term, the 3D limb direction term, the IUV term, the silhouette term, the joint visibility term, as well as the prior terms and the smoothness term. The data term penalizes the difference between the multiple measurements from the network and the synthetic body model controlled by shape parameters α, β and pose parameters θ. E_{prior} is the priors term, penalizing the implausible solutions of pose parameters and shape parameters.

4   Experiments

In this section, we demonstrate the power and effectiveness of our system by capturing a wide range of human movements using a single camera, including an RGBD camera as well as an RGB camera. In the first subsection, we compare the performance of our method against various alternative methods (Sect. 4.1) to showcase the capabilities of our method with RGB inputs. However, there are still numerous failure cases with RGB inputs. Consequently, in the second subsection, We evaluate the effectiveness of our RGBD fusenet by examining failure cases in RGB or depth networks and the advantages of multi-task regression in the RGBD fusenet. (Sect. 4.2). Our system employs an Intel Core i7 CPU and a 1080ti graphics card, achieving frame rates of approximately 20.39 fps and 17.46 fps for RGB and RGBD image inputs, respectively.

4.1   Comparison Against Alternative Methods

We have evaluated the effectiveness of our RGB system against state-of-the-art methods.

Comparison Against SPIN [12]. Our method is compared against the state-of-the-art regression-based method: SPIN [12], which directly regress the shape parameters and pose parameters of the body model from a single RGB image using a CNN. Figure 4 presents a side-by-side comparison of results in both the original and novel views. It is evident that our method achieves superior accuracy and image-model alignment compared to SPIN.

Comparison Against Vnect [17]. Since neither SPIN [12] or SMPLify [1] offer a fully self-contained and complete system for real-time 3D pose capture, we compare our system against a recent real-time system, Vnect [17], which only captures 3D skeletal pose. Figure 5 (b) provides side-by-side comparison

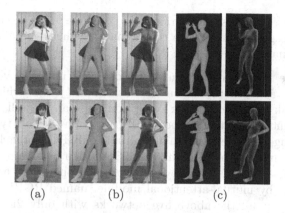

Fig. 4. Comparison of SPIN [12] (left) and our method (right). (a) input; (b) results in original view; (c) results in novel view.

of raw 3D predictions from the CNN of Vnect and our method. We apply 3D limb direction to a default limb length for visualization, demonstrating that our multi-task CNN yields more accurate 3D estimation. Figure 5 (c) and (d) further compare the final optimization results in two views of Vnect and our method, illustrating that our approach achieves a more accurate 3D pose.

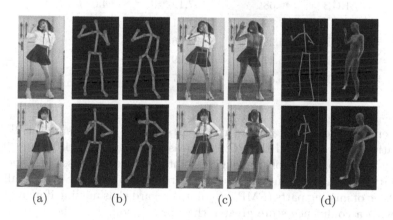

Fig. 5. Comparison of Vnect [17] (left) and our method (right). (a) input; (b) raw 3D prediction from CNN; (c) optimized 3D pose in the original view; (d) optimized 3D pose in a novel view.

4.2   Evaluation on RGBD FuseNet

Although the RGB system attains state-of-the-art results, it still encounters numerous failures. We introduce the RGBD fusenet to address these failure cases and test the performance of three types of input: RGB, depth, and RGBD.

For RGBD input, we assess the performance of three types of cross-modal feature fusion strategies: channel-wise concatenate, element-wise summation, and mutual-attentional module.

Impact on the Accuracy of the 2D Pose. We initially evaluate the performance of the above networks on the task of 2D joints, which is the most fundamental task of our multi-task regression and can be well evaluated both quantitatively and qualitatively. Specifically, we train the five types of network with the following feature extraction modules: 1) only RGB branch, named RGB; 2) only depth branch, named Depth; 3) RGBD fusion by summation operation, named RGBD-s; 4) RGBD fusion by concatenation operation, named RGBD-c; 5) RGBD fusion by mutual-attentional module, named RGBD-m. Noted that in this experiment, all the above five networks with only 2D joint tasks are trained on the dataset collected by the Kinect camera without any initialization. The collected data are divided into a training set (327 actors), validation set (20 actors), and testing set (20 actors), with each actor including 1000 frames covering various actions.

Table 1. The impact of different feature extraction modules on the accuracy of the 2D pose. The evaluation metric is PCKh (%) and PMP (‰)

network	PCKh@0.1 (%)	PCKh@0.5 (%)	PMP (‰)
RGB	46.68	97.12	4.0
Depth	47.72	97.81	3.0
RGBD-s	54.28	98.36	1.9
RGBD-c	55.17	98.29	1.7
RGBD-m	60.82	98.47	1.2

We employ the percentage of correct parts (PCKh) to measure the 2D joints localization accuracy[1] and the PCK is measured at threshold 0.1 and 0.5. To evaluate the recognition of challenging joints, such as in cases of appearance ambiguity, occlusion and motion blur, we introduce a new error metric called the percentage of missing parts (PMP). A joint is regarded as missing if no maximum point with a confidence score greater than 0.03 is found on the corresponding confidence map. We computed the PMP as the number of missing joints divided by the total number of joints. Table 1 summarizes the evaluation results of the testing set. Compared with the single-modal input, RGB/Depth network, the RGBD (-s/-c/-m) network significantly improves the estimation quality. The best results are achieved by RGBD-m, that is RGBD fusion by a mutual-attentional module. This result demonstrates that geometric information in depth images can help reduce the ambiguity and uncertainty of appearance in RGB images,

---

[1] The evaluation code is the same as the MPII human pose benchmark: http://human-pose.mpi-inf.mpg.de/#evaluation.

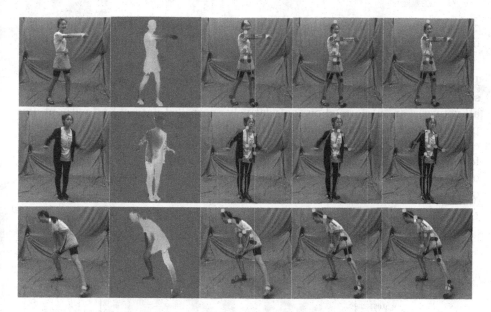

Fig. 6. Comparison of the results of the 2D pose from RGB, Depth, and RGBD-m networks on the testing dataset. From left to right are RGB input, depth input, results of RGB network, Depth network, and RGBD-m network.

and vice versa. In comparison with the fixed RGBD fusing operation (-s/-c), the learnable and adaptive fusing operation (-m), dynamically fuses the features of RGB and depth according to the attributes of the input image, learns richer cross-modality features, and achieves optimal performance.

It is worth noting that the Depth network outperforms the RGB network. The reason is that all the networks in this experiment are trained on our collected dataset, which lacks sufficient diversity in appearance, texture, and actors. Consequently, the generalization ability of the RGB network is limited. In contrast, the depth network shields the diversity of appearance and texture between different people, focusing on structural information and thus exhibiting better generalization ability.

Figure 6 compares the visualized results of 2D pose predicted by RGB, Depth, and RGBD-m networks. The following conclusion can be drawn: (i) For highly distinguished joint points, the RGB, Depth, and RGBD networks can all predict the correct joint positions; (ii) The results from the RGB network are easily affected by the motion blur (the 2nd row) and left/right limb ambiguity (the 3nd row), while the Depth and RGBD networks provide correct predictions due to the clear geometry information in depth images. (iii) When depth images are disrupted by noise or clothing, the Depth network may produce incorrect estimations. In such cases, the RGB image with rich texture information plays a critical role in accurate identification (the 1st row). Generally, the RGBD network can fuse the advantages of the RGB input and the depth input while compensating for their missing or ambiguous information. Overall, the RGBD network gives the best results compared with the RGB network and the Depth network.

Impact on the Validation Loss of Each Task. The above experiment demonstrates the effectiveness of the depth information. Since training and testing of all networks are performed on the relatively controlled dataset and without any pre-training, their generalization ability on the wild image is limited. In this experiment, we train the RGB network and RGBD network with all seven tasks following the training details described in Sect. 3.2, and evaluate the performance of all tasks by comparing the validation loss of each task and the visualized results on wild images.

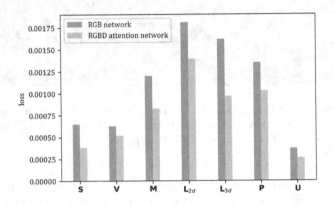

Fig. 7. Comparison of validation loss for RGB network and RGBD network with mutual-attentional fusion.

Figure 7 reveals that, for each task, the RGBD network reduces the validation loss compared with the RGB network, particularly for joint confidence maps **S** and part segmentation maps **P**.

As expected, RGB images contain rich appearance features and texture details of objects, while depth images contain relatively sparse geometric information to describe the structure of objects. Due to the complex environment and diverse object appearances, depth information can be used to reduce the uncertainty caused by the ambiguous RGB information during CNN regression. High-quality predictions from the network form the foundation for subsequent 3D body geometry and pose reconstruction; the more accurate human body features predicted by the RGBD network, the more precise 3D human body pose optimization.

5   Conclusion

This paper presents an approach for 3D human body geometry and pose reconstruction from a single RGBD image. We introduce a mutual-attentional RGBD fusion network to generate multiple predictions, representing the first instance of utilizing an RGBD image as input for a CNN to learn multiple human pose-related tasks. Experimental results demonstrate that incorporating depth information considerably enhances system robustness, particularly in challenging scenarios such as appearance ambiguity, partial occlusion, and motion blur, when compared to single-modal input. Based on the network's predictions, we employ an optimization-based algorithm to reconstruct full-body geometry and kinematic pose. Consequently, we realize a self-contained and near-real-time system that reconstructs 3D human poses and full-body geometry models from a single RGBD image, which facilitates the retargeting of reconstructed 3D poses for real-time character animation.

Acknowledgment. We would like to express our sincere gratitude to the reviewers for their invaluable insights and constructive feedback. This work is supported by National Natural Science Foundation of China (Grant No. 61872317).

References

1. Bogo, F., Kanazawa, A., Lassner, C., Gehler, P., Romero, J., Black, M.J.: Keep it SMPL: automatic estimation of 3D human pose and shape from a single image. In: Leibe, B., Matas, J., Sebe, N., Welling, M. (eds.) ECCV 2016. LNCS, vol. 9909, pp. 561–578. Springer, Cham (2016). https://doi.org/10.1007/978-3-319-46454-1_34
2. Carion, N., Massa, F., Synnaeve, G., Usunier, N., Kirillov, A., Zagoruyko, S.: End-to-end object detection with transformers. In: Vedaldi, A., Bischof, H., Brox, T., Frahm, J.-M. (eds.) ECCV 2020. LNCS, vol. 12346, pp. 213–229. Springer, Cham (2020). https://doi.org/10.1007/978-3-030-58452-8_13
3. Chen, H., et al.: Pre-trained image processing transformer. In: Proceedings of the IEEE/CVF Conference on Computer Vision and Pattern Recognition, pp. 12299–12310 (2021)
4. Couprie, C., Farabet, C., Najman, L., Lecun, Y.: Indoor semantic segmentation using depth information. In: First International Conference on Learning Representations (ICLR 2013), pp. 1–8 (2013)
5. Deng, L., Yang, M., Li, T., He, Y., Wang, C.: Rfbnet: deep multimodal networks with residual fusion blocks for RGB-d semantic segmentation. arXiv preprint arXiv:1907.00135 (2019)
6. Gupta, S., Girshick, R., Arbeláez, P., Malik, J.: Learning rich features from rgb-d images for object detection and segmentation. In: Fleet, D., Pajdla, T., Schiele, B., Tuytelaars, T. (eds.) ECCV 2014. LNCS, vol. 8695, pp. 345–360. Springer, Cham (2014). https://doi.org/10.1007/978-3-319-10584-0_23
7. Habermann, M., Xu, W., Zollhoefer, M., Pons-Moll, G., Theobalt, C.: Livecap: real-time human performance capture from monocular video. ACM Trans. Graph. (TOG) **38**(2), 1–17 (2019)
8. Hazirbas, C., Ma, L., Domokos, C., Cremers, D.: FuseNet: incorporating depth into semantic segmentation via fusion-based CNN architecture. In: Lai, S.-H., Lepetit, V., Nishino, K., Sato, Y. (eds.) ACCV 2016. LNCS, vol. 10111, pp. 213–228. Springer, Cham (2017). https://doi.org/10.1007/978-3-319-54181-5_14
9. He, K., Zhang, X., Ren, S., Sun, J.: Deep residual learning for image recognition. In: Proceedings of the IEEE Conference on Computer Vision and Pattern Recognition, pp. 770–778 (2016)

10. Jiang, L., et al.: Deep3dpose: realtime reconstruction of arbitrarily posed human bodies from single RGB images. arXiv preprint arXiv:2106.11536 (2021)

11. Kanazawa, A., Black, M.J., Jacobs, D.W., Malik, J.: End-to-end recovery of human shape and pose. In: Proceedings of the IEEE Conference on Computer Vision and Pattern Recognition, pp. 7122–7131 (2018)

12. Kolotouros, N., Pavlakos, G., Black, M.J., Daniilidis, K.: Learning to reconstruct 3D human pose and shape via model-fitting in the loop. In: Proceedings of the IEEE/CVF International Conference on Computer Vision, pp. 2252–2261 (2019)

13. Li, J., Xu, C., Chen, Z., Bian, S., Yang, L., Lu, C.: Hybrik: a hybrid analytical-neural inverse kinematics solution for 3d human pose and shape estimation. In: Proceedings of the IEEE/CVF Conference on Computer Vision and Pattern Recognition, pp. 3383–3393 (2021)

14. Li, X., Hou, Y., Wang, P., Gao, Z., Xu, M., Li, W.: Trear: transformer-based RGB-D egocentric action recognition. IEEE Trans. Cogn. Dev. Syst. **14**(1), 246–252 (2022)

15. Li, Z., Liu, J., Zhang, Z., Xu, S., Yan, Y.: Cliff: carrying location information in full frames into human pose and shape estimation. In: Avidan, S., Brostow, G., Cissé, M., Farinella, G.M., Hassner, T. (eds.) ECCV 2022. LNCS, vol. 13665, pp. 590–606. Springer, Cham (2022). https://doi.org/10.1007/978-3-031-20065-6_34

16. Liu, C., Zhou, W., Chen, Y., Lei, J.: Asymmetric deeply fused network for detecting salient objects in RGB-D images. IEEE Sig. Process. Lett. **27**, 1620–1624 (2020)

17. Mehta, D., et al.: Vnect: real-time 3D human pose estimation with a single RGB camera. ACM Trans. Graph. (TOG) **36**(4), 1–14 (2017)

18. Obdržálek, Š., et al.: Accuracy and robustness of kinect pose estimation in the context of coaching of elderly population. In: 2012 Annual International Conference of the IEEE Engineering in Medicine and Biology Society, pp. 1188–1193. IEEE (2012)

19. Park, S.J., Hong, K.S., Lee, S.: RDFnet: RGB-D multi-level residual feature fusion for indoor semantic segmentation. In: Proceedings of the IEEE International Conference on Computer Vision, pp. 4980–4989 (2017)

20. Parmar, N., et al.: Image transformer. In: International Conference on Machine Learning, pp. 4055–4064. PMLR (2018)

21. Tung, H.Y., Tung, H.W., Yumer, E., Fragkiadaki, K.: Self-supervised learning of motion capture. In: Advances in Neural Information Processing Systems, pp. 5236–5246 (2017)

22. Valada, A., Mohan, R., Burgard, W.: Self-supervised model adaptation for multi-modal semantic segmentation. Int. J. Comput. Vision, 1–47 (2019)

23. Vaswani, A., et al.: Attention is all you need. In: Advances in Neural Information Processing Systems, pp. 5998–6008 (2017)

24. Wang, H., Zhu, Y., Adam, H., Yuille, A., Chen, L.C.: Max-deeplab: end-to-end panoptic segmentation with mask transformers. In: Proceedings of the IEEE/CVF Conference on Computer Vision and Pattern Recognition, pp. 5463–5474 (2021)

25. Xu, Y., Zhu, S.C., Tung, T.: Denserac: joint 3D pose and shape estimation by dense render-and-compare. In: Proceedings of the IEEE/CVF International Conference on Computer Vision, pp. 7760–7770 (2019)

Distortion-Aware Mutual Constraint for Screen Content Image Quality Assessment

Ye Yao, Jintong Hu, Wengming Yang[✉], and Qingmin Liao

Shenzhen International Graduate School, Tsinghua University, Beijing, China
{yaoy20,hujt22}@mails.tsinghua.edu.cn, yang.wenming@sz.tsinghua.edu.cn,
liaoqm@tsinghua.edu.cn

Abstract. The relationship between image distortion and image quality exhibits a strong correlation. Various methods incorporate auxiliary tasks such as the classification of distortion types and levels to address this issue. However, these tasks tend to be relatively independent and do not exert significant mutual influence. To tackle this challenge, we propose a novel method called the distortion-aware mutual constraint (DAMC) for full-reference screen content image quality assessment. Our approach consists of a feature extraction network and a multi-task network, with the DAMC loss function facilitating positive feedback and entanglement among all tasks to achieve simultaneous optimization. To transform the origin image features space for the following main and auxiliary tasks, we propose a selective similarity fusion (SSF) module which weights different similarities in accordance with the origin image features. The experimental results demonstrate the excellent performance and generalization capability of our method.

Keywords: Image Quality Assessment · Screen Content Image · Mutual Constraint · Selective Similarity Fusion

1 Introduction

Nowadays, people spend a considerable amount of time using terminal devices such as mobile phones and computers for both work and entertainment. Since all the information is displayed on screens, research on screen content image quality assessment (SC-IQA) is crucial. Compared to natural scene images (NSIs), screen content images (SCIs) have different structural and statistical characteristics due to the greater diversity of content compositions, which include text, graphics, NSIs, charts, and so on [17]. SC-IQA methods can be categorized into three

---

This work was partly supported by the National Natural Science Foundation of China (Nos. 62171251 & 62311530100), the Special Foundations for the Development of Strategic Emerging Industries of Shenzhen (Nos. JCYJ20200109143010272 & CJGJZD20210408092804011) and Oversea Cooperation Foundation of Tsinghua.

H. Lu et al. (Eds.): ICIG 2023, LNCS 14355, pp. 403–414, 2023.
https://doi.org/10.1007/978-3-031-46305-1_33

types based on the existence of a reference image: full-reference (FR), reduced-reference (RR), and no-reference (NR).

FR-IQA aims to assess the image quality by computing the similarity (or difference) between the reference image and distorted image. Traditional methods like SSIM [21] try to extract some hand-craft features in accordance with the human visual system (HVS). To better assess the SCIs specifically, [8,10,17–19,22] have been proposed. However, traditional methods are limited by the HVS's cognitive ability and the complexity of the hand-crafted algorithm, making it challenging to improve their performance. To overcome this challenge, some researchers have employed traditional machine learning methods such as SVR to map the extracted features into a score [2–4,6,7,26]. Since Deep learning methods like convolutional neural network (CNN) have great success in many vision tasks, more methods based on CNN have been proposed. [5,12,23,24,28] use CNN for end-to-end learning, score regression, contents classification or NSIQA domain adaptation. Multi-task learning employs auxiliary tasks to assist the score prediction task. [9,27] employ histogram of oriented gradient (HOG) prediction as auxiliary task.

Distorted or low-quality images are produced by various distortion processing from reference or high-quality images. Different combinations of image contents and distortions may exhibit unpredictable differences in quality. Some researchers employ distortion type and level classification as auxiliary tasks to obtain more prior knowledge [13,14,16,25] for score prediction ability enhancement. However, in these methods distortion (including distortion type and level) classification auxiliary tasks do not have enough correlation to the score prediction main task. The auxiliary tasks assist the main task by sharing part of the network or passing on the features from the auxiliary branch to the main branch, which makes the distortion classification can not constrain the score prediction directly. Meanwhile, the main task lacks direct positive feedback to the auxiliary tasks. This motivates us to design a method that can entangle the distortion classifications and score prediction. Hence we propose the distortion-aware mutual constraint (DAMC) loss. DAMC loss integrates the outputs of distortion classification tasks and score prediction task, the result of each task will directly affect the other tasks. It would generate positive feedback between all tasks in training, resulting in simultaneous optimization for distortion classification and score prediction tasks.

It is ill-posed for FR-IQA to map the similarity between the reference image and distorted image into the quality score. In order to provide more relatively explicit prior knowledge, we generate hand-crafted similarity images using traditional methods designed specifically for SC-IQA and employ them as an extra input. As analyzed above, the hand-craft method and feature have their limitation, which motivate us we proposed a selective similarity fusion (SSF) module. Under the guidance of the deep origin image feature, the SSF module selectively extracts meaningful features from both the deep hand-craft similarity and deep network difference features by assigning different weights. Then the weighted similarity feature is then used to transform the deep origin feature space to better fit the following tasks.

The main contributions of this paper are summarized as follows: First, we propose the DAMC method for full-reference screen content image quality assessment. The DAMC loss is employed to enhance the mutual constraint for distortion classifications and score prediction task. Second, the SSF module is proposed to select different similarities and transform the origin feature space for each task branch. Finally, extensive experiments demonstrate the state-of-the-art performance of our method.

2   Proposed Method

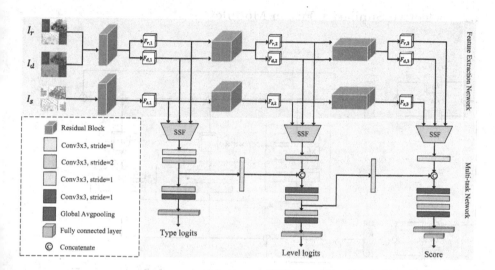

Fig. 1. The architecture of our proposed method.

The architecture of our proposed method is illustrated in Fig. 1. It consists of a feature extraction network and a multi-task network. In this paper, we use GFM feature map [18] as hand-craft similarity image I_s. Distorted image and reference image are denoted as I_d and I_r respectively. In the feature extraction network, we employ pre-trained siamese ResNet18 [11] to extract deep reference feature $F_{r,i}$ and deep distorted feature $F_{d,i}$ from I_r and I_d respectively at different layers. Similarly, Another pre-trained ResNet18 is used to extract deep hand-craft similarity feature $F_{s,i}$ from I_s, where $i = 1, 2, 3$ denotes the layers of conv3_x, conv4_x, conv5_x in ResNet18 respectively.

In the multi-task network, we adopt the progressive multi-task learning strategy [14]. Distortion type classification, distortion level classification, and score prediction branches are set from shallow to deep layers. For each branch, A SSF module is used to fuse $F_{r,i}$, $F_{d,i}$ and $F_{s,i}$, sequentially followed by a conv3x3 (stride=1), two conv3x3 (stride=2) for reducing the spatial size, a global average pooling. Conv3x3 (stride=1) denotes the convolutional layer with kernel size 3 ×

3 and stride 1. Channel dimension of the feature between two conv3x3 (stride=2) will be expanded by a conv3x3 (stride=1, shown in light blue in Fig. 1). Then the expanded feature will be concatenated with the feature in the next branch. After concatenating, a conv3x3 (stride=1, shown in purple in Fig. 1) is used to reduce the channel dimension before two conv3x3 (stride=2). Each conv in the multi-task network is followed by batch normalization and ReLU. At the end of each branch, a fully connected layer (two for the score prediction branch) is used to output distortion type logits, distortion level logits, and predicted quality score, respectively. The details of the proposed SSF module, DAMC loss, and other training loss will be described in the following subsections.

2.1   Selective Similarity Fusion Module

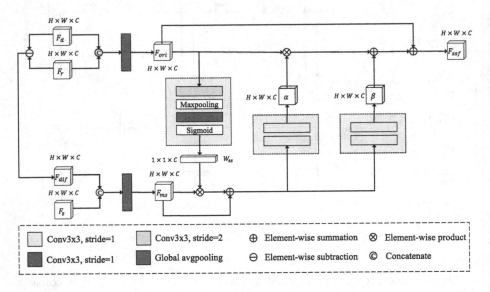

Fig. 2. The structure of the SSF module.

The structure of the SSF module is shown in Fig. 2. To obtain the similarity information between deep reference feature F_r and deep distorted feature F_d from different layers, we employ Deep network difference feature F_{dif} which can be calculated as follows:

$$F_{dif} = |F_r - F_d| \tag{1}$$

We concatenate F_r and F_d, and use a conv3x3 (stride=1) to get deep origin feature F_{ori}. The same process is conducted to generate deep mixed similarity feature F_{ms} from F_s and F_{dif}:

$$\begin{cases} F_{ori} = Conv(Concat(F_r, F_d)) \\ F_{ms} = Conv(Concat(F_s, F_{dif})) \end{cases} \tag{2}$$

We use the block composed of a conv3x3 (stride=2), a maxpooling2x2 (stride=2), a global average pooling, and a Sigmoid to generate selective similarity weights W_{ss} from F_{ori}. Each conv in SSF is followed by LeakyReLU with 0.2 negative slope. W_{ss} is employed to weight the deep mixed similarity F_{ms} with shortcut connection. Then, the weighted deep mixed similarity feature is mapped into the transformation parameters α, β by two conv3x3 (stride=1) respectively [20].

$$\alpha, \beta = Conv((F_{ms} \otimes W_{ss}) + F_{ms}) \tag{3}$$

where $\otimes$ means Element-wise product. Finally, α, β are employed to transform feature space of F_{ori} for the following distortion classifications and score prediction tasks:

$$F_{ssf} = (F_{ori} \otimes \alpha + \beta) + F_{ori} \tag{4}$$

where F_{ssf} is the output of SSF module.

2.2 Distortion-Aware Mutual Constraint Loss

Compared to the commonly used $\mathcal{L}_1$ (MAE) and $\mathcal{L}_2$ (MSE) score prediction loss, the proposed DAMC loss would simultaneously enhance the distortion classifications and score prediction tasks. DAMC loss can be formulated as follows:

$$L_{damc} = \frac{1}{N} \sum_{i}^{N} C_i |y_i - \hat{y}_i| \tag{5}$$

where N is the number of samples in a batch, i means the i-th sample in a batch, y_i denotes the ground-truth quality score, $\hat{y}_i$ represents the predicted quality score. C_i is the mutual constraint factor:

$$C_i = \frac{\gamma}{\delta e^{c_{type,i}} + \epsilon e^{c_{level,i}}} \tag{6}$$

where δ, ϵ, and γ are the parameters to adjust the mutual constraint intensity between distortion type classification, distortion level classification, and quality score prediction. We find that the classification of distortion level is more difficult than distortion type through experiments. Thus, distortion level classification should relatively make more contributions to DAMC loss for better training. We finally set $\delta = 10$, $\epsilon = 1$, and $\gamma = 1$. $c_{type,i}$ and $c_{level,i}$ denote the distortion type constraint factor and distortion level constraint factor, respectively. Higher classification precision should lead to lower DAMC loss for backpropagation. Hence we formulate them by the Softmax of ground-truth class logits:

$$\begin{cases} c_{type,i} = \dfrac{e^{logits_{gt,i}}}{\sum_m^{M_{type}} e^{logits_{m,i}}} \\[4mm] c_{level,i} = \dfrac{e^{logits_{gt,i}}}{\sum_m^{M_{level}} e^{logits_{m,i}}} \end{cases} \tag{7}$$

where M_{type} and M_{level} are the number of distortion types and levels respectively. $logits_{m,i}$ means the m-th class logits of the model. $logits_{gt,i}$ is the ground-truth class logits.

In order to improve the consistency between the model and the human visual system, Pearson linear correlation coefficient (PLCC) loss is used during the training:

$$L_{plcc} = 1 - PLCC(\boldsymbol{Y}, \hat{\boldsymbol{Y}}) \tag{8}$$

where $\boldsymbol{Y}$ is the ground-truth quality scores of a batch, and $\hat{\boldsymbol{Y}}$ is the predicted quality scores of the batch. PLCC is a metric to measure the linear correlation between two Sequences:

$$PLCC = \frac{Cov\left(Y, \hat{Y}\right)}{\sigma(Y)\,\sigma(\hat{Y})} \tag{9}$$

For distortion type classification and distortion level classification tasks, we employ cross-entropy loss L_{type} and L_{level} respectively during the training.

Finally, the overall training loss function L can be expressed by:

$$L = \lambda_1 L_{damc} + \lambda_2 L_{type} + \lambda_3 L_{level} + \lambda_4 L_{plcc} \tag{10}$$

where λ_1, λ_2, λ_3 and λ_4 are the weight of each loss, we set them as 1, 0.1, 0.1 and 1 respectively in the experiments.

3   Experiments

3.1   Experimental Settings

Datasets. The experiments are conducted on SCID [22] and SIQAD [17] dataset.

SIQAD has 20 reference images and 980 distorted images for 7 distortion types. Each type has 7 distortion levels. The distortion types include Gaussian noise (GN), Gaussian blurring (GB), motion blurring (MB), contrast change (CC), JPEG compression (JC), JPEG2000 compression (J2C), and layer-segmentation-based compression (LSC).

SCID is a larger SCI dataset with more distortion types and higher resolution (1280 × 720), which consists of 40 reference images and 1800 distorted images. SCID has 9 distortion types at 5 distortion levels, including GN, GB, MB, CC, JC, J2C, color saturation change (CSC), high-efficiency video coding (HEVC), and color quantization with dithering (CQD).

Table 1. Performance comparison on two datasets (Red and Blue numbers represent the best and second best respectively)

Method	SCID			SIQAD		
	PLCC	SROCC	KROCC	PLCC	SROCC	KROCC
GFM (FR)	0.8760	0.8759	0.6844	0.8828	0.8735	0.6876
EMD (FR)	0.903	0.904	–	0.887	0.885	–
CNN-SQE (FR)	0.9147	0.9139	0.7352	0.9042	0.8943	0.7152
DDEGSM (FR)	0.9137	0.9147	–	0.9001	0.8967	–
QODCNN (FR)	0.882	0.876	–	0.914	0.907	–
SPSIM (FR)	0.8713	0.8456	–	0.8920	0.8810	–
HAMTL (NR)	0.8613	0.8569	0.6679	0.9000	0.8962	0.7265
FVC (NR)	0.8681	0.8550	–	0.9014	0.8915	–
PQSC (NR)	0.9179	0.9147	–	0.9164	0.9069	–
MSDL (NR)	0.8935	0.8891	–	0.9191	0.9112	–
MtDl (NR)	0.9248	0.9233	–	0.9281	0.9214	–
DCMTC (NR)	0.9133	0.9050	–	0.9260	0.9242	–
Ours (FR)	0.9617	0.9617	0.8280	0.9373	0.9304	0.7691

Evaluation Metrics. Three metrics are used for performance comparison: PLCC, Spearman rank-order correlation coefficient (SROCC), and Kendall rank-order correlation coefficient (KROCC). As suggested in [1], we employ 5 parameters nonlinear mapping function to adjust the prediction quality score before computing PLCC:

$$p = \beta_1 \left(\frac{1}{2} - \frac{1}{\exp(\beta_2(q - \beta_3))} \right) + \beta_4 q + \beta_5 \qquad (11)$$

where p and q denote the origin prediction score and the mapped score respectively.

Implementation Details. We randomly crop 384×384 patches from the same position of distorted image, reference image, and similarity image for training. For testing, 8 group of patches are sampled and the mean quality scores of them are reported as the final quality score.

Our model is implemented by PyTorch with NVIDIA 1080Ti GPUs. For training, the learning rate is set to 0.0001 and reduced to 1/10 of the previous at the interval of 20 epochs. Adam optimizer is used for 50 epochs with 0.0005 weight decay, and the batch size is set to 32.

We follow the commonly used experimental protocol. For each dataset, We randomly divide 80% of the images for training, and the rest 20% for testing based on the reference images. The random divisions are conducted 10 times, the median performance is taken as reported result.

Table 2. Performance of different distortion types on SCID

Metric	GN	GB	MB	CC	JC	J2C	CSC	HEVC	CQD
PLCC	0.9777	0.9502	0.9457	0.9036	0.9739	0.9706	0.9332	0.9442	0.9247
SROCC	0.9701	0.9480	0.9378	0.8455	0.9711	0.9564	0.9370	0.9269	0.9180
KROCC	0.8654	0.8141	0.7885	0.6615	0.8564	0.8321	0.7782	0.7705	0.7590

Table 3. Performance of different distortion types on SIQAD

Metric	GN	GB	MB	CC	JC	J2C	LSC
PLCC	0.9375	0.9491	0.9538	0.8779	0.8825	0.8960	0.8893
SROCC	0.9420	0.9540	0.9595	0.7876	0.8741	0.9064	0.9026
KROCC	0.8042	0.8307	0.8360	0.5979	0.6931	0.7407	0.7460

3.2 Single Dataset Evaluation

Our method is compared with state-of-the-art FR-IQA and NR-IQA methods including: GFM [18], EMD [15], CNN-SQE [28], DDEGSM [19], QODCNN [12], SPSIM [24], HAMTL [9], FVC [3], PQSC [6], MTD [2], MSDL [4], MtDl [25] and DCMTC [27]. The results are shown in Table 1, our method outperforms all the methods on both datasets. We also conduct experiments on individual distortion types. As shown in Table 2 and Table 3, our method achieves good performance on both traditionally simple distortions like GN, GB, MB, and relatively complicated image processing distortions like JC, J2C, HEVC, except contrast change (CC).

Table 4. Ablation experiments on SCID

DAMC	SSF	PLCC	SROCC	KROCC
×	×	0.9497	0.9495	0.8010
×	✓	0.9545	0.9555	0.8138
✓	×	0.9569	0.9571	0.8185
✓	✓	**0.9617**	**0.9617**	**0.8280**

3.3 Ablation and Cross-Dataset Studies

We conduct the ablation experiments on SCID dataset to analyze the effectiveness of the proposed DAMC loss and SSF module. The results are shown in Table 4, in which we replace DAMC loss with $\mathcal{L}_1$ loss if "DAMC" is "×", and replace SSF module with Concatenate if "SSF" is "×". It can be observed that both DAMC and SSF would significantly improve the performance, and the combination of them would achieve superior performance.

Table 5. Performance comparison with different fusion method and similarity input on SCID (Numbers in bold represent the best)

Fusion	Similarity	PLCC	SROCC	KROCC
Concatenate	–	0.9284	0.9273	0.7635
SSF	–	0.9592	0.9587	0.8198
Concatenate	SSIM	0.9403	0.9404	0.7868
SSF	SSIM	0.9589	0.9594	0.8210
Concatenate	GFM	0.9569	0.9571	0.8185
SSF	GFM	**0.9617**	**0.9617**	**0.8280**

Selective Similarity Fusion Module. We conduct additional experiments to further investigate the efficiency of different fusion methods (SSF, Concatenate) and different similarity input (GFM, SSIM [21], None) combinations. The results are presented in Table 5. In this experiments, DAMC loss is replaced with $\mathcal{L}_1$ loss. Among the different similarity input methods, "GFM" outperformed "SSIM" and "None", as "SSIM" was not specifically designed for SC-IQA, and "None" lacked the hand-craft prior knowledge. For similarity input of "SSIM" and "None", they have comparable performance in the case of "SSF", and both are significantly better than the "Concatenate" counterparts. "SSF" achieves stable and excellent performance across all hand-crafted similarity inputs. It indicates that the SSF module can selectively obtain and aggregate the important similarity information from either deep hand-craft similarity feature map or deep network difference feature map for the following tasks.

Table 6. Performance comparison with different score prediction loss on SCID (Numbers in bold represent the best)

Loss	PLCC	SROCC	TYPE ACC	LEVEL ACC
$\mathcal{L}_1$	0.9497	0.9495	83.06%	52.08%
$\mathcal{L}_2$	0.9454	0.9462	66.39%	27.92%
Smooth $\mathcal{L}_1$	0.9488	0.9484	83.19%	52.50%
DAMC	**0.9569**	**0.9571**	**92.92%**	**71.81%**

Distortion-Aware Mutual Constraint Loss. We conduct more ablation experiments to compare DAMC loss with other commonly used score prediction loss, including $\mathcal{L}_1$, $\mathcal{L}_2$, and smooth $\mathcal{L}_1$ loss. To verify the mutual constraint efficiency on the three tasks (score prediction, distortion type classification, and distortion level classification), we employ two metrics of "TYPE ACC" and "LEVEL ACC", which mean the classification accuracy of distortion type and distortion level respectively. It should be noted that "LEVEL ACC" requires correctly predicting both distortion type and distortion level. The SSF module is not used in this experiments. As shown in Table 6, DAMC loss has a significant performance improvement compared to the other loss on all three tasks, indicating the effectiveness of the DAMC loss.

Table 7. Performance of cross-dataset experiments with different score prediction loss (Numbers in bold represent the best)

Loss	Training on SCID		Training on SIQAD	
	PLCC	SROCC	PLCC	SROCC
$\mathcal{L}_1$	0.8791	0.8823	0.8816	0.8881
$\mathcal{L}_2$	0.8866	0.8814	0.8809	0.8853
Smooth $\mathcal{L}_1$	0.8732	0.8794	0.8815	0.8906
DAMC	**0.8901**	**0.8877**	**0.8935**	**0.8933**

Cross-Datset Evaluation for DAMC. To evaluate the generalization ability and robustness of the proposed method and DAMC loss, we conduct cross-dataset experiments on SCID and SIQAD. We train on one dataset and test on the other dataset. All the experiments employ the SSF module. The results are shown in Table 7. Compared to other score prediction loss, the proposed DAMC loss achieves the best performance on both datasets. Since SCID and SIQAD have partially different distortion types and levels, the results demonstrate the competent generalization ability and robustness of the proposed DAMC loss.

4   Conclusion

In this paper, we proposed a DAMC method for the full-reference screen content image quality assessment. Specifically, DAMC loss is introduced to conduct joint optimization for distortion classification and score prediction tasks by enhancing the constraint between them. Additionally, the SSF module is proposed to select the similarity features and transform the origin features space to fit the following tasks. We conduct experiments on two benchmark datasets, our method achieves state-of-the-art performance. Extensive ablation and cross-dataset experiments demonstrate the promising efficiency and robustness of our method.

References

1. Antkowiak, J., et al.: Final report from the video quality experts group on the validation of objective models of video quality assessment march 2000 (2000)
2. Bai, Y., Zhu, Z., Jiang, G., Sun, H.: Blind quality assessment of screen content images via macro-micro modeling of tensor domain dictionary. IEEE Trans. Multimedia **23**, 4259–4271 (2020)

3. Bai, Y., Zhu, Z., Zhu, C., Wang, Y.: Blind image quality assessment of screen content images via fisher vector coding. IEEE Access **10**, 13174–13181 (2022)
4. Chang, Y., Li, S., Liu, A., Jin, J.: Quality assessment of screen content images based on multi-stage dictionary learning. J. Vis. Commun. Image Represent. **79**, 103248 (2021)
5. Chen, B., Li, H., Fan, H., Wang, S.: No-reference screen content image quality assessment with unsupervised domain adaptation. IEEE Trans. Image Process. **30**, 5463–5476 (2021)
6. Fang, Y., Du, R., Zuo, Y., Wen, W., Li, L.: Perceptual quality assessment for screen content images by spatial continuity. IEEE Trans. Circuits Syst. Video Technol. **30**(11), 4050–4063 (2019)
7. Fang, Y., Yan, J., Li, L., Wu, J., Lin, W.: No reference quality assessment for screen content images with both local and global feature representation. IEEE Trans. Image Process. **27**(4), 1600–1610 (2017)
8. Fang, Y., Yan, J., Liu, J., Wang, S., Li, Q., Guo, Z.: Objective quality assessment of screen content images by uncertainty weighting. IEEE Trans. Image Process. **26**(4), 2016–2027 (2017)
9. Gao, R., Huang, Z., Liu, S.: Multi-task deep learning for no-reference screen content image quality assessment. In: Lokoč, J., et al. (eds.) Multi-task deep learning for no-reference screen content image quality assessment. LNCS, vol. 12572, pp. 213–226. Springer, Cham (2021). https://doi.org/10.1007/978-3-030-67832-6_18
10. Gu, K., et al.: Saliency-guided quality assessment of screen content images. IEEE Trans. Multimedia **18**(6), 1098–1110 (2016)
11. He, K., Zhang, X., Ren, S., Sun, J.: Deep residual learning for image recognition. In: Proceedings of the IEEE Conference on Computer Vision and Pattern Recognition, pp. 770–778 (2016)
12. Jiang, X., Shen, L., Feng, G., Yu, L., An, P.: An optimized CNN-based quality assessment model for screen content image. Signal Process. Image Commun. **94**, 116181 (2021)
13. Jiang, X., Shen, L., Yu, L., Jiang, M., Feng, G.: No-reference screen content image quality assessment based on multi-region features. Neurocomputing **386**, 30–41 (2020)
14. Li, A., Wu, J., Tian, S., Li, L., Dong, W., Shi, G.: Blind image quality assessment based on progressive multi-task learning. Neurocomputing **500**, 307–318 (2022)
15. Loh, W.T., Bong, D.B.: A generalized quality assessment method for natural and screen content images. IET Image Proc. **15**(1), 166–179 (2021)
16. Ma, K., Liu, W., Zhang, K., Duanmu, Z., Wang, Z., Zuo, W.: End-to-end blind image quality assessment using deep neural networks. IEEE Trans. Image Process. **27**(3), 1202–1213 (2018). https://doi.org/10.1109/TIP.2017.2774045
17. Ni, Z., Ma, L., Zeng, H., Chen, J., Cai, C., Ma, K.K.: ESIM: edge similarity for screen content image quality assessment. IEEE Trans. Image Process. **26**(10), 4818–4831 (2017)
18. Ni, Z., Zeng, H., Ma, L., Hou, J., Chen, J., Ma, K.K.: A Gabor feature-based quality assessment model for the screen content images. IEEE Trans. Image Process. **27**(9), 4516–4528 (2018)
19. Tolie, H.F., Faraji, M.R.: Screen content image quality assessment using distortion-based directional edge and gradient similarity maps. Signal Process. Image Commun. **101**, 116562 (2022)
20. Wang, X., Yu, K., Dong, C., Loy, C.C.: Recovering realistic texture in image super-resolution by deep spatial feature transform. In: Proceedings of the IEEE Conference on Computer Vision and Pattern Recognition, pp. 606–615 (2018)

21. Wang, Z., Bovik, A.C., Sheikh, H.R., Simoncelli, E.P.: Image quality assessment: from error visibility to structural similarity. IEEE Trans. Image Process. **13**(4), 600–612 (2004)
22. Yang, H., Fang, Y., Lin, W.: Perceptual quality assessment of screen content images. IEEE Trans. Image Process. **24**(11), 4408–4421 (2015)
23. Yang, J., et al.: No-reference quality assessment for screen content images using visual edge model and adaboosting neural network. IEEE Trans. Image Process. **30**, 6801–6814 (2021)
24. Yang, J., Bian, Z., Zhao, Y., Lu, W., Gao, X.: Full-reference quality assessment for screen content images based on the concept of global-guidance and local-adjustment. IEEE Trans. Broadcast. **67**(3), 696–709 (2021)
25. Yang, J., Bian, Z., Zhao, Y., Lu, W., Gao, X.: Staged-learning: assessing the quality of screen content images from distortion information. IEEE Signal Process. Lett. **28**, 1480–1484 (2021)
26. Yang, J., et al.: No reference quality assessment for screen content images using stacked autoencoders in pictorial and textual regions. IEEE Trans. Cybernet. **52**, 2798–2810 (2020)
27. Zhang, C., Huang, Z., Liu, S., Xiao, J.: Dual-channel multi-task CNN for no-reference screen content image quality assessment. IEEE Trans. Circuits Syst. Video Technol. **32**, 5011–5025 (2022)
28. Zhang, Y., Chandler, D.M., Mou, X.: Quality assessment of screen content images via convolutional-neural-network-based synthetic/natural segmentation. IEEE Trans. Image Process. **27**(10), 5113–5128 (2018)

Visual Realism Assessment for Face-Swap Videos

Xianyun Sun[1], Beibei Dong[2], Caiyong Wang[1], Bo Peng[2(✉)], and Jing Dong[2]

[1] Beijing Key Laboratory of Robot Bionics and Function Research, Beijing University of Civil Engineering and Architecture, Beijing, People's Republic of China
`sunxianyun@stu.bucea.edu.cn, wangcaiyong@bucea.edu.cn`
[2] Center for Research on Intelligent Perception and Computing, Institute of Automation, Chinese Academy of Sciences, Beijing, People's Republic of China
`dongbeibei2022@ia.ac.cn, {bo.peng,jdong}@nlpr.ia.ac.cn`

Abstract. Deep-learning-based face-swap videos, also known as deep-fakes, are becoming more and more realistic and deceiving. The malicious usage of these face-swap videos has caused wide concerns. The research community has been focusing on the automatic detection of these fake videos, but the assessment of their visual realism, as perceived by human eyes, is still an unexplored dimension. Visual realism assessment, or VRA, is essential for assessing the potential impact that may be brought by a specific face-swap video, and it is also important as a quality assessment metric to compare different face-swap methods. In this paper, we make a small step towards this new VRA direction by building a benchmark for evaluating the effectiveness of different automatic VRA models, which range from using traditional handcrafted features to different kinds of deep-learning features. The evaluations are based on a recent competition dataset named DFGC-2022, which contains 1400 diverse face-swap videos that are annotated with Mean Opinion Scores (MOS) on visual realism. Comprehensive experiment results using 11 models and 3 protocols are shown and discussed. We demonstrate the feasibility of devising effective VRA models for assessing face-swap videos and methods. The particular usefulness of existing deepfake detection features for VRA is also noted. The code can be found at https://github.com/XianyunSun/VRA.git.

Keywords: Deepfake · Face-swap · Realism Assessment · benchmark

1 Introduction

Face-swap videos, as the name indicates, are videos in which the appearance of a face is manipulated using computer programs (especially deep learning based methods) so that audiences may recognize the face as another individual. This technology has contributed a lot to filming and other entertainment industries, yet holding a high risk of being abused. The detection methods against face-swap

---

This work is done while Xianyun Sun is an intern at CASIA.

H. Lu et al. (Eds.): ICIG 2023, LNCS 14355, pp. 415–426, 2023.
https://doi.org/10.1007/978-3-031-46305-1_34

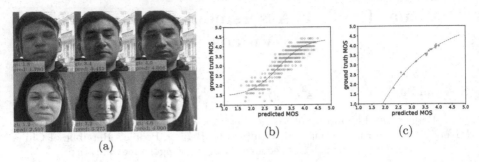

Fig. 1. (a) Face-swap videos with different degrees of realism, annotated with the ground truth MOS (*gt*) vs predicted MOS (*pred*) by the DFGC-1st VRA model. (b) and (c) are scatter plots with the fitted logistic curves (see Subsect. 4.1). (b) is the video-level plot and (c) is the method-level plot.

videos, or deepfakes, have improved a lot with intense attention being drawn [10]. Since the ultimate goal of face-swapping is to serve human viewers, subjective realism assessment could play a critical role not only in estimating the influence of fake videos on social networks, but also in evaluating the performance of face-swapping models during their development.

Several studies have been carried out to explore the subjective opinions on the persuasiveness of deepfake media. Deep models such as MOSNet [14] and MOSA-Net [31] are developed for assessing the naturalness of converted speeches. Compared with deepfake audios, relatively fewer studies have been carried out on deepfake images or videos.

Nightingale et al. [16,17] conduct subjective evaluations on StyleGAN2-generated images and find that the synthetic faces are indistinguishable from and even more trustworthy than real faces. Korshunov and Marcel [12] conduct a subjective study on face-swap videos from the DFDC dataset [5] and find that human perception is very different from the machine perception, and they are both successfully but in different ways fooled by deepfakes. All these studies, however, only demonstrate human performance in deepfake detection, with none of them providing any quantitative method to estimate the realism degree of deepfakes. A model proposed in [25] is trained to predict subjective quality for GAN-generated facial images, which is the only model of its kind to the best of our knowledge. There is an obvious vacant position for models assessing the visual realism of deepfake videos.

Here in this paper, we build the first visual realism assessment (VRA) benchmark for face-swap videos as an attempt to fill this gap. In our proposed method, models from related fields are employed as feature extractors, with support vector regression (SVR) as the regressor mapping features to a predicted subjective realism score. Figure 1a shows a demo of some frames from fake videos with the ground-truth mean opinion score (MOS) and predicted MOS. Figure 1b and Fig. 1c show a general view of the correlation between the prediction and the groundtruth on the DFGC-2022 dataset, in video-level and method-level (i.e. face-swap methods assessed) respectively.

In the following parts, Sect. 2 gives a brief overview of the DFGC-2022 dataset, on which our work is based. Section 3 introduces the proposed VRA method. Experiment details and results are discussed in Sect. 4, and Sect. 5 summarizes this work.

2   Dataset Analysis

Originated from the Second DeepFake Game Competition (DFGC) [19] held with the IJCB-2022 conference, the DFGC-2022 dataset contains a total of 2799 face-swap videos and 1595 real videos, all about 5 s in length. Fake clips in the dataset are generated by various face-swap methods (e.g. DeepFaceLab [20], SimSwap [3], FaceShifter [13]) and post-processing operations, and they are submitted by the participants through three separate submission sessions, i.e., C1, C2, and C3. This forms three subsets, with their details shown in Table 1. Each submission is associated with a submit-id and contains 80 swap videos for 20 pairs of facial IDs. The fake clips from the same submit-id are deemed to be created by the same method or process. 40 clips in each submission are annotated by 5 human raters independently in the aspect of video realism, apart from some other aspects. The rating is from 1 (very bad) to 5 (very good). The mean opinion score (MOS) and the standard deviation of each video's ratings are calculated and their distributions are shown in Fig. 2.

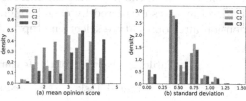

Table 1. Details of C1, C2, and C3 subset in DFGC-2022

subset	annotated fake clips	facial-ids	submit-ids
C1	240	20 pairs	6
C2	520	20 pairs	13
C3	640	20 pairs	16

Fig. 2. Histograms of the mean and standard deviation of each video's realism rating in DFGC-2022.

3   VRA Methods

In this section, we will go through the workflow of the VRA methods. First, we crop the face area from each frame in the data pre-processing step. Then, per-frame features are extracted using existing handcrafted or deep-learning models. And finally, the per-frame features are fused into video-level feature, which goes through a feature selection step before it is used to regress the video realism score. Here we follow the classical video quality assessment workflow [26] to construct our own, which is in contrast to learning end-to-end deep models for VRA, e.g. using LSTM [9] and GRU [4] models. This is because deep models heavily rely on the amount of training data, which is not suitable in our case, considering that there are only several hundreds of annotated training videos in the DFGC-2022 dataset.

3.1   Data Pre-processing

The videos in DFGC-2022 dataset have the resolution of 1080×1920, with the speaker's face taking over less than 25% of the area. Since VRA for face-swap should focus more on the facial area than the backgrounds, we crop each video according to detected face bounding boxes. For the fairness of comparing different face-swap methods, the face detection is only performed on the original target videos, and the result boxes are shared by all face-swap videos that originate from the same target video.

Specifically, we first enlarge the detected boxes by 1.3 times to include the full head region. We then obtain the smallest box that encapsulate all face boxes in the video and use it to crop all the video frames. This cropping strategy prevents the jittering of consecutive cropped frames. Cropped videos shrunk to about 600×600, which is also beneficial for the time efficiency of following processes.

3.2   Feature Extraction

For feature extractors, we employ several representative models from the subjective image/video quality assessment (I/VQA), image recognition, face recognition, and deepfake detection fields, with the consideration of potential feature sharing between VRA and these tasks. Table 2 summarises the included models. The *original* part in the *feats dim* column refers to the dimension of the original video-level features extracted by each model, and the *selected* part denotes the dimension after our feature selection step.

Table 2. Overview of the feature extraction models.

Model	Original Task	feats dim		Training Data
		original	selected	
BRISQUE	IQA	72	72	handcrafted
GM-LOG	IQA	80	80	handcrafted
FRIQUEE	IQA	1120	1120	handcrafted
TLVQM	VQA	75	75	handcrafted
V-BLIINDS	VQA	46	46	handcrafted
VIDEVAL	VQA	60	60	handcrafted
ensemble	VQA	3229	240	handcrafted
ResNet50	image recognition	4096	160	ImageNet
VGG-Face	face recognition	8192	280	VGG-Face
DFDC-ispl	deepfake detection	3584	100	FF++, DFDC
DFGC-1st	deepfake detection	11264	260	9 deepfake datasets

IQA Features. BRISQUE [15] is a typical IQA model under the natural scene statistics (NSS) framework, adopting mean subtracted contrast normalized (MSCN) coefficients as its band-pass filter. The FRIQUEE model [6] further extends the application of NSS model from gray scale to multiple color spaces including RGB, LAB and LMS. GM-LOG [30] uses isotropic differential operators in replacement of band-pass transforms, including the Gradient Magnitude (GM) and Laplacian of Gaussian (LOG) operators.

VQA Features. Different from IQA features that only focus on single frames, VQA features also represent the temporal information. TL-VQM [11] includes statistical features of the motion vectors between every two consecutive frames. V-BLIINDIS [22] also includes features of the motion vectors and includes DCT features extracted from frame differences.

VIDEVAL [26] is a SOTA VQA model which packs up features from BRISQUE, GMLOG, FRIQUEE and TLVQM and employs an additional feature selection process. Inspired by VIDEVAL, we propose a new *ensemble* model that extends VIDEVAL's feature candidates to also include features from V-BLIINDS and the handcraft features in RAPIQUE [27]. Similarly, the feature selection process is conducted, as will be introduced in Sect. 3.3.

General Image Recognition Features. In existing VQA literature, it has been shown that features extracted by general-purpose image recognition models like VGG [24] and ResNet [7] pre-trained on ImageNet can be potential video quality indicators with an additional regressor on top. This makes it a natural choice for us to also include the image recognition features in our evaluation. A pre-trained ResNet-50 is adopted, and we resize the images according to its input requirements.

Face Recognition Features. VGG-Face [18] are selected as the representative face recognition model for feature extraction. VGG-Face achieves a remarkable face recognition accuracy using a VGG-19 model finetuned on the VGG-Face dataset including 2622 identities. We select it for its simplicity and high performance.

Deepfake Detection Features. Since our VRA benchmark is based on the DFGC-2022 dataset, the 1st-place solution [1] in DFGC-2022 detection track (referred to as DFGC-1st) is a natural candidate for evaluation. Two ConvNext at different epochs and a Swin-Transformer are employed in this solution, and they are trained on an abundant collection of 9 deepfake datasets with data augmentation and two-class classification loss. Note that the DFGC-2022 dataset itself is not in the training data of this model.

As a comparison, we also include a top 2% solution from the ISPL team in the DFDC challenge [2] (referred to as DFDC-ispl). This solution employs a single EfficientNet with extra attention blocks, which is trained on two datasets, i.e., FaceForensics++ [21] and DFDC.

3.3   Realism Score Regression

Video-level Feature Fusion. Apart from the VQA features, i.e., TLVQM, V-BLIINDS, VIDEVAL and ensemble, which are already extracted as video-level features following their original fusion designs, the rest are per-frame features and need to be fused to video-level features. With frame features $f_1, f_2, ..., f_n$

extracted from n sampled frames, average pooling (f_{mean}) and standard deviation pooling (f_{std}) are the two most popular feature aggregation methods in the VQA field, which are also adopted in our work.

Note that f_{mean} and f_{std} each has the same feature dimension as the frame features, and they are concatenated to form the video-level features. Take the ResNet50 model in Table 2 as example, the dimension of frame features extracted by the model is 2048, then the fused video-level feature dimension becomes 4096 after concatenating the mean and std.

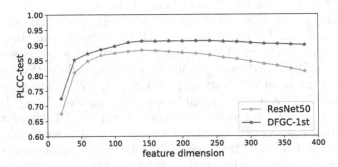

Fig. 3. PLCC under different selected feature dimensions.

Feature Selection. The performance and efficiency of our regressor, which is a SVR here, drop prominently when feature dimension grows too large, indicating a need for feature selection. Figure 3 shows how the accuracy of ResNet50 and DFGC-1st changes with the dimension of selected features. Our feature selections are conducted for the ensemble, ResNet50, VGG-Face, DFDC-ispl, and DFGC-1st models, as their original feature dimensions are relatively high, as shown in Table 2.

Following the VQA work presented in [26], we implement a similar two-stage feature selection strategy. In both selection stages, feature importance is ranked by a SVR with the linear kernel. In the first stage, the optimal number of features k is selected by gird-search over the range of total feature dimensions in a step of 20. The k giving the best average PLCC in 10 random train-test iterations is chosen. Each feature extraction model has its own optimal k, as shown in the *selected* sub-column of Table 2. In the second stage, 100 iterations are preformed with the optimal k, resulting in 100 subsets of chosen features. The frequency of each feature being selected over these iterations is recorded, and the top-k most frequent features are selected as the final selected features. More details can be found in [26].

Score Regression. With each model's selected features as the input, support vector regression (SVR) models are trained to regress the groundtruth MOS of video realism, using L2 loss. For this score regression step, we use the SVR model with RBF kernel, and set its hyper-parameters C and γ by grid-search using a random 20% of the training data as the validation set. Finally, the regressor is trained again on the whole training set with the searched hyper-parameters.

Table 3. Performance comparison of VRA models

(a) Performance under video level facial-id split			
Metric	SRCC↑(std)	PLCC↑(std)	RMSE ↓(std)
BRISQUE	0.2646(.104)	0.4185(.124)	0.6473(.055)
GM-LOG	0.4324(.097)	0.5630(.088)	0.5907(.053)
FRIQUEE	0.5281(.084)	0.6926(.078)	0.5134(.059)
TLVQM	0.3988(.081)	0.5586(.096)	0.5923(.058)
V-BLIINDS	0.4042(.114)	0.6251(.123)	0.5502(.071)
VIDEVAL	0.3277(.124)	0.4521(.104)	0.6376(.054)
ensemble	0.6364(.063)	0.7979(.052)	0.4298(.052)
ResNet50	0.6006(.083)	0.7827(.059)	0.4420(.049)
VGGFace	0.5814(.111)	0.7710(.078)	0.4486(.054)
DFDC-ispl	0.5641(.092)	0.7868(.061)	0.4380(.047)
DFGC-1st	**0.7952(.051)**	**0.8975(.028)**	**0.3132(.030)**
(b) Performance under video level submit-id split			
Metric	SRCC↑(std)	PLCC↑(std)	RMSE↓(std)
BRISQUE	0.5379(.202)	0.5803(.198)	0.4208(.135)
GM-LOG	0.5160(.229)	0.5657(.226)	0.4152(.114)
FRIQUEE	0.6481(.165)	0.6928(.175)	0.3536(.082)
TLVQM	0.5593(.195)	0.6165(.203)	0.3097(.096)
V-BLIINDS	0.4851(.235)	0.5316(.247)	0.4166(.096)
VIDEVAL	0.5438(.201)	0.6014(.202)	0.4047(.119)
ensemble	0.7211(.142)	0.7628(.152)	0.3020(.048)
ResNet50	0.7423(.126)	0.7868(.132)	0.2905(.043)
VGGFace	0.7673(.100)	0.7922(.113)	0.3049(.094)
DFDC-ispl	0.7582(.115)	0.8009(.129)	0.2825(.050)
DFGC-1st	**0.8081(.096)**	**0.8356(.106)**	**0.2540(.037)**
(c) Performance under method level submit-id split			
Metric	SRCC↑(std)	PLCC↑(std)	RMSE↓(std)
BRISQUE	0.6906(.453)	0.7687(.453)	0.2730(.226)
GM-LOG	0.6970(.476)	0.7500(.472)	0.2887(.209)
FRIQUEE	0.8120(.347)	0.8712(.312)	0.2073(.181)
TLVQM	0.7170(.428)	0.7749(.432)	0.2578(.175)
V-BLIINDS	0.6833(.510)	0.7263(.506)	0.2428(.146)
VIDEVAL	0.7633(.418)	0.8109(.383)	0.2696(.210)
ensemble	0.8756(.271)	0.9168(.276)	0.1281(.107)
ResNet50	0.8370(.342)	0.9048(.295)	0.1362(.106)
VGGFace	0.9496(.144)	**0.9746(.056)**	0.1840(.189)
DFDC-ispl	0.8656(.275)	0.9407(.250)	0.1401(.097)
DFGC-1st	**0.9556(.129)**	0.9715(.082)	**0.1141(.105)**

4   Experiment Results

4.1   Evaluation Protocols and Metrics

Since C3 is the session with the largest number of submissions, as shown in Table 1, we train our models exclusively on the C3 subset of DFGC-2022. We report both intra-subset and inter-subset performances, where the former trains on a portion of C3 videos and tests on the rest C3 videos, while the latter trains on C3 and tests on C1 and C2.

For the intra-subset evaluation, we report model performances using three different protocols: the *video level facial-id* split, the *video level submit-id* split, and the *method level submit-id* split. In the facial-id split, 4 out of 20 ID pairs (128 out of 640 videos) are chosen as the test set, and the rest are the train set. In the submit-id spits, 3 out of 16 submit-IDs (120 out of 640 videos) are chosen as the test set. To reduce the impact of randomness, 100 train-test iterations are preformed with different choices of facial-ids or submit-ids across iterations. A random seed equals to the iteration number is set to ensure the uniformity of splits when testing different models.

Different from the video level protocols that calculate prediction accuracy for videos, the method level protocol aims to evaluate the overall quality of different face-swap methods with respect to the realism of their created videos. For method level evaluation, the groundtruth method MOS is calculated by the average of groundtruth MOS of videos in the same submit-id, and the predicted method MOS is the average of predicted MOS of these videos.

For the inter-subset evaluations, the models are trained on all C3 videos and tested on all C1 or C2 videos. It is a more challenging protocol that can reflect the generalization ability of evaluated models. This is because C2 and C1 videos are created by different face-swap methods from C3 and their MOS has different distributions. Note that, in the inter-subset setting, the selected features and hyper-parameters are all the same from those in the intra-subset setting, meaning that the models are not fine-tuned from sets to sets.

Following the VQA literature, SRCC (Spearman rank-order correlation coefficient), PLCC (Pearson linear correlation coefficient) and RMSE (root mean square error) are employed as evaluation metrics in our benchmark. The average value over all testing iterations is reported to reflect model performances, and the standard deviation is also shown, which can imply the robustness of the models. As suggested in [23,26], a nonlinear logistic function with four parameters is fitted to the predicted MOS before calculating the final metrics to improve prediction accuracy.

4.2   Intra-subset Evaluation

Table 3 shows a general image comparing different VRA models under our intra-subset evaluation protocols. As can be seen, the DFGC-1st model outperforms the others under nearly all metrics and protocols. The ensemble, VGG-Face, and DFDC-ispl models have the second-rank under some metrics and protocols.

Table 4. Inter-subsets evaluation results

(a) Training on C3 and testing on C1

model	SRCC↑		PLCC↑		RMSE↓	
	video	method	video	method	video	method
random	-0.0091		-0.0084		1.3727	
ResNet50	0.2384	0.4857	0.2978	0.7818	0.6834	0.3158
VGG Face	0.2512	0.6571	0.2939	0.8315	0.6843	0.2813
DFDC-ispl	0.3367	**0.9428**	0.3595	**0.9406**	0.6680	0.1719
DFGC-1st	**0.3743**	0.6571	**0.4222**	0.7818	**0.6489**	**0.3158**

(b) Training on C3 and testing on C2

model	SRCC↑		PLCC↑		RMSE↓	
	video	method	video	method	video	method
random	0.0083		0.0083		1.411	
ResNet50	0.4173	0.6044	0.4027	0.7607	0.7460	0.4582
VGG Face	0.4522	0.6813	0.4350	0.7580	0.7339	0.4605
DFDC-ispl	0.3554	0.6978	0.3477	0.7698	0.7642	0.4507
DFGC-1st	**0.5045**	**0.8846**	**0.4844**	**0.9088**	**0.7130**	**0.2946**

While the other handcrafted IQA and VQA models suffer from obliviously lower accuracy. The result of the DFGC-1st model leading the board implies that deepfake detection features may relate most to the VRA problem at hand.

Comparing with the video level results, it is clear that the method level counterparts are much more accurate for all models and metrics. This shows that evaluating the realism performance for different face-swap methods are more tractable than that for individual videos. This result is not so unexpected, considering that method level evaluations can average out prediction noises on video instances.

4.3 Inter-subsets Evaluation

Table 4 demonstrates the results of the prediction accuracy of models when trained and tested on different data subsets. Handcrafted models are not tested here due to their high computational cost in feature extraction. The DFGC-1st model again surpasses the other models in terms of generalization ability. Although much better than a random guesser (random prediction in [1, 5]), all models have a clear performance degradation at video level compared to the intra-subset setting. The situation improves when coming to method level evaluations, but the accuracy gap between intra- and inter-subsets is still obvious. This calls for further study on improving the generalization ability of VRA models.

Table 5. Video level performance comparison of popular objective quality metrics on C3

metric	SRCC↑	PLCC↑	RMSE↓
SSIM	−0.0814	0.1789	0.7256
LPIPS	−0.1312	0.2918	0.6941
FAST-VQA	0.1094	0.1104	0.9679
DFGC-1st detection score	0.2651	0.3232	0.6867
DFGC-1st VRA score	0.8081	0.8356	0.2540

4.4 Comparison with Popular Objective Quality Metrics

Table 5 demonstrates the performance of several existing objective quality metrics: SSIM [28] and LPIPS [32] are commonly used for evaluating deepfake generation models, FAST-VQA [29] is a SOTA VQA model, the detection score of DFGC-1st reflects the probability of a video being a fake one predicted by the model. FID [8] cannot be applied here since it is a metric for evaluating the quality of a set of samples instead of a single one. It can be seen that comparing with the VRA scores predicted by DFGC-1st, none of these existing metrics can perform well as a predictor for human perception of deepfake realism. Also, since VRA and anti-detection scores originate from the same DFGC-1st features in this example, the result indicates that our feature selection and regression process play an important role in extracting VRA-related information.

5   Conclusions

In this paper, we propose a benchmark for the new visual realism assessment (VRA) problem of face-swap videos. This benchmark is based on the DFGC-2022 dataset and includes several models from related fields which are used as feature extractors. An SVR is trained as the regressor to predict realism scores for fake videos. We find that deep features beat most handcrafted ones in this VRA task, with a deepfake detection model trained on diverse datasets, i.e., the DFGC-1st model, achieving the best performance, implying the close relation between deepfake realism assessment and its detection. However, improving VRA's generalization ability under new datasets is still an open problem that requires further research. This work serves as a reference for future studies.

Acknowledgment. This work is supported by Beijing Natural Science Foundation under Grant No. 4232037, the National Natural Science Foundation of China (NSFC) under Grants 62272460, U19B2038, 62106015, a grant from Young Elite Scientists Sponsorship Program by CAST (YESS), CAAI-Huawei MindSpore Open Fund, the Pyramid Talent Training Project of Beijing University of Civil Engineering and Architecture (JDYC20220819), the 2023-2025 Young Elite Scientist Sponsorship Program by BAST (BYESS2023130), and the BUCEA Post Graduate Innovation Project (PG2023090).

References

1. Dfgc-2022 first-place solution of the detection track. https://github.com/chenhanch/DFGC-2022-1st-place
2. Bonettini, N., Cannas, E.D., Mandelli, S., Bondi, L., Bestagini, P., Tubaro, S.: Video face manipulation detection through ensemble of CNNs. In: 2020 25th International Conference on Pattern Recognition (ICPR), pp. 5012–5019. IEEE (2021)
3. Chen, R., Chen, X., Ni, B., Ge, Y.: Simswap: an efficient framework for high fidelity face swapping. In: Proceedings of the 28th ACM International Conference on Multimedia, pp. 2003–2011 (2020)
4. Chung, J., Gulcehre, C., Cho, K., Bengio, Y.: Empirical evaluation of gated recurrent neural networks on sequence modeling. arXiv preprint arXiv:1412.3555 (2014)
5. Dolhansky, B., et al.: The deepfake detection challenge (dfdc) dataset. arXiv preprint arXiv:2006.07397 (2020)
6. Ghadiyaram, D., Bovik, A.C.: Perceptual quality prediction on authentically distorted images using a bag of features approach. J. Vis. **17**(1), 32–32 (2017)
7. He, K., Zhang, X., Ren, S., Sun, J.: Deep residual learning for image recognition. In: Proceedings of the IEEE Conference on Computer Vision and Pattern Recognition (CVPR), pp. 770–778 (2016)
8. Heusel, M., Ramsauer, H., Unterthiner, T., Nessler, B., Hochreiter, S.: Gans trained by a two time-scale update rule converge to a local nash equilibrium. Advances in neural information processing systems 30 (2017)
9. Hochreiter, S., Schmidhuber, J.: Long short-term memory. Neural Comput. **9**(8), 1735–1780 (1997)
10. Juefei-Xu, F., Wang, R., Huang, Y., Guo, Q., Ma, L., Liu, Y.: Countering malicious deepfakes: Survey, battleground, and horizon. Int. J. Comput. Vis., 1–57 (2022)
11. Korhonen, J.: Two-level approach for no-reference consumer video quality assessment. IEEE Trans. Image Process. **28**(12), 5923–5938 (2019)
12. Korshunov, P., Marcel, S.: Deepfake detection: humans vs. machines. arXiv preprint arXiv:2009.03155 (2020)
13. Li, L., Bao, J., Yang, H., Chen, D., Wen, F.: Advancing high fidelity identity swapping for forgery detection. In: Proceedings of the IEEE/CVF Conference on Computer Vision and Pattern Recognition (CVPR), pp. 5074–5083 (2020)
14. Lo, C.C., Fu, S.W., Huang, W.C., Wang, X., Yamagishi, J., Tsao, Y., Wang, H.M.: MOSNet: deep learning-based objective assessment for voice conversion. In: Proceedings of Interspeech 2019, pp. 1541–1545 (2019). 10.21437/Interspeech. 2019–2003
15. Mittal, A., Moorthy, A.K., Bovik, A.C.: No-reference image quality assessment in the spatial domain. IEEE Trans. Image Process. **21**(12), 4695–4708 (2012)
16. Nightingale, S., Agarwal, S., Härkönen, E., Lehtinen, J., Farid, H.: Synthetic faces: how perceptually convincing are they? J. Vis. **21**(9), 2015–2015 (2021)
17. Nightingale, S.J., Farid, H.: Ai-synthesized faces are indistinguishable from real faces and more trustworthy. Proc. Natl. Acad. Sci. **119**(8), e2120481119 (2022)
18. Parkhi, O., Vedaldi, A., Zisserman, A.: Deep face recognition. In: Proceedings of the British Machine Vision Conference, pp. 1–12 (2015)
19. Peng, B., Xiang, W., Jiang, Y., Wang, W., Dong, J., Sun, Z., Lei, Z., Lyu, S.: Dfgc 2022: the second deepfake game competition. In: 2022 IEEE International Joint Conference on Biometrics (IJCB), pp. 1–10 (2022)
20. Perov, I., et al.: Deepfacelab: Integrated, flexible and extensible face-swapping framework. arXiv preprint arXiv:2005.05535 (2020)

21. Rossler, A., Cozzolino, D., Verdoliva, L., Riess, C., Thies, J., Nießner, M.: Face-forensics++: learning to detect manipulated facial images. In: Proceedings of the IEEE/CVF International Conference on Computer Vision (ICCV), pp. 1–11 (2019)

22. Saad, M.A., Bovik, A.C., Charrier, C.: Blind prediction of natural video quality. IEEE Trans. Image Process. **23**(3), 1352–1365 (2014)

23. Seshadrinathan, K., Soundararajan, R., Bovik, A.C., Cormack, L.K.: Study of subjective and objective quality assessment of video. IEEE Trans. Image Process. **19**(6), 1427–1441 (2010)

24. Simonyan, K., Zisserman, A.: Very deep convolutional networks for large-scale image recognition. In: Proceedings of the 3rd International Conference on Learning Representations (2015). https://arxiv.org/abs/1409.1556

25. Tian, Y., Ni, Z., Chen, B., Wang, S., Wang, H., Kwong, S.: Generalized visual quality assessment of gan-generated face images. arXiv preprint arXiv:2201.11975 (2022)

26. Tu, Z., Wang, Y., Birkbeck, N., Adsumilli, B., Bovik, A.C.: Ugc-vqa: benchmarking blind video quality assessment for user generated content. IEEE Trans. Image Process. **30**, 4449–4464 (2021)

27. Tu, Z., Yu, X., Wang, Y., Birkbeck, N., Adsumilli, B., Bovik, A.C.: Rapique: rapid and accurate video quality prediction of user generated content. IEEE Open J. Signal Process. **2**, 425–440 (2021)

28. Wang, Z., Bovik, A.C., Sheikh, H.R., Simoncelli, E.P.: Image quality assessment: from error visibility to structural similarity. IEEE Trans. Image Process. **13**(4), 600–612 (2004)

29. Wu, H., Chen, C., Hou, J., Liao, L., Wang, A., Sun, W., Yan, Q., Lin, W.: Fast-vqa: efficient end-to-end video quality assessment with fragment sampling. Proceedings of European Conference of Computer Vision (ECCV) (2022)

30. Xue, W., Mou, X., Zhang, L., Bovik, A.C., Feng, X.: Blind image quality assessment using joint statistics of gradient magnitude and Laplacian features. IEEE Trans. Image Process. **23**(11), 4850–4862 (2014)

31. Zezario, R.E., Fu, S.W., Chen, F., Fuh, C.S., Wang, H.M., Tsao, Y.: Deep learning-based non-intrusive multi-objective speech assessment model with cross-domain features. IEEE/ACM Trans. Audio Speech Lang. Process. **31**, 54–70 (2023). https://doi.org/10.1109/TASLP.2022.3205757

32. Zhang, R., Isola, P., Efros, A.A., Shechtman, E., Wang, O.: The unreasonable effectiveness of deep features as a perceptual metric. In: Proceedings of the IEEE Conference on Computer Vision and Pattern Recognition (CVPR) (2018)

360° Omnidirectional Salient Object Detection with Multi-scale Interaction and Densely-Connected Prediction

Haowei Dai[1], Liuxin Bao[1], Kunye Shen[2], Xiaofei Zhou[1(✉)], and Jiyong Zhang[1(✉)]

[1] School of Automation, Hangzhou Dianzi University, Hangzhou 310018, China
tengye84@gmail.com, {lxbao,jzhang}@hdu.edu.cn, zxforchid@outlook.com
[2] School of Communication and Information Engineering, Shanghai University, Shanghai 200444, China
kunyeshen@outlook.com

Abstract. Despite the fact that 360° cameras have become affordable, the efforts in salient object detection (SOD) of 360° omnidirectional images are still relatively few. The performance of the SOD task is significantly hindered by the severe distortion and the large range of object sizes in omnidirectional images. Therefore, we propose a Multi-scale Interaction and Densely-connected Prediction network (MIDP-Net) to counteract distortion and extract multi-scale information in 360° omnidirectional images. Specifically, we introduce a Multi-Level Features Interaction (MLFI) module that firstly integrates the features with different receptive fields from adjacent levels, and then fuses the semantic cues from upper-level decoder to obtain the accurate multi-scale information. In addition, to overcome the distortion of 360° omnidirectional image, we design a Two-Pass Decoder (TPD) module, which further strengthen the semantic information by secondary decoding and combines the edge cues and saliency cues to optimizes the details of prediction map. The comprehensive experiments on two public 360° omnidirectional datasets indicate that the proposed MIDP-Net outperforms the state-of-the-art methods.

Keywords: 360° omnidirectional images · salient edge cues · multi-scale deep features · salient object detection

1 Introduction

Salient object detection (SOD), which aims to simulate human visual effects and extract the most attractive objects of the image according to human vision [1,2], is a crucial first step for various visual tasks and has been widely used in many domains, including image/video segmentation [3–7], image retargeting [8], and visual tracking [9].

H. Dai and L. Bao—Equal contribution.

H. Lu et al. (Eds.): ICIG 2023, LNCS 14355, pp. 427–438, 2023.
https://doi.org/10.1007/978-3-031-46305-1_35

Although the existing SOD models based on Convolutional Neural Networks (CNNs) have achieved remarkable processes in normal 2D planar images with a limited field of view (FoV) [10–20], they find it challenging to produce satisfactory results in the SOD task of 360° Omnidirectional images due to the distortion caused by the projection from sphere to plane. On the one hand, the traditional models frequently fail to appropriately segment the targets which have changed significantly in size due to distortion in the panoramic image. On the other hand, the traditional model is severely hampered by the changes in semantics brought about by the distortion of the object and the division in the perspective.

In recent years, several deep learning methods have been proposed for the SOD of 360° omnidirectional images. Li et al. [21] proposed the first SOD dataset on 360° omnidirectional images and introduce a baseline model to address the fundamental issues in omnidirectional images. Zhang et al. [22] collected 107 equirectangular panoramas to build a fixation-based 360° image dataset and evaluate the newly proposed state-of-the-art 2D SOD models on the dataset. Huang et al. [23] combined the features generated from 360° equirectangular images and cube-map images, respectively. They also proposed a multi-Level features adaptation module to weight and integrate features for better prediction. However, the severe distortion in omnidirectional images and the large distribution of object size still remained problems.

To address the above problems, we propose a Multi-scale Interaction and Densely-connected Prediction network (MIDP-Net), which contains a multi-level features interaction (MLFI) model that aggregates the features from multiple layers to extract accurate multi-scale information and a two-pass decoder (TPD) model to refine the salient objects from rough to precise.

Overall, our main contributions can be summarized as follows:

1. We propose an end-to-end MIDP-Net to segment the 2D equirectangular 360° image robustly for 360° omnidirectional image SOD task.
2. To introduce sufficient multi-scale information, we design a MLFI module to extract multi-scale features, aggregating information with different receptive fields from adjacent encoder layers and fusing the semantic cues from upper-level decoder layer.
3. To resists image distortion, we propose a TPD module which enhance the semantic information by secondary decoding and densely connects the edge information and saliency information to improve the details of the prediction map.
4. Extensive experiments on two benchmark 360° omnidirectional images datasets demonstrate that the proposed MIDP-Net outperforms 8 SOTA methods.

The remaining of this paper is organized as follows. Section 2 gives a detailed description of the proposed MIDP-Net. In Sect. 3, comprehensive experiments and the detailed analysis are presented. Finally, the conclusion is detailed in Sect. 4.

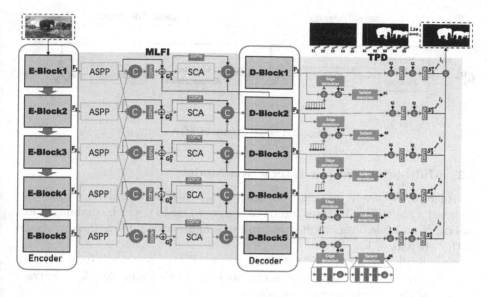

Fig. 1. The architecture of the proposed MIDP-Net: The whole model contains two modules: MLFI module and TPD module, which are represented by different background colors.

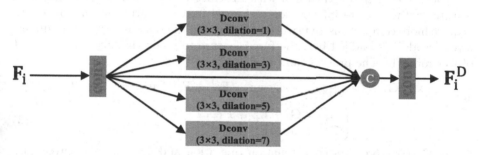

Fig. 2. The structure of ASPP

2 Methodology

2.1 Feature Extraction Network

As shown in Fig. 1, to extract the abundant multi-scale features, we build a feature extraction module based on VGG-19 [24]. Different from the original VGG-19, we discard the last max-pooling layer and three fully connected layers of the VGG-19 network, for fitting the pixel-wise SOD task. Our encoder utilizes five convolutional layers (*i.e. E-Block*1 to *E-Block*5) to provides individual features with different scales, which are successively denoted as $\{\mathbf{F}_1, \mathbf{F}_2, \mathbf{F}_3, \mathbf{F}_4, \mathbf{F}_5\}$.

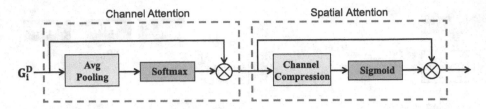

Fig. 3. The structure of SCA

2.2 Multi-level Features Interaction Model

In order to effectively integrate the feature information of different scales, we designed a multi-level features interaction model (MLFI), which combines information of multiple layers to fuse and enhance multi-scale information, as shown in the left part of Fig. 1.

Specifically, as shown in Fig. 2, the features $\{\mathbf{F}_i\}_{i=1}^5$ generated from VGG-19 are fed into the atrous spatial pyramid pooling (ASPP) module [25] to extract features with different receptive fields:

$$\mathbf{F}_i^D = ASPP(\mathbf{F}_i) \tag{1}$$

Then, the high-level features with abstract information and the low-level features with concrete information are fused into the current-level features to acquire more comprehensive features. Meanwhile, the semantic cues from upper-level decoder also added into the fused feature to guide the location of salient object robustly. The process can be defined as:

$$\mathbf{G}_i = Conv_{3\times3}(Cat(Down_{\times2}(\mathbf{F}_{i-1}^D), \mathbf{F}_i^D, Up_{\times2}(\mathbf{F}_{i+1}^D))) \tag{2}$$

$$\begin{cases} \mathbf{G}_i^D = \mathbf{G}_i \oplus \mathbf{F}_i^D \oplus \mathbf{P}_{i+1} & i = 1,2,3,4 \\ \mathbf{G}_5^D = \mathbf{G}_i \oplus \mathbf{F}_i^D & i = 5 \end{cases} \tag{3}$$

where $Cat(\cdot)$ represents concatenation operation and $Conv_{3\times3}(\cdot)$ represents a 3×3 convolutional layer which reduces the concatenated channels to 64. $\mathbf{P}_{i+1}$ means the output of upper-level decoder block. $Down_{\times2}(\cdot)$ denotes the max-pooling operation and $Up_{\times2}(\cdot)$ denotes the bilinear interpolation upsampling operation. Besides, $\oplus$ means the element-wise summation.

In addition, attention mechanism [26] is applied to enhance the important feature information in each layer. As presented in Fig. 3, the Spatial and Channel Attention(SCA) module filters out the noise information along both spatial and channel dimensions, preserving the most critical features for subsequent processing. Besides, a residual branch is utilized to prevent overfitting. The overall process can be written as:

$$\begin{cases} \mathbf{H}_i = Cat(Conv(\mathbf{G}_i^D), SCA(\mathbf{G}_i^D), \mathbf{P}_{i+1}) & i = 1,2,3,4 \\ \mathbf{H}_i = Cat(Conv(\mathbf{G}_i^D), SCA(\mathbf{G}_i^D)) & i = 5 \end{cases} \tag{4}$$

where $Conv(\cdot)$ denotes the 3×3 convolution layer with a ReLU layer, and $SCA(\cdot)$ means execute the SCA module.

2.3 Two-Pass Decoder

In traditional U-shaped networks, a symmetric decoder block will follow the encoder block and transfers information with some bridge modules. Such a structure can usually extract most of the information and roughly segment the target in nature images SOD task. However, for 360° omnidirectional images which have distorted semantics information, deformed edges and irregular contours, this structure failed to obtain a satisfactory result. Therefore, we designed a Two-Pass Decoder(TPD) module. The first stage of decoder will find out the outline and generate an approximate salient object mask, while the second stage further enhance the semantic information and refines the prediction map from approximate to precise. The whole process is shown in the right part of Fig. 1.

Similar to traditional U-shaped networks, our first stage of decoder, which stacks four 3×3 convolution blocks in each decoder layer, is symmetrical to the encoder in structure. Five decoder's features $\{\mathbf{P}_i\}_{i=1}^5$ will be generated by the first stage of decoder and sent to both the second stage of decoder and the lower layer of MLFI module.

To improve the accuracy of prediction maps in detail, our second stage of decoder applies the edge detection module and the saliency detection module to refine the feature details. The outputs of each edge and saliency detection module will be supervised by the ground truth of the edge and the salient object, respectively. Besides, they will also be sent into the lower decoder block for information aggregation. The whole process is as follows:

$$\mathbf{E}_i = \mathrm{Convs_P}(\mathrm{Convs}_{3\times3}(\mathrm{Cat}(\mathbf{P}_i, \sum_{j=i+1}^{5} \{\mathbf{E}_j, \mathbf{S}_j\}))) \tag{5}$$

$$\mathbf{S}_i = \mathrm{Convs_P}(\mathrm{Convs}_{1\times1}(\mathrm{Convs}_{3\times3}(\mathrm{Cat}(\mathbf{P}_i, \mathbf{E}_i)))) \tag{6}$$

where $\mathrm{Convs}_{3\times3}(\cdot)$ and $\mathrm{Convs}_{1\times1}(\cdot)$ donate 3×3 and 1×1 convolution layer followed by a batch normalization (BN) layer and a ReLU layer. $\mathrm{Convs_P}(\cdot)$ generates the prediction masks by a 1×1 convolution operation with sigmoid activation function. $\mathbf{E}_i$ and $\mathbf{S}_i$ represent the masks obtained by edge detection module and saliency detection module, respectively.

Finally, we obtain the ultimate saliency cue $\mathbf{S}_1$ and edge cue $\mathbf{E}_1$ which contain the most comprehensive and precise multi-level information. We combine the $\mathbf{E}_1$ and $\mathbf{S}_1$ with $\{\mathbf{P}_i\}_{i=1}^5$ to guide the generation of prediction maps in each layer. Besides, to further aggregate multiple-level information, we merge the outputs of five layers to generate the final prediction map:

$$\mathbf{S}_i^o = \mathrm{Up}(\mathrm{Conv}_{1\times1}(\mathrm{Cat}(\mathbf{E}_1, \mathrm{Conv}_{3\times3}(\mathrm{Cat}(\mathbf{P}_i, \mathbf{S}_1))))) \tag{7}$$

$$\mathbf{S}_{final}^o = \mathrm{Conv}_{1\times1}(\mathrm{Cat}(\mathbf{S}_1^o, \mathbf{S}_2^o, \mathbf{S}_3^o, \mathbf{S}_4^o, \mathbf{S}_5^o)) \tag{8}$$

where $\mathrm{Conv}_{1\times1}(\cdot)$ and $\mathrm{Conv}_{3\times3}(\cdot)$ represent a 1×1 convolution layer and 3×3 convolution layer that reduce the channel to 1, respectively. $\mathrm{Up}(\cdot)$ denotes upsampling the prediction map to the original resolution.

To better supervise prediction maps, we adopt the binary cross-entropy loss l as the loss function. We also deploy supervision to all the side-outputs of the decoder, the total loss function can be written as $\mathcal{L}_{total} = \sum_{i=1}^{5} l_i$.

Table 1. Quantitative comparison results of S, F_β^{max}, E_ξ^{max} and MAE on the 360-SOD and F-360iSOD datasets. The best three results in each row are marked in red, green, and blue, respectively.

Methods	360-SOD				F-360iSOD			
	S	MAE	E_ξ^{max}	F_β^{max}	S	MAE	E_ξ^{max}	F_β^{max}
CPD	0.6703	0.0861	0.6774	0.4700	0.5205	0.1699	0.5687	0.2137
U2Net	0.6395	0.1220	0.6773	0.4549	0.4884	0.2440	0.5667	0.2022
U2Netp	0.6207	0.1279	0.6430	0.4010	0.5204	0.2027	0.5732	0.2108
BASNet	0.6298	0.1113	0.6505	0.4137	0.4877	0.2372	0.5485	0.1964
MINet	0.6418	0.1013	0.6626	0.4461	0.5099	0.2158	0.5248	0.2144
SCRN	0.6599	0.0841	0.7092	0.4654	0.5436	0.1771	0.5867	0.2469
EGNet	0.6948	0.0778	0.7310	0.5312	0.6193	0.1161	0.7101	0.3382
FANet	0.8260	0.0208	0.9002	0.7699	0.6456	0.0378	0.7521	0.3887
Ours	0.8310	0.0220	0.9101	0.7799	0.6657	0.0463	0.7705	0.4099

3   Experimental Results

3.1   Datasets and Evaluation Metrics

Datasets. To comprehensively validate our model, we conduct extensive comparisons on two public datasets. **360-SOD** [21] consists of 500 equirectangular 360° images and corresponding ground truths, of which 400 images are used for training and 100 images are used for testing. **F-360iSOD** [22] contains 107 equirectangular 360° images with challenging scenes and multiple object classes.

Evaluation Metrics. We adopted five common measures as the quantitative evaluation metrics to evaluate our model: S-measure (S) [27], max F-measure (F_β^{max}) [28], max E-measure (E_ξ^{max}) [29], Mean Absolute Error (MAE) [30], and Precision-Recall(PR) curve.

3.2   Implementation Details

Our experiments were implemented in the PyTorch [31] framework using a computer equipped with two GeForce RTX 2080Ti GPUs. We trained our model on the training set of 360-SOD dataset, and test our model on the F-360iSOD and the testing set of 360-SOD dataset. During the training phase, each image is resized to 512×256 pixels. VGG-19 is utilized for model initialization. We applied multiple data augmentation operations to extend training dataset with different strategies, such as flipping and rotation. In addition, Adam optimizer [32] is used to optimize our network with a batch size of 1 and initial rate 1e-4.

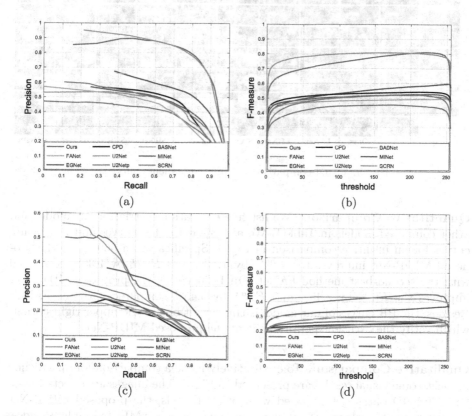

Fig. 4. (better viewed in color) Quantitative evaluation of different saliency models: (a) presents PR curves and (b) presents F-measure curves on 360-SOD dataset, (c) presents PR curves and (d) presents F-measure curves on F-360iSOD dataset.

3.3   Comparison with the State-of-the-Art Methods

On the F-360iSOD and 360-SOD, we compared the proposed MIDP-Net with eight state-of-the-art SOD models: CPD [15], U2Net [16], U2Netp [16], BASNet [17], MINet [18], SCRN [19], EGNet [20], and FANet [23]. For a fair comparison, we tested the trained model provided by the authors on two datasets to obtain the prediction maps.

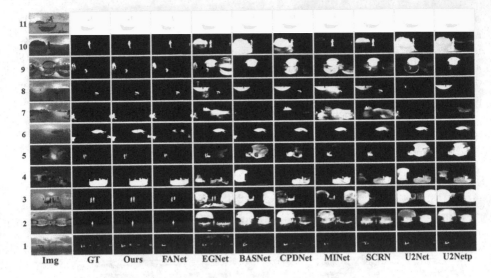

Fig. 5. Visual comparison of different saliency models.

Quantitative Comparison. We list five evaluation metrics of our model and other compared models in Table 1. We also show the PR curves and F-measure curves for an intuitive comparison in Fig. 4. Specifically, on 360-SOD, the proposed MIDP-Net improves the E_ξ^{max} by 1.10% and F_β^{max} by 1.30% compared with the second-best method FANet. On F-360iSOD, the proposed MIDP-Net improves the E_ξ^{max} by 2.45% and F_β^{max} by 5.45% compared with the FANet. Besides, the PR curves of our model is the closest one to the upper right corner, which verify the excellent performance of the proposed MIDP-Net.

Qualitative Comparison. To qualitatively make a comparison for all saliency models, some visual results are presented in Fig. 5. The images are selected from the 360-SOD dataset. Compared with other models, the proposed MIDP-Net can locate multi-scale targets more accurately due to our MLFI module. Besides, through the combination of edge information and salient information, the proposed MIDP-Net shows a strong ability in the segmentation of marginal details. It demonstrates that the prediction results of our model are more complete and accurate than other models.

3.4   Ablation Studies

We designed eight ablation experiments on 360-SOD dataset to verify the effectiveness of each part of our model. The results are listed in Table 2 and Fig. 6. Specifically, w/o NC deletes the connections of neighboring levels after ASPP block in MLFI module, w/o SCA deletes the SCA block in MLFI module, and w/o $NC\&SCA$ deletes both of them. Similarly, w/o $Salient$ removes the

Table 2. Ablation studies are performed on 360-SOD dataset, where the best result in each column is bold.

Methods	S	MAE	E_ξ^{max}	F_β^{max}
w/o NC	0.8278	0.0232	0.8976	0.7636
w/o SCA	0.8209	0.0237	0.9040	0.7593
w/o NC&SCA	0.8134	0.0248	0.8938	0.7349
w/o Salient	0.8120	0.0233	0.8874	0.7505
w/o Edge	0.8160	0.0232	0.9053	0.7615
w/o Sal&Eg	0.8179	0.0235	0.8865	0.7454
w/o 2nd De	0.7968	0.0286	0.8968	0.7445
w/o Fusion	0.7993	0.0284	0.8887	0.7500
Ours	**0.8310**	**0.0220**	**0.9101**	**0.7799**

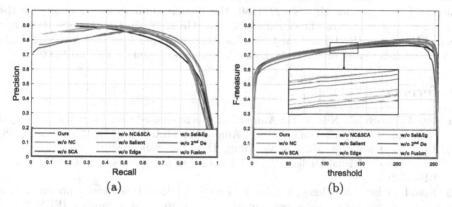

(a)   (b)

Fig. 6. (better viewed in color) Quantitative evaluation for the ablation study: (a) presents PR curves and (b) presents F-measure curves.

saliency detection module in TPD module, *w/o Edge* removes the edge detection module in TPD module, and *w/o Sal&Eg* removes both of them. Besides, *w/o 2nd De* delete the second stage of decoder, utilizing P_1 to generate the prediction map directly after the *D-Block*1. *w/o Fusion* cancels the merging of the outputs of five decoder layers, using the output of the last layer of TPD module S_1^o as the final prediction map. The results prove that the proposed MIDP-Net with all its modules outperforms the architectures of the ablation experiments on 360-SOD dataset.

4   Conclusion

In this paper, we attempt to overcome the severe distortion and the large distribution of object size in omnidirectional images by designing MIDP-Net, which contains two significant modules. The multi-level features interaction (MLFI) module combines the features with different receptive fields from adjacent layers and fuses the semantic cues from the upper-level decoder layer to gather comprehensive multi-scale information. Then, the two-pass decoder (TPD) module utilizes secondary decoding to combat the distortion and combines the edge information and saliency information to refine the prediction map from approximate to precise. Extensive experiments on two benchmark 360° omnidirectional images datasets demonstrate that the proposed MIDP-Net outperforms 8 SOTA methods.

Acknowledgement. This work was supported by the National Natural Science Foundation of China under Grants 62271180; the Fundamental Research Funds for the Provincial Universities of Zhejiang under Grants GK229909299001-009; the Hangzhou Dianzi University (HDU) and the China Electronics Corporation DATA (CECDATA) Joint Research Center of Big Data Technologies under Grants KYH063120009.

References

1. Itti, L., Koch, C., Niebur, E.: A model of saliency-based visual attention for rapid scene analysis. IEEE Trans. Pattern Anal. Mach. Intell. **20**(11), 1254–1259 (1998)
2. Borji, A., Cheng, M.-M., Hou, Q., Jiang, H., Li, J.: Salient object detection: a survey. Comput. Visual Media **5**(2), 117–150 (2019). https://doi.org/10.1007/s41095-019-0149-9
3. Sun, L., Cheng, S., Zheng, Y., Wu, Z., Zhang, J.: Spanet: successive pooling attention network for semantic segmentation of remote sensing images. IEEE J. Sel. Top. Appl. Earth Observ. Remote Sens. (2022)
4. Zeng, Y., Zhuge, Y., Lu, H., Zhang, L.: Joint learning of saliency detection and weakly supervised semantic segmentation. In: International Conference on Computer Vision (ICCV), pp. 7223–7233 (2019)
5. Ye, L., Rochan, M., Liu, Z., Wang, Y.: Cross-modal self-attention network for referring image segmentation. In: Proceedings of the IEEE Conference on Computer Vision and Pattern Recognition (CVPR), pp. 10502–10511 (2019)
6. Li, G., Liu, Z., Shi, R., Wei, W.: Constrained fixation point based segmentation via deep neural network. Neurocomputing **368**, 180–187 (2019)
7. Liu, Z., Zou, W., Li, L., Shen, L., Le Meur, O.: Co-saliency detection based on hierarchical segmentation. IEEE Signal Process. Lett. **21**(1), 88–92 (2013)
8. Ahmadi, M., Karimi, N., Samavi, S.: Context-aware saliency detection for image retargeting using convolutional neural networks. Multimed. Tools Appl. **80**(8), 11917–11941 (2021). https://doi.org/10.1007/s11042-020-10185-0
9. Hong, S., You, T., Kwak, S., Han, B.: Online tracking by learning discriminative saliency map with convolutional neural network. In: International Conference on Machine Learning, pp. 597–606. PMLR (2015)
10. Wei, J., Wang, S., Wu, Z., Su, C., Huang, Q., Tian, Q.: Label decoupling framework for salient object detection. In: Proceedings of the IEEE Conference on Computer Vision and Pattern Recognition (CVPR), June 2020

11. Qin, X., et al.: Boundary-aware segmentation network for mobile and web applications. CoRR abs/2101.04704 (2021). https://arxiv.org/abs/2101.04704

12. Feng, M., Lu, H., Yu, Y.: Residual learning for salient object detection. IEEE Trans. Image Process. **29**, 4696–4708 (2020). https://doi.org/10.1109/TIP.2020. 2975919

13. Zhao, T., Wu, X.: Pyramid feature attention network for saliency detection. In: Proceedings of the IEEE Conference on Computer Vision and Pattern Recognition (CVPR), pp. 3085–3094 (2019)

14. Wang, W., Zhao, S., Shen, J., Hoi, S.C., Borji, A.: Salient object detection with pyramid attention and salient edges. In: Proceedings of the IEEE Conference on Computer Vision and Pattern Recognition (CVPR), pp. 1448–1457 (2019)

15. Wu, Z., Su, L., Huang, Q.: Cascaded partial decoder for fast and accurate salient object detection. In: Proceedings of the IEEE Conference on Computer Vision and Pattern Recognition (CVPR), pp. 3907–3916 (2019)

16. Qin, X., Zhang, Z., Huang, C., Dehghan, M., Zaiane, O.R., Jagersand, M.: U2-net: going deeper with nested u-structure for salient object detection. Pattern Recogn. **106**, 107404 (2020)

17. Qin, X., Zhang, Z., Huang, C., Gao, C., Dehghan, M., Jagersand, M.: Basnet: boundary-aware salient object detection. In: Proceedings of the IEEE Conference on Computer Vision and Pattern Recognition (CVPR), pp. 7479–7489 (2019)

18. Pang, Y., Zhao, X., Zhang, L., Lu, H.: Multi-scale interactive network for salient object detection, June 2020

19. Wu, Z., Su, L., Huang, Q.: Stacked cross refinement network for edge-aware salient object detection. In: International Conference on Computer Vision (ICCV), pp. 7264–7273 (2019)

20. Zhao, J.X., Liu, J.J., Fan, D.P., Cao, Y., Yang, J., Cheng, M.M.: Egnet: Edge guidance network for salient object detection. In: Proceedings of the IEEE Conference on Computer Vision and Pattern Recognition (CVPR), pp. 8779–8788 (2019)

21. Li, J., Su, J., Xia, C., Tian, Y.: Distortion-adaptive salient object detection in 360° omnidirectional images. IEEE J. Sel. Top. Signal Process. **14**(1), 38–48 (2019)

22. Zhang, Y., Zhang, L., Hamidouche, W., Deforges, O.: A fixation-based 360 benchmark dataset for salient object detection. In: 2020 IEEE International Conference on Image Processing (ICIP), pp. 3458–3462. IEEE (2020)

23. Huang, M., Liu, Z., Li, G., Zhou, X., Le Meur, O.: Fanet: features adaptation network for 360° omnidirectional salient object detection. IEEE Signal Process. Lett. **27**, 1819–1823 (2020)

24. Simonyan, K., Zisserman, A.: Very deep convolutional networks for large-scale image recognition. arXiv preprint arXiv:1409.1556 (2014)

25. Chen, L.C., Papandreou, G., Kokkinos, I., Murphy, K., Yuille, A.L.: Deeplab: semantic image segmentation with deep convolutional nets, atrous convolution, and fully connected crfs. IEEE Trans. Pattern Anal. Mach. Intell. **40**(4), 834–848 (2017)

26. Woo, S., Park, J., Lee, J.Y., Kweon, I.S.: Cbam: convolutional block attention module. In: Proceedings of the European Conference on Computer Vision (ECCV), pp. 3–19 (2018)

27. Fan, D.P., Cheng, M.M., Liu, Y., Li, T., Borji, A.: Structure-measure: a new way to evaluate foreground maps. In: International Conference on Computer Vision (ICCV), pp. 4548–4557 (2017)

28. Achanta, R., Hemami, S., Estrada, F., Susstrunk, S.: Frequency-tuned salient region detection. In: Proceedings of the IEEE Conference on Computer Vision and Pattern Recognition (CVPR), pp. 1597–1604. IEEE (2009)

29. Fan, D.P., Gong, C., Cao, Y., Ren, B., Cheng, M.M., Borji, A.: Enhanced-alignment measure for binary foreground map evaluation. arXiv preprint arXiv:1805.10421 (2018)
30. Borji, A., Cheng, M.M., Jiang, H., Li, J.: Salient object detection: a benchmark. IEEE Trans. Image Process. **24**(12), 5706–5722 (2015)
31. Paszke, A., et al.: Pytorch: an imperative style, high-performance deep learning library. Advances in Neural Information Processing Systems 32 (2019)
32. Kingma, D.P., Ba, J.: Adam: a method for stochastic optimization. arXiv preprint arXiv:1412.6980 (2014)

Author Index

H. Lu et al. (Eds.): ICIG 2023, LNCS 14355, pp. 439–440, 2023.
https://doi.org/10.1007/978-3-031-46305-1

Printed in the United States
by Baker & Taylor Publisher Services